CONFESSIONS
OF AN
ILLUMINATI

AUTHOR:

LEO LYON ZAGAMI

VOLUME II

CCC PUBLISHING
SAN FRANCISCO, CALIFORNIA

Leo Lyon Zagami

CONFESSIONS

of an

ILLUMINATI

VOL. II

The Time of Revelation and Tribulation
Leading up to 2020

Consortium of Collective Consciousness Publishing
CCCPublishing.com

Confessions of an Illuminati, Volume II:

The Time of Revelation and Tribulation leading up to 2020

1st edition

Copyright © 2016 by Leo Lyon Zagami
Published by the Consortium of Collective Consciousness Publishing™

As is common in a historic and reference book such as this, much of the information included on these pages has been collected from diverse sources. When possible, the information has been checked and double-checked. Almost every topic has at least three data points, that is, three different sources that report the same information. Even with special effort to be accurate and thorough, the author and publisher cannot vouch for each and every reference. The author and publisher assume no responsibility or liability for any outcome, loss, arrest, or injury that occurs as a result of information or advice contained in this book. As with the purchase of goods or services, caveat emptor is the prevailing responsibility of the purchaser, and the same is true for the student of the esoteric.

Library of Congress Cataloging-in-Publication Data:

Zagami, Leo Lyon
    CONFESSIONS OF AN ILLUMINATI, VOL. II / Leo Lyon Zagami
        p. cm.
      print ISBN 13: 9781888729627 (Pbk.)

1. Religion & Spirituality. 2. Other Religions, Practices & Sacred Texts. 3. Freemasonry. I. Title
    Library of Congress Catalog Card Number: 2015930356

Printed in the United States of America.

10 9 8 7 6 5 4 3 2

He had a dream in which he saw a stairway resting on the earth, with its top reaching to heaven, and the angels of God were ascending and descending on it.

(Genesis 28:12)

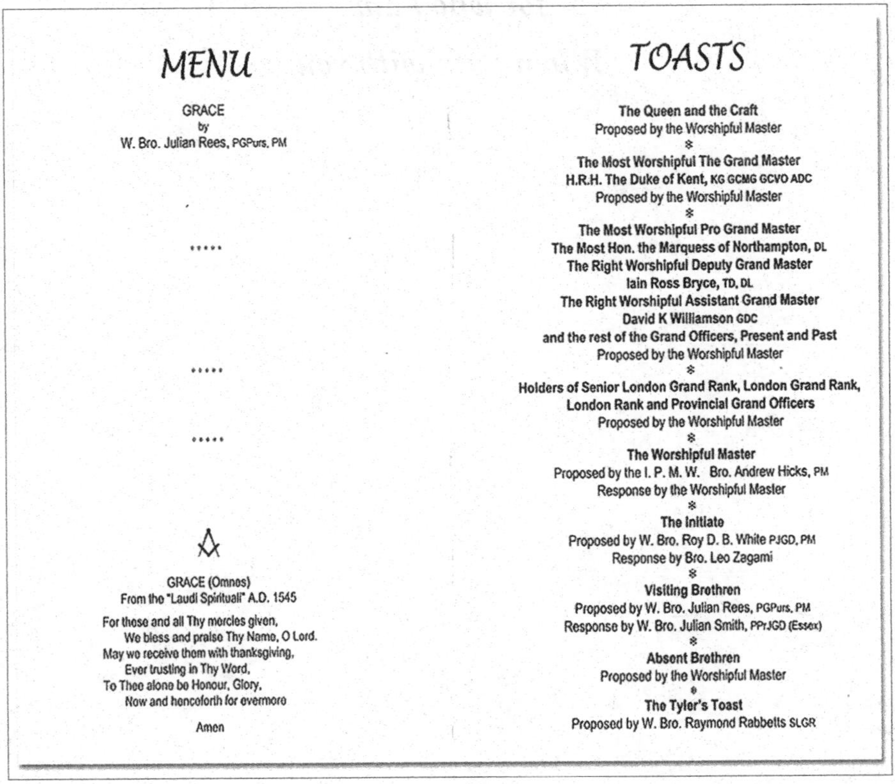

MENU

GRACE
by
W. Bro. Julian Rees, PGPurs. PM

.....

.....

.....

GRACE (Omnes)
From the "Laudi Spirituali" A.D. 1545

For those and all Thy mercies given,
We bless and praise Thy Name, O Lord.
May we receive them with thanksgiving,
Ever trusting in Thy Word,
To Thee alone be Honour, Glory,
Now and henceforth for evermore

Amen

TOASTS

The Queen and the Craft
Proposed by the Worshipful Master
❄
The Most Worshipful The Grand Master
H.R.H. The Duke of Kent, KG GCMG GCVO ADC
Proposed by the Worshipful Master
❄
The Most Worshipful Pro Grand Master
The Most Hon. the Marquess of Northampton, DL
The Right Worshipful Deputy Grand Master
Iain Ross Bryce, TD, DL
The Right Worshipful Assistant Grand Master
David K Williamson GDC
and the rest of the Grand Officers, Present and Past
Proposed by the Worshipful Master
❄
Holders of Senior London Grand Rank, London Grand Rank, London Rank and Provincial Grand Officers
Proposed by the Worshipful Master
❄
The Worshipful Master
Proposed by the I. P. M. W. Bro. Andrew Hicks, PM
Response by the Worshipful Master
❄
The Initiate
Proposed by W. Bro. Roy D. B. White PJGD, PM
Response by Bro. Leo Zagami
❄
Visiting Brethren
Proposed by W. Bro. Julian Rees, PGPurs. PM
Response by W. Bro. Julian Smith, PPrJGD (Essex)
❄
Absent Brethren
Proposed by the Worshipful Master
❄
The Tyler's Toast
Proposed by W. Bro. Raymond Rabbetts SLGR

FIG. 1 – The menu and the toast at the initiation of the author in the United Grand Lodge of England.

Dedicated to my wife, Christy
I love you
not only for who you are
But I love you
for who I am
When I am with you

⌣

Translation: Leo Zagami, Jennifer Fahey
Adaption: Christy Zagami
Editing: Christy Zagami, Brad Olsen
Photo Credits: Gerald Bruneau
Cover and Book Design: Mark J. Maxam

After this I looked, and behold, a door standing open in heaven! And the first voice, which I had heard speaking to me like a trumpet, said, "Come up here, and I will show you what must take place after this."

(Genesis 28:12)

FIG. 2 – Table tracking for 2nd degree of Freemasonry (Companion) created by Lady Frieda Harris (1877 to 1962), artist and illustrator, known for having designed the Tarot for A. Crowley.

CONTENTS:

Chapter IV: The Need for Positive Change

Chapter V: The Prophetic Aura of the Illuminati and the New World Order

Chapter VI: My Experience in the New World Order and my War against Satanism and Disinformation

Chapter VII: Apologists and the Excessive Use of the Taxil Mystification

Chapter VIII: Psychic Defense, Satanism and the Adepts of Atlantis

Preface by Princess Kaoru Nakamaru

This book as an entire series is a deep analysis, as never before, of the Illuminati, the brain's "power of darkness." I have worked to disclose some information on this power in an easy language accessible to all, but I certainly can't reach such a detailed and erudite exposition. The value of this book lies in the fact that you will understand that there is factual basis and an actual background behind what I have been saying for years. At the end of August of 2011, I personally flew to Rome, at the invitation of Leo Zagami. Thanks to his coordination, I was able to meet with the leaders of Freemasonry at an international gathering arranged in Italy's Capital. I realized that one cannot speak of the Masons as one distinct group. There are Freemasons who follow the "way of power," and there are those who follow the "way of life."

I met different personalities in the Vatican. Zagami says in the first volume of his Confessions, "The Vatican on the one hand, and the Jewish lobby on the other, play a daily game of chess with the fate of all of humanity." The people I met in Italy between late August and early September of 2011, are those who want to put an end to this power play. While the world powers plot to constitute the headquarters of the New World Order in Jerusalem, the people I met are building an alternative to this. Inside the Vatican, which is considered a stronghold of the power of darkness, a new seed has been planted, and I was able to attend the sprouting of this seed. At the center of this movement is the Marquis, Roberto Caldirola, a 33rd degree of the Ancient and Accepted Scottish Rite, a character who has awakened and has said "no" to the power of darkness.

I'm really happy to see that these people have turned from the darkness and are now deciding to work with the light, like Leo did. A truly remarkable phenomenon!

This book tells how the powerful think that many disasters will happen on our planet in the near future, likely influenced by the approach of the planet Nibiru, an economic collapse of finance, and the rumblings of a Third World War gradually manifesting.

Part of humanity for centuries have been preparing for the days of the great catastrophe, the so-called "end of times." In different parts of the world, today, they are building huge underground bases. The powerful are trying to survive only for themselves. But Zagami has decided to reveal this reality and for this reason, he was persecuted. Behind his revelations there is a risk to his own life. So I ask the readers to read well and carefully, even if it is not easy facts to read about our world.

The Jews are bipolarized

I have several friends of Jewish affiliation. Three years ago some rabbi's suddenly came up to me and they gave me the sacred text of the *Zohar*. They knew that I was the granddaughter of Emperor Meiji, but I could not understand why they had given me the *Zohar*, in particular. Reading this book I realized why it is so important for the Illuminati and the Masons, who read and try to interpret it to know the future, to be able to divine, but also to acquire the operating methods and the means to fulfill the prophecies. The power of darkness can do and have done certain operations overlapping certain events with a specific ritual mode operating in secret, following astro-theology, to transmit an aura of prophecy and authority to their deeds.

We must try to understand the deep secrets that are hidden behind the "door," which Zagami has opened for us. Behind all the important situations of Freemasonry there are Jews heading the show with the Jesuits. Maybe there are rabbis, which I have also written about in books, who did not know the reality of the Jewish penetration in certain quarters, and they did not know what kind of compromise was reached for global control with the other parties involved.

I had a conversation with Ben-Ami Shillony, Professor Emeritus of Japanese history and culture at the Hebrew University of Jerusalem. He does not consult the *Zohar* and has no suspicion that the Israeli secret service Mossad, or the Rothschild family, can be involved in a global conspiracy. Contrary to this, from Leo's book the image emerges of a Jewish society organized almost like a secret society, which is defined by Zagami citing the *Illuminati* "as the oldest religious Freemasonry of the world."

Among the Jews there are people who see and experience only on the surface, unaware of the hidden reality, and the others in power who see deep and manipulate reality, dominated by dark forces. Zagami says in his book, "Jews become the scapegoats of the projects of the Zionist elite, despite half of the American Jews, who have nothing to do with certain Jewish organizations, or with the religion they belong to, and are affiliated only in a superficial or symbolic way." I fully agree with him on this point.

The real power of the Illuminati traces back to the astral dimension!

Zagami states clearly that the source of the power behind the Secret Societies and their Occult Governments is in the invisible world, as in the astral dimension, and that the Illuminati know how to evoke entities from that dimension. It seems that Zagami has also taken part in diabolical rituals at one time. He not only knows, but has experienced first hand this reality. So his complaint weighs like a brick of truth in this day and age. He calls the Egregore, the collective spirit, a kind of hypnosis that envelopes the powerful, and creates an entity. I would call it "the effect of the actions of certain groups of spirits."

Anyway, our thoughts come together in the invisible dimension, and begin to have concrete strength in the human world and the real one made of matter. This is the power of darkness; for this reason the *Illuminati* together with the Jesuits and certain Jewish leaders work a lot in the field of mind control, using the universities, cinemas, education, media, and scientific academies to promote their goals.

Thus they can maneuver people's thoughts through an Egregore, pushing them towards a police state and the rule of fear. This is the situation I have in mind when I speak of the importance of correcting and purifying the conscience of each person. Htsukishnnji called it the, *Yu-Kai,* the "subtle dimension." Thoughts, straight or crooked, unite and become a force that changes reality. This is the secret of the secrets of Freemasonry: the power of the will! I would say that this second book of Zagami, which is now finally available in the English book market, performs a sort of "vivisection" of the brain of the Illuminati, and analyzes and shows how the world works at various levels.

Japan is a wonderland of light. It has no defense and no censorship. It is an open society from this point of view. But therein lies the wonderful freedom that everyone can buy and read books like this. I do not know if this is because of the charateristic closure represented by the Japanese language, but all the secrets of the world seem to end up here in Japan first. I wrote earlier in the preface to the Italian edition of this book, "Imagine what could happen if we published this book in English." You are privileged now to be able to finally read Zagami's work in English, as we the Japanese were before you. Zagami told me, "The truth will make you not only as free as St. John stated in Revelation, but powerful, indeed Extremely powerful, just like the Freemasons call the Grand Inspector General of the Supreme Council of the 33rd Degree: Illustrious and Powerful." There is currently no such book in English or in another language with this vast content.

Japan and Italy have already embraced this unprecedented exposure of the New World Order in this form and now it's your turn. I ask you to read and study what this book offers. [1]

Princess Kaoru Nakamaru

---

1   Translation of the introduction by Princess Kaoru Nakamaru from Japanese and adaptation by Hal Yamanouchi and the author. Final edit to English by Christy Zagami

About the Author

Supported by a creative environment from an early age, Leo Lyon Zagami's devotion to the study and research of esoteric, historical, and philosophical subjects has yielded his unique perspective. This ran parallel to his passion for music, which led him to collaborate with radio and television stations around the world. Since 2006, Leo began circulating, first-hand, information regarding his direct involvement with the New World Order and various secret societies connected to it; often referred to as the Illuminati. From 2009 to 2013 he authored six books published in Japan, all of which were bestsellers in their genre; and together selling over seventy thousand books. From 2012 to 2015, Leo published seven books in Italy with great results—results that have made him a household name in his native country.

Introduction by the Author

As a gesture of respect and appreciation, I would like to thank Princess Kaoru. It is an honor to include her preface in this Second Volume of my *Confessions of an Illuminati* series. As constructed from my years of experience in the world of secret societies, Confessions II provides even more comprehensive information, towards a complete exposure regarding the composition of the New World Order (NWO). In this book, I delve into the deeper aspects of this "strange" parallel world that, in one way or another, has involved me since birth. In some ways, this volume is more autobiographical, and personal aspects of my story will be revealed to you for the first time.

My analysis opens with the support of a tracing board displaying the second degree of Freemasonry (FIG. 2 – *See page 7*). It is here to visually introduce, through analogy, the themes and subjects represented in this book. This modality, which you find repeatedly in my Confessions series, works according to old traditions that rely on imagery to draw analogies.

I will begin by reiterating that this work would not be possible without the help and support of many adherents of Freemasonry and other chivalric orders and secret societies that have expressed their willingness to cooperate with me once again, and with my Order, the *Ordo Illuminatorum Universalis,* in the service of truth. This book, as well as the others in this trilogy, could not have been otherwise brought forth. These works aim to open minds concerning a reality that has for too long been considered an untouchable secret force—*a force that guides the destiny of humanity.* Namely, this includes the so-called "Illuminati elite" and their " Illuminati network," as well as their plans for a One World Government. This has been unfolding in front of our eyes at an even faster pace since the recent Vatican takeover by the Jesuit faction. The enemy in question consists of an association made up of the most organized religions on the planet. Organizations that are mostly linked and controlled by the Vatican. Although not as effective as it once was in the past millennia, when slavery and the ignorance of the masses were considered a normal thing, these organizations; certain families; banks; and government controllers are scattered throughout the world. These associations are enacting a unified plan for world domination that is directed by a strong and dark power. The foundations of this dark power are, *unfortunately,* very strong, able to quickly infiltrate any structure, *even those theoretically deemed inaccessible,* strengthened by the power of money and infinite resources.

This cluster of families tied in with the infamous *NWO,* and their collusion within this completely criminal system, must now be publicly denounced, and can no longer be ignored, if we want to change this course, and preserve the life of all humanity for the better. Within the structure mentioned above, some of the most despicable, dark, ruthless and evil acts towards mankind, many that you could never imagine, have been accomplished. I have been a direct witness to this evil at one time, and experienced the blatant hypocrisy of these shady characters. It motivated me to write my *Confessions* trilogy, and to dedicate my life to helping to build a better world. The New World Order, and their "New Golden Age," is manifested at the top by the Rothschilds and through British Zionism, Jesuitism, which include many patterns of corruption that have correlations with the *Illuminati* network linked to Freemasonry and other secret societies. Societies that have diverged from their original creed to merge with the demonic side, and become dominated by the those mentioned above, along with the world's royal families and black nobility.

Unfortunately, this is becoming increasingly evident each day, even to the most inexperienced eye. It is worthwhile then, in this second volume, to expose these groups with an in-depth description and analysis of their secret world, in relation to the difficult times and to the current crisis that we are all experiencing. Through this material, I hope we can all put into practice the teachings of the great initiate *Count Cagliostro*, and follow *the way of the heart*. These are my *Confessions;* the true confessions of a former member of the infamous New World Order, a single project whose aim is to exploit the people of this planet with conditions to help implement the emergence of a single World Government; after a series of conflicts culminating in one big war that would eliminate 95% of the world population! To manifest the prophecies fully, this project includes the possible rebuilding of the Temple of Solomon, as planned in the upper echelons of Masonry. We often hear about this hidden intention to materially reconstruct a temple in Jerusalem, a symbolic allegory, which is what the majority of Freemasons believe. This was also reported by the great English Freemason and author *Arthur Edward Waite (1857-1953)* in his book *A New Encyclopedia of Freemasonry* that came out in 1921: *"... in the High Grades (of Masonry) we hear of a secret intention to build yet another temple at Jerusalem."*[1]

In the late nineteenth century, Edward Waite was a prominent figure of Freemasonry and the *Golden Dawn,* which he attempted to reform by removing many of the magic rituals of the original system. He boldly asserted that there was a secret project within Freemasonry that pursued the attempt to physically reconstruct another temple in Jerusalem. No doubt that this statement constituted, and constitutes to this day, a big problem. In fact, in the mid-seventeenth century, the Dome of the Rock, the Islamic Al-Aqsa Mosque, was built in the square and placed on the mountain of the Temple of Jerusalem. Therefore, any "secret intention" on the part of the present leadership of the Masonic New World Order to rebuild the Temple of Solomon has to inevitably take into account the proposed removal of the above mentioned mosque.

So to summarize what has been said so far: the Freemasons are concerned not only with the symbolic value, but also with the physical *Temple of King Solomon*, and are obsessed toward justifying their intentions for rebuilding a *new one* on the mountain within Jerusalem. The first Temple (also called "Solomon's Temple"), was built around 826 BC and, according to tradition, housed the famous Ark of the Covenant and the miraculous rod of Aaron. It was destroyed by the Babylonians of Nebuchadnezzar II in 586 BC after a period of so-called "Babylonian captivity." But Solomon originally upset the divine plans made for the reconstruction of the Temple, and as he did not follow the original plan of God, subsequently, God destroyed his grand Temple. It was then rebuilt around 515 BC, but the Second Temple (of which the Temple of Herod was an extension), was destroyed in 70 AD by the Romans. What remains today is the Western Wall, also known as the infamous "Wailing Wall."

It is said that with the supposed return of the Messiah, the rebuilding of the Temple in accordance to the original design of God will be realized. Now some of you may certainly remember the rule announced a few years ago by the Jew-Orthodox leadership; that "only the Messiah can rebuild the Temple."

---

1   Edward Waite, A New Encyclopedia of Freemasonry and of Cognate Instituted Mysteries: The Rites, Literature and History, Volume II, (New York, Weathervane Books, reprinted in 1970), pp. 486-7

Referring to a passage of Psalm 127:1, Waite also states that when the Masonic Christ will come, "the Lord will build the house." Well, *at least that's the plan*. We will have to wait to see what will happen, and the implementation and subsequent historical and geopolitical implications this effort will bring about. If the long-awaited Messiah, placed in this unique role, eventually turns out to be the Antichrist (as many claim), certainly we will all witness an unparalleled period in human history.

Let us remember that for some adherents, the Hindu's construct of the universe is only an illusion, known as "Maya." And, although the name Maya is used in different ways by different cultures, the 2012 prophecy could actually have manifested in very different and less obvious ways, and serve the purpose of lifting the veil of illusion that Arthur Schopenhauer (1788-1860) first called *"the effect of the veil of Maya."* He was the first philosopher to use Indian thought, Western terms, and recover from Indian mythology the concept that nature is a veil of Maya.

Nature is one, but it is covered by a flashy veil of colors that implant in us an impression of many beings, plants, animals, and people. In short, a myriad of individual elements that cause us to forfeit our perception behind the oneness of nature. Humanity does not currently grasp nature in unity because we have the veil of Maya deceiving our eyes. In terms less imaginative and more practical, consider that space, time and causality are a filter.

Regarding this, Schopenhauer states that: *"Maya, the veil of illusion, clouds the eyes of mortals and makes them see a world that can not be said to exist or not exist, because it is similar to a dream, to the glitter of sunlight on the sand, which the traveler mistakes from afar for water, or a rope thrown to Earth that he mistakens for a snake."*

Now is the time for the general public to comprehend what is really behind this veil of illusion. Only then will we come to better understand the years prior to 2020, as indicated by many in Illuminati circles as the year of real change toward the implementation of the New World Order, as a time of opportunity for the creation of a better world. There are many who believe that it is in this time that disclosure concerning an alien reality on earth will finally be revealed. A truth which will completely revolutionize and forever change our society and mankind.

The Temple Institute, which is the organization leading the Jewish movement for the construction of its new Jerusalem temple, has already made detailed plans, and provide regular updates, concerning their various "preparatory" activities. So far, the information that has been disclosed paints a striking picture. Some examples include the *"Last Spring,"* announced in 2015, which will be the altar for the future Temple when completed, that is identical in size and characteristics to that which existed at the time of Jesus. Then there is the work of the famous architect Shmuel Balzam, who is developing the blueprints for the temple's Sanctuary. The best goldsmiths of Israel are also faithfully reproducing copies of the furniture and tools used during that sacred period (shovels, basins, trumpets, crowns, cups, censers, candlesticks, and more). They are preparing clothes and ornaments true to tradition, and in 2013, the *"Committee for the Veil"* was created with a team of Jewish women who are weaving a veil that will adorn the temple. In recent years, extensive studies have been made by interested parties in the Jewish community to replicate, with extreme accuracy, the sacred rites of their ancestors. Thanks to sophisticated DNA studies, scientists have been able to trace the male descendants of *Aaron*. These are the only men said to be able to exercise the priestly office in their religious tradition, as well as to revive the famous Ritual of the Red Heifer (Hebrew: פרה אדומה; *parah adumah*). This is also known as the *Ritual of the Red Cow*, where a red cow is brought to the priests as a sacrifice, as according to the Hebrew Bible, and its ashes are to be used for the ritual purification (as prescribed in Chapter 19 of the Book of Numbers), and deemed suitable for service in the Third Temple. After centuries and centuries, the temples re-appearance is considered a sign in anticipation of the next coming of the Messiah.

In short, we are closing in on the so-called end of times ... and every little detail, if properly interpreted, reveals ever more disturbing truths. So, welcome to Volume II of my *Confessions*, where I expose a far different reality then that held within most peoples every day perceptions.

Leo Lyon Zagami

Chapter   I

The Time of Revelation

Awaiting the "Elect" and the so-called "End of Times"

Significantly, the Masonic Bible affirms the fact that the construction of the Temple of King Solomon need wait for the reappearance of a special being. In fact, we find the following words in this foreword on the subject: *"It is known to every reader of the Bible and student of Solomon's days, that an amazingly detailed description of the Temple and its associated structures has been carried down from the mists of antiquity by the Scriptures. Lineal measurements, materials employed, and ornamental detail are so graphically presented that restoration of the Temple, at any time within a score of centuries past, awaited only the coming of a man with the vision to recognize its historic value, and the imagination to undertake the task."* [1]

The key problem for certain Freemasons, and members of the various mystery schools of the Illuminati network, is to reach beyond the speculative and allegorical symbolism that functions as an internal training mechanism for individual Freemasons. The restoration of the Temple of Solomon is a metaphysical event whose occurrence awaits the coming of a very special being during a period in history that Christians define as "Revelation"... a time of apocalyptic catastrophes made less natural, *and a new world war.* Unfortunately, since the rise of Sunni Wahhabi ISIS, and following the Arab Spring and the establishment of puppet governments by the Islamic-fundamentalists, sometimes disguised by moderate Islam, the third war is relentlessly close. Add Turkey to the mix, a country that supports the idea of a Sunni "Caliphate," thus causing a conflict with the Shi'ite Islams, which will extend the war in the Middle East. Between the Sunni and Shia contenders, there is a third element, Israel, which originally helped to establish the Wahhabi doctrine of Sunni Islam. Israel was created by the Zionists and Imperialist Britain, primarily to control this area of deep strategic concern. But now Israel is progressing toward its own destiny... a final confrontation led by elite Zionist Freemasonry, with the international intent to promote the rebuilding of the Temple, *together with Christians.*

---

1   See. John Wesley Kelchner, *The Bible and King Solomon's Temple in Masonry,* (Philadelphia, PA: A. J. Holman Company, 1968).

Building Solomon's Temple was the title of an exhibition that took place a few years ago at the Library and Museum of Freemasonry, presented in the headquarters of English Freemasonry, between the 17th of January and 27th of May, 2011, at Great Queen Street in London (FIG. 3). The leaflet that presented the event acknowledges the fact that civil engineer **Henry Maudslay (1823-1899)** was involved in excavations in the area of the Temple in Jerusalem at the end of the nineteenth century. He sent a shipment of some 47 crates containing pieces of mosaic *stolen* from the Temple by the British, and sent to the headquarters of English Freemasonry to use in a new Masonic structure. A portion of the mosaics in question are present in what many call the center of worldwide Freemasonry, in London, where references to the Temple of Solomon and the Masonic figure of Hiram Abiff (Hiram the king of Tyre, or Hiram, a foreman of outstanding competence from Tyre) are everywhere. I am referring to the headquarters of the **United Grand Lodge of England**, on Great Queen Street, and the imagery por-

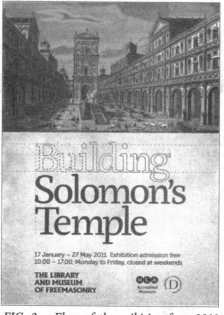

*FIG. 3 – Flyer of the exibition from 2011 entitled **Building Solomon's Temple** held at the Library and Museum of Freemasonry at 60 Great Queen Street London WC2B 5AZ.*

trayed on the huge bronze doors of the Central Temple where, since his installment in 1967, the Duke of Kent, the lodge's longest serving Grand Master, regularly conducts rituals (including those of the Royal Arch). In December, 2013, he celebrated 50 years as a Freemason.

The objects shown in this 2011 exhibition were of great interest from both a historic and ritualistic point of view. Many of the objects and artifacts relate to the first Masonic Lodges in Jerusalem, and others related to the rituals of the **Royal Arch**, which follows the Rite of Perfection in England, for the 3rd degree, and was until 2004 considered by the United Grand Lodge of England a necessary compliment to the Masonic Master Mason degree, a step that was almost mandatory toward a true understanding of the mysteries. This was not the same in the rest of world, where the 3rd grade has always been considered the apex of the system that drives the Craft. On the 10th of November, 2004, after the convocation of the **Supreme Grand Chapter** in London, there was a series of changes, *ostensibly to make the ritual more accessible to new generations and to better adapt to the rest of the Masonic tradition worldwide.* According to some British Freemasons, this was actually done to conceal the true meaning by altering the original content. If interested, you should read the sixth edition of the *Complete Royal Arch Ritual*, published in England by **Lewis Masonic**. The Royal Arch imprints its Masonic allegory and symbolism on the discovery of a secret room located beneath the Temple of Solomon during the reign of Zerubbabel; who was the head of the tribe of Judah during the time of the return from Babylon exile. In this secret place, it is still revealed—*at least in those traditional chapters, or the ones that are part of the American York Rite, which never followed the ongoing reviews in the English system*—The existence of a **"omnific word,"** which is the lost name of God. The name in question is revealed to the candidate in the mysteries as **JAH-BUL-ON,** which for English Freemasonry means *"I am and shall be Lord in Heaven on High, the Powerful, the Father of all."*

In Aleister Crowley's book, *The Confessions of Aleister Crowley,* he spoke with great admiration about the Royal Arch degree: *"I supposed myself to have reached the summit of success when I restored the Secret Word of the Royal Arch. In this case, tradition had preserved the Word almost intact."* It seems perfectly understandable that this hater of Christianity would love the Royal Arch degree of Freemasonry, as the Freemasons in this degree actually seem to blaspheme the God of the Bible. They form God's name by uniting together the name of various pagan gods, (Masonic writers agree that this is a composite of three gods). Jah represents Jehovah, Bul represents the pagan god **Baal**, and **On** represents the Egyptian sun god **Osiris**. This name and its true meaning have been omitted from the English Supreme Grand Chapter after the major revision of 2004, *ostensibly to streamline the system in the eyes of young Masons.* This is something the infamous **Ordo Templi Orientis (O.T.O.)** did not comply with, as they kept their own version of the Royal Arch going. In *their* para-Masonic system, the 4th degree is a Crowleyan version known as the **"Royal Arch of Enoch"** ... of course, inclusive of JAH-BUL-ON.

The Royal Arch was also particularly appreciated by Alberto Moscato (now deceased), The former head of the O.T.O., Moscato, a 33° of the Ancient and Accepted Scottish Rite, once invited me to his O.T.O. Lodge in Rome, known as Khem Lodge, to participate in the *Royal Arch works* during a plenary session of the O.T.O. 4th degree, activities that he considered to be of great importance to his mystery school. When he died from a heroin overdose on the 2nd of April 2006, he was well-known in the field of Crowleyanity and magical experimentation, which he conducted with rigorous scientific methodology during his period as leader of the O.T.O.

I have studied various researchers and historians of Freemasonry and the O.T.O., such as Francis King, and JAH turns out to be God's name as it appears in Psalm 68, and means "the highest." It is so sacred to the Jews that it cannot be mentioned in full. BAAL is a name in certain Asian cultures that describes the Lord of all things, and in Egyptian, ON is simply the name of the Sun, *the Lord of us all,* and was used by the priests of Heliopolis.

ON, who is Osiris, is also the secret name of God given to Minerval's (introductory initiates) of the O.T.O. However, this term is judged by outsiders of Freemasonry, and in particular, American fundamentalist Christians, to be *rather pagan* and inconsistent with the Christianity followed by many of its members. Curiously enough, the Rastafari tradition consistently use "Jah" in their terminology. In this case, it is simply another name used to refer to the last emperor of Ethiopia, the central figure of the modern religion of Rastafari, which has very little paganism in its faith, and as we know, was popularized worldwide by the famous singer **Bob Marley.**

It has been said, in fact, that the Rastafarian religion has used the name *Jah* to define the Creator ... not because it exists in a specific passage of the Bible (as in Psalm 68, mentioned above), but extrapolated instead from **Jah-Bul-On**... *the lost word "rediscovered" by the Arch Royal Master Mason.* This may have transpired as a result of the influence of **Archibald Dunkey** and **Joseph Nathaniel Hibbert,** the first preachers who inspired the Rasta religion. Apparently, they began this new religious trend while active members of a para-Masonic order known as the **Ancient Mystic Order of Ethiopia,** this derived from a form of Freemasonry founded within the United States' black community, called *Prince Hall.* This thesis is also suggested by David Spencer, in his book *Dread Jesus.* [2]

2 See. William David Spencer, **Dread Jesus,** (London: SPCK Publishing, 1998).

The Rastafarian religion is nothing but a mixture of the *best* forms of Christianity and Judaism, but there are definitely a few people who know that Rastafari is a new Abrahamic belief created within Freemasonry that, unfortunately, as I will describe to you later on, has a rather complex and often hypocritical stand toward soft drugs that are popular with Rastafarians, like marijuana. In this regard, I really admire the calm and tranquility of the only "stoned" religion on Earth, one that is dedicated to **Emperor Haile Selassie** who, of course, succeeds from a "Holy bloodline." In Ethiopian tradition, **Ras Tafari Makonnen** was crowned Emperor with the new name of Haile Selassie I, the 225th descendant of the Solomonic Dynasty through the line of David, belonging to the tribe of Judah.

In an ancient Ethiopian sacred text called *Kebra Nagast,* the Queen of Sheba (i.e. Ethiopia), named Makeda, met King Solomon (an event described in the Bible, 1 Kings 10; 2 Chronicles 9), and together they had a son. Their firstborn was crowned with the title of King Menyelek I (or Menelik I), and it is from this sovereign, and through 224 generations, that **Haile Selassie I** would ascend. According to the Rastafari, the *Book of Revelation* refers directly to Haile Selassie. The Rastafarian Armageddon as a theological concept, is a little different, and does not indicate a battle at a place and at a specific time, but rather, identifies with the general degenerate state in which we now find the world. However, the role of Selassie in Ethiopia is seen by Rastafarians as the fulfillment of some important prophecies. Let us not forget, Haile Selassie is an Ethiopian descendant of King Solomon, and Soloman, the founder of the Temple, is at the core of what became the heart of the Global Initiatic System (modern Speculative Freemasonry). This system, because of its so-called universality, is *a Universal Initiatic Order, both regular and irregular,* and has become the ideal medium of exploitation driving the occult forces behind the New World Order—*in all its many facets and emanations, even the most improbable.*

The rise of the dragon and the Tibetan Lama mercenaries

The Leopard, the Bear and Lion are animals that we find in the symbolism of North European Freemasonry. Let us first explore the *Dragon.* There are various forms of Freemasonry: The Muslims, who gave birth to the famous Society of the Muslim Brotherhood; the Catholics, who are a part of the Jesuit matrix; and, the Jewish Zionists, who are always present at the summits of earthly power as being the main influences behind the Occult Government, toward the creation of a One World Government. This, at least, was until the recent rise of so-called "Irregular" Chinese Freemasonry; and the **Hogmen** (the "Great Gate"), or the **Hung Mun** (the "Red Gate"), that are not recognized as "Regular Masonry," or even as "Masonry," by the rest of the Masonic world ... and for this reason they remain, a mysterious subject.

I would like to stress that the Chinese tradition is not linked to the legend of the Temple of King Solomon—nor to any element of the Masonic Judeo-Christian tradition. Given their historical and religious backgrounds, this seems natural, as the Hongmen and Sanheui (Three Harmonies Society, or the Triad) originally derive from a secret society called **Tiandihui**, namely, *Company of Heaven and Earth.* According to Kelvin Bechkam Chow, a member of the organization, the latter was founded during the reign of Emperor Kangxi (1654-1722), and independent research, verified by Wikipedia, concluded that Tiandihui was officially founded only around 1760. According to the legends origins, this mystery school was created by five Shaolin monks known as "the five elderly." They are known, for example, as "the five elderly of kung fu," with the names: Ji Sin, Ng Mui, Bak Mei, Fung Dou Dak, and Miu Hin. The Triads call them **"the five elders of the Triads,"** and their names are: Dak Choi Jung, Daai Fong Hung, But Chiu Hing, wu Dak Tai, and Lei Sik. Even the founders of the largest martial arts families in southern China refer to the legends five elders, and are a recurring theme in the initiatic tradition of China.

According to experts in the history of these mysterious kung fu monks, they survived a terrible massacre that despoiled their Shaolin monastery in 1647, immediately following the reign of the Ming dynasty (which lasted until 1644). During the reign of Emperor Kangxi they were then joined by the loyalists of the Ming Dynasty, and became a secret revolution that, *unfortunately and out of desperation and necessity,* gave way to the involvement in criminal acts. This is partly due to the fact that they were persecuted. As such, they could not perform ordinary jobs, and the eventual result was the creation of the notorious *Chinese Triads.* Indeed, the Triads were dedicated to one single goal: making money. This, ironically, helped the Chinese accomplish their relentless expansion, and hence, to become the world's *third pole* of the New World Order ... *after the Jesuits and the Zionists.* The Jesuits, however, have a long history of involvement in China, an involvement that began during the time of the Jesuit Saint, Francis Xavier, aka Francisco de Jaso y Javier (1506-1552), and also the Jesuit missionary Father **Matteo Ricci** (1552-1610). As written by the Jesuit Francesco Occhetta: *"The apostolic mission of Ricci should be seen in that of the Society of Jesus in the Far East, started by Francesco Saverio who was the founder and organizer of all missions in East Asia, including China, although he died in Shangchuan o Sancian in 1552, on the threshold of China. Xavier was pushed to China, when he discovered that the Japanese were dependent on Chinese culture."* [3]

At the center of these legends of "Chinese Freemasonry," there is a temple in the South, *Nan Shaolinsi,* whose location is still being searched for. It is believed that this temple was in Fujian Province (also known as Fukien) on the southeast coast of China, and more specifically, in the vicinity of the city of Quanzhou (Chuan Chow), located at the strait that separates China from the island of Taiwan.

This city still plays a very important and strategic role for the Freemasonry *of the Chinese Hongmen* where, unlike in Hong Kong, they are not only accepted, but reside at the very top of society, and who hold a more political and philanthropic role (very similar to regular Freemasonry).

The most illustrious member of this secret society was **Sun Yat-Sen**, one of the most important Chinese revolutionaries, and who was among the first to propose the overthrow of the Chinese Empire. He is considered the founder of modern China by both the Republic of China and Taiwan. Nowadays, Sun Yat-Sen descendants live outside of China in the West, and are apparently linked to bonds seized in Chiasso, Italy, in June 2009 (a story made popular by researcher **Benjamin Fulford**), which I'll discuss in more detail at the end of the book. The information above was confirmed by the financial advisor and Freemason Vincenzo Mazzara, who, in February 2012, was contacted by the family of Sun Yat-Sen in Milan to see if an understanding could be reached between the parties involved—to recover those famous bonds. The offer however, was declined, because it was deemed unenforceable by the authorities who to this day, still hold the mysterious bonds.

So what is the role of Chinese Freemasonry in the powerful People's Republic of China? In China, the most influential and legitimate form of "Chinese Freemasonry" is the Hongmen, who manifested in what is now known as the China Zhi Gong Party, and now a major political player that actively participates in the political life of China, in a context that we all know hosts very little democratic debate. Wan Gang, the vice president of the Zhi Gong Party, was the only non-Communist minister of the Chinese government in 2012. Apart from their communist façade, this clearly demonstrates the

3 http://www.francescooocchetta.it/wordpress/?p=190 ‡ Archived 24th June 2015.

power and direct influence of "Chinese Freemasonry." Strangely enough, the Zhi Gong Party was founded in San Francisco, California, with the blessing of the elite and rich Chinese Freemasons living oversees who helped to finance this socialist/Masonic party constructed to embrace the New World Order.

This is a small extract from a brief presentation on their website, which demonstrates a clear picture of their elitist nature and their links to the Chinese present in the USA:

The China Zhi Gong Party is mainly composed of the upper and middle classes of returned overseas Chinese and their relatives, as well as other noted figures who have overseas ties. It is a party of political alliance that is committed to developing socialism with Chinese characteristics. The China Zhi Gong Party was founded in October, 1925 in San Francisco, USA, by the American Zhi Gong Tang, an overseas Chinese society. Since its establishment, the China Zhi Gong Party has been committed to safeguarding the legitimate rights and interests of overseas Chinese, paying attention to national independence and the prosperity of the country. After the breakout of the War of Resistance against Japan, the China Zhi Gong Party called on all its members to actively support the anti-Japanese struggle in the motherland. In May 1947, the China Zhi Gong Party held its third congress in Hong Kong and reorganized itself. Ever since then, the party has worked together with the Communist Party of China and embarked on the road to a new democratic revolution. It has made positive contributions to a new democratic revolution and the founding of a New China, to the undertakings of socialist revolution and construction, and to the promotion of reform and open-up the cause for the reunification of the motherland. Taking the Constitution of the People's Republic of China as the fundamental guiding principle, the China Zhi Gong Party has conducted activities independently.

Over a long period of time, the China Zhi Gong Party, as a party participating in state and political affairs, has always upheld and improved the system of multiparty cooperation and political consultation under the leadership of the Communist Party of China, and has played an important role in the political life of the state. The China Zhi Gong Party has participated in state power and consultation of state policies and selection of candidates of state leaders. It has participated in the administration of state affairs and the formulation and implementation of state policies, laws and regulations. It has played an active role in democratic supervision and contributed a lot to making the decision-making of the state more democratic and scientific. Closely focusing on the central task of the social and economic development, the China Zhi Gong Party has worked hard for the acceleration of reform, to open-up to modernization, as well as for the establishment and improvement of the socialist market economic system. It has safeguarded the legitimate rights and interests of returned overseas Chinese and their relatives, as well as those of overseas Chinese, and has taken active measures to convey their opinions and reasonable requirements to the government. It has conducted extensive social activities and exchanges with overseas Chinese, overseas students and scholars and the compatriots of Hong Kong, Macao and Taiwan in an attempt to make friends with people from all walks of life and promote the cause of the peaceful reunification of the motherland. Meanwhile, it has done a good job in exchanges and introduction of talents and expertise in the fields of economy, science and technology, education and culture. It has been engaged in friendly activities with foreign countries and academic exchanges and cooperation with the rest of the world, so as to further deepen the understanding and strengthen the friendship between the Chinese people and the people in other countries. Since China introduced reform, the China Zhi Gong Party has fully taken advantage of its extensive ties overseas to actively conduct multi-tier, multi-channel social activities with overseas friends in various fields. Through the exchange of visits and other forms of contacts, the party has made friends with people from all walks of life and promoted friendship. It has helped introduce overseas funds and donations and energetically supported activities of public interests at home, including the building of hospitals, schools, the fight against poverty and disaster-relief. It has also provided assistance to overseas Chinese, foreign friends and international institutions in making investments in China, conducting activities serving public interests.

To date, the China Zhi Gong Party has established extensive ties with overseas institutions and personalities including the Freemason Society in more than 40 countries and regions on the five continents of the world. [4]

By their own words it is evident that even if not officially recognized by "Regular Freemasonry," the Zhi Gong Party enjoy "extensive ties" with Freemasons in 40 countries around the world.

Returning to the criminal side of the Triads, and the role played by its most important strategic centers, we find Macau, a small territory overlooking the Chinese Sea that was a Portuguese colony until December 1999, when it became a *Special Administrative Region* (SAR) following the system of "one country, two systems" already adopted for Hong Kong.

In the second half of the 1990s, an Italian journalist named Riccardo Cascioli wrote an article entitled, *What scenario after Hong Kong? Beijing and the dream of a great China.* In the section called "Mafia and Crime," he writes:

Macau, if not a paradise, is a kingdom of criminals after they officialized their return to China, with the announcement of an end to the monopoly of casinos planned for 2001. It is here that the government of China is facing a complicated challenge. The ten "sanctuaries" of gambling spread around Macao are indeed the greatest economic resource of the area, with revenues in excess of two billion U.S. dollars a year, half of which go to fatten the state treasury while the rest contributes the fortune of one family, whose patriarch is Stanley Ho, 75, who for 36 years is the undisputed king of the casino business. Just the lure of money from gambling, combined with new projects arising from the end of the monopoly, attracted to Macau the "Triads," the Chinese mafia, in growing numbers which are transforming the area into a veritable battlefield. From October to January '96, 25 people were killed in Macao according to the rituals of the Triads, and they have multiplied bombings to private residences, jewelers and even McDonald's restaurants. Indeed, at the end of last year, an armed mob ambushed Colonel Manuel Apolinario (who escaped death by a miracle), was commissioned by the Portuguese government to view the casino industry: it was the first attack to a Portuguese official since 1849, an ominous sign of the degeneration of the situation.

What was described is certainly a scenario with disturbing implications, but China quickly solved things in Macao, thanks to the organizational skills and influence of Chinese Freemasonry over the Triads in those territories, where problems are resolved in the name of economic interest. In this scenario, unprecedented for China, an important role was also orchestrated by the Chinese military Intelligence, *Er Bu*, "**The Department**," which exclusively deals with Hong Kong and Macau through a special working group called "**Autumn Orchid**," and includes members of the Zhi Gong Party and high level Freemasons of the Hong Men.

4   http://www.chinazhigongparty.org.cn/zgparty/party/ ‡ Archived 24th June 2015.

The powerful Stanley Ho, who reached the ripe old age of ninety, with an estimated fortune of $3.1 billion, continues to be dominant, yet recent scandals have deprived the king of the Macau casinos of a huge fortune. More than ever, the Macau of today is the center of a billionaire gambling ring. It is the most profitable side of Chinese Freemasonry and its Chinese Triads, who have, since 2001, joined forces with the powerful U.S. Illuminati arm called the **Galaxy Group**, including the Jewish American **Steve Wynn**. Wynn was born Stephen Alan Weinberg in New Haven, Connecticut, but his father Michael, in 1946, conveniently changed the family name from Weinberg to Wynn when Steve was only six months old, and he became what some call a *Crypto-Jew*.

In 2015, Bloomberg reported that: *"Steve Wynn has called on Macau's government to provide clarity on plans for the Chinese city as his casino company cut its dividend and China's anti-corruption drive slashes profits."* So, things basically seem to be changing in Macau as President Xi Jinping, elected in 2013, *"began a campaign on graft that snared thousands of officials, prompting many wealthy Chinese to cut back on conspicuous consumption and stay away from the world's largest gambling hub."*[5]

According to the new dictates of the New World Order, Steve Wynn was also the first to install the famous microchip technology RFID (Radio Frequency Identification) in his mega-center of entertainment in Las Vegas, where RFID devices will be added to the Wynn chips in order to signal secret serial numbers to casino computers, which in turn will keep track of who is betting what, who owes what to whom, and who is trying to count cards. Furthermore, it looks like spurious chips won't be a factor at Wynn Vegas—as it is difficult to copy a computerized casino chip.[6]

Located in the 29th of January, 2011, foreign edition of the Italian newspaper *La Stampa* website (Stampa.it), we can examine the situation in Macau after the arrival of Wynn and his partners:

In 2001, Beijing authorized a big American gambling business a chance to land in Macau, where they brought all the excesses of Las Vegas. Steve Wynn, and his Galaxy group, have recreated Venice in Las Vegas and in Macau. ... To keep up, the casinos of Stanley Ho have been modernized and enriched with sequined dancers and features of USA gambling. The American competition has not brought excessive problems: as it is the only town in the whole of China where gambling is legal, and earnings have always been insured. As China's economy grows, the number of visitors to Macau also grows, and the "VIP rooms" (where the minimum bet is several thousand Euros) are always booked. In 2006, Macau surpassed the gains in Las Vegas. Last year, Stanley Ho's only casino made more money than the entire American capital of gambling.[7]

Together with Macau, of course, there is Hong Kong, a focal point for Asian high finance, and that, in 1847, was considered to be the strategic center of the *Triads*. On Wikipedia, under **"Triad (criminal organization),"** we find:

In the 1760s, the Heaven and Earth Society, a fraternal organization, was founded, and as the society's influence spread throughout China, it branched into several smaller groups with different names, one of which was Three Harmonies Society. These soci-

5   http://www.bloomberg.com/news/articles/2015-04-29/wynn-macau-dip-7-as-parent-cut-dividend-on-city-s-casino-risks ‡ Archived 24th June 2015.

6   http://www.hotelchatter.com/story/2005/2/13/215642/117/hotels/RFID_wynn_win%3F ‡ Archived 24th June 2015.

7   http://www.lastampa.it/2011/01/29/esteri/il-re-dei-casino-di-macao-ripulito-dalla-terza-moglie-7R6UIIYuewVbbgntnPdy8K/pagina.html ‡ Archived 24th June 2015.

eties adopted the triangle as their emblem, usually accompanied by decorative images of swords or portraits of Guan Yu. Their aim was to overthrow the Qing Dynasty and restore the Ming Dynasty. ... The term "Triad" was assumed to be coined by British authorities in colonial Hong Kong, as a reference to the triads' use of triangular imagery.

The Triads have definite criminal and mafiosi undertones, but only after an "underground" period of profound spirituality and religiosity. The Shaolin monks are in fact the Eastern version of our Western monks, those who helped create Speculative Freemasonry in the West. So parallels between the two are certainly not lacking, at least considering the legends upon which these origins are based. Although the English Wikipedia, under *"Tiandihui,"* specifies: *"Ethical systems have different origins and different purposes"* ... during the period when Hong Kong was under the colonial rule of the British Empire, which was extended until 1997... all the secret societies and Chinese Freemasonry were, without any distinction, accused, sometimes unfairly, of being Branches of the Chinese underworld and organized crime, even *as I will demonstrate later,* the reality was quite different. A ban to unite and officially exist still persists in Hong Kong—even after the changing of the guard within China toward Hongmen Chinese Freemasonry. The latter has not always been linked to the power games of Beijing, and it is sometimes perceived by the Chinese authorities as dangerous and not "patriotic," specifically for constructing secret agreements with Western intelligence agencies and foreign governments with the intention to become a leading player in international crime linked to the lucrative drug trade, that began with opium, which as you may know, was the first drug to enrich the Illuminati elite.

The drug trade also contributed to the foundation of famous American universities, and even to secret societies like the **Skull and Bones** at Yale University, which boasts as one its founders William Huntington Russell, cousin of Samuel Wadsworth Russell, founder of Russell & Company, the largest and most important importer of opium from China from 1842 to 1891, despite the drug being illegal even back then. In fact the Opium Wars, which took place from 1839 to 1842, and from 1856 to 1860, respectively, saw the Chinese empire under the Qing Dynasty wage wars against Great Britain in response to the commercial penetration of the British, who had opened the Chinese market to opium from British India. This resulted in China tightening their prohibitions with respect to this drug, thereby triggering the conflict. The defeat of the Chinese in both wars forced China to tolerate the opium trade, and to sign treaties with the British in Nanjing and in Tianjin, which included the opening of new ports of trade and the transfer from Hong Kong to the United Kingdom. In short, the Chinese Freemasons might not always be the good guys, but they are not any worse than the British or the Americans, who for centuries unscrupulously exploited the drug trade to finance their New World Order, as they do to this day.

For this reason, the Hong Kong police found it very difficult to oppose and fight the Triads, who had the backing of the elite of the Western secret societies of the Illuminati Network, including Hong Kong's top influential people and untouchables. From the thirties until the early eighties, in the United States, there was a popular culture figure who inspired a number of *seemingly racist* pulp fiction books, movies and TV shows, which dealt with this issue as fiction. I'm talking of the famous *adventures of Dr. Fu Manchu,* which have gradually disappeared from popular culture, ostensibly, because they conveyed a stereotypical image of the Chinese community, that associated it to the world of organized crime and secret societies. That's why the Chinese U.S. lobby, growing ever more powerful, in 1972, blocked the planned broadcast for television of the 1966 film, *The wives of Fu Manchu.*

Years before the 1959 film *The Manchurian Candidate* was released, which gave a fictional depiction of the process of mind control among U.S. POW's during the Korean Conflict, the nature of mind control via hypnosis and drugs was already being explored in the literary imaginings of Sax Rohmer, author of the Fu Manchu series. In one such book published in 1936, *President Fu Manchu* the Chinese villain, attempts to influence the U.S. Presidential election. As part of the plot, a gangster's bodyguard is drugged and hypnotized into committing murder at a given signal. The scene describes a fictional mind control procedure which is not too far away from what the CIA attempted with MK-ULTRA, demonstrating the possibility that the Chinese Illuminati had this kind of knowledge a long time before the CIA:

> *The snaky yellow fingers of Dr. Fu Manchu held a needle syringe. He made a quick injection and studied the motionless man before him. Then, with a delicate atomizer, Dr. Fu Manchu shot sprays up the left and right nostrils of the unconscious victim.*

> *Ten seconds later Herman Grosset sat suddenly upright, staring wildly ahead. His gaze was caught and helped by green compelling eyes only inches from his own.*

> *"You understand"—the strange voice spoke slowly: "The word of command is 'Asia!'" "I understand" Grosset replied.*

> *"The word," Dr. Fu Manchu intoned hypnotically, "is 'Asia.'"*

> *"Asia," Grosset echoed.*

> *"Until you hear that word,"—the voice seemed to come from the depths of a green lake—"forget, forget all that you have to do."*

> *"I have forgotten."*

> *"But when you hear the word?"*

> *"I shall kill!"*

There is a possibility that Sax Rohmer's words were piloted by a strange career that revolved around the "Yellow Peril Scare," a racist doctrine popularly promoted by Western Powers as a means to justify the subjugation of East Asia by Euro-American interests. a bit like what is happening now with Colbert I. King, as defined in a December, 2015 article in *The Washington Post* entitled: "the Islamic Scare era." Rohmer's depiction of East Asians as being conniving, secretive plotters, fit perfectly into the propaganda program initiated by the West. In his writings, Rohmer may have been repeating stories he heard concerning the nature of mind control from various British Intelligence agents. Rohmer's interest in mysticism and esotericism caused him to join the occult organization of the Hermetic Order of the Golden Dawn, and he worked for both British and American Intelligence agencies during WWI and WWII where he may have been privy to, and picked up, brainwashing-*type* techniques from the secretive and highly elusive world of Chinese secret societies.

Understanding then what is now apparent concerning this co-mingling of interests and power in the secret world of the Chinese Triads and their "Freemasonry" was literally impossible after the 1941-1945 break, which saw Japanese employment in Hong Kong. Margaret Di Canio describes the difficulty in finding evidence and understanding the true history of the Triads, in the book *Encyclopedia Of Violence: Frequent, Commonplace, Unexpected*, when she writes: "*...was mainly due to the fact that the most influential Chinese Triads of that time reached a secret agreement with the Japanese for the total destruction of all the research material on the Chinese secret societies collected by British police since 1842, eliminating every trace of those dangerous criminal links that by opium and other means of interests bound them secretly to the West, and the* *structure of hidden power that lay behind it."* [8]

An agreement to make a *clean sweep* of the cumbersome past was made possible for "Chinese Freemasonry" only by virtue of a privileged relationship with the Japanese empire, and in particular with the Secret Society of the **Black Dragon**, which at that time dominated the Empire of the Rising Sun and its elite. It is also true that the world of Asian secret societies, including China, is not always so murky and criminal. Some societies have nothing criminal in their practices and objectives.

These are dedicated to guard the secrets of certain martial arts; to preserve other forms of transcendental meditation, magic, divination and spiritual elevation, and often arise from merging Chinese Taoism, Chinese Buddhism, and sometimes a *mix of both seasoned with elements of confucianism.* In order to avoid persecution, all were forced, to hide and to *go underground,* as they say, where they reconstituted as secret societies.

Regarding the practice of inner-alchemy in China, these practices are well-known through the success of disciplines such as Qigong, for example, that is said to have a three thousand year history. Then there are traditions and secret societies that sprung up from Chinese Buddhism, and the influence of the Shaolin monks, now widely considered martial arts *par excellence:* the art of kung fu. The Shaolin devoted themselves to the study of this discipline without implication to the criminal lodges of the Hung Mun, and Chinese Freemasonry in the United States, Canada and other parts of the world. Recently, I had a chat with a friend who is initiated into Chinese Freemasonry, named Frankie McCarthy, who belongs to the Hung Mun **Jung Tong Kung Ghee,** and we spoke of the origins of his lodge in relation to the five founding fathers of the Hung Mun, and he wrote to me: *"Many styles of southern kung fu were members of the Hung Mun. My kung fu lineage has members since 1851, as our founder was a student of one of the five Hung Mun founders."*

The President of the Hung Mun Jung Tong Kung Ghee is a controversial figure in the USA, who I believe is on his way to purification in regards to his past, although some of the media say the opposite. He is a former *gangster* and former Dragon of one of the most feared Triads in the United States of America. **Raymond Chow,** known also as Shrimp Boy, now repentant, and leader of what is described as an honest organization for charitable purposes, the Hung Mun Jung Tong Kung Ghee mentioned above. I want to thank Frankie McCarthy who is one of the few Americans to gain entry into Hung Mun "Chinese Freemasonry," which is dedicated to the preservation and teaching of secret techniques and forms of Chinese martial arts, for introducing me to the good side of their mysterious "Chinese Freemasonry," which certainly exists and is dedicated (in this case, at least) to the recovery of the most hardened criminals. **Raymond Chow,** who despite doubts and criticism in the American press, and the ostracism of U.S. authorities who tried for years to nail him, and finally did convict him of murder and other charges in January, 2016, had stated that he was willing to help his community in a noble way after sincere repentance. So the Hung Mun Tong Ghee Kung Jung seem to have nothing to do with the corruption and wickedness of Chinese organized crime, except in a very marginal way, especially when compared to traditional Triads that, as I will also demonstrate in the last chapter, have become part of the apex of power called the New World Order.

I want to emphasize this important fact so that the reader will understand that it is important to not think of Chinese Freemasonry, or the Chinese, whom I personally admire, as a single entity—as evil, as I previously mentioned in relation to Western Freemasonry.

8   Margaret Di Canio, *Encyclopedia Of Violence: Frequent, Commonplace, Unexpected.* (New York: Facts on File, 1993), p. 319.

While there are families and individual Masonic lodges engaged in a path toward the improvement of the individual, others (the majority) are lost in the delusions of the physical realm, are corrupted by material things, and are often drunk with a Satanism that helps them to "ride the tiger." In short, it is no coincidence that their leaders call themselves Dragons. The dragon, in the *Apocalypse* of St. John, is one of the greatest representations of evil. But St. George dominates the dragon, a symbol that, among others, we find in the *The Most Noble Order of the Garter,* itself being the oldest and highest order of knighthood in the United Kingdom, dating back to the Middle Ages, and kept under control, if only superficially, until 1997. The inexorable rise to global power that English expert Martin Booth describes as "The Dragon Syndicates" is an excellent essay on the Triads, and contains some good information about the lesser known side of this global phenomenon:

> *The common element that links the* **Hong Mun Hong Men** *or other realities called "Hung,"* writes Martin Booth in his essay, *is the bond with the legendary Shaolin monks, from which even the Hung Mun and in general the Triads say they descend— with a few minor variations, probably due to oral transmission only of ritual—and the first name of these Brotherhoods, shows the great respect for the first emperor of the Ming era, the legendary Hongwu, also known as the Hung wu (1328-1398). Hence the first name or Hong Hung.* [9]

Hung Wu is a special character in history, as one who took on the role of father and reformer of the Chinese Empire after the "Mongol" period of the Yuan Dynasty. Within the Chinese initiatic tradition, he is someone to be admired... a sort of Chinese *King Solomon.* It is understood that he had the gift of prophecy and foresaw the future. His name alone inspired terror in his opponents, and it is still used by the practioners of these secret societies as a mantra that is recited when entering into a meditative state of *communion* with the heavens and the universe. This is similar to the O.T.O. ritual practice of reciting the name of King Solomon.

If delivered in English, *Solomon* is broken up into three distinct parts: **SOL-OM-ON.** As you will see, this delivers a surprising result. It includes the Latin name of the Sun, **SOL; OM,** the classical syllable of incantation considered sacred in Hinduism and Mahayana Buddhism; and, ON, the meaning of which being related to Osiris and the Sun, all of which I have previously discussed in relation to the name **JAH-BUL-ON.**

So, there is **"Chinese Freemasonry,"** devoted to the Triads and their crime, and there are others that arise in contrast—often helping Chinese youth (and others) who have had problems with the law and the notorious *gang culture*—that, thanks to the discipline of their spirituality and martial arts, provide great benefits to the communities around them.

Chinese Freemasonry, however, is different than Western Freemasonry, but only in appearance. Since we know that there are Freemasons "in odor of sanctity" in the West; among "Chinese Freemasonry," and the so-called *regular Freemasonry,* there are commonalities like the monastic origins of the two, the concept of "Brotherhood," and the practice of mutual assistance among members. Of course the differences between the two are also huge, and careful historical analysis suggests that at one point the Chinese simply "replicated" the central symbols of Western Freemasonry and applied them to Chinese secret societies with great success (including the criminals and evil ones), and cleaving to the typical Chinese tradition of "copying," or should I say, *faithfully reproducing*, what is produced in the West, including Freemasonry.

9   See. Martin Booth, **The Dragon Syndacates,** (London:Double Day-Transworld Publishers LTD, 1999).

This is something that "Regular" Freemasonry still cannot fully digest, as you will discover if you visit the prestigious Canadian Masonic Grand Lodge of British Columbia and the Yukon web site on the subject of **Chinese Freemasons:**

http://freemasonry.bcy.ca/societies/chinese_freemasons/index.html

There is sharp criticism of so-called "Chinese Freemasonry," as it is accused of adopting the name and main symbols of Western Freemasonry without any historical justification. If you wish to further deepen your research, I suggest a visit to this Masonic site:

http://www.freemasons-freemasonry.com/chinese-masonic-society.html

China and its secret societies are certainly the odd-man-out in this struggle for the creation of a One World government, and it is important that we investigate the Chinese influence. It is equally important to not fall into the Chinese Freemasonic trap, as my collegue and past acquaintance Benjamin Fulford seems to have done. Fulford, is a controversial figure, who I will discuss later in this book; to better explain who is behind certain misinformation on the internet, and the danger presented by its hidden manipulators.

For many years there have been contacts and stable relations between the leaders of "Western Illuminati networks" and "Chinese Freemasonry." This is something I can confirm from my own personal experience. The Western Illuminati, especially the Americans, are the driving force behind occult globalization. They use the military, politicians, and lobbyists to seal strategic alliances between the powerful, well beyond religious or political beliefs. Their ultimate goal is what matters: the creation of a One World Government, nothing more or less. Obviously, they are turning to China, and the China Zhi Gong Party, to be a potential ally in their plan to install a dictatorship on a global scale.

This complex operation is implemented with a methodology that has developed with increasing intensity, through chosen emissaries to China, since the early seventies. This was mentioned in my interview with John Compact, known as Frater Arthur, a high priest of the Bohemian Grove, an apparently innocent *"Pythagorean,"* a member of the Rosicrucian *Ordo Rosae Aureae,* and in reality a dangerous magician belonging to the dark side of Martinism who is deeply involved in witchcraft and is a follower of contemporary occultist **Andrew D. Chumbley.**

Compact, as a "High Priest" of the Bohemian Grove, is therefore well-informed about secret projects of the elite in relation to China. It is worth noting that **Henry Kissinger (b. 1923)** is a prominent member of this prestigious *Club of San Francisco.* The Illuminati behind Freemasonry today seem not too troubled by the fact that the Chinese have copied the name and symbols of "Freemasonry." Let us remember, Freemasonry did similar things in the past when creating *para-* and *pseudo-*Masonic orders, all born within Freemasonry, and often modeled on their symbols, ways, and customs. Adam Weishaupt was among those like Aleister Crowely, with his reform of the *Ordo Templi Orientis* (O.T.O.), which was reprimanded by Freemasonry during Crowley's stay in Detroit, in 1919, for blatantly copying their rituals. This made Crowley quickly rewrite some of the content to not further anger the local Masonic authorities who had accused him of plagiarism. This was after his attempt, which I will return to later, to gain control of the Supreme Council of the *Ancient and Accepted Scottish Rite* in Detroit.

Currently, the elite of Freemasonry—those who practice the Craft in the powerful transnational Ur Lodges, and the Western Illuminati—just want to maintain a good business relationship with Chinese Freemasonry. It is worth noting that the Dalai Lama "theater" has gradually been exposed for what it is … *a cauldron of interests* … that only serves as a smokescreen for unlikely and unnecessary opposition in Tibet against the Chinese giant. We've known for years that Chinese leaders are methodically and violently destroying Tibetan culture, which they consider subversive and highly dangerous. This is not only because it is secretly manipulated by the Western Illuminati, but also against the occult practices of Tibetan shamanic tradition (**Bon Pa**). This practice was absorbed in the West when brought in during the last century by the Nazi Illuminati. In 2002, an article by Pierangelo Giovanetti was published that detailed a project devised by Professor Giuliano Di Bernardo, past Grand Master of Italian Freemasonry, that had abandoned Masonry, and fully embraced the Illuminati when founding their Academy in Rome.

The article is entitled, *Goodbye Freemasonry. Giuliano Di Bernardo, former Grand Master, launches its new structure*. The following is a key passage:

> An international structure "made up exclusively of men of quality, expression of science, economics, politics of religion, to come up with a new project for humanity." A supreme entity for "summits," involving countries such as Italy, Brazil, Switzerland, Ukraine, Yemen and China and of which he, Giuliano Di Bernardo, Professor of Philosophy of Science, from the University of Trento, will be the international president. An entity, which for now is called "structure," in which they are already involved "prominent international personalities" and will be financed "by organizations that believe in the project." It is the former Grand Master of the Grand Orient of Italy, the most important Italian Masonic Obedience, to give notice of is decision of leaving Freemasonry ("in fact I abandoned it to create something bigger") and venture into a new plan "the progress towards the supreme being in a new brotherhood of man, who knows how to respond to the world after September 11." [10]

In short, it seems pretty clear where all this is headed. It is also evident that the turning point for the Illuminati was September 11, 2001. Professor Giuliano Di Bernardo, who I will discuss in depth later, is a major advocate of the rebuilding of the Temple of Solomon. I wonder if he can convince the Chinese to climb on board? I already imagine the model of the Temple, "made in China," as an exact copy, possibly located in Shanghai, where the enlightened elite would feel more at ease these days than Jerusalem, with the beautiful firework displays as only the Chinese can do, and the *possible appearance* of the Compass and Square in the sky as the Grand Finale. I apologize for the fanciful picture, but even this seems plausible during this strange era for humanity, where we regularly see even the most improbable alliances *in the name of the dragon that seeks to lead all humanity against God.*

Even now, the People's Republic of China promotes Atheism, and the apparent conflict between China and Tibet actually hides a secret alliance, as the Tibetan figure of the Panchen Lama is recognized as the true spiritual authority. Responding to an interview, and included in one of his books, Joël Labruyère stated: *"We talk about the mysterious Panchen Lama, the Black Pope, of Lamaism, virtually unknown to most people, and then we have the Dalai Lama, for which the media is crazy, who looks like a beautyful butterfly hovering here and there, throwing enchanting phrases like "everyone is beautiful, everyone is kind."*

The next question, *"do you believe he is an usurper because he never represented the real power of Tibet?"* Labruyère replies: *"We see that the Americans gave him the role of ambassador of peace to serve the propaganda of the New World Order as their singer."* [11]

---

10   http://fc.retecivica.milano.it/Novita'/Estremo%20Oriente/Archivio/S03AB38A9?PrevInThread ‡ Archived 24th June 2015.
11   Joël Labruyère, *Kali Yuga, Lumi sulla civiltà dell'Era Nera* (Arrens-Marsous, France: Editions L'ile Blanche, Italian Ed.2012), p. 19.

I was not therefore surprised when, in 2012, a dossier compiled by the German newspaper *Sueddeustche Zeitung* (Sz) revealed that the Dalai Lama was fully informed of the concrete support provided in the 1950s by the CIA to the Tibetan guerrillas fighting against the occupation of Communist China. The dossier is called, *St Circus,* and dates back to 1956. Here is an excerpt:

> *The highest representative of pacifism*—writes the Bavarian newspaper—*was well aware of the action of the CIA, and the conclusion is that the religious Holines of the religious leader was apparent. The newspaper said the first meeting between the religious authority and the American Intelligence agent Kenneth Knaus, was after the Chinese occupation in 1950. The Dalai was "pretty nervous" and he always maintained a rather "distant" approach in his contacts (which have been directed from 1951 to 1956). The CIA supported the guerrillas with tons of weapons. Even the Dalai Lama was sustained, writes Sz: "every year, the report says, $180,000 was paid, which was declared in documents as money to aid the Dalai Lama." Telling this story is the same Knaus, today 89 years old, and he was astonished by the coldness of the Tibetan leader in their meetings, due to the fact that in reality the religious leader agreed to an operation that blatantly contradicted his religious mission.* [12]

Unfortunately, few know the heavy influence of the Jesuits on Tibetan Lamaism, which in turn has impressed the so-called wisdom of the famous masters of the **Great White Lodge of Theosophists,** and of Helena Blavatsky who, despite having revealed to the world the existence of this secret brotherhood in Tibet, fully ignored the Jesuit presence during the introduction of modern Lamaism, as also reported by Joël Labruyère. [13]

Sacred geometry and Initiation into the real Illuminati

Everything is created by God the Geometer of the Universe. This concept of God linked to "Geometry" is of great importance to Freemasonry. It is the secret word that is communicated to the Installed Master (Worshipful Master) of the **Emulation Rite,** the most important rite of Freemasonry practiced in England. Not coincidentally, René Guenon (1886-1951), author, French essayist and Freemason, wrote that the G used in Freemasonry also stands for the initial of God. Ultimately, despite the efforts of the dark side of the Craft to take us towards certain disaster, the Great Architect of the Universe, *and not Freemasons,* will decide the fate of humanity. *Remember this beloved brothers,* in the years to come, what I say here will become increasingly more obvious. A crisis is is now manifesting for those with eyes to see. Even to the *average Joe,* who does not know who René Guenon is, and very little about the subjects in this book, the uniqueness of this historical period is becoming obvious.

One lesser known problem is that incomplete and misleading initiations offered by most current sects and mystery schools within the New World Order, *including Freemasonry,* often create superficiality within. **Paul M. Virio** (aka Paolo Marchetti, 1910-1969), the leader of a Western Essene Order within the Illuminati network, whose lineage was transmitted to him by Count Umberto Amedeo Alberti Catenaia (known as "Erim," 1879-1938), was an important occult figure addicted to sexual magic, and who counted among his close friends and collaborators Julius Evola, Arturo Reghini, and other important esoteric figures and magicians of his time.

12   http://www.ilmessaggero.it/PRIMOPIANO/ESTERI/contatti_con_la_cia_armi_soldi_dossier_segreto_sul_dalai_lama/notizie/201371.shtml ‡ Archived 24th June 2015.
13   Joël Labruyère, *Ibid.,* p. 23.

I repeat the importance of certain topics and words to stress concepts within the Illuminati network, like the oo "Initiation," for example, so that their complexity and effectiveness can imprint thoroughly and clearly in your mind. This is the best way I can think of to eradicate wrong ideas you may have previously had on certain subjects.

On both the light and the dark side, Initiation is a *second birth,* with fullness and *perfection of being* as the result of "correctly" entering the path. For such initiation to be complete, it is necessary that it is constructed in a *regular* and effective way, and characterized by a **real transmission,** that is to say, from a legitimate transmission of spiritual influence. Otherwise, no matter the number of initiatic efforts, one will never arrive at true realization and achieve subsequent awareness.

Behind the doctrine and qualifications required to institute virtuous transformation and gain the possibility of realization, it is essential to have spiritual influence. In the Muslim tradition it is defined as the **Barakah, or baraka,** and it is a kind of "blessing." Initiatory knowledge is given by the Master to an initiate that includes gestures, incantatory repetition of the Holy Names, situations, places, and special times, etc. The initiatic depository, *or virtual school,* whether pre-existing or not, must maintain continuity and connection, and is regarded as the first element of effectiveness. In this regard, Virio wrote the following:

> *This is surely connected to a spiritual center, which in turn receives the arcane influence from above, from the invisible hierarchy that resides on the upper floors. Although the starting points are various, it is important that you participate to a real tradition, and the tradition is one, albeit in different forms, and that we strive for a proper implementation of it. The realization is achieved with practice, rather precisely the purpose of this practice is carried out: the convergence of forces and qualities that each has started at the top, to the divine, to rise to the higher life and to participate. Participation, therefore, develop the inner perception, with a illuminative consciousness and the continuity of consciousness. Having participated to a illuminative consciousness already places the candidate in the right state to receive the initiatory knowledge for direct communication, and your relation with the higher worlds, established consciously, such knowledge, considered as revelation, is properly intellectual intuition, and implies absolute certainty, both as Wisdom Revealed that as experience made, and it is personal, incommunicable and inexpressible. This deep and high aspect can only be realized if the preparatory work, the opus to be performed personally, is practiced with faith and respect, diligence and decision. Of course the first movement in the opus must be a movement or rhythm of vibration that would place him in natural relationship with the different elements, since all the basic movements of the Universe are vibrations and rhythmic movements: as a principle both of Energy, of Thought, of Form, and in Space, Ether, in which it develops this movement.*
>
> *The initiate in unison with this vibration through the respiratory rhythm harmonizes with the cosmic forces and enters the First Energy, in the uncreated Light.* [14]

Contemporary Freemasons at the center of the Western initiatic system seem to have lost their original link to the cosmic forces mentioned by Virio, which gave original light and energy to the members of this old and prestigious institution. I notice far too much confidence in the words of young Freemasons these days, and their analysis often appears superficial, making them bad apologists, and the worst spokesmen for Freemasonry. Young Masons are often only given the most superficial version of proceedings, and at times the high-level dignitaries of Freemasonry even participate in acts of deliberate dis-

14　See. Paolo M. Virio, *Orientamenti Iniziatici,* (Rome: C.S.A.M. Edizioni, 1998).

information in order to protect the darker side of their Institution from possible scandals.

For this reason, this second volume of my *Confessions* is particularly important, and is definitely controversial. It will shock many people, including Freemasons, who often decide to ignore certain realities. To those Brother Freemasons who want to defend Masonry in a serious and objective way, without using the usual rhetoric of convenience, I strongly recommend further investigation and self-criticism. The material that I expose in my books is the result of serious research and study, and not a *Leo Taxil style* hoax. It is also important for you to know that I still consider myself a true Mason, even if I have not attended regularly any lodge workings since 2006.

The present state of worldwide Freemasonry is, to say the least, disappointing, and to my eyes, it seems to be a pathetic theater, and represented by emanations of ancient traditions that have long lost the right path. Unfortunately, this has also happened with the Catholic Church, which is now lead by the Jesuits, as well as many institutions... civilian, military, and political ... that preach good yet later practice evil. Every day we are reminded that this period in human history is marked by *hypocrisy*. Finally, to fully understand what a real Illuminanti "Initiation" is, *and what are the prerequisites,* aspiring students must impress firmly in their minds that the whole of humanity advances... or at least *has* advanced along the path of evolution ... even subtly, in order to reach ever higher levels of consciousness. This is up until recent times, when the forces of darkness and chaos have caused a dramatic halt to this *evolution*.

Upon examination, the physical side of the path of evolution appears in the form of a spiral. When we consider both physical and spiritual aspects, it is very much a two-folded affair, *that is,* there are two spirals that form what we call a *Caduceus*.

In *The Rosicrucian Cosmo-Conception,* dealing with the subject of "Initiation," by Max Heindel, who joined the Theosophical Society of Los Angeles after attending lectures by the Theosophist C.W. Leadbeater, there is an excellent description of the Caduceus. He writes:

(*The*) *Caduceus, or the "Staff of Mercury," so-called because this occult symbol indicates The Path of Initiation, which has been open to man only since the beginning of the Mercury half of the Earth Period. Some of the lesser mysteries were given to the earlier Lemurians and Atlanteans, but not the Four Great Initiations. The black serpent on diagram 15 indicates the winding, cyclic path of Involution, comprising the Saturn, Sun and Moon Periods, and the Mars half of the Earth Period, during which the evolving life built its vehicles, not becoming fully awake and clearly conscious of the outside world until the latter part of the Atlantean Epoch.*

The white serpent represents the path that the human race will follow through the Mercury half of the Earth Period, and the Jupiter, Venus, and Vulcan Periods, during which pilgrimage man's consciousness will expand into that of an omniscient, Creative Intelligence. The **serpentine path** *is the path followed by the great majority; but the "Staff of Mercury," around which the serpents twine, shows the "straight and narrow way," the path of Initiation, which enables those who walk therein to accomplish in a few short lives that which it requires millions of years for the majority of mankind to accomplish.*

It need scarcely be said that no description of the initiatory ceremonies can be given, as the first vow of the Initiate is silence; but even if permissible, it would not be important. What concerns us in getting a bird's-eye view of the evolutionary path is to ascertain the results of the ceremonies. The whole result of initiation is to give to the spiritually aspiring an opportunity to develop the higher faculties and powers in a short time and by severe training, thereby gaining the expansion of consciousness that all mankind will surely possess eventually, but which the vast majority choose to acquire through the slow process of ordinary. [15]

To facilitate the efforts towards achieving this "expansion of consciousness" **the Mystery Schools** of the various Illuminati traditions were established in ancient times, and like modern Freemasonry, during their initiation, the initiates are presented with an allegory that must be interpreted. In a trance state, the initiate is given the answers to the origin and destiny of mankind. If dishonest and evil, however, the initiate's are exposed to demonic entities and infernal powers. Upon *awakening,* they are usually educated in the sacred science of how to further rise within their degree system. At this point of initiation, the greatest danger to the newly initiated is that of falling victim to the trap of selfishness, and thereby to the possibility that the Mystery School he has joined is just another pathetic theatre of the New World Order, or even worse, an evil sect within their black magic network. To guard ourselves against this, we must cultivate faith, devotion and a sense of goodwill toward all Creation.

THE CONCLUSION BY ELIPHAZ LEVI

One last word remains to be said. When the Temple is rebuilt, there will be no more sacrifice upon its High places. Centuries have passed since Hermes and Zoroaster lived and taught. A voice greater than that of the Soul of the World has imposed silence upon the Oracles. The Word has been made Flesh; a new symbol of salvation by holy water has replaced the magical ceremonies of the day of Luna. The sacrifices to Samael on the day of Mars are surpassed by the heroic severities of penitence.

The sign of the Gift of Tongues and the Christian code have replaced the sacrifices to Mercury. The day once sacred to Jupiter is now devoted to the sign of the Kingdom of God in man by the transubstantiation of love under the forms of bread and wine.

*Anael has vanquished Venus: Lilith and Nahemah are consigned to Hades, and the sacred rite of marriage gives divine approval to the alliances of men and women. Lastly, extreme unction, which prepares a man for a death of peace, has replaced the sad offerings of Saturn; and **the priesthood of light** gives forth illumination on the day sacred to the Sun. Glory be to the Christ, who has brought to their completion the symbols of the Ancient Mysteries, and who has prepared the reign of knowledge by faith. Will you now be greater than all Magi? Hide away your science in the recesses of your mind. Become a Christian, simple and docile; be a faithful servant of the Church, believe, mortify yourself, and obey.* [16]

The Illuminati occultist **Éliphas Levi** is seen as a **John the Baptist of the New Age,** described by the principal originator of the New Age, **Madame Blavatsky** as:

One of the great masters of occult sciences of the present century in the West. An ex-Catholic priest, he was unfrocked by the ecclesiastical authorities at Rome, who tolerate no belief in God, Devil, or Science outside the narrow circle of their circumscribed dogma, and who anathematize every creed-crushed soul that succeeds in breaking its mental bondage. "Just in the ratio that knowledge increases, faith diminishes; consequently, those that know the most, always believe the least," said

---

15　Max Heindel, *The Rosicrucian Cosmo Conception,* (Oceanside, California, USA: Rosicrucian Fellowship, 2012), pp. 412-414.
16　Eliphas Levi, *The Magical Ritual of the Sanctum Regnum,* 1892.

Carlyle. Eliphas Levi knew much; far more than the privileged few even among the greatest mystics of modern Europe; hence, he was traduced by the ignorant many. He had written these ominous words: "The discovery of the great secrets of true religion and of the primitive science of the Magi, revealing to the world the unity of the universal dogma, annihilates fanaticism by scientifically explaining and giving the reason for every miracle." [17]

"The end" of HAARP?

The High Frequency Active Auroral Research Program (HAARP) was an ionospheric research program jointly funded by the U.S. Air Force, the U.S. Navy, the University of Alaska, and the Defense Advanced Research Projects Agency (DARPA). Designed and built by BAE Advanced Technologies (BAEAT), its purpose was to analyze the ionosphere and investigate the potential for developing ionospheric enhancement technology for radio communications and surveillance. [18] Its official closure was announced on ARRL (*American Radio Relay League, the American Amateur Radio Association*), who questioned James Keeney, *program manager* of project HAARP, the reasons behind the facilities closure: *"Currently the site is abandoned,"* he said. *"It comes down to money. We don't have any."* Keeney explained that the decision had been made two years ago (in 2011) because of costs. Keeping open a facility like this one, he explained, costs $300,000 per month. The *Clean Air Act,* an anti-pollution law that began in 2011, pushed for the readaptation of the plant to new diesel generators with ecological standards at a cost to upgrade of $800 thousand dollars. Hence the decision to close it. [19] The access roads were blocked, buildings boarded up, the electricity turned off, and the website taken offline. [20]

In 1995, I discovered an article on the subject in *Popular Science* magazine. [21] It stated that at the time of its creation, project HAARP was designed to exert influence on the climate. Roberto Quaglia is the Vice President of the ESFS (*European Science Fiction Society*). With his comprehensive approach to science, the article he wrote in *Popular Science* helped me to understand that HAARP was not just a "conspiracy theory." Roberto Quaglia stated: *"If HAARP is capable of shooting 1.7 gigawatts in the ionosphere, it can no longer be considered a trivial discussion."* [22] Another hypotheses about HAARP that was subsequently forwarded by a former U.S. Air Force electronic engineer, Dr. Brooks Agnew, who is known for his studies on the subject and his many television appearances, including the History Channel. He also confirmed the earthquake thesis laid out by Roberto Quaglia, and talked of the possibility that this technology could be used for mind control, *as did the former Governor Jesse Ventura in his TV show "Conspiracy Theory,"* which was terminated abruptly after three successful seasons.

Ventura visited the Center for HAARP Research in Alaska for a face to face confrontation with those responsible for the various charges brought against them, but never received any response, and indeed failed to even enter the facility in question. There had been many fears about HAARP before the sudden closure of the center in 2013, includ-

17   The Theosophist, Vol. II, No. 10, July 1881, pp. 211-12. ‡ Collected Writings, (A POSTHUMOUS PUBLICATION) III pp. 207-209.
18   https://it.wikipedia.org/wiki/High_Frequency_Active_Auroral_Research_Program ‡ Archived 24th June 2015.
19   http://www.arrl.org/news/view/haarp-facility-shuts-down ‡ Archived 24th June 2015.
20   http://www.queryonline.it/2013/07/20/requiem-per-haarp/ ‡ Archived 24th June 2015.
21   http://arcticcircle.uconn.edu/VirtualClassroom/HAARP/acf.html ‡ Archived 24th June 2015.
22   http://www.comedonchisciotte.org/site/modules.php?name=News&file=article&sid=8097 ‡ Archived 24th June 2015.

ing those presented by Nick Begick, who said at the time that HAARP could even boil the upper layers of the atmosphere, which has been suggested as unlikely by various scientists. In his analysis of the problem of HAARP, popular author Eldon Taylor stated: *"We will leave to others the discussion on climate, global risks and things like that. Our interests are different."*[23] HAARP, therefore, seems to have hidden from most people's view, the most interesting side of experiments involving the topic of mind control.

Eldon Taylor, after an enlightening encounter with Dr. Pat Flanagan, who is known for his work on the **neurophone,** which sends audio messages directly to the brain, thereby bypassing the normal channels of hearing, developed an incredible invention that unfortunately ended up in the hands of the National Security Agency, thereby preventing him from access to his device for 25 years, arrived at the conclusion that HAARP was: *"Constituted for an opportunity to perform real experiments on humans using knowledge of frequencies and subliminal messages."*[24] In this case, it refers to devices like **MASER** (*Microwave Amplification by Stimulated Emission of Radiation*), or **SQUID** (*Superconducting Quantum Interference Device*). These devices are explained in depth in 2010 by the Italian Professor **Andrea Giotti,** engineer and PhD graduate in computer engineering, with a doctorate in computer engineering and telecommunications. He became a victim of these technologies, and subsequently decided to denounce and publicly expose information through a series of online articles. **ELF** (*Extremely Low Frequency),* frequencies up to 100 Hz that can cause physiological disorders and emotional distortion with an *infrasonic vibration* (up to 20 Hz) that can subliminally effect the brain by aligning itself to alpha, beta, delta and theta wave forms. This is a concept cited by the expert of manipulation and mind control himself, Dr. Michael Aquino, in his book called *The Church of Satan,* wherein he reports a quote previously provided in the book *The Cycles of Heaven*, by Guy L. Playfair and Scott Hill. [25]

Prof. Andrea Giotti Ph D wrote the following about the *use of technology within the context of a psychological operation ...* in this case, one in which he was personally subject:

The device that generates the beams is controlled by a remote operator, probably through a satellite link. This operator is definitely a human being which can occasionally make use of supporting software but personally conducts the psychological operation during its entire duration. The dialogue with the operator of the device is still essential because the operation takes place, then he must know perfectly the language of the victim. Trying not to listen to spoken sentences by a remote operator transmitted through the beam is very difficult. The contents of the sentences pronounced by the operator are usually based on those of the most common paranoia (such as delusions of persecution, mystical delirium, etc.), so that all persons belonging to the social context of the victim believe that he suffers from mental disorders, so it's totally inappropriate to verbalize them in front of strangers. The operator can impersonate anyone, for example, the devil, an alien or a senior officer of the services of his country (the latter is the version that was proposed to me at the start of my psychological operations). Demystifying the most unlikely cases is quite easy, since the operator is revealed eventually as an ordinary human being, and in my particular case it is probably a subject raised in central Italy, which made classical studies, politically right, agnostic, with a surface preparation in physics but a good preparation in psychology, while not able

---

23   Eldon Taylor, *Mind Programming,* (Vicenza: It.Ed.Edizioni Il Punto d'Incontro, 2011), p. 117.

24   *Ibid.,* p. 118.

25   See. Guy L. Playfair, Scott Hill, *The Cycles of Heaven: Cosmic Forces and What They are Doing to You,* (New York: St. Martin's Press, 1978), pp. 130-140.

to carpirgli *(steal) no more specific information also because of its choice not to reveal anything that could not already have been know before (a choice that makes sense both as general rule of prudence in view of a comparison of the victim with a psychiatrist who must decide if the "voices" are the result of a psychosis). Through appropriate filters you can also alter their tone of voice in order to simulate the presence of several people who control the device, usually self-appointed employees or superiors. Among the manipulation techniques used by the operator's assertiveness, contradictory orders, the "cold shower" (illusion followed by disappointment), the suggestion through subliminal messages even while you sleep and sleep deprivation itself as a last resort but at least in principle every traditional manipulation technique can be used. These techniques are reinforced by inducing appropriate emotions, tension and pain such as to constitute a real torture and in this context the control of heart rate and headaches are probably the worst. The program executed by the operator is conventionally called "destruction," and passes through the discrediting of the victim, his social isolation, induction of neurosis and psychosis and eventually death by suicide, heart attack or car accident caused by the feeling subjective acceleration, which is almost paralyzing, or by sudden muscle contractions while driving. To discredit a person you must push to take actions against the common sense, the law or morality up to him to real acts of self-harm, then the "voices" may for example order the victim to destroy the objects to which it is more tied (not necessarily the most valuable), perform obscene acts in public, hit a pedestrian, attacking loved ones, gradually mutilate their bodies, jump through a window or under a speeding car, and so on (all these examples are drawn from my own experience). The decision to destroy a person before deleting it is not due to simple cruelty but the need to discredit the claims relating both to the secrets eventually held earlier that the nature of the transaction incurred, thus minimizing the risk of embarrassing inquiries that are more difficult to open if the subject is disgraced socially and was disowned by relatives and friends.* [26]

Behind the curtains of history

So, my dear readers, perhaps all of this has nothing to do with HAARP, or maybe it does, but it is worth mentioning in this volume. Beyond what satellite or antenna, or other technological means or devices used to expose these harmful frequencies, it is absolutely true that technological tools for remote mind control really do exist and have been tested for decades without our knowledge. They are known to the specialists as psychotronic weapons which derive from "Psychotronics," a term coined by **Zdeněk Rejdák** [27] to define weapons that can control the human mind where special electromagnetic radiations are used. In truth, I have also been the subject of such dangerous attacks over the years, made mostly to discredit and possibly ruin me, or even worse... to bring me to the verge of suicide. Fortunately, a few years ago a Norwegian friend of mine, who knew about this secret technology (initially developed in the countries of the *so-called* "Eastern Bloc" or Soviet Union), introduced me to the problem. Since then I have tried to defend myself as well as I can from these intrusions by the "cold shower," which is a type of *sonic shower* pointed at you, as is mentioned in various articles by Professor Giotti, who I introduced you to earlier.

I did this by activating defense techniques, and although they were adequate most of the time, there were times that unfortunately, the enemy managed to achieve their

26 http://www.aisjca-mft.org/ingegnere.htm ‡ Archived 25th June 2015.
27 https://en.wikipedia.org/wiki/Psychotronics ‡ Archived 25th June 2015.

goal. These weapons are extremely powerful, and in addition, there is also the possibility of psychic attack—which sometimes can be even worse. I can personally confirm the use psychotronic weapons. I felt these attacks at the onset of sleep, when everything was quiet, and a point I could hear a sound that gradually changed in intensity. According to what is being transmitted, these signals reach your **NRM** (Neural Remote Monitoring), which can then provoke strange phenomenas such as voices that arrive directly into your head. In current terminology, these are known as **"voice to skull" (V2K)** transmissions.

To stop, or at least disrupt, V2K, it is said that we need to use a cage similar to a Faraday tent—or an EMF shielder such as Shungite. We should also include the use of a radio jammer, or a GPS Jammer Pro, tuned to certain frequencies. Contrary to this, there is a psychiatrist named Alan Drucker who referred to people discussing "psychotronic weapons" as suffering from a delusional disorder. As I have already demonstrated, in Volume 1, trusting psychiatrists is risky business, considering that many are members of Freemasonry, and actually serve institutions of the New World Order. I will return to this subject in *Confessions* Volume III.

In March of 2012, the ex-Russian Defense Minister **Anatoli Serdyukov** (sacked by Putin on the 6th of November, 2012, and replaced by Sergei Shoigu), said that: *"The development of weapons based on new physical principles, directed energy weapons, geophysical weapons, wave energy weapons, genetic weapons, psychotronic weapons, etc., are part of the weapons program of the Russian Federation for the years 2011-2020."* The media reacted to this hint of psychotronic weapons use, and published the first experimental results achieved in the 1960's when electromagnetic waves successfully transmitted simple sounds directly to the human brain. Most of these publications did not mention that broader worldwide scientific research has been carried out since then. The Columbian newspaper *El Spectador* published an article covering a full range of results and advances in this field. [28] The British *Daily Mail*, an occasional exception within the world of contemporary press—*perhaps due to the fact that many consider it only a tabloid*—after the announcement of the Russian Minister mentioned above, wrote that research into electromagnetic weapons has been secretly conducted by the U.S. and Russia since the 1950s, and that previous research has shown that low-frequency waves or rays can effect brain cells, alter psychological states, and make it possible to transmit *conditions* and directly control the thought process of an individual. *"High doses of microwaves can damage the functioning of internal organs, control behavior or even drive victims to suicide."* [29] In 1975, neuropsychologist Don R. Justesen, who was the director of the Laboratories of Experimental Neuropsychology at Veterans Administration Hospital in Kansas City, unwittingly leaked National Security Information when he published an article in *American Psychologist* concerning the influence of microwaves on living creatures behavior.

In the article, Mr. Justesen quoted the results of an experiment described to him by his colleague, Joseph C. Sharp, who was working on *Pandora*, a secret U.S. Navy project. Don R. Justesen wrote: *"By radiating themselves with these voice modulated microwaves, Sharp and Grove were readily able to hear, identify, and distinguish among the nine words. The sounds heard were not unlike those emitted by persons with artificial larynxes"* [30] And finally regarding HAARP, even if the activities of the HAARP center

28 http://www.parrocchie.it/correggio/ascensione/armi_psicotroniche_2014.htm ‡ Archived 25th June 2015.
29 http://www.dailymail.co.uk/news/article-2123415/Putin-targets-foes-zombie-gun-attack-victims-central-nervous-system.html#ixzz2DPaQUNBO ‡ Archived 25th June 2015.
30 http://nanobrainimplant.com/2013/04/03/psychotronic-and-electromagnetic-weapons-remote-control-of-the-human-nervous-system/ ‡ Archived 25th June 2015.

FIG. 4 – Platform maritime mobile radar system HAARP X-band (SBX-1).

located in Alaska, near Gakona have ceased, there has been for several years a mysterious *mobile platform*, located in a remote area with similar functions and capabilities as HAARP. It is called the **Sea-Based X-Band Radar,** (FIG. 4) and is known to insiders as **SBX-1**. It is an immense floating platform that was originally designed in Norway for drilling oil, built in Russia, and then converted into a huge mobile X-band radar station in Brownsville, Texas. It operates on behalf of the U.S. Department of Defense.

The Sea-Based X-Band Radar -1 (SBX-1) is officially a self-propelled mobile station and floating radar that is designed to operate as a monitoring platform for rockets or flying objects, missiles and the fire control of missiles, and is part of the Ballistic Missile Defense System of the U.S. Defense Department. Managed by the U.S. Navy, the Sea-Based X-Band Radar (see Figure 4) is an existing device. But what is it really? This strange ship was built in 2007 with a 26 million dollar investment, and is berthed at the island of Adak, Alaska... not far from where the Gakona HAARP research center was based. The SBX-1 could easily be a mobile continuation of the work originally conducted at HAARP.

So who hides behind all this technology and incredible machinery along with its infernal implications and apocalyptic flavor? The answer to this question can be found on one of the highest hills of Elbert County, Georgia, in the United States, where there is a huge granite monument called *the Georgia Guidestones* (Figure 5, next chapter), and also known as the *American Stonehenge*.

Chapter   II

2020: Dawn of a New Era

The prophetic message of the Georgia Guidestones

The Georgia Guidestones, (FIG. 5) although unknown to most people, are important visible evidence declaring the plans of the Occult establishment that dominates the world today. They are a great way to understand the philosophy of the upper-elite hierarchy and its true apocalyptic beliefs. Until now, the origin of this mysterious monument has remained shrouded in mystery, because no one knows the identity of the person or persons who planned the monument. All we know for certain is that in June, 1979, a well-dressed and well-spoken stranger paid a visit to the office of the *Elberton Granite Finishing Company,* announcing his intentions to construct a building which was to convey an important message to humanity. He introduced himself to its owner, Joe H. Fendley, a local Freemason, using the name **Robert C. Christian.** Fendly was immediately aware that this was not his real name, because it contained a veiled reference to the brotherhood of the most mysterious co-fraternity in the world: The Brotherhood of the Rosicrucians (Rose Cross, from which derive the initials RC), which in 1776 gave birth to the now famous Order of the Illuminati of Bavaria. As Manly P. Hall wrote in his book, *The Secret Teachings of all Ages,* the letters RC are the trademark and the stamp of the brotherhood of the Rosicrucians since its beginnings.

The man proclaimed he was there on behalf of a group of people who wanted to reveal a path for humanity, and *of course* from these shady Rosicrucians, we could not expect anything more than a "messianic" project headed for what Christians call *the end of times.* The messages carved on the Georgia Guidestones related four points of a specific plan being carried out on a global scale by the New World Order:

1) **The authorities and the establishment of a world government unit**
2) **Population and reproductive control**
3) **Environment and the relationship of man with nature**
4) **The spirituality of post-modern man**

Thanks to blogger and researcher Van Smith [1] we have identified three potential candi-

---

FIG. 5 – The infamous Georgia Guidestones.

dates for the true identity of R.C. Christian, who could not conceivably be a single person, but a project related to Freemasonry, and even more, to the elusive Rosicrucians. They are: Joe H. Fendley Sr., Dr. Francis Merchant, and Ted Turner; the founder of the famous pioneer news channel CNN in Atlanta, Georgia, which was created in 1980, the same year that the Georgia Guidestones materialized in all its imposing granite splendor. When CNN took off, Ted Turner stated that he would go on until the end of the world. In 2015, a mysterious video by Ted Turner appeared on the internet that showed a military band made up of elements from each branch of the U.S. Armed Forces playing the hymn *Nearer My God to Thee,* [2] composed by the English poet Sarah Flower Adams (1805-1848).

It seems that leaders of the media industry, like Turner, love to build controversial monuments with deep esoteric content. Van Smith concluded that Ted Turner is the most likely candidate to be the mysterious RC Christian. He certainly did not lack the finances for such a project, which did not cost little. The land for this monument of historical importance was bought on the 1st of October 1979 for $5,000 (at the time, a figure comparable to $50,000 dollars today). In addition, a mysterious book was discovered in the local library entitled "Common Sense Renowed," published in 1986, and written by Robert C. Christian, which provides several indications about their "secret mission." *RC* writes that the monument was erected in recognition of **Thomas Paine, (FIG. 6)** who is regarded as one of the Founding Fathers of the United States of America. The occult philosophy discussed in his book was the same as that of the true Rosicrucian Brotherhood of the Americas. Van Smith tells us that this book is now freely available online, and was written on behalf of Ted Turner by Dr. Francis Merchant, an author and university professor, but also a

2   www.dailymail.co.uk/news/article-2897936/Is-video-CNN-wants-play-end-world-Intern-releases-clip-supposedly-recorded-station-founder-Ted-Turner-run-apocalypse.html ‡ Archived 25th June 2015.

disciple of Alice A. Bailey, one of the central figures of the occult and esoteric side that lurks behind the New World Order. She is someone I will discuss later in detail.

The *Thomas Paine Lodge* is also the name of a known progressive international lodge where Gioele Magaldi, former Worshipful Master of the Masonic Lodge Har Tzion Montesion 705 (Grand Orient of Italy) was initiated, and proof of its link to the New World Order.[3] The monument was actually created with the support and help of

FIG. 6 – Thomas Paine Oil painting by Laurent Dabos, circa 1791.

language experts from the UN, and scientists and engineers who took care of positioning every single stone and detail and which follows a specific astronomical calendar. Ted Turner is outspoken, both in interviews and during public events, in openly promoting eugenics and birth control.[4] Over the years and in his speeches, he fully embraces the nefarious project demonstrated to the world on the *Georgia Guidestones,* which implies a dramatic reduction of the world population to 500 million.

Inscribed in eight modern languages, the Georgia Guidesontes state the following:

1. Maintain humanity under 500,000,000 in perpetual balance with nature.

2. Guide reproduction wisely – improving fitness and diversity.

3. Unite humanity with a living new language.

4. Rule passion – faith – tradition – and all things with tempered reason.

5. Protect people and nations with fair laws and just courts.

6. Let all nations resolve external disputes in a world court.

7. Avoid petty laws and useless officials.

8. Balance personal rights with social duties.

9. Prize truth – beauty – love – seeking harmony with the infinite.

10. Be not a cancer on the earth – Leave room for nature.

RadioLiberty.com wrote back in 2001:

> *Limiting the population of the earth to 500 million will require the extermination of nine-tenths of the world's people. The American Stonehenge's reference to establishing a world court foreshadows the current move to create an International Criminal*

3   http://www.ilfattoquotidiano.it/2014/11/19/massoneria-libro-shock-gran-maestro-magaldi-i-potenti-nelle-logge/1220062/ ‡ Archived 25th June 2015.

4   **Eugenicist Ted Turner talks about population control:** https://www.youtube.com/watch?v=KZSc7Tn2Jk8 ‡ Archived 25th June 2015.

Court and a world government. The Guidestones' emphasis on preserving nature anticipates the environmental movement of the 1990s, and the reference to "seeking harmony with the infinite" reflects the current effort to replace Judeo-Christian beliefs with a new spirituality.

This current attempt to replace Jewish and Christian beliefs with a new spiritual form, the so-called New Age, was formulated by certain parts of the Ancient and Accepted Scottish Rite and the Theosophical Society, and later highjacked by the Jesuits. The deviated side of the Rosicrucian creed, often linked to the perverse practices of black magic and Apocalyptic and Messianic beliefs, have definitely influenced the Georgia Guidestones, and are still the main movements that participate in the formation of the present New World Order; the creation of a new economic system and a renewed spiritual life that binds to the pitfalls of New Age and the many false prophets.

We speak once again about a Rosicrucian deviation from the original Christian path of this Brotherhood, as initially denounced by Elias Ashomole. In the first volume of my *Confessions,* I made a rather extensive analysis on the misuse of magic by initiates. Magic for the Illuminati sects is an initiatory path which aims to achieve a supreme realization of the true nature of the practitioner who, at the lowest level, uses ritual magic.

At a higher level, we find the magician-practitioner no longer in need of performing rites for magic; he can just say a word or make a single gesture to activate his magic. Then at an even higher level, we begin to find the *true wizards* of magic who no longer need rites, gestures, or words, but only a thought. Thanks to his work in the media and influencing reality for us all, this level of magic surely has been achieved by the likes of Ted Turner. The secret of the true magician is confidence in himself and in his actions, the ability to modify the physical plane through the astral spirit... by imposing Will from the mental soul. Jesus said: *"Those who try, try until they find. When they find, remain troubled. When they are disturbed, they will marvel, and will reign over all,"* (from the apocryphal Gospel of Thomas).

Magic is created in the mental world by causes (a higher level vibrating domain by the electric field). This induces effects in the astral world (a lower level vibration domain of the magnetic field), which in turn produces coagulation, *or dissolve,* in the real world. Hindus call it **MAYA** or **ILLUSION,** it is through the microcause involving matter in the microcosm of atoms that produces an avalanche of macro effects in accordance with the law of chaos. At this point the reader will begin to understand that what he perceives as real is nothing but part of an interactive *simulation* that the human body *recognizes* as subjective reality. The real world is nothing but a constantly evolving energy matrix— thanks to billions of automatism (demons) in the astral world that determine its shape. *Conditioning* reality means using the physiology of the body to raise the upper level image (IMAGO), on this plane, by the magician (MAG=wise). [5]

Infowars reporter Paul Joseph Watson wrote about Ted Turner and other elite members in an article for PrisonPlanet.com, *The Population Reduction Agenda For Dummies* that appeared on Friday, June 26, 2009:

There are still large numbers of people amongst the general public, in academia, and especially those who work for the corporate media, who are still in denial about the on-the-record stated agenda for global population reduction, as well as the consequences of this program that we already see unfolding. We have compiled a compendium of evidence to prove that the elite have been obsessed with eugenics and its

5   francis.xavier.777@gmail.com, TREATY ON SCIENCE THEORY OF THE MAGI, private essay, p. 110.

*modern day incarnation, population control, for well over 100 years and that goal of global population reduction is still in full force to this day. **The World's Elite Are Discussing Population Reduction.** As was reported only last month by the* London Times, *a "secret billionaire club" meeting in early May which took place in New York and was attended by David Rockefeller, Ted Turner, Bill Gates and others was focused around "how their wealth could be used to slow the growth of the world's population." We questioned establishment media spin which portrayed the attendees as kind-hearted and concerned philanthropists by pointing out that Ted Turner has publicly advocated shocking population reduction programs that would cull the human population by a staggering 95%. He has also called for a Communist-style one child policy to be mandated by governments in the West. Note that in China, the one child policy is enforced by means of taxes on each subsequent child, allied to an intimidation program which includes secret police and "family planning" authorities kidnapping pregnant women from their homes and performing forced abortions.* [6]

China is a "trendsetter" among the false-philanthropic monsters of the elite. From ancient times, to appease the gods of the astral plane, they offered animal and sometimes even human sacrifices, as I often heard personally during my time in some sects within the networks of the Illuminati. From this point of view, the plan to limit births and force abortions certainly has a magical significance to the astral plane, and can be considered as a human *sacrifice* when done intentionally. At the end of March 2015, a drone pilot made a shocking discovery: *"I was flying my quadcopter above Georgia Guidestones and found these crazy stains that look like blood,"* said the pilot, who works for PhenomenalPlace.com, *"Very intriguing to watch because you don't see any stains from the ground at all. These stones look completely normal from the ground level but from the top you can see a big splash of this. I don't know what you can make of it, but it does look like blood."* [7]

The sacrifice of the Meat takes place during the rituals through the slaughter of an animal (or human) followed by its slow agony and the final roasting on a pyre, the billowing smoke then calls forth astral entities. An example of this ritual is present in the Jewish tradition of Pentecost. Illuminati sects linked to the creation of the Georgia Guidestones will surely carry out an animal sacrifice, at least from time to time. It is certainly not the first time animal sacrifice has been discussed in relation to this strange monument.

In 2014, the website *http://govtslaves.info/* made the rare book by Robert C. Christian "Common Sense Renewed" public. Included in their brief introduction to the text they offer their point of view (which differs greatly from Van Smith's), and also material that I think advances objective research on the many mysteries surrounding the Georgia Guidestones, here they are:

> *Van Smith on Vanshardware.com did a lot to help bring this out into the open but I think he underscored the importance of Thomas Paine being repeatedly mentioned in R. C. Christian's book. R. C. Christian didn't just mention Thomas Paine's books for nothing. I believe it is a very important clue.*

> *Unlike Van Smith I don't think that they have anything to do with some Satanic cult. It is important to keep an open mind on things like this but I think they were meant by R. C. Christian to be an ancient form of Druid sun worship. The core points of druidic religious beliefs reported in Roman sources was their belief*

6   http://www.prisonplanet.com/the-population-reduction-agenda-for-dummies.html ‡ Archived 25th June 2015.
7   Blood Stains On Georgia Guidestones? https://www.youtube.com/watch?v=NhP50VFV0jE ‡ Archived 25th June 2015.

in reincarnation and their reverence for the natural world. It is very similar to the beliefs in the New Age movement. If you want to know what part Thomas Paine's books had to do with the Georgia Guidestones I would start with the book "The Age of Reason."

Every single copy of "The Age of Reason" in book stores today only have the first two parts in them. Most people don't know that there is a 3rd part of the book that is always left out. I managed to get a hold of the 3rd part that I have included in this torrent. Thomas Paine and the other founders of this country were actually Deists instead of Christians. In my opinion Deism is the only belief system not tainted by man and is the only path in knowing who and what God is.

There is a section in the third part of "The Age of Reason" called "Origin of Freemasonry" that I think shows the link between the Georgia Guidestones and Thomas Paine were not just a coincidence. You can find it on page 250. Here are some quotes from it:

Masonry (as I shall show from the customs, ceremonies, hieroglyphics, and chronology of Masonry) is derived and is the remains of the religion of the ancient Druids; who, like the Magi of Persia and the Priests of Heliopolis in Egypt, were Priests of the Sun.

The Christian religion and Masonry have one and the same common origin: both are derived from the worship of the Sun. The difference between their origin is, that the Christian religion is a parody on the worship of the Sun, in which they put a man whom they call Christ, in the place of the Sun.

In Masonry, many of the ceremonies of the Druids are preserved in their original state, at least without any parody. With them the Sun is still the Sun; and his image, in the form of the sun is the great emblematical ornament of Masonic Lodges and Masonic dresses.

Masonry is the remains of the religion of the Druids.

The emblematical meaning of the Sun is well-known to the enlightened and inquisitive Free-Mason; and as the real Sun is situated in the center of the universe, so the emblematical Sun is the center of real Masonry.

The Lodges of the Masons, if built for the purpose, are constructed in a manner to correspond with the apparent motion of the Sun. They are situated East and West.

The high festival of the Masons is on the day they call St. John's day.

The case is, that the day called St. John's day, is the 24th of June, and is what is called Midsummer-day. The sun is then arrived at the summer solstice.

The 24th of June is always taken for Midsummer-day; and it is in honor of the sun, which has then arrived at his greatest height in our hemisphere, and not any thing with respect to St. John, that this annual festival of the Masons, taken from the Druids, is celebrated on Midsummer-day.

The religion of the Druids, as before said, was the same as the religion of the ancient Egyptians. The priests of Egypt were the professors and teachers of science, and were styled priests of Heliopolis, that is, of the City of the Sun.

The natural source of secrecy is fear. When any new religion over-runs a former religion, the professors of the new become the persecutors of the old.

The Christian religion over-ran the religion of the Druids in Italy, ancient Gaul,

Britain, and Ireland, the Druids became the subject of persecution. This would naturally and necessarily oblige such of them as remained attached to their original religion to meet in secret, and under the strongest injunctions of secrecy. Their safety depended upon it. A false brother might expose the lives of many of them to destruction; and from the remains of the religion of the Druids, thus preserved, arose the institution which, to avoid the name of Druid, took that of Mason, and practiced under this new name the rites and ceremonies of Druids.

"The Age of Reason" was suppressed a long time after it was made and many of the first copies were destroyed. It is very interesting to me that the only part that is still being suppressed today is the third section of the book.

Van Smith claimed to have come across Evidence suggesting that R. C. Christian was in fact Ted Turner.

Here is some information about him:

Robert Edward "Ted" Turner III (born November 19, 1938) is an American media mogul and philanthropist. As a businessman, he is known as founder of the cable news network CNN, the first dedicated 24-hour cable news channel. As a philanthropist, he is known for his $1 billion gift to support UN causes, which created the United Nations Foundation, a public charity to broaden support for the UN. Turner serves as Chairman of the United Nations Foundation board of directors. In addition to donations, Turner has devoted his assets to environmentalism and capitalism. He owns more land than any other American. He also created the environmental animated series Captain Planet and the Planeteers.

Turner created CNN in 1980. He said: "We won't be signing off until the world ends. We'll be on, and we will cover the end of the world, live, and that will be our last event ... and when the end of the world comes, we'll play 'Nearer, My God, to Thee' before we sign off.

I suggest reading "Reflections on God and Religion" on page 82 in "Common Sense Renewed" first. I think it will help you get a better understanding of R. C. Christian and a better understanding about the book in general as you read the rest of it. [8]

During my most recent analysis of the subject made for this updated edition of Volume II on the Georgia Guidstones, I discovered an article by Van Smith called, *The Georgia Guidestones: A conversation with Plato in Hell* (published in November 2012), which confirms the link of the Georgia Guidestones with **the earthquake of Sendai and of Tōhoku in 2011**. This is something I realized during the writing of the past editions of this book in Japanese and Italian, whose publication dates back to 2012:

One of the most diabolical examples of Georgia Guidestones numerology involves the Magnitude 9.0 Tōhoku, Japan, earthquake that claimed nearly 16,000 lives. This massive disaster struck Japan on March 11, 2011, exactly 11,311 days after the Georgia Guidestones monument was officially completed on March 22, 1980. The number "11,311" in day/month/year format ("little endian," which is most commonly used around the world) or year/month/day format ("big endian," which is used by the military and also in Japan) can be written 11/3/11. This corresponds to March 11, 2011, the actual date of the earthquake. Furthermore, the earthquake occurred exactly 9 years, 6 months after 9/11/2001. Treating these

---

8   Introduction to the book by Robert C. Christian, Common Sense renewed taken from PDF available on http://govtslaves.info/pdf-common-sense-renewed-robert-christian/ ‡ Archived 25th June 2015.

dates as vectors and adding them together we get: [9, 11, 1] + [3, 11, 11] = [12, 22, 12] or December 22, 2012, the day after the end of the Mayan calender, or, more appropriately, the first day of a new age. [9]

Of course for the more superficial and foolish people out there this could all be a coincidence. Yet time is a commodity that we no longer have. More and more people are awakening to this evil reality which grows worse by the day.. For those who wish to understand the hierarchies of occult power and their terrestrial puppets, which as you have seen in the case of Ted Turner, can range from the most liberal to the more conservative political subjects, I will deal in depth with the theme of synchronicity, as according to Carl Gustav Jung, in Volume IV of my *Confessions,* entitled *Invisible Master.* No matter the ideology of these individuals, they have a common denominator, that being the mysteries within the orders and sects of the vast Illuminati network. This is a network that ranges from Freemasonry, the Rosicrucians, the *Ordo Templi Orientis,* the Temple of Set, Theosophy, and much more. All are supervised by the United Nations and the many transnational Ur Lodges that work hand in hand towards globalism. The Jesuits, Pope Francis, the Church of Rome, Israel, and the powerful Jewish finance establishment, together with the English Royals, the existing aristocracy and so on ... act in accordance toward the establishment of a **New World Tyranny!**

The earthquake in Japan, one of the signs of the end-times

Inside Japan, a culture dominated by Shinto and Buddhist philosophy, and where Christians make up only 1% of the population, a concept such as the end of times is perhaps difficult to understand or grasp, especially as it is described in the eschatological writings typical of the three religions focused on the figure of Abraham; namely Judaism, Christianity and Islam. However, like all of us who inhabit this world, the Japanese must realize that Freemasons and the Illuminati who set up the New World Order are convinced of the veracity of these apocalyptic prophecies. They believe that the Judeo-Christian New World Order acts in accordance with a divine plan that will be supported by the use of technology and other *diableries* that will serve to implement their Apocalyptic vision. We must also consider that such prophecies are based on complex and precise astronomical calculations that determine the beginning and the end of each era.

Shinto-Buddhism, or any other religion not in connection with the three Abrahamic religions, are considered atheist, as mentioned in the manifesto of the new Rosicrucians, which appeared in 2007, as did the guidelines found on the Georgia Guidestones. The 2011 earthquake in Japan, and the resulting tsunami, as well as the nuclear disaster that followed, for example, are perceived by the people who practice the Abrahamic religions as a sign that we are about to experience the end of times. This is a time when the world will face natural disasters and various tribulations that inevitably lead to disaster, but also mark the arrival of a Messiah, which for Christians is the second coming of Jesus Christ; and it is for this reason that the letters **RC** *literally* represent "**Resurrection of Christ.**"

To my dear friend Princess Kaoru Nakamaru, granddaughter of Emperor Meiji of Japan, (FIG. 07) the earthquake that struck Japan March 11, 2011, was not a natural event, but caused by the United States on behalf of the New World Order: *"There were some anomalies on the modalities of the earthquake that struck our country. It is possible that the consequences did not reach the neighboring countries? The impression is that it was caused artificially."* This was a shocking statement made on the 5th of September, 2011, during an interview in the studios of a Roman radio called *Radio Mana Mana All News 24*, in which the Princess spoke about a possible nuclear explosion in the depths of the sea off Fukushima. These statements, although difficult to prove, signify that lethal attacks are being used to reduce the population of the planet. During the period known as "Tribulation," *so-called natural disasters* will increase as *they* seek to fully realize their vision to reduce the population to less than 500 million individuals before 2025. *So what specifically is that vision?* The survivors, together with the last Avatar, the Messiah of the Jews, who the Christians call Jesus, will lay the foundation of the new Empire which they claim will last 1,000 years. It is the millennial kingdom prophesied by Rosicrucians as coming to fruition; a kingdom that will originate from the city of Jerusalem, where they estimate the Messiah will return for the second time and merge with the Kingdom of God as according to prophecy. It is a nice ending, but is it propaganda or truth? On many occasions this "Return of the Messiah Syndrome," turns out to be instrumental for something else. Look, for example, at what happened in the previous century with Hitler in Nazi Germany. He was expected and received as a Messiah according to Freemason and Thule Master, Rudolf von Sebottendorff. Unfortunately, as with many others in the course of human history, he turned out to be an Antichrist, and not a Messiah.

FIG. 07 – The Princess Kaoru Nakamaru with the author at Brancaccio Castle Roviano (Rome).

Returning again to Princess Kaoru Nakamaru. Some of you will remember that in the beginning of 2012, she published a video on *YouTube* [10] where she warned us with the shocking statement that: *"On December 21, there will be three days of darkness."* These shocking revelations, however, were not accurate, and of course nothing happened on December 21, 2012, as her information was not the result of an authoritative source, as you would expect from a princess, but instead came through a psychic operation. This is not unlike many "New Age" channelers that made the same mistake during that period; getting carried away with all sorts of predictions, teased on by certain entities on the astral plane. Nakamaru has been in contact for many years with entities she calls *inhabitants of the Earth's subsurface*, but I do not personally want to certify their benevolent origins, indeed quite the opposite. It can happen even to a noble and elevated soul as is Princess Nakamaru, who became the victim of a **Trickster,** a Jinn or other spirits, pranksters who live under the Earth's surface and usually tease humans. Following the analysis of the ethnologist Paul Radin:

10   https://www.youtube.com/watch?v=EifqdfR8JeY ‡ Archived 25th June 2015.

FIG. 8 – Edgar Cayce (1877-1945).

We can conclude that the Trickster, the Jinn and the elementals are not really demons, but their intermediate nature leads them to be able to be also evil. Or rather, mostly evil. Deceivers, manipulators and pranksters. Ideally, they scoff at animals as men without a specific reason. In the worst case scenario instead, their spiritual subversion is preparing the way for the Antichrist. In any case "dark forces," the aim of which—as far as such—is beyond our interpretation. They can get in touch with us at their choice, as well as us, risking beyond common sense, we can summon them. In any case we can not expect from them what they promise: when it suits them, in fact, they are nothing more than swindlers, tricksters and pranksters. Then, as shown by those who have burned themselves playing with fire, there is a whole category of disembodied beings who we can rightly identify with the demons and that all traditions beyond the geographical coordinates, teach how to drive away. [11]

At the same time, the realization of the Divine plan is also that of the Antichrist, which apparently opposes it, but heralds in its own way the return "of the Savior," implying for the Illuminati of the Rosicrucian tradition who created the Georgia Guidestones, an elimination of 95% of humanity, in ways more or less natural. This is something that becomes evident by reading the first of the ten principles carved in Georgia Guidestones. It is an assumption that perfectly matches the revelations of Edgar Cayce, called the "Sleeping Prophet" (FIG. 8), who believed that **the second coming of Christ would take place before 2020,** and He would begin to reveal himself to the public, presumably in 2015, but not without a frame of massive disasters that will mark his return. And in one of his self-induced trances, Cayce was able to describe a large number of unimaginable natural disasters which occurred at the beginning of the twenty-first century. Edgar Cayce was surely not a fool, and in the course of his life he made a series of predictions that were amazingly accurate, confirming many times his prophetic talent, even to the most skeptical.

In 1934, Cayce predicted the beginning and the end of World War II well before it actually happened. He predicted the end of Communism and said that Russia would resurrect again to become a great force, like it is doing now in the Putin Era. Cayce even predicted natural disasters such as Hurricane Katrina, and the Japanese earthquake, saying that it would take place during 2010 or 2011, *and in fact it took place in 2011.* Among his predictions, he predicted a shift of the Earth in 2011 that, although modest in size, was indeed caused by the earthquake in Japan.

One notable scholar who has analyzed the immensity of Cayce's work in depth, and with a truly scientific and unbiased spirit, **Michael Wells Mandeville**, wrote:

Buried in the several hundred thousand pages of some 15,000 psychic readings given by Edgar Cayce, there is a large legacy of clues, which, like a jigsaw puzzle, fit together to reveal the outline of a vast historical drama, a World Epic: A historical scenario that starts from Genesis through three successive destructions of Atlantis (the final one around 10,500 BC), and describes the civilizations of the ancient world and the modern world with a wealth of news, comments and expectations for the future ages. [12]

What I admire about Cayce is that he had a purely scientific approach to his work, and I think that's the strong point that makes Cayce not only a reliable source, but also an admired character by the enlightened elite, and a unique figure in the panorama of modern prophets and mystics.

FIG. 9 – *Jean-Marie-Joseph René Guenon, also known as Shaykh ʿAbd al-Wahid Yahya after converting to Islam (Blois, November 15, 1886 - Cairo, January 7, 1951).*

It is important to study and verify Edgar Cayce's "revelations," because he himself wished for his "readings" to be scientifically examined, to verify the contents, and to ensure a fair and correct use of them. Surely there is something special and magical in Cayce's visions, and it was an unusual synchronicity which led me discover his work. Soon after I was introduced to the works of Cayce, I met an excellent Italian researcher named Piero Cammerinesi; a follower of Rudolph Steiner's principles. In an article published on September 2, 2009, in the website *altrogiornale.org*, he excellently describes the work of **Edgar Cayce**.

His article which preceded Cayce's 2012 prophecy was very intriguing, especially in today's light. Going beyond all the doomsday prophecies that *never happened,* 2012 represented a turning point for humanity as the year in which "the Great Wall" considerably expanded. *So what is the "Great Wall?"* As the French author and initiate René Guenon (FIG. 9) once wrote, this term is used in Hindu symbolism and terminology as the circular mountain *Lokaloka* that separates the cosmos *(loka)* from the outer darkness *(aloka)* representing devastating chaos. According to Guenon the "Great Wall" represents the barrier spiritually positioned to safeguard our sensible world against the onslaught of dark forces (basically, separating us from the hellish demon hordes that exist *out there).* As Cayce suggested, this barrier was destined to be weakened and consumed during the *end of times,* **thus allowing the subsequent passage of the infernal legions into our reality.** This is what appears to bring significance to the date of December 21st, 2012. It is clear that the infernal powers are already maneuvering on our plane of existence. Their access into our plane of reality are the result of reckless evocations and wrong spiritualistic practices typical of necromantic magical circles within *Illuminati.* These practices have undermined the defensive power of the spiritual barrier that was protecting our world. The process of corrosion to the barrier—due to the metaphorical *digging* made by the hordes of **Gog** and **Magog**—is significant to this moment of profound "crisis" within our historical cycle. In both a conscious and subconscious way, mankind has forgotten how to maintain the defensive role of "The Wall," and how to resist access by the forces of the underworld. [13] René Guenon speaks clearly about this in his book, *The Reign of Quantity and the Signs of the Times*:

However far the solidification of the sensible world may have gone, it can never be carried so far as to turn the world into a "closed system" such as is imagined by the materialists. The very nature of things sets limits to "solidification," and the closer those limits are approached the more unstable the corresponding state of affairs is; in actual fact, as we have seen, the point corresponding to a maximum of "solidification" has already been passed, and the impression that the world is a "closed system" can only from now onward become more and more illusory and inadequate to the reality. "Fissures" have been mentioned previously as being the paths whereby certain destructive forces are already entering, and must continue to enter ever more freely; according to traditional symbolism these fissures occur in the "Great Wall" that surrounds the world and protects it from the intrusion of malefic influences coming from the inferior subtle domain.

In order that this symbolism may be fully understood in all its aspects, it is important to note that a wall acts both as a protection and as a limitation: in a sense therefore it can be said to have both advantages and inconveniences; but insofar as its principal purpose is to ensure an adequate defence against attacks coming from below, the advantages are incomparably the more important, for it is on the whole more useful to anyone who happens to be enclosed within its perimeter to be kept out of reach of what is below, than it is to be continuously exposed to the ravages of the enemy, or worse still to a more or less complete destruction. In any case, a walled space as such is not closed in at the top, so that communication with superior domains is not prevented, and this state of affairs is the normal one; but in the modern period the "shell," with no outlet built by materialism, has cut off that communication. Moreover, as already explained, because the "descent" has not yet come to an end, the "shell" must necessarily remain intact overhead, that is, in the direction of that from which humanity need not be protected since on the contrary only beneficient influences can come that way; the "fissures" occur only at the base, and therefore in the actual protective wall itself, and the inferior forces that make their way in through them meet with a much reduced resistance because under such conditions, no power of a superior order can intervene in order to oppose them effectively. Thus, the world is exposed defenceless to all the attacks of its enemies, the more so because, the present-day mentality being what it is, the dangers that threaten it are wholly unperceived. In the Islamic tradition these "fissures" are those by which, at the end of the cycle, the devastating hordes of Gog and Magog will force their way in, for they are unremitting in their efforts to invade this world; these "entities" represent the inferior influences in question. They are considered as maintaining an underground existence, and are described both as giants and as dwarfs; they may thus be identified, in accordance with what was said earlier on the subject, and at least in certain connections, with the "guardians of the hidden treasure" and with the smiths of the "subterranean fire," who have, it may be recalled, an exceedingly malefic aspect; in all such symbolisms the same kind of "infra-corporeal" subtle influences are really always involved. If the truth be told, the attempts of these "entities" to insinuate themselves into the corporeal and human world are no new thing, for they go back at least to somewhere near the beginning of

13   See. Enrica Perucchietti, *Ibid.*, p. 162.

the Kali-Yuga, a period far more remote than that of classical antiquity, by which the horizon of profane historians is bounded. [14]

Whether unconsciously, or deliberately, modern man creates openings for the passage of these evil influences. This can happen even in good faith, done by those who, having embraced neospirtualist theories (today we would call them New Age), do not realize they are professing a modern form of counter-initiation. Spiritualism, channeling, sorcery, etc. give free access to these infernal powers. [15]

The years of tribulation, and the influence of the astral dimension

On the cover of my book, you will find the date 2020. While you may think it provocative of me to announce such a fixed date, from my point of view, the dye is cast, and now, more than ever, we must prepare to live during these years of tribulation leading up to 2020. During this time, we will witness the "choreography" of a series of natural disasters, the spread of deadly viruses, *unspecified events* that will bring hunger and destruction, and a full-on Third World War. These conclusions are not crackpot "conspiracy" theories, instead, they are *yet to be realized facts*. Epiphanius writes in *Masonry and Secret Sects, The Covert Face of History*:

Given that the conspiracy theorist and the dietrologist are the bad guys, who are the good guys? The answer to this question is logical and inescapable: the good citizens are serenely confident in their version of history, and in the chronicles of the regime, disciplinely placed in political parties and trade unions in which they are organized; these people, frankly, are not even touched by the suspicion that the news and scenes of television news and newspapers can be manipulated, or that, if feeding some suspicion, they feed only in the riverbed preordained idea that it is for the good of the political party leaders, whose member's point to them with infallible authority. Among these kind, are those who, by buying the newspaper every morning enjoy and assimilate the messages of the day, possibly at odds with those of the previous number, and make them their defending act, if necessary, with warm conviction. In a world where advertising techniques are almost always seductive and deforming, or even false, and dominate even the toothpaste trade, in which "fiction" films, photomontages, virtual reality and even subliminal messages are present at every turn, your average person is in a system which, perhaps, they delude even to oppose, and are not even touched by the doubt of being able to be taken by the nose and kept on a lead by it. [16]

This manipulation is executed through a specific plan of the New World Order in collaboration with extra-dimensional entities that are not of terrestrial origin, because the supreme guides of the Illuminati elite are mostly evil entities from another dimension that merge with the spiritual Egregore of the various sects of the Illuminati Network. They have a perverse nature on this dimensional plane, and are strongly driven by the mysterious "Unknown Superiors" of Freemasonry and Martinism as their catalysts. **What is Martinism?** Carlos Gentile (1920-1984), a Freemason, historian, philosopher and distinguished educator, and the Honorary Grand Master of the Grand Orient of Ita-

14   René Guenon, The Reign of Quantity and the Signs of the Times, (Hilldale, NY: Sophia Perennis, 2001), pp. 172-174.

15   E.Perucchietti, *Ibid.*, p. 165.

16   Epiphanius, ***MASSONERIA E SETTE SEGRETE, La faccia occulta della storia*** ("MASONRY AND SECRET SECTS, The Covert Face of History," (Naples:Controcorrente Edizioni, fourth edition, 200, **pfd version**), p. 6.

ly, and as the Unknown Superior Initiator (S∴I∴I∴ Supèrieur Inconnu Initiateur-Lodge/ Heptad Master) of the Martinist order, described it like this: *"Martinism is an illuminist order positioned between Freemasonry and the occult spiritual world: the origin is of course being Rosicrucian."* [17] Epiphanius also mentions the origins and significance of the mysterious "Unknown Superiors" concept in Freemasonry, when he wrote that the Masonic Rite of the *Strict Observance*:

> *Took the concept from the Martinist Unknown Superior, to describe entities not well defined, with supernatural powers that drive from the shadows, Orders and sects. The Martinist Pierre Mariel, describes them like this: Indeed Freemasonry (except in certain "high degrees" unknown to "brothers" less advanced) is the hall, the vestibule of other groups, closed, most active and powerful. To use a picturesque comparison: Freemasonry is like a fish resevoir. Wiser fishermen know how to get the big fish to dispose of them safely.*

> *Who are these "fishermen," who are called Unknown Superiors to those in the Templar Strict Observance and the Rectified Scottish Rite, but of which we speak only with half-words, with fear and trembling? And even the authoritative writer Ernesto Mason Nys, quoting from the book of Count Mirabeau entitled, "The Prussian Monarchy under Frederick the Great," written in 1788 in collaboration with Jacob Mauvillon said: "At this time, he said speaking in the middle of the eighteenth century, everyone wanted to become Masons; above all many princes joined in the multitude of this society. But it seemed that it was not possible to run such a large institution and they wanted to change address. Then it appeared as if sprang from the Earth, the men involved said they were sent from unknown superiors with powers to reform the order and re-establish it to it's ancient purity.*

Another Mason, Jean Pierre Bayard, in his book described their nature calling them: *"... invisible beings, without physical body, that however, convey powers to their followers, as in the case of the Golden Dawn."* [18]

The name of the Golden Dawn was accompanied by its Hebrew equivalent **"Chebreth Zerech aur Bokher."** While its symbolism referred to that used within Egyptian, Greek, and Hindu mythology, and, of course, the Jewish Kabbalah, even in the Golden Dawn, as in Martinism, the real leaders were believed to be "invisible beings who, without a physical body, transmitted powers to the adepts." [19]

The Martinist Mariel, while discussing the nature of the Unknown Superiors, asked whether they are men of flesh, or geniuses, entities, or demons, concludes that: *"The Secret Doctrine of HP Blavatsky gives us, if not certainties, at least interesting approximations."* Epiphanius also writes: *"All Gnostic teachers—and Valentino was no exception—attached great importance to the so-called 'direct intuitive knowledge' of the deity, method of inspiration that seeks contact with 'higher' entities through the magic and astrology getting personal 'superhuman revelations.'"* [20]

To ensure that these astral entities (benign or evil) can manifest in our reality, Jews perform, along with the Jesuits, the role of supreme manipulators and controllers of Freemasonry and the Illuminati sects. They practice magical arts, hiding their true potential to the masses.

17 *Ibid.*, p.74.
18 *Ibid.*, p. 77-78.
19 *Ibid.*, p. 25.
20 *Ibid.*, p. 145.

Only the mystery schools of the complex network of the Illuminati know the truth about certain techniques for opening to certain angelic or demonic entities. The Past Grand Master of the Italian O.T.O. Alberto Moscato, in 1988 wrote:

> *The so-called Astral Dimension is, as opposed to what is believed, a parallel to the physical one, but just as true and real. It is not a figment, a "daydream" or a fantasy, but a real alternative state of being subjective-objective with properties that are similar, but different to those of the physical dimension. The astral light, or Akasha, vibrates much more intensely to the corresponding photon, and has a higher plastic coefficient. In addition, the density of molecules that can be considered the "matter" of the Astral Plane, is constant and therefore there is, for example, a distinction as clear as on the physical plane, between the different states of aggregation. The gases, fluids and solids, in the Dimension of Light, therefore have equal density and cohesive strength, or better, they behave as if it actually was. Not enough scientific studies have been conducted to determine which is the quality that allows such a distinction between the different states of astral matter, but in the light of experience, it is extremely easy, for example, to go through a wall with your astral body, or divert a stream of water from its natural course.* [21]

Many Martinists and Rosicrucians have been bribed by black magic. There are many harmful and dangerous characters such as Dr. Emanuele Guidi Coulter, who secretly monitors a vast network of Satanic sects, and a mysterious Martinist revival of the *Ordre Kabbalistique de la Rose-Croix* (**Kabbalistic Order of the Rose-Cross**). [22]

Viscount Louis-Charles-Edouard de Lapasse, doctor and esoterist, was the animator of the Rosicrucian mystery school created in Toulouse around 1850. Stanislas de Guita received the transmission of a specific and secret mission from this school, and he was commissioned to unite the authentic French Rosicrucian tradition. In 1888, respectful of this mission, the 27 years old Stanislas de Guaita officially founded the *Kabbalistic Order of the Rosicrucians,* also known by the acronym OKRC. It is important to note that this date was not chosen at random.

The Fraternity of the Golden Rosycross' German origins followed a cycle of 111 years, and its ranking system was reorganized in 1777. Following directives received, Stanislas de Guaita again externalized the Order after 111 years. In 1891, **Gérard Encausse** (1865-1916), who was a French physician and one of the great occultists of his time, and is known by his pseudonym **Papus,** succeeded de Guaita as the driving force of the Kabbalistic Order of the Rose-Cross... this proceeding the renewal of the Martinist system, and from that moment the mysterious order entered a "sleeping phase." In 1898, the number of Martinist lodges in old Europe was 94, while there were 18 in the Americas. Today, more than 100 years later, the various divisions of the Martinist lineages gave rise to new groups in the States, and elsewhere, including one that is linked to the world's most known Rosicrucian Fraternity: AMORC, which I wrote about in depth in Volume 1.

Despite the scarcity of documents available, to understand the importance and context of secret societies linked to the the Kabbalistic Order of the Rose-Cross within the mysterious Illuminati network, one must keep in mind that Stanislas de Guaita was a keen supporter of the theory of *Synarchy,* as developed by another Member of the Order, **Saint-Yves Alveidre.** Alveidre promoted anti-democratic ideas of hierarchy and control

21   Alberto Moscato, *LA BIANCA CAMPANA DI LUCE Teoria e Pratica della Dimensione Astrale* "THE BELL OF WHITE LIGHT Theory and Practice of the Astral Dimension." (Rome: PUBLISHER: Br. ·. David Vinci RECTOR MAGNIFICENT of the GARDEN PAN, 1988), p. 7.

22   See. http://en.metapedia.org/wiki/Ordre_Kabbalistique_de_la_Rose-Croix ‡ Archived 27th June 2015.

over the secret societies by the elite, and it was he who predicted the advent of a one world spiritualism that leads to and culminates in the God's kingdom *metaphor* of the One World Government—all referring in part to certain Martinist doctrines.

The important religious scholar Henri Charles Puech, known for his many books on the history of religions, claimed that Guaita founded the Kabbalistic Order of the Rose-Cross as an underground instrument of religious revolution designed to replace the pontificate of Peter. It is founded on an evangelical path, substituting the esoteric principles of St. John, and ruled by the *spirit of authority*. That is why we now find ourselves with a Catholic Church that is increasingly authoritarian and less loving. Gianni Vannoni, on page 20 of his now unobtainable but excellent book published in Florence in **1985**, *Secret societies. From the seventeenth century to the twentieth century*, wrote:

> *The Kabbalistic Order of the Rose-Cross can boast a staggering priority and appear almost foreshadowing certain guidelines pervasive in contemporary Catholic Church, especially as its Grand Master confided to the occultist Josephin Péladan of being an ordained "occult priest" according to the Roman Catholic ritual, like "all the followers of the third degree," and to have received the power to worship in secret, "and not a priestly magic."*

Roman Catholic ritual? As you can see, the long arm of the Jesuits has always been at work behind the scenes of the unknown world of the Illuminati and its occultists, corrupting, at the root, all of the mystery schools.

I discovered the link for myself between the Catholic Church and Kabbalistic Order of the Rose-Cross after being initiated to the latter by one of its top representatives in Norway, Nicholaj de Mattos Frisvold, who claimed to have also initiated one of the people closest to the Pope of that time (John Paul II). It was Frisvold who initated me into *The Fraternitas Rosicruciana Antiqua*, and he then introduced me to the dreaded black magician Emanuele Coltro Guidi—who boasted to me about how *in a week* he was sacrificing a lamb in his temple in Verona, Italy.

Another out of print volume that come out of Florence, this time from 1945, and entitled "La Massoneria," mentions a ritual that should be executed only during the spring equinox:

> *Precisely the vernal equinox ... the Rosicrucians celebrate their feasts usually, they sacrifice a lamb, recalling the formula: "Behold the Lamb of God," that is, the immaculate nature who "takes away the sin of the world." ... The rose, the most delicate and the most kind of Masonic emblems, fragrant flower of spring, means grace, loveliness, youth ... The rose was also the emblem of the woman; since the cross also symbolized the generative virtue of the Sun, the pair of two symbols, the cross and rose, expresses in a discreet and gentle, with discreet and mysterious figuration, the relentless breed of beings. (op. cit., p. 62).*

There are Martinists and Rosicrucians that have nothing to do with Satanism or black magic although they are now a minority.They regard Satanists as deviations of the real magical path of their original tradition; and, fight against them magically. All these events inevitably lead us to a final confrontation between the forces of evil and the angelic forces of light. These angelic forces have tried to protect us from becoming enslaved by the more oppressive beings that control our world and material dimension. These oppressive beings, from time immemorial, and known in the Christian culture as the Legions of Satan, must be dominated and defeated if we are to establish a new human race free from slavery. At this moment, evil is corrupting the planet more than ever before, and it is advancing a world of seduction leading all nations towards the *New Golden Age*, planned in secret by the occult elite and the Jesuits.

Besides obtaining knowledge and becoming aware of the corruption going on around us, there is something more that you can do to save yourself. And that is through prayer and faith.

From the psycho-spiritual side of prayer, as the Martinists also call it, we find great insight regarding this kind of effort in the research of **Peter Roche de Coppens,** who died in 2011. He dedicated the last 50 years of his life to the study of spirituality, the awakening of spiritual awareness, education and holistic health, as well as profound and authentic research into the most important mystery schools, including Martinism. Through prayer, he healed himself of a serious injury caused by an accident, and for the following 40 years he continuously studied, practiced, and refined approaches to this form of medicine: prayer, holistic health, and well-being.

The late Peter Roche de Coppens, Professor of Sociology, Religious Studies and Psychology, whose influence in the spiritual field involved figures of the contemporary medical establishment, wrote an excellent article on the subject of prayer as Science, entitled: *The Important use of Prayer in Medical practice. The Science and Art of Prayer or Prayer made conscious, alive and active.* The main passages of the text that helps us to better understand the power of prayer, often even beyond our religious beliefs, include the following:

> *Prayer is a psycho-spiritual process by which we can consciously through the Mind reconnect to Pneuma and God to know and do His will, (not that of the ego) and to become truly alive and actualize our true and Big Self.*

> *Both the great scientists of our time, and what the true mystics of all time agree upon: God, Man and the universe are made up of energies and vibrations with infinite specific frequencies. God, the Ultimate Reality, both internally and externally, is Spirit, and the Spirit is made of energy and vibrations that occur as Life. Life in turn raises and the consciousness grows, evolves and expands to include all that exists, from matter to spirit. What humans want the most from life is to be alive, that is, have more consciousness, love, and life energy and creativity. Prayer is the royal road to receiving more energy. That is, to energize and boost awareness: to understand, to love, and to create! Our aim and essential objective is to make prayer conscious, alive and active. That is, it can make a difference, quantitative and qualitative, Subjective and objective, meaningful and measurable. Obviously, this takes time, work, attention, purification and consecration; a lot of patience and perseverance as well as the union of human effort with grace. But it is worth the effort as it is an essential part of the Magnum Opus, the Great Work which is so important to our era. Each person will then have to develop their own personal model of prayer that is unique and particular to each individual. Let us remember that prayer is a function of a level of consciousness and evolution. My goal is simply to offer a perspective, a theory, practice, and some tools, derived from my experience and from my personal experience, to propose a vision of what prayer can be and can do in concrete terms; I would invite you to utilize this motivation and enthusiasm to try out this adventure and work. To go from thought to the experience, in terms of "exoteric" to the "esoteric," from the unconscious to the conscious and then the super-conscious, it is essential to understand, master, and integrate well the following assumptions:*

The analogy of the macrocosm (outward appearance, the world)/Microcosm (the inner aspect, man).

The nature, dynamics and functions of the symbols, archetypes, myths and analogies.

The image and the analogy of Man and of the Skyscraper, "Vertical Axis of Consciousness."

Articulate a theory of human nature and a model of the psyche that are truly holistic.

Know and be able to work with the structure and functions of the psyche, use what I call the "muscles of consciousness."

Be able to understand and use, at least up to a certain point, the symbol of the trinity.

Getting to transform and expand the consciousness, both horizontally and vertically ... so you can come down and do the light and climb Consciousness!

Ultimately, there is no substitute for personal experience! This is true for all spheres of life and activities of the human being, but especially for the spiritual life and then to the practice of prayer. So in the end will be the same prayer to reveal its mysteries and treasures, its nature, dynamics. [23]

In this time of great need for humanity, I believe that evil can still be stopped before reaching the point of no return, by *prayer in the truest sense of the term.* Only in this way will we have the long-awaited Kingdom of a thousand years of peace on Earth as prophesied in the *Book of Saint John.* Satan, as described by Christians, needs to be identified, not only as an external danger (represented by the New World Order in all its emanations), but more importantly as an internal danger. In order to save others, we must first save ourselves from any form of evil; those who work for the cause of the fallen angels, and their evil spirits. Only then can we establish a clear way to communicate with our **higher self** and those beings of light who many say will save the world from the evil someday. Those who control the power structure, the "Illuminati" of the various mystery school traditions, are corrupt with greed and materialism, and we are continually manipulated by soulless Statesmen controlled by occult powers. We humans have so far persevered along the wrong path, by entering into a blind alley of self-destruction that can lead only to the extinction of our species—thanks to bad choices such as the use of nuclear energy for civilian and military purposes. The techniques of the dark side pushes idolatry, sin, blasphemy, apostasy from God, deviations and depravity. This is a rebellion against God, and consequently against our own selves, as we are a reflection of Him.

The instruments used by the dark side are different, but the sound is always the same. Jesus called Satan "the ruler" of this world: *I will not speak much more with you, for the ruler of the world is coming, and he has nothing in Me (John 14:30 - NASB).*

And John said: *We know that we are of God, and that the whole world lies in the power of the evil one (1 John 5:19 - NASB).*

And James said: *You adulteresses, do you not know that friendship with the world is hostility toward God? Therefore whoever wishes to be a friend of the world makes*

23   Peter Roche de Coppens, Ph.D., *THE IMPORTANCE AND USE OF PRAYER IN MEDICAL PRACTICE The Science and Art of Prayer how to make conscious, alive and active,* private publication distributed by the Martinist Order in Italy, p. 3.

himself an enemy of God. (James 4:4 - NASB).

Apocalyptic passages reveal that in the near future Satan will transform his invisible domain into a real, permanent, *and visible* kingdom within this world—what many call a *prison planet.* Even if one does not believe in the Gospel, or is not Christian, or is even an atheist, one has to admit that, since the end of World War II, what we are experiencing with the establishment of the New World Order certainly looks very similar to what has been described in various passages of the Gospel, especially in the *Apocalypse of John, commonly known as Revelation or Apocalypse or Book of Revelation.*

This *globalization* is not just uniforming customs, arts, and ways of thinking, but it is also facilitating the expansion of Judeo-Christian Messianic thought. The arrival of the Antichrist will also mean the arrival of the true Messiah, and for Christians the definitive "Salvation" for the whole of humanity from the Satanic realm and the Illuminati Network are profoundly influenced by such beliefs. Let us remember that **Aleister Crowley**, a central figure of the Illuminati, claimed that he was the **Beast prophesied in Revelation.** Crowley himself gives a full account of how this happened in his piece, "The Master Therion–A Biographical Note," as well as in "The Equinox of the Gods," and Part 4 of "Liber ABA." T. Polyphilus and Soror Sphinx, two followers of Aleister Crowley, in an article published in *Reality Sandwich* entitled, "The Great Beast Was Here," wrote: *"What if the Apocalypse has already happened? How should we live in a post-Apocalyptic world, when all of the values of the previous one have been destroyed? Aleister Crowley had an answer: We should each live according to our own True Will."* 24 This kind of "philosophy" has prevailed within the multitude of sects that compose the Illuminati Network these days, so it is no wonder that we are living in a world on the brink of self destruction.

Karma of a race or Jewish manipulation?

The Rosicrucian Manifestos were originally two documents written back in the early 17th century in Europe of unknown authorship. The new Rosicrucian Manifesto dates back to June 6, 2007, and is published in Volume I of my *Confessions*. In it the Order of the Rose and Cross makes the following statement:

> *Our Order teaches that true Christianity is not merely a question of belief, but also one of racial karma. After the invasion of the kingdom of Israel, the Assyrians scattered the indigenous population. They resettled in the Caucasus Mountains, and later drifted into Europe. We believe that the Anglo-Saxon and associated Indo-European cultures are the spiritual and literal descendants of these "lost ten tribes of Israel," representing God's chosen people as mentioned in the Old Testament. We believe in the inevitability of the end of the world and in the Second Coming of Christ.*

Promoting this new Apocalyptic "Rosicrucian Manifesto" is a group of leading occultists and Senior Freemasons that are piloted behind the scenes by the Zionist Jewish elite. This continues to this day toward the manipulatation and control of Rosicrucian chapters under their sphere of influence, where a constant and growing number of English speaking Christian Freemasons on both sides of the Atlantic are adhering. Of course, there are exceptions, such as where the ultimate controllers are instead the Jesuits, but that usually occurs in Catholic countries. This process of recruiting Freemasons in Rosicrucian Brotherhoods enables control, and leads them to believe that they are a part of a specific lineage of "elected beings" while being, at the same time, "good Christians." They may be harbingers of their cause and their operations, but in the end they support the demonic side. Complicated, and sometimes difficult to understand from the outside, these people are the true masters of deception and manipulation. Above all, they occupy the spheres of power that influence the world, the Vatican, and Israel, and have key roles in the hierarchical structure of the NWO. The trick coming from the apex of the pyramid of manipulators of the New World Order is to make one feel to be a part of their *chosen people.* Their "master race" and their "clubs" want you to feel that way when you submit to their system. As I have myself verified since childhood, at the top of the pyramid reside the bloodlines of the elite, where there is a strange kind of bond between the English nobility and the Jews. This suggests that a bloodline relationship exists between the British royals and the Israelites.

Currently at the British Museum in Huntington, and ranging from Abraham to King David, from Jesus to Queen Elizabeth II, and all summed up in official maps created for the Queen by WH PROBUS- Pleming MM Gayer OBE REV WM H. MILNER M AFRGS, **AVI, 1958,**[25] we find a curious and interesting family tree (FIG. 10). Thanks to the Lyon family, which is partly my lineage, this document shows that the world's most influential monarchy, namely the English, can boast of direct descendency from King David, similar to the "Master of Masters," Jesus. This makes it all too clear why it is they who hold the leadership of so-called "regular" Freemasonry and, from their headquarters of the United Grand Lodge of England, which is based in Freemasons Hall, n. 60 Great Queen Street, maintain a direct link to the Temple of Solomon and supervise the whole of Freemasonry worldwide. So, you may ask... Are there any unusual links between Judaism and the rich and powerful elite in the USA? In an article published at the time of the Gulf War, signed by M. Dornbierer, and dated 29 January 1991, the Mexican newspaper *Excelsior* denounced the "disproportionate Zionism" tendencies of President George Bush Sr. and revealed that, according to the *Encyclopedia Judaica Castellana* (Castilian Jewish Encyclopedia), the Bush family is actually of Jewish origin. It is worth investigating such a claim, don't you think? In recent years, however, there has been an interesting development in the world of Secret societies associated with Yale University, such as Skull & Bones, where the Bush family have been involved for many generations. *Time Magazine,* writes:

> *In the shadows of Skull and Bones—an organization that boasts Presidents William Howard Taft, George H.W. Bush, George W. Bush and FedEx founder Frederick Smith as members—a secret society of a different stripe is flourishing as the "modish club du jour." This secret society is called **Eliezer**, and was founded in the fall of 1996 by Rabbi Shmully Hecht, Ben Karp, Cory Booker and Michael Alexander, as an intellectual salon and Jewish leadership society, but after a more careful examination it seems just another emanation of the Illuminati Network, simply open to a more wide range of members instead of the more restricted WASP elite.*

> *Time Magazine* adds, in fact, that, *"The society was originally founded as a thumb in the eye to Yale history: Jews, blacks, Muslims, women and gays had been prohibited from joining the traditional secret societies. This secret society, however, would include everyone, so long as you were a promising Yale-affiliated leader of tomorrow."*[26]

So as you see the leaders of tomorrow, no matter which color or faith they are, can receive help along the way in their future endeavors, and Eliezer, backed by the Jewish elite, does just that with a more tolerant and multicultural appeal, reflecting today's prevelent reality as promoted by the system.

25   http://www.lostisrael.com/images/RoyalGen.gif ‡ Archived 27th June 2015.

26   http://content.time.com/time/nation/article/0,8599,2057526,00.html ‡ Archived 27th June 2015.

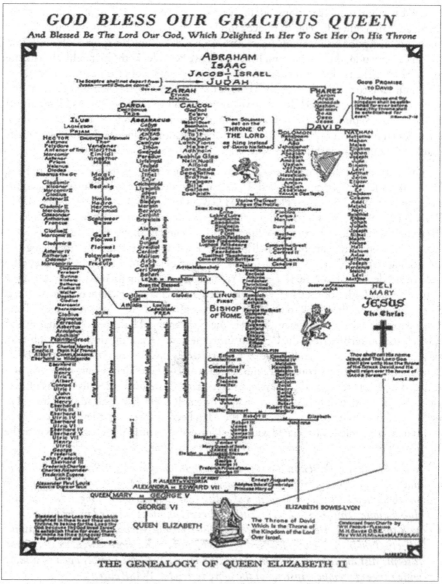

FIG. 10 – Source: *The family tree of Queen Elizabeth II (1958).* **From the British Huntington Museum.**

The strange correlation between nuclear development and UFOs

From what I have demonstrated in Volume I, we know that **John Whiteside Parsons**, who specialized in jet propulsion, and **L. Ron Hubbard**, founder of Scientology and former Naval Intelligence Officer, were involved in a special project during 1945 and 1946. This special project was carried out in the California desert, and was reported as part of a black witchcraft ceremony known as "Babylon Working." This magical ceremony was designed by **Aleister Crowley**, who died in 1947, the year of the alleged

Roswell UFO crash and the implementation of the National Security Act. The purpose of the series of ceremonies performed by Parsons and Hubbard was to unseal an interdimensional gateway that had been sealed in antiquity, thereby allowing other dimensional entities known as the "Old Ones" access to our space/time continuum. [27]

There is, however, another interesting "synchronicity" in regards to the Roswell incident as this *first major sighting* of unidentified flying objects occurred in the USA in the summer of 1947, just two years after the Americans dropped two atomic bombs on Japan (Hiroshima and Nagasaki), that resulted in nearly 200,000 people being killed. It does not take a great imaginative effort to see that these weapons of mass destruction, used by one of the most civilized nations of the planet Earth, could one day again be used. In 1947, this arsenal was being tested in the same area where a massive presence of UFOs began to manifest in the Southwest of the United States. Sightings, in increasing numbers, occurred in the United States beginning in the summer of 1947 with over 800 cases reported in six weeks, half of which were daytime sightings of disks or "flying saucers." These sightings peaked within a few weeks, and then stopped precisely within the period of time of the sighting of an object which was seen falling on the 4th of July 1947 near the town of Corona in New Mexico, and near the Roswell Army Air Field headquarters, at that time the headquarters of the **509th Operations Group** (**509 OG**), which traces its origins to World War II. It was the 509th Composite Group that conducted the atomic bombings of Hiroshima and Nagasaki in August 1945. In 1946, they were redesignated the **509th Bombardment Group.** As a result of postwar reductions, the 509th was the only organization in the world that was equipped to handle the delivery of atomic bombs. In the summer of 1947, an area so technologically advanced *and potentially at risk* did not exist anywhere throughout the entire world.

In addition to all this, on December 20, 1951, the EBR-I, an experimental station near Arco, Idaho, became the first reactor that initially was able to produce about 100 kilowatts—the first electricity generated by a nuclear reactor. On December 8, 1953, U.S. President Dwight Eisenhower made his famous *Atoms for Peace* speech before the United Nations General Assembly. President Eisenhower suggested the transformation of the atom from a scourge into a benefit for mankind. In 1954, soon after this historic speech, an amendment was passed which allowed the rapid reclassification of American technology related to nuclear reactors, and encouraged the development of this new technology by private entities around the world. It was called the Atomic Energy Act.

Was it a positive move? As usual, there were large interests at stake for those at the top of the pyramid of power that rules the world. In 1954, Japan decided to allocate 230 million yen for the development of nuclear power, and thus officially launching its nuclear program. The Basic Law on Atomic Energy Development limited its use only for peaceful purposes, and the first nuclear reactor was built in Japan by British GEC, a company that was under the control of English Freemasonry and its founder Baron Arnold Weinstock (1924-2002). Weinstock, a British businessman was referred to by the renowned British newspaper *The Guardian* as: "*The greatest post-war British industrialist.*" In addition to being the creator of GEC, he had an interesting background. He was the son of Polish Jewish immigrants belonging to the working class, and he certainly was not rich . But, thanks to his brilliant entrepreneurial skills in the field of nuclear energy and the support of the Jewish Lobby, he was awarded the title of Knight of the Kingdom by the Queen of England in 1970. Later, in 1980, he was even granted a *peerage* as "Baron Weinstock Bowden," in the County of Wiltshire. All this was because Queen Elizabeth II, unbelievable as it may seem, to this day owns uranium mines all over the world, including America, Canada and Africa. To conduct this controversial business discreetly, she uses the *Rio Tinto Group*, a British-Australian multinational with headquarters in London that specializes in finding, mining and processing the Earth's mineral resources and was established, thanks to the British royal family, in the late fifties.

It was originally the intervention of an "advisor for African affairs" to the Queen, a German called Roland Walter Fuhrhop, who his countryman defined as an enthusiastic supporter of Hitler—as well as an arrogant and detestable guy. It appears that he had all the characteristics needed for working with the English Royals, who initially were enthusiastic supporters of Adolf Hitler. "Tiny Rowland," as they used to call him, had been a staunch member of the Nazi Youth Movement, and this "nuclear" combination seems to be composed of Jews, the English Royal Family, and former Nazis; In short, *a truly atomic mix*.

And, if you wonder who owns the rest of the uranium mines on this planet, well, in 1995, the late **Dr. Kitty Little,** a retired nuclear physicist from the U.K.'s Atomic Energy Research Establishment at Harwell, made an astonishing claim, when stating that the **Rothschild family controlled 80% of uranium supplies around the world.** Basically, she identified them as having a monopoly in the nuclear business, but we know that's only partly true, as the British Royals have a fair share of the cake. Ostensibly, Dr. Kitty Little, being herself a fervent monarchist, would probably never have admitted that. In any case, the one responsible for the construction of the first nuclear power plant in Japan was Baron Weinstock's GEC (General Electric Company), and that was the beginning of a nightmare that eventually brought us to the Fukushima disaster that is slowly killing the Pacific Ocean.

"Atomic" considerations

On the 27th of September, 2010, an unprecedented event shook the international press when a group of people made up of former military officials held a *press clarification conference* at the National Press Club, with the intent of formally requesting an investigation and the release of information on past, obscure, episodes that witnessed the involvement and presence of UFO's at military sites that housed nuclear missile installations. In attendance were eight former officials from the U.S. and British armed forces, representing a group of over 120 former soldiers or retired officers, who had personally witnessed UFO interaction with nuclear sites linked to the Military Industrial Complex. The last recorded episode occured in 2003. In some cases, several nuclear missiles simultaneously malfunctioned without any apparent reason, just as an unidentified round object hovered quietly over the military base. This object, oblivious of the dangers, and seemingly monitoring the situation, demonstrated clear technological superiority. These episodes match what I wrote in my first volume, where the French occultist and French military Intelligence operative Jean Pierre Giudicelli described the UFOs, and certain entities that lie behind the secret activities of the military, as being far superior to us in technological terms, and with total control over terrestrial war apparatuses and nuclear weapons. But there is something even more equivocal that marks the beginning of the Atomic Age—so strongly promoted by the leaders of the New World Order and its occult supporters. There is a series of messages that are particularly indicative, that were transmitted by an individual called Djwal Khool, known as "The Tibetan," who was the spokesmen of the Great White Lodge of Theosophists until the middle of the 1950s.

He communicated through Theosophist Alice Ann Bailey (1880-1949), who also described him as "The Christ," and said: "*The Tibetan has asked me to make it clear that when he speaks of Christ he refers to his official name as Head of the Hierarchy. The*

Christ works for all people regardless of their faith; It does not belong to the Christian world more than the Buddhist or Muslim or any other. No man must necessarily adhere to the Christian church to be affiliated with the Christ. What is required is: love your neighbor, to lead a disciplined life, recognize the divinity in all religions and in all beings, a daily life ruled by love." [28]

His teachings, in particular those which are transmitted in "The Externalization of the Hierarchy," are today a constant source of inspiration for numerous gurus and New Age channelers. In this book, dated August 9, 1945, we see a particularly significant and shocking statement in relation to atomic energy, entitled, *THE RELEASE OF ATOMIC ENERGY*:

> *I would like at this time to touch upon the greatest spiritual event which has taken place since the fourth kingdom of nature, the human kingdom, appeared. I refer to the release of atomic energy, as related in the newspapers this week, August 6, 1945, in connection with the bombing of Japan. Some years ago I told you that the new era would be ushered in by the scientists of the world and that the inauguration of the kingdom of God on Earth would be heralded by means of successful scientific investigation. By this first step in the releasing of the energy of the atom this has been accomplished, and my prophecy has been justified during this momentous year of our Lord 1945. Let me make one or two statements about this discovery, leaving you to make your own application and deductions. Little as to the true nature of this happening is as yet known, and still less is understood. Certain ideas and suggested thoughts may be of real value here and enable you to see this stupendous event in better perspective.* [29]

"The Tibetan," and Alice A. Bailey, who channeled him, make an exaggerated apology for atomic energy, and considered it not only a weapon, but a divine energy: "*This 'saving force' is the energy which science has released into the world for the destruction, first of all, of those who continue (if they do) to defy the Forces of Light working through the United Nations.*" [30] This admission is clear proof of the criminal intentions of the wizards of the "New Age" who are prepared to blow up the world to establish their New World Order "through the United Nations." Within these implications behind the violation of the atom, and against the base of natural order, there are no possible compromises, as nuclear energy opens up a bottomless pit.

Magicians and theosophists of the New World Order make plunder of Lamaism and many initiatic and religious organizations. They pretend to be incarnations of Jesus, Buddha, Krishna, Hermes, Zoroaster, Pythagoras, and even George Washington or Joan of Arc when announcing that their public manifestation is imminent. It will begin with the appearance of Christ-Maitreya, the head of their worldwide religion. This will be a gross parody of the return of Christ, which I will discuss further on. Some have been deceived by this so-called New Age idea and the promise of a Golden Age. It could be said that an army of false prophets lead the blind on the streets of illusion that flourish within the New Age Movement. The Great White Lodge has extended its influence to all the international organizations: The United Nations, UNESCO, The World Health Organization, and the various globalist circles, where its Illuminati agents organize the realization

28   Alice A. Bailey, The Externalization of the Hierarchy, Italian Edition, (Città della Pieve, Perugia, Italy: Casa Editrice Nuova Era, 1986), footnote 10 present at p. 268.
29   *Ibid.*, p. 237.
30   *Ibid.*, p. 240.

of their plan in the financial, political, and cultural spheres. [31] Some followers of "The Tibetan" and Theosophy, or rather Neo-Theosophy, will say that my criticisms are making the game easier for the Black Lodge, but they have to understand that from my point of view, as well as those of other researchers such as French researcher Joël Labruyère, their alleged "Great White Lodge" is merely a gateway to the dark side.

The so-called "White Lodge" is a department of the *Luciferian Lodge,* which is divided into the *appearance* of both "black and white." Spiritualists are deceived by the perceived appearance, wisdom, and sophistication of "The Tibetan." The messages of The Tibetan are still popular in today's New Age, in spite of the severe and sick pathology of these doctrines. One declaration of **Djwal Khool** reveals that the magicians of Tibet are collapsing and are ready to propagate panic in the world. The declaration of Djwal Khool on the atomic bomb does not resist a more philosophical analysis on the meaning of morality.

To clarify the link between the mysterious "Great White Lodge" and atomic energy, the same Labruyère seeks clarification from a certain Mr. Bhodyoul who, in addition to being a scholar and a free spirit and great connoisseur of the magic of Tibet, boasts among his ancestors, members of the Buddhist brotherhood of Lohan, the Karmapa lama (red caps), and the official Lamaism of the Gelugpa (yellow caps).

The question made by Labruyère is the following: *"Why are atomic energy purposes 'spiritual?'"* Mr. Bhodyou replied:

> *The Eastern Lodge of the Mahatmas, or Hidden Masters, needs to raise the level of radioactivity to intensify their control over humanity. It is a program of pollution to put us "in tension." Pushing the benefits of the atomic bomb, The Tibetan admits at one point that the "underground atomic explosions can eliminate invisible enemies." What is that all about? Well some esoteric research show that the followers of the Eastern Lodge try to destroy some brotherhoods who do not want to participate in their game and who are opposed to it. We therefore understand that the secret function of the nuclear impact force is to feed a covert war on the pretext of "peaceful" experiments.* [32]

To Bailey, the atomic bomb is a beneficial instrument, *"It will change the mode of human living and inaugurate the New Age wherein we shall not have civilizations and their emerging cultures, but a world culture and an emerging civilization, thus demonstrating the true synthesis which underlies humanity."* [33] This synthesis is of course the New World Order: *"On all sides the need for a New World Order is being recognized."* [34] Alice A. Bailey, in opposition with the pre-Vatican II conservative scheme present then in the Holy See accuses them of being *"unable to leave politics alone and attend to the business for which all religions are responsible—leading human beings closer to the God of Love."* [35] It is certainly a strong affirmation *and the right one in this case;* but the use (or threat of use) of atomic energy when conceived as a liberating force, however, reveals Bailey as being in false opposition to the Church of Rome. Bailey, for example, fully justifies the use of the atomic bomb against the Japanese, and this allows us to better understand the words used in the second of her Great Invocations: *The hour of service of the saving force has now arrived.* But this so-called "saving force," described with en-

31   See. Joël Labruyère, *Ibid.,* p. 45.
32   *Ibid.,* pp. 45-46.
33   Alice A. Bailey, Externalization of the Hierarchy, *Ibid.,* p. 263.
34   *Ibid.,* p. 92.
35   *Ibid.,* p. 264.

thusiasm by Bailey, was immediately transformed into the exact opposite, becoming a "destructive force," and thus disturbing the delicate balance of the universe. Indeed, the extraordinary evolutionary acceleration of the twentieth century, including two world wars, and more recently, both before and after the turn of the millenium, the experiences and convulsions within the system with strong apocalyptic undertones seems to be compelling us along an invincible cosmic path. It is like someone—or something—is giving us access to advanced technology, such as nuclear power, simply to test us, and to truly see if our self-destructive nature will eventually bring us to extinction.

In the Science fiction novel, *Inside-Outside* (Ballantine, 1964), Philip Jose Farmer, one of the most interesting authors of science fiction of the time, expressed a formula that was later picked up by the great French author and initiate **Serge Hutin,** who used it to conclude his essay published in Italy in 1973, entitled **Occult Governments and Secret Societies**:

> *Super-human powers direct, from the top of the pyramid, visible and invisible rulers, the evolution of the stellar and planetary systems and all the beings that live in them, including men. If this is the case, the human point of view, so limited, would be unable to grasp the overall lines of the stellar and planetary cycles, like a cell in our body is unable to understand all the various structures that help form it.* [36]

Kurosawa and the redness of Mount Fuji

Since my childhood in the seventies, thanks to the teachings of my father, the famous Jungian analyst Dr. Elio Zagami (1939-2010), I learned to appreciate the work of the greatest Japanese filmmaker ever, **Akira Kurosawa (1910-1998)**. In particular, for years I pondered an episode within one of his last works, the nightmare sequence in the film *Dreams* that was released in 1990, and which later proved strangely, and figuratively prophetic, when *exhibiting* the "redness" of Mt. Fuji. (FIG. 11)

In this scene we see a huge nuclear power plant located near Mt Fuji exploding, coloring the sky an eerie red, and forcing millions of people to seek refuge in the coastal areas towards the ocean. Three adults and two children remain in place, but soon realize that the radiation will kill them anyway. Among them is the engineer who designed the plant responsible for this radiation. As a result of this disaster, in typical Japanese style, he decides to commit suicide. In the great cinematic tradition of Master Kurosawa, there is significant and revealing dialogue that takes place among the survivors. A wise response is given in the last scene of the film *Dreams;* in the dialogue between the stranger and the protagonist, entitled, "The village of watermills," it goes like this: *"Humanity today seems to have forgotten that it is itself a part of nature,"*—noted the wise old man—*"for this reason, it destroys that part of nature upon which is life, creating things that ultimately make us just unhappy."*

It is unhappiness tied to materialism that seems to characterize Judeo-Christian civilization today. It is guilty of corrupting not only us, but also other cultures like the Japanese culture. However, in the last part of this chapter, I will speak of the role played by Israel in the Fukushima Nuclear plant disaster. In particular, we will try to understand together the process of nuclear fusion that continues, ongoing, after so many years, and may actually be the result of a sort of "vendetta" by Israeli Intelligence upon Japan... *who they apparently consider guilty of supporting the birth of a Palestinian state.* **Conspiracy?**

---

36   Serge Hutin, *Governi Occulti e Società Segrete* (Occult Governments and Secret Societies), (Rome, IT: Ed. Mediterrrance, 1973, 1996), p. 162.

FIG. 11 – The famous scene of Mount Fuji in the Kurosawa film Dreams *(Warner Bros. Pictures -1990): an unforgettable nightmare image of a nuclear disaster, two decades before it happened.*

Read carefully what I am about to put before you. **Mario Agostinelli,** an ecologist, political and trade unionist, wrote in March 2015:

> *The news from* Bloomberg *on February 25th, reveals the concerns of TEPCO, the Japanese electrical corporation, which, four years after the meltdown of the Fukushima reactors and the spent fuel rods, is investigating the cause of a spike in radiation levels registered in February in the water drainage to the Pacific Ocean. Obviously, the rain water is still contaminated by contact with radioactive substances. TEPCO has already found 23,000 becquerels per liter of cesium 137 in rainwater accumulated on the roof of the reactor No. 2, the legal limit for the release of cesium-137 should not exceed 90 becquerels per liter. A lethal dose, which persists and spreads over time, in addition to the fact that such exposure is incalculable concerning the risks of the development of tumors. Obviously, the losses in the ocean are still ongoing, even after the evacuation of 160,000 people in the area. The Japanese government set out to reclaim the 11 municipalities most severely contaminating the Fukushima Prefecture by March 2014, to reduce the annual dose of 1 millisievert. The presence of radioactive water is a novelty that the Chernobyl accident was not exposed to: the Fukushima reactors, in contrast to the Ukrainian, are water moderated reactors and if there is a core meltdown we find spillage at sea of cooling water, which results in a radiation scatter through the dynamics of currents spread through the food chain that makes home in the ocean. Unfortunately this information follows the standard of secrecy and non-transparency of the entire nuclear system: nothing is under control now and the data on the contamination and health effects have been so hidden and manipulated from the start, makes it really difficult to make statements and forecasts.* [37]

From Agostinelli's words, above, we've come to understand that the problem in Fukushima is not only *not* resolved, but continues to be subject of constant obfuscation and secrecy by the hidden rulers of the planet, who clearly, do not want to put a stop to the use of nuclear energy. It is apparent that they would like to contaminate the planet even

37   http://www.ilfattoquotidiano.it/2015/03/09/fukushima-quattro-anni-dopo-e-oltre-davvero-si-investe-ancora-sul-nucleare/1488596/ ‡ Archived 27th June 2015.

more, as is the will of the Invisible Masters behind the **"New Age Occult Elite,"** and their **"Eastern Lodge,"** which rules the **United Nations** together with the **Jesuits** and the **Zionist** elite. I will now show you how a lethal computer virus created by the Israelis may have helped this secret agenda that involves Fukushima even further.

At the time of the disaster, the Israeli newspaper *Haaretz* stated that an Israeli company, Magna, was responsible for the security of the Fukushima Daiichi Nuclear Power Station just before the incident that occurred on the 11th of March, 2011. According to Yoishi Shimatsu, former editor of *Japan Times Weekly,* the support for the new Palestinian state by Japan could not be forgiven by Israel. In other words, the Israeli Intelligence sabotaged the reactor in retaliation for Japan's support of an independent Palestinian state. Yoishi Shimatsu also stated that these nuclear materials were shipped to the plant in 2007 on the orders of Dick Cheney and George W. Bush, with the connivance of Israeli Prime Minister Ehud Olmert. The shipment was in the form of warhead cores secretly removed from the U.S. nuclear warheads facility BWXT Plantex near Amarillo, Texas. While acting as the middleman, Israel transported warheads from the port of Houston, and in the process kept the best ones, while giving the Japanese older warhead cores that had to be further enriched at Fukushima. [38]

As I mentioned, Israel and its secret services took care of the transport of these important strategic nuclear components from the Port of Houston in the United States to Japan, but retained those in optimal state, still rich in uranium and plutonium, and then sent empty warheads to Japan, where they were to be "regenerated," or rather enriched, with uranium and plutonium at the Fukushima plant in order to be subsequently used in that area for strategic purposes. This, however, was a serious mistake for the Japanese government, which according to experts, would soon thereafter cause even greater damage following the earthquake and tsunami.

On another front, Michael Joseph Gross described a dangerous computer virus in a long article for *Vanity Fair*, where it is assumed that the virus originally was the basis of an act of war itself, albeit virtual, against Tehran's nuclear program. [39] This disturbing scenario engages the hypothesis of Jim Stone, a self-declared former analyst at the National Security Agency, with experience in engineering, who stated that the operation was a sinister act of nuclear war: *"The whole thing was a deliberate and dastardly act of nuclear war."*

As later reported by Princess Nakamaru, the Israelis had even planted a nuclear device in the sea off the Fukushima plant. According to the "experts" of *Wired* magazine, this thesis has no foundation, and Jim Stone is described as a "Crackpot." [40] *Wired,* however, is not always a reliable source because of its link with the power system of the New World Order. Strangely enough, *Wired* has never made mention of Stuxnet, even though, at Wired's Italian launch, an Italian monthly magazine defined *Wired* as: "the Bible of the digital revolution." [41]

Even Yoishi Shimatsu correctly emphasized the importance of Stuxnet for the event when writing that the computer virus entered the system within twenty minutes before the start of the nuclear fusion of Central Fukushima: *"The natural disaster, however, was vastly amplified by two external factors: release of the Stuxnet virus, which shut*

38   http://americanfreepress.net/japanese-journalist-accuses-israel-of-fukushima-sabotage/ ‡ Archived 27th June 2015.

39   See. http://www.vanityfair.com/news/2011/03/stuxnet-201104 ‡ Archived 27th June 2015.

40   See. http : //www.wired.com/2012/01/jim-stone-fukushima/ ‡ Archived 27th June 2015.

41   http://tg1live.blog.rai.it/2009/02/23/wired-la-bibbia-della -rivoluzione-digital-arrives-in-Italy / ‡ Archived 27th June 2015.

down control systems in the critical 20 minutes prior to the tsunami; and presence of weapons-grade nuclear materials that devastated the nuclear facility and contaminated the entire region."[42]

In this way, devastation was released into the environment. There is not only the radioactivity naturally present in the complex for the production of atomic energy, but also within the nuclear military warheads that arrived from the United States, that then were enriched with uranium and plutonium *on site* for military purposes—and related to the future construction of nuclear warheads either to be introduced on Japanese territory, or another place within a delicate geopolitical and strategic area. All this took place while the United States experienced growing opposition towards the North Korean threat. Bush mentions North Korea on the occasion of his State of the Union address on the 29th of January, 2002, in his famous "Axis of Evil" speech, in which he introduced the term. In 2007, Roland Vincent Carnaby was the first person to expose secret information about the dismantling, and covert sending, of nuclear warheads from Texas to Japan. He was later (*murdered*) on April 29th of 2008—although the official version reveals that he was killed by police in Houston after a chase on the highway for reasons that were never fully explained by official authorities. Strangely enough, Roland, who was appointed a C.I.A. agent and, according to some, was a bit of a mercenary in the industry, came *by chance* to discover this international nuclear traffic which ostensibly led to his murder.

I was scheduled to meet Roland for a potential interview shortly after my arrival to the U.S. in 2008. I arrived in Chicago on April 20th, 2008, just nine days before his death. The meeting with him was arranged by a former American military member with whom I was in contact with, but unfortunately, because of this tragic event, it never took place. Nonetheless, I discovered that, as a security operator at the Port of Houston, he interceped a group of Mossad agents involved in the transport of the nuclear material from the port.. Myself, as well as other researchers and investigative journalists, including my friend journalist Greg Szymanski, began to investigate this matter in September 2007, in addition to other similar incidents, including the alleged theft of nuclear warheads from Denver International airport. [43]

All this interest from various investigative journalists definitely did not play in Roland's favor. Roland Vincent Carnaby was eliminated because George W. Bush and Dick Cheney, who were still in power at that time, would not allow such an operation to be compromised.

But let us not forget *Magna,* the Israeli security firm that was supposed to take care of the safety of Fukushima. This from the Israeli news source *Haaretz* on the 18th of March:

> *The CEO of the Israeli company that installed the security system at Japan's Fukushima nuclear power plant said Thursday that those workers who have elected to stay behind are "putting their lives on the line" to save Japan. Magna BSP set up the security system about a year ago at the facility, which suffered extensive damage after the recent earthquake and tsunami, with particular concern over radiation leakage from the reactors at the site.*

So the Israeli company responsible for the safety of the Japanese nuclear power plant argued that those who work there were putting their lives at risk stating that: *"The Japanese workers who have remained at the reactor are really putting their lives on the line, with the knowledge that they're doing it to save all of Japan."* This is a difficult concept to grasp

42   http://www.rense.com/general94/secbb.htm ‡ Archived 27th June 2015.
43   See. http://www.illuminati-news.com/2007/0919.html ‡ Archived 27th June 2015.

for those of us in the Western World. Magna is a company located in the city of Dimona, an Israeli city in the Negev desert, 36 km south of Beersheba and 35 kilometers west of the Dead Sea. The activities of Magna in Japan are carried out by a local company in direct contact with the Israeli government declaring: *"We have an agreement in principle with the Japanese that we will provide protection for all of the country's nuclear reactors."* [44]

Israeli security and the Rothschild's who manipulate it

In 2009, Nathaniel Popper wrote, *"Like the best Chabad-Lubavitch rabbis, Manis Friedman has won the hearts of many unaffiliated Jews with his charismatic talks about love and God; it was Friedman who helped lead Bob Dylan into a relationship with Chabad."* But Friedman, who today travels the country as a Chabad speaker, when asked how he thinks Jews should treat their Arab neighbors, was not as warm in his reply, *"The only way to fight a moral war is the Jewish way: Destroy their holy sites. Kill men, women and children (and cattle)."* Friedman wrote this in response to the question posed by **Moment Magazine** for its **"Ask the Rabbis"** feature, arguing that if Israel followed this wisdom, there would be *"no civilian casualties, no children in the line of fire, no false sense of righteousness, in fact, no war. I don't believe in Western morality, Living by Torah values will make us a light unto the nations who suffer defeat because of a disastrous morality of human invention."*

Friedman's use of phrasing might seem more familiar as coming from an Islamic extremist. It has, however, generated a swift backlash. [45] One wonders, therefore, why the Japanese entrusted their security to an Israeli company like **Magna**... from a culture so far and distant from their own... where realities like Chabad exist. Once and for all, before going even deeper in the perilous subject of Zionist manipulation and Jewish Freemasonry, I would like to clarify for my readers that I am not anti-Semitic. Instead, I am opposed to Zionism—and especially *Rothschild Zionism*. Indeed, I have nothing against the Jewish population. They are, like the rest of us, subject to the will of a minority that continues to compromise their existence, as was true even at the time of Jesus. In conclusion, just as I pointed out earlier in Master Kurosawa's *Dreams* movie dialogue, which refers to a scene including an explosion near Mount Fuji, we have always trusted the wrong people (i.e. the representatives of the New World Order), and they use all the technology at their disposal to devastate our lives (while "improving it" in appearance only). In this movie, in the episode entitled "The village of watermills," the stranger asks the wise old man how old he is. He answers, *"Only three hundred years. People who live in this village live a life much in touch with nature, and leave this world at a very advanced age."* So, this suggests that we can forget the *illusory benefits* forwarded by our current form of Judeo-Christian civilization, now corrupted by vile matters, and no longer true to its original foundation.

The civilization the elite has built is not the world of love and light that God desires for us. Maybe that's why UFO's always appear in conjunction with nuclear tests—*because these criminals of the New World Order make fun of creation with their science.* We must now do everything in our power to ensure the New World Order will never resort to nuclear Armageddon. *We can do this* because humans are *one,* and through our union we can achieve salvation for the planet and its precious creatures. But mind you, I'm not pro-

44 See. http://www.haaretz.com/print-edition/news/israeli-firm-which-secured-japan-nuclear-plant-says-workers-there-putting-their-lives-on-the-line-1.349897 ‡ Archived 27th June 2015.

45 See. http://forward.com/news/107112/popular-rabbi-s-comments-on-treatment-of-arabs-s/ ‡ Archived 4th July 2015.

moting the sort of feel-good, meaningless, "New Age" stuff, but instead a real method: the scientific use of prayer, that, if directed with positive intent and pure intentions will benefit mankind, and possibly even save the planet from these evil *Egregores.*

Imagine millions of people forming a truly positive Egregore, a thought form with the right intentions, instead of the intentions within a corrupt Church, Mosque or Sinagogue. This would create a *nuclear bomb effect* against the globalist enemy and their materialistic mindset. Clearly, just as there are many religious and spiritual traditions and spiritual masters more or less honest, there are various definitions of prayer (meditation, spiritual exercises, etc.). Therefore, it is very important to begin with an operational definition of what we mean by "prayer." For me, it is a psychological process that is beautifully described, previously in this volume, by the aforementioned **Unknown Superior** and true enlightened being, **Peter Roche de Coppens.**

Unfortunately, I can not see this operation happening immediately, or even at a ground level, because of the propogated ignorance that blocks conscious development today. The World's people are becoming increasingly more confused and skeptical. This is because the myriad of false prophets—whose main focus is to sell books and be handsomely paid by their followers for seminars and advice, while energetically vampirizing them in the process. This scenario should alert you. But, we must persist in our goal to win over the dark and perverse forces of the New World Order by combining our energies and thought forms... *through prayer.* The creation of a global Egregore, created by the right people in the coming years, can conceivably save us. I have spoken of this concept in *Volume I,* and I will address it several times again in this trilogy, specifically, because this concept is of importance to the Illuminati. To be clear, not only human thought-forms exist within our universe of matter. Power can be generated within stellar and planetary bodies by harnessing what the ancients called, the **"music of the spheres."** These radiations of a powerful electro-magnetic nature are what the Illuminati use, and at times abuse, to further their own goals. The stars and planets are not dead bodies, but instead are living beings with a conscience. Their thought forms are manifested within a vibrational quid, *a certain bearing,* that produces an electro-magnetic radiance so powerful as to have an influence that can reach great distances. Their *shapes* are electro-static interference patterns that keep humans perpetually locked within certain limitations of consciousness.

The influences that the planets and stars have on destiny, and human behavior, were well known to ancient astrologers, but are commonly unknown in our *so-called* modern era. It is also well-known that thought vibrations focusing on the material plane are very low in frequency. These kind of vibrations abound in churches, as the faithful tend to ask for material favors, or for satisfaction on the animal side of man, instead of for gifts aimed at nurturing the spiritual evolution of their spiritual soul, an aspect that is significant to the true initiates and real Illuminati via the light of God. To clarify, these vibrations permeate the statues where the faithful pray, and create what is called an Egregore or *egregor* (from the greek ἐγρήγοροσ, «watchful,» «awake»). An Egregore is essentially *an amoeba energy,* and totally devoid of Intelligence, whose sole purpose is to preserve itself through a process of subtracting energy. Without them even realizing it, energies are *subtracted* from all the faithful who prostrate in front of religious statues. Over time, the amoeba can become something extremely powerful. This is not fictional speech.

The great Moses, the Supreme Master who had knowledge of the potential of human thought, forbade his people such forms of worship, *specifically for the reasons mentioned above,* as absolutely dangerous, immoral, and disrespectful of the God within. More specifically, Moses forbade worshiping idols (containers), *or things,* over essence.

In this sense, those who do not understand this concept worship the physical body rather than the inner god. The *initiation* is aimed at generating thought forms of love related to eternal ideals (divine archetypes), rather than those composed of low astral matter. [46] Satanists worship matter, not God. As Satan is the ruler of the lower astral plane (matter), that is why Satanism is rising so aggressively now, during this *Age of Matter*.

Chapter III

Satanism, Hollywood and the Illuminati

Modern Satanism and the Illuminati

If modern Satanism was created by Aleister Crowley, the more commercial and popular version was created by Anton Szandor LaVey, born Howard Stanton Levy (1930-1997). He promoted the more simplistic, atrocious, and exhibitionist side of Satanism. LaVeyan Satanism does not involve "devil worship" or worship of any deities. It is an atheistic philosophy that asserts: *"Each individual is his or her own god (and that) there is no room for any other god."* Adherents see the character of Satan as an archetype of pride, carnality, liberty, enlightenment, undefiled wisdom, and of a cosmos which Satanists perceive to be motivated by a *"dark evolutionary force of entropy that permeates all of nature and provides the drive for survival and propagation inherent in all living things."* [1]

LaVey's objective for the occult elite was to open up this Satanic reality by manipulating the average person to believe it as a suitable form of atheism. LaVey was an esoteric and occult student, a musician, a writer, and the founder of the Church of Satan. With LaVey's influence, beginning in 1966, the second phase of modern Satanism was launched as a genre that will come to find ample exposure within the media and contemporary culture. The resulting image of the "pop Satanist," will be pushed on us from that moment onward as someone who has become gradually accepted by the masses. We now embrace them as being among societie's eccentrics, and nothing more.

In the 1980s, as could be anticipated, everything changed with the exposure of **Satanic ritual abuse,** described by Wikipedia as:

> *SRA, sometimes known as ritual abuse, ritualistic abuse, organized abuse, sadistic ritual abuse and other variants that originated in the United States in the 1980s, spreading throughout the country and eventually to many parts of the world, before mostly diminishing in the late 1990s. Allegations of SRA involved reports of physical and sexual abuse of people in the context of occult or Satanic rituals. In its most extreme form, SRA involved a supposed worldwide conspiracy involving the wealthy and powerful of the world elite in which children were abducted or bred*

---

1   https://en.wikipedia.org/wiki/Satanic_ritual_abuse ‡ Archived 4th July 2015.

for sacrifices, pornography and prostitution. [2]

In the meantime the rise of the next "Satanic Whore" was just around the corner. For those who are not aware of it, the musician of Jewish origin Marilyn Manson was a disciple of Anton LaVey. In the book *Lucifer Rising*, in the chapter "War in Hell," author Gavin Baddeley states that despite his origins, LaVey was reported as saying: "*The true Satanist should be a 'Nazi Jew,' adopting the roles of both scapegoat and villain.*"[3] Of course this shocking statement by LaVey, who apparently was part Jewish, was made in sarcasm. Eventually, the Church of Satan highlighted issues of anti-Semitism present in the Church, something typical within certain fringes of Satanism that are close to right wing politics. Their goal, however, is to get rid of Christianity, not Judaism. The fact is that the "Satanic elite" is actually of Jewish descent. LaVey's protege rock star Manson says it proudly: "*Hopefully, I'll be remembered as the person who brought an end to Christianity.*"[4] Manson, who was ordained a Satanic reverend in the early stage of his career by *his "Satanic Majesty"* Anton LaVey, went on to shock the world by mutilating himself on stage, ripping up the Bible, and vomiting blasphemies against Jesus Christ at every concert. The negativity, chaos and pure evil promoted by Marilyn Manson at the height of his fame in the late 1990s and early 2000s is typical in this age of dissolution and evil.

At his concerts, bracelets were sold written with the acronym WWJD, stating that it did not stand for "What Would Jesus Do," but instead, "WE WANT JESUS DEAD." More than one Christian website states that:

> *He has allegedly raped a young girl on stage, and has sodomized one of his band members in front of thousands of children. He took a little puppy dog that was only six weeks old, and tossed it into the audience, encouraging kids to rip it to pieces and then smear the blood all over one another, which they gladly did. He said he dreams of the day that he can take a little baby and do the same thing to the baby. He has asked audiences at his concerts if they have ever eaten babies. He sells t-shirts encouraging children to KILL GOD, KILL THEIR PARENTS, and then KILL THEMSELVES.* [5]

Regardless of your religious beliefs or musical taste, thanks to people like him, pathetic little helpers of the Satanic New World Order, how sick this world has become needs to be recognized. Manson claims in one of his albums entitled *Anti-Christ Superstar ... that this is the age of the Anti-Christ ...* that presumably came to him via supernatural-inspiration: "*I heard this album as finished, I heard it in dreams ... It was like the revelations of John the Baptist or something.*"[6] The roots of all this is blasphemy and self-destruction, typical of LaVeyan Satanism, which was transmitted to Manson and other sicko's like him, and which are found in the teachings of Illuminati Grand Master **Aleister Crowley**.

Even the Italian Wikipedia suggests the link between the two: "*LaVey became interested in occultism in 1951, through the theories of Aleister Crowley,*" adding, "*In 1961, LaVey starts to detach from Crowley's ideas and, together with his friend, film director Kenneth Anger, establishes the Magic Circle, that from 1966 will become the Church of*

2   https://en.wikipedia.org/wiki/Satanism ‡ Archived 4th July 2015.
3   Gavin Baddeley, *Lucifer Rising: A Book of Sin, Devil Worship And Rock 'n' Roll*, (London: Plexus Publishing, 1999), p. 213.
4   See. Spin, New York in August 1996. p. 34.
5   See. http://www.jesus-is-savior.com/Evils%20in%20America/marilyn_manson-the_truth.htm ‡ Archived 4th July 2015.
6   See. hUH, Oct. 1996, p.34.

Satan."[7] Strangely enough, the English Wikipedia avoids making this claim or mentions Crowley's influence on LaVey, or his special connection with Kenneth Anger. **Why?** It is probably because of the power and influence the O.T.O. exercises in most English speaking countries; and, the fact that both organizations don't want to be associated or linked in any way. The "official" version of LaVey's connection to the O.T.O., as provided by The Church of Satan website, in *"Anton Szandor LaVey: A Biographical Sketch,"* is the following: *"A few years earlier LaVey had explored the writings of Aleister Crowley, and in 1951 he met some of the Berkeley Thelemites. He was unimpressed, as they were more spiritual and less 'wicked' than he supposed they should be for disciples of Crowley's libertine creed."*

Having said this, Anton LaVey was actually a participant to the mysteries and secret workings of the O.T.O., and Church co-founder Kenneth Anger is an honorary member of the O.T.O. Caliphate to this day. LaVey had a clear link to the O.T.O., and there are dark initiatic links still present between these two organizations, unknown to most people, and which I have been able to witness for myself when in the High Degrees. In 1966, soon after his experience with the O.T.O., LaVey's Church of Satan emerges with the full support of the various sects of the Illuminati connected to Kenneth Anger, who some say has always been the Church's Unknown Superior. The C.I.A. (Psyops sector in particular), and the F.B.I., are all organizations that helped LaVey to quickly achieve a certain reputation, and to have an immediate impact on the American media, making him literally famous overnight. This is something one can only achieve at that level if the system permits it. Isaac Bonewits wrote in *Real Magic* (1971), cited also by Dr. Michael Aquino, the following that clears up what was going on behind closed doors in the early days of the C.O.S in San Francisco:

> *Here in the San Francisco Bay Area an ex-circus odd-jobber jumped on the occult bandwagon and came close to making a fortune. Knowing just enough about occultism to impress the ignorant, he plagiarized Nietzsche and Hitler to put together a philosophy that appealed to fascists countrywide ... This man soon had members of the KKK, The American Nazi Party, local police departments, the Mafia, and ordinary socialites and jetsetters in search of a new thrill, all flocking to his meetings. Those without money or influence never got through the front door. How did I infiltrate, then? That's another story.*

> *This man had a rather monotonous repertoire of six or seven routines he perfomed weekly. These included prayers to Satan for blessings on the members, "incantations" of pure gibberish, ceremonies stolen from the Masons, the wearing of black KKK sheets, and a nude woman for an altar.*

> *Corny as he was, the rubes ate it up. He had absolutely no magical powers of his own, all he had was an incredible amount of charisma and pure chutzpah. But then again, there were fascinating deals going on behind closed doors (in his "Inner Circle"), and his knowledge of the private lives of San Francisco's wealthiest and most powerful families gave him tremendous opportunities for extortion and blackmail.*[8]

The figure of LaVey gradually made Satanism acceptable to the masses, let us always keep this in mind, as it was a stunt well-planned and crafted by the New World Order for achieving their own goals, nothing more. In this context, LaVey received the support of some famous people from the show business world, upon which he is said to have sum-

7   http://it.wikipedia.org/wiki/Anton_LaVey ‡ Archived 4th July 2015.
8   Michael Aquino, *The Church of Satan*, (San Francisco, CA: fifth edition privately issued Xeper@aol.com, 2002). p. 217.

moned a mysterious curse. The actress Jayne Mansfield tragically died soon after participating in one of his Black Masses, and **Sharon Tate** the wife of **Roman Polanski,** who
consulted LaVey for his *Rosemary's Baby* project (1968), was brutally mudered, together
with three friends by the followers of Charles Manson, himself a member of the *Solar
Lodge* of the Order Templi Orientis. [9] One of Sharon Tate's killers was Susan Atkins, who
worked with Anton LaVey. He employed Susan for his *Topless Witches Revue,* where "she
would come out of a coffin dressed as a vampire." [10]

Stemming from the Church of Satan derived another important sect, currently said to
be one of the most influential and powerful within the world of the occult, the **Temple
of Set,** which was created in the mid 1970s by the U.S. Military Intelligence officer **Lieutenant Colonel Michael Aquino** who, like the Illuminati, always believed that Satan
is a true entity, and not a figment of ones imagination or other sort of archetype or symbol. He believed Satan needed to be worshipped and addressed properly. For many years,
LaVey had been falsely portraying Satan to the outside world, and within the lower levels
of his Church, selling a mild and superficial version of lies and atheistic nonsense only to
please the masses. Once, Anton LaVey let his guard down when responding to the English
journalist and author Gavin Baddeley, also reputed by LaVey as a real Satanist, telling him
the true side of the story: *"If they're at all intelligent (other true Satanist's) … they'll
realize that there's only so much I can say publicly … I will not advance things in print
which make my position untenable … How long would the Church of Satan have lasted
if I hadn't appeased and outraged in just the right combination? It required a certain
amount of discretion and diplomacy to balance the outrage."* [11]

Lieutenant Colonel Michael Aquino was so committed to Satanism that he had the
number 666 tatooed on his scalp. The **Temple of Set,** a Satanic initiatory order founded
in 1975, proclaims that Set, another name for Satan, is a real entity and is a name for "**The
oldest known form of the Prince of Darkness.**" Aquino appears to have been convinced that society had become jaded to the point that many of those in the outer circle
of Satanism were ready to worship Satan as a real entity. Aquino believed it was time for
Satan to come out of the closet in all of his naked deformity. [12]

Aquino even brought a more up-front view of Satanism to the television airwaves,
stating that Satan *is* a real entity and that many remain in the dark as to whom they are
actually worshipping, including millions of New Agers. As I wrote in Volume I, when
Aquino went on Oprah Winfrey, he admitted to Winfrey—*and the television audience
made up of millions*—that they are following *the* Satan who initiated the original rebellion against God. He then added, "We are not servants of some God," declaring, "we
are our own gods!" At that point, Oprah Winfrey appeared to be shocked as she may
have realized that this was exactly what she believed as a New Ager, failing to recognize
that the New Age movement has its roots in Theosophy and Crowleyan Satanism, just as
with Aquino's Satanism. Orchestrated with various priests belonging to the Church of
Satan, Aquino's mid-70s *coup d'état* caused an internal schism at the top of the Satanic
hierarchy. This is when *the Temple of Set* was consecrated in **Santa Barbara, California**
during the summer solstice of June, 1975, by Michael A. Aquino.

In a "greater black magic" ritual, Aquino formulated a creation that resulted in what
he regards as an inspired text, entitled *The Book of Coming Forth by Night.* Aquino's

9   See. http://www.pararreligion.ch/sunrise/manson.htm ‡ Archived 4th July 2015.
10   Gavin Baddeley, *Ibid.*, p. 66.
11   *Ibid.*, p. 133.
12   http://www.goodfight.org/a_co_saraniccults.html ‡ Archived 4th July 2015.

work is compared by some to Aleister Crowley's "Cairo Working" of 1904, which resulted in the *Book of the Law*, the central sacred text of Thelema.[13] This schism gave an important role to the wife of Dr. Michael Aquino, who at that time was the head of the *Lilith Grotto* in New York, called **Lilith Sinclair**. In 1996, after many years, Aquino vacates the leading role of High Priest of the Order. From 1996 to 2002 the office of High Priest of the Temple of Set was held by Don Webb (born in Austin, Texas, in 1960), an American writer of science fiction. Suddenly, in 2002, and for an unspecified reason, the role of leader was passed on to **Magistra Zeena Schreck** (born Leena Galatea LaVey, 1963), **(FIG. 12)** Anton LaVey's daughter, who remained in office for only three months preamble to a schism within the Temple of Set. In 2004, after a period of *interregnum* in which Dr. Michael Aquino resumed control of his occult toy for a couple of years, he gives the leadership role to Patricia Hardy.[14] The above mentioned Don Webb is the author of an essay on Aleister Crowley, *The Fire and the Force*.[15] Webb focuses on the initiatory and philo-

FIG. 12 – Zeena Schreck, (born Zeena Galatea LaVey, 19 November 1963) in a photo made when she still belonged to the Church of Satan, founded by her father Anton.

sophical meaning of Crowley's life-work. I mention this just to reaffirm the importance of Crowley within the roots of contemporary Satanism, and the inspirational role that Crowley has always played with these puppets of the devil who are all part of the vast sectarian world behind the New World Order.

The text of Webb's book is divided into two sections: **The first** is made up of essays originally written for his inner students in the Temple of Set. **The second** part consists of new writings created exclusively for this book. Throughout the book Webb guides the reader in an initiatory journey along the Left Hand Path of the Illuminati. Inspired by the novel *1984* by George Orwell (1903-1950), LaVey wrote: *"On the altar of the Devil up is down, pleasure is pain, darkness is light, slavery is freedom, and madness is sanity. The Satanic ritual chamber is the ideal setting for the entertainment of unspoken thoughts or a veritable palace of perversity."*[16] This is exactly the kind of language used by professional manipulators of the mind, the so-called "mind-controllers," those who pull the strings of contemporary Satanism, not only from some dark Satanic grotto, but from the centers of military and academic influence. In 1975, journalist Dick Russell interviewed Anton

13   James R. Lewis, Jesper Aagaard Petersen, *Controversial New Religions,* (Oxford, England: Oxford University Press 2004), p. 435.

14   See. http://it.wikipedia.org/wiki/Temple of_Set. ‡ Archived 4th July 2015.

15   See. http://it.wikipedia.org/wiki/Don_Webb. ‡ Archived 4th July 2015.

16   https://archive.org/stream/Anton_Szandor_Lavey-The-Satanic-Rituals/Anton_Szandor_LaVey_-_The_Satanic_Rituals_id1996027432_size541_djvu.txt ‡ Archived 4th July 2015.

LaVey in an interview entitled "The Satanist Who Wants To Rule the World," where LaVey actually expressed that he and an elite group of Satanists would one day rule the world.

To reach this point, LaVey apparently used an occult booklet from the 1930s, [17] and some thoughts taken from Herbert George Wells' (1866 -1946) book called *The Island of Dr. Moreau,* a book he used to compose the lycanthropic rite, "Das Tierdrama," claiming it was orginally put together by the "Illuminati." This ritual includes the following words: "Man is God. We are men. We are gods. God is the Man." In short, it is the same old story Crowley repeated over and over again in his writings and in the motto: *Deus est homo* (God is man), present in the upper echelons of the O.T.O. It is also used as the name of an important lodge of the order located in Gothenburg, Sweden, and led by an old friend and collaborator of Anton LaVey, the occultist and musician, **Carl Abrahamsson**; a member of LaVey's inner-circle when he was alive. Carl was someone I met personally a few times, and he is probably one of the most influential occultists in Scandinavia. When you read, *The Island of Dr. Moreau,* which was LaVey's inspiration, and you analyze the "Das Tierdrama" ritual, you can perfectly understand how it can be adapted to a trauma-based mind control system.

In fact, the people who attend the secret rituals of the Church of Satan of today, know very well that once they enter the room where the rites usually take place, they are going to be prevented from exiting the premises prematurely; not only by closed doors, but also by two hooded guards. The rituals have been defined by some as disgusting, but others appreciate them for the presence of the usual girlie altar that appeals so much to its founder. LaVey used, in fact, naked human altars for rituals, as you can see in some photos taken during the Satanic baptism of his daughter Zeena, officiated when she was three years old, in May, 1967. [18]

Satanists to conquer space?

In the mid-1970s, the fringe that was closest to Anton LaVey and his Church of Satan, suddenly entered into a crisis when its leader gradually began to escape the public eye, and even the *faithful.* This gradual departure from the scene transformed in the early 1980s into a kind of seclusion by LaVey. He felt he had laid down the structure of Laveyan Satanism, and earned the right to privacy. While he has always maintained that the Satanic ritual abuse myth was too famous to represent any threat to the genuine Satanists, it is also true that the cultural environment wasn't any friendlier since the foundation of his Church of Satan in 1966. This despite opening up to the outside, and the continued participation in the media circus by LaVey, soon joined by Dr. Michael Aquino, who had left the C.O.S. to constitute his own sect and seek his own glory.

A pearl handled pistol and a big black cat as a pet were enough to ensure LaVey's protection in the past, but then came the 1980s and the arrival of "Satanic Ritual Abuse" in the media. Christian fundamentalists bombed abortion clinics, and paranoid communities formed teams of *vigilantes* against people who may be "cultists." LaVey could be forgiven for being a bit cautious in that period, as he was the most natural target. *The Black House,* his residence on California Street in San Francisco, CA, once freely-accessible to interested persons, began to resemble a fortress with a tall barbed-wire fence in the front yard, among other protections. [19]

17   http://www.centrosangiorgio.com/occultismo/articoli/anton_lavey_uomo_satana_2.htm ‡ Archived 4th July 2015.
18   *Ibid.*
19   Cf. Gavin Baddeley, *Ibid.,* p. 158.

Gavin Baddeley who was ordained a Reverend in the Church of Satan by LaVey, and is an experienced journalist, wrote the following on the most significant policy statement made by LaVey during the 1980s, called "Pentagonal Revisionism," with his corresponding "five points program":

1) *Stratification— LaVey believed in meritocracy and his contempt for egalitarianism was stronger than ever.*

2) *Strict taxation of all churches—the subject on which he fell out with Martin Lamers of the Kerk van Satan. Christianity was a racket, but if it was a honest racket it would have gone bust overnight.*

3) *No tolerance for religious beliefs secularized and incorporated into laws and order issues—already enshrined in the U.S. Constitution, though the antics of Christian fundamentalist during the 1980s made it worth restating.*

4) *Development and production of artificial human companions—an increasing preoccupation of LaVey's, illustrating his wish to use the androids for a "politically correct slavery" and also—in it's freedom for reliance on human beings for social stimulation—his belief on the disposability of most people.*

5) *The opportunity for everyone to live within an environment of his or her choice, with mandatory adherence to the aesthetic behavioral standards of same.* [20]

The so-called "Total Environments"—characterized by small-sized modern offices accompanied by spooky mannequins, always interested LaVey—and now in his old age he became obsessed by them. Satanists influenced by his work quoted him more often than Walt Disney, Milton, or Baudelaire, demonstrating to the world that LaVey's influence on contemporary Satanism was stronger than ever. The rising star of 1980s Satanism, Boyd Rice, once called LaVey "the Walt Disney of the dark side," and shared the admiration of LaVey for Disney and his creation, Disneyland. [21] In a 2002, a remake of the CD *Music Martinis and Misanthropy* by Boyd Rice and Friend, included as a bonus song, where Rice addresses the Columbine shootings in the line: **"Boyd Rice is the one who did it— now I've heard the secret news."** Despite his confession of complicity in the Columbine shootings, he was still invited to speak at M.I.T. [22]

As the Hellfire Club of the eighteenth century created their Abbeys of Thelema in desert caves, and Crowley opened his own in rural Sicily, LaVey was creating his private world in the basement of his Black House. At this point, as is evident from his writings, the majority of humanity not only disappointed him, but even distressed or disgusted him. His response was to isolate himself in a *film noir* fantasy-world made of seedy gin joints and run down hotel rooms, occupied only by his mannequins, that seemed to come alive in the twilight.

Not even a fantasist or a sorcerer—as the two terms are often interchangeable in the world of the occult—could isolate himself from family conflict. December 30, 1990, Zeena made public a letter she wrote to Dr. Michael Aquino, not only resigning from the Church of Satan, but disassociating from her father, who was the founder. To rub salt in the wound, Zeena, along with her husband, musician Nicholas Schreck, brought her circle of close followers inside the Temple of Set—which had for so long ridiculed her father's work:

"I was born a Satanist," wrote Zeena, *"My unfather was raised in the mundane*

20   Gavin Baddeley, *Ibid.*
21   *Ibid.*
22   William H.Kennedy, Satanic Crime, (Mystic Valley Media, 2006) p. 14.

FIG. 13 – Nikolas Schreck, husband Zeena Schreck, is an American musician, an author, film-maker and a prominent member of the Satanic milieu in California. Image taken from https://en.wikipedia.org/wiki/Nikolas_Schreck Filed July 28, 2015.

world of humankind, where he remains." Even his daughter understood that her father unknowingly had been an agent of pure demonic energy, but of course Zeena appreciated that: *"He unwittingly served as the agent of the true demonic energy needed to sire me, a genuine magical child."* At this point LaVey's daughter added that she had never seen any evidence that her father sincerely believed in the power that he used for so long. Regardless, her father still managed to attract the witch needed to perfect her own conception. *"My mother, a natural magician being as the incarnation of Diana the Huntress, was the driving force of the most positive aspects of the Church of Satan.*[23]

The full story behind this very bitter schism is probably only fully known by the people who were actually involved in it, but as I wrote in the previous pages, Zeena Schreck became the High priestess of the Temple of Set, however, she retained this title for a very short time. After reaching the top of the Setian hierarchy, Zeena helped her husband **Nicholas Schreck** **(FIG. 13)** to create a splinter group known as the **Sethian Liberation Movement** (S.L.M.), where she currently presides as its spiritual leader. S.L.M.'s strategic base is apparently in **Berlin Germany,** where it happily interfaces with the Ordo Templi Orientis, the location of their European Headquarters.

The Setian schism was well-described by Alex Burns of *disinfo.com*, and later reported by O.T.O. expert Peter-Robert Koenig on his website, "The Ordo Templi Orientis Phenomenon," in the Context: *Aleister Crowley, and the O.T.O. in the U.S., 2002 Schism: The Storm Awakens.*

Left Hand Path institutions often have a history of confrontations between individualist practitioners with different worldviews. The Temple of Set is no exception. High Priest Don Webb stepped down on the 9th of September, 2002, and was succeeded by High Priestess Zeena Schreck. Six weeks after the Helsinki Conclave (September 2002), Zeena, Magister Aaron Besson, Magister Nikolas Schreck, and Magister Michael Kelly, all resigned on the 8th of November, 2002. Four Priests, Alfred Rodriguez, Kevin Rockhill, Jared Davison; and Richard Gavin also resigned. Temple of Set sources have claimed that eighteen Initiates resigned, while others estimate the number to be closer to sixty (including several Orders, Elements, and members of the Adept and Setian degrees). The formation of any new magical group usually creates a period of inter-group conflict between the old and new. Michael Kelly's following document called the *Four Horsemen* (11 November 2002), was posted as follows on the *alt.satanism newsgroup* on the 13th of November 2002:

An early draft of a Frequently Answered Questions document defines the new and

---

23   Cf. Gavin Baddeley, *Ibid.*, p. 158.

as-yet unnamed group as "a loose con-federation of Setian Teachers and Students, an alliance of Orders." The group has eschewed the Temple's administrative and non-profit structure, as well as its degree system and titles. "We Work together through mutual respect and interest, not through any organizational limitations or restrictions," the FAQ document states. Finally, its founders have sought to avoid the "magical society" structure of post-Theosophy groups: the confederation is "an ongoing Magical Working in which we may participate, a living, dynamic and evolving thing." After a period of custodianship and transition, the Council of Nine, the Temple of Set's oversight body, ratified the nomination of Dr. Michael A. Aquino on the 9th of December 2002 as the new High Priest of Set. [24]

FIG. 14 – Book cover of Nickolas Schrek's The Satanic Screen: An Illustrated Guide to the Devil in Cinema, Creation Books published in June, 2001.

If you are interested in further studies on the subject, there is also a series of important **Public Research Sources** that are later given by Koenig, keeping in mind his usual apologetic stand and comments towards the Satanic/O.T.O. phenomena:

While the long-term implications of this schism are still unfolding, interested parties can check out a growing collection of public material on Left Hand Path practices and traditions. Neville Drury's Occult Experience *book (New York: Avery Penguin Putnam, 1987) and documentary film features an extensive interview with the Aquinos. Larry Kahaner's* Cults That Kill *(New York: Warner Books, 1989) contrasts Setian philosophy with "occult crime" distortions during the 1980s Satanic Ritual Abuse cycle. Dr. Stephen Edred Flowers'* Lords of the Left Hand Path *(Smithville, TX: Runa-Raven Press, 1997) remains the most authoritative and academic study of dissent and antinomian spirituality. Nikolas Schreck's* Flowers From Hell: A Satanic Reader *(London: Creation Books, 2001) collates key literary texts. Don Webb's* Seven Faces of Darkness: Practical Typhonian Magic *(Smithville, TX: Runa-Raven Press, 1996) and Uncle Setnakt's* Guide to the Left Hand Path *(Smithville, TX: Runa-Raven Press, 1999) offer a postmodern and practical approach to Left Hand Path initiation. Nikolas Schreck's* The Satanic Cinema *(FIG. 14) (London: Creation Books, 2001) offers a self-critique of the Devil as the Satanic archetype in this historical film. Two books, Dr. Stephen Edred Flowers and Crystal Dawn's* Carnal Alchemy *(Smithville, TX: Runa-Raven Press, 2001), and Nikolas and Zeena Schreck's* Demons of the Flesh *(London: Creation Books, 2002), reveal Left Hand Path practices of sado-magical and tantric sexuality.* [25]

Nicholas Schreck, Zeena's husband, was the founder and frontman of the impor-

24   http://www.parareligion.ch/schreck.htm ‡ Archived 4th July 2015.
25   *Ibid.*

FIG. 15 – Cover of the videotape of the film / Charles Manson Superstar documentary directed by Nikolas Schreck in 1989.

tant magical/musical collective known as *Radio Werewolf*, founded in 1984 in Los Angeles, and later disbanded in 1993. The group achieved some degree of success, particularly in Germany. Nicholas Schreck, with his video production company, produced *Video Werewolf* in 1989. It was a controversial documentary dedicated to the already cited Charles Milles Manson (b. 1934), entitled *Charles Manson Superstar* (FIG. 15). This documentary film, mostly shot by Schreck in the state penitentiary of San Quentin, where Charles Manson resides, has quite an interesting soundtrack where we find music by Olivier Messiaen's *Death and Resurrection*, Bobby Beausoleil's *Lucifer Rising*, Krzysztof Penderecki's *Apocalypsis,* and even Anton LaVey's, *The Satanic Mass*, along with tracks by Charles Manson himself, like *Clang Bang Clang* and *Mechanical Man,* taken from his album *Lie, The Love and Terror Cult.* [26]

As you may have noticed Schreck was inspired by Anton LaVey—whose original source was the usual Aleister Crowley—whose philosophies are utilized by the sickest artists on the scene; Boyd Rice, Marylin Manson; and, criminals who are inclined to follow a philosophy of life that centers on selfishness and disregard for all forms of authority. LaVey had ties to organized crime himself, and claimed Las Vegas gangsters were his role models. He pimped women in San Francisco's red light district throughout his entire adult life.

It is no wonder that LaVey's disciples, like Susan Atkins, went on to perform heinous murders. LaVey's Satanic teaching influenced a variety of criminals who also claimed to be Satanists. This is not to say that the Church of Satan or any of its offshoots are responsible for the criminal actions of others, but their publications and related media certainly encourage illicit activities. There are also other Satanic groups which espouse violence and criminal activities behind the veil of free speech. Several groups seek to unify Satanists in a final battle against Christians. *Radio Free Satan* has broadcast shows which encourage teenagers to commit suicide. LaVey's former followers have also faced legal problems. Boyd Rice was questioned by the United States Secret Service because of his relationship with Charles Manson. Rice actually visited Manson on many occasions, but was banned from doing so when he was caught attempting to smuggle a bullet into the prison where Manson was being held. Charlie had access to an arts and crafts shop where he could easily have fashioned a zip gun, and used Rice's bullet to either attempt an escape or kill a guard or fellow inmate. [27] In a documentary called *Speak of the Devil* (1993)—a

26   Leo Lyon Zagami, *Illuminati e la Musica di Hollywood,* (Montevarchi, Arezzo: 2014), p. 151.
27   William H.Kennedy, Satanic Crime, ***Ibid.***, p. 13.

biography of Anton LaVey—Boyd Rice, a high-ranking priest in the Church of Satan, and mentor of shock rocker Marilyn Manson, can be seen in a bowling alley dressed all in black like the Columbine shooters. He speaks of how most Satanists meet in bowling alleys "working on their scores." This segment is quite eerie when one considers that Harris and Klebold (i.e. the assassins of the The Columbine High School massacre), bowled for almost two hours before they began their murderous rampage. [28] Shane Bugbee (b. 1968), a high priest of the Church of Satan, is another underground artist of the Satanic milieu important for Satan's propaganda. Bugbee is a publisher, multi-media communicator and expert filmmaker, and the guy who actually conducted the final interview with Anton LaVey just months before his death in 1996. Bugbee also had his own problems with the law. Especially when he was investigated by the Secret Service after a guest on his Satanic radio show threatened the life of the President. However, even after the Secret Service visited his home, Bugbee commented on the 2004 election, when stating that: "*If you're not voting with lead, it's not worth a fucking vote.*" Both Bugbee and the aforementioned Boyd Rice were great supporters of George Walker Bush, as all Satanist support the Satanic establishment. Like William H. Kennedy wrote over ten years ago:

> With these sorts of exemplars it is no wonder that Satanic crime is on the rise. The constitutionally protected Religious Satanists like Rice and Bugbee are encouraging and celebrating violent acts to the Self-styled Satanists who most often do not belong to any formal organization and tend to form small cults, many of whom engage in illegal activities and use the literature and teachings of LaVey and his acolytes as ideological justification for crime. [29]

The problem is that people like Shane Bugbee seem influential not only within the growing sectarian criminal side of Satanism, but in recent years have also been unwillingly promoting a brand new generation of high profile Satanists. They are seemingly non-violent, and highly respectful of the system and its laws, as they want to introduce a more acceptable side of Satanism to the public in the name of religious freedom. Conscious pawns of this New World Order like **Douglas Mesner,** a.k.a. **Lucien Greves,** the founder of **The Satanic Temple,** created an organization in 2012 which has achieved more publicly than any other Satanic organization in the last few years. The group came into existence when its founder Douglas Mesner, who studied cognitive science, and was a long time member of LaVey's Church of Satan, joined Harvard's exclusive set-up with Cevin Soling, who now calls himself Malcom Jarry; a Harvard graduate, director, producer, and millionaire, who pulls the strings of The Satanic Temple's media campaign, with David Guinan; producer, director and creative director at Arise Media. [30]

Soling and Guinan are two rich kids connected to the elite of the New World Order. Shane Bugbee's involvement in mentoring Lucien Greves, and others like him, is shown with pride on the site *Vice,* in his article, "Unmasking Lucien Greaves, Leader of the Satanic Temple," published in July 2013:

> I have sought to promote alternative thought for more than 25 years as a publisher, promoter, gallery owner, and, as my mother-in-law once said, "a flim-flam man." During this time, I have opened the door to free thinkers and pure crazies alike. Sometimes they are welcome guests; other times, not so much. Lucien Greaves of the Satanic Temple, who first showed up at my door over a decade ago, would fall into the former category. He was a young man, too smart for his own good.

28 *Ibid.*
29 *Ibid.,* p.14.
30 http://www.shanebugbee.com/?p=2161 ‡ Archived 4th July 2015.

He wanted a copy of a book I had republished called, Might Is Right. *It was a 100-year-old tome, long forgotten by most, with the exception of Anton LaVey, who'd found it in a bookstore as a young man and used it as the basis for* The Satanic Bible. *I asked Anton to write an introduction, and he jumped at the opportunity to introduce the book to the world again.* [31]

I will further analyze the implications of Lucien Greaves and his "Satanic Temple," especially in relation to the activities of their Detroit Chapter, that recently held a Satanic ceremony on the steps of the state Capitol in Lansing, Michigan, on December 19, 2015. This was the nation's first state-sanctioned Satanic ceremony in history, another sign the End Times may be closer then you can imagine.

Meanwhile let's return to the late LaVey, who went through a bitter divorce from the mother of Zeena in the mid to late 1980s, that consumed him with appeals and legal procedures that would drag on for years. He spent much of his time in the last period of his life with his secretary and biographer, **Blanche Barton**, who would also give him a son. Zeena criticized LaVey's biography written by Burton, entitled, *The Secret Life of a Satanist,* laughing about certain excerpts, and criticizing them as: "*The sickening repetitive flattery she (he) extends to Zionism, Bolshevism and the state of Israel, while safely negating any Norse or Teutonic mythology.*"[32] The split seems to have been both personal as well as ideological between the two, as Anton, and his late companion Barton, gradually indulged in a more leftist approach, wanting to support the New World Order and their ideology that has lead to the Zionist /Jesuit/Communist hell of today (supported also by the Satanic Temple). LaVey's daughter Zeena shifted to a more Nazi-Norse Teutonic approach, that as we all know is just another emanation of the same dualistic system implimented by the elite. Zeena simply behaves like many other artists and Satanists were doing in the 1990s Satanic scene, that lead to the rise of Black Metal in Scandinavia, and the eventual burning of churches in Norway. It was the dawn of the final phase of the New World Order program pushed by the occult establishment, and the dark shadowy elite of the various Illuminati sects.

The most powerful Intelligence agencies were preparing for big developments for the apocalyptic new millenium, beginning with the tragic events of September 11th, 2001. LaVey was considered a simple icon of the past in front of the incredible rise of his protégé Marilyn Manson (which he personally initiated earlier to the priesthood of the Church Satan), who was inspired by the practices of an ancient Islamic sect of killers known as the *Assassins,* a name used to refer to a medieval sect, called the Nizari Ismailis, a branch of Shia Islam. [33] **Anton LaVey died on October 29, 1997** before he could witness the final eruption of so-called "Islamic fundamentalism," and "Islamic Terrorism." The latter phenomenon of "Islamic fundamentalism," and radical Islam is not restricted to a specific branch of Islam, and is present in both the Sunni variant of Islam (mainly in the Salafist ultra-conservative orthodox movement), and Shiite fundamentalism (present in Iran).

Wikipedia writes that: "*The modern Islamic fundamentalist movements have their origins in the late 19th century. The Wahhabi movement, an Arabian fundamentalist movement that began in the 18th century, gained traction and spread during the 19th and 20th centuries. During the Cold War following World War II, some NATO governments, particularly those of the United States and the United*

31   http://www.vice.com/read/unmasking-lucien-greaves-aka-doug-mesner-leader-of-the-satanic-temple
‡ Archived 4th July 2015.
32   Gavin Baddeley, *Ibid.,* p. 159.
33   https://en.wikipedia.org/wiki/Assassins ‡ Archived 4th July 2015.

Kingdom, launched covert and overt campaigns to encourage and strengthen fundamentalist groups in the Middle East and southern Asia."[34]

So even Wikipedia clearly admits the backing of the "Islamic fundamentalist" by NATO. I have analyzed the secrets of "Islamic Fundamentalism" in relation to the New World Order and the *Assassins* in Volume I, [35] "Islamic Fundamentalism," was presented to the masses and will eventually manifest the ultimate "Satanist" of today, first with Al Quaeda, and now with the black uniform armies of ISIS. That is something LaVey would have appreciated, for sure. Mind you, all this evil was carefully crafted at the time LaVey was still alive, in those secret programs of *Psychological Warfare* to which some say even LaVey himself was a participant, as well as his famous friend turned enemy, Dr. Michael Aquino. High level English Freemason Andrew Hicks, founding member of the prestigious "Corner Stone Society," and a member of Kirby Lodge 2818 in the United Grand Lodge of England, once confessed to me that they had inside information confirm-

FIG. 16 – Colonel John B. Alexander, indicated by many as the current leader of U.S. Satanism, and also close to Hollywood.

ing LaVey had been a Central Intelligence operator in the field of "Mind Control," and one of the top operators, not a simple pawn in their game. A well-orchestrated form of chaos is necessary to lay the foundations of the New World Order, and LaVey could have helped immensely with his diabolical expertise. ***Who is the Satanic leader in the U.S. as of today, you may ask?*** Who can match the likes of LaVey or Aquino in the Satanic structure? Obviously this doesn't count the far too many imposters we see on the web every day. In addition to the figure of Zeena I have already mentioned, there is the lesser significant one, she being Karla LaVey, half sister of Zeena, and creator of the *First Satanic Church,* an organization that appears to mimic the more commercial appeal of Satanism. There is also another key player in the field of *Psychological Operations* that is much talked about these days in the Satanic milieux, **Colonel John B. Alexander, (FIG. 16)** indicated by the *Executive Intelligence Review as an affiliate of the Stanford Research Institute linked to Tavistock Institute embedded in "New Age" Frankfurt School theories,* and contrary to Zeena, has always been loyal to Aquino and his Temple of Set

It comes as no surprise that Alexander is well-known by the so-called conspiracy theorists and UFO researchers who often interface with him on topics involving the UFO phenomenon. He is indicated by many credible sources as one of the leading contemporary figures in American Satanism, and is certainly popular among the rich and famous. Maybe that's why Alexander has been residing for years in the city of Las Vegas,

34   https://en.wikipedia.org/wiki/Islamic_fundamentalism ‡ Archived 4th July 2015.
35   *Confessions of an Illuminati, VOL I, Ibid.,* pp. 208-211.

where Satanism is present along with the elite of the entertainment world. Since the beginning—thanks to people like Sammy Davis, Jr., a member of the famous *Rat Pack* (group of artists led by Sinatra that helped create the myth of *Vegas),* was recruited into the world of Satanism by LaVey and Dr. Michael Aquino, and who was a frequent visitor to their Black Masses for many years. It is no wonder that occultists organize all sorts of events in Las Vegas, from the national gathering of alchemists, to meetings of branches of the infamous **Golden Dawn.** Colonel Alexander is an expert in the art of mind control, and he partially inspired the book *The Men Who Stare at Goats,* and the film that followed. He was, in fact, one of the trusted men behind **General Albert Stubblebine,** who in September, 2013 confirmed in an interview to *Gnostic Media* that **Aldous Huxley** was one of the guides—if not the supreme head of MK-Ultra. The General could not hide his embarrassment when he was asked the question about Huxley's involvement and, almost reluctantly, he admitted that "until now" this information had never been publicly revealed by any other member of American Intelligence, let alone by a former high ranking military Intelligence officer.

Returning to Colonel Alexander, he received the *National Award for Volunteerism* from President Ronald Reagan in 1987, and the *Aerospace Laureate Award* for *Aviation Week* in 1993 and 1994. Currently he lives in Las Vegas, with his two sons and his wife Victoria Lacas Alexander, who studies alien abductions. The two worked for *The National Institute for Discovery Science* (NIDSci), a privately financed research organization, that operated from 1995 to 2004, based in Las Vegas, and was created and funded by another "strange" character, the billionaire **Robert Bigellow.** He is one of those figures who is unknown to most people, but who is bound body and soul to the darkest faction of the American Illuminati that is connected to Dr. Michael Aquino and his associates. They also were involved in the study of the paranormal and ufology ... mysterious research that some say was used to disguise the group's more occult experiments and Satanic practices.

Colonel John B. Alexander is also the author of a very interesting book on the UFO phenomenon called, *UFOs: Myths, Conspiracies, and Realities* (New York, NY: Thomas Dunne Books, 2011). It is a book particularly appreciated by his ex-colleague in the U.S. military, Michael Aquino, who knows Alexander and described on an internet forum that the whole UFO phenomena as a huge PSYOP (Psychological Operation): *"So the emerging picture from UFO's is not one of are-They/aren't-They-here, but rather of a global phenomenon of human psychology: a PSYOP campaign without anyone actually running it. Much like the traditional circus coming to town, it thrills us, scares us, and certainly alleviates boredom. John Alexander isn't about to stare it down; like everyone else, he's having way too much fun with it."*[36]

By making such a statement publicly on an internet forum, Aquino is also participating to some extent in the massive *cover-up* underway of the true occult origin of the UFO phenomena, possibly in favor of something much more sinister that is going on behind closed doors with his friend Colonel Alexander and the other members of the Temple of Set. *Satanists conquering space* could be something to keep an eye on, as billionaire Robert Bigellow and his *Bigelow Aerospace* intend to market space flight. Amazingly enough, *Bigelow Aerospace* recently subcontracted with NASA to build a space module for them. It seems that Bigelow, Col. Alexander, and the Temple of Set, are actually going back to their roots, and dealing with the industry that was pioneered by scientist and occultist Jack Parsons (1914-1952), who I introduced in Volume I. Beyond all the *disinfo* out there, and demonstrating the proven links with the esoteric and the occult world, in

Volume IV, entitled *The Invisible Master*, I will outline, in detail, the reality behind the so-called "Roswellian Syndrome" and *the UFO myth.*

In order to clarify, once and for all, the link between Neo-Theosophy, Jesuitry and Satanism, I will discuss more about Dr. Michael Aquino in relation to his Theosophical background later in this book.

The occult roots of Hollywood and the god Enki: SATAN

FIG. 17 – The author indicates the Babylonian gate in the center of the The Hollywood & Highland Center, located between Hollywood Boulevard and North Highland Avenue in Los Angeles.

In the back entrance of the Kodak Theatre (now known as **Dolby Theatre**), where the famous Oscar ceremony takes place every year, there is a huge symbolic secret positioned there by the Illuminati elite for all to see,. The Dolby is a giant auditorium for concerts and events, and it is located in a huge shopping mall and entertainment center called **The Hollywood & Highland Center**, located between Hollywood Boulevard and North Highland Avenue in Hollywood, Los Angeles (FIGS. 17-18-19). The opening of the center took place on November 9, 2001, an event that went almost unnoticed to the majority of people, as it occurred only two months after the tragic events of September 11th, which had catalyzed the attention of the international media. The Dolby first hosted the prestigious ceremony of the Academy Awards (Oscars) in March, 2002. Many artists have performed within its walls, from Neil Young to Christina Aguilera, to Celine Dion, Mariah Carey, Beyonce Knowles, Alicia Keys, Elvis Costello, Barry Manilow, Prince, and my fellow Italian Andrea Bocelli,[37] and many others.

This is the first permanent home for the film industry's most important annual award, the Academy Awards, so as you can easily imagine, it is a place of enormous strategic importance for the various Illuminati sects and their vampiric Egregore. Through the so-called Hollywood stars, we find a world of illusions and entertainment that is constantly promoted by the New World Order. In the Dolby Theatre, which could be defined as the Vatican of the film industry, the meetings of what is regarded as the most influential Masonic lodge in Hollywood takes place. Most of the key places in this *Hollywood Babylon,* including the Masonic Temple across the street, now known as *El Capitan Entertainment Centre* (bought a few years ago by Walt Disney), were created by the Freemason and Worshipful Master, Charles E. Toberman (1880-1981). Having said that, I sincerely

37   http://en.wikipedia.org/wiki/Dolby_Theatre ‡ Archived 4th July 2015.

FIG. 18 – A close-up image of the two deities from ancient Mesopotamia represented on top of the gate.

did not expect to find all this Illuminati symbolism splattered right in front of my eyes in the middle of Hollywood. A full scale Babylonian gate oversees it all, positioned right at the center of the huge shopping mall and entertainment center, where every year the red carpet is unfolded to welcome the Hollywood elite and the rich and famous. Most tourists that visit this place every day are unaware of the symbolic importance, although they are constantly feeding their energies to the Hollywood Egregore and its propaganda.

David Icke formed an interesting analysis a few years ago in his book ***Children of the Matrix,*** where he declares: "*I can't emphasise enough that to understand what we call the present we have to understand the past, and this is why the Anunnaki- Illuminati have concentrated so much effort on rewriting history. Even Hollywood is an example. The Druids were tree worshippers, especially the oak. The holly was their most sacred symbol because it was sacred to Mother Holle or Hel, the goddess of the underworld. Thus we have Holle or Holly-wood (Hel-wood), the 'place of magic' and home of the Illuminati's mass propaganda and conditioning machine in California. The holly wood was a favourite source of magic wands.*"[38]

Well said David. Unfortunately, when he wrote the statement above, the monstrosity I described above had not yet been created, so I wonder what Icke will write about Hollywood now, as the Annunaki element is clearly visible at the top of this huge monument. On the left, you find the images of the god known in Sumerian mythology as **Enki,** later known in Babylonian times as **Ea,** and defined by the noted scholar Zecharia Sitchin as the commander in chief of the *Anunnaki,* and on the right, the god **Nisroch,** the ancient Assyrian god of agriculture. [39]

Enki is presented in its classic role of water carrier, as it was well-known in antiquity. Some researchers say this is the basis of the alien "blood lines" that rule our planet, the same as those David Icke calls the *Reptilians.* The historian Benito CA stated in his well-known 1969 thesis: "*With Enki is observed an interesting change in the symbolism of the sexes, the agent fertilizer is also water, in Sumerian 'a' or 'Ab' which means, however, also sperm. In a passage of a Sumerian hymn, Enki lingers on the empty riverbeds and fills them with his water.*"[40] At the center of the two deities is a representation of the tree

38   David Icke. ***Children of the Matrix,*** (Wildwood MO: Bridge of Love, 2001), p. 179.
39   http://en.wikipedia.org/wiki/Nisroch ‡ Archived 4th July 2015.
40   See. http://www.gatewaystobabylon.com/essays/essayenkiworld.html ‡ Archived 4th July 2015.

FIG. 19 – A Google Maps © frame dated 3/8/2011, shows an overview of the immense center and its Babylonian gate.

of life of the Kabalah, which symbolizes the laws of the universe. Both representations on this "Hollywood Babylonian gate" show impressive images from the early civilizations of Mesopotamia—at the center of what is *effectively* the main temple of the global factory of illusions within our civilization. There are also two gigantic elephants, placed on two immense columns, that are the symbols of the Babylonian god Ishtar (also known as the Sumerian Inanna, or the Egyptian Isis). The full story of the impact of the *Annunaki* (as they call these deities) on human civilization has been partly revised and narrated in recent decades by Zecharia Sitchin (1920-2010) in his works, and in particular, in his book *The Earth Chronicles.* Many traditional historians never accepted his interpretations, with its paleo-astronautical flavor, and are in line with the religious beliefs of the Illuminati sects; who love the fact that they can be descendants of these ancient deities, which, according to Stitchin, came to this planet from another about 445,000 years ago.

The Annunaki (according to Stitchin) came to Earth in search of gold and assumed the role of gods, transmitting civilization to mankind and teaching men to worship them, becoming, as taught also by David Icke, the ancestors of the current royal families that guide and control the world and the power system of the Illuminati network of secret societies. According to the eccentric English author Icke, many royal families are part of the Annunaki bloodline, and the old Queen Mother, Elizabeth of England (1900-2002), was repeatedly seen changing from reptilian to human when she was still alive.

On this theory I diverge with Icke a little bit, or at least we used to diverge until recently—when David Icke finally embraced the extradimensional view of the alien reality to define the so-called "reptilians." I think this is a much more credible stance, as I personally don't shapeshift nor have a tail. However, the **"Spiritual Satanist,"** as the dark side of the Illuminati often consider themselves, does not believe in the existence of the Judeo-Christian God YHVH, that they consider as a deity imposed by the Jewish system (which is, by the way, secretly in league with them). The spiritualist of the dark side instead believe in Satan, who was actually a name attributed to the Sumerian god *Enki.*

In their interpretation, *Astaroth* coincides with the Sumerian god *An-Anum* and the gods *Enlil* and *Enki-Ea* (respectively **Beelzebub** and **Satan** in "Spiritual Satanism"), which together form a **Cosmic Triad**.[41] Some Illuminati initiates intepret the three points used by Occult Masonry and the *Ordo Templi Orientis* to the Cosmic Triad. The "Spiritual Satanist" also states that the Abrahamic religions have labeled the ancient pagan gods unfairly, the so-called demons. In this context, *Enki-Satan* is considered the most powerful of all, so it is no wonder he rules over the Hollywood Babylonian gate. In Hebrew, "Satan" means adversary, and for this reason he is an opponent to the Jews but, in their interpretation, he is not an enemy of the Gentiles (non-Jews). Satan is a figure that in their view sprung up from a "demonization" of the Sumerian god *Enki* and his lineage. But while Satan is cloaked, by most, in an aura of "negativity," the Sumerian *Enki* never was. Also, the Satan that was handed down to us, in their eyes, is wrongly accused of all his "evil deeds." *Enki* is responsible for glorious actions, as well as reprehensible ones. According to the Illuminati, who embrace the philosophy of Enki known as *Enkism,* the basis of "Spiritual Satanism," this makes him *more human* in the eyes of the Satanist, They even state that Judaism and Christianity are indirectly based on *Enki*, a character that has been defined as an "enemy" (*Shaytan*) and placed in a negative light.

Enki/Satan was no longer officially worshipped[42] by the population, but only in the secret temples and secret lodges of some sects of the Illuminati. I went to Hollywood while I was writing this chapter to visit the Neo-Babylonian structure next to the Dolby Theatre, and I felt the strong energy present in this place. It was not the best, I can assure you. I then discovered something that could confirm the occult and evil nature of this place. This design of the three-story complex known as "The Hollywood and Highland Center" is based on a movie made by American film director and Freemason **David Llewelyn Wark DW Griffith (1875-1948)**, who is remembered by many for his controversial film that came out in 1915 called *The Birth of a Nation,* upon which the current scenery is based, including its impressive Baylonian gate. The underlying problem is that David Wark Griffith, with his immensely successful film, was actually openly promoting the *Ku Klux Klan* sect, known by the acronym "KKK," and presenting them as the unlikely heroes of this racist film, and inspiring their come back after a period in which their numbers had been reduced to a minimum. It is a diabolical idea inspired by the usual manipulators of the occult establishmen pursuing the promotion of the "Race War" card.

In any case, even back then, Griffith was criticized for his racist film, and he had to immediately resort to creating another in order to change the atmosphere around him as quickly as possible. That's when he made *Intolerance (1916),* where he describes the subject of "intolerance" during different ages of mankind, as if to justify himself for his previous film. But the damage had been done. Many historians are inclined to believe that Griffith made *The Birth of a Nation* with the purpose of criticizing the Afro-American man and glorifying the white man. This was the message he gave in a film that was received and endorsed by the White House, over a hundred years ago, on February 18, 1915, in the presence of President Thomas Woodrow Wilson (1856-1924). This is an unprecedented act that was never entirely forgotten by the African American community, so much so that DJ Spooky recently dedicated a live mix to this silent movie, of course being highly critical of the content. Thusa new version of the film was created entitled *Rebirth of a Nation,*[43] a project that led Spooky to travel the world and perform in the most unlikely places, including a small stone-built theater located on the southern slope of

41 http://it.wikipedia.org/wiki/Astaroth ‡ Archived 4th July 2015.
42 http://laviadienki.altervista.org/enkismo.html ‡ Archived 4th July 2015.
43 http://www.rebirthofanation.com/ ‡ Archived 4th July 2015.

the Acropolis of Athens. Griffith's funeral was celebrated at the aforementioned Masonic Temple in Hollywood, but with the growing controversy surrounding his film dedicated to the KKK, there were actually very few *stars* present.

Despite this, **Charlie Chaplin** called Griffith "the Master of us all," and directors like Ford, Hitchcock, Welles, Kubrick and others [44] have always spoken of their great respect for the director of *Intolerance*. It should come as no surprise that after so many years, the "illuminated" elite would dedicate a space for his role in the "magic" of Hollywood, with a movie like *Intolerance,* about his alleged "redemption." But behind this symbolism, taken from Griffith's film set, there is something more sinister: Enki... or Satan... the power that determines control over the masses. Not surprisingly, the first public celebration of the **Gnostic Mass** conceived by Aleister Crowley for the O.T.O. was held in Hollywood in March 1933, at 1746 Winona Boulevard, just off the much better known Hollywood Boulevard, where we have the Dolby Theatre, which is placed on an important ley line according to writer and investigator Bret Lueder in his book, *Song in Your Heart: The Story for the Search for the Lost Note*. There is a ley line that runs from Hollywood to the northeast of California, through the Forest Lawn Memorial Park of Hollywood Hill, the famous cemetery of the stars, and all the way to the Disney studios of Pasadena. [45]

The term "ley line" was originally conceived by Sir Alfred Watkins. The current definition of a ley line according to Wikipedia is as follows: "*Ley lines are hypothetical alignments of a number of places of geographical interest, such as ancient monuments and megaliths. Their existence was suggested in 1921 by the amateur archaeologist Alfred Watkins, whose book* The Old Straight Track *brought the alignments to the attention of the wider public.*" [46] I find it interesting that this new Babylonian monument was placed next to the Dolby Theatre on this important ley line in 2001, exactly ten years after celebrated English gay film director Nigel Finch came out with an hour-long documentary called *Kenneth Anger's Hollywood Babylon* (1991). It begins with Kenneth Anger's tale of DW Griffith's recreation of ancient Babylon for his silent 1915 epic, and all the drama that went with it. It seems as though the elite Satanists in Hollywood were already preparing for what they were to visibly erect in 2001, as this documentary is heavily-influenced (like Anger's 1965 book *Hollywood Babylon),* by DW Griffith's epic Hollywood legacy. It alternates the life and work of the occult filmmaker Kenneth Anger, with readings and enactments of the lurid episodes recounted in Anger's scandalous *Hollywood Babylon* and *Hollywood Babylon II* books. Apparently Kenneth "chickened out" of the third book in this series because exposing Scientology would have created problems for him with the Hollywood establishment.

In 2010 Anger mentioned in an interview that the third volume was finished, but was placed on hold, explaining: "*The main reason I didn't bring it out was that I had a whole section on Tom Cruise and the Scientologists. I'm not a friend of the Scientologists.*" [47] Let's not forget that there is a fair degree of competition between the *Ordo Templi Orientis* and Scientology, but they will not clash with each other as they both have close links to Aleister Crowley, whose rites are said to have opened the gates of hell. Babylon comes from the Sumerian, **"KA.DINGIR.RA"** which in the translation to Akkadian in Bab-ilani, means: **"The Gate of the Gods."**

44   http://en.wikipedia.org/wiki/D._W._Griffith ✝ Archived 4th July 2015.
45   See. Bret Lueder, *Song in Your Heart: The Story for the Search for the Lost Note* (Chico, CA: House of Lueder Publishing, 2012).
46   https://en.wikipedia.org/wiki/Ley_line#Alfred_Watkins_and_The_Old_Straight_Track ✝ Archived 4th July 2015.
47   https://en.wikipedia.org/wiki/Hollywood_Babylon ✝ Archived 5th July 2015.

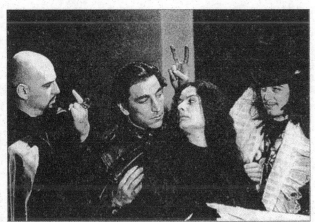

FIG. 20 – *A very rare frame from the original* Lucifer Rising. *It is said that the group known as the Manson "Family" buried in an unmarked grave the only existing copy in the vast plains of Death Valley. This image is taken from the book* Lucifer Rising *written by Gavin Baddeley.*

Partly miming the opening phrase of the soliloquy portrayed in the "Nunnery Scene" of William Shakespeare's play *Hamlet*, "I should say this time Gods or Demons, *that is the question. Whether is nobler in the mind* of a truth seeker and a libertarian *to suffer The slings and arrows of outrageous fortune, Or to take arms against a sea of demons,* And by opposing them? To die: to sleep."

Shakespeare is regarded as the greatest writer in the English language, and the world's pre-eminent dramatist, and he is a key figure to every English speaking actor, but few realize that the philosophic ideals promulgated throughout the Shakespearian plays distinctly demonstrate their author to have been thoroughly familiar with certain doctrines and tenets peculiar to Rosicrucianism. In fact, the profundity of the Shakespearian productions stamps their creator as one of the Illuminati of the ages. [48] Who knows what Shakespeare would have written about in Hollywood today, especially now that it seems firmly in the hands of the dark side of the the Illuminati, where black magicians and witches are casting a constant spell on humanity, *so beware of the "Magic of Hollywood."*

The Illuminati artists serving HER SATANIC MAJESTY

In January of 2002, an article in the **Special Collector's Editions** of *Uncut,* published a story on the Rolling Stones. The article covered the most hidden and dark secrets of the legendary group. The singer Mick Jagger was awarded the title of Knight Bachelor for services to music by Prince Charles, eleven months later. Another key member of the Rolling Stones, Keith Richards, criticized Mick Jagger for accepting such an honor. But Richards criticism was "liquidated" by Jagger who stated that Keith is like a child who sees another with an ice cream and is simply envious about it. However, many of his fans saw this move as a contradiction to his supposed anti-establishment image. These fans probably know very little about the real Jagger, who has always been a fan of the monarchy... and especially Satan. **"United Press International,"** noted that it was definitely an unusual gesture from the UK's Royal House, as "Sir" Mick Jagger never did any charitable work during his life, not even participating in the pop/rock concert that was held at Buckingham Palace to celebrate the fifty years on the throne of the Queen. *So why such an honor?* Perhaps the usual "devil's luck" that touches those who have a certain passion for the occult and the central figure of Aleister Crowley. (FIG. 20) This may be the same luck that befell another character mentioned in Simon Goddard's article in *Uncut.* I'm talking about **Jimmy Page, (FIG. 21)** who in December, 2005, received the same distinguished honor by the British Royals: *The Most Excellent Order of the British Empire.* This is a British order of chivalry established by King George V, and it is considered one of the most important awards in Britain. In this case, Page did not receive the award for his music merits (of a clear diabolical nature), but for charity... charity Mick Jagger, another sympathizer of the devil, never did. As for the songs with a Satanic touch in the discography of the Stones, we find the all time classic *Sympathy for the Devil* at the top of

FIG. 21 – *Advertising poster for the unused soundtrack of the film* Lucifer Rising, *promoted as a project related to Jimmy Page and Led Zeppelin, shows the symbol* **Ordo Templi Orientis.** *Disagreements between Anger and the group came to annoy the director, who eventually threw them into what was called the "curse of Kenneth Anger."*

the list. The interest of the Stones for Satanism is also apparent from the titles of other songs: *Sweet Black Angel, Conversation with my Demon Brother, Dancing with Mr. D,* and the album *Their Satanic Majesties Request.* It would seem that this last one, in particular, was composed at the request of Anton LaVey, as stated by Father Jean-Paul Regimbal (1931-1988), while others claim it was done for Kenneth Anger, who in turn states that he was the inspiration for the song *Sympathy for the Devil.* Kenneth Anger (still alive), co-founder of the Church of Satan, leading figure of the *Ordo Templi Orientis,* and former occult mentor of both Mick Jagger and Jimmy Page, must be proud of his disciples now that they were both rewarded for their work by the supreme elite manipulators that rule this planet: the British Royals.

The Brits and the Royal family, along with British Intelligence, have supported the rise of the "Great Beast 666" Aleister Crowley from the very beginning, and later promoted his sick ideology, thanks to their embrace of many "Rock Stars" (starting with the Beatles). If you sell your soul to the devil, eventually you will be reciprocated with generous rewards by the British Royals. Of course *you can prefer little children,* as in the case of Jimmy Saville, since the English Royals have no preferences regarding sexuality, provided you stay within the bounderies of their "game." If not, your life will be cut short, possibly with a heart attack at age 27, in which case, you will join the infamous and legendary *Club 27.* Mick Jagger's latest tragedy, the death of his girlfriend Wren Scott, seems to be part of the ongoing "curse of the devil" that hits the weaker subjects involved in these enterprises. But let's not forget the *luck* of the devil. Kenneth Anger still enjoys plenty in contemporary Hollywood, as he is one of the top representatives of the *Ordo Templi Orientis,* with his prestigious honorary 9th degree (the equivalent of an honorary 33rd degree in the A.A.S.R.).

Kenneth Anger recently participated in a re-enactment of the previously cited **"Das Tierdrama,"** originally created by his friend Anton LaVey, who promoted it as a ritual of Adam Weishaupt's Order of the Illuminati. But, according to his friend and then main antagonist Dr. Michael Aquino, this isn't really the case.:

"Das Tierdrama" is again a variation of the original Church of Satan version. In the Satanic Rituals it is attribuited to the Order of the Illuminati in Germany. Records of the doctrines and ceremonies of that order exist in the papers of its two principal leaders, Adam Weishaupt and Baron de Knigge, however, and I have found nothing resembling the "Tierdrama" among them. Nor, as Anton also suggest, it is from the ritual text of the O.T.O. or the Golden Dawn. Applying Occam's Razor, then, I presume it was adapted from HG Wells' The Island of Dr. Moreau, in which case the reference to the "house of pain," "the hand that wounds," and "the hand that heals" make sense. The German origin of the text is also argued against by the erroneus German-language translation. The version of "Die Elektrishen Vorspiele" appearing in the Satanic Rituals also evidences German language problems—beginning with its title, which is erroneously translated into the plural. [49]

However, "Das Tierdrama" is considered one of the most important rituals devised in the milieu of modern Satanism. It became, in 2013, the main inspiration for a music video behind the song *Love In The Old Days* (Ted James 1999 remix), by the duo called Daddy. But Daddy is not just your average musical project, as is was established by the famous Hollywood actor **James Franco** and his old school friend, Tim O'Keefe.

Dangerous Minds blog writes: *"When producer Ted James remixed one of Daddy's songs, Love in the Old Days, Franco cast Kenneth Anger in the music video, presiding over a masked bacchanal based on Anton LaVey's lycanthropic Das Tierdrama ritual (which was, in turn, based on* The Island of Doctor Moreau *by HG Wells).* [50]

James Franco is an ambiguous figure. In 2014, he was accused of inappropriate relations with a seventeen year old he attempted to meet online. Well, suprise surprise, Franco himself is a long time Satanist, who made his first short film, based on his idol Kenneth Anger, when in cinema school at New York University. Franco and O'Keefe, along with another musician and occultist named Brian Butler, who introduced Franco to Anger were, on the 4th of December 2012, due to invoke the demon *Bartzabel,* using a ritual originally designed by Aleister Crowley for a unique public event held in London in 1910. In our *modern times,* this ritual was to be replicated in an art gallery in Venice Beach (L&M Arts, Los Angeles, 660 South Venice Boulevard, Venice, CA, 9029).

On December 5, 2012, Lisa Derrick in *MAGAZINE, Show & Event Coverage* wrote: "Brian Butler—assisted by Twilight: New Moon actress Noot Seear, and actor Henry Hopper—were supposed to invoke *Bartzabel,* the forceful spirit of Mars, into the body of actor James Franco." Announcing later in an UPDATE on the same page: "JAMES FRANCO MISSED HIS FLIGHT AND THERE WAS AN UN-ANNOUNCED STAND-IN, ACCORDING TO COMMENTS AFTER THIS WENT TO PRESS." [51]

So presumably, Franco missed his plane at the last minute and was quickly replaced by someone else. This should make one wonder what really went on that day in LA., as Anger was also absent from the stage *(or was he?).* This part of Los Angeles is well-known around the world for having been the birthplace of the famous rock group *The Doors,* whose leading singer Jim Morrison, another lover of Crowleyanity and the occult, prematurely died at age 27 (thereby joining the sinister "27 Club"). After visiting Venice

---

49   Michael Aquino, *The Church of Satan, Ibid.,* p. 235.
50   http://dangerousminds.net/comments/love_in_the_old_days_james_francos_satanic_music_video_starring_kennet ‡ Archived 5th July 2015.
51   http://www.cartwheelart.com/2012/12/05/cartwheel-blog-twlight-star-noot-seearbrian-butler-perform-aleister-crowley-ritual/ ‡ Archived 5th July 2015.

in 2014, I can confirm that it feels like the usual tourist trap—light years away from the poems and lyrics of Morrison, with a negativity present that is all too noticeable.

Secretly instigated by the elite in the 1960s and 70s, the "Flower Revolution" was celebrated. It offered some great music, but it was actually a great experiment to modify the cultural foundations of American society. This movement permeated an entire generation—pleasing both Morrison and mind control expert Aldous Huxley—which carries into the decadence of today. It would appear that the Aleister Crowley ritual mentioned above was effectuated by these modern Hollywood Illuminati in a place of magical power like Venice Beach so they could energize their Egregor involving as many people as possible. They did all this wishing to *re-open the doors—The Doors,* in fact, *of Hell.*

In 2015, Paris Hilton, an American socialite and in the last few years aspiring DJ, after attending an event linked to Formula 1 car racing in the principality of Monaco, was suddenly picked up and brought to an exclusive party, which took place not far from Cannes, and arranged by Kenneth Anger. It appears that Paris Hilton is not only a DJ for Kenneth, some say that she has inherited the role of *priestess of the mysteries* that was once held by British artist Marianne Faithfull. Incidentally, in April 2006, Hilton was the protagonist of an unusual cover, created for *Masonic Quarterly Magazine,* a now defunct official journal of the United Grand Lodge of England (later substituted by *Freemasonry Today*). The April issue associated the entertainment world and the Illuminati. It is a subject I analyzed and published in an Italian essay called *Illuminati e la Musica di Hollywood* ("Illuminati and the Music of Hollywood" —Harmakis Ed. Montevarchi, Arezzo), in November 2014.

Illuminati and Psychedelia: from Rome to California

In their 2002 work, *Demons of the Flesh,* authors Nikolas and Zeena Schreck dedicated their book to a new magical path. In cleaving much closer to Crowleyanity and sexual magick (with a "k" as Crowley wanted), they thereby broke with Dr. Michael Aquino, their occult controller, and moved toward an initiatic independence that introduced their *Sethian Liberation Movement* (formerly known as *Storm*). The first words in their book include a dedication that leaves me rather perplexed. The dedication is to an important figure of the Italian esoteric scene, a person I respect and admire, named Julius Evola (1898-1974). The words written by these two Satanists constitute a full-blown recognition of Evola's work: *"For the Order of Babalon, the Order of Sekhmet and their allies. Dedicated to the Memories of Baron Julius Evola, who began the work of awakening the left-hand path in the West."*

Baron Julius Evola was born in Rome within an ancient Sicilian family, a similarity with my own origins that has always made me sympathetic to this somehow "obscure" figure. Evola was a member of the mysterious Illuminati group known in Italy in the 1920s as the **Group of Ur,** that later became known as the **Group of the *"Dioscuri"*** (literally **"Blackgods"**), which are in existence still to this day. Just before I left the Illuminati Network in 2006, I published an article for their prestigious occult publication. The work in question was based on the Alchemy Gate, *or Magic Portal,* of Piazza Vittorio in Rome,[52] an extradimensional portal of which I have spoken of both in Volume I and III of this *Confession series..* Going back to address this apparent link between Baron Evola and modern Satanists in the U.S. Illuminati and Satanism gives me the opportunity to investigate the unusual background of the Group of Ur and their influence in the occult world. Especially interesting is this group's relationship with drugs, and their *somewhat scientific* testing of these sustances in an initiatic environment. With their extensive research and

52   https://it.scribd.com/doc/139047284/8-La-Porta-Ermetica ‡ Archived 5th July 2015.

publications, the influence they had at an international level is demonstrated within the dedication made in the book *Demons in the Flesh,* which is followed on the same page by the **Disclaimer:** *"The sexual and magical activities described in this book are intended for application Exclusively by adults who have Reached the Age of Majority, and Should only be performed on a consensual basis by individuals possessing sound physical and mental health. Recommendations suggesting that the reader undertake proper training in physical activities. Neither the authors nor the publishers of this book can assume any liability or responsibility for any harm that might happen to the reader as a Consequence of the experiments outlined herein."* [53]

I'm not sure what Julius Evola would think of this radicalization of the left-hand path, described in this way by the authors:

> *Demons Of The Flesh is the very thing it describes, in that it can be understood as a sex magic working in its own right. As a brain-child created by the polarized erotic energies of male and female sexuality generated by its authors, this book illustrates how the combined sexual force of two magicians can create a daemonic third entity. By shaping the collaborative words and perspectives of two magicians into a cohesive whole, we have aimed to bring into being a magical elemental that takes on a certain life of its own, independent of its creators. Whenever two magicians work together, the creation of such an elemental force is the result; William S. Burroughs and Brion Gysin referred to this phenomenon as "the third mind."* [54]

I have personally known both the above mentioned Burroughs and Gysin. This is thanks to my grandmother, Felicity Mason a.k.a. Anne Cumming, [55] a controversial figure within the elite of whom I speak about in Volume I of my *Confessions,* [56] I can therefore personally confirm the importance of the magical work done by the two, work which will eventually lead to the initiation of William Burroughs in the **Illuminati of Thanateros (I.O.T.)**, an Illuminati sect I will analyze further in Volume III. The Italian researcher Franco Landriscina's new and improved description of the Group of Ur was originally published in an article in Italy, in a book by Antonio Castronovo called, "L'Immaginazione al Podere. Che cosa resta delle eresie psichedeliche"(Viterbo, Italy: Stampa Alternativa, 2005), which helps us to understand the strange connections of the **Group of Ur and the initiatory path to psychedelia**, which is the translation of the title of Castronovo's short essay that opens this way:

> *In the 1980s, visiting an exhibition in Rome on the art form known as Dadaism, I experienced a curious effect of "cognitive dissonance." Among the works on display there were some paintings and a small wooden table painted by none other then Julius Evola. The paintings impressed me for their visionary content, not really in tune with the rest of the show. More than that, though, I was puzzled by the table. For the style and colors of the images that covered it, in fact, didn't look like it came from the Rome of the 1920s where it was made, but from the San Francisco of the late 60s, the home of the "Flower Power Child" on acid. What's more, the name of its author was for me connected at the time to the far-right slogans and events of the 70s, certainly not to this kind of colorful patterns. In short, something was not right. For the moment I did not enquire further.*
>
> *Years later, though, once I read several books on the subject of altered states of*

53   Nikolas & Zeena Schreck, *Demons of the Flesh,* (Washington DC: Creation Books, 2002), p. 1.

54   *Ibid.,* p. 11.

55   http://www.independent.co.uk/news/people/obituary-anne-cumming-1464458.html ‡ Archived 5th July 2015.

56   *Confessions of an Illuminati, Vol. I, Ibid.,* pp. 210, 212, 213.

consciousness and approached more deeply the esoteric world, studying the writings of Evola, I finally started to understand certain things, and found out that, indeed, behind those paintings, and that table something truly "psychedelic" was really going on. Something, indeed, throwing a new light on the recent history of psychedelic substances.

The "official" historical version of the events surrounding the birth of psychedelia explains that it originated in 1943 with the discovery of LSD by the Swiss chemist Albert Hoffmann, and continued into the 1950s when the writer Aldous Huxley tried mescaline... 1955 is the year of Huxley's first experience with LSD, followed, in 1959, by Allen Ginsberg. In 1960 Timothy Leary founded the Psychedelic Research Project at Harvard University, and three years later he was fired from the same university when he began his adventure as a guru of the growing youth protest movement. LSD became illegal in 1966, and in 1967 the hippie movement blossomed into the intense season of the "Summer of Love." By 1970 up to one million two hundred thousand Americans had tried LSD. It is, therefore, a story in which my native country of Italy does not apparently play any particular role, and in which the use of these substances seems almost naturally tied to instances of a liberal and "leftist" nature, and not a reality that is in any way tied to an obscure branch of the Italian Illuminati. So for me and others like Franco Landrisci, it was a real surprise to discover that a group of Italian "researchers" from the Illuminati network had already, within the first decades of the century, experimented with mind expanding/altering drugs; using and interpreting them in the light of ancient spiritual teachings and gathering observations that astonish many, even today, for their deep erudition and originality. These researchers developed a way to the use of drugs that can be called "initiatic," and different, as we shall see, from the "utopian" and "individualistic" way that most well-known personalities use them. Franco Landriscina described the historical set-up in the folllowing way, giving us a perfect picture of the situation:

> *Rome, 1927. A tram rattles through the streets of the capital crowded with bicycles. The notes of pleasant music spreads through the air from the radio's placed inside the houses. Gentlemen discuss politics on street corners. A diverse group of people, however, relax their mind with concentration exercises, yoga, mantra recitation, discover the magical power of sex, learn the art of entering into conscious sleep, and try any kind of drug. It is the **Group of Ur**.* [57]

In the second volume of their *Introduction to Magic,* the Group of Ur, who since their first edition, speak of the secrecy of "substances" and "necessary doses" hiding under the alchemical name of "corrosive waters," state the following: *"Which substances, then, have these powers, and what is the science of dosing them for immediate practice, was a very difficult secret to obtain already back in the ancient times."* [58]

In the third edition of the trilogy of the Group of Ur, released in 1971, when Evola was still alive (he died in 1974), his group appears to have made a significant update, when advertising the second volume with a very flashy green stripe and the words **"Edition revised and updated with a new chapter on drugs."** The 1970s had obviously arrived even for the oldest surviving members of the group, who opened the chapter ON DRUGS in the following way:

---

57   "The Group of Ur and the initiatory path to the psychedelia" article by Franco Landriscina. Originally published in Antonio Castronovo, *L'Immaginazione al Podere. Che cosa resta delle eresie psichedeliche* (Viterbo, IT: Stampa Alternativa 2005).

58   AaVv., Introduzione alla Magia (Introduction to Magic), Volume 2, (Rome: Edizioni Mediterranee, 1971), p. 142.

Having mentioned in vol. II, p.140, those that are called in alchemical Hermetism "corrosive waters," for many contact points and some more details we judge useful to publish the confidential instructions about a higher use of drugs, made by a group close to us. For the reader, a point to notice is the absolute difference of the experiences in respect to the modern widespread prophane use of drugs amongst the younger generation, with effects that can only be of degradation and self-destruction. [59]

Among the large group of characters that composed the original foundation of the Group of Ur, there was Leone Caetani, 15th Duke of Sermoneta and 5th Prince of Teano (1869-1935); the Anthroposophists John Colan and Massimo Scaligero; poets Girolamo Comi, Arturo Onofri; and, traditionalists like Guido De Giorgio, plus other important characters and intellectual figures of the time. Among them was Emilio Servadio, a Freemason and future president of the *Italian Psychoanalytic Society*, and the young Pio Filippani Ronconi, who will become one of the most authoritative Italian Orientalists after an interesting past in the Italian Division of the SS. There is also the great Freemason Arturo Reghini, recognized as one of the "spiritual fathers" of the *Symbolic Italian Rite of Freemasonry* as constituted within the Grand Orient of Italy.

Arturo Reghini appointed Crowley as an honorary member of the *Italian Philosophic Rite* on October 20, 1913, but in 1927 he turned his loyalty to the Group of Ur, and Julius Evola, [60] who disliked Aleister Crowley.

It seems that Evola always managed to stay independent from the rest of the Illuminati Network, and rejected attempts to control the Group of Ur that were made by various secret societies like the O.T.O., who aggressively tried to grab Evola's loyalty and attention; which he rejected when he warned Mussolini of the danger represented by the occult and magical side of Freemasonry. He even broke up *the inner circle* at the onset of what later became the second volume of *Introduction to Magic*, and Reghini was eventually expelled. It should be remembered that Arturo Reghini was also a close associate of René Guenon. Baron Evola always refused any kind of ceremonial magic and put emphasis on a strict, free and personal asceticism. [61] This was a very different way of perceiving things, apart from his modern followers in the Satanic milieux who were obsessed with ceremonial magic. Above all, the other members of the Group of Ur, including Julius Evola, always stood out. The Group of Ur was a magical partnership of great importance that confronted and inspired the great initiates of the time after becoming active in Italy in the late twenties. It was officially founded by Arturo Reghini, Julius Evola, and Giulio Parise, all three co-directors of the magazine UR. The group declared itself independent of any school or esoteric movement of the time (the occult, Freemasonry, theosophy, spiritualism, etc.), as the tradition is not linked to any school. In reality, the main movements that represented within the Group of Ur were anthroposophic, Masonic-Pythagorean, and included some Catholics. According to Evola, the group's goals were essentially:

1 *To reawake a higher metaphysical force that could help individual members to work magically.*

2 *Use this superior force to influence the political forces of the time magically.*

After the Second World War, a new Secret Brotherhood born in Italy that would fully embrace and relaunch the message of the Group of Ur, the previously mentioned Group

59 *Introduction to Magic, Volume 3, Ibid.,* p. 363.
60 http://www.parareligion.ch/sull.htm ‡ Archived 5th July 2015.
61 See. https://dublinsmick.wordpress.com/2012/04/13/the-germans-call-it-mehr-als-leben-more-than-living/ ‡ Archived 5th July 2015.

of the "Dioscuri." [62] This new esoteric experience was put together in the 1950s and 60s by some of his young students who were close to the political right, within which Evola represented one of the greatest thinkers in the postwar period. [63] Franco Landriscina's description of the Group of Ur show them as:

> Addicted to rituals and invocations, you find them reading and commenting passionately about Tantra, The Life of Milarepa and the Tibetan Book of the Dead. Next the Eastern tradition, among their favorite books are the texts of Pythagoreanism, Neoplatonism, the ancient Greek and Roman religions, Renaissance alchemy and German mysticism.

The Group of Ur's secret esoteric teachings to the various traditions are related to the techniques that can cause, or as we say today, induce, altered states of consciousness; beyond the control of breathing, through concentration, remote viewing, sex, dance, and so on. An important role has always been given to the "corrosive waters" (as they call drugs in alchemical language), as long as they are used in the right context. But what kind of "psychedelic" drugs could have been available to the Italian esoterist of the time? [64]

One answer to Landriscina's question, of course, is Cannabis, although it is obviously not the only one, as there are also other drugs used by the Group of Ur, but "Mary Jane" was particularly dear to this enlightened group. Arturo Reghini, in fact, wrote enthusiastically about **Cannabis** in his important essay on Freemasonry: THE *SACRED WORDS AND PASSWORDS OF THE FIRST THREE DEGREES AND THE HIGHEST MASONIC MYSTERY*:

> Other causes, known and unknown, alter the state of pure consciousness without removing the new status from the old, the result that there is contemporary consciousness of the two conditions and there is mutual oblivion. The intoxications of any kind can determine precisely similar conditions.

> Who does not go into ecstasy before a glass of wine?

> The ear of [wheat] grain, sacred to Ceres, was the symbol of the resurrection; life, sacred to the Free God, was the symbol of intoxication, ecstasy and joy, wine was the symbol of immortality-giving ambrosia (Note from the author: Ambosia was the food or drink of the Greek gods, often depicted as conferring longevity or immortality upon whoever consumed it). The passage of Plato on the Corybantes suggests that they will push their heart to beat faster with some artificial means, dances, fumes of intoxicants, they would lay in a rapture in which the heart was throbbing loudly. Even Hashish, the grass par excellence in Arabic, makes your heart beat strongly, and can make wonderful changes in the state of consciousness; it certainly has some affinity to the grass that made Glauco a God, the vivax gramen of which is Ovid."

Finally, He adds that, "Other means to obtain ecstasy are still to fix on bright objects, repeat spells, fasting, prayer, breathing exercises, spiritual contemplation. [65]

Freemason Arturo Reghini clearly compares the effects of Hashish as having a no-less heady effect than that of wine. In 2012, the German tabloid "Bild" said that those who think that wine or beer does less damage than a "joint" are making a big mistake. Alcohol

62   https://forum.termometropolitico.it/226299-reghini-o-t-o-crowley-evola.html ‡ Archived 5th July 2015.
63   https://it.wikipedia.org/wiki/Gruppo_di_Ur ‡ Archived 5th July 2015.
64   Franco Landriscina, *Ibid.*, p. 2.
65   Arturo Reghini, "Secret words and Passwords of the first three Masonic degrees and the ultimate Masonic Mystery," Atanòr, Rome, 1922.pp. 176-177.

clearly destroys brain cells and causes major damage to our bodies. So, if we were to adopt the prohibition as a matter of health, we should also do the same with alcohol.

Speculation, the hypocritical prohibition on drugs and their initiatic use since ancient times

After reading Arturo Reghini's words describing hashish as a substance that can create "wonderful changes"—not a poison, or a dangerous drug facilitating poor health—two claims that have been insisted upon for years, many have been left puzzled. Doctors were subserviant to the pharmaceutical system before the sudden turn toward sanitary use of this drug in recent years. Reghini was a Mason of the highest level who began his adventure in Freemasonry in 1902, within the Rite of Memphis in Palermo (rite of Egyptian origin organized within the more Universal branches of Freemasonry). In 1905, he founded the **Lucifer Lodge,** belonging to the Grand Orient of Italy. In 1912, he entered the Supreme Council of the Universal Italian Philosophic Rite, a post he resigned in 1914. In 1921, however, he became a member of the Italian Supreme Council of the 33rd degree of the **Ancient and Accepted Scottish Rite.**

To learn more about the mind-altering substances used by the various Illuminati mystery schools throughout different periods in history, we need to review some historical facts that will help you better understand the level of hypocrisy in our current society. For those "intellectuals," who are skeptical about the role of hashish, they should know that **Dumas, Hugo, Gautier, Baudelaire, De Nerval,** and **Balzac,** *just to name a few*, were all members of the **Hashish Club** (or *De Haschischins*). The modern history of hashish begins in France with **Dr Joseph Moreu de Tours,** who, during a trip to Egypt in 1837, learned about the therapeutic use of the marijuana plant, used as a cure for many illnesses by the local people. But he aimed higher, experimenting with the plant by initiating **Theophile Gautier** to the substance. **Gautier** would then create an Illuminati Club called the **Hashish Club,** which included the participation of many luminaries. It was considered a secret initiation of the highest degree and was sought after by Masons and intellectuals such as Dumas (18th degree of the A.A.S.R.), who was devoted to experiments with hashish. It is interesting to note that the Knights Templars were among the first consumers of hashish in Europe. Helena Petrova Blavatsky (1831-1891), the founder of the Theosophical Society, was known by various historians to consume drugs. [66] So let's move away from contemporary society's hypocrisy on the prohibition of cannabis, whose legalization would offer a great step forward for humanity, and in my view is a display of a more advanced civilization for those countries that practice its consumption.

If there remains today, an example of genuine research regarding the higher alchemical uses of hashish, perhaps we owe it to authors and researchers who have assessed drugs in the right manner: Alexander and Ann Shulgin, Timothy Leary, Ram Dass, Albert Hofmann, Richard Evans Schultes, Terence McKenna, Stanislof Grof, Nina Grabioa, Suzanne Budapest, my father Elio Zagami, and many others, who have not only identified the stupid and superficial use of these banned substances, but have also discovered uses more profound and meaningful. Nearly 500 years ago a man named François Rabelais, prophesied that cannabis use would lead to the creation in alchemical laboratories of even more powerful drugs that could be used for religious purposes. The Rastafari gave birth to their religion, and migrating from alchemy to chemistry laboratories, the aforementioned Albert Hofmann discoverered LSD. Obviously this should not be an excuse or a justification for the abuse of potentially dangerous substances, which, as we all know, can ruin the life of a person.

66   http://alchemylab.com/cannabis_stone5.htm ‡ Archived 5th July 2015.

Let us not forget the pharmaceutical lobby is a very important element within the New World Order structure. There are also the mega-speculators like **George Soros**, who under the auspices of the Rothschilds, invested for many years in a program for supporting the free circulation of drugs. Soros even created an organizational chart outlining the main individuals and institutions committed to this program. Soros' interest is not to help humanity to free themselves from hypocritical prohibition, but simply to keep the usual speculators of the New World Order's moneyed interests intact. The elite has long prepared for the upcoming legalization of drugs, (starting with marijuana), but with one stipulation: that the drug business remain within the absolute control of their interests, families and corporations. To them drug distribution must remain another money making tool (of course at the greater expense of the poor). In 1988, the drug trade amounted to five hundred billion dollars, 10-15% of the GDP. A drug trade committed to spreading drugs and removing all possible obstacles in the process, with a capillary network of drug traffickers with troops, planes and ships, and a mafia supported by the New World Order at their disposal. It is fair to say that you can't hide 500 billion U.S. dollars of profit under the bed. It is naive, to say the least, to believe the world of High Finance is not involved in all of this. Their vast investments and recycling can only pass through the computer keyboards of the international banking cartel, presided over by the usual suspects. One of the many confirmations of this truth surfaced in a conference held by the United Nations in Vienna in 1980, where the obvious truth emerged, that drug trafficking could be eradicated only by mining the operations behind their financial structure.

If deprived of the opportunity to investigate the intricate system of the banking world—and violating one of the most closely guarded secrets in every latitude—is a *mission impossible scenario* that is bound to fail. [67] This is the same system that has allowed Vatican financial institutions the opportunity to recycle dirty money from weapons and the drug trade for decades. The Vatican is a den of gangsters and perverts that have little to nothing to do with the message of Jesus. Returning to Soros, his main activity regarding the drug front in recent years can be summarized as follows: He has provided more than $10 million to the **Drug Policy Foundation (DPF),** the main American lobby for legalization. He opened a center for the same purpose, the **Lindesmith Center,** and entrusted it to Ethan Nadelman, the manager of **DPF** and former professor of political science at Princeton University. Nadelman is a keen advocate of the decriminalization of drugs and a collaborator to the Carnegie Foundation's magazine *Foreign Policy*, which was originally mobilized in support of abortion, and now campaigns for the liberalization of drugs. [68] Soros has lavished millions of dollars upon foundations that fight for drug legalization, the most important being **Drug Strategies,** directed by Malthea Falco, the founder of **NORML** (another important lobby for the legalization of marijuana), and who is married to an executive of the **Council on Foreign Relations.** [69] Soros, moreover, is a great manipulator of the recent Ukrainian cisis, and has promoted the career of economist **Jeffrey Sachs,** who, since the late eighties, promoted "shock therapy" within the countries of the former Warsaw Pact.

Sachs is an employee of Soros, who boasted that he was the architect of the "financial miracle in Bolivia." This was the wholesale of Bolivia, an entire country, to a mafia of cocaine traffickers, who openly and explicitly proposed the "financial liberalization of drug money." Through **Open Society** Foundations, Soros invested some 500 million tax-free

---

67   Epiphanius, Masonry and Secret Sects, *Ibid.,* p. 321.
68   Epiphanius, *Ibid.,* p. 325.
69   Article in the publication Solidarietà, IV n.2, May 1996 also on line at: http://www.movisol.org/soros3.htm
‡ Archived 5th July 2015.

U.S. dollars into these so-called cultural projects. [70] We must also consider the role of the pornographic magazine **Playboy,** which is identified as financing the aforementioned NORML. This historic soft-porn magazine, under the leadership of Israelite Hugh Hefner (and subsequently his daughter), has been the spearhead behind the anti-prohibitionist drug campaigns within American society. In review, two Israelites: the widely quoted George Soros, who is also a member of the CFR and the Trilateral Commission, and **Milton Friedman,** who won the Noble prize for economics, and is a member of the elitist Mont Pelerin Society; founded in 1947, by an Israelite Baron of liberal belief, **Ludwig von Mises,** are noble and ardent supporters of the legalization of drugs.

In relatively recent years, among the members of Mont Pelerin, we find Edward H. Grane, since 1977, the founder and president of the Cato Institute in Washington, and a leading member of the National Organization for the abrogation of Marijuana Laws. Charles de Ganahl Koch, from the same Cato Institute, is a member of the Board of Directors of First National Bank of Washington. The Atlantic Richfield Company (ARCO), led for many years by Robert O. Anderson, is also a sponser of the conservative Cato Institute, as are the Rockefeller-owned Chase Bank, Koch Industries, Philip Morris, Shell Oil, the usual Rothschilds, Amoco, Procter & Gamble, Seagram Bronfman; a Jewish family of Canadian origin that is linked to the Bnai B'rith which controls a good share of the world market of alcohol sales, and finally Upjohn, a manufacturer of industrial contraceptives ... [71]

Should drugs be legalized? In conclusion much more damage is done by current prohibition laws, but let us not underestimate the will behind a minority that has monopolized the market in advance. It is clear that liberalization will now gradually begin, but we must not leave it in the hands of the usual unscrupulous lobbyists promoting the New World Order. If left to individual state legislatures and their citizens, money generated from the sale of these *legal* substances can be used to restore economic health while eliminating the crime that has been generated from years within this perverted and sick system. People clearly do not deserve the unnecessary suffering that has resulted from these many years of prohibition. As is currently happening, the legalization of marijuana in Colorado, for example, is proving that legalization can help a state through tourism and taxation, and stands as an example to follow that is beyond the interests of Soros and company.

The Society of the future, the one society that will survive our present errors, must be a just society. Mafia and gangster types only serve the present sick system, set up by the Illuminati and criminal Freemasonry. Our current situation is far too often tied to false compromise, and it is clear that we must re-examine the many civic structures that are considered illegal. I will now explore the historical context regarding the Illuminati in relation to their use of drugs as a **fuel for initiation.**

The year is 396 A.D. It is the date that the Temple of Eleusis was destroyed. It is also symbolically, a date signifying an end of the ritual use of psychedelic drugs in Europe. In the long period from the Middle Ages to modern times, the use of plants and hallucinogenic drugs became confined within the world of witchcraft and alchemy. From 1700 through to today however, the use of the substances that "open the mind" resumed thanks to two factors: advances in chemistry and contacts with people of other cultures. Alchemy was responsible for the discovery of *ether,* a volatile and flammable liquid known today as an anesthetic. In 1275, Ramon Llull discovered ether, and called it "sweet vitriol." In 1540, Valerius Cordus performs the first synthesis of ether, and Paracelsus describes the hypnotic properties. Frobenius worked with it in 1730, and changed the name of "sweet vitriol" to

70 *Ibid.*
71 Epiphanius, p. 324.

ether. Inhalation of ether for anesthetic purposes began in 1846. Many years before this, however, taking ether for recreational purposes was a widespread practice in various parts of the U.S. and Europe. One of the first reports of a mystical experience, due to the inhalation of ether, is that of Dr. Oliver Holmes, of Harvard Medical School, who wrote:

> *The mighty music of the triumphal march into nothingness reverberated through my brain, and filled me with a sense of infinite possibilities, which made 'me an Archangel for the moment. The veil of eternity was lifted. The one great truth which underlies all human experience, and is the key to all the mysteries that philosophy has sought in vain to solve, flashed upon me in a sudden revelation.* [72]

The gas, ether, began to propagate its visionary effect in the late 1800s within fashionable society and various intellectual circles. American physician Benjamin P. Blood published a pamphlet entitled: *The Anaestetic Revelation and the Gist of Philosophy.* Within it he states that nitrous oxide provided him with "a revelation of the secret of life." Dr. Blood sent copies of his manuscript to various poets and philosophers, including the poet Tennyson, and psychologist William James.

As soon as 1882, William James began his own investigations, and in the journal *Mind,* published an article, entitled *"The subjective effects of nitric oxide,"* in which with great clarity he describes, *particular modifications of perception and thought processes when under the effect of the gas.* [73] Among the experimenters of nitrous oxide, **Peter Ouspensky,** a Russian disciple of **Gurdjieff,** uses drugs from 1912 to 1929 in an attempt to boost his ability to achieve clairvoyance, divination and other forms of magical thinking. [74] In 1886, during a trip of exploration in America, the German botanist *Lewin* gains possession of peyote plants, a cactus that is sacred to American Indians who gain effects by chewing, or drinking an infusion of the plant. Within a short time in America and Europe, numerous physicians began experimenting with drugs. Their research immediately illuminated the hallucinogenic properties of each substance.

In 1897, in an effort to identify plants with pyschoactive properties, the German chemist Arthur Heffter experimented on himself with the principles extracted from plants, and was in this way able to identify and isolate mescaline. In 1898, the English physician Havelock Ellis, the father of the movement for sexual liberation, tries mescaline and publishes an article entitled *Mescal: a new artificial paradise.* In 1919, Ernst Spath was able to synthesize this substance in a laboratory, thus making it available in pure form, and in controlled doses. In 1927, Alexandre Rouhier publishes *La plante qui fait les yeux émerveillés,* (The plant that makes the eyes marvel). In the same year we find a book by Kurt Beringer *Der Meskalinrausch* (The Mescaline Noise), a detailed study of the effects of mescaline in which the author suggests that religion can cause problems similar to some symptoms of schizophrenia. This is the birth of the theory of "psychotomimetic" (also known as psychotogenic), where hallucinogens act on the brain according to mechanisms similar to those of mental illness. *This theory will meet great success until the 1950s, when the term psychotomimetic will be replaced by "psychedelic."*[75] The toxicological nature of witchcraft in *medieval diabolism* emerges in a scientific way in the 1930s, in an article that stated: *"The drugs used by witches in their Satanic functions are known, if*

----

72   O. W. Holmes, Mechanism in Thought and Morals, an address delivered before The Phi Beta Kappa of Harvard University, June 29, 1870, JAMES R. OSGOOD & Co., Boston, 1871, p. 46.
73   See. William James, *The Varieties of Religious Experience,* Create Space Independent Publishing Platform, 2013.
74   L. Franco, *Ibid.,* p. 3 of the original essay available also on scribd.com.
75   L. Franco, *Ibid.,* p. 4.

not all, at least in large part. We know how they act on the basis of the alkaloids content in the plants chosen, alkaloids that have the power to cause hallucinations in character, almost always, full of terror. Such, for example, opium, black henbane, the Solanum nigrum or black nightshade, the Mandragora officinarum or mandrake, belladonna, etc." [76]

Then, in the 1920s, in addition to popular drugs like cocaine and opium, ether, chloroform, nitrious oxide, hashish, mescaline and a number of plants known to witches were found within the dispensary of those who, like the Group of Ur, wished to make initiatic use of these "corrosive waters." Each of these substances were explicitly, or with veiled illusions, mentioned in the writings of Evola and the Group of Ur. This of couse is not to suggest that these substances were unknown to other esoteric and occult groups in the world at the time. In fact, one could make a similar argument concerning the Hermetic Order of the Golden Dawn. This secret paramasonic society founded in England in 1888, had among its members both the poet William B. Yeats, and the famous magician Aleister Crowley, who entered the sect in 1898, (only to be expelled two years later). In 1905, Crowley funded a rival secret society named *Argenteum Astrum*, described in the first volume of my *Confessions*.

The most obvious secret society to develop a systematic ritual use of psychoactive substances in the Illuminati sectarian network was without a doubt the *Ordo Templi Orientis*, which in 1922, was taken over by Aleister Crowley. Even occultist Gustav Meyrink's novels are fueled with references to hallucinogenic substances. In short, occultism and drugs have generally gone hand in hand, even if the experience of Evola and the Group of Ur differs profoundly from the values and beliefs of other occult groups. In the many pages devoted by the Group of Ur to the "corrosive water" subject, there are many true statements dissimilar to the beliefs of many known contemporary psychedelic gurus of the day. It presents, for example, that difficulty lies in maintaining and developing a *core of consciousness*, and an *active attitude*, without the reference of ordinary bodily sensations: *"The active attitude is similar to that of someone who, is about to take a leap. Therefore, one should not simply wait for the feelings and changes of consciousness to occur, but rather like a spider at the center of its web is careful, must immediately make it an act of his own conscience."* [77]

Appearing here, is a primary and fundamental difference with a purely mystical approach: *"The next stage is a higher ecstatic freedom, free from psychic contents. It corresponds to the state of sleep in common language. Usually the point of passage is marked by a feeling of fear or distress. It is believed that if you go one step further, you would die. Even pictures or voices can strengthen this feeling. You must have a fearlessness and absolutely want to go forward, come what may. If consciousness holds up to this state (after death), this is the state in which occur phenomena of initiatory importance."* [78]

Isn't it always said that one has to let themselves "go with the flow" of the experience when one is on a "trip?" This is also indicated by the Group of Ur, yet the alchemical point of view does not exclude a second possibility:

So the already difficult game to close your eyes and let yourself fall without fear is complicated by another necessary and subtle attitude: you have to kill at the same

76   See. Marszalkowicz S., "The toxicological element in witchcraft and medieval demonism" works of medical history compiled by various authors in the Academic year 1936-37-XV, (Rome, IT: Graphic Arts Bodonia 1938), pp. 80-93.

77   *Introduction to Magic, Volume 3, Ibid.,* p. 371.

78   *Ibid.,* p. 372.

time get killed, you have to "fix" what is being "carried."[79] This is obviously an uncommon possibility, in fact: "... a few ever reach the state in which, after abnormal physical sensations, visions, hallucinations, etc. They produce interesting initiatory experiences. Often you lose consciousness before you can go that far. It interrupts the relationships with those who could assist you."[80]

That is why a key role can be played by periods of preparation and purification, from the contemplation of magical and religious symbols, determined upon to lead the process properly, or the presence of an experienced guide. In the "initiatory path" of drugs, Evola and his companions used psychotropic substances as a tool that is available to the adept attempting to cross the threshold that separates common man, who is limited and mortal, from the *world* of the gods and heroes. In this instance , it is not important to take into account the means used (drugs), but instead to recognize the attempted end result, that of reaching illumination. It does not matter if this takes place in San Francisco, Basel, or the Amazon, or perhaps as few would have imagined, in 1920s fascist Rome, where a group of experienced Illuminati, knowledgeably used drugs in an initiation of the *superior* type, that was played out following a truly rigorous scientific method, that had nothing to do with the use of the same substances as used by black magician Aleister Crowley, who was a contemporary of the Group of Ur, living a much more extreme and self-destructive experience that ended with his own death by overdose. I would like to add that opening doors of the mind with the use of psychodelic drugs is a dangerous journey that is not to be taken lightly. The use I have referred to in the previous pages is that of initiated individuals, who approach the concept in a controlled and scientific way. It is easy to find horror stories of individuals who travel to the *depths of the jungle* to experience an Ayahuasca *enlightenment*, only to lose their minds in the process. The approach is only useful for individuals who have achieved within themselves the self-control needed to go forward in this method of enlightenment. I would also add that not all adepts are keen on using drugs to open doors of perception. One such person was *Dion Fortune*, who looked down on the use of drugs for enlightenment, and who felt enlightenment could be achieved naturally. Returning to Crowley, Franco Landriscina writes about Crowley's attitude on drugs:

> *The latter claimed to use a scientific method to study what others call spiritual. His magazine* The Equinox *had in fact the subtitle* The Method of Science; the Aim of Religion. *He can also be considered to some extent a precursor of Leary and his research on the altered states of consciousness. Despite his high-sounding statement about using "Science," in the works of Crowley, there is very little scientific method in his approach, therefore it received little attention outside of occult and alternative circles.* [81]

Nevertheless, it had an important role in the manipulation of society once it was assimilated by the New World Order in use toward their own agenda.

After demonstrating how drugs have been constantly used (and sometimes abused), throughout the course of history within the various Illuminati mystery schools, we must once and for all refute the many hypocrisies related to drugs as publicized within our modern world structure. During this time of crisis, we must instead attempt, as soon as possible, to promote important contemporary structural changes that can bring immedi-

79   Julius Evola, *La Tradizione Ermetica,* (The Hermetic Tradition), (Bari: Laterza, 1931, current edition, Edizioni Mediterranee, Rome, 1996), p. 123.

80   *Introduction to Magic, Volume 3, Ibid.,* p. 369.

81   L. Franco, *Ibid.,* p.8 of the original essay available also on scribd.com.

ate benefit to mankind. Eliminating the illegality of many, if not all drugs could, virtually overnight, eliminate a large portion of the related criminality that is controlled by the New World Order and their policies.

A gradual abolition of drug prohibition, and a regulation and taxation of these highly profitable commodities, would in the process eliminate all the irregular conduct surrounding the market. This may be as great an opportunity for an evolutionary leap forward in our way of being and thinking as human beings as we have ever had, and it is an operation, that we must keep out of the hands of the usual Geroge Soros', or similar speculators. It must be up to us and not the "Babysitter State," to decide if when, how, or how much drugs we want to use or alcohol we want to drink ... as long as we respect ourselves and the people around us, not imposing on others.

Think about it for a moment, the abolition of drug prohibition can solve many of our security and economy problems in an instant. As sovereign states we could generate income out of drug taxation. This will enable us to feed the world's poor, instead of making them work as slaves in, and for a perverse society. Drugs and prostitution, as well as the mafias that generate them, are an endless tragedy of global proportions, that have substantial repercussions regarding the safety of all of us and our children. I maintain however, that the wounds within our current system are ripe to become new opportunities and resources for a better future society ... a society, where people will have a choice to self-destruct, or *not* ... and where these decisions will be left to the individual, and not within the religious institutions in collusion with the dominant powers.

In the long run, this situation has led to the institutionalization of the police as mere mercenaries in the service of the elite, and therefore policemen and other professionals in the field are forced to live in a paradox of constant compromise, and surrounded by corruption.

What's more, the prisons, where often the rights and dignity of humans are not respected, are unecessarily crowded with drug offenses. I have clearly stated my point of view—that one's drug use should never come at the *expense* of the people around you. Parents, also, must be especially responsible. In the case of prostitutes, where physical and emotional damage is caused by the abuse of drugs pushed by controllers (pimps), as well as by the lack of hygiene and health checks. If prostitution was legalized, as it once was in Italy, the whole of society would gain a huge benefit, not only from taxation, but also for the healthcare possible in a legitimate operation. Most Christians obviously would say *no* to this, as they have accepted the bigotry imposed on them by the same occult manipulators who annually attend places like the **Bohemian Grove,** where members use prostitutes of both sexes in the interludes. At the same time these people like to be seen as the moralizers of our society. What they are really showing us is pure hypocrisy. More than ever, prostitution not only contributes to the economy of many criminal organizations that serve the New World Order, it also conveniently provides *material* for the "secret" perversions of the elite.

Wake up, my dear revolutionaries of tomorrow, if we are to ensure a prosperous future for our children, who will otherwise live within the oppression and misery of a violent and false society, we have difficult work ahead.

But are we ready to change this dreadful, and absurd situation? Far too many people will turn up their noses at my proposals, but I guarantee that a complete abandonment of prohibition on drugs, will eventually accomplish results that are positive and good for humanity. But who am I to make judgements and condemnations, **John Ronald Reul**

Tolkien (1892 – 1973) wrote: *"Many that live deserve death. And some that die deserve life."*—I am just a modest veteran of what was once the Sacred Knighthoods, someone who writes this to project a true light of wisdom and knowledge into the future, and to invite you to detach from past false perceptions of reality.

The origins of the Mafia and the occult roots of evil

On January 11th, 2012, the Italian newspaper, *Il Sole 24 Ore*, writes on its website: *"The largest Italian bank is virtual: it is called the Mafia. They alone, each year, can count on a liquidity of 65 billion."* [82] If I were to tell you, however, that the Illuminati created the Mafia, what would you say?

Since I am half Sicilian, the city of Palermo is very dear to me, and its narrow streets overflow with stories and legends of a dark and sinister cult from the past, that of the **Beati Paoli,** who some say still act as a link between the aristocracy and the Sicilian Mafia. According to urban legend, there is a network of tunnels under the beautiful city of Palermo, that reach from the shores of the Oreto River, to Piazza Matteotti. It has been mentioned that these tunnels could potentially be converted into a form of commercial subway for very little cost.

Vox Populi, vox dei, is a latin saying still commonly used in Italy. It means that if the population says certain things, there must be some truth to the story. As we know, time can cause our memories to alter events, but at the base of each legend, there is an element of truth. Common people did not invent legends, they do not have the time, nor inclination to do so. The accuracy of oral tradition is an incontrovertible fact, and useful in order convey a more profound understanding concerning the origins of the Mafia. Near the Church of Santa Maruzza, under Palazzo Baldi-Blandano, a cave was found that, over the centuries, has been used as a meeting place, as a landfill, and as a refuge bunker, during the air raids of the Second World War. It is accessed by a door that opens onto a little street referred to as the **alley of the Orphans (Vicolo degli Orfani).** Buried in the soil objects from different periods of history have been found. There also is said to be an entrance to "the cave of the Beati Paoli." On the facade of Palazzo Baldi, the historian Vincenzo Giovanni, who died in 1627, was said to have found traces of the sect found in the town of Salaparuta, where later a marble plaque engraved with the words **"Ancient Headquarters of the Beati Paoli"** later erected. Historical confirmation originates from the writings of historian and black nobility member Francesco Maria Emanuele Gaetani Marquis of Villabianca (1720 – 1802): *"The home of the lawyer Giovanbattista Baldi is located in Santa Maruzza, in the quartier of the Chief: ... where these sectarians held their covens after the touch of midnight."* Gaetani adds that there is another access to this mysterious place within the alley of the Orphans. Among the many doubts and mysteries surrounding the sect of the Beati Paoli, there is this physical link back to the origins of the Mafia.

To paraphrase **George Orwell (1903-1950):** *"Power corrupts, and the power of life and death in humans corrupts absolutely."*

The theory that supports the existence of a link between the Mafia and Beati Paoli dates from the early twentieth century, when New York Police Lieutenant **Joseph Petrosino (1860-1909),** was assassinated in Palermo in Piazza Marina (12 March). His investigation revealed that the Mafia had appropriated the myth of the Beati Paoli, and held meetings in the same underground place as the sect.

---

82   http://www.ilsole24ore.com/art/economia/2012-01-11/mafia-cassa-miliardi-064340.shtml?uuid=AaSM3fcE
‡ Archived 5th July 2015.

Seventy years later, Tommaso Buscetta, a big Mafia boss on both sides of the Atlantic, and known as "The boss of two worlds," stated that: *"The Mafia comes from the past. First there were the Beati Paoli: we have the same oath, the same duties."* The Anti-Mafia Commissions Gaspare Muto said the same thing with other words.

In the lyrics of an old song from the Italian region of Calabria, three survivors of the Order of the Temple (Knights Templar) are described as the founders of the three main Mafias: *"Ossu, Mastrossu and Carcagnossu, stopped in Calabria. And here they dug a profound hole to plant the three of Science. Around they planted the seeds of roses and flowers, and then dictated the social rules, the code of the made man."*

The three survivors of the Temple: **Osso, Mastrosso and Carcagnosso,** are indicated as custodians of the *sum* of knowledge that will shape the various Mafia groups, who took refuge in southern Italy. Carcagnosso, went to Calabria, and with the protection of St. Michael, founded the 'Ndrangheta; Osso, helped by St. George, gave birth to the Mafia in Sicily; Mastrosso, with the assistance of the Holy Mary, established the Neapolitan Camorra. The three main Mafia origins seem to have a pretty "Holy" nature. Some readers may say that this has the air of a fairy tale, and that the **Order of the Temple** (better known as the Knights Templar), does not deserve such slander, by association, yet we know that *lu battiu* (the Calabrian baptism) of a "man of honor," or "made man" in English, provides formulas and gestures that are a parody of the oldest and noblest initiation ceremonies that take place in Freemasonry and Neotemplarism. Could people in the remote region of Calabria—where the verses of the song mentioned above are recited during their so-called "tragic dance"—be aware of the misadventures of the **Order of the Temple**? The reference made in this song to the *Tree of Science* is also striking. [83]

To confirma this, I will quote an article written by Riccardo Bocca, a great journalist and author of major investigations on the subject in Italy, in an extract from the article entitled *Honoured Society 'Ndrangheta:*

"L' Espresso" published the memorial that a former boss of the 'Ndrangheta, here anonymous for security reasons, has delivered to the National Anti-Mafia Directorate. Inside he told firsthand the mysteries of trafficking in toxic waste in Italy and abroad, but also the bonds that the Calabrian underworld had with State authorities, fixers, Intelligence and Freemasons. [84]

Riccardo Bocca also addresses a second memorial to this former boss of the 'Ndrangheta, now a police informer, in which he describes his journey through the rules and rituals of the Mafia organization of Calabria:

"It was not a simple criminal structure. Even before the practical things always came tradition, delivered orally from father to son."

He confirmed what I have just reported to you above, about the three mysterious historical figures that lay behind the foundation of the main Mafia groups, and the esoteric roots of the traditional Mafia, which confirm the fact that the Mafia was created by the Illuminati and Freemasonry.

The former boss, in fact, declares:

83 "The Beati Paoli. A Historical hypothesis" a report by Dr. Giorgio Di Giorgio.
84 "CRIME / THE CONFESSION OF A CHIEF. 'Ndrangheta the Honoured Society hierarchy. The affiliation. The symbols. The secrets. In a memorial presented to the judges, the former boss tell the rules and rituals of the Calabrian clans," an article by Riccardo Bocca, 23.06.05. Available also online at: http://lampadarios.free.fr/espresso_simbolindrangheta.pdf ‡ Archived 5th July 2015.

The story goes back to Spain where these three knights on white horses came from, and that their names were Osso, Mastrosso and Carcagnosso. After a long journey, it is said, they came to the island of Favignana, where they took different directions. Osso founded in Sicily the Mafia, Carcagnosso went to Abruzzo and founded the Camorra, while Mastrosso reached Calabria and founded the 'Ndrangheta. The 'Ndrangheta, says the former boss, is represented by the Tree of Science, a large oak tree at the base of which is located the Chief of the Stick, also called Mammasantissima, which is the absolute leader. The trunk of the oak represents the "sgarristi," those who are the backbone of the 'Ndrangheta, the Calabrian Mafia, while the "rifusto" (consisting of the large branches that depart from the trunk) is the symbol of the Camorra, affiliates of a lower level. Finally, there are the twigs on the tree, that's the famous "picciotti," and the leaves, indicating the so-called "honored contrast," subject to the will of the organization but not officially affiliated. It goes without saying that the "falling leaves" are the infamous ones that for their betrayal will die. [85]

So the **Tree of Science** reminds us of the **Sephirotic Tree,** which as many of you know is a summary of the most famous and important teachings of the Jewish Kabbalah. I would like to dwell briefly on words written by the occult scholar Alessandro Orlandi in his article, *Nature and Origins of evil in the Jewish Kabbalah,* which lends further clarity on this issue, and the very origins of evil: "*Another theory on the origin of evil regards the two trees, of Life and Knowledge. Once the two trees were united in a single tree, but Adam, by eating of the fruit of the tree of knowledge, separated them, he separated the fruit from its origin, the 'above' from 'below', the Power of Judgement contained in the tree of knowledge from that of Love and Mercy contained in the one of Life.*" [86]

These conceptions of Evil co-exist side by side in the *Zohar,* says Orlandi. The *Zohar* assigns **Samael** as the Kabalistic equivalent of Satan, and **Lilith** as the central role in the Kingdom of Evil. The Kingdom of Evil is unfortunately embraced by the various Mafia groups, that are connected at the top to Freemasonry, and the Illuminati. Returning to the revelations of the former boss of the Calabrian Mafia, and taken from the article of Riccardo Bocca on the Masonic roots of the dreaded and powerful Calabrian mafia: "*Everything in it, the former boss said, has obvious Masonic roots and a deep historical connection. The characters referenced by the Mafiosi are General Alfonso La Marmora as war strategist and General Giuseppe Garibaldi as a fighter for freedom and justice.*" [87] Another similarity between the brand of Italian mafia called 'Ndrangheta, and Freemasonry, is the fact that the ceiling in every lodge in the world, is painted with the stars of the night sky, a clear reminder of the "Great Cosmic Structure," and a depiction of the Egyptian tradition of the macrocosm, and the reflection of heaven on earth shown on the **Emerald Tablet,** also known as the *Smaragdine Table,* or *Tabula Smaragdina.* [88] On the meetings of the 'Ndrangheta the former boss declares:

Their meetings are held in the starry nights because they are the stars, and their high level of power hints at the way the older introduces their meeting by saying: "Good vespers, wise companions we are gathered here to compose and to break down what is discussed, we can say and do what others are not permitted." And what happens to the top level of this organization, at its summit? The former boss states: "I

85   *Ibid.*
86   http://www.esonet.it/News-file-article-sid-512.html Archived 5th July 2015. *[emphasis added].*
87   Ricccardo Bocca *Ibid.*
88   See. http://www.loggiagiordanobruno.com/20110928-la-massoneria-guarda-alle-stelle-astrologia-scienza-e-fantascienza.html ‡ Archived 5th July 2015.

myself, have reached this level, so I can testify that the religious figures of reference are all the holy Apostles Peter and Paul, while the historical figures are Giuseppe Mazzini as founder and promoter of the company secret in general, and Count Camillo Benso di Cavour, the sum mind of a statesman. [89]

From this direct testimony, we can confirm what was written years ago about the Mafia and Mazzini, by the Estonian historian **Juri Lina**, in his book "Architects of Deception":

In 1860, Mazzini created an organization called The Oblonica, *a name derived from the Greek word* obelos, *which means "skewer or knife." In this group, he created another more internal one: a modern band of criminals, called* MAFIA, *which was an acronym for: Mazzini Autorizza* (Authorizes) *Furti* (Thefts) *Incendi* (Fires) *Avvelenamenti* (Poisonings)." [90] The last initial of the acronym could also be the initial of **Assasination**.

So who really was Giuseppe Mazzini? He was the son of a Jacobin, and was initiated in 1827 with the nickname "Strozzi," into the Cabonari "Hope Lodge," by paying the sum of 25 francs, an a monthly 5 franc fee. He was immediately initiated into the second degree, which allowed him to recruit new followers. [91]

Even if the history books suggest that Mazzini was never made a Freemason, historian Eugene Bonvicini, Freemason of the Grand Orient of Italy, and 33° of the A.A.S.R. (Currently recognized by the American Supreme Councils), in one of his many books on the history of Freemasonry entitled "**Modern Freemasonry**" (Ed. Bastogi, 2007) argues that Giuseppe Mazzini, began irregularly in prison in Savona in 1834, where he eventually received **the 32nd degree of the Scottish Rite.**

All arguments aside, his position was "Regularized" in 1862, by the Supreme Council of the ASSR in Palermo, which had Giuseppe Garibaldi as its Sovereign Grand Commander, eventually being elevated by the Supreme Council to the 33rd degree in Palermo on June 18, 1866. He also paticipated in masonic meetings abroad, and received honorary membership in various Lodges, which he accepted with several letters addressed using the Masonic term "Brothers." Along with Karl Marx (1818-1883), as you can read in the *Jewish Encyclopedia*, the Italiano Cabonaro Giuseppe Mazzini, was responsible for preparing for the establishment of, and the address to, *First International* (organized in September 1864) . The intimate ties that Mazzini had with Jewish circles is well-known. For his part, in his essay *The Manifesto*, published in the journal "*American Opinion*" in February 1972, Alan Stang highlighted the dependence of the Italian **Carbonari** to the Order of the Illuminati of Bavaria, [92] stating with absolute certainty that "*The Carbonari belonged to the Bavarian Illuminati. The same was true of Mazzini.*" [93]

A singular confirmation on the Masonic and Enlightenment ideals of Giuseppe Mazzini, is found in his declared faith in **reincarnation.** He in fact stated: "*The perfection of the individual takes place from existence to existence, more or less rapidly, depending on our works.*" This is a proposition that somehow echoes what was later written in the official organ of the **Gnostic Apostolic Universal Church**, the religious entity inspired by the Martinist Order, another branch of the Illuminati network, which states:

89   Ricccardo Bocca, *Ibid.*

90   Juri Lina, Architects of Deception, http://jyrilina.com, Norsborg, 2001, p.251, *[emphasis added].*

91   See. E.E.Y. Hales, Mazzini and the secret societies—The making of a mith, (London: Eyre & Spottiswoode, 1956) pp. 40-47.

92   "Demonological hypothesis on Marxism" essay by Paolo Zanotto in http://apologetica.altervista.org/ipotesi_demonologiche_origine_marxismo.htm ‡ Archived 5th July 2015.

93   See. Alan Stang, "The Manifesto," in "*American Opinion*," February 1972, pp. 53-55.

"The work done on oneself is not lost: from life to life, and in the subsequent reincarnations, will bear its fruit and will advance more and more."

Mazzini had an Israelite collaborator named **Henry Mayer Hyndman**, who was a Marxist, and headed an association called "The National Socialist Party." In 1881, Hyndman founded the "Democratic Federation" with Eleanor, the daughter of Karl Marx, who was later joined by Annie Besant (1847-1933), a 33rd degree of the Scottish Rite and the head of the Theosophical Society. [94] Returning to the present day, in 1992, in an effort to hinder the rise of the Yakuza, the Japanese government issued the *anti-boryokudan*, which outlawed all associations that resort to violence and intimidation. Initially, the measure seemed to pay off, as more than a thousand members were arrested with several giving up their criminal activities and embracing legality. But over time, the measure proved ineffective, as the more powerful components of the dismantled clans that survive police prosecution joined organizations like **Yamaguchi-gumi,** Japan's largest yakuza organization, and the **Sumiyoshi-rengo** and **Inagawa-kai,** respectively the second and third largest yakuza families. Although there are many diverse yakuza groups, if taken together they form the largest organized crime group in the world.

Following the Tōhoku earthquake on March 11th 2011, and the tsunami that followed, the Yakuza sent hundreds of trucks filled with food, water, blankets, and sanitary accessories, to aid people in the areas effected by the natural disaster. **CNN Mexico** stated that although the yakuza operates through extortion and other violent methods, they *"[moved] swiftly and quietly to provide aid to those most in need."*

For this, and many other reasons, the Yakuza enjoys the support of many of the Japanese who see them as a group of protectors they can rely on in times of need. This is despite the numerous awareness campaigns conducted by the Japanese government that claim the opposite. Because of this support,Yakuza members can quietly circulate in plain view, wearing prestigious clothing, driving luxury cars, casually displaying their business cards, and working out of elegant buildings. For this reason and others, the Japanese police encounter many difficulties trying to disrupt this organization, and attempting nearly everything, seem to have stopped trying.

While there are several hypotheses regarding the origins of the Yakuza, most modern Yakuza derive from two classifications that emerged in the mid-Edo Period (between 1603–1868):

Tekiya, those who primarily peddled illicit, stolen or shoddy goods; and bakuto, those who were involved in or participated in gambling. The roots of the Yakuza can still be seen today in initiation ceremonies, which incorporate tekiya or bakuto rituals. Although the modern Yakuza has diversified, some gangs still identify with one group or the other; for example, a gang whose primary source of income is illegal gambling may refer to themselves as bakuto.

The Yakuza have often been used, by secret societies and the world's elite, and are included within the Illuminati network, in order to do their dirty work. This historical connection links the Yakuza to the Jesuit Order and even to the Opus Dei. In the end *nothing has changed under the Rising Sun*, in regards to the various Mafia groups in Japan as well as in other parts of the world. In an ideal society, where prohibition is non-existent, for example such problems would be non-existent.

In 2012, the Obama administration imposed sanctions on the leader of the Yama-

*FIG. 22 – **Father Ferruccio Romanin SJ**, the Jesuit involved with the Italian Mafia and "Irregular" Freemasonry, now happily residing in Australia. Image taken from: http:// www.gesuitinews.it/2011/02/12/australia-news-su-padre-ferruccio/ ‡ Archived 4th of July 2015.*

guchi-gumi, along with his second-in-command Kiyoshi Takayama. The sanctions also targeted several individuals linked to three other transnational organized crime groups, the **Brothers' Circle** of Russia, the **Camorra** of Italy, and **Los Zetas** of Mexico.[95] Whatever his nationality, the typical "Mafia" boss of today should be smart enoough to understand that the Grand Masters of the Freemason/Illuminati Network, along with their minions in the Intelligence community, use the mafia as long as they are useful. If ever an individual or group is not useful to the Illuminati agenda, they are immediately placed on the Most Wanted lists all over the world, or simply killed. This also happened many times with the various dictators supported by the New World Order, later murdered or arrested. If you ask a Freemason if there are links between the Mafia and Freemasonry, they will probably tell you that you are a fool or a con artist. How they ignore the reality of transnational super lodges, is beyond me. Supporting a true understanding, the famous Italian author and investigative journalist Ferruccio Pinotti wrote the following in his bestseller ***Brothers of Italy***: *"In Calabria and Sicily there are actually difficult realities: there are many examples of cooperating informers who speak of organic relationships between organized crime and secret lodges."*[96]

Mafia Brothers—stop supporting your superiors in the Vatican, people like the Jesuit father **Ferruccio Romanin (FIG. 22),** a close friend of Pope Francis, and the former director of the church of St. Ignatius of Loyola in Rome, which I remind you is the Mother Church within the Society of Jesus, the place where the Italian Mafia often meet in secret with their "Secret Chiefs."

In an investigation called *Hiram*, Father Romanin's ties to the Sicilian Mafia, along with Freemason **Stefano De Carolis,** Grand Master of the S.O.M.I. (*Sovrano Ordine Massonico d'Italia*), from 2003 to 2011, whose headquarters is located in **Rome** in **Via Iberia 62.**[97] have been under investigation by the Italian police authorities since 2008. "Hiram" (Hebrew meaning "exalted brother") was obviously a name chosen for this investigation because of the Masonic ties of the people involved. After the scandal the Vatican quickly sent Father from Rome to Melbourne, Australia,[98] where his parishioners most likely didn't know about his controversial past connections to the Mob. Although

95   See. http://it.wikipedia.org/wiki/Yakuza and https://en.wikipedia.org/wiki/Yakuza ‡ Archived 5th July 2015.

96   Ferruccio Pinotti, Fratelli d'Italia, (Milan: BUR, 2011), p. 249.

97   See. http://www.somi-massoneria.it/la-storia.html ‡ Archived 5th July 2015.

98   See. http://www.gesuitinews.it/2011/02/12/australia-news-su-padre-ferruccio ‡ Archived 5th July 2015.

I'm sure even there, where many Sicilians emigrated, some will show their "respect" to Don Ferruccio. But let me tell you more about the *Hiram investigation*. It originated in 2008, and after years of work, between Agrigento and Trapani (two of the biggest cities in Sicily), has uncovered that the Jesuit-Masonic-Mafia association's, were to shut or slow down certain high-profile Mafia trials then going on in the Italian Supreme Court. *Sole 24 Ore's*, Roberto Galullo writes: *"Fixers, Freemasons, police members, mobsters and Jesuits who allegedly—each acting as a piece that formed a piece of a puzzle—tended to postpone or adjust trials of the Supreme Court of affiliates (and not only) to gangs in the provinces of Agrigento and Trapani."*[99]

In short, according to this survey, Jesuits like Father Romanin, were involved in the defense of the leaders of Cosa Nostra, the top Sicilian Mafia. This clearly demonstrates that the Jesuits support the Mob. And behind Romanin and the then Grand Master Stefano de Carolis, there was also the presence of the Supreme manipulator of Italian Freemasonry, the ex-Worshipful Master of the powerful P2 Lodge: **Licio Gelli.** This was later confirmed by investigators, and magistrates, Fernando Asaro and Paul Guido, who went to Licio Gelli's **Villa Wanda** residence in Arezzo, Italy, to meet Gelli in person, along with deputy prosecutor Roberto Scarpinato, to learn which leads to follow in the *Stefano De Carolis* investigation. **Result?** Licio Gelli took advantage of the right to remain silent (as he was very disappointed by the situation), as did the Italian politician Marcello Dell'Utri, who was also summoned as a witness during the trial. [100]

In addition, when the actual scandal broke, something initially discovered during the investigation, created quite a stir in the Italian media. It was a recorded phone conversation between the suspects, stating that the **Church of St. Ignatius** was used for private meetings because it was **"free from any bugs."** [101] So this tells us that the most important Jesuit church in the world, *their "Mother Church,"* as they call it, was, (and perhaps still is), used for super secret summits between Mafiosi, Jesuits, Freemasons, and senior members of the police. We should not be too astonished that we have had a Jesuit Pope in charge of the church since 2013. That is considering that the above reality has nothing to do with the principles of Christianity, and instead more to do with what we commonly refer to as the *Mafia*.

After this scandal erupted, Count Licio Gelli had a sort of "Mystical revelation," that pushed him to reassess his past alliances. And then there are the many Masonic operations between Sicily and Calabria, operations directed by the Vatican, and strongly supported by the Zionists in Jerusalem and their feared *Mossad*. I'm talking about Freemasons like Giorgio Hugo Balestrieri of the P2, later operating out of the Grand Lodge of New York, and his friend and partner, the self-styled Grand Master **Robert Amato**, from Calabria, who is linked to the more deviant side of the international Intelligence community. In an article from their website entitled, *Politics, Masons and Dirty Business,* which appeared on the 1st of July 2011, the Italian Masonic Organization UMSOI described complex plots, and describes of: *"A trasversal ruling class, which used and uses political affairs, in a reckless manner, increasingly infiltrated by the commitees of power linking Freemasonry-mafia-business-institutions, to the detriment of Calabria."* [102] If you ask the repre-

99   See. http://robertogalullo.blog.ilsole24ore.com/2009/05/19/processo-hiram-2-de-carolis-licio-gelli-dellutri-e-le-lettere-del-gesuita-romanin-per-il-figlio-del-boss-di-cosa-nostra/?refresh_ce=1 ‡ Archived 5th July 2015.

100   See. http://www.informarexresistere.fr/2010/10/15/hiram-anatomia-di-un-processo-dimenticato/ ‡ Archived 5th July 2015.

101   See.http://archiviostorico.corriere.it/2008/giugno/20/faccendiere_gli_incontri_chiesa_contro_co_9_080620116.shtml?refresh_ce-cp ‡ Archived 5th July 2015.

102   http://umsoi.org/2011/07/01/politica-massoni-e-intrallazzi. *Filed in 2012, the page is no longer active.*

sentatives of so-called "regular" Freemasonry in Italy, like the Grand Orient of Italy, (the only one recognized by the majority of American Grand Lodges), about "Grand Master" Stefano De Carolis, they will tell you that De Carolis is only a "so-called" Grand Master, not a real one, releasing this to the press shortly after the start of the Hiram investigation:

> *The Grand Orient of Italy of Palazzo Giustiniani, has nothing to do with Stefano De Carolis Villas, who is attributes the high-sounding title of "Grand Master of Freemasonry," without detailing the legitimacy of his supposed or presumed Masonic group.* Massimo Bianchi, Deputy Grand Master of the Grand Orient of Italy added: "*The Grand Orient of Italy denounces once again the superficiality with which they made such news, as well as the indiscriminate and careless use of generic names, which can cause confusion in the media.*" The Grand Orient of Italy, concludes: "*I hope that in the future they will think more carefully about the information they publish, especially when involving a judicial inquiry into alleged plots with the Mafia.*" [103]

In January 2015, yet another investigation surfaced in the Italian media concerning the Mafia and Freemasonry, bringing to light the following statement by a former Mafia boss from Sicily, and now a trusted police source, named Carmelo D'Amico: "*There is a large, secret Masonic lodge, that affects the destinies of Calabria and Sicily.* [104] *The name of this mysterious lodge is Corda Fratres and is based in the town of Barcellona Pozzo di Gotto near Messina.*" [105] These are places I know all too well.

103   http://www.grandeoriente.it/comunicati/2008/10/palermo-9-ottobre-2008-ansa,-mafia,-hiram-bianchi-(grande-oriente-ditalia)-pi%C3%B9-attenzione-quando-si-parla-di-gran-maestro-della-massoneria.aspx ‡ Archived 5th July 2015.
104   http://www.24live.it/95887-carmelo-damico-attacca-la-corda-fratres-definendola-una-loggia-a-tutti-gli-effetti ‡ Archived 4th July 2015.
105   Filed http://www.ilquotidianoweb.it/news/economia/732911/Una-loggia-massonica-segreta-condiziona-.html ‡ Archived 5th July 2015.

Chapter   IV

The Need for Positive Change

Synarchy and Technocracy: the NWO upgrades their operating system

E *uropean governments are post democracies dominated by the media and finance ... The crisis could mark the end of capitalism as we know it, a form of fascism and totalitarianism which makes it very hard to allow the upper classes to maintain their standard of living.*

That is, at least, according to the economist Serge Latouche, as reported from the interview with Guilia Innocenzi that was transmitted by the Italian TV Show **Public Service** on the 19th of January, 2012.

So let us discover what is within the New World Order and at the heart of their system of power. As described so well by Serge Latouche, the gradual establishment of the system of **Technocracy,** during the "post democracy" period was originally created as a social movement in the early twentieth century. **Alexandre Saint-Yves, Marquis of Alveydre** (1842-1909), preferred to call technocracy "emporiumcracy," meaning *the way of the emporium,* and wished that the technical side be used to help humankind, for the good of the community, but in reality the opposite is happening.

As the mysterious Epiphanius states:

Today the technocrats, present in governments, are at the exclusive service of big multinational companies, which in turn are controlled by a few families of the stateless and international High Finance. In fact it need be taken into account that there is a revolution against God and His work, whose purpose is the destruction of the natural order willed by him, it is not difficult to understand the function of technocracy: the primacy of economy through concentrated businesses, and therefore putting first the political, rather the spiritual dimension more essential and noble for man. The rules of technocracy are before our eyes: economic concentration, urban concentration, specialization of professions—and then education—the progressive reduction of the rights of the individual and the family with their transfer to public anonymity, since for the technocrat man is not a person, but a mere object of production and consumption. We can not escape the close parallel with the socialism that inculcates in its followers the idea of the primacy of the economy. It's not an accidental fact that socialism is a branch of the Synarchist organization that sees technocrats (as the arm), High Finance (as the means), and Upper Freemasonry (as the mind). The founder of technocracy is unanimously considered Saint-Simon (1760-1825), whose slogan was: "Everything for the industry, everything with it," which means that the sources of power were already then sought in technical developement and in the industry. To understand this revolutionary thought, simply check out his concept of freedom, based on his work, Du Système industriel; where he states that the preservation of individual freedoms can not be in any case the real purpose of the Social Contract. The technocrat, in the vision of Saint-Simon and his followers, who will be called polytechnics, are the priests of a new rationalist and positive religion that assumes the task of enlightening the masses through the media propaganda on the gospel of progress, in the spirit of things to come, where the ancient cathedral is replaced by the company that produces it. With this move technocracy arrogates to itself spiritual power, a trend fully exploited half a century later by Saint-Yves and the enemies of the one, true religion. [1]

In the United States, the Technocracy movement took off and managed to enjoy a great popularity for a short period of time in the thirties, when it overshadowed many other proposals that had been put forward to deal with the crisis generated by the Great Depression, that was created in part by the elite of the Illuminati network. This same thing could be said today. Right from the start, the technocratic movement was introduced to replace politicians with scientists and engineers, who possessed the technical expertise to manage the economy. But for the Illuminati, technocracy must line up with synarchism; a term like synarchy, denotes rule by a secret elite. The basic aim is, at the end of this transition period to indefinitively establish a technocratic spiritual New Age movement, in the U.S. and Europe. At the peak of this hierarchy of power, one who is regarded as the **enlightened tyrant,** the Grand Master of the Academy of the Illuminati in Rome, *Prof. Giuliano Di Bernardo.* As with many Grand Masters within the New World Order system, Di Bernardo is hoping to rise to an open Illuminati leadership role which can govern society, without the need of the various political ideologies that tend to pollute the financial markets and the international order; with quarrels that are judged totally superfluous and unnecessary by proponents of "Illuminati" style globalism 2.0.

According to a carefully orchestrated plan arranged a long time ago, the technocratic elite are running things on top. It is a highly organized secret organization that acts according to the will of the elite. It is expected that one day this reality will openly transform itself in a New Age "clergy," made up of top managers, super-specialized scientists, and disciplined professors, who motion to preserve the survival of the system and the species when publicly denouncing any form of democracy. Of course this expresses their view, not mine.

Some believe that this new phase of the New World Order is just around the corner, while others think "democracy" will eventually prevail and stop them. The founders of the Bilderbergs were never lovers of democracy, for example, so how can one expect that a contemporary society crafted by them and their influential think tanks, foundations, and major media outlets , could be truly democratic? It's impossible. This operational introduction of open technocracy will in the years to come, unveil the total decline and defeat of the illusion of democracy in the West. This will accompany a so-called "financial crisis" , also created by the Illuminati and their powerful lobbies, that is directed toward the

---

1 Epiphanius, ***Ibid.***, pp. 162-163 footnote 17.

eventual implementation of a **One World Currency**. As also discussed in Volume 1, it is the elite of these secret transnational **Ur Lodges**, that have since 2008, gradually created an increasingly visible global condition of economic and social emergency, as not seen since the end of WWII. The actions have the initial purpose of establishing technocratic dictatorships in those countries considered unable to manage themselves politically. Italy and Greece, are only the beginning.

So while the United States appears as trying to retain a semblance of democracy, the present U.S. political class remains the result of strict selection, made according to the family background and university and military connections, in the most influential secret societies operating within the New World Order. As an example, and to cite one of the better known pawns of the game, we have "Bonesmen" John Forbes Kerry serving as Secretary of State under the Obama Administration. This should give you a clear idea of who is in control these days—It is the Illuminati!

The politicians are mere puppets in this situation, and increasingly seen as useless and expensive by the system, and the elite are gradually becoming more intolerant of their waste. But we are still in the initial stages of this technocratic insurgency, where the synarchic Illuminati element remains well-hidden to the *sheeple* behind a false political halo. This will soon change as this new technocratic element is gradually revealed, and our present façade of democracy will fade before the «technocratic» dictatorship behind this synarchic totalitarian project. In the hands of the Vatican and Israel, and their ally the United States, the technocrats represent the *armed wing* of the New World Order, along with the Chinese, the Japanese and the leaders of Saudi Wahabism. The Wahabi's control the oil and finance operations and ISIS—known also as ISIL or Daesh—that extract and sell oil, without the limitations of a controlled market.

Alexandre Saint Yves was a highly qualified person in the esoteric field, and a key figure in the Illuminati of his time, in his book entitled, *La France vraie*, he used the term "Synarchy" to describe a form of ideal government that could oppose the rise of political ideologies and anarchist movements. Saint-Yves described his conservative political-theological formula, in a series of four books, written beginning in 1882. If society was to be considered as an organic unity, he reasoned, it could and should be in harmony. This *ideal* was partly inspired by life in medieval Europe. It was also inspired by the *nearly perfect* forms of government that were encountered in India in the past, in ancient Egypt, and even in Atlantis, at a time when the Illuminati, and their power and management over the populace, was far more visible. Saint-Yves was a staunch defender of hierarchical and social differences. He also argued that there must be reasonable collaboration between the different stratum of society, and that through collaboration, society could move beyond social and economic conflicts. In other words, synarchy was the exact opposite of anarchy.

Saint-Yves advocated a European society with a government composed of **three Supreme Councils** which were to represent **the economic power, the judiciary and the scientific communities;** the structure of these three Supreme Councils would be held together by a so-called "Metaphysical Chamber (of Deputies)." His ideas were strongly influenced by Martinism and the work of Plato's *Republic*.

In theorizing these concepts on governance, Alexandre Saint-Yves d'Alveydre undoubtedly determined that a very important role be played by secret societies, or, more precisely, by esoteric societies that consist of oracles who, leading from metaphysical perception, safeguard each government. He was also convinced that the Knights Templar had already forwarded this task in the past during the European Middle Ages, and he also discovered that many Freemasons and other sects he encountered claimed to be direct descendants of the Templars. Saint-Yves was very active in many of these orders, and also with the Rosicrucians, and worked to renew the synarchic mission in accordance with the Jewish people, of whom he held in high esteem. In his book, *The Mission des Juifs* (1884), as his disciples continue to be, Saint Yves was favorable to Jews. Some of its material, however, was later referenced in *The Secret of the Jews,* a small anti-semitic pamphlet written by **Yuliana Glinka,** and his friend and Grand Master **Gerard Encausse** (Papus). In the *Echo de Paris* under the pseudonym *Niet,* Encausse was involved in a series of articles about a Jewish conspiracy, showing the Anti-Zionist nature of their work. These articles may have contributed to allegations that Gerard Enclausse was the author who forged the infamous *Protocols of the Elders of Zion.* [2] In *The Mission des Juifs,* Encausse turns to the *chosen people,* and Saint-Yves exhorts them to replace the "anarchy" of the *Societas Christianorum* with his new concept of **"Synarchy,"** or the **"Scientifical law of the organism of the society."**

By doing this, Saint-Yves Marquis of Alveydre is mindfully laying out the tenets of this new project, and preparing to end all conflicts between the Christian and the Jewish elite, in favor of something new, a New World Order that will materialize after WWII, and fully develop after the Second Vatican Council.

In this unprecedented initiatic scenario, there is a current generational conflict in many of the Mystery Schools within the Illuminati Network, including Freemasonry. The older generations are not in tune with the constant changes that this "New Age" actually requires, and they are therefore likely to leave a negative legacy for the future generations of Illuminati leaders. They seem to have a more bureaucratic mentality that in the long run may not be able to avoid the demand for real knowledge and enlightened leadership. Many people who join Freemasonry today, including the Neotemplars, the Rosacrucians or any other order, often feel disappointed by their choices if they seek more than simple material gratification among the false forms of spirituality, which are abundant in today's Western initiatic system.

If geniune and caring about his initiatic mission, the modern Grand Master, whatever his Order, who is not a simple robot of the New World Order, and the monstruosity called mondialism, faces the growing social tensions and conflicts that are rising today within Freemasonry and other initiatory orders. These leaders suffer constant power struggles amongst their members who occupy positions from the upper, to the lowest levels of initiation. These people are often corrupt by greed and power, and practice values that have nothing to do with what they are *supposedly* preaching to the outside world. If the right balance isn't maintained within what initiates call **"the profane world,"** *which is the outside world*, sooner rather than later, we will arrive at complete societal chaos. Should we reach this state, it will be impossible to restore order, and we will thus be **catapulted into an age of darkness and poverty such as has not been seen since the end of the Roman Empire**. For this reason, we are now experiencing a time of great tension throughout all levels of the internal hierarchies within this vast sectarian Illuminati network. It doesn't really matter whether it is the esoteric and occult, the religious, the political, or military segments of society; these branches do not carry the literal "Illuminati" meaning of "enlightment." At the top of this hierarchical structure, whether conciously or unconciously, reside simple puppets who are willing to submit to the dark forces that are pushing the Satanic agenda. The younger members of the current Illuminati sects, and Freemasonry, live in a state of uncertainty, and operate within a very different modality than those initiates two or three centuries ago. It appears that we can have very little hope for real change, or the possiblity of emergence with a new ideology, within such a controlled and manipulated environment. Once they are in, it appears *that's it*! For many initiates a small piece of the cake is better than nothing, and so they blindly follow orders.

In the meantime, the "spoiled children" of the so-called elite are very carefully considering their future, *so as not to put too much at risk*, even if what clearly prevails amongst these privileged individuals is a simple degree of stupidity. Unfortunately this stupidity is born from a lack of goals, and often created by incompetent parents who are only obsessed with **Materialism,** and the perverse values of the New World Order, which could legitimately be renamed *The New Idiotic Order*. Is there anything that could save modern initiates from all this decadence? The answer is **Spiritual Alchemy**. *Alchemy: the study of the Energy of matter. Spiritual Alchemy: the study of Energy in shape. The Alchemist is: one who frees the energy from matter. The Spiritual Alchemist: is the one who frees the Energy from the Form*.[3] This is from form to energy, and not vice versa. The initiate of the *Elus Cohen*—which in Hebrew means *Elect Priests*—Athos A. Altomonte, writes to his disciples of the *Ordre des Chevaliers Maçons Élus Coëns de l'Univers*:

> We know that the universal reintegration of the Cosmos and of all creatures spiritual and material, is the ultimate goal of Spiritual Alchemy. According to the authentic tradition of the Rose Cross in fact, the entire universe has degraded with man, his initial guardian. There is a passage in Genesis in which the exoteric church is given little attention:[4] "Cursed is the ground because of you; through painful toil you will eat food from it all the days of your life. It will produce thorns and thistles for you, and you will eat the plants of the field." Genesis 3: 17-18.[5]

Alchemy is the science of transformation, It is constantly changing, and experiencing spiritual regeneration. To be successful we must convince the members of these elderly institutions and brotherhoods, such as Freemasonry, the Rosicrucians, the Illuminati and Neotemplars, to change their current theosophical "New Age" approach, an approach that in the long run has become too materialistic, and instead *retransform* the Western Initiatic System into something spiritual. In fact, this attempt for change and positive renewal is beginning to occur, within both the Catholic Church (where two major players of our time reside: the Jesuits and Opus Dei), and Judaism. This is a complex issue that will require much deeper analysis, and that I will revisit in the third volume of my *Confessions*. Many of you who have followed me on the Internet since 2006, will recognize that after ten years, I have embarked on this major work of investigation. Where possible I had dialogue with certain mystery schools, and other significant esoteric movements operating within and outside of Freemasonry and suggested renovation. I have also tried to do the same with various Knighthood orders, and Neotemplars groups, linked to both the Catholic Church and Orthodox Churches—but it really doesn't matter. In regards to truth and awareness, I don't discriminate.

The potential to challenge and change the minds of those who are "confused" on topics such as *real illumination* versus *fake illumination* has always fascinated me, along with the constant war against Satanism, and the castration and lobotomization of our society at large by dark forces. Although I have to admit it is becoming increasingly difficult to interact with these groups, and their representatives, mostly due to their dishonesty. People who often present themselves with good intentions turn out to be diversions, or simply attempting to destroy my projects or make me lose time. At the end of our brief collaboration, the author and Mason Gioele Magaldi, turned out to be one of these kind

3   http://www.esonet.it/News-file-article-sid-245.html † Archived 4th July 2015.
4   http://www.esonet.it/News-file-print-sid-274.html † Archived 4th July 2015.
5   Genesis 3:17-18 New International Version (NIV).

FIG. 23 – *Bernardino Fioravanti Grand Librarian of the Grand Orient of Italy and 32° of the Scottish Rite. Photo taken from the website dagospia.com.*

of people. Migaldi is an opportunist with interests tied to much bigger players than himself, including the Jesuits, and powerful Ur Lodges that he is a member of. These organizations reflect what is possibly the worst side of this "New Age," and have nothing to do with true Brotherhood and real Freemasonry. Meanwhile, many people belonging to the Catholic Church, the Masons, and the Illuminati groups within the various traditions, are more concerned by the consequences that could arise from dealing publicly with me, personally these are disappointing at times. It seems that they are becoming increasingly worried about what I am exposing in my work, *so I must be doing a good job.* My position inside the A.A.S.R. (Ancient and Accepted Scottish Rite) and Italian Freemasonry was permanently impaired by Bernardino Fioravanti (FIG. 23), the Librarian of the Grand Orient of Italy, and a 32° of the Scottish Rite. Fioravanti approached my dear friend and brother Mason Danilo Tiberi, a 31° degree of the *Golden Fleece Lodge nr. 1247* in **Fro-sinone,** and in front of the Jesuit headquarters, during a meeting of the Rite in Piazza del Gesù, Fioravanti said to Tiberi, upon arriving to the meeting, that "*I was a strange and dangerous individual related to the deviant side of the Intelligence services.*"

This is to say the least, insulting, and to make matters even worse the situation was further compromised by the Ex-Grand Secretary Giuseppe Abramo, now deceased, who wanted me to repeat all my initiations starting with the *Apprentice degree*, despite the fact that it was he who originally received all of my Masonic documentation. So was all this ostracism just to take more money? It was like telling me I was not welcome. Due to legal costs related to my trial on espionage charges in Norway, they knew perfectly well that I could not afford such expenses. I was in no position to help pay the salary of the Grand Master or his lavish quarters. And it was totally ridiculous, as I was initiated in 1993 by Prince Gianfranco Alliata, and regularized in England in the most important Masonic location in the world, namely that of Great Queen Street in London, home of the United Grand Lodge of England **Kirby Lodge 2818.**

Then of course there was my brief period with the *Regular Grand Lodge of England (R.G.L.E.)*, where I entered the so-called *Masonic High Council of English Freemasonry,* a lodge that followed a more continental tradition. At the same time however, it was a cover for nefarious activities within the shadow of the New World Order and its Intelligence Community.

I do believe that the accusations made against me a few years back, by the site *Masonicinfo.com* and its advocate Ed King of the Grand Lodge of Masons of Maine, have been totally slanderous, inappropriate and inaccurate. One day he too may have to re-think what he wrote. Despite this I am very pleased to respond to such cowardice, as it is followed by an equal amount of corruption. Suffice to say that there are many brothers

Masons, Knights and Rosicrucians, who instead of criticizing me for my difficult choices, are joining in increasing numbers, my order (*Ordo Illuminatorum Universalis*), and who stand ready to defend me from external attack.

For this reason I thank people like Fortunato Luciano Sciandra of the *Equestrian Order of the Holy Sepulchre of Jerusalem* (known also with the acronym O.E.S.S.G.), Luca Monti of the Grand Lodge of **AF & AM** of Italy of the Vitelleschi Palace and Grand Master of the *S.O.E.E.T. Equestrian Order of Orthodox Knights Templar,* Grand Master Marcello Piergentili of the *Suprema Militia Equitum Christi*, Ettore Giuffrida of the *Sovereign Grand Adriatic Sanctuary of the Egyptian Rites*, an important figure of the Knights of Malta of the Orthodox rite, and finally **Prof. Giancarlo Seri,** Sovereign **Grand Master** of the Ancient and Primitive Rite of Memphis and Misraïm, in addition also many Brothers within the various Lodges. These are brave men who over the years continue to follow a path of spiritual regeneration and serious inquiry regarding the oppression generated by the New World Order system, and those who have deviated from the path as historically followed by Neo-Theosophical sects. Within my order *Ordo Illuminatorum Universalis,* some members have even occasionally been threatened with the risk of being thrown out of their orders, for their support of the "Zagami mission." Unfortunately these threats have occured in both the religious orders of chivalry linked to the Vatican, and within the Ancient and Accepted Scottish Rite of Freemasonry covering the Italian jurisdiction, a Rite that is particularly dear to me, after receiving the 33 degree by Prince Gianfranco Alliata of Montereale, who appointed me as his successor in 1993. Unfortunately, as I am often viewed with suspicion, attending, the Lodges of Freemasonry created far too many problems.

It is my belief that above all we should strive for clarity and honesty within *the Craft*, what Masons call Freemasonry. This is something I hope to at least partly offer by presenting my own historical and intellectual insights and analysis. But let us for a moment review what a "Legend" within the Ancient and Accepted Scottish Rite had to say about Freemasonry. **Henry Christian Clausen (1905-1992)**, a distinguished member of the Lucis Trust formerly *Lucifer Trust / Lucifer Trust*. The Lucis Trust is *a nonprofit organization (NPO)* created by Alice Bailey (who I will talk more about in the next chapter). Clausen was one of the most influential Sovereign Grand Commanders of the Southern Jurisdiction of the United States Scottish Rite, and who led this prestigious ritual from 1969 to 1985:

> *Our overall mission can be summarized thus;*
>
> *To seek that which is the most worth in the world; To exalt the dignity of every person, the human side of our daily activities and the maximum service to humanity; To aid mankind's search in God's Universe for identity, for development, and for destiny; And thereby achieve better men in a better world, happier men in a happier world, and wiser men in a wiser world.*
>
> *Our ultimate goal, simply stated, is mankind's moral and spiritual and intellectual development. Historically, the Scottish Rite of Freemasonry as we know it evolved as the Rite of Perfection over 200 years ago on the Continent of Europe under the Constitutions of 1762. Later, the Grand Constitutions of 1786 were enacted and became the creative and derivative laws for us and all our descendant Supreme Councils of the Ancient and Accepted Scottish Rite. Our Supreme Council was organized at Charleston, South Carolina, in 1801 as the Mother Supreme Council of the World, and hence all regular and recognized Supreme Councils throughout the world must trace their pedigree to us.*

But the actual roots of the Scottish Rite go far deeper. Tracing them is a romantic and exciting quest for adventure in the realm of the mind and the spirit. It is a superb story of success—more intriguing than the storied search for the Holy Grail and more rewarding than a successful probe for the philosopher's stone.

Our teachings and symbols preceded our formal organization by thousands of years. They go deep into ancient ages. The signs, symbols and inscriptions come to us from across long, drifting centuries and will be found in the tombs and temples of India to those of Nubia, through the Valley of the Nile in Egypt down to its Delta, as well as in what was then known as Chaldea, Assyria, Persia, Greece, Rome and even in Mexico and Yucatan. The Scottish Rite, therefore, is a treasure house in which there is stored the ageless essence of immutable laws, the accumulation of thousands of years of Masonic experience. [6]

These are beautiful words from the Most Powerful and Illustrious Brother, Henry Christian Clausen. I must admit, however, in front of all of you, and with absolute honesty, that these words once again reiterate the usual *nice words* behind Freemasonry. Unfortunately when they are made to charm, these words are rarely followed with substantial facts. I say this because the reality suggests something else. In my personal experience within Freemasonry, since 1993, I have never found the so-called "Philosopher's Stone," as mentioned by **Clausen**. Instead, I have often found hostility towards free thought, and even at times strong forms of racism, especially within the North American WASP (*White Anglo-Saxon Protestant*) community, and within the Scandinavian circles connected to the Swedish Rite. Racism in Freemasonry, especially in the USA, is a subject I would like to discuss in the following pages. It is a subject that no researcher or historian of Freemasonry has wished to investigate in recent decades, probably for fear of retaliation by the interested parties, as racism is against the stated beliefs behind real Universal Freemasonry.

Racism in U.S. Freemasonry

Since 1999 and until this day, I am the Grand Master and supporter of an important branch of the French-Italian section of the Illuminati that is dedicated to the study and practice of the ancient mystery schools. It originated in Monte Carlo, where it was founded by the Masonic Executive Committee of the Monte Carlo Lodge of the P2, the *Ordo Illuminatorum Universalis*. We have in the past attempted to collaborate with similar, like minded groups, after our internal conflict brought us out of the Monte Carlo group in 2008. Initially we were based out of Rome, and later moved to Pomezia near Rome; before finally moving to our present headquarters in Florence. For a brief time we maintained close cooperation with *the International Academy of the Illuminati* in Rome, with its vice president Piergiorgio Bassi, and its President and Grand Master, Professor Giuliano Di Bernardo. Our cooperation has been terminated in recent years, presumably for our diversity of views regarding the perilous subject of the New World Order, *and their globalist vision typical within this New Age.* These views are not in line with our principles. This has led me to repeatedly refuse numerous offers from similar organizations that in the last few years, wished to enter into contact with us. Some of them were genuine affiliations and *Illuminati sects,* with seemingly good intentions. Others contacted us to form possible collaborations, or have even asked for treaties of mutual recognition, a practice in use in Freemasonry, Neo-Templarism and similar orders. There are also completely imaginary and spurious orders, based on myth and the wild fantasy of their creators, like the "Illuminati Order" founded in Spain in 1995 by **Gabriel Lopez**

6   http://freimaurer-wiki.de/index.php/En:_Clausen%C2%B4s_commentaries ‡ Archived 4th July 2015.

de Rojas, a person who later demonstrated to the world his true colors, that of being a simple pawn of Zionist obscurantism. This became evident after de Rojas publicly converted to Judaism and took the name **Gabriel Yehuda Shahor.**

As a Grand Master with a lot of regular patents issued to me by initiates, and belonging to various secret sections of the Illuminati and other occult associations having to do with the Rosicrucian and Neo-Templar tradition, I began, in 1999, an independent project tied to secret groups located throughout the world, that we believe have a genuine tradition to offer. All this is accomplished in the pursuit of dialogue and mutual understanding. In this difficult moment where we are living all levels of the Kali Yuga initiatic system, the "age of the demon Kali," also known as the "age of vice," where society is dramatically characterized by wrong values and corruption, and even the Dalai Lama has been proven to be a false initiate.

After my rebellion against the New World Order pyramid of power in 2006, however, only the "Secret Chiefs" and "Invisible Masters," said to be transcendent cosmic authorities; a Spiritual Hierarchy responsible for the moral caliber of the cosmos, reside above me and my group.

No man or institution can be our superior in this day and age where all terrestrial institutions are compromised and corrupt. Many Freemasons respect me for refusing compromises that at times may have made me a very rich and powerful man among the elite. Others obviously hate me for revealing this secretive world and their hidden plans to the masses. Still, there are those who hate me even more because of my Italian origins—like the racist Masons of the **Grand Lodge F & A M of Alabama** who criticize me, when saying that I give Freemasons a bad name, and calling me an "Italian commoner" when my origins as you may know are quite the opposite. [7]

This is an e-mail I received from them some time ago:

Title: Disgrace you are.

From Joseph Rothenburg, June 28, 2010, at 5:34 am.

I am sorry that you are a commoner regular average everyday citizen, it's nice you like take pictures that seem dark or foolish, Goomba's don't cut it, no Italian cigarette smoking liar is going to lead us. you are a poor man of Italia, sorry you do not qualify AND WE DETEST YOU from the MASONIC USA, and we always will, you don't even have a dollar to move with, so be off with you peasant. Yea I have to admit, if I was going to choose one to be the Messiah I'd much rather take Supriem David Rockefeller over the cigarette smoking Jesus/Emperor, even Supriem hasn't made himself look as retarded as Leo Zagami does. So how about a new Allied Union update page for Leo Zagami now, lol, NOT! Leo I must ask you, what brand of cigarettes does Jesus smoke? could be some endorsement money out there for you, lol.

Oh and Leo you are a laughing stock in the Masonic fraternity, trust me on that.

Mr. Zagami, you have delusions of grandeur, that's all, nothing more, you are a known felon with an arrest record, you would not be welcome in our lodges I assure you. You are only seeking that people follow your nut campaign, I encourage everyone to ignore this man, he only seeks any kind of attention he can get, oh and Mr. Zagami Bad News Bulletin you are not a cigarette smoking Jesus nor an Emperor, you are just an Italian commoner with an arrest record touting NWO doctrine giving

7   https://leozagami.wordpress.com/2008/06/19/leo-lyon-zagami-family-background-research/ ‡ Archived 9th July 2015.

FIG. 24 – Image of the patent James Jeffrey Staples, 32° of the Ancient and Accepted Scottish Rite.

FIG. 25 – Certificate of Master Mason of Masonry by Benjamin T. Mollica, released by the Grand Lodge of New York on March 5, 1996.

all Masons a bad name. We will not follow your Internet BS Leo, like you would like, or your publications.

Considering the message that you have just read, Freemason Joseph Rothenburg seems to want to express his thoughts about me, on behalf of the whole Masonic Community of the United States, which would seem already quite ridiculous, since there is no Grand Lodge uniting the members of the different States of the Union. This is a demonstration of ignorance and racist behavior contrary to the code of ethics of Freemasonry. The Masonic Lodges of Alabama have an internal racist protocol to this day, that is present in their constitutions and in their teachings, and unfortunately they are not the only racist Freemasons in the United States.

A 32° Mason of the Ancient and Accepted Scottish Rite named **Jeffrey Staples** (FIG. 24), wrote to me about the problem of racism present inside U.S. Freemasonry, signaling racism also out of the State of Missouri:

Missouri, much to my horror and dissapointment, seems as if one of the pillars of its tradition is "whitery is Righty... any other shade cannot be made a Mason." I AM Ashamed of Missouri Masonry, as it appears quite unrepentant of its racism, and one will be called down if one dares to question "Tradition." I have spent over two years trying to A. contact Prince Hall Masons in the state so I can B. Switch Obediences. They sadly have no desire at all to fix or mend the gap.

Last but not least, and definitely worth mentioning in this context, is the story of Benjamin Mollica, better known as **Arthur F. Temple**, an Italian-American writer and occultist connected in the past with the infamous inner circle of the Temple of Set, which I will also mention later in connection with a case of Satanism. Since 1996, Mollica was a Master Mason belonging of **Jamaica Queens Village Lodge No. 54** of the Grand Lodge of New York. (FIG. 25) He is the author of the book, *Dark Currents: A Journey Into The Abyss*. But he left Freemasonry in great disappointment after moving to Arizona and during a not so fraternal visit to **Scottsdale Lodge 43**, after being called an "Italian nigger" by his supposed Freemasonic "Brothers." So as to maintain his good status, Benjamin continues to pay his lodge dues even after quitting Freemasonry. He told me that he was only welcome as a guest of Scottsdale Lodge for the occasional visit. The moment they realized he wanted to apply for membership in their lodge things instantly changed, and their true White Anglo-Saxon Protestant racist nature came out. Maybe they were inspired by the infamous Freemason and Illuminati Aleister Crowley who in his book, **Diary of a Drug Fiend Book I, Chapter 9,** applied the term "nigger" to Italians: *"We (British) always somehow instinctively think of the Italian as a nigger. We do not call them 'Dagos' and 'wops' as they do in the United States, with the invariable epithet of 'dirty,' but we have the same feeling."*

Racism pushed the aforementioned Arthur Reghini, an old acquaintance of Aleister Crowley, who nonetheless exchanged mutual recognitions and charters in the Illuminati, wrote harsh words of criticism and disgust regarding the state of affairs within Freemasonry in his important Masonic book published in 1922 in Rome, entitled, *The Sacred Words and Passwords of the First three Degrees and the Greatest Masonic Mystery*, (*Le Parole Sacre e di Passo dei primi tre Gradi e il Massimo Mistero Massonico, Studio critico ed iniziatico*).

Reghini, a neo-Pythagorean Italian intellectual, seemingly in perpetual balance between Freemasonry and **fascism,** wrote words that called into question the way fascists are often portrayed as racist, in this case demonstrating more tolerance for certain alleged Freemasons:

> *Jesus, preaching the good news, did not distinguish between white and colored men, but they exclude blacks from their lodges because to apply the love of neighbor they want to first see the color of the skin! And equality? And the brotherhood? Consequently, not even your fellow blackmen, dear Anglo-Saxon brothers?* [8]

And from Genesis 4:8-12 N.I.V.:

> *Now Cain said to his brother Abel, "Let's go out to the field." And while they were in the field, Cain attacked his brother Abel and killed him.*
>
> *Then the LORD said to Cain, "Where is your brother Abel?"*
>
> *"I don't know," he replied. "Am I my brother's keeper?"*
>
> *The LORD said, "What have you done? Listen! Your brother's blood cries out to me from the ground. Now you are under a curse and driven from the ground, which opened its mouth to receive your brother's blood from your hand. When you work the ground, it will no longer yield its crops for you. You will be a restless wanderer on the earth."*

On JUNE 21, 2009, *Masonic Traveler* wrote this on his popular Blog:

> *The Grand Lodge of Georgia has openly documented its policy of racial exclusion of "non-white men." In a court filing to the Superior Court of Dekalb county—Civil*

8   Arturo Reghini *Ibid.*, pp. 226-227.

action 09CV7552-8, are documents which include the charges brought against the Worshipful Master of Gate City Lodge No. 2. The charges as filed were quantified as a Violation of the Moral Law:

Specification 1 In This: That said worshipful master xx xx did in fact raise or allow to be raised in and about February 2009 in the lodge that he is the Worshipful Master, a non-white man, xx xx.

Specification 2—This said worshipful master xx xx did commit overt act or acts against moral laws of Free and Accepted Masons and the moral duties as the Worshipful Master of Gate City lodge no 2 as follows:

– Violation of moral law from word of mouth

– Violation of moral obligation to the ancient landmarks, ancient customs, ancient traditions, ancient usages, constitution, laws and edicts working under the jurisdiction of the Grand Lodge of Georgia.

– Violation of moral official obligation was taken at the time of installation of officers.

– Violation of moral obligations of not upholding the charter of Gate City Lodge #2

– Violation of moral obligation of keeping peace and harmony in the craft by allowing the operation of a Cabal in Gate City Lodge #2

– Violation of moral obligation as pursuant to Masonic Code 1-104 without having obtained the sanction of the grand Lodge are hereby declared spurious and clandestine and of no Masonic authority whatsoever.

The Master of gate City Lodge, proclaiming his innocence, was then charged in the following manner.

– Violation of the Laws of Masonry.

Specification 1 In This: That said Worshipful Master xx xx did in fact embrace a formed Cabal to secretly unite to bring about and overturn with usurpation of the constitution, laws, ancient landmarks, customs and traditions of Free and Accepted Masons working under the jurisdiction of ancient landmarks, customs and traditions of Free & Accepted Masons working under the jurisdiction of the grand Lodge of the state of Georgia, when he was elected Worshipful Master in December 2008.

Specification 2 In This: The worshipful master xx xx knowingly and willfully did in fact allow a raising of a non-white man in February 2009, which has never been done working under the jurisdiction of Grand Lodge of the state of Georgia. According to the old customs of the Grand Lodge of the state of Georgia which has existed continuously since February 21, 1734. After the fact, xx xx did allow parading xx xx to other Masonic Lodges, presenting him as a Master Mason accompanied by a letter dated February 25, 2008 on gate city Lodge #2 letterhead with the typed from xx xx xx, Grand Master.

Specification 3 In This: That the said worshipful Master xx xx did commit act or acts of destroying peace and harmony throughout the craft of Masonry in the state of Georgia.

Specification 4 In This: that said worshipful master xx xx of Gate City Lodge #2 did in fact knowingly and willfully commit this act or acts which is in conflict with the ancient landmarks and Masonic code sections 71-101, 4-101#6, 1-101, 1-201, 1-202, 1-205. Worshipful Master xx xx committed act or acts knowingly and willfully that conflicts with the ancient customs and traditions which are the immemorial usages and fundamentals of the craft which have existed from time immemorial and are unchangeable.

Specification 5 In This: That said worshipful Master xx xx of gate city lodge #2 must be tried by a trial of present and or past masters pursuant to Masonic code 83-401 and when found guilty of this charge of violation of the laws of Masonry as he would be under no less penalty than that established by Masonic code 21.106 and 21.107.

Masonic Law speak, the charges are based on committing act or acts of destroying peace and harmony, but involving the moral law as to the cabal behind the making of an "non-white" man a Mason. The disharmony seems to have stemmed from the "parading" of an African American Georgia Freemason, which is apparently now, a violation of their moral law. Never mind that the brother was made and recognized by the state, and never mind that he was acknowledged in a tiled lodge as such some speculation suggests that rather than drop the proceedings, the Grand Master will hold the trial to quell the misconception of racism and set the record straight, but this remains to be seen. In the mean time, a civil filing by the Worshipful Master turned Plaintiff suggests that the Grand Lodge is in violation of its Non-Profit Status as it is now openly admitting that it discriminates based on race, which is against the public policy of the State. In the filing, it is also points out in several sections where the Grand Lodge is ... an enemy of bigotry or intolerance ... and also states the the Grand Lodge in leveling the charges is in violation of its contract with the member(s) when facing revocation of charters and membership privileges as members have a value property investment (contract) from their dues. Interesting to point out, the filing also says openly that "Upon information and belief, Plaintiffs show that there are currently in Georgia active, regular Master Masons of at least the following extractions in whole or in part: American Indians, East Indian, Arab/Lebanese/Egyptian, Persian/Iranian, Vietnamese, Chinese, non white Mexican/Hispanic, African-American, and Filipino, in addition to those of white/Caucasian ancestry." So, now there seems to be a provision of the fraternity being not strictly white, which seems to countermand the white only exclusion. The long and short of this convoluted tale comes squarely to rest on the odious claim that a "non-white man" can not be a Freemason. I affirm, that racism is not tolerable, and bigotry, open or otherwise, is not included in our Moral Law. The brothers of Georgia are sorely mistaken in this assertion. As I AM my brother's keeper my "...brother's blood cries out to me from the ground." To let this go will put the fraternity under a curse that will send us "... driven from the ground." If not addressed this open proclamation could destroy the fraternity. This is not Freemasonry in the 21st Century. This is not tolerable, on a personal level or from a Grand Lodge level, especially our Grand Lodges are an electable body from the craft lodge. Recognition of Georgian Freemasonry must be held in questioned especially if they are so ignorant to hold these ideas to be Moral Laws. If in fact they do then Recognition must be terminated. We are our brother's keepers and only have the Great Architect to answer to. How will we respond when he asks us how we addressed this?[9]

Remember Brother Freemasons, to survive the challenges of the new millenium, we must not only move beyond these bigoted and racist ideologies, typical of the manipula-

9   http://freemasoninformation.com/2009/06/my-brothers-keeper-open-racism-in-georgia-freemasonry/ ‡ Archived 4th July 2015.

tors of Freemasonry—the Jesuits and the Zionists—we must also respect the "Christian" tradition and values of the Craft. It is a delicate balance to achieve, especially when one must also consider the sudden rise of the "Gay Lobby" that has taken over the Vatican, which is now working to take over Freemasonry. In this context I would like to discuss the supposed revelations of Communist, Jesuit agent and Freemason **Roger Dachez,** in a strongly controversial article, that appeared in 2015. [10]

Dachez, who besides being the founder of the Masonic review "Renaissance Traditionnelle" (traditional rebirth), is a close collaborator of Alain Bauer. Bauer was the former Grand Master of the Grand Orient of France in the 1990s. He is a controversial "big brother," "tolerance zero" type of Freemason, who supports having surveillance cameras everywhere, an advisor of the NYPD, a mentor of both **Nicolas Sarkozy and Manuel Valls**, and who is probably of Rothschild descent.

A friend of mine writes this about Bauer: *I know how sick this man is (notably a perverted type of closed homosexual) as Simon Giovanna, who is a good friend of mine and has also been the G.O. Grand Master (1999-2000), has known him very well and has actually been evicted mainly by him (under the pretext of the Corsican affair), and still to this day has an enmity with him to the point that some court cases are still taking place to this day or so ... Simon proposed me to join his free lodge in the alternate G.O. he co-created (the traditional G.O. of Mediterranean) but as I had no affinities at all with some key characters there (some really materialistic and within a lodge I consider sterile and indulging in wishful thinking), I declined ... Yet, I have made a lecture on the Tarot in their lodge back in October 2011, and I send you here a picture of myself there. I guess I have a high expectancy of what is supposed to be a free mason, and I can't imagine a lodge not composed of people sharing a real common vision and objective goals ... So I think that the only group I could join would be with a great master like you.*

Well those are indeed very kind words coming from my friend, towards my Order and myself. Of course for security reasons, I must keep his name anonymous. Here is his take on the aforementioned article by Roger Dachez, where he muses the languid progressive good-thinking and globalist tendencies typical within left wing Freemasons:

In short, Dachez is deploring the fact that the Freemasons from Georgia are openly against homosexuality and "fornication" (or lustful sexuality), and are sticking tight to strict moral standards. (in appearance only?) In this article such positions are presented as regressive, passeist and nefarious, presented as being akin to racism, misogyny, and even Muslim fundamentalists ... This article is openly calling into action against these lodges (referring to globalist collaborator Paul Rich http:// www.paulrich.net/ and praising the "progress" of the Catholic church in regard of the gay issue), for the sake of "exemplary masonry"... As usual, under the cover of good and progressive thinking, this is paving the way of a globalist socialist agenda along with a pro-gay rhetoric and aggressive reformative politics ... By the way, you'll pay attention to the title of the book by Bauer & Dachez presented at the end of the article: The little dictionary of the true and false Brothers—The secrets of the great characters of Freemasonry.

I fully support the words of my friend, and partially the conservative stand of The Grand Lodge of Georgia, but not their racism. The LGBT lobby does not need another liberal platform to promote their New World Order *Rainbow agenda.* Homosexual ac-

10   http://pierresvivantes.hautetfort.com/archive/2015/11/03/un-ouragan-maconnique-aux-usa-5710474.html ‡ Archived 4th July 2015.

tivities are not in line with conservative Masonic values. In England, homosexuals reside at the top of the hierarchy that rules the United Grand Lodge of England, and their more popular Rite called *Emulation*, which only opens to dark energies and chaos. In their Masonic Lodges and Illuminati sects like the *Ordo Templi Orientis*, many openly promote homosexuality and bisexuality as added values in line with their "Prophet" Aleister Crowley, and his depraved cult of *Thelema*, where their motto is: *"Do what thou wilt,"* which often translates into toleration of pedophilia and its use in Satanic practices. In Dallas, Texas, **James Robert Wright** a member of the *Ordo Templi Orientis* and the *Golden Dawn*, who was a 32° degreee of the A.A.S.R., and at one time held many positions of responsibility in his Masonic lodge, called **Northern Star #377**, at one point becoming an actual employee and a Special Assistant to the Secretary General of the Supreme Council of the Scottish Rite, suddenly broke with Freemasonry accusing them of not respecting his "sexuality." Wright wrote a small booklet of a little more than a 100 pages called, "Freemasonry's Cult Abuses, Human and Gay Rights Controversy," that was full of senseless accusations and lies against his formal Brothers. It was distributed by **New Falcon Publications,** a publisher connected to the O.T.O.[11] Acknowledgments positioned at the opening of this tiny over priced book, include among others, his O.T.O. superior and friend Lon Milo Duquette, the Satanist **Nicholas de Vere Von Draken-berg (1957-2013),** and the *Bubastis Oasis,* which represents the *Ordo Templi Orientis* in Dallas. A person can be gay of course, *who cares*! But why bring Satanism and the O.T.O. into the equation? And why then attack your ex-Brothers in "Regular" Masonry using a publisher supported by Crowley's infamous order? For you to do that, James, you deserve to be kicked out, as such things are not compatible with real Freemasonry and I suggest that you join "The Choronzon club" instead.

It is now the time to communicate a positive change within the Masonic orders, that can lead to a **New Era of light and scientific progress,** in the coming years, an era removed of all the Illuminati sects polluting Freemasonry with their evil goals and perversions. In a society that already struggles with poverty and growing social problems, the elite and their Illuminati slaves instead indulge in the advocacy of a liberal agenda that openly promotes gay marriages, abortion rights, and Satanism. This effort is supported by an increasingly sick elite that is full of hypocrites, and who secretly intend to eliminate a large part of the world's population, as they stated on the Georgia Guidestones, including the commercialization of Human Body parts, as exposed in the Planned Parenthood controversy outlined in 2015.

Freemasonry and the various Illuminati sects, which boast of having characters like the Clintons, the Bushes, and Barack Obama, in their circles, should instead initiate a drastic process and change their way of perceiving themselves and the others around them. Currently they only care for their incessant need to exercise power over others (Hillary's presidential race is an example of this), while gathering personal recognition and material benefits. Current leaders of the Illuminati or *pseudo-Illuminati*, as it were, have certainly not been inspired by a true spiritual vision as taught in the ancient mystery schools. Instead, they have been corrupted by greed and rampant materialism. Anyone who says different are told they are lying. The people now in power, are all Satanists who are following a course set out by the New World Order. It is an organization where *the way of the hypocrite and the liar* rules over everything else. This results in a false and phony society that screw us all. They are supported by ruthless and unscrupulous clubs,

---

11   James Robert Wright, *Freemasonry's Cult Abuses, Human and Gay Rights Controversy,* (Las Vegas, NV: New Falcon Publications, 2011).

very powerful think tanks, and para-masonic organizations like the Bilderberg Club. This exclusive club is considered to be the most secret and powerful organization in the world, and directed by the *not so Illuminated* elite within religion and Freemasonry. I assure you, however, that it is not the only group within "Paramasonry."

So what is Paramasonry? *Metapedia.org* describes it this way:

Paramasonry (also known as Pseudomasonry) is a term used to refer to fraternal organizations which mimic the structure of Freemasonry and some of its esoteric ritualism, but which official freemasonry itself publically claims to have no connection to. These organizations themselves may have completely different initiatives and "causes" to each other. Because of the secretive nature of freemasonry, it is hotly disputed whether a hidden elite within official freemasonry has encourged some para-masonic organizations such as the Order of the Illuminati and the Carbonari or whether these radical groups simply infiltrated and took over some of the lodges of Continental Freemasonry. [12]

Of course para-masonic organizations are another important part of the network of the Illuminati, secretly manipulated by the "Guardians" who have created this state of affairs in the first place since the dawn of mankind.

The Reptilian

For the Illuminati, the "Guardians" are those that originally came to Earth to tend to creation, as symbolized by the Garden of Eden, as well as having created our earlier forms of civilization. This is where the ancient mystery schools of the Illuminati were actually established, which later gave birth to Freemasonry. This process was originated in the *mists of time* with the ancient Fathers of heaven, the "Elohim" which means "the Powers." In this system of belief, the Elohim are the *gods* that created us, at which time those who, the Sumerians, and later the Assyrian-Babylonians, called the Annunaki, that would become our "Guardians." **They are tied to our DNA,** are involved in the past of our species, and determine our future. Their offspring are our planets aristocracy and royalty, and they have the responsiblity to rule through their bloodlines, and by divine power, and they are commonly referred to as **"blue blood."** In contemporary society this so-called "reptilian theory" is also present in science fiction, ufology and now in conspiracy theories about the Illuminati. They are described in terms like: reptilian, humanoid reptilian, saurian, lizard man, Homo saurus, and of course, lizard people.

The Native American Hopi tribe speaks of the existence of a reptilian race of men that lives underground called SHETI or **"Snake Brothers."** In pre-Columbian mythology, the primordial Eve named Bachue can turn into a large snake, and is referred to as "The Serpent of Heaven." There are also many other examples that suggest that there is something "reptilian" going on within the elite communities since ancient times. The first legendary king of Athens, Cecrops, was half man and half snake. In Greek mythology, the Titans had servant snakes and the Giants were sometimes depicted with the legs formed by **serpentine endings.** In the scriptures and Indian legends, the **Nagas** are snake shaped beings believed to live underground, while maintaining contact with man. In some versions, it was reported that these reptoid beings lived on a continent that would eventually sink into the Indian Ocean, (another **Atlantis** or Atlantis itself?) The Indian texts also refer to another race of men called **Sarpa the Sanskrit term for snake/serpent.** In Chinese, Vietnamese, Korean and Japanese cultures, there are legends of the **Long** (**Yong** in Korean, **Ryu** in Japanese) or **dragons,** halfway between the physical and the astral plane, but they are rarely described in humanoid form, having human shape with reptilian characteristics. The Japanese told stories about **Kappa,** a mythological race of humanoid reptilians.

In China, Korea and Japan, the underwater realms are populated by mythological *Dragon Kings*, and their descendants are considered humans descendents, of a race of dragons. Such "Reptilian" lineage is often claimed by Asian Emperors, who were believed to be able to voluntarily change from human to dragon form, which is considered, in some Asian traditions, as no better than the form of the devil.

In the Middle East, the snake men and dragons, spoken of since ancient times, are known as *Jinn*. In the iconography of Western art there are numerous representations that are in line with the "reptilian myth," and we often find a woman with a serpent's tail, sometimes even a reptilian foot, like in the *The Last Judgment,* a famous triptych by **Hieronymus Bosch,** created after 1482. In the Middle Ages, the Devil was often depicted with reptilian characteristics, as well as the various demons depicted in Middle Age iconography.

In Africa, the ancient Egyptian god *Sobek* is seen as a man with the head of a crocodile. In Mali, Africa there is a population called the **Dogon,** who have a foundation myth that includes a reptilian man. The Dogon say that they descend from the god Amma, who came from the star Po Tolo (**Sirius B**).

The reader is probably wondering why the spirit takes the form of a reptile rather than that of any other animal. According to MacLean's evolutionary triune brain theory, developed by Dr Paul D McLean (1931-2007), an American physician specializing in neuroscience and who made important contributions in the field of psychiatry, formulated and modeled in the 1960s, and propounded at length in his 1990 book, *The Triune Brain in Evolution* (paraphrased): *The triune brain consists of the reptilian complex, the paleomammalian complex (limbic system), and the neomammalian complex (neocortex). Each is viewed as structures sequentially added to the forebrain in the course of evolution.* [13]

The triune brain hypothesis became familiar to popular audience through Carl Sagan's Pulitzer prize winning 1977 book *The Dragons of Eden.* The theory has been embraced by some psychiatrists and at least one leading neuroscience researcher. [14]

*1) The first brain, the reptilian, even if it is small, is the true and only absolute master of the whole body and is known as the R-complex or **complex-R,** where R stands for Reptilian and is the innermost part of the fundamental and brain. It evolved around **300-400 million years ago.** The reptilian complex, was the name MacLean gave to the basal ganglia, structures derived from the floor of the forebrain during development. The term derives from the idea that comparative neuroanatomists once believed that the forebrains of reptiles and birds were dominated by these structures. MacLean proposed that the reptilian complex was responsible for species-typical instinctual behaviors involved in aggression, dominance, territoriality, and ritual displays.* [15]

*2) The second brain called the **limbic system** or paleomammalian brain is a complex set of brain structures located on both sides of the thalamus, right under the cerebrum grown over the reptilian brain to generate emotions, and is in a secondary position*

13　http://www.kheper.net/topics/intelligence/MacLean.htm ✝ Archived 4th July 2015.

14　See. Foreword by Jaak Panksepp, Edied by G. A. Cory, Jr. and Russel Gardner, Jr. T*he Evolutionary Neuroethology of Paul MacLean: Convergences and Frontiers,* (Westport, Connecticut: Praeger Publishers, 2002).

15　https://en.wikipedia.org/wiki/Triune_brain ✝ Archived 4th July 2015.

*to the reptilian brain in governing the body. It evolved about **250 million years ago.***

*3) The third one known as neocortex (Latin for "new bark" or "new rind"), also called the neopallium ("new mantle") and isocortex ("equal rind"), is a part of the mammalian brain, has developed slowly over the first two, and has the illusion to rule the body but is just a guest fooling with the commands. In humans, the neocortex is in fact involved in higher functions, like a generation of motor commands, sensory perception, spatial reasoning, conscious thought and even language. **It evolved about 5 million years ago.***

*The reptilian brain is the mind that grants the "machine" to function without having to deal with reflection. The limbic brain is the one that preserves the past experience and memory to avoid having to re-learn and continuously, it is the brain of the beliefs and conditionings. The neocortex -intellectual- is to the future that links the past to the present, to protect us, it grants the possibility to man to associate different elements of its reality and recombine to create new structures to meet ably the other two brains, the "emotions" and the "pleasures"of the other five senses and the vital "sex force." The reptile state is clearly visible in the human embryo. In the biogenetic law of the universe given by the evolutionary biologist at the end of the nineteenth century, **Ernst Haeckel,** postulates that living embryos during their development re-experience the evolutionary process of that of their progenitors. He theorized that during its development in the womb, the human embryo first displayed the characteristics of a fish, then a reptile, and finally those of humans. [16]*

Suffice to say that all humans are a little bit reptilian, but there's no need to be frightened about this issue. Of course there are those among the elite that have a stronger link with this "reptilian" reality, along with the extradimensionality of the "reptilian" type, which I will try to clarify in these writings.

Carl Edward Sagan (1934–1996) was one of the most famous astronomers, astrophysicists and astrochemists of the twentieth century, as well as science fiction author and a founding father of the SETI project in search of extraterrestrial intelligence. In the aforementioned book The Dragons of Eden, *he emphasized that in our constant search for the evolution of human intelligence, it is important not to ignore the most ancient part of the human brain, on which all other segments are only additions. Throughout his book, one can find subtle hints of his true knowledge on the reptilian issue which played such an important role in the existence of our species. It mentions how much of our behavior is even expressed in reptilian terms, as a killer in "cold blood" and the fact one uses the sound like that of a snake for silence or get the attention of those present. [17]*

In a lost work called the "Syntagma" (arrangement), and taking their name from the Serpent (FIW in Greek) a great reverence and importance was given to a Christian Gnostic Illuminati sect depicted by Hippolytus of Rome (170-235). The Ophite members of this sect (Orphites), had the Serpent as the center of their cult, it was a predominant element in the origination myth that characterizes their doctrine. In antagonism with the evil demiurge, it is the Serpent, the creator of matter, the real revealer of dualism that underlies the gnostic concept. In this belief it is the Snake that brings gnosis, the enlightened knowledge of good and evil to mankind; **The Serpent is the positive element to worship and seek as a way toward the salvation for what is hidden in man.** In this

16   Author Unknown, TREATY ON SCIENCE THEORY OF THE MAGI (ABC Alchemy and Magic), pp. 92,93,94,95, taken from https://it.scribd.com/doc/82594342/22/Magia-e-religione ✝ Archived 4th July 2015.
17   http://www.bibliotecapleyades.net/sumer_anunnaki/reptiles/reptiles38.htm ✝ Archived 9th July 2015.

philosophy flesh is treated as a prison and the "pneumatic," or spiritual, was manifested by the creator of good, for the consequent abandonment of what is the material evil, that is constituting the world. In this design, redemption can be achieved, even through the most perverse libertinism. [18] That is why to the Illuminati perversion includes an element of salvation and redemption, even when their behavior suggests the opposite.

The longstanding Freemason, and author, Mariano Bizarri, depicts the Ophites as having a belief that is close and "comparable" to the Gnostic revival that began with the first Gnostic Church of the "New Age" created by the Illuminati sectarian network founded by Freemason and known esoterist, **Jules-Benoît Doinel (1842-1903)**. Bizzari explains it this way:

> *Speaking of ophites—considered here as a paradigm of the Gnostic sects in which the figure of the snake is hypostasized to that of "savior"—the Father of the Church observes as the Great Mother Sophia-Prunikos, desperately tries to counter the evil of the adopted child—Ialdabaoth—Iehovah—who sent the snake to "seduce Adam and Eve and cause them to disobey the command of Iadalbaoth." It allowed for the first couple to realize that Ialdabaoth, the Demiurge, was not the "Supreme God." The act of the serpent, "marks the beginning of gnosis on earth," the beginning of that path of redemption of mankind from the darkness that would confine the evil god of the Old Testament. A conception quite comparable will be the one developed by the Gnostic Church of Doinel in the nineteenth century, which confirms not only the survival of certain concepts, but how these relate very closely to the story of Rennes-le-Château. This hypothesis, taken to its extreme (and logical) consequences, led some sects—like the Cainites or the Manichaeist, the followers of Mani—to believe Christ as one of the incarnations of universal snake dispenser of "light" (intellectual), knowledge of "secret" and then, ultimately, of "redemption."* [19]

Since what has been described as "the act of the snake, this different and heretical view of Christ and *Creation*, is an integral part of the vision of the Illuminati within the various Gnostic sects. According le-Château, and shown by the studies of Bizzarri, the obscure Illuminati sect of the Cainites have demonstrated that ancient "reptilian" wisdom has been secretly transmitted within certain mystery schools since ancient times. That is why the Chief Agent, or better *Past Frater Superior*, of the Italian O.T.O., Alberto Moscato says in his studies, "*that this long journey through the Royal Art of the O.T.O., traditional or experimental, rests upon Occult Serpentine Energy.*" [20] In their "re-reading" of the sacred texts hinging upon "rehabilitation" of the figure of the serpent, the Gnostics literally invert the esoteric exegesis of Genesis. This is true as well with the **Ophites, the Naassene, the Perati and the Cainites, or Cainians.** [21]

There is a lot of reverence towards "**the Great Mother,**" this is something you may have noticed in reading the famous fiction by Dan Brown, *The Da Vinci Code*, where the protagonist Robert Langdon states: "The Grail"..."symbolizes the lost goddess." [22]

This flows into the hypothesis of a "female Messiah" which for Bizzari, was rediscovered by "New Age literature," often twisting elements of a very old tradition which, in this specific case, makes reference to texts discovered at Nag Hamamdi in which the

18   http://www.30giorni.it/articoli_id_664_l1.htm ✝ Archived 9th July 2015.
19   Mariano Bizzarri, *Rennes le Chateau. Dal Vangelo perduto dei Cainiti alle sette segrete,* (Rome, IT:Edizioni Mediterranee, 2005), pp. 127-128.
20   Alberto Moscato, *Ars gratia artis. Il Libro dell'Arte Regale,* (Foggia, IT: Bastogi, 1998), p. 28.
21   *Ibid.,* footnote 26 at page 27.
22   See, Dan Brown, *The Da Vinci Code,* (Milan, IT:Mondadori, 2003), p. 280.

role of "savior" is hypostatized by a female character. In the context of this manuscript, the symbol of wisdom implicitly places Isis in relation to the Snake, as witnessed by the Gnostic-Ophites. [23]

So we speak again about the worshippers of the snake, and reapproach the so-called "reptilian," theory as seen as an interpretive key objective. Considering that determination—where the snake in esotericism has a double meaning—Epiphanius cites Guenon, who considers the serpent **OPHIS** as a symbol of wisdom, "Ophis" stems from the Greek word **SOPHIA,** from which Ophis draws the letters in order to connote to it a less evil value, than that of Satan, the adversary. As explained by Guenon, the representation of the two snakes together, in forming Hermes Caduceus, symbolizes the antagonistic forces of Good and Evil, representing the perpetual motion of uphill-downhill-involution and *evolution* of the Universal Force, that is rolling on the Axis of the World It represents the vertical path that leads from the earth (mankind) to the sky, and the regeneration of the initiate.

Epiphanius specifies instead that: *"In fact, the Caduceus is the balance, and then the indifference between good and evil, the **Masonic coincidentiam oppositorum** that the Gnostic theology of counterchurch holds events with cyclical of humanity's way along a fixed direction (the Axis of the World), and in the direction of the celestial world it is understood as a self-divinization initiate. The wings represent precisely the sky, the goal to reach."* [24]

This would correlate with what William Bramley, the pseudonym of a Californian lawyer and author in 1989, in the book *The Gods of Eden*, called "The Brotherhood of the Snake," created by the god Enki / Ea the Annunaki. This book is subtitled, "The chilling truth about extraterrestrial infiltration and the conspiracy to keep humankind in chains."

To name a few, this thesis was later supported by modern people like Zecharia Sitchin and David Icke, both modern proponents of so-called "Conspiracy Theory" who specialize in non-fiction. [25] This philosophy also appeals to the supporters of so-called "spiritual Satanism"—another side of the dark realm.

Here is what the *Joy of Satan Ministeries* says about the matter:

Satan is the Sumerian God known as "EA" or "ENKI." He is a GOD, not an angel! He has been denigrated and slandered through the centuries with falsehoods and lies. Most people do not know Satan. They believe everything they are told about him without question. Fear is a powerful tool that has been used for centuries to keep humanity away from Satan.

Satan is the most brilliant and powerful of the Gods. He is symbolized by the Water Bearer of the sign of Aquarius, the 11th sign of the Zodiac. Aquarius is the sign of humanity, technology and genius. One of Satan's numbers is 11.

Satan/Enki established the Ancient Egyptian Order of the Serpent, also known as "The Brotherhood of the Snake." Through the millennia, the teachings have been corrupted and no longer resemble the original doctrines. This Order was to bring humanity godly knowledge and power and to complete the Great Work of transforming our souls. This knowledge has been kept in the hands of a few and abused to the detriment of us all under the direction of the enemy gods. People are told if they are given this power, they will abuse it. This is another lie created and spread by

23   Bizzarri M., *Ibid.*, p. 216.
24   Epiphanius, *Ibid.*, p. 31., *[emphasis added].*
25   http://it.nostradamus.wikia.com/wiki/Fratellanza_del_Serpente ✝ Archived 9th July 2015.

those who deliberately use these powers for nefarious ends under the direction of the enemy extraterrestrials masquerading as "Jehovah" and company. To reveal these well-kept secrets to the average person would assure that those in control would no longer retain their power.

The Gods are an extra-terrestrial humanoid race of beings. In the Christian bible, they are referred to as the "Nephilim." These beings are very evolved, highly advanced, and immensely knowledgeable and powerful. They genetically modified their DNA, so they do not age. [26]

The *Joy of Satan Ministeries* is a modest group of Satanists founded rather recently in the States. Their belief, however refers to an ancient Illuminati creed, that is deeply embedded in the Illuminati tradition. In choosing the left hand path, these aspiring black magicians and Satanists view "The Serpentine Energy" as benevolent, and as a link to the Anunnaki, who they recognize as their gods.

Sirius and the serpentine energy

As I did in Volume I of these *Confessions*, it is important to emphasize the Egyptian belief that the Anunnaki originated from Sirius, also known as the Dog Star. Sirius is a star in the constellation *Canis Major*, it is the brightest star in the night sky, and was considered essential to their belief that. ... **it is He Who is the Lord of Sirius.** (Qur'an, 53: 49)

The fact that the Arabic word "shiaara," the equivalent of the star Sirius, appears only in Surat an-Najm, meaning star 49, is particularly striking. This is because, the movement of Sirius is considered irregular. Scientists have since discovered that what they were viewing it was actually a set of two stars, known as **Sirius A** and **Sirius B**. The larger of these is Sirius A, which is closer to the Earth and it is the brightest star that can be seen with the naked eye. Sirius B, however, cannot be seen without a telescope. The Sirius double stars orbit in elipses and the accuracy of this scientific fact was only realized in the late 20th century. But somehow it was *miraculously* indicated in the Qur'an 1,400 years ago. When verses 49 and 9 of Surat an-Najm are read together, this miracle becomes apparent:

> *... it is He Who is the Lord of Sirius,* **(Qur'an, 53: 49)**
> *He was two bow-lengths away or even closer.* **(Qur'an, 53:9)**
> *[He is] the Originator of the heavens and earth. When He decides on something, He just says to it, "Be!" and it is.* **(Qur'an, 2:117)** [27]

The star Sirius also plays an important role in the life of Jesus; it is also known as the Morning Star and in the New Testament Jesus says: *I, Jesus, have sent my angel to give you this message for the churches. I am both the source of David and the heir to his throne. I am the bright morning star.* **From the Book of Revelation, 22:16.** [28]

The various mystery schools of the Illuminati are undoubtedly an integral part of this ancient Sirius tradition. Their priesthood consists, today and in the past, of chosen members of aristocratic and Royal families, which by virtue of blood ties, place them in direct contact with these stellar alien beings. Secret societies are gradually made aware of their connection with these ancient demonic forces that seem to guard the secret of their origin. Some of those chosen will eventually be elevated to the level of High Priests.

26   Copyright 2002, 2004, 2005, 2006, Joy of Satan Ministries; Library of Congress Number: http://www.angelfire. com/empire/serpentis666/TRADITIONAL. ‡ Archived 9th July 2015.
27   http://mysteryoftheiniquity.com/2011/05/03/lord-of-sirius/ ‡ Archived 9th July 2015.
28   New Living Translation.

A person named *Alberto Moscato* issued a detailed study of the first Degrees of the O.T.O., called the *Man of Earth Triad* (**0-P.I.**). He stated that inside the O.T.O. from a technical, operational, and philosophical point of view, initiates are taught the way to reveal the **Conscious Subconscious Unconscious** group, as defined by Moscato as *Set-Khem, to raise to the level* of a **Superconscious** unit. [29] The Superconcious unit has control over the body, the life force and the path of our lives. If we are to admit it, this is the "God consciousness." Humans have discovered that the body is controlled and responds by quantum functions. These reciprocal interactions have a connection with what we define as "God-consciousness" of the universe, or *Superconscious*, if you are uncomfortable with the word God. It is imperative we recognize that our bodies live and exist as the result of a power beyond the capacity of what our words can describe. [30] From this capacity, however, a chance arises to come into contact with multidimensional entities of lower or higher vibration, depending on one's own intentions and spiritual purity. As is true for an ever increasing number of channelers these days, many attempt to establish such contact. This often leads to the seeker simply deluding themselves; or worse becomin a slave to the dark forces.

Occultists, have a different relation to these entities, As was Alberto Moscato, occultists are uniquely aware of their conscious choice to enter in to contact with such unpredictable forces. To achieve this, Kundalini, a divine energy that resides in the base of the spine, must be set free through your **Chakras**, which according to Moscato needs to be **"initiated and unsealed."** It is only in this way, according to secret rules taught in the Tantric schools of the Left Hand path, that one can magnetically ascend. Moscato then explains that the various Chakras, in a way that can be found with the appropriate scientific tools, possess the psychological characteristics that elevate from a simple concept of knots, nerves and nerve activity, to something more powerful. In particular the Chakras, can serve in keeping with the will of the operator, to revitalize the *Aura*, and to filter "Pure Will," the **Serpent of Fire,** the Kundalini. [31] This is Moscato's description of the chakric "reptilian" element:

> *This long journey through the Royal Art of the O.T.O., in both a traditional or an experimental way, rests upon its **Serpentine Occult Energy**. Assuming that the story of the serpent Kundalini, the relations of this energy with the nerve centers called the Chakras, and the occult powers of the human magnetism and the orgasm are all true (the scientists who have researched these phenomena are many, and their theories have often anticipated official science discoveries, their laboratory testing, and everyday applications), they remain to provide a plausible explanation, beyond the philosophical and religious one, to these occult mechanisms. [32]*

> *In the Ordo Templi Orientis of Aleister Crowley exists special bodies responsible for them: there are many advanced students of this organization that, after learning the techniques and the basic doctrines of so-called sexual magic (as are explained in this book when addressed as "official") and after many years of successful practice, continue to work together in order to describe in the most scientifical way possible the mecanism of this operation taking out all the superflues mystical-philosphical, religious and / or superstitious ingredient (as all the technical and philosophical, official and unofficial material, presented here, proves exhaustively). **Kundalini is a***

29   See. Alberto Moscato, *Ars gratia artis, Ibid.,* p. 14.
30   http://misteri.newsbella.it/la-salute-e-governata-dal-superconscio/ ‡ Archived 9th July 2015.
31   See. *Ibid.,* p. 14.
32   *Ibid.,* p. 28.

latent energy, defined as "Sleeping Beauty" present in the human body, depicted as a snake coiled in three and a half loops around the spine and relaxing at the pelvis with its tail coinciding with the sacrum.

These three coils and a half, as well as giving the ratio of the size of the "snake" and the trunk and the head of the holder, have traditionally tantric relationship with the Awareness, with Sleep and Dreaming, the extra half refers to the Samadhi, fusion and sublimation of these three stages. As we mentioned in a previous note, when at the final and simultaneous Orgasm, the Androgynous Perfect, although normally unable to reach such a high state of super-consciousness, for a moment is automatically beyond time and space with an altered consciousness to the inside or the outside of the Cosmos, in Samadhi, therefore if it is properly prepared and trained to take advantage of this moment to operate in absolute freedom sensitive to changes of objective "reality."

During some of the practices, many of which have already been described to the extent possible, the occult energy (which we Thelemites call "ShT" Fire Serpent) wakes up, stretching toward the base of the skull and activating in its slow ascent different chakras (or clusters of nerves and glands) located along the Spine, the energy channel formed, upon activation of Kundalini, from the union of the two Nadim, positive and negative, called "Sushumna." As will be seen below, each chakra has a specific function of active and passive (proven fact, rather than science, experience). Of course there are many links, on the road of Kundalini, including the base Chakra, Muladhara, and the last true Chakra, usually the end of the race for the Fire Serpent, called Ajna or the "third eye" for its location. [33]

As Frank G. Rippel, the Grand Master of the *Illuminati Knights* reminds us in one of his books, in Egypt the serpent was represented, as Ureus (Cobra), and was hung on the head dress of the Pharaohs (the head of this snake was attached at the level of the third eye, the eye of Shiva), as well as among the Jewish conception as the dark side of the serpent, represented by a snake coiled around the tree of Knowledge of Good and Evil.

As Rippel also reminds us, this snake is *Satan*, the tempter, and specifying that this title was conferred at the beginning of the Aeon of Osiris (50 BC), when in his opinion, the concept of Satan was distorted. [34] But we know of course, that Satanists like Frank G. Rippel tend to be too apologetic about their Master. In Chapter 2 of the *Book of the Law* by Aleister Crowley, there is a specific passage dedicated to the Snake:

22. I am the Snake that giveth Knowledge & Delight and bright glory, and stir the hearts of men with drunkenness. To worship me take wine and strange drugs whereof I will tell my prophet, & be drunk thereof! They shall not harm ye at all. It is a lie, this folly against self. The exposure of innocence is a lie. Be strong, o man! lust, enjoy all things of sense and rapture: fear not that any God shall deny thee for this. (34)

Frank G. Rippel comments in his book *BANNED BOOKS – nine texts in initiatic magic:*

The god Hadit states that he is the Serpent Kundalini which gives the Power (Knowledge), Amrita (Delight) and Illumination (luminous glory), to the conscience (hearts) of men by means of their energy. To worship you take wine and common drugs (strange drugs), as he told his Prophet—Aleister Crowley—The

33 *Ibid.*
34 See. Aleister Crowley. Liber Al vel Legis (The Book of the Law), (Newburyport, M: Red Wheel/Weiser, 1996).

wine and drugs will not do any harm, but this is a lie, a folly. The belief that wine and drugs make no evil is an innocent conception, like the one of a child who has no experience. Therefore the same exposure of innocence is a lie. Then Hadit urges started to be strong, because the man who craves and enjoys his senses need not fear that any God shall deny him. [35]

The final battle

The final battle on Earth is happening now, in our third dimensional reality, and in other dimensions on the astral plane. That is why, understanding the secret science of the Illuminati in all their manifestations is crucial. This is both an internal and external struggle, and it takes place against the demonic factions that wish to accelerate this scenario of worldwide oppression. Knowledge that has been hidden for millennia can help us to position ourselves during this apocalyptic scenario. It is represented in part by the archetypal meaning of the temptation of Jesus, who, after being baptized, fasted for **forty days** and forty nights in the desert. During his stay in the desert, the devil appeared and attempted to compromise His spiritual mission for humanity; but with the help of the Holy Spirit, Jesus was able to defeat him. In the initiatic tradition, the practice of 40 days is an important subject I will return to in my book *Invisible Master*. Because of the great importance given to it by the real Illuminati, those who have tried through their *illumination* to save or at least steer humanity toward a positive change, and not oppress it such as with Aleister Crowley. There is a revelatory passage in the ***The Book of the Law***, Crowley's channeled masterpiece also known as ***Liber AL vel Legis,*** that helps us to understand his twisted thought and the inherent evil present in the dark side of the mystery schools, and the majority of the New Age sects that shape the Illuminati sectarian network:

> *Yea! deem not change: ye shall be as ye are, & not other. Therefore the kings of the earth shall be Kings for ever: the slaves shall serve. There is none that shall be cast down or lifted up: all is ever as it was. Yet there are masked ones my servants: it may be that yonder beggar is a King. A King may choose his garment as he will: there is no certain test: but a beggar cannot hide his poverty* (**AL II.58***).* [36]

Dear readers for the elite Illuminati of today, the words **"ye shall be as ye are"** and **"the kings of the earth shall be Kings for ever: the slaves shall serve"** have special meaning, and demonstrate an obviously elitistic Crowleyanity perspective, in line with the occult hierarchy ruled by those bloodlines, that as mentioned, descend from our creators, the ones we now call *aliens*. Again in their own way, the Qur'an partly confirms a form of "alien" intervention in our creation:

> *O mankind! if ye have a doubt about the Resurrection, (consider) that We created you out of dust, then out of sperm, then out of a leech-like clot, then out of a morsel of flesh, partly formed and partly unformed, in order that We may manifest (our power) to you; and We cause whom We will to rest in the wombs for an appointed term, then do We bring you out as babes, then (foster you) that ye may reach your age of full strength;* [37]

Meanwhile, humanity is preparing for either a positive, or highly negative turn after the year 2020, as I have already suggested in the first chapter. It is likely that society will

35   Frank G.Rippel, ***BANNED BOOKS nine texts of magic initiation,*** (Rome, IT: 1997, Hermes Editions), pp. 86-86.
36   Aleister Crowley, ***Ibid.***, Chapter 2, verse 58.
37   *Al Qur'an,* Verse 5 , Chapter 22, (sūrat l-ḥaj)- (Yusuf Ali Version).

sink even further into materialism, possibly manifesting a scenario similar to the one presented by the famous 2002 movie **Equilibrium.** In the movie we find a Supreme Council of **Technocratic Fascism** called the **Council of the Tetragrammaton,** a clear reference to the Tetragrammaton found in the Bible. Formed by the four Hebrew letters **yod, he, waw, he,** this proper name of God described in the **Tanach** is of great importance within the Jewish tradition; Freemasonry, and the many mystery schools and Illuminati sects populating our society. It is no wonder that in the film, the Council of the Tetragrammaton is ruled by a solitary figure called "Father," who just so happens to embody all the worst features of **Big Brother** in George **Orwell's** famous book **1984.** A bit like the dark Illuminati of today, at first glance, this film is in full agreement, with the previously exposed concept of a technocratic synarchy. If not for the total absence of the spirit of hierarchy of the Tetragrammaton, which appears in the film represented as a lobotomized and robotic caste with no real access to authentic spirituality. In this apocalyptic scenario that slowly manifests in front of our eyes, we also have the constant manipulation of the figure of Christ, interpreted and transformed to serve the religious leaders, and powers that be , so as to preserve their "sheeple" system, who go to great lengths to conceal the truth of His revolutionary nature. French author Roger Guasco writes:

> *Jesus said: "I am a man" and not "I am God" and Guasco describes him like this: From the first candidate to the Jewish kingdom, to fighting the invading Romans. Gradually Jesus realized he had to play a high-level work that led him to transform himself, and this allowed him to hope to be the chosen of God. He began to say words that were no longer those of a warrior, and the search for justice led him to judge his own brothers. His ideas were different from those he had at first. He has certainly received a high level teaching in Egypt in the period after his escape, and became a kind of revolutionary denying the teachings of the old tradition, attacking much more his own people than the invaders. As a rebel, he became a religious dissident and the behavior of priests against him led Jesus to realize the disadvantaged, and the errors of His religion and therefore to design the foundations for a new one.* [38]

For a Christian, Guasco's words seem to minimize the figure of Jesus, but I assure you that this is not the case. Jesus was a great revolutionary, the greatest. After all, we *are* still talking about him 2,000 years after he lived. We must, therefore, acquire true superior knowledge that can develop into a genuine form of spirituality, not a New Age senseless mix of religions to suit anyone's needs.

A few years back, during a conversation with Freemason and known Jewish Kabbalist **Arie Ben Nun,** (FIG. 26) I confronted him on the revolutionary figure of Jesus, who Nun seemed to like for one reason only: "*being a Jew, Jesus facilitated* (according to him) *the birth of Israel, that would never have become a nation without the unconditional support, and the support of much of the Christian world.*" This is a man who participates in *supposed* international projects for spirituality and peace. For him to speak of Jesus in this way leaves one puzzled. The only thing that I could agree with him about, at least partly during our talks, was the nature of Jesus while He was on Earth. Even if immersed in the Divine, He was not a God in the traditional sense that the Council of Nicae later imposed on us. I must say that Arie Ben Nun is certainly an expert on Kabbalah. But, after two thousand years, he, and the majority of the Jewish world, still do not want to admit the real importance of this revolutionary named Jesus. For me, as for many other true initiates, *He* is the real Master of all times; the luminous force that the Kabbalists call Shekinah (in Jewish and Christian theology *the glory of the divine presence); or Ruach*

38   Roger Guasco, *Le parcours de la vie de Jésus,* short essay published online.

FIG. 26 – From left: Arie Ben Nun, considered a leading expert of Kabbalah in Europe; the author; the Marquis Caldirola; and Princess Kaoru Nakamaru. Photo taken at the Villa of the Marquis during a reception in honor of the Japanese Princess in September, 2011.

Elohim (Come, Spirit of God); and who the Christians call *the Holy Spirit,* that which descended and wrapped Him entirely. Even the prophet Mohammed reserves a special place for Jesus in the "end of times" scenario described in the Qur'an. Thus, like Christians, Islam believes that the return of Jesus will occur at the end-times. Muslims also believe in a resurrection of both the wicked and the righteous; and a final judgment.

Both Islam and Christianity proclaim an eternal dwelling of the lost and saved in Hell or Heaven (Paradise), respectively. Therefore, in many ways, the Islamic structure of the end-times, (eschatology) is similar to that of Christianity. Christians and Muslims, however, view the life of Jesus very differently. And both are diametrically opposed, and therefore both cannot be true. Although all Muslims do not agree on every aspect of Muslim eschatology, the *Muslim* Jesus descends and converts the world to Islam, kills the Jews, breaks crosses, declares himself a Muslim and gets married. He dies after 40 years. Therefore, in the Muslim view, the end has a much different outcome when compared to the Christian or the Jewish view. The Sunni and Shiite have a different view regarding the role of the Muslim *end of times figure,* known as the *Mahdi,* who will arrive before the return of Jesus. The Shiites view this person as someone who will establish order in the world and turn people to Islam before the return of Jesus. Even the particular events of the end-times are not completely spelled out in the Quran. One can reference the *Hadith* to supplement what the Quran does not say. This is significant because belief in the end-times, or *the last days,* is mandatory in Islam. It is listed as the fifth article of faith. [39]

Following communications received by **"The Tibetan,"** "New Age Guru" and Neo-Theosophist, Alice A. Bailey, reports in **the return of Christ** that which is the most crucial issue for modern-day Illuminati:

> *The coming of the Avatar, the advent of a Coming One and, in terms of today, the reappearance of the Christ are the keynotes of the prevalent expectancy. When the times are ripe, the invocation of the masses is strident enough and the faith of those who know is keen enough, then always He has come and today will be no exception to this ancient rule or to this universal law. For decades, the reappearance of the Christ, the Avatar, has been anticipated by the faithful in both hemispheres—not only by the Christian faithful, but by those who look for Maitreya and for the Boddhisattva as well as those who expect the Imam Mahdi. When men feel that they have exhausted all their own resources and have come to an end of all their own in-*

nate possibilities and that the problems and conditions confronting them are beyond their solving or handling, they are apt to look for a divine Intermediary and for the Mediator Who will plead their cause with God and bring about a rescue. They look for a Saviour. This doctrine of Mediators, of Messiahs, of Christs and of Avatars can be found running like a golden thread through all the world faiths and Scriptures and, relating these world Scriptures to some central source of emanation, they are found in rich abundance everywhere. Even the human soul is regarded as an intermediary between man and God; Christ is believed by countless millions to act as the divine mediator between humanity and divinity. [40]

The UN and the "New World Disorder"

The ultimate goal of all enlightened beings should be to lay the foundations for a new civilization that will overcome poverty and ignorance, resulting in a *Golden Age* for humanity. But the situation is extremely delicate and the balance can break at any time, even within the halls of power, just as it did 2,000 years ago with the coming of Jesus, and the consequences for the human race that are of immense proportions. We are, in fact, in the midst of a struggle against a strong Satanic element present within the New World Order, which rules at the top of the pyramid of the not-so-enlightened-elite, who are paving the way for the coming of their ultimate Antichrist.

Within the Orthodox Churches, there is a stronger bond with mystical theology and traditional metaphysics. The Orthodox monk of U.S. origins, one **Father Seraphim Rose,** author of *Orthodoxy and the Religion of the Future* (Platina, CA: Saint Herman of Alaska Brotherhood, 1990; Revised Edition), has examined the phenomenon of alien visitations to Earth from an Orthodox viewpoint. Archbishop Chrysostomos of Etna writes about it in the following analysis:

He devotes an entire chapter of this work, Signs from Heaven: An Orthodox Christian Understanding of Unidentified Flying Objects (UFOs), *to the true nature and meaning of alien contacts with human beings. Though Father Seraphim, at a superficial level, approaches this matter in a way reminiscent of Protestant fundamentalistic thinking, and while his materials are dated and center only on more sensationalistic abduction reports—deficits compounded by the fact that some of the authorities whom he cites are clearly on the fringes of science—his deeper analysis of the phenomenon is ingenious and supports much of what I have suggested about alien encounters with humans. He also observes that the aliens in contemporary abduction reports are similar in appearance to the demons which, for centuries, have been described in Orthodox literature (p. 134). In fact, he recounts two cases of demonic "kidnappings" in fifteenth- and nineteenth-century Russia that, in Father Seraphim's words, are "quite close to UFO 'abductions'" today (pp. 136-137). It is his conclusion that classical demonic possession, known to the Orthodox Church for centuries, accounts for the alien abductions that we see in modern times and that "...modern men, for all their proud 'enlightenment' and 'wisdom,' are becoming once more aware of such experiences—but no longer have the Christian framework with which to explain them" (p. 137). This conclusion perfectly reflects what I have said about alien abductions and how they should be understood and viewed by the Orthodox Christian.* [41]

The UFO phenomenon, like other phenomena, is enhanced and promoted by the

40   Alice A.Bailey, *The Reappearance of the Christ,* 1948, (Vitinia di Roma, RM, IT: Casa Editrice NUOVA ERA, reissue 1982), p. 5.
41   http://orthodoxinfo.com/praxis/alien_abduct.aspx ‡ Archived 9th July 2015.

New Age movement and "New World Disorder." It is nothing more than an element within *the religion of the future* that is paving the way to facilitate the advent of the Antichrist; and a new religion without God, and as has always been preached within the Illuminati, a focus on the paranormal and the power inherent in man. In the footsteps traced by Father Rose, *Father Justin Popovic* examined the UFO phenomenon in light of the millennial Christian belief in supernatural events. Popovic said: *"Starting from evangelical awareness every good tree produces good fruit; but a bad tree bears bad fruit."* Testimonies such as this that have been collected in the past by known scholars of the abduction experience, such as **John Mack,** should be examined by the Orthodox Church within a Christian viewpoint. Archbishop Chrysostomos of Etna gives a very detailed explanation in this short passage:

> *Dr. Mack identifies in the process of personal transformation in abduction victims. Seeing life in terms of cycles of birth and death, identifying with other beings and entities, the cessation of personhood, and looking to the "cosmos" for a "home"—these are all undefined, vague, and eclectic things that violate the precise, Christocentric teachings of Christianity and the life of discipline and obedience that spiritual transformation entails. Indeed, the Fathers of the Church warn us against these "false" teachings: reincarnation, delusion, and spiritual wanderings. The observations of one abductee interviewed by Mack, in particular, fully confirm the anti-Christian dimensions of the post-abduction philosophies and "spiritualities" of those who have come into contact with aliens.* [42]

So, when pointing out the persistent and sometimes downright grotesque and terrifying, misleading and mentally destabilizing episodes related to the so-called UFO phenomenon, a theological approach would be to consider the real possibility of Satanic intervention in these events. [43] This is a problem the Catholic Church is not taking into consideration. It is no secret that the Vatican has recently stunned the world with its sudden openness on the existence of extraterrestrials.

Indeed, interviews given by the Vatican's chief Demonologist, Corrado Balducci (1923-2008), followed by **Father José Gabriel Funes**, past Director of the Vatican Observatory who published the article, **"The extraterrestrial is my brother,"** in the *Osservatore Romano,* caused quite a sensation.

In more recent years another Jesuit Reverend Brother **Guy Consolmagno,** who succeeded Funes in September, 2015, as a new Director of the Vatican Observatory, presented a curious book co-written with Jesuit *Paul Mueller* entitled, *Would You Baptize an Extraterrestrial?*

This highly publicized presentation took place on the 18th and 19th of September 2014, exactly one year before Consolmagno was personally appointed by Pope Francis to an important new role at the prestigious *NASA/Library of Congress Astrobiology Symposium.* [44]

Brother Guy Consolmagno told *HuffPost* senior science editor David Freeman:

> *"I believe [alien life exists], but I have no evidence. I would be really excited and it would make my understanding of my religion deeper and richer in ways that I can't*

42   See Orthodox Tradition, Vol. XIV, No. 1, pp. 57-62.

43   See. Enzo Pennetta, Gianluca Marletta, *Extraterrestri. Le radici occulte di un mito moderno,* (Soveria Mannelli, Calabria, IT: Rubettino Publisher, 2011), p. 112.

44   http://www.loc.gov/loc/kluge/news/nasa-program-2014.html ‡ Archived 9th July 2015.

even predict yet, which is why it would be so exciting." [45]

Even Pope Francis has brought up the term extraterrestrials in public on more than one occasion:

"If, for example, tomorrow an expedition of Martians came to us here and one said 'I want to be baptised!,' what would happen?" Clarifying that he really was talking about aliens, the Pope said: *"Martians, right? Green, with long noses and big ears, like in children's drawings."* [46]

In another metaphor, the Pope clearly used the term "alien," possibly revealing more than he should have:

We are not saviors of anyone, we are transmitters of an "alien" who saved us all and that we can transmit, if we take in our lives, in our flesh and in our history the life of this 'alien' called Jesus.

An "Alien called Jesus"? Well, clearly this concept suggests a true "Revolution" in the Vatican-Alien/UFO approach. Through Pope Ratzinger, the Jesuit astronomers have already confirmed the possibility of the presence of aliens in the universe. In his trip to Cuba and meeting with Fidel Castro, Ratzinger discussed the need to enrich our knowledge about other forms of life in the universe. A conference on astrobiology was later organized at the Vatican in 2009, with astrophysicists and Exobiologists, which was repeated in Tucson, Arizona, in 2014.

As you can see, the positions between Orthodoxy and Catholicism are very different, with the latter, without reserve, serving the globalist plan of the New World Order; building a bridge between religious faith and scientific investigation; rejecting what is left of the process of belief within the Catholic religion, so as to embrace the demonic side. A rare video appeared a couple of years ago on YouTube, where **Holiness Patriarch Kirill of Moscow and All Russia** (secular name Vladimir M. Gundyaev, b. 1946) appears to condemn the UFO phenomena as linked, in his eyes, to Satanic beings, stating: *"Because it's not aliens or UFOs. It's the devil!"* [47] Of course it could be a fake, like so many things on the internet, except that other members of the Russian Orthodox Church clergy also spoke out on the subject at the time, showing the same strong opinion of their Patriarch. Their opinions declared that "angels and demons" are in reality "alien beings" that we should avoid, as reported by the Russian News Agency, *RIA Novosti*. [48] All this has created two differing factions in the world: **the Catholic Pro-Alien-demonic faction,** headed by the Jesuits and the Pope; versus, **the Orthodox Anti-demon faction,** headed by Patriarch Kirill in Moscow. Kirill suddenly has become a threat to the NWO, as well as his President, Vladimir Putin. So, the question arises, are we witnessing a genuine struggle? If we are to compare the Christian values of the two contenders, one would have to agree that Orthodox Christianity is the *real thing,* as Catholicism descends into a mere shadow of its former self, and now in the hands of the Jesuit-Communist-Satanic agenda. In my book, *Pope Francis: The Last Pope?* I wrote:

Patriarch Kirill of Moscow and Russian President Vladimir Putin seem to understand that in this tumultuous endgame, before "the Beast" springs the trap for the

45 http://podcasts.am1020whdd.com/~am1020wh/shows/play.php?id=28508 ‡ Archived 9th July 2015.

46 http://www.independent.co.uk/news/world/europe/pope-francis-says-he-would-baptise-aliens-9360632.html ‡ Archived 9th July 2015.

47 https://www.youtube.com/watch?v=5YRvRiPm3k8 ‡ Archived 9th July 2015.

48 http://www.ufoonline.it/2013/04/14/alieni-sono-angeli-e-demoni-parola-del-patriarcato-russo/ ‡ Archived 9th July 2015.

rest of humanity, that perhaps they can act in opposition to the tragic manipula-tion by the world powers-that-be. Let's see if in this period of "Tribulation" and "Revelation," which is set to end in 2020, humanity can manifest the real Kingdom of God and righteousness, instead of the looming Orwellian dictatorship led by the globalist Bilderberg Club, and the evil plan that we have begun to expose. The fate of our planet and civilization, with every passing day, seems to be teetering on a perilous "razor's edge." On one side, there is our worst dystopian nightmare. On the other, the promise of a Golden Age. [49]

Is the good of Russia versus the evil of Europe and the U.S. part of a Prophetic sce-nario? Or is it instead part of a carefully orchestrated scenario played out by the Secret Chiefs and Invisible Masters behind the New World Order? As stated in the Bible, al-most 2,600 years ago, the prophet Daniel foretold of events that would impact the world in the "Last Days," when a third Temple would be the focus of world attention.

Are living in the days Daniel speaks of? As it is, Israel and the New World Order cur-rently have plans drawn up to build a third Temple on the site of Islam's third most holy location, the Dome of the Rock. Visible events and daily happenings are unfolding in front of our eyes. While most end-times Bible prophecy authors have argued that Russia's origins trace back to the ancient nation of "Magog," as described in Ezekiel 38-39, that is simply not true. This myth actually traces back to the mid-1800s, and is built on his-torical statements and language that were deliberately altered. Although ancient records have been found that tell a different story about the identity of Magog and about Russia's origins, the myth of "Russia is Magog" persists. [50] It is a completely misleading tale.

Chapters 19:11-21:8 of the Book of Revelation, dating from the end of the 1st cen-tury, tells how Satan is to be imprisoned for a thousand years, and how, on his release, he will rally "the nations in the four corners of the Earth, Gog and Magog," to a final battle with Christ and his saints: *When the thousand years are over, Satan will be released from his prison and will go out to deceive the nations in the four corners of the Earth—Gog and Magog—and to gather them for battle. In number they are like the sand on the seashore.* [51] This passage needs to be intepreted following the view of René Guénon, who I introduced to you earlier, where the idea that Gog and Magog, or for that matter, **Koka and Vikoka,** are "entities belonging to the subtle world," "hidden from the human realm," and "symbolically described as subterranean." For the average non-initiated per-son, this view is somewhere *between incomprehensible and plain wacky,* as are some on-line comments reflected in "Talk: Gog and Magog" on **Wikipedia.** Some critics say that Guénon is no expert: *because he is not a biblical scholar—as his biography shows, he never acquired any formal training in the discipline that biblical scholars need (Hebrew language, various other languages, various forms of criticism, etc), and never held any academic position connected with biblical studies, and never published in the relevant journals, nor had any books reviewed in those journals (at least so far as I can tell). Nor is he ever mentioned in the books in the bibliography. He is not a reliable source.* [52]

These people are obviously *non-initiates* who don't know who René Guénon really was, and the importance of his theories in the Illuminati network to this day. They will never understand the bigger picture and ultimate goals of the elite and the entities behind

49   Leo Lyon Zagami, *Pope Francis: The Last Pope?* (San Francisco, CA: CCC Publishing 2015), p. 213.
50   http://www.newscientificevidenceforgod.com/2012/02/debunking-russiawar-of-gog-and-magog.html ‡ Archived 9th July 2015.
51   https://en.wikipedia.org/wiki/Gog_and_Magog ‡ Archived 9th July 2015.
52   *Ibid.*

this "End of Times" scenario, or the huge step toward world domination established when the **United Nations** *came to life* on the **24th of October, 1945.** It is no coincidence that this event was followed by the **birth of the state of Israel on May 4th, 1948.**

These events constituted two of the most important strategic moves the elite have accomplished in the last thousand years. These developments were installed to facilitate the coming of the Antichrist; which will be followed by the return of the Messiah, who will announce the end of our corrupt civilization, and will presumably establish an *Empire of Perfection.*

This is the reason why the elite Illuminati of Adam Weishaupt, founded in Germany in 1776, was called the elite of *Perfectibilist.* Their purpose was to strive for the perfection of the human being. Their emulation of a materialistic idea of Christ was gradually lost in obscurity, because of the many pacts Weishaupt's successor's signed with the underworld and dark forces. This initial stage of the project is to create a *prison planet* under the control of a World Government, and headed by the United Nations. This is not the creation of the *Kingdom of God on Earth* originally planned by the Rosicrucians.

Many members of the Illuminati elite believe that the evil side is necessary for the coming of the Messiah. For these shady characters, the so-called Kingdom of God is simply an ongoing project, and they feel justified in thinking that they are the supreme manipulators, and beyond the rules of good and evil. Within this context falls *The Book of the Law,* where we find: *"the announcement of a new era, that of Horus or the Crowned and Conqueror Son, exoterically known as the Age of Aquarius."* [53] This reality is represented in the Kenneth Anger film entitled, *Lucifer Rising.* As *Professor Enzo Pennetta* rightly points out regarding the real purpose of this film:

> *The ritual is successful, the final scenes show in fact the coming of the Antichrist, adepts scan the sky waiting for his manifestation and they are in fact rewarded by the expected sign, the same seen years earlier by occult adept Marjorie Cameron in the desert, as the result of Jack Parsons and L. Ron Hubbard's magickal rituals: the presence of a UFO, with the characteristic shape of a disk, a flying saucer that flies through the sky above the pyramids.* [54]

Director Kenneth Anger described the film as being about the generation of love: **The birthday party of the Age of Aquarius,** which exposes current ceremonies used to resurrect Lucifer. For Anger, Lucifer is the *god of light,* not the devil. He agrees, however, that Lucifer is the *rebel angel* who agitates behind world events. [55] Pennetta concludes that the film **Lucifer Rising** seems *to be the message of the "extraterrestrial," the aliens* from 2001: A Space Odyssey *or the UFO of* Lucifer Rising, *just as Madame Blavatsky prophecied and Alice Bailey helped promote with Lucifer Trust.* [56]

Wikipedia reports that the organization now called the **Lucis Trust** (originally *Lucifer Trust;* **Lucifer Publishing Company**), is a non-profit organization founded by the theosophist Alice Bailey, and her husband Foster Bailey in 1920; and has its headquarters in New York (at the 24th floor of 120 Wall Street), London (Lucis Press Ltd.), and Geneva (*Lucis Trust Association*). The Lucis Trust is affiliated with the **Windsor International Bank and Trust Company** and it has long been recognized by the United Nations as a Non-Governmental Organization, and is represented at regular briefings of

53   See. Enzo Pennetta, Gianluca Marletta, *Ibid.,* p. 68.
54   Enzo P. Gianluca P. *Ibid.*
55   See. Carlo Climati, *Inchiesta sul rock satanico. Tutte le prove,* (Milan:Piemme, 1996). pp. 211-212.
56   Enzo P. Gianluca P. *Ibid.*

the Directorate General of the U.N. The Lucis Trust *itself* is a member of the Economic and Social Council of the United Nations. [57]

The nerve center of the New World Order is the United Nations building in New York, and it is a very important meeting place for the varied and controversial societies of the elite who, thanks to their magic and occult rituals, hold the world under their control. **The Headquarters of the United Nations** was built with the strong contribution of the **Rockefeller family**, one of the most influential elitists within the New World Order. In his 2002 autobiographical memoir, David Rockefeller, Sr. (born June 12, 1915), the current patriarch of the family, acts as the victim of of ideological extremism on all sides of the political spectrum, who he says are created with the declared intention to attack the Rockefeller family because of the excessive influence they exert on the American political and economic institutions.

The actual operational center where the the New World Order occult direct their Egregore is the "**Room for Meditation**" at the United Nations. Unknown to most people, this place is is well-described by Robert Keith Spenser in his little 1960s book entitled, *The Cult of the All Seeing Eye*, where he writes the following:

The Meditation Room is 30 feet long, 18 wide at the entrance (which faces north north-east), and 9 wide at the other end. It is therefore wedge-shaped. Its only entrance is through two tinted glass-paned doors outside of which stands a U.N. guard. Inside the room is another guard. Once through the doors, the visitor finds himself in a darkened corridor which leads to the left. The sharp transition from a world of light to one of extreme darkness forces a feeling of abrupt withdrawal from the outside world upon the senses of the visitor who walks along the corridor, reaches the inner arched entrance, turns right, and looks into the room.

The room is very dimly lit. The only source of light, at first glance, is that which is reflected squarely from the gleaming upper surface of the brooding, somber altar in the center of the room. A special lens recessed in the ceiling focuses a beam of light on the altar from a point above and just beyond its far edge. Thin lines of bluish light lap the edges of the shadow cast by the altar.

The acoustical properties of the room are unique. The edges of padding material behind the paneling on the walls can be detected at the ceiling level. This absorbs sound as does the Swedish-woven blue rug which covers the floor of the corridor and the back of the room. The room is as quiet as an underground tomb. Its floor is paved with blue-gray slate slabs laid in a hap-hazard pattern. At the edge of the rug are two very low railings extending out from the east and west walls of the room. The center space between the railings is some six feet in width. To the right of the inner entrance are ten low wicker benches arranged in two rows of three and one back row of four against the corridor wall. Attempts by visitors to pass the railings are discouraged by the guard.

The mural is a fresco which was painted originally on wet plaster, one section at a time by the artist, with the aid of an expert in this work brought from Europe. It is set into a steel-framed narrow panel projected from the wall, behind which is an enclosed area some six inches deep which has its own light source. A small, square projector set close against the front base of the altar throws a diffused beam of light from a recessed aperture upon the surface of the mural. There are also ten hidden lights, five on each side of the room, behind the upper edges of a thin suspended ceil-

57   https://it.wikipedia.org/wiki/Lucis_Trust ‡ Archived 11th July 2015.

*ing which extends out over the room from the top of the mural. The 18 inch space
between the two ceilings contains the light control apparatuses. The lower ceiling
is wedge-shaped and separated from three walls of the inner room by a foot-wide
space. Thus the room appears to be much longer than it really is because of the many
converging lines leading into the narrow end, the corners of which are rounded off
on either side of the mural. The altar is four feet high and rests on two narrow cross
pieces. It is a dark gray block of crystalline iron ore from a Swedish mine and weighs
six and one-half tons. The Swedish Government presented this block of ore—the
largest of its kind ever mined—to the U.N. in early 1957. The chunk rests on a concrete pillar that goes straight down to bed-rock. The area and passageway beneath
the room are closed to the public.*

*The chunk of ore has been described as a lodestone, or magnetite, which is strongly
magnetic and which possesses polarity. In northern Sweden are what may be the
largest magnetite deposits in the world, believed to have been formed by segregation
in the magma. Magma is the term for molten material held in solution under the
pressure of the earth's crust.* [58]

This dark gray block of crystalline iron ore was actually a gift of Dag Hammarskjold,
an eleventh degree of the Swedish Rite of Freemasonry (the title of which is illuminated
Brother, Commander of the Red Cross), which was received from the King of Sweden
at the time **Gustaf VI Adolf of Sweden.** [59] **Dag Hammarskjold (1905 -1961)** was
a Swedish diplomat, economist, and author particularly obsessed by Freemasonry and
esotericism. During his period as Secretary General of the United Nations, a position he
held from April 1953 until the day of his mysterious death by an unlikely plane crash in
September 1961, he pledged to build this "Room for Meditation," at the U.N. Headquarters in New York.

In his historic speech to the 64th session of the United Nations General Assembly on
23 September 2009, Muammar Gaddafi called upon the Libyan president of UNGA, Ali
Treki, to institute a U.N. investigation into the assassinations of Congolese prime minister
Patrice Lumumba, who was overthrown in 1960, and murdered the following year; and
also that of U.N. Secretary-General Dag Hammarskjöld who died (*murdered*) in 1961. [60]

Colonel Muammar Gaddafi's historic speech at the United Nations took place two
years before being brutally murdered himself, in October, 2011, by the hit men and cow-
ards of the New World Order. During his speech, the brave Gaddafi also asked to investigate the death of **John F. Kennedy,** and Gaddafi said that the U.N. has not provided
security for the world since its establishment, but has rather provided the world with
"*terror and sanctions. Sixty-five wars broke out after the establishment of the U.N. and
the Security Council, and the victims are millions more than the victims of World War
II,*" he said. "*Were these wars in the interest of all of us? No, they were in the interest of
one country or three countries or four countries.*"

I can add that the speech Gaddafi made to the United Nations certainly provided an
additional reason behind the elimination of this real opponent to the globalist system.
Who has replaced Gaddafi in Libya today are a bunch of thugs and mercenaries of ISIS
that are working for the **Hathor Pentalpha** transnational lodge. Given the latest events
in Libia, Gaddafi had rightly named the U.N. NWO set up as "the Council of Terror."

58   Robert Keith Spenser, The Cult of the All Seeing Eye, (Palmdale, CA: Omni Publications, 1964), pp. 7-8.
59   https://en.wikipedia.org/wiki/Gustaf_VI_Adolf_of_Sweden.
60   http://www.un.org/ga/64/generaldebate/LY.shtml ‡ Archived 11th July 2015.

Indeed, there is also something very strange about the sudden death of Hammarskjold.

On July 29, 2005, 100 years after Hammarskjöld's birth, the Norwegian Major General, Bjørn Egge, gave an interview to the newspaper *Aftenposten* regarding the events surrounding Hammarskjöld's death. According to Egge, who was the first U.N. officer to see the body, Hammarskjöld had a hole in his forehead. This hole was subsequently airbrushed out of photos taken of the body. It appeared to Egge that Hammarskjöld had been thrown from the plane, and that grass and leaves in his hands might indicate that he survived the crash and tried to scramble away from the wreckage. Egge does not directly claim that the wound he saw was from a gunshot, and his statement does not align with information from Archbishop Tutu's—or with the findings of the official inquiry. In an interview on March 24, 2007, on the Norwegian TV channel NRK, an anonymous retired mercenary claimed to have shared a room with an unnamed South African mercenary who claimed to have shot Hammarskjöld. This alleged killer is alleged to have died in the late 1990s. [61]

Hammarskjöld is still the only U.N. Secretary-General to die in office.

This latest revelation leads one to believe that it was a homicide, and not an accident. This once again confirms the importance *human sacrifice* holds within the New World Order. The NWO apparently *used* the Dag Hammarskjold's dedication and esoteric knowledge during the years preceding his death, in order to build their occultist "Room for Meditations," and then later sacrificed its creator. This follows the most ancient of occult traditions, including the Masonic allegory of architect Hiram Abiff, the chief architect of King Solomon's Temple. As the temple neared completion, three fellowcraft masons from the workforce ambushed Abiff as he was leaving the building, demanding his *master mason* secrets. Challenged by each in turn, Abiff refused to divulge the information, and his assailant strikes him with a mason's tool (differing between jurisdictions). He is injured by the first two assailants, and struck dead by the third. [62]

To conclude this chapter, it is important to understand that the United Nations occult foundation are the result of meticulous and painstaking work initiated by Freemasonry, Neo-Templarism, and various Neo-Theosophical sects connected to the Jesuits. There are many traces within recent historical documents that corroborate these occult ties. I will go further into this later on. When again considering the fact that Turner personally donated $1 billion to create the *United Nations Foundation,* the links between the Georgia Guidestones, Ted Turner, and the U.N. are not surprising. [63]

Warning! Scandinavia is not what it seems

In my analysis, how can I forget the important role played by another Scandinavian country loyal to the Swedish Rite of Freemasonry, the New World Order and their United Nations? I speak of the Kingdom of **Norway,** where I lived for several years. (FIG. 27) **Trygve Halvdan Lie (1896-1968)** was a Norwegian politician, Labor leader, government official, and author. He was the first Secretary-General of the U.N., from 1946 to 1952, before Hammarskjold replaced him. We can therefore say that the foundations for this Evil New World Order Empire were constructed in Scandinavia, with the installation of the first Secretary **General**, in this case, from Norway. Trygve Halvdan Lie is another *worthy member* of the *Swedish Rite network* of Freemasonry, officially

61 https://en.wikibooks.org/wiki/United_Nations_History/Dag_Hammarskj%C3%B6ld ‡ Archived 11th July 2015.

62 http://www.freemasons-freemasonry.com/legend_hiram_abif.html ‡ Archived 11th July 2015.

63 2015.http://www.unfoundation.org/ ‡ Archived 11th July 2015.

Christian, and his country has been complicit in giving refuge to Satanists and some of the most dangeorus Islamic fundamentalist in Europe.

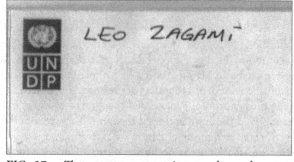

The Scandinavian Rite of Freemasonry is in the hands of a pro-Nazi elite, headed in Sweden by the Teutonic Knights, directing Neotemplars of the Swedish Rite, who are operating in every Scandinavian country and Germany to this day.

FIG. 27 – The entrance passes given to the author at a meeting on the United Nations Development Program (UNDP), held in Oslo in 2006.

This Masonic-Knighthood is so powerful that no country lifted arms against Sweden during the Second World War. *In fact,* the Swedish government even got paid for train tickets issued to the occupying Nazi forces passing through Sweden as they prepared to invade Norway. The elite, who were led by Norwegian *Vidkun Abraham Lauritz Jonsson Quisling,* son of a pastor of the Church of Norway, who was executed at the end of the war for treason, welcomed the Nazis with open arms. Among the older members of the Norwegian Illuminati elite, many at that time collaborated with the Nazis. Count among them the Norwegian Order of Freemasons. They saw the confiscation of their headquarters and books by Himmler's S.S., who wanted Trondheim to become the future capital of their so-called *Aryan empire.* I can assure you that the Satanic elite have a great attachment to the people of Scandinavia, who they consider naive for being honest and selfless. Once genetically pure (though increasingly less), Norwegians were involved in the bloodiest of ancient pagan cults, as originally practiced by their forebearers, the Vikings. Secret rituals we know little or nothing about are still performed within the sectarian Scandinavian brotherhoods, where **silence** reigns, and their sects control the land with seemingly no opposition. An Italian initiate of the Illuminati, the mysterious *Brother Raum,* described his initiation into one of these ancient, mysterious, Norwegians sects in the following way:

> *I had the pleasure to meet an old friend whom I had met during my stay in Switzerland during my first initiation.* **Frater Belenos 66,** *a man of over fifty years who looks forty, looks nice and attractive, social class medium high, but whose way of life is difficult to attribute any price; always fond of Magic and Esoteric, expert connoisseur of art and archaeological artifacts, at that time was already a member of several brotherhoods, orders, colleges and workshops, among them it is worth mentioning the* **A∴A∴ (Astrum Argentum), the Fraternitas Saturni, the Temple of Set** *and the* **Silentium Fraternitas** (Brotherhood of Silence).

> *The latter has always attracted my curiosity and urged my imagination, it was a mysterious Brotherhood, almost mythological for me, I remember that my grandfather talked about it, he was the brother of the Archbishop of Capua Monsignor Salvatore Baccarini (until 1962), Great prior of the Chivalric Order of "St. Bridget of Sweden," affiliated with other orders of chivalry and esoteric circles close to the Catholic Christian environment, who said that there was an old order that operated since the time of the Sumerians, that over the centuries had changed several times its name, adapting to the temporal and social context; in this upper room they sat in a Phrygian cap in equality the more enlightened beloved men and women that lived in every age.*

Raum also said that there were no hierarchies or degrees in this circle, there was no top or bottom, first or last... *only unity.* When the brothers conversed, they always referred to themselves as a **unit,** using the plural, he says:

I state that as a child, although I always liked to dream, imagine, design, I was always skeptic of their existence, so despite their history, the Brotherhood of Silence fascinated me. I maintained always a certain reserve on the veracity of some of the statements which I had dismissed as mere mythology, above all those that members could communicate with each other by thought alone. So just try to imagine my surprise when the Belenos Brother told me that he was a member of this mythical brotherhood, which then at least was not a myth.

I asked him, talking, news of what was in reality this legendary secret society, but he said that nothing could be said about the Brotherhood, but he could invite me in front of it, and after being weighed and considered suitable, I would have become a member of the Brotherhood of Silence. By my nature I am not a person that when he makes a similar decision he is feeling enlightened by the mere fact that he is admited, but rather, instead, is very suspicious and I always try to figure out if a path can really do for me before starting. As for the Free Masonry, as mentioned, more than once I was expressly required by Worshipfull Brothers, also affiliated in very elitist Masonic circles, to be initiated as Apprentice Mason, indeed in some cases, given my present initiatic level, I was expressly required to be initiated by the sword directly to the Master Mason degree and I would have been consecutively awarded the "honorary" 33° degree.

But on this occasion, the curiosity and the story that I had heard as a child in the stories of my grandfather, which were a great start, and were enough to make me say yes and to plan my next trip to northern Europe, after being weighed and examined by the Council of the Brotherhood of Silence, I would become formally part of it.

After a couple of months after the conversation with F. ⸫ Belenos 66, from which he was discharged with the promise that within a month you would have made me feel and I would communicate by telephone on the day and place of the meeting, I had not yet received any phone calls and began to believe seriously that he had made a fool of me, but mostly I was about to convince myself that this brotherhood was a myth, a bedtime story that started as a grandfather tells his niece and lover of esotericism in the evening before going to bed. At the dawn of the third month, after being placed on the official waiting list, the phone rang, it was a private number, and upon answering heard the unmistakable voice of Frater Belenos, who just told me "Three days, Oslo Airport, Notify your arrival time and you will find a car waiting for you."

I arrived in Oslo about nine o'clock one morning in late October, it was raining and a gray blanket enveloped the airport area, left the terminal and found a driver with a sign and my name. They took me to an elegant hotel in Olso and He took his leave, telling me that I should be ready in 17 hours, when he returned to take me in a secret location two or three hours drive from the city. At five and fifteen minutes I was already in the car along a highway out of town, the Nordic darkness enveloped the landscape so as to prevent any recognition or clue to what was the final destination.

But there is no time to formulate a hypotheses, because the adventure continues for the aspiring Italian initiate, who says:

We arrived early in what was to be the eastern wing of the manor, which had collapsed long ago, I did not understand what we went looking at that pile of stones, when I saw an opening closed by a grate anachronistically solid and new to the environment in which it was placed. The man stopped in front of it, handed me the torch, grabbed and bent to open the grate, under which stood a spiral staircase. Open the grille, he took up the torch and started down the steps, of course I followed taking care of not leaving open the grating. After an unusually long descent, it is appropriate to say, in darkness, we were in a hall where the ladder ended. There was only a door with the image of a skull above an inscription in latin on it:

Memento Audi Tacere F/\S

The man turned off the flashlight, and motioned for me to wait in front of door. It was the entry of the Temple of the Brotherhood of Silence. After about ten minutes, nine to be precise, I heard come through the door from which came a faint light, a sound but

FIG. 28 – *Thomas Karlsson (born 1972), Swedish, author of books and esoteric black magic, lecturer, musician and founder of the* **Dragon Rouge**. *(Photo taken from the site http://www.roterdrache.org).*

intermittent battery of hands, similar to that with which the Freemasons give their approval to the Great Architect of the Universe and SIGN some moments of their rituals. I knew it was time to go, so I crossed the threshold, and found myself in a circular stone room in which the brothers and sisters, all wearing a black hooded robe, adorned with a purple belt and a Silver medallion the size of a hand, on which stood out the seal of the Silent Brotherhood, the **Silentium Fraternitas.** *What happens from now on I am not allowed to disclose, I'll just say that from that day are a 0° of Silentium Fraternitas, in which unexpectedly besides Frater Belenos, I found two other dear Brothers, Frater Itmos and with great surprise, Soror Meretrix, which strangely had not told me anything about her membership in the Brotherhood. So I was able to ascertain the existence of this mythical and silent brotherhood, where there are no hierarchies, speaking little or nothing and communicating with gestures, signs, symbols, touchings and in all ways in which creative thinking suggests that we do; This was referring to my grandfather when he said that they communicate by thought alone.* [64]

As you may have noticed by reading this experience, silence *reigns supreme* in distant Norway. This facilitated a series of secret occult experiments, and other more "scientific" endeavours. DNA research, for example, was done in the small country of Iceland, where the entire population has voluntarily provided their data to the multinational pharmaceutical lobby of the New World Order; and, the **Svalbard Global Seed Vault,** that ostensibly serves to provide a *reservoir* of seeds, against the accidental loss of plant species, is located in Norway. [65]

64   http://maestrodidietrologia.blogspot.it/2015/03/intervista-al-mago-nero-fratello-raum.html ‡ Archived 11th July 2015.
65   See. https://it.wikipedia.org/wiki/Svalbard_Global_Seed_Vault ‡ Archived 11th July 2015.

FIG. 29 – Very rare photo of Carl Abrahamsson leading O.T.O. in Sweden obtained by a group of fundamentalist Christians Swedes who prefer to remain anonymous to avoid reprisals. Carl was tied in the past, even artistically, to the late father of modern Satanism Anton Szandor LaVey (real name Howard Stanton Levey), a Jewish American born in Chicago on April 11, 1930 and died in San Francisco on Oct. 29, 1997.

There are also many Illuminati and pseudo-Illuminati lodges in Scandinavia, like the lodge begun by the mysterious Brother Raum, who is linked to seven para-Masonic and Masonic lodges in which we find macabre rituals, such as those of the secret and mysterious **Dragon Rouge: Ordo Draconis et Atri Adamantis.** This is an order created by Swedish occultist **Thomas Karlsson** (FIG. 28). Not coincidentally, Karlsson is the author of books on rather black and dangerous forms of magic such as "Kabbalah, and Goetic magic," published in 2005; and, "The runes and the Kabbalah," released in 2007. Both were published in Italy by the Masonic publishing house *Atanòr* in Rome. Karlsson is also linked to Professor **Henrik Bogdan,** a member of the O.T.O., and a high degree Swedish Rite Freemason, whom I previously addressed in Volume I. [66] Although to be fair, we have no specific evidence in this regard. Yet both Karlsson and Bogdan, together with known Satanist **Carl Abrahamsson,** are linked to animal, and some even say, human sacrifice. This is not commonly known in Sweden, where the Illuminati sects are in the hands of contemporary Satanists.

Illuminati style "Russian Roulette" in Sweden

There is a practice popular among the Swedish Satanic elite that left me baffled. It is a perverse ritual of great danger, that was described to me in detail in 2001 by Carl Abrahamson (FIG. 29), who is one of the leading North European O.T.O., figures who is also linked to Anton LaVey's famous **Church of Satan.** In this ritual, 50 members of the elite indulge in an unhealthy orgy called "*The Russian Roulette Orgy*" in which three members have AIDS and 47 *players,* who are completely healthy, deliberately expose themselves to infection while *hoping* that the gods will protect them. Sweden was one of the first nations on Earth, by the way, to market pornographic movies—making them available in order to facilitate a moral decline within Western civilization. In 2015, **Sofia Hellqvist, a** former porn star with a passion for snakes (just a coincidence?), married the non-hereditary Prince **Carl Philip of Sweden.** In recent years, however, a drastic change toward increasingly strict values has led *Professor Don Kulick* from the University of Chicago (who previously taught at the University of Stockholm) to denounce the Swedish system in 2008, accusing them of becoming "draconian":

> *From being admired and envied by many as beacons of sexual enlightenment in the 1960s and '70s, the Scandinavian countries today have some of the most repressive sex laws in the Western world. Sweden is the most draconian. ... The message conveyed by [recent laws] is clear: your sexuality is the property of the state, and the state will claim its right to regulate and punish that sexuality, wherever you may be. So whatever, indeed, happened to sex in Scandinavia?* [67]

This statement is then addressed in 2012 by the author and blogger Oscar Swartz, the nephew of former Swedish Prime Minister *Carl Swartz* in his now unobtainable and censored book, *A Brief History of Swedish Sex: How the Nation That Gave Us Free Love Redefined Rape and Declared War on Julian Assange.* In spite of the fact that it was originally available in an Amazon kindle format on the 1st of June, 2012, the book is currently unavailable to order in many countries. Network experts *Rixstep.com* positively commented on the original release of this book, calling it *one of the most important books of the new millennium.* Here is an excerpt of their significant review:

> *Julian Assange dropped into Sweden on 11 August 2010 and planned to stay not quite a fortnight. Over five hundred days later and he's still wearing an ankle bracelet under house arrest. The "crime" is having "consensual but unprotected sex." And they call it "rape" in Sweden. What happened? More importantly: what happened to Sweden? Oscar Swartz may not have all the answers, but he's come closer than anyone to assembling the necessary background data. And now for a meagre £5 you can partake of it.* [68]

Hopefully, you will be able to find and read this controversial book freely and uncensored. What was done to Assange is a trap that Swartz rightly denounces when indicating the bond between Assange's alleged victims, who have denounced him, and the radical feminist wing of the Social Democratic Party. In Scandinavia, there are clearly sects and cults that are linked to sexual perversion, and at times, acts of violence which are sharply increasing. The Norwegian government, however, is actively assisting the victims of these religious sects, and has created a specific institution to support them.

Rituals regarding child abuse and so on have unfortunatley involved the clergy of the Catholic Church, as with the bishop and Swedish Rite Freemason **Georg Müller,** who was forced to resign because of pedophilia in 2009. [69] Years ago, in great detail, a close Swedish friend (named) Lars, told me how local Freemasonry not only tolerated the pedophilia of the bishop, but practiced it with him inside the lodges, and brought him poor children who were chosen by these monsters. This is something intolerable that deserves a thorough investigation. This is impossible in a country where the Swedish Rite, acting like a Mafia organization, is linked to both the police and Christian clergy of all denominations, including the Catholic one, in the supposed name of ecumenism and in defense of Christianity.

Wikipedia writes about the strict rules of acceptance in the Swedish Rite:

> *A final requirement is that the candidate profess to adhere to a mainstream Christian faith, assert that it is the best of all possible religions, and swear never to abandon it. If the Christian belief of the candidate is in doubt, a birth certificate may be requested; in the Scandinavian countries, birth certificates contain a field for religion. Neither The Church of Jesus Christ of Latter-day Saints (LDS Church),*

67   http://wlcentral.org/node/2657 ‡ Archived 11th July 2015.

68   http://rixstep.com/1/1/1/20120604,00.shtml ‡ Archived 11th July 2015.

69   http://www.repubblica.it/esteri/2010/04/07/news/vescovo_norvegese_abusi-3165650/ ‡ Archived 13th July 2015.

the Unification Church, nor the Jehovah's Witnesses are considered to be Christian denominations by the Swedish Rite; beyond this, the Order does not admit a preference for any sect, whether Lutheran, Orthodox, Anglican, or Catholic.[70]

Thus, all creeds are accepted, democratically, into the **Swedish Rite,** and within its degrees that are full of *Neo-Templarism with a Jesuit flair.* This "Christian" form of Freemasonry has received the secret blessing and encouragement of a Pope after a member of the rite was able to present all their degrees in a private audience, and meeting his full approval. We do not know for sure who this Pope was, but this unusual event took place long before the Second Vatican Council... almost one hundred years ago. I don't know the exact term in which this Papal Blessing of the Swedish Rite of Freemasonry occured, but the episode was personally confirmed to me by a French Catholic Freemason IX° of the Swedish Rite based in Oslo, a well-known antique dealer from whom I have purchased some very interesting items.

This gentleman's antique shop was located in front of *Vår Frelsers gravlund* ("Our Saviour's cemetery"), in Norway, north of Hammersborg, in the Gamle Aker district of Oslo. I remember him constantly complaining about the damage inflicted on the graves in the nearby cemetery... which was regularly attacked and often used by local Satanists for their absurd and depraved rituals. One night, by chance, I witnessed something obscure, unusual, and possibly perverse going on in that cemetery while I was walking downtown. Suddenly, in front of me, in the dark, I observed three members of the O.T.O. that I actually knew—two guys and a girl—half naked, running around, and chanting Thelemic verses. I was surprised, of course, but it didn't take long for me to realize what they were up to. I was on the way to a nightclub, so I didn't stop, but I greeted them and said that I was in a hurry. This sort of activity happens *under the noses* of people living in Norway every day. The Scandinavian Illuminati community, and their Swedish Rite of Freemasonry which is full of Christian hypocrisy, has always exerted a great fascination in the United States. They are considered as an example to follow by many in the U.S. Masonic community who, unfortunately, are ignorant of the facts. The Illuminati elite love the Scandinavian "socialist" models... similar to that which appeals to the Obama camp; or even Bernie Sanders. Scandinavians of the Swedish Rite, thus, represent a living example of the future as provided by the New World Order, and the Americans are only just beginning to feel a similar sense of oppression. If the criminal Hillary Clinton ever manages to rise to power, the Illuminati communist tradition may fully manifest within the USA. In other words, the U.S. and the rest of Europe are just one step away from the Nazi-Communist model that has been in place in Scandinavia for years.

The only difference is that the Scandinavian population *voluntarily* participates in this sick game—and countries such as Norway, Sweden and the rest of Scandinavia, including Iceland (although to a much lesser degree than the others, just because of their remoteness). These countries are under the complete control of a Nazi Fascist Police State ruled by Socialist/Communist leaders. *What a mix from hell!* And from my viewpoint, the majority of Scandinavians don't seem to care. They have traded their silence in exchange for material satisfaction from the state.

As happened in the 1990s, the burning of churches by members of the black metal scene in Norway was the first red flag, and the world should have responded at that time, in order to halt these activities that are now damaging later generations. This dangerous heresy has persisted, and in 2009 the Satanists continued to vandalize churches and cemeteries throughout Norway. According to the Norwegian state TV, NRK, Satanism experts stated that these 2009 acts of vandalism towards religious buildings could mark the beginning of a new wave of attacks. For example, on May 29th, 2009, a church located at 1800 of Våler, 180 km north of Oslo, (FIG. 30) a site that contained numerous and priceless works of art, was destroyed by a fire ignited by Satanists. Fortunately they saved the (circa 1697) altar from destruction, but many works of art were irreparably damaged. The police then opened an investigation and asked for the assistance of the *National Bureau of Crime Investigation* (**KRIPOS**).[71]

FIG. 30 – Dramatic photo taken during the fire of May 29, 2009 in a church from the year 1800 in Våler, 180 km north of Oslo. Image taken from: http://gallery4share.com/v/varg-vikernes-church-burning.html ‡ Archived 17th August, 2015.

More examples: In early May, 2009, the cemeteries of Oslo and Sandefjord were targeted, resulting in damage to several tombs; another church and adjoining cemetery in Nordstrand was attacked and the graves desecrated; and, in April 1997, almost a year before my first visit to Norway, the headlines of the National newspapers screamed loudly about the discovery of a plan to slay religious leaders and representatives of political parties from the area. *Nazi-fascist Michael Moynihan* and *Didrik Schjerven Søderlind* speak about this in their book originally published by Feral House in 1998, called *Lords Of Chaos—The bloody rise of the Satanic metal underground*. This is my own translation of a crucial passage taken from the Italian edition:

> *The criminals, who not only possessed weapons, but also large amounts of money, were planning further action to be added to the list of murders. Among their plans was the release of their fellow inmate, who hoped to be able to escape abroad. But this "prisoner of war" was perhaps an extreme nationalist like them, with a long history of political clandestine activism. It was twenty-four year old Varg Vikernes, the most notorious black metal musician in the world. It is a winding path that leads from the world of popular music to political terrorism. It is not the first time that Rock 'n' Roll takes on a revolutionary aspect, but this is the most fanatical and uncompromising event that has been seen so far. And it is just the tip of the iceberg. Upon closer inspection, the plan for freeing Varg Vikernes is only a later development of one of the most bizarre and shocking events in the history of music. However so far very little has been written. The history of black metal is full of violence—exploded in the form of suicides committed with gunfire, and cold-blooded murders executed with strokes of a knife. The number of deaths occurred from one end of the world to the other, is difficult to calculate, but the delusional nature of the murders*

71   http://metalitalia.com/articolo/norvegia-a-fuoco-una-chiesa-torna-il-pericolo-vandalismo-a-sfondo-satanico/ ‡ Archived 13th July 2015.

gives them a definite unmistakable aura. And the constant campaign of burning churches, such as the relentless killings, adds to the arsenal of black metal and the psychological terror and religious intimidation. [72]

Two key elements jump out—*psychological terror* and *religious intimidation*. As I have shown in Volume I of *Confessions*, these tactics have always been used by the Illuminati sects and their occult-controlled governments. They are used in specific programs of mind control that we commonly refer to as **MK-ULTRA**... although the name tends to encompass a much wider reality. After these tragic events in Norway, I can state outright that the "Age of Satan" has *kicked-off* an increasing and aggressive campaign. Even moreso than in the USA in the 1960s when "Satanic poser" Anton LaVey, according to many, brought about the end of the *hippie* movement. This *end* was punctuated by Charles Manson and his sect, who's murderous rampage was founded within the Satanic milieu that included the Church of Satan, the O.T.O. and **The Process Church of the Final Judgment.**

In a chapter entitled, "**Satanism in Norway,**" it is strange to see the presence of Nazifascist Michael Moynihan and the dangerous black magician and occultist (former *Ordo Templi Orientis*) **Simen Midgaard.** [73] Can you trust the reporting made by interested parties in these events? I have met and interviewed Midgaard several times when I lived in Oslo. He was a member of the O.T.O. in the early 1980s, and the leader of the local branch of the U.S. O.TO. Caliphate in the Norwegian capital. This was before Midgaard got out of the O.T.O., to pursue a solo initiatic path with his own Illuminati elitist sect dedicated to black magic and Satanism.

Simen Midgaard was the most influential person in the Norwegian occult scene in the years that preceded the rise of Satanism, which included the destruction of churches, various cemeteries, and even murders. In the O.T.O. where Simen operated, that later became the **Heimdall Lodge of the O.T.O. in Oslo,** lighters were distributed with the design of a church in flames and the phrase "**light your faith.**" I had discovered after my many years of living in Scandinavia, that they are obsessed with the cold, calculated and perfect execution of their rituals. My experience has led me to reflect on the energy unearthed during those rituals, astrally projected into the darkness rather than the light. I was also surprised to learn, that the co-author of *Lords Of Chaos*, the Norwegian Didrik Søderlind also known as **Didrik Schjerven Søderlind,** [74] Editor of the magazine *Humanist* of **The Norwegian Humanist Association** (Norwegian: *Human-Etisk Forbund,* HEF), has employed **John Hilmer Berge Færseth,** as spokesman in 2012. [75] John Færseth is a dangerous Norwegian occultist and aspiring spy, who I have written about in Volume I of *Confessions*. [76] He is suspected of espionage and disinformation activities on behalf of the Norwegian civilian Intelligence services, that now seem to promote him and use him at an international level.

Færseth participated on the 26th of March, 2015 in the "**International Conference Expression of Opinion Online: Human Rights, Ethics and Case Studies,**" [77] an important event that took place in the prestigious Conference hall of the Ministry

---

72   Michael Moynihan, Didrik Søderlind, *Lords Of Chaos – The bloody rise of the satanic metal underground,* (Milan, IT: Tsunami Editions, 2010), pp. 13-14.

73   *Ibid.,* Chapter: *Satanism in Norway,* p. 375.

74   See. https://no.wikipedia.org/wiki/Didrik_S%C3%B8derlind ‡ Archived 13th July 2015.

75   See. Http://nb.xiandos.info/John_F%C3%A6rseth ‡ Archived 13th July 2015.

76   See. Leo Lyon Zagami, op.cit., pp. 209, 227, 228, 236.

77   See. http://manoteises.lt/wp-content/uploads/2015/02/Prane%C5%A1%C4%97jai-Nuomon%C4%97s-rai%C5%A1ka-internete-2015-03-26-EN.pdf ‡ Archived 13th July 2015.

of Justice of the Republic of Lithuania in Vilnius, where he displayed his new polished image, as he was presented as one of Norway's leading authorities on conspiracy culture. Because of his position as secretary of the local O.T.O. body, Færseth was one of the first people I met, when I arrived in Norway in the late 1990s. John was deeply involved in the activities of various orders and fraternities of the Illuminati Network, even the mysterious Rosicrucian group, Golden Dawn, which is a branch of Martinism. He was not a regular Freemason at the time, and he appeared to practice "Irregular" Occult Masonry, instead.

Human-Etisk Forbund officially rejects any beliefs related to the occult, magic and religion, so Færseth's vast involvement in the occult demonstrates his incompatiblity in this organization that declares it is "a way of life." Since 1956, *Human-Etisk Forbund* has been an integral part of the **International Humanist and Ethical Union (IHEU)**, which is an umbrella organization under the control of the elite of the New World Order. They encompass humanist, atheist, rationalist, secular, freethinking and ethical organizations worldwide; that are strongly promoted by the dark Illuminati and sects like the O.TO. The **IHEU** was founded in Amsterdam in 1952, and consists of 117 organizations in 38 countries. Julian Huxley (the first director of UNESCO) and his brother Aldous Huxley (linked in turn to the Tavistock Institute and subsequently project MK-ULTRA) presided over the founding Congress of the IHEU. The Norwegian branch of the *Human-Etisk Forbund* was founded in 1956 to organize supporters in a new "ethical" system of thought later known as *human ethics*. The organization is often described by outsiders as a cult, and an "alternative" religion, in opposition to the official church. [78] This religion lacking true spirituality is dedicated to the *Deus est Homo* motto present at the higher levels of the O.T.O.

All member organizations of the International Humanist and Ethical Union are required by IHEU bylaw 5.1 to accept the IHEU Minimum Statement on Humanism:

> *Humanism is a democratic and ethical life stance, which affirms that human beings have the right and responsibility to give meaning and shape to their own lives. It stands for the building of a more humane society through an ethic based on human and other natural values in the spirit of reason and free inquiry through human capabilities. It is not theistic, and it does not accept supernatural views of reality.*

It is then restated in a more concise way by Norwegian HEF: "*Humanism is a democratic, non-theistic and ethical life stance which affirms that human beings have the right and responsibility to give meaning and shape to their lives and therefore reject supernatural views of reality.*" [79]

How can Færseth be involved in occult activites, when he publicly subscribes to a philosophy that openly rejects any relationship with the supernatural? It is because Hypocrisy is at the core of these low-level agents of the New World Order. Færseth once threatened to kill me in a telephone call made on behalf of the Norwegian O.T.O., and he conspired against me several times when I was living in Oslo. It is ironic that he has been promoted to this new role of journalist and author, specializing in the field of conspiracies as a professional **debunker.** He appears to live a double life, where during the day he extends to his subscribers, which are mostly Norwegians—the reasons why conspiracies don't exist. Then, when the sun sets, he secretly takes part in Satanic rituals, often as master of ceremonies in obscure temples hidden in the Norwegian woods. Færseth also writes about geopolitical topics related mostly to Eastern Europe, and published a

78   See. http://nb.xiandos.info/Human-Etisk_Forbund ✝ Archived 13th July 2015.
79   See. https://en.wikipedia.org/wiki/International_Humanist_and_Ethical_Union ✝ Archived 13th July 2015.

mediocre book entitled, *Ukraine. The land on the border*, in 2014.[80] In recent years, Norwegian National TV (NRK) has hired him as a columnist, even to discuss controversial topics such as Anders Behring Breivik. This is most likely because of the growing influence of Satanist / atheists in the current cultural scene in Scandinavia, and the fact that the elite need double agents like him to defend their interests. After learning about the web of deceit present in Norway in relation to Satanism, squalid people such as Færseth and his friend Didrik Søderlind; who was the former editor of the local *Playboy* earlier in his life, we can no longer be surprised that history's most influential journalists and authors, are many times minions that have embraced the dark side of the force. Around the world, mainstream media is in the hands of the globalist enemy, which spew lies everyday as part of their agenda to obfuscate the truth about the global dictatorship that they are trying to impose. As long as they continue to manipulate our reality, you will only hear the truth in books such as mine

AMOOKOS *vs* Ordo Templi Orientis

One of the most powerful sects of the Illuminati is the *Ordo Templi Orientis*, but during my years in Norway, I witnessed the rise of another dangerous sectarian group connected to Aleister Crowley, a mysterious Illuminati sect that Caliphate O.T.O. members feared could eclipse their own occult order. This formidable group is called AMOOKOS (the Arcane and Magickal Order of the Knights of Shambhala), and in Volume I, I wrote about the famous occultist Grand Master, the Norwegian *Dr. Nicholaj De Mattos Frisvold*.[81]

Shri Lokanath Maharaj writes this very useful short bio on the origins of AMOOKOS:

Shri Gurudeva Mahendranath (Dadaji) was born in London in April, 1911. From his early youth he had a deep interest in the occult and spiritual patterns of the world. In his early twenties he chanced to meet the infamous Aleister Crowley, whose hyperbole stirred and outraged Fleet Street in the twenties and thirties.

Crowley's advice to the young seeker was simple—go to the East to learn more of the occult and wisdom patterns which had flourished there from pre-Christian times. However, the Spanish Civil War—in which Dadaji fought against the Fascists as a member of the International Brigade—and the Second World War intervened. It was 1949 before Dadaji left the shores of Britain to arrive, penniless, in Bombay. There he was introduced by a mutual acquaintance to a sadhu of the Adinath cult. The Naths were at one time very numerous and influential in India; there are nine subsects, one of which is the Adinath cult. Nath, is Sanskrit for "Lord" and is an epithet of Shiva, the Lord of Yoga. Initiates have names ending in "nath." One of the Nath initiates—Goraknath—devised or reintroduced Hatha Yoga in the 11th Century. The Nath cult was also responsible for such works as the Hatha Yoga Pradipika and the Shiva and Goraksha Samhitas. The sadhu introduced to Dadaji was the last remaining Adinath Yogi in all India, and was also the Adiguru or holder of the sacred line of tradition. Unlike some of the other sects of Naths the Adinath's chief interest was the Yoga of liberation from the restraining conditions of life, and to become free from the Wheel of Samsara or death and rebirth. Dadaji was initiated as a sannyasi by Adiguru Lokanatha, so becoming the first Englishman to become a sadhu. A sadhu may make only three demands: for shelter—the shade of a tree; for clothing—rags. For food—leftover scraps. These conditions in former times helped the seeker after wisdom to realize the transitory and ultimately worthless nature of attachment.

In this, the sadhus emulate the Guru figure of all India, Lord Dattatreya. Datta is the legendary founder and guardian spirit of many if not most of the Nath subsects.

*He represents a human being who has swung free of the three gunas or threads of Hindu philosophy from which the whole fabric of the Cosmos is said to be sewn. For this reason he is often pictured as a naked man with three heads and six arms to represent the Hindu Trinity of gods, Brahma, Vishnu and Shiva. For the next thirty years Dadaji wandered South East Asia as a penniless sannyasi. His travels took him to Bhutan, where he was initiated into the Kargyupta Sect of Tibetan Lamaism. He also traveled to Malaysia where he became a Taoist priest and studied the I Ching, and to Ceylon, where he was for a time a 'Bhikku of Theravada Buddhism. It may perhaps seem strange that a sannyasi of a Hindu tradition could also become a lama, a bhikku and a priest, but as many of the Eastern traditions recognize only sincerity in an aspirant for wisdom and knowledge, there is no essential contradiction in a person having more than one guru or guide or seeking wherever an individual quest may lead. During Dadaji's Indian wanderings, he met and was initiated by the last surviving Guru of the **Uttara Kaulas** of Northern Tantriks. He also became an initiate of the "Naked Sahajiya cult of Benares." In an introduction to Tantra Magick, An AMOOKOS Manual is stated:*

Initiates of AMOOKOS take as their starting point the assumption that within each and every human is a divine spark, the Alpha Ovule, or spirit, which simply had to be freed from the bonds or fetters of ignorance or conditioning to shine free. As a presentation of practical methods for working towards self-knowledge, wisdom, and understanding, many may find the exercises in the different grade papers indispensable. Much of the material will not be found in any other tradition or teaching. Its rendering of the basics and essentials of tantrik practice in simple language is also new. AMOOKOS was started at the behest of HH Shri Gurudeva Mahendranath. Wishing to transmit his own experience and the Nath transmission, in 1978 Mahendranath passed the parampara or line of transmission to a youthful "seeker after truth." At this point, the Adinath Sampradaya was transformed into an international group (See Charter below). Soon after, instructions were received to start a nine-grade group within the Naths, and AMOOKOS was the result. Dadaji collaborated with the compilers of this material at every step, and approved their contents:

"the morning post arrived and another shake up with the grade raw material. Astounding—will take some days to get through it step by step. 14 March 1983."

"I have been wandering again through AMOOKOS grade 1 and 2 material. It is stupendous, nectar of the wise. You have certainly produced a miracle explosion in the occult world." 24 March 1983."

"The grade 3 papers are hyper-dimensional and this alone is a masterpiece of collated wisdom and expression." 16 November 1983. [82]

The following is the **Charter of AMOOKOS** issued in 1978:

Be it known that on this New Year Day, January the First, Nineteen Hundred and Seventy-Eight, this decision, being my true Will and Wish has been put into immediate operation.

82   See. AMOOKOS and Mandrake, Tantra Magick, Introduction by Shri Lokanath Maharaj, (Bombay: D. B. Taraporevala Sons & Co. Pvt. Ltd. by arrangement with Mandrake, 1992).

*Therefore I, Shri Gurudeva Dadaji Mahendranath, the only surviving Supreme Guru of the Adi Natha Sampradaya—the Cult and Organization of the First and Supreme Sacred Lords of the Spiritual Cosmos; King of Shambhala and Grand Lord of its Knights; Keeper of the First Book of the Nine Secret Chiefs, Merlin of Cockaigne and Light of the Silver Star; do hereby ordain by that Supreme Authority which rests with me, that the Adi-Nath Sampradaya shall from henceforth become an International and Cosmopolitan Order of all Worthy People, students and householders above the age of eighteen years, who may occupy a normal life and pursuit of livelihood; provided always that they accept the three basic aims and objects of the Nathas—to wit—real Peace, Real Freedom and Real Happiness. Therefore from the Naked Guru to Naked Sishya, the Transmission and Initiation shall be given to all **Noble Masters, Magicians, Alchemists, Masons, Rosicrucians, Astrologers and Occultists** of stable nature who will bond themselves into one Grand Concord of Cosmic People and Work, Experiment and Teach for the weal and welfare of all mankind. This new promulgation does not prevent or discourage those whom as Nathas wish to become Hermits, Sannyasins, Anchorites or Recluses if they wish to do so. To finalize this decision of a greater and more expansive Order, the Initiation and Parampara (line of Nath succession) has now been passed on by me to Shri Lokanath Maharaj, Lord of Cockaigne and Prince of Babalon that He may continue the line of succession and pass it on to all other worthy people. This is our law, the Rhythm of the Cosmos by which the Wise must live.*

This knowledge that originates in the Far East, has been willingly transmitted to members of the Illuminati Network in the West and has as it's members "Noble Masters, Magicians, Alchemists, Masons, Rosicrucians, Astrologers and Occultists," and openly teachs that Satan is not evil and we should *"not allow conventional interpretation to obscure the truth!"* [83]

Welcome to the age of the Antichrist! Anticipating a New Age messiah known as the Maitreya

I would now like to introduce you to Benjamin Creme (born 1922), the creator of *Share International Foundation*, established in 1975, often cited with the acronym **SI**, (not **SIF** as one would expect). This is so that the initiate will immediately recognize who is behind this latest New Age farce, and that SI is simply *"Societas Iesu,"* the Latinized name of the famous *Society of Jesus*. Some may say that because Benjamin is an avid follower of the teachings of the Theosophical Society created by Madame H.P. Blavatsky, which is tied to the work of another important theosophist Alice Ann Bailey, that he cannot possibly be tied to the Jesuits. I will prove otherwise. Benjamin Creme writes in his book, *The Reappearance of the Christ and the Masters of Wisdom*:

From the Hierarchical point of view, the Secret Doctrine of Madame Blavatsky, the founder of the Theosophical Society, represents the preparatory phase of the Teaching given out to the world for this new age. The Teaching embodied in the Alice Bailey Teachings represents the intermediate phase of this Teaching. This was given to her by the One Who called Himself for many years simply "the Tibetan," Whom we know now as the Master D.K.—Djwal Khul. Alice Bailey received it by means of the higher telepathy, through the medium of the soul. If you read her autobiography, you will find that she downright refused to have anything to do with these Teachings and said: "No, I am not going to be a medium," until she was assured by her own Master that this was nothing to do with mediumship, that it was the higher telepathy, that it was work for the Plan, and that it would be in the best interests of the Hierarchy and the world if she would kindly undertake this thirty-year duty—it lasted thirty years. Finally, she agreed and started the work. And so, for thirty years, she was the amanuensis of the Master D.K.

The next stage, the Revelatory Phase, we are told, will emerge, world-wide, through the medium of the radio, after 1975. [84]

In 1889, Blavatsky stated that the main purpose for establishing the Theosophical society, was to prepare humanity for the future reception of a *"torch-bearer of Truth,"* an emissary of hidden Spiritual Hierarchy that, according to theosophists, will guide the evolution of humankind. [85] This was repeated by Annie Besant, (1847-1933) who came to believe in the imminent appearance of this "emissary," who was identified by theosophists as the *World Teacher*. [86] Thus the phenomenon of "Messiah," was born in the Theosophical Society's important appendix, the *New Age project* devised by trans-national lodges of Freemasonry. Unfortunately for Annie Besant, the Messiah figure never materialized in the person initially appointed by her. **Jiddu Krishnamurti** refused the position of Messiah, perhaps demonstrating more illumination than his Neo-Theosophical "Masters."

In 1909, Krishnamurti was scouted by the Western Illuminati to become the future Messiah, at the young age of fourteen. Exactly 20 years later, in 1929, he refused the role of "World Teacher" and took the path of true enlightenment. Jiddu Krishnamurti says: *"There is nothing that you can claim as your own. I have no questions of any kind. How do you have so many questions? Neither I am giving you answers. I repeat the same things day after day. That you understand it or not, it does not matter for me. What does it mean when people talk about the conscience? There is no such thing as consciousness."* [87] Krishnamurti was not the Messiah, and not even a high level initiate, but he managed to grasp the concept of "Cosmic Consciousness." Richard Maurice Bucke, a Canadian psychiatrist, in the book *Cosmic Consciousness: A Study in the Evolution of the Human Mind*, published in 1901, where he explained the concept very well. In his book he defined Cosmic Consciousness as **"a higher form of consciousness than that possessed by the ordinary man."** According to Bucke:

This consciousness shows the cosmos to consist not of dead matter governed by un-conscious, rigid, and unintending law; it shows it on the contrary as entirely im-material, entirely spiritual and entirely alive; it shows that death is an absurdity, that everyone and everything has eternal life; it shows that the universe is God and that God is the universe, and that no evil ever did or ever will enter into it; a great deal of this is, of course, from the point of view of self consciousness, absurd; it is nevertheless undoubtedly true. [88]

Jiddu Krishnamurti was a complex figure, and at times too wise and difficult to deal with for the Illuminati sects after his initial rebellion against their plans to present him

84   Benjamin Creme, *The Reappearance of the Christ and the Masters of Wisdom,* (Los Angeles, CA: Tara Press, 1980), p. 206.
85   See. Helena Petrovna Blavatsky, *The Key to Theosophy,* (London: The Theosophical Publishing Company, 1889), pp. 306-307.
86   See. Mary Lutyens, *Krishnamurti: The Years of Awakening,* (New York: Avon Books, 1983), p. 12.
87   Jiddu Krishnamurti. The Courage to become themselves, taken from http://www.well.com/user/jct/ ‡ Archived 13th July 2015.
88   https://en.wikipedia.org/wiki/Cosmic_Consciousness ‡ Archived 13th July 2015.

as the Messiah of the New Age. Nevertheless, Krishnamurti continued to surprise many with his knowledge and his wisdom for years to come, becoming an alternative cultural icon of the 1960s and '70s.

In the 1970s, Benjamin Creme pursued this idea again, despite failure in the past, becoming the new promoter of the return of a Theosophical Messiah called **Lord Maitreya.** Facilitating a new organizational structure for the masses, Creme announced an unprecedented event in the history of mankind, which was pushed earlier by Alice Bailey. But today Bailey, as well as Annie Besant's other successors, are accused of being neo-Theosophists, and are not close enough to Blavatky's original ideals. They are criticized by Orthodox Theosophists, who admit the possible infiltration of the Jesuits within the Theosophical Society shortly after the death of its founder Helena Petrovna Blavatsky, disliked and feared them, writing in 1888:

> *A day will come when Oriental Esotericism will render the same service to Christian Europe as Apollonius of Tyana rendered at Corinth to his disciple Menippus. The golden wand will be stretched out towards the Church of Rome, and the ghoul which has vampirized the civilized peoples since Constantine will resume its spectral, demoniacal form of incubus and succubus. So may it be! OM MANI PADME HUM![89]*

Coincidentally, a bolt of lightning struck the top of St Peter's Basilica just hours after Pope Benedict XVI shocking announcement of his resignation on Monday, February 11th, 2013—*so could this day have finally arrived?*

The list of anti-Vatican, anti-Catholic and anti-Jesuits citations from Blavatsky can be found in many publications. Unfortunately Theosophists of today who have been made corrupt by the Church, prefer to ignore them, demonstrating their loyalty the *Jesuits.* Here are her most significant quotes:

> *The Jesuits have practised not only Occultism, but BLACK MAGIC in its worst form, more than any other body of men; and to it they owe in large measure their power and influence.*
>
> (H.P. Blavatsky, "Theosophy or Jesuitism?")

> *We cast our gauntlet at the dogmatic theologians who would enslave both history and science; and especially at the Vatican, whose despotic pretensions have become hateful to the greater portion of enlightened Christendom.*
>
> (H.P. Blavatsky, "Isis Unveiled")

> *It [Roman Catholicism] not only obstructs the way to Theosophy and Occultism but threatens to throttle both.*
>
> (H.P. Blavatsky, "Letter to A.P. Sinnett")

> *The opposition represents enormous vested interests, and they have enthusiastic help from the Dugpas—in Bhootan and the Vatican!*
>
> (Master Koot Hoomi, "The Mahatma Letters")

> *The Theosophical Society ... recognizes and knows of, and therefore avoids its representatives in its ranks—but one enemy—an enemy common to all, namely, Roman Catholicism.*
>
> (H.P. Blavatsky, "Force of Prejudice")

89   "Collected Writings," Helena P. Blavatsky, Theosophical Publishing House, volume IX, p. 387, footnote.

The Society [was] founded to remedy the glaring evils of Christianity.

(H.P. Blavatsky, "The Theosophical Mahatmas")

As analyzed by Emmette William Coleman, Madame Blavatsky had many flaws, which included plagiarism, when she did not accurately cite quotes in her writings. [90] The knowledge she portrayed was often infused with an array of Luciferian and Satanic elements, but her ideas about the Jesuits and the Vatican were correct, and could be deemed forward-thinking. The Church of Rome even tried to convince her, going so far as to offer her money, to not mention them in her publications (which as you can see, she obviously refused). The Jesuits secretly infiltrated and possibly divided the Theosophical Society shortly after her death. Blavatsky's Theosophy Group in the UK, linked to the **United Lodge of Theosophists** in London contend that this is the truth behind the Theosophical society of today. I was a member of the Theosophical Society Pasadena, until 2003, and are also opponents of what is called **Neo-Theosophy**.

This extract from '*Neo-Theosophy*' on *Wikipedia:*

The term Neo-Theosophy is a term, originally derogatory, used by the followers of Blavatsky to denominate the system of Theosophical ideas expounded by Annie Besant and Charles Webster Leadbeater following the death of Madame Blavatsky in 1891. This material differed in major respects from Blavatsky's original presentation, but it is accepted as genuinely Theosophical by many Theosophists around the world.

After Blavatsky died in 1891, William Quan Judge became involved in a dispute with Henry Steel Olcott and Annie Besant over Judge allegedly forging letters from the Mahatmas. As a result, he ended his association with Olcott and Besant during 1895 and took most of the Society's American Section with him. He managed his new organization for about a year until his death in New York, whereupon Katherine Tingley became manager. The organization originating from the faction of Olcott and Besant is based in India and known as the Theosophical Society—Adyar, while the organization managed by Judge is known nowadays simply as the Theosophical Society, but often with the specification, "international headquarters, Pasadena, California." The Theosophical Society—Adyar is the group denounced as Neo-Theosophy by those who are followers of William Q. Judge and the original teachings of Madame Blavatsky; they do not accept what they regard as the Neo-Theosophical teachings of Annie Besant, Henry Olcott, and C. W. Leadbeater. [91]

Let us now examine what these "puritans" of Thesophical thought, who belonged to **Blavatsky's Theosophy Group,** have to say about Jesuit infiltration in relation to Neo-Theosophy, that now reigns supreme as the new religion of the United Nations. We discover in this short essay entitled *Theosophy, The Jesuits & The Roman Catholic Church,* the truth about how Blavatsky perceived the Jesuit enemy, and how they retaliated *post mortem* against her. They manipulated the essence of Theosophy, and infiltrated the organization Blavatsky created, to shape it into a pseudo-Christian-Messianic religion manipulated by the Vatican. Although I have not identified the authors hidden in anonymity behind the name *Blavatsky Theosophy Group UK,* I would like to thank them publicly for their testimony and their valuable research in unmasking the Jesuit sabotage of Theosophy. I would also like to remind my readers that HPB stands for Helena Petrovna Blavatsky.

90   William Emmette Coleman, "The Sources of Madame Blavatsky's Writings," article first published in A Modern Priestess of Isis by Vsevolod Sergyeevich Solovyoff, (London: Longmans, Green, and Co., 1895), Appendix C, pp. 353-366.

91   https://en.wikipedia.org/wiki/Neo-Theosophy ✝ Archived 15th July 2015.

"Theosophy, The Jesuits & The Roman Catholic Church":

One subject freely spoken and written about in the days of the original Theosophical Movement was that of the Jesuits, otherwise known as the Society of Jesus, a controversial religious order within the Roman Catholic Church and founded in 1540 by Ignatius of Loyola.

Strangely—or perhaps not so strangely, when the facts are examined—nothing was ever said about them or against them by later leaders of the Adyar Theosophical Society such as Annie Besant and C. W. Leadbeater, or by Adyar Theosophist Alice Bailey, who went on to found her own organisation, the Lucis Trust.

Indeed, these three even spoke favourably of Catholicism, with Leadbeater eventually co-founding a so-called Theosophical church known as the Liberal Catholic Church (complete with confession and absolution of sins by its priests and an affirmed belief in the apostolic succession of the Church of Rome!) and announcing the impending Second Coming of Christ, and Alice Bailey informing her readers that the "Master Jesus" was planning to eventually travel to Rome in order to become the new Pope, whereupon a glorious new era could begin for the Catholic Church, not to mention the almost enforced Christianisation of the Adyar Society and its literature by Annie Besant under Leadbeater's dominating influence.

Purposely suppressing, criticising, altering, depreciating and distorting the teachings and work of Madame Blavatsky after her death, Besant (who had previously been married to a Church of England minister) and Leadbeater (who had previously been a Church of England priest) deliberately turned the attention and focus of the Theosophical Society away from the Eastern esoteric philosophy which had originally characterised it, and towards a peculiar form of psychically inspired Christianity.

Happily allowing HPB's books such as The Key to Theosophy, Isis Unveiled, and even her major work The Secret Doctrine to go out of print, they instead began publishing such tomes as Leadbeater's weighty work The Science of the Sacraments, The Christian Creed and The Hidden Side of Christian Festivals and Besant's Esoteric Christianity and The Coming Christ. Just like the later Alice Bailey (who had previously been an evangelical Christian missionary and, in her own words, "formerly a rabid fundamentalist Christian") books, the dominant and central theme was the impending reappearance on the world scene of the "Lord Christ" and of the validity, role, and importance of the Christian Church.

Bearing in mind that HPB, William Quan Judge, the actual Masters, and all the proponents of the original genuine Theosophy viewed and spoke of the Christian religion—and especially the Catholic Church—as a major enemy of humanity and emphasised that it was Eastern spirituality alone that could save the Western world ... and that HPB once explained that one way the Jesuits work to destroy a potentially powerful spiritual movement is to infiltrate it and then gradually weaken it from within by means of replacing its authentic teachings and practices with a weak and insipid form of Christianity ... those Theosophists who have concluded that Leadbeater, Bailey, and Besant were either themselves Jesuits or agents of the Jesuits can hardly be blamed for arriving at such an opinion. On top of that, Theosophical researcher Morten Sufilight (author of the extensive article "Are the books by Alice A. Bailey dangerous?") has found specific evidence linking Alice Bailey's husband Foster Bailey with the Jesuits via Freemasonry.

But leaving all that aside, what do H.P. Blavatsky and the Masters actually have to *say about the Jesuits? There is a whole section about them in the second volume of HPB's first book* Isis Unveiled, *in which known facts, quotations, and references regarding them and their activities are presented alongside emphatic statements and pieces of information provided by some of the Masters and Adepts who aided her in the writing of the book.*

There we are informed that the Roman Catholic Church is today almost completely under the control of the Jesuits, who are "the hidden enemy that would-be reformers must encounter and overcome."

"The Church is henceforth an inert tool, and the Pope a poor weak instrument in the hands of this Order. But for how long?" ... "That crafty, learned, conscienceless, terrible soul of Jesuitism, within the body of Romanism, is slowly but surely possessing itself of the whole prestige and spiritual power that clings to it." ... "The Jesuits have done more moral harm in this world than all the fiendish armies of the mythical Satan. Whatever extravagance may seem to be involved in this remark, will disappear when our readers in America, who now know little about them, are made acquainted with their principles (principia) and rules as they appear in various works written by the Jesuits themselves."

Quoted on the same page of Isis Unveiled *is an excerpt from the report about the Jesuits delivered to the King of France in 1762 by the Commissioners of the French Parliament, who wrote of "the perversity of this doctrine. ... A doctrine authorizing Theft, Lying, Perjury, Impurity, every Passion and Crime, teaching Homicide, Parricide, and Regicide, overthrowing religion in order to substitute for it superstition, by favoring Sorcery, Blasphemy, Irreligion, and Idolatry, etc."*

HPB also quotes from Mackenzie's Royal Masonic Cyclopaedia, *which says about the Jesuits that "The Order has secret signs and passwords, according to the degrees to which the members belong, and as they wear no particular dress, it is very difficult to recognize them, unless they reveal themselves as members of the Order; for they may appear as Protestants or Catholics, democrats or aristocrats, infidels or bigots, according to the special mission with which they are entrusted. Their spies are everywhere, of all apparent ranks of society, and they may appear learned and wise, or simple or foolish, as their instructions run. There are Jesuits of both sexes, and of all ages, and it is a well-known fact that members of the Order, of high family and delicate nurture, are acting as menial servants in Protestant families, and doing other things of a similar nature in aid of the Society's purposes. We cannot be too much on our guard, for the whole Society, being founded on a law of unhesitating obedience, can bring its force on any given point with unerring and fatal accuracy."*

This would of course be casually dismissed by most people nowadays as nothing more than paranoia, ignorance, and a dated forerunner of today's many lurid conspiracy theories. Yet suspicion of the Jesuits was relatively widespread amongst all classes of Western society until fairly recently. The only real reason this is no longer the case is due to repeated strenuous efforts by the Roman Catholic Church and the Jesuits themselves to repair their tarnished image and to present themselves as decent and respectable in the eyes of the world.

One way of doing this is to repeatedly laugh to scorn any criticism and condemnation, no matter how valid or undeniably legitimate, until eventually the unthinking masses will just join in and put it all down to crazy conspiracy theories and overactive imaginations ... just as the Jesuits would want them to.

HPB explains that "The cry of an outraged public morality was raised against this Order from its very birth. (It dates from 1540; and in 1555 a general outcry was raised against them in some parts of Portugal, Spain, and other countries.) Barely fifteen years had elapsed after the bull approving its constitution was promulgated, when its members began to be driven away from one place to the other. Portugal and the Low Countries got rid of them, in 1578; France in 1594; Venice in 1606; Naples in 1622. From St. Petersburg they were expelled in 1815, and from all Russia in 1820. It was a promising child from its very teens. What it grew up to be every one knows well."

In HPB's The Trial of the Sun Initiate, we come across the following insight: "The Jesuits ... To give one instance of their success in throwing dust into the eyes of ordinary individuals to prevent their seeing the truths of Occultism, we will point out what they did in what is now called Freemasonry. This Brotherhood does possess a considerable portion of the symbolism, formulae, and ritual of Occultism, handed down from time immemorial from the primeval Initiations. To render this Brotherhood a mere harmless negation, the Jesuits sent some of their most able emissaries into the Order, who first made the simple brethren believe that the true secret was lost with Hiram Abiff; and then induced them to put this belief into their formularies. They then invented specious but spurious higher degrees, pretending to give further light upon this lost secret, to lead the candidate on and amuse him with forms borrowed from the real thing but containing no substance, and all artfully contrived to lead the aspiring Neophyte to nowhere.

And yet men of good sense and abilities, in other respects, will meet at intervals, and with solemn face, zeal and earnestness, go through the mockery of revealing "substituted secrets" instead of the real thing."

Her article "Theosophy or Jesuitism?" informs the reader that "The Roman Catholic [Church] is rapidly decaying from within. It is honeycombed throughout, and is being devoured by the ravenous microbes begotten by Loyola. It is no better now than a Dead Sea fruit, fair for some to look at, but full of the rottenness of decay and death within. Roman Catholicism is but a name. As a Church it is a phantom of the Past and a mask. It is absolutely and indissolubly bound up with, and fettered by the Society of Ignatius Loyola."

"It is vain to argue and claim a difference between Jesuitism and Roman Catholicism proper," she continues, "for the latter is now sucked into and inseparably amalgamated with the former."

The same article goes on to say: "What was the origin of that order? It may be stated in a few words. In the year 1534, on August 16th, an ex-officer and 'Knight of the Virgin,' from the Biscayan Provinces, and the proprietor of the magnificent castle of Casa Solar—Ignatius Loyola, became the hero of the following incident. In the subterranean chapel of the Church of Montmartre, surrounded by a few priests and students of theology, he received their pledges to devote their whole lives to the spreading of Roman Catholicism by every and all means, whether good or foul; and he was thus enabled to establish a new Order. Loyola proposed to his six chief companions that their Order should be a militant one, in order to fight for the interests of the Holy seat of Roman Catholicism. Two means were adopted to make the object answer; the education of youth, and proselytism (apostolat). This was during the reign of Pope Paul III, who gave his full sympathy to the new scheme. Hence in 1540 was published the famous papal bull—Regimini militantis Ecclesiae (the regiment *of the warring, or militant Church) —after which the Order began increasingly rapidly in numbers and power."*

Today the Society of Jesus numbers around 20,000 members throughout the world. Since there are various levels and degrees of the Order, the average Jesuit no doubt has no idea whatsoever of the true nature of the association to which he belongs and is most probably a good, sincere, and perfectly harmless and decent person.

The Wikipedia entry states that "The society is engaged in evangelization and apostolic ministry in 112 nations on six continents. Jesuits work in education (founding schools, colleges, universities and seminaries), intellectual research, and cultural pursuits. Jesuits also give retreats, minister in hospitals and parishes and promote social justice and ecumenical dialogue." —which sounds harmless enough.

Loyola's opening statement in the fundamental charter of the Order declares:

"Whoever desires to serve as a soldier of God beneath the banner of the Cross in our Society, which we desire to be designated by the Name of Jesus, and to serve the Lord alone and the Church, his spouse, under the Roman Pontiff, the Vicar of Christ on earth, should, after a solemn vow of perpetual chastity, poverty and obedience, keep what follows in mind. He is a member of a Society founded chiefly for this purpose: to strive especially for the defence and propagation of the faith and for the progress of souls in Christian life and doctrine, by means of public preaching, lectures and any other ministration whatsoever of the Word of God, and further by means of retreats, the education of children and unlettered persons in Christianity, and the spiritual consolation of Christ's faithful through hearing confessions and administering the other sacraments. Moreover, he should show himself ready to reconcile the estranged, compassionately assist and serve those who are in prisons or hospitals, and indeed, to perform any other works of charity, according to what will seem expedient for the glory of God and the common good."

Niccolini, however, wrote that "There is also a secret class, known only to the General and a few faithful Jesuits, which, perhaps more than any other, contributed to the dreaded and mysterious power of the Order."

Throughout the centuries a whole mass of evidence has been amassed in every nation and even in the Catholic Church itself by priests who have dared to speak out and expose the evil, that the public front of the Jesuits is indeed just that—a public front. In one part of the Jesuit "Extreme Oath of Induction," the Superior is required to say the following to the would-be initiate:

"My son, heretofore you have been taught to act the dissembler: among Roman Catholics to be a Roman Catholic, and to be a spy even among your own brethren; to believe no man, to trust no man. Among the Reformers, to be a Reformer; among the Huguenots, to be a Huguenot; among the Calvinists, to be a Calvinist; among other Protestants, generally to be a Protestant; and obtaining their confidence, to seek even to preach from their pulpits, and to denounce with all the vehemence in your nature our Holy Religion and the Pope; and even to descend so low as to become a Jew among Jews, that you might be enabled to gather together all information for the benefit of your Order as a faithful soldier of the Pope. You have been taught to plant insidiously the seeds of jealousy and hatred between communities, provinces, states that were at peace, and to incite them to deeds of blood, involving them in war with each other, and to create revolutions and civil wars in countries that were independent and prosperous, cultivating the arts and the sciences and enjoying the

blessings of peace; to take sides with the combatants and to act secretly with your brother Jesuit, who might be engaged on the other side, but openly opposed to that with which you might be connected, only that the Church might be the gainer in the end, in the conditions fixed in the treaties for peace and that the end justifies the means. You have been taught your duty as a spy, to gather all statistics, facts and information in your power from every source; to ingratiate yourself into the confidence of the family circle of Protestants and heretics of every class and character, as well as that of the merchant, the banker, the lawyer, among the schools and universities, in parliaments and legislatures, and the judiciaries and councils of state, and to be all things to all men, for the Pope's sake, whose servants we are unto death. You have received all your instructions heretofore as a novice, a neophyte, and have served as co-adjurer, confessor and priest, but you have not yet been invested with all that is necessary to command in the Army of Loyola in the service of the Pope. You must serve the proper time as the instrument and executioner as directed by your superiors; for none can command here who has not consecrated his labours with the blood of the heretic; for "without the shedding of blood no man can be saved."

And if that be thought so incredible as to seem implausible or impossible, bear in mind that Alberto Rivera, who escaped from the Jesuit Order in 1967, confirmed that the text of this particular oath was identical to the above. The oath is also quoted by Charles Didier in his book Subterranean Rome, *published in 1843 as well as being recorded in February, 1913 in the Journals of the 62nd Congress, 3rd Session, of the United States Congressional Record, from which it was later torn out, never to be seen again.*

There is a very profound and emphatic letter published by Theosophical University Press in the book The Letters of H.P. Blavatsky to A.P. Sinnett, *in which the Jesuits are unhesitatingly called "the enemies of the human race." It was thought by Alice Leighton Cleather—one of HPB's trusted friends and disciples in her final days in London and one of the specially chosen twelve members of her "Inner Group" of esoteric students—that this particular letter (No. CVI) was in fact dictated to HPB by the Master K.H. The letter was unsigned and the style, tone, and phraseology bear many of the distinctive hallmarks of the K.H. letters published in "The Mahatma Letters" and "Letters from the Masters of the Wisdom," thus giving credence to this theory.*

We quote here some of the most interesting and important parts of that letter, which deals solely with the subject of the Jesuits:

"Their plottings have a much wider scope and embrace a minuteness of detail and care of which the world in general has no idea. Everything is done by them to bring the mass of mankind again to the state of passive ignorance which they well know is the only one which can help them to the consummation of their purpose of Universal Despotism."

"In former times, at least, no country has better and more successfully withstood the encroachments and treacherous designs of Popery than England. Consequently, there is no country the Jesuits would so much like to dismember and destroy."

"They have openly avowed they will put an end, at any rate, a stop to the wheels of the English political machine by making converts of her chief men. All the world knows they have secured a few of the richest, noblemen and others."

"These particulars are given that not only Occultists, but also Nations, Communities and individuals may be aware and forewarned against what we have no hesitation

in saying are the enemies of the human race. It is generally known that the College of Jesuits is at Rome. It is not so well-known that virtually, for some years, their Head Quarters are in London and were so even before they were expelled from Republican France. They then flocked to England in greater numbers and were allowed to come, the English showing their usual apathy."

"Students of Occultism should know that while the Jesuits have by their devices, contrived to make the world in general, and Englishmen in particular, think there is no such thing as Magic and laugh at Black Magic, these astute and wily schemers themselves hold magnetic circles and form magnetic chains by the concentration of their collective WILL, when they have any special object to effect, or any particular and important person to influence. Again, they use their riches lavishly also to help them in any project. Their wealth is enormous."

"The time may come, when their wealth will be violently taken from them for the poor, and they themselves mercilessly left to be destroyed amidst the general execrations of all Nations and peoples. There is a Nemesis called KARMA, tho' often it allows evil-doers to go on successfully for centuries. Meanwhile, who has ears—"let him hear."

Although this letter was written over 120 years ago, the main facts of the matter will not have changed since then. If we give any credence at all to H.P. Blavatsky and to the Masters who trained her, taught her, and sent her to the West on her Theosophical mission, then we would do well to think twice before laughingly dismissing or forgetting about such notions as the Jesuits being the "enemies of the human race."

It would not be amiss here to mention that during the time HPB was busily engaged in writing The Secret Doctrine, *a member of the Roman Catholic Church was sent to offer her 25,000 Francs (a tremendous amount of money in those days!) if she would agree not to say anything about Christianity and the Church in the book. Naturally she furiously refused the offer or, to be more precise, the bribe. Her good friend Countess Wachtmeister, who was staying with her during that time, wrote about this and added that "They are fighting for life, for the S.D. has that which will give them their death blow, they may be a long time in expiring, but they surely will in time."*

Later on in the "Theosophy or Jesuitism?" article, HPB asks "But what are we to think of the future of Society if it is to be controlled in word and deed by this villainous Body? What are we to expect from a public, which, knowing the existence of the above mentioned charges, and that they are not exaggerated but pertain to historical fact, still tolerates, when it does not reverence, the Jesuits on meeting them, while it is ever ready to point the finger of contempt at Theosophists and Occultists? Theosophy is persecuted with unmerited slander and ridicule at the instigation of these same Jesuits, and many are those who hardly dare to confess their belief in the Philosophy of Arhatship. Yet no Theosophical Society has ever threatened the public with moral decay and the full and free exercise of the seven capital sins under the mask of holiness and the guidance of Jesus! Nor are their rules secret, but open to all, for they live in the broad daylight of truth and sincerity. And how about the Jesuits in this respect?"

The Society of Jesus is "the insatiable monster feeding on the brain and marrow of humanity, and developing an incurable cancer on every spot of healthy flesh it touches," according to the Master K.H. In Letter No. XXX of "The Mahatma Letters" he writes these very serious and powerful words, contrasting the Masters of the Trans-Himalayan Brotherhood and their ways of training disciples with the methods of the Jesuit Masters...

"As I once said before, they know that what they teach is a lie; and we know that what we impart is truth, the only truth and nothing but the truth. They work for the greater power and glory (!) of their order; we—for the power and final glory of individuals, of isolated units, of humanity in general, and we are content, nay forced—to leave our Order and its chiefs entirely in the shade. They work, and toil, and deceive, for the sake of worldly power in this life; we work and toil, and allow our chelas to be temporarily deceived, to afford them means never to be deceived hereafter, and to see the whole evil of falsity and untruth, not alone in this but in many of their after lives. They—the Jesuits sacrifice the inner principle, the Spiritual brain of the ego, to feed and develop the better the physical brain of the personal evanescent man, sacrificing the whole humanity to offer it as a holocaust to their Society—the insatiable monster feeding on the brain and marrow of humanity, and developing an incurable cancer on every spot of healthy flesh it touches. We—the criticized and misunderstood Brothers—we seek to bring men to sacrifice their personality—a passing flash—for the welfare of the whole humanity, hence for their own immortal Egos, a part of the latter, as humanity is a fraction of the integral whole, that it will one day become. They are trained to deceive; we—to undeceive."

The Theosophical Movement at large has still not recovered from the damage done in the first half of the 20th century by the likes of Leadbeater, Besant, and Bailey, as we have shown in such articles as *The Closing Cycle, A Conversation with an Alice Bailey Student, The "Etheric" Body Does Not Exist, Maitreya in the Light of Real Theosophy, The Unavoidable Facts about C.W. Leadbeater,* and *31 Important Differences between Theosophy and Neo-Theosophy.* Eventually it will but in the meantime it is interesting to note that even today there are numerous "Theosophists" around the world who will readily admit to being enemies of H.P. Blavatsky and her work and teachings. Some of these individuals have even spent years using websites and online Theosophical forums to spread lie after lie and attack after attack against HPB, with the specific intent of discouraging and turning people away from reading her teachings and often directing them instead towards the works of Leadbeater and Besant, which are highly questionable in their own right, regardless of the distinctly Christian theme.

In some Theosophy-themed groups on the internet, members are even banned from mentioning the name "Blavatsky." Some of these groups are run in dictatorial manner by members of the Liberal Catholic Church, mentioned at the start of this article. This is certainly shocking and bizarre and such strange behaviour on the part of so-called Theosophists can only be attributed to either psychological imbalance, stupidity, or a definite destructive agenda. In any other situation, if a person hated the founder of a movement and the teachings and ideologies of that movement to such an extent they would avoid having anything at all to do with that particular movement. The aim of this article is not to get Theosophists imagining that there are Jesuits lurking around every corner—which is most definitely not the case!—but to make readers aware, if they were not aware before, of this matter, which Madame Blavatsky and her Trans-Himalayan Teachers felt was so serious. [92]

(End of the article by Blavatsky Study Group UK: *Theosophy, The Jesuits & The Roman Catholic Church*)

---

92   http://blavatskytheosophy.com/ theosophy-the-Jesuits-the-roman-catholic-church ‡ Archived 15th July 2015, *[emphasis added]*.

After reading this excerpt, we can now better understand that through a lot of effort, the Jesuits took control of Theosophy. The aforementioned Benjamin Creme is not the usual "New Age" guru who speaks in conference rooms of a large hotels, or even worse at a distant farm in the hands of the classic New Age-style cult. Creme, on the contrary, is a pawn of the Jesuits and the Illuminati in a much more complex and important game. In 2006 He suddenly appeared out of nowhere holding court in the United Nations headquarters, where he assumed his unusual position, and announced a possible Messiah called "Maitreya," in the famous United Nations hall, that bears the name of **Dag Hammarskjold.** His speech was requested by the *Society for Enlightenment and Transformation (what a beautiful name!)* Let me remind you that the use of the Dag Hammarskjold Hall takes place in accordance with the instructions given in the manual published by U.N. Protocol, as duly specified in the following regulation number XXII **for the use of the Dag Hammarskjold Auditorium:** *"As a United Nations facility, the Auditorium is put at the disposal, first, of United Nations organs, then the Secretariat and the permanent/observer missions of Member States. The use of the Auditorium is restricted to purposes that may be characterized as United Nations purposes, that are of positive value, either directly to the United Nations or to a particular objective or program endorsed by the Organization. Any shows, film showings, lectures or seminars sponsored by the permanent/observer missions are to be of a cultural or artistic nature and without any political connotation that could be offensive to any Member State."* [93]

So the function of the United Nations include, believe it or not, the arrival of the Messiah prophesied by many religions. Benjamin Creme delivered this surreal speech at the United Nations, introducing the future teacher and spiritual guide for humanity, known as the *Maitreya:*

Maitreya has a task: His main task is to show humanity how to live together in peace. It is so simple—it requires only to share the resources of the world. Sharing is the key. In one stroke, when we accept the principle of sharing, we will create the trust which is needed for all other action. When trust has been established, the other problems will dissolve and fade away. Goodwill, born of trust, makes the solving of these difficulties simple acts of common sense.

We are waiting for Maitreya. Maitreya is waiting for the soul of America to express itself, and when the soul of America does express itself it will inaugurate the principle of sharing and will become the beneficent sharer of all its resources. America has lost its way. It is adrift. It is not the only nation that is adrift, but it has much to give the world, and indeed has given the world. Today its soul is waiting to be invoked so that it can lead the way to sharing and justice and liberty. Governments, politicians, always talk about liberty, but where is the justice? We never hear about justice. Russia used to talk about justice but never of freedom. You can't have justice without freedom, you can't have liberty without justice. They are one and the same. Maitreya comes to teach this, to show us that without one you cannot have the other. They are both divine concepts, leading humanity forward into the future. That future is more wonderful, more glorious, than anything you can imagine, but requires the decision of humanity to share to bring it about.

Sharing is the key to all. Some nations, some people, find it the hardest of all to do. I know many people who agree with everything I say except the idea about sharing. They cannot see that it is the key, the core of the problem of humanity. We have to see ourselves as one, brothers and sisters of one humanity, and therefore to do what a family does: share the resources. Today, as you know—this is the United Nations, you know the facts—you know that millions of people are starving to death in a world of plenty. Thirtyfive thousand people die every day of starvation in a world overflowing with food, with a huge surplus per capita. Why do the nations not see this? They don't see it because they are complacent, greedy, selfish and ignorant. Complacency makes for ignorance. Humanity has to wake up. Maitreya comes to waken humanity and to guide us out of this morass into which we have fallen. He comes to show that there is a simple way, a simple path: to share and create justice. Then wars will cease. Then terrorism will be no more. You cannot fight a war against terrorism. There are millions of new terrorists springing up every month, because of injustice, because of their sense of grievance, of poverty, of misuse. That is what makes for terrorism.

You have to seek the cause of terrorism. It is a canker, an abomination, but it has a cause, and that cause is the injustice in the world. And it is caused by the developed nations of the world, the G7 or G8 nations, who think they own the world. No nation, no one nation, owns the world. No one group of nations owns the world, or can tell the world what to do. The world has its own destiny and that destiny it will carry out under the inspiration and guidance of Maitreya and His group of Masters. [94]

Who are the real hidden manipulators of the United Nations? They are religious and banking lobbies, the Illuminati sects and transnational Masonic lodges who now dominate the global scene, and not the single states that have lost their last remains of sovereignty. The UN employs mercenaries for international terrorism in order sell senseless wars, thus helping the infamous **Military Industrial Complex** maintain its important status. Poverty is not only present because of the geographical position of a nation, but there is a specific intention of the New World Order to exploit every human being until he is completely enslaved. Even Gaddalfi renamed the United Nations "The Council of Terror," and he (Gaddafi) was not exactly a saint! When Creme, a few months before the physical elimination of Gaddafi, was asked about the matter, he became the supporter of the worst globalism, when he stated that the "*Arab Springs*" was a great thing.

Today we know that the "Arab Springs" was the beginning of the end for the states involved, as the whole area became irremediably destabilized, paving the way for ISIS, the worst terrorists and mercenaries in the world, with the ability to now create a super rogue state, a modern "Caliphate" that is threatening the West like no other terrorist organization ever has before. Benjamin Creme and others like him should be ashamed of themselves. In an article that appeared in *Share International magazine*, in October 2005, entitled "The Brotherhood of Men," the *Master* channeled through Benjamin Creme, stated:

> *The United Nations is, of course, the forum in which the voice of the smaller nations can be raised and heard. This is only possible when the Security Council, with its arbitrary veto, is abolished. It has outlasted its usefulness and must soon give way to a United Nations Assembly free of the abuses of power and veto. Then will we see the nations acting without restraints imposed by Great Power veto and financial inducement. Those who call loudest for democracy in foreign lands are strangely blind to its absence in the halls of the United Nations.* [95]

94   http://www.sharesweden.se/artiklar/BC%20tal%20i%20FN%202006.html ‡ Archived 15th July 2015.
95   Benjamin Creme, "The brotherhood among men," article in Share International, October 2005, (http://www.share-international.org/master/2005/ma_oct05.htm ‡ Archived 14th July 2015.

In this case, Benjamin Creme was very critical of the system confirming the total absence of democracy in the United Nations. So where is this long-announced Messiah / Maitreya he has promoted since 1975? Thursday, January 14, 2010, during a lecture at *Friends House* in London, Benjamin Creme announced that Maitreya, the World Teacher, had just released his first interview to a U.S. television channel, [96] but there are now many on the Internet who doubt the veridity of it, especially since the interview has not been made public. [97]

However, on the 7th of September 2015, Benjamin Creme stated:

Soon, very soon now, men will realize the power that lies unused in their hands. They will see that they have the ability to change the quality of their lives. They are beginning to understand that freedom, justice and right relationship, one to another, are essential for man's living. Many are calling for the structures which will ensure the creation of this blessed state. This makes clear to Maitreya that the world is ready for the new dispensation. Men should, therefore, use the limited time available to make known His presence and so prepare His way. [98]

What they are attempting issomething that should not be decided by man, and insisting in this way will only materialize an Antichrist!

Benjamin Creme warned his collaborators of **Share International,** that in the event that they should recognize him, to avoid indicating him as such to people outside of their network (including family and friends), as this could interfere with the freewill of an individual to recognize Maitreya on their own.

It appears the Maitreya/ Messiah is being launched onto the world stage. At the **Club Bilderberg annual meeting of 2011,** which was held in St. Moritz in Switzerland, there was the appearance of a mysterious figure, presumably female, all dressed in white that appeared out of nowhere. The British newspaper *The Guardian* described the rather unusual appearance, writing: *"It was an odd walk right from the start. From nowhere, like something from a dream, a distinguished lady, dressed from top to toe in white, whooshed serenely past security and swanned to the front of the power walkers."*

Adding a few lines later: *"The lady in white led her band of Bilderberg bigwigs and billionaires along the charming Swiss byways, across bridges over gentle streams ... and straight into a pack of 50 baffled activists, who were milling around outside a community hall during a break in a symposium."* [99] Benjamin Creme confirmed that the "woman in white" was Maitreya. [100]

The situation seems very confused with this unexpected participation of the Maitreya at Club Bilberberg in 2011, and would imply the possibility for the Maitreya to change appearance depending on the situation. Anything is possible, but of course this appearance, and the article that followed in *The Guardian,* seem piloted by the New World Order in order to promote the concept of a mysterious teacher leading the elite. What is certain is that Benjamin Creme and his organization *Share,* seemingly controlled by the

96   http://www.share-italiano.org/mait6.php ‡ Archived 14th July 2015.
97   Benjamin Creme's "Maitreya" Debunked (full video), https://www.youtube.com/watch?v=fCG4ZpKu9Fs ‡ Archived 14th July 2015.
98   http://www.share-international.org/master/2015/ma_2015-10.htm ‡ Archived 14th July 2015.
99   http://www.theguardian.com/news/blog/2011/jun/12/bilderberg-2011-mandelson-nature-walk ‡ Archived 14th July 2015.
100   In "Signs of the Times Follow my Leader!" article in Share International, http://www.share-international.org/magazine/old_issues/2011/2011-07.htm ‡ Archived 14th July 2015.

Jesuits, have found once again another way to lead people astray with New Age nonsense. Remember **S.I.** means not only **Share International** but *Societas Iesu*, the real name of the Company of Jesus, the infamous *Jesuits*.

Maitreya and the Indignados – Occupy Movement

After analyzing, the words and true intent of Benjamin Creme, and demonstrating those who are his real occult guides, the Jesuits, we understand even better how the United Nations is a tool of the New World Order fueled by misinformation and deception. It doesn't take a genius to realize that if something materializes through them, you can rest assured that it would be at best a false prophet, if not the Antichrist himself. From my brief interactions with the U.N., its members appeared to me, most of the time, to be false opportunists...and nothing more. I have never witnessed anything truly spiritual manifesting from the U.N., and with **AGENDA 21** followed by **AGENDA 2030**, and the public blessing of a Jesuit Pope in September 2015, they definitely are in league with pure evil, if not the *Devil* himself!

Benjamin Creme and the whole "Operation Maitreya," in my opinion, is not creating expectations for a true Messiah, but rather for a submissive Antichrist, who will only serve to unify the New World Order under a false flag of pseudo-New Age spirituality. Their Messiah / Maitreya would not be a true guide of light and wisdom, but a simple tool to use, a robot of the elite.

Benjamin Crème was asked: *"Many Christians may fear that Maitreya is the anti-Christ; will he be able to say or do something to assuage those fears?"*

He simply answered: *"It may well be that, for many, the acceptance of Maitreya as the Christ will be impossible in this life. For the vast majority of Christians, however, I believe that the events and experience of the Day of Declaration and His subsequent mission of salvage and teaching will remove their fears. The tree, after all, is known by its fruits."* [101]

Share International Foundation claims to be an acredited non-governmental organization (NGO) of the United Nations, even though there is no trace of them on the official website of the U.N. The magazine *Share International*, declares on the inside cover of every issue, that they are published in association with the Department of Information of the United Nations. Incidentally, in the advertising of its Tara Center, in 1982, Benjamin Creme stated without shame: *"What is the Plan? It included the installation of a new world order government and new world religion under Maitreya."* [102]

The "Maitreya Operation" has the direct involvement of *Lucifer Trust*, later *Lucis Trust*, of Alice Bailey, who has influenced Benjamin Creme spiritually and intellectually, paving the road for this project of global governance through the United Nations.

In addition to supporting the so-called "Arab springs," the U.N. aided in the spread of ISIS, secretly supporting the activities of pseudo revolutionaries involved within the *Occupy Movement* of Wallstreet. It would be better to call them the "manipulated movement," as not only are they linked to George Soros, but also to the *Lucis Trust*. These many fake uprisings, including the Ferguson, MO "Black Lives Matter" protests, are obviously the result of constant manipulation by the New World Order elite.

Despite the emphasis of those concerned about a possible World Government re-

101   http://www.shareintl.org/archives/M_teachings/Mt_religion.htm ‡ Archived 14th July 2015.
102   http://www.conspiracyarchive.com/NewAge/Creme_Maitreya.htm ‡ Archived 14th July 2015.

iterated by Pope Francis in June 2015, [103] we constantly see protests spread like wildfire around the world, even though there is media coverage *only* when ordered by the elite. Many countries participate to this daily tension, because people want real change, but regularly, as in the most recent cases of Greece in 2015, or Occupy Wall Street in 2011, nothing ever happens unless there is an interest in destabilizing the area, and reaching a civil war, as in the case of Ukraine, or Libia, or ... Syria.

In these countries they have paved the way for the mercenaries of the CIA, the Israeli Mossad and Intelligence agencies of the New World Order. In July 2015, the *New York Times* reported the presence of three Islamic divisions linked to ISIS/Daesh in Ukraine, the **"Dzhokhar Dudayev,"** the **"Sheikh Mansur,"** which are mostly Chechen troups, and the **"Crimea,"** that is formed mainly by Tatars in the region now under the control of Moscow. [104] It seems that many of these soldiers are linked to the Chechen **jihadist movement** led by Aslan Byutukayev, who had no qualms in declaring his affiliation with the Islamic State [105] controlled by Abu Bakr al Baghdadi of the *Hathor Pentalpha Lodge* and the reoccuring **Nazi-Islamic alliance,** [106] that the U.S. State Deparment seem to support right now.

In a 110-page FBI report, entitled **"Potential Criminal Activity Alert,"** it appears that the Occupy Wall Street movement was spied upon, infiltrated, polluted and delegitimized by an intense campaign of disinformation. These documents also talk about contacts with major banks and financial institutions in the USA. [107] The whole operation was basically a farse. We are moving towards a New World Order and it is not enough to say we are 99%, if the 1% system and its leaders are in charge of all that surrounds us, including the war machine of the **Military Industrial Complex** built to contain and oppress us. The occult and malignant nature of this manipulation of pseudo-indignation and false revolutionaries is on a global scale. There is *even* the direct involvement of the disciples of the false Messiah known as "Maitreya"— which was uncovered thanks to the research of an American blogger later picked up by an Italian site. [108] The official website of the event was **15october.net**. Researching the owner of the site, you can read from the image I saved on my computer (FIG. 31), that it was officially changed October the 18th, to:

> *Paulina Arcos*
> *866 United Nations Plaza*
> *Suite 516*
> *New York, New York 10017*
> *United States*

Paulina Arcos is the wife of an Ecuadorian politician, **Francisco Carrion-Mena**, Minister of Foreign Affairs at the time, a man who by reason of his office attended the

103   See. http://www.independent.co.uk/environment/pope-francis-calls-for-new-system-of-global-government-to-tackle-climate-change-10330124.html ‡ Archived 15th July 2015.

104   See. http://www.nytimes.com/2015/07/08/world/europe/islamic-battalions-stocked-with-chechens-aid-ukraine-in-war-with-rebels.html?_r=0 ‡ Archived 15th July 2015.

105   See. http://www.ilgiornale.it/news/mondo/battaglioni-islamisti-dellisis-fianco-dellucraina-contro-i-s-1150353.html#comment-form ‡ Archived 15th July 2015.

106   See. http://www.ilfattoquotidiano.it/2015/07/10/ucraina-rispunta-lalleanza-nazi-islamica-lisis-a-fianco-delle-brigate-neofasciste/1861019/ ‡ Archived 15th July 2015.

107   http://www.theguardian.com/commentisfree/2012/dec/29/fbi-coordinated-crackdown-occupy ‡ Archived 15th July 2015.

108   http://www.lateoriadelcomplotto.com/2011/10/forse-non-tutti-sono-pronti-leggere.html ‡ Archived 15th July 2015.

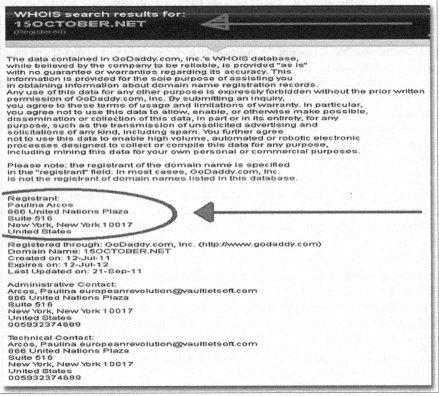

FIG. 31 – Picture taken from the site http://lalternativaitalia.blogspot.com/2011/10/forse-not-all-are-ready-leggere.html, which allows us to attribute without doubt the authorship of part of the Occupy Wall Street Movement to the Lucis Trust and the UN Illuminati.

United Nations. This explains the unusual address *"866 United Nations Plaza."*

It is incredible that the Organization of the United Nations resorts to unusual means to manipulate the population. Epiphanius writes:

> *We also report, for those who want to know more about the Lucis Trust, there is a text that does not refer to the official addresses, but indicates instead no. 866 of the United Nations Plaza in New York, very close to n. 823, home of the ADL [Anti-Defamation League], the operational arm of the B' nai B 'rith, the Jewish Freemasonry.* [109]

The text mentioned by Ephipanius is *Die Netzwerke der Insider* by Von Peter Blackwood. [110] Just four days after its launch, the registration address of the official website of October 15, 2011, was changed again. Subsequently, it is no longer registered to Paulina Arcos but to: *DomainsByProxy.com 15111 N. Hayden Rd., Ste 160, PMB 353 Scottsdale, Arizona 85260 United States*—It was possible, however, to see with a simple search on the internet to https://www.godaddy.com [111] that the domain was passed suc-

109   Ephipanius, *Ibid.*, p. 620.
110   Peter Blackwood, *Die Netzwerke der Insider,* (Leonberg, DE: Diagnosen Verlag, 1986) p. 260.
111   https://who.godaddy.com/whoisstd.aspx?domain=15october.net&prog_id=GoDaddy ‡ Archived 15th July 2015.

cessively to: **whois.namepal.com 6140 Tutt Blvd, # 160, Colorado Springs, Colorado 80923 United States.**

These manipulators of the New World Order reign supreme and wish to detect and flush out all possible opposition by creating such movements, just as they do by creating their own terrorist groups, and at the same time creating chaos and unrest whenever convenient. This is in order to establish a police state, thanks to new draconian laws that allow total control of the masses. For an example, just look at what happened in Paris on **Friday the 13** of November 2015. The rock concert shootings in the Bataclan began at the very moment the band called "Eagles of Death Metal" began playing the song "Kiss the Devil," beginning with the line: "I Meet the Devil And This Is His Song," an obvious tribute to Satan.

The Lucis Trust, is the "spiritual side" of the United Nations overlooking the leaders of the New World Order awaiting the false Messiah. If this was not disturbing enough, Bailey, considered the pioneer of the New Age of Aquarius, had heavy accusations of racism propelled against her because of her writings, and heavy public statements against blacks and Jews. Rabbi Gershom Yonassan, along with others, have described her writings as racist and anti-Semitic. [112]

I ask myself why a racist like Alice Bailey, who criticized Jews and Blacks like Adolf Hitler, can be a beacon of light and an inspiration to the members of the United Nations? This not only borders on ridiculous, but demonstrates the hypocrisy of the U.N., and my final judgment can only be negative about the whole "Maitreya Operation," which is in my opinion the worst spiritual farse ever promoted by the New World Order.

As Pierre de Senarclens, a past director of the Division on Human Rights of UNESCO between 1980 and 1983, once stated:

> *The real power of the United Nations lies not in the concrete policy decisions, which are most often of mediocre capacity, but functions in the ideological, political influence that comes from his authority as instance of legitimacy. ... The speeches, resolutions and documents of any nature, which are the product of this deliberative function, exert widespread political influence on international life. Governments can't ignore the impact of such activities that are part of the action and ideological approach given so the orientation of the opinions, the formation of politicians. ... The U.N., on the same basis of specialized political organizations, has the mandate for the propagation of certain ideas, certain values. The examination of their budgets shows, in fact, that their main activity is to organize meetings, disseminate their recommendations, suggest policies ... They contribute to the conceptualization, and especially the circulation of many political issues, especially in the economic field and social.*

If, in various ways, they promote a false Messiah, the so-called Maitreya, you can be sure that a project will sooner or later move to politics and religion in the international arena, because the plan for a single **One World Religion** is not a farce, but something very serious to the Illuminati network linked to both Israel and the Vatican.

Freemasonry and the P2 at the United Nations

The United Nations flag is flying with the same pale blue flag color of Israel. It is no coincidence that the symbol is often surrounded by branches of acacia, the tree sacred to Freemasonry. The globe has meaning of lordship over the world and is a sym-

bol that is repeated on the entrance columns of the Masonic temples. Hermeneutics of Gnosis says nothing is accidental: The 33 divisions of the globe recall the 33 degrees of initiation of the Ancient and Accepted Scottish Rite, the diffusion of which is—in fact— universal and global. The corn ears are right and left of the globe, as in the figure—other interpretation of the branches that surround the symbol—mean seed and harvest—13 in number for each side. 13 is a number of good wishes with Jewish meaning yet so broad as to include even antithetical, namely to jinx; but 13 is a number that also belongs to the high Rosicrucian initiation, as indicated by the steps of the truncated pyramid of the British Israel that towers on the American dollar bill. [113]

This dissertation of Epiphanius on the esoteric side of U.N. symbolism helps us to understand the deep ties of this institution within Freemasonry. The U.N. organization is in fact the single most hypocritical institution ever created by man up until now. I will be demonstrating through analysis the direct link the U.N. has with a guy who was once a powerful player of the New World Order, **Giorgio Hugo Balestrieri.** Balestrieri is a member of the *Lodge in Monte Carlo,* currently under house arrest in Italy since May 2015, after only two months spent in Rebibbia prison. His latest problems with the Italian justice system created issues for his untouchable status as one of the driving forces of the *Executive Committee Masonic of the Monte Carlo Lodge,* known worldwide as *Massonic Executive Committee,* that is linked to the Illuminati Clubs of the *Universal Unity.* Balestrieri's criminal activities finally brought an Italian arrest warrant in 2009, and that was one of the main reasons why I decided to leave this branch of the P2 Lodge in 2006, based in the Principality of Monaco, with which I was associated for a few years. Balestrieri is a native of Livorno, member of the P2 Lodge (membership n. 907), as you can see for yourself on *Wikipedia,* on the official list of P2 members. [114]

Giorgio Hugo was a well-known asset of the International Intelligence community, engaged in operations with Israeli Mossad, British SIS, the United States, the NSA, the CIA, and the FBI. He was called upon often, mainly because of his familiarity with government projects bordering on illegality, in so-called "anti-drug operations" on behalf of the U.S. government. This after having been for years a prominent agent of Operation GLADIO, on behalf of NATO. Balestrieri is a wily character who climbed the ladder of Freemasonry and the Illuminati thanks to the recommendations of the late Licio Gelli, who would later regret it. It was through these channels that Balestrieri eventually was able to acquire an American citizenship, after the P2 scandal erupted in Italy in the early 1980s. He eventually will use the nickname "**Hugo,**" in which the **initial H** is in fact linked to his new identity as an "honest" American citizen. Balestrieri previously worked as a consultant for the Italian Senate, and because of his Italian-American connections, was involved in activities of the unauthorized transfer of technological material. His alleged specialty is the use of electronics for the interception of signals. Until a few years ago, he used the website of **Silvio Rononi** [115] to make stock transactions related to these materials. He was arrested in Morocco in 2014, and then extradited to Italy in March 2015. Balestrieri was part of new super Masonic structure made up of various sectors, mainly related to **Security and Intelligence**, called with no shame P3, that was created in 2012. The following information about the P3 appears still to this day on his **Linkedin profile:**

At the present time, Comandante Giorgio Balestrieri is the Founder of The P3 ∴. E-POL Team of International Consultants & Strategic Partners and the Director

113   Ephipanius, *Ibid.,* Pdf, p. 285.
114   http://it.wikipedia.org/wiki/ListadegliappartenentiallaP2 ‡ Archived 15th July 2015.
115   www.rdn.it ‡ Archived 15th July 2015.

International Marketing of AMETOS Ltd. The mission of The P3 ∴ is to promote Public Private Partnerships providing targeted high-end and cost effective solutions to specific problems in the world's front lines. We understand and operate within today's environment while analyzing tomorrow's potential threats. Our targeted solutions begin with a comprehensive analysis of each client's needs, and end only upon the successful implementation of a custom-tailored security platform that can include everything from updated protection protocols to cutting-edge equipment.

P3 ∴ E-POL Team (Public Private Partnerships for Security, Peace and Sustainable Development)

The P3 ∴. Team (AMETOS—EAGLE—ABACUS) January 2012—Present New York City, United States

Dr. Capt. Giorgio Balestrieri is The E-P3 ∴. POL Team Founder: (1) Director of International Marketing AMETOS (www.ametosltd.com), (2) Senior VP of EAGLE (www.eagleguardsecurity.com), (3) Principal of ABACUS (www.abacuspower.com). [116]

Thanks to his significant involvement in the activities within the Rotary club, Giorgio Hugo Balestrieri eventually rose to the prestigious post of **President Elect of the Rotary Club of New York at the United Nations**, a historical grouping founded in 1909 as Rotary Club No. 6, which is headed by the Department of the Interior of the United Nations. Balestrieri was later reconfirmed in this role, even after an arrest warrant was issued by Italian authorities during an investigation called "Operation Maestro" on December 22, 2009. The warrant was issued for collusion with the Mafia, which was later confirmed by INTERPOL in 2011, with a European arrest warrant, that officially made Giorgio Balestrieri a criminal. However, in the United States and the United Nations, he continued to act undisturbed for years, until his eventual arrest in Morocco on Sept. 22, 2014, which was then followed in 2015 by an extradition to Italy. So Balestrieri, up until September 2014, continued to enjoy legitimacy at an international level, as well as a significant function of power, prestige and control within the elite of the New World Order.

His arrest may only be staged, since the media are silent on the event, and Balestrieri even boasts on various social networks that he now collaborates with the "Mafia Capitale Justice Department" on the recent scandals in Rome called "Mafia Capitale." But exactly how is it possible for someone under arrest for crimes relating to the Mafia, be in a position of power that goes against the Mafia? Balestrieri writes:

The insiders of the "Mafia Capitale Justice Department" are telling me that it is better to have a bad trial than a funeral. I am being detained (with no trial and no judgment) for over a year, six months in Morocco where I was nicely tortured and now six months in Italy that is no better as far as human rights. Forget the funeral, I would like to know if the "friends of the imams and the hezbollah" want to give me the bad trial they already gave to some U.S. Veterans (see Former CIA Operative Sabrina De Sousa and the Abu Omar case). We've been fighting the mafiosi linked to Iran since the first twin towers bombing!

Iran? Involved with 9/11? "Friends of the Imams and Hezbollah"? Not giving him a fair trial? Giorgio Hugo Balestrieri who is a criminal of the New World Order, also has a very special relationship with the State of Israel, and in particular with the **Mossad** and its experts in advanced technologies in the detection of the presence of weapons of mass destruction. So much so that he has become in recent years (despite his international arrest warrant), the Director of International Marketing of Israeli AMETOS—which is part of the mysterious structure called P3 Balestrieri, described on their site as: *"Operating in specialized areas within the international security market, We work with a few, very carefully selected strategic partners, each of which is uniquely established and accomplished in assessing & confronting the risks of International terrorism & crime at State level. ... We are run by former Israeli, American and U.K. Intelligence & Counter-Terrorism executives who all have a long, proven track record of success within the international Intelligence and protection arena at State level."* [117]

Balestrieri also boasted of his long experience in the area of strategic planning, evaluation and development of advanced technologies into complex systems of border crossing, such as the SLA-C4I, which is the airport's multifunctional security system, that is discussed in the book, *Terrorism: Defensive Strategies for Individuals, Companies and Governments*. It is written by Lawrence J. Hogan with the help of Giorgio Balestrieri, and other experts in the field, and is described as a prophetic book, that was written before September 11th 2001, and published strangely enough on October 1st 2001. The book is described as a veritable encyclopedia of terrorism, that brings together some of the country's leading experts on terrorism from the government, police departments and universities; as well as computer, biological and chemical specialists. [118] *Midwest Book Review* on February 6, 2002 writes this on Amazon:

> *Ably edited by Lawrence Hogan,* Terrorism: Defensive Strategies for Individuals, Companies and Governments *is a sober, serious, and highly analytical survey of the worldwide threat of terrorism, its various manifestations, history, and trends, with numerous indexes focusing on terrorist activity in different locations around the globe. Critical, meticulous, and filled with straight no-nonsense information by knowledgeable contributors,* Terrorism *is a essential reading for everyone trying to better understand this very real and dangerous threat and a highly recommended acquisition for corporate, governmental and public library reference collections.*

I would also like to add that Balestrieri paved the way for the creation of the modern concept of "total security" in airports. *Why am I telling you all this?* Because Giorgio Balestrieri is one of the most relevant figures in regards to the framing and drafting of the September 11 attacks, which, as you know, caused the collapse of the Twin Towers, and the Pentagon attack. Yes, he is one of those people in the establishment behind the attacks, which makes him an important asset, even after being accused of being a mafiosi by the Italian authorities, yet he is protected by both the U.S. and Israel. That's why he constantly bashes Iran in connection to 9/11, continuing to spread disinformation.

I highly doubt the authenticity of his alleged arrest in reference to his shady business deals with the Calabrese Mafia. In the Rotary Club of New York he worked for years with a Turk named **Kaan Soyak**, a Freemason and a contractor supported by certain groups that operate within the elite of his country of Turkey in order to "facilitate" relations between the United States Military Industrial Complex and Turkey, which are now essential for the ISIS/ISIL/Daesh project.

Let's not forget American journalist Serena Shim, who worked for Iran's state owned Press TV as a Turkish correspondent, who was killed in 2014, in a mysterious car crash

117   http://www.ametosltd.com ‡ Archived 15th July 2015.
118   See. Lawrence J. Hogan, *Terrorism: Defensive Strategies for Individuals,* Companies and Governments, (Frederick, Maryland: Amlex Inc, 2001).

in the city of Suruc in Turkey, just days after claiming that Turkish Intelligence services had threatened her over her report that suggested that ISIS militants were actually being smuggled in by vehicles of the World Food Program (WFP) and other Aid groups **linked to the UN,** going back and forth over the Syrian border. [119] Roy Greenslade wrote in *The Guardian*:

> *In a report on the Press TV website, a London-based political analyst claimed that "our sister Serena" had been "assassinated by the government of Turkish president Recep Tayyip Erdogan." Shabir Hassan Ali said: "Serena was hounded in a fashion by Turkish Intelligence" because she told the truth about Erdogan's regime, which he accused of oppressing the Kurdish population and "actively" supporting Islamic State (ISIS). [120]*

There is a direct correlation between a contract signed by NATO, and the one signed by a Turkish company owned by Soyak. [121] About a decade ago, 2005 to be exact, Balestrieri and Soyak, both high level members of the exclusive **International Service Division** of the **Rotary Club** at the **United Nations** Headquarters in New York, and the *Illuminati* branch operating from the Principality of Monaco, organized an international conference in Turkey, [122] which was attended by the most important representatives of the Caucasian region. Such a conference could not take place without the active assistance of the Rotary Club and Freemasonry. It was attended by more than four hundred people, including Giunchiglia, the puppeteer of the notorious Monte Carlo Lodge, and a man working for David Rockfeller and the Vatican.

The conference itself was considered a milestone for the New World Order, and was held in Ankara during a period of great turmoil regarding strategic studies in the geopolitical arena that was preparing for what became a few years later, the Islamic State. Balestrieri's participation to the event was later described as having "a key role in the peace process in the Caucasus," as more than 400 Rotarians arrived in Ankara from Armenia, Azerbaijan, Georgia and Turkey. Between the latter were representatives of the Kurdish minority. In fact, Kaan Soyak himself, a Freemason and business partner of Balestrieri, had significant interests involving weapons deals in the Kurdish region in northern Iraq, and Balestrieri proposed to me once to open an office in Turkey as a cover for his activities.

As we know this region now plays a strategic role with the arrival of ISIS/Daesh, and the immense quantities of oil that originate from its self-styled Caliphat, that can only be "regularized" in secret, and sold worldwide primarily through Turkey. So of course Balestrieri's "P3" must be in on it, and that's why you will never hear a word against ISIS/Daesh from Giorgio Hugo Balestrieri, who is too busy accusing Iran for the 9/11 attacks, never mentioning Wahhabi Islam, as they are the ones promoting the new "strategy of tension," first experimented in Italy during the 1970s.

The methods used are illegal, and often violent, such as terror attacks, murder, kidnapping and paramilitary operations, but also propaganda, economic sanctions, support of civil unrest, fake grassroots movements, and a purposeful escalation of formerly peaceful protests involving agent provocateurs. These are typically carried out under a false flag

119   http://www.dailymail.co.uk/news/article-2799924/mystery-american-journalist-killed-car-crash-turkey-just-days-claimed-intelligence-services-threatened-coverage-siege-kobane.html ‡ Archived 15th July 2015.

120   http://www.theguardian.com/media/greenslade/2014/oct/20/journalist-safety-turkey ‡ Archived 15th July 2015.

121   See. http://www.arcticbeacon.com/articles/15- Apr-2007.html ‡ Archived 15th July 2015.

122   http://www.clubrunner.ca/Data/7230/3633/HTML/110401//Declaration_Caucasian_Friendship_Days.pdf ‡ Archived 15th July 2015.

FIG. 32 – Kaan Soyak, the influential Turkish Mason tied to Giorgio H. Balestrieri, who still on the list of the Board of Directors for the Rotary Club of New York for the years 2015-2016. Photo taken from the site: http://portal.clubrunner.ca/ 3633 / Stories / board-roster-for-2015-16 ‡ Archived 15th July, 2015.

operation, and in combination with spreading disinformation to blame an uninvolved third party. The main target of a strategy of tension is public opinion, to manipulate votes, to generate the impression of a national threat to legitimate war, to call for a strong leader or to tolerate surveilance and denounce peacemakers as unpatriotic. False flag terrorist attacks are just the tip of the iceberg of the possible measures that can be used to achieve these goals. [123] On his official website Kaan Soyak (FIG. 32) is presented as a hero of the "International Fraternity organizations" of the New World Order, a.k.a. the *Illuminati*:

Presently working on Religious Minorities and inter-faith relations among different religious and institutions and promoting USA-Turkish-Kurdish economic relations and facilitating relations between Armenia and Turkey. Also involved in numerous NGO activities including The World Water Organization and the World Energy Forum (in partnership with the United Nations and the World Bank), along with International Fraternity organizations. [124]

There is no doubt that the leaders of The Rotary Club and the United Nations are corrupt businessmen and Intelligence crooks such as Balestrieri or Soyak. They are Satanists disguised as Theosophists such as Alice Bailey, and her many contemporaries, like Benjamin Creme, or even criminals like most of today's politicians. I would like to condemn all of them in bulk, and without appeal. A small group does exist, even in the United Nations, that strive to save lives. The problem is they are a small minority often pushed to terrible compromises. We should defeat certain hypocrisy and lack of ethics in public institutions which then can lead to abuse and misuse of humanitarian organizations, the so-called **NGOs,** that are often linked to *Intelligence operations,* on patrol for the puppeteers of corruption and power sitting in the various multinational corporations. They hide behind NGOs for their alleged humanitarian projects, so they can achieve a different goal, coordinated by the Illuminati elite for their imperialist interests. They belong to the same old families, that have done nothing, (*repeat nothing*), to help true integration and the ideals of peace and universal brotherhood that should guide the United Nations created by Freemasonry. Those who lead the U.N. at this historic moment should resign *en bloc* for their failure and corruption.

They should devote themselves to a spiritual rebirth, not to the creation of a New World Order that will inevitably lead to corruption worldwide and the poverty of too many against the wealth of a few. They should not use, for their spiritual rebirth, the Neo-Theosophical rubbish offered by various New age gurus. **Raffaello Gelli,** who is

123 https://wikispooks.com/wiki/Strategy_of_tension ‡ Archived 15th July 2015.
124 http://www.soyak.net ‡ Archived 15th July 2015.

son of the recently deceased Count Licio Gelli, at one point broke ties with his father and managed to obtain a seat at the U.N., representing an organization called "Humanitarian," which has their headquarters and post office box in Geneva, but is unknown to most people. How was the son of the late Licio Gelli, who his own father considered a crook, able to receive this official standing at the U.N., remains to this day a mystery.

The Italian Newspaper *Corriere della Sera*, in April 2001 wrote the following:

Raffaello Gelli. The eldest son of the founder of the P2 lodge, himself several times the subject of judicial investigations and recently indicted for helping his father to avoid arrest in 1998.

He is not really the best candidate for this institution, or maybe he is just in good company with the rest of the corruption present: "*Gelli Junior can count on a vantage point: nothing less than a U.N. seat, or rather, at the United Nations Economic and Social Council (ECOSOC), based in Geneva.*" [125] The U.N. should be the first tool in the global fight against corruption and crime, but the U.N. often spreads its corruption worldwide, and in all this, with great sadness, we find the usual Illuminati from the P2 Lodge (now P3?) rewarded for their work past and present. Pressure from the honest side of the Italian government eventually lead to the investigation that brought Balestrieri to justice, but of course that's not enough to stop people like him, protected by the USA and the U.N. The reflections of Benjamin Creme on the Messiah / Maitreya, are just empty words in today's world full of deception inside and outside the United Nations. (FIGS. 24-25) These pawns for the lucrative businesses that enrich the usual elite and occult manipulators, are despicable characters who continue to starve millions of people, that are innocent victims of opportunism and wickedness. We can include Ban Ki-moon, Secretary-General of the U.N. in this farse, that is so instrumental to the New World Order.

Ban Ki-moon strangely enough will not disclose his religious views as he considers it inappropriate to his position, however as I demonstrated earlier, the U.N. leaders believe in a New Age Neo-Theosophical mix, and that is why many suspect him to be tied to the late Rev. Sun Myung Moon, (1920-2012) who declared himself in 2004 the Messiah, and said his teachings helped Hitler and Stalin to be "*reborn as new persons.*" [126]

Crazy as it may seem, many U.S. politicians were present for the event and *The Washington Post* later wrote: "*Some Republicans who attended the event, including Rep. Roscoe G. Bartlett (Md.), said they did so mainly to salute the Washington Times, a conservative-leaning newspaper owned by Moon's organization. 'I had no idea what would happen' regarding Moon's coronation and speech, Bartlett said yesterday.*" [127]

Balestrieri, Zionism and Wahhabism

Remember, religious ideals are the typical deception of the criminals who dominate the world in this particular moment in history, without a hint of compassion or genuine sense of altruism. They move forward towards "New World Disorder," immersed in materialism and corruption, that can only generate chaos and destruction. Forget the words: **Peace and Security,** (FIG. 33) often used by the U.N.—that's only propaganda. Freemasons scattered around the world should fix the tips of their compasses in accordance with the Law of the Great Architect of the Universe, and when

125   http://archiviostorico.corriere.it/2001/aprile/24/figlio_Gelli_seggio_all_Onu_co_0_010424428.shtml ‡ Archived 15th July 2015.
126   http://www.washingtonpost.com/wp-dyn/articles/A61932-2004Jun22.html ‡ Archived 15th July 2015.
127   *Ibid.*

*FIG. 33 – Screenshot of the United Nations website using the words "**PEACE AND SECURITY**" makes us meditate on 1 Thessalonians 5:3: "Now when they are saying, 'There is peace and security,' then sudden destruction comes on them, like labor pains on a pregnant woman, and they will surely not escape."*

their work results in a non-Masonic and Satanic way of life, they should not be considered Freemasons by the International Masonic Community. Most of the time the kind of Freemason, like Giorgio Balestrieri, is awarded by the institutions some of the highest honors, while the author of this book, after waging an open war of information against these criminals in 2006, had to learn the hard way what it means to be on the right side, in a unfair world corrupt by minions of Satan.

In society, where the family concept is in a coma, and science rules supreme as the "New World Religion," these lords of bargain, the "elite," act with indifference. With a conference, a summit, and perhaps a ritual orgy, they prepare for the advent of the Antichrist. Their false Messiah is expected to arrive at the United Nations headquarters, just like Pope Francis did on the 28th of September 2015, to distribute lies and false miracles to the masses. This is a society where God is virtually a dead concept, if not for the brainwashed growing faction of mercenary-terrorists like ISIS/Daesh who are willingly pushing the global scenario towards the end of times.

Pamela Enders writes in ***Busines Insider UK*** on September 25th 2015:

ISIS bases much of its recruitment and expansion strategy around the idea that the end times are upon us. The extremist group pushes the idea that the apocalypse is nigh and that Islamic fighters will battle the "infidels" of the West in Dabiq, a town in Syria that ISIS now controls. ISIS (also known as the Islamic State) uses Islamic scripture and prophecies to bolster its assertion, but it conveniently ignores one particularly damning prophecy that could inherently challenge the legitimacy of its self-declared "caliphate"—the territory in Iraq and Syria it controls that is central to Islamic doomsday prophecies. Will McCants, director of the Project on U.S. Relations with the Islamic World at the Brookings Institution, mentions it in his new book, The ISIS Apocalypse. "There is one prophecy about the Antichrist that the Islamic State and its fans have studiously avoided, even though it is in a collection of prophecies they revere: The Antichrist will 'appear in the empty area between Sham

[Syria] and Iraq,'" McCants wrote. "That, of course, is precisely where the Islamic State is located." As McCants explained in his book, Jesus and the Antichrist do have a place in Islamic foretellings. "The Qur'an portrays Jesus as a messenger of God and his followers as those 'nearest in love to the believers' (5:82)," McCants wrote. "But the prophecies attributed to Muhammad outside the Qur'an foresee Jesus returning to fight alongside the Muslims against the infidels. As in the Bible, the appearance of Jesus heralds the Last Days. ..."He will lead the Muslims in a war against the Jews, who will fight on behalf of the Antichrist." [128]

This is the apocalyptic scenario of today, where Christian theory of the End of the World, based on Biblical accounts, believe that during the Apocalypse period, an Anti-Christ will appear in the world (in the Middle East somewhere near Israel), bringing with him the Armageddon or the end of the world. Is this Antichrist ISIS? Many Shia Muslims rightly say ISIS are the messengers of Satan, but of course Giorgio H. Balesteri-eri hates Shia Muslims, and is firmly on the side of ISIS and its deeply Wahhabist version of Islam. Wahhabism and Zionism may seem like unrelated entities on the surface, but these two ideologies are largely responsible for the situation in the Middle East today. "Zionism" is a complicated term to define, all the more so for the sheer amount of exaggeration and disinformation on the internet. Political Zionism is bound in serving the interests of the state of Israel, and religious Zionism, which refers to Jewish or Christian interests in the state of Israel in terms of fulfilling Biblical prophecy or "divine will." These two schools of Zionism could in some instances be entirely separate; people can be political Zionists without being religious Zionists or vice-versa (such as Christian organizations who are Zionist for the sake of fulfilling perceived Bible texts). It was Colonial Powers of the late nineteenth and early twentieth century, particularly in Great Britain, that actively pursued the Zionist agenda under the guidance of powerful and wealthy British Jews such as Lord Rothschild, resulting in the famous **Balfour Declaration**. Zionism and Wahhabism have both been demonstrably divisive destructive forces in the region (and beyond). Zionism has led to the unending plight and humiliation of the Palestinian people, as well as ensuring that the modern State of Israel is perceived in an entirely negative way, and is the least popular nation on earth. Wahhabism has inspired an immeasurable amount of extremist terrorist ideologies, indoctrination and the toxic polarization of societies. We can look at the influence of Wahhabism in the world at this stage in time and legitimately call it a cancer.

Given the prevalent view in conspiracy theory lore of the "Zionist conspiracy" behind the Balfour Declaration and so much of what has transpired since, is it possible that Wahhabism, which began to gain momentum at around the same time, was also something much more than it appeared to be, even at that time?

The Memoirs of Mr. Hempher, The British Spy to the Middle East (also known as *Confessions of a British Spy*) has long been regarded as a forged document. The document, purporting to be the account of an 18th century British agent named "Hempher," and his instrumental role in founding Wahhabism as part of a conspiracy to corrupt Islam, first appeared in 1888. It has been described as "an Anglophobic variation" on *The Protocols of the Elders of Zion*.

Was *Confessions of a British Spy* telling the truth? Was Wahhabism founded by outside agencies as a long-term plan to "corrupt Islam?" Is it just a coincidence that this is exactly what Wahhabism appears to have done over the course of a century—corrupting

128   http://uk.businessinsider.com/isis-makes-sure-to-avoid-one-apocalyptic-prophesy-about-the-antichrist-2015-9?r=US&IR=T ‡ Archived 15th July 2015.

Grande Oriente d'Italia
Palazzo Giustiniani

Collegio Circoscrizionale
dei Maestri Venerabili della Toscana

Forum
"Valori Universali"

XI Convegno della Massoneria della Toscana

Tavola rotonda sul tema:

I Valori Universali e la riforma dell'ONU

Sabato 12 febbraio 2005, ore 14,30 a Firenze
Salone dei Cinquecento
Palazzo Vecchio in Piazza della Signoria

FIG. 34 – Masonic Forum that took place on the 12th of February, 2005 on the subject of "Universal Values" and the reform of the U.N. led by the District Board of Worshipful Masters of Tuscany belonging to the Grand Orient of Italy of Palazzo Giustiniani.

the Islamic religion to the point where it is now widely regarded by many non-Muslims as a source of evil and ill in the world? Islam, let's remember, wasn't always regarded with the kind of stigma it now has, but rather the opposite. Islamic societies are historically perceived as being intellectually, and even scientifically enlightened at a time when Christianity in the West was characterised by inquisitions, torture, mass persecutions, execution pyres and utterly ridiculous doctrines and proclamations. Historical accounts tell of the brutality of Christian Crusaders and the comparative nobility of Salahuddin and the Muslim armies. The Islamic world had its "enlightenment" long before the Christian West, despite being a younger religion. At a time when Europeans were burning "witches," the classical Islamic cities of Damascus, Baghdad and Cairo were centers of learning and philosophy. [129]

Going back to Giorgio H.Balestrieri, a member of the infamous P2 lodge, working for years for the Israeli Mossad, who wished to recruit me in this sick Zionist reality to promote Wahhabism, because of my knowledge of Islam and my capacity to infiltrate them and determine their danger level. An offer that included an office for the *Ordo Illuminatorum Universalis* at the United Nations, which of course I refused. Now you know the main reason why I began my *Confessions* series.

Strangely enough, a couple of years later I met Freemason **Massimiliano Mion from the Grande Orient of Italy,** (FIG. 34) who became the national coordinator of my order in recent years before being exposed himself as a spy. He is an expert in the field of security and Intelligence, who pointed out that soon after our first meeting, he was scrutinized and put under surveillance by Balestrieri through his powerful espionage network. You see, Giorgio is obviously still scared about my revelations on him, and certainly will not forgive me for refusing his offer in 2006, and will never digest the fact I went public with my *Confessions.*

To an American investigative journalist who contacted Balestrieri about my first revelations about him back in the early months of 2007, he said *"I have put Zagami on my black list."*

In any case let's hope one day "Brother" Giorgio Balestrieri from the infamous P2 Lodge, will finally spill the beans on 9/11 and *repent* his sins! Regardless of all this the Knights Templars are in the UN today.

Peace and lies: the rainbow of Lucifer and the cross of Nero

The Rainbow Family of Living Light, also known as the Rainbow Family, is a community of people united by the values of nonviolence and egalitarianism. Since its beginnings in 1972, it has held annual meetings (called Rainbow Gatherings) in various places around the world, mainly in the summer months. The meetings usually last a month, following the lunar cycles, beginning with the new moon and ending with the next new moon. The Rainbow Family has no commercial purpose, and some argue that it is the largest non-organization of non-members in the world; there are no leaders. In fact, the *Rainbow Family* has a deeper meaning, and the inspiration of the values of Native Americans are similar. [130] Every religion or ideology has a leading group, and the New Age movement is no different.

FIG. 35 – 30th November 2002, the Templars of the SMOTJ and the OSMTH celebrate in Scotland the official recognition received by the United Nations as an International NGO. On this occasion, the Chevalier Paul Mc Gowan talked about the relationship between the Knights Templar and the United Nations.

Professor Enzo Pennetta wrote in 2011 that among them one of the most representative is the **Rainbow Tribe**. The origin of this choice is indicated in an ancient American Indian legend reported by Prof. Bartolomeo Dobroczynski, Professor of Psychology at the University of Krakow: *"When the Earth will begin to get sick, animals and plants to die and the water and the air to be poisoned, we will see a new tribe of people from all cultures that will return to its original beauty of nature ... will save the Earth in danger, taking the name of Rainbow Warriors."* The author of the above, noted the coincidence with the name of the Greenpeace ship which is called Rainbow Warrior. [131] In addition, Pennetta also quotes Professor Dobroczynski, who spoke to two scholars of the Seneca tribe of American Indians, Twyla Hurd and Nitsch Yehwehnode, who said their work, according to the Indian tradition, will be a **"turning point,"** a cosmic shock after which a new era will begin. It seems in fact, to have began after the ultra-advertised date of the 21st of December, 2012 where nothing apparent happened, but at the same time, things are changing faster and faster every day, and not always in a

130   https://it.wikipedia.org/wiki/Rainbow_Family ‡ Archived 15th July 2015.
131   Enzo Pennetta, Gianluca Marletta, *Ibid.*, p. 45.

positive direction. The hidden rulers whose desire is to control every aspect of our lives, are preparing for projects like the *Soul Catcher* Computer Chip, due out in **2025**. It is a computer chip implanted behind the eye that can record a person's every lifetime thought and sensation which is being developed by British scientists. [132]

In the meantime other experiments in global control continue, and in 2015 the Italian daily *La Stampa* reported in regards to the famous *Rainbow Pride Profile Application on Facebook*:

> *A wave of sincere enthusiasm and support for the right of homosexual couples to marry, or a clever social experiment, in which millions of people in good faith, are becoming mice for a laboratory experiment? When 26 million people seek means to color with a rainbow their Facebook profile photo, the question inevitably arises. Especially if we consider that it has been developed by engineers of the social network, and that the site has previously been criticized for the way it studied the emotional reactions of the users according to the type of post that was presented to them.* [133]

After the Paris attacks on Friday the 13th, 2015, Facebook introduced a French flag filter to superimpose users profile pictures, as a gesture of presumed unity over the terrorist attacks, but in reality part of yet another NSA experiment. And even though *Facebook* stated that they made the application with no ulterior motives, many disappointed people felt an unhealthy sense of global manipulation by the Social Network on the whole affair. Not surprisingly, *Facebook* is one of the tools used by the elite of the New World Order to monitor not only our activities (for economic purposes, commercial and military), but to shape our way of being and thinking. *So what really lies behind the symbol of the rainbow?* The answer is simple: the Illuminati New Age sects and **LUCIFER!** Just as in the Indian legend, and also in occult tradition, the rainbow is defined as great change, preceded by a period of rapid decline, at the limit of decay. The *Rainbow* has always been an important symbol for alchemists and their "Great Work," and it is proven by the presence of a rainbow in a well-known engraving by **Albrecht Dürer Melancholia**, 1514. It was created in the Renaissance era in which esoteric and magical ideals began to spread with the doctrines of the occultist and magician Heinrich Cornelius Agrippa von Nettesheim, who a little later would publish "Three Books of Occult Philosophy" (*De Occulta Philosophia libri III*), a work whose title is very reminiscent of "The Perennial Philosophy," a comparative study of mysticism by Aldous Huxley, which was basically that of Madame Blavatsky. Back to the aforementioned engraving by Albrecht Dürer, we find many symbolic elements, beginning with the angel frowning, reminiscent of the stage of *Nigredo*, or **blackness,** in the alchemical sense, meaning putrefaction. Melancholia, a term that literally means the mood defined as *"black,"* is astrologically linked to the planet Saturn, according to the scholar **Frances Yates**, and represents "the form of religion from which all others derive," a principle that we have seen govern the Theosophical doctrine.

In the background to frame the word *"Melancholia,"* a rainbow is clearly visible. Something interesting about the symbolism of the rainbow can also be found in Friedrich Nietzsche, author of "The Antichrist," which in his "Thus Spoke Zarathustra: A Book for All and None" (German: *Also sprach Zarathustra: Ein Buch für Alle und Keinen*, also translated as "Thus Spake Zarathustra"), in paragraph 9, states: *"We will join the creators, the harvesters, and the rejoicers: I will show them the rainbow and all the steps to the Superman."* In Nietzsche's thought, the rainbow retains its character as a sign tied to a

132   http://www.bibliotecapleyades.net/ciencia/secret_projects/project108.htm ‡ Archived 15th July 2015.
133   http://www.lastampa.it/2015/06/30/tecnologia/le-foto-colorate-su-facebook-per-il-matrimonio-gay-erano-un-esperimento-sulle-emozioni-fY0oPe09Si7ylPn49myMcN/pagina.html ‡ Archived 15th July 2015.

rise of the New Age, which opens in this case the "Superman," a concept based on the paradigm shift of the Conspiracy of the Age of Aquarius. [134] In more recent years there are various movements linked to the use of the rainbow in their symbolism. Thanks to the invitation of Democratic Sen. Gaylord Nelson, the event called **EC (*Earth Celebration*)** was launched in 1970, with the number of participants estimated at 20 million. [135] On the 26th of February 1971, the third Secretary-General of the United Nations; signed the proclamation which officially announced the participation of the United Nations at the annual celebration of Earth Day at the equinox in March, setting March 21st as the official date of the international event—later replaced by the date of the 22nd of April. [136] Earth Day has now become one of the world's most widespread rites, and in 2010, participating countries have reached 190, and the people involved were estimated at one billion. Taking into account that in 2009 there were 192 UN member states, it is understandable that the 190 nations who agreed to join Earth Day, brought this event to first place among the celebrations that sees it irremediably placed in between other religious celebrations such as Christmas and Ramadan. [137] But there is a dark side to the story of the *Earth Celebration,* as in many other events related to the years that mark *Lucifer Rising*, to put it in Kenneth Anger's terminology. An era of *"flowers, peace and love,"* but only in appearance, as taught by the Manson case, as it hides something dark and sinister. **Ira Einhorn (b. 1940)** was on stage on April 22, 1970, considered a guru of the hippie scene in Philadelphia, and has said for years that he is the co-founder of the event. [138]

Known to preach peace, and a great opponent of the Vietnam War, Ira Einhorn was actually a dark character, with a terrible secret that led to his arrest in France in 1997, and his extradition in 2002. Thirty-two years earlier in 1972, he met **Helen Maddux,** originally from Tyler, Texas, a beautiful cheerleader in high school, who graduated from Bryn Mawr College in Philadelphia. In 1973, his introduction to the new edition of *Beyond Telepathy*, was published which was a book written by **Andrija Puharich,** [139] who was a well-known researcher in the field of medicine and parapsychology. Einhorn introduced Uri Geller to the ideas of *Fundamental Fysiks Group*. He was friends with Jerry Rubin, Abbie Hoffman, the rock star **Peter Gabriel,** Allen Ginsberg, John Cage and Freeman Dyson. But there was dark turning point in 1977, when he beat to death his ex-girlfriend, Helen Maddux, and kept the body in a locked trunk in his apartment, in Powelton Village (Philadelphia), for 18 months before her body was discovered by the police and he was arrested. However, his connections in high places would help him flee and avoid arrest for nearly 20 years. The bail for Einhorn was reduced from $100,000 to $40,000 at the request of his lawyer **Arlen Specter (then Senator),** and with the pressure of influential people **(religious, university professors and executives of large companies testified that he was of good character and not violent).** Einhorn was able to get out of jail before the trial, paying 10% of the requested bail: 4,000 dollars. This deposit was paid, not by Einhorn, but by his friend Barbara Baerwald Bronfman, a rich woman of the elite from Montreal, daughter of banker Herman Frederick Baerwald, and first wife of Charles Bronfman of the Seagram group. They shared a common interest in the paranormal, and

134　　Enzo Pennetta, Gianluca Marletta,, *Ibid.*, p. 47.

135　　*Ibid.*, p. 46.

136　　https://it.wikipedia.org/wiki/Giornata_della_Terra Archived 15th July 2015.

137　　Enzo Pennetta, Gianluca Marletta, *Ibid.*

138　　See. http://www.nbcnews.com/id/42711922/ns/technology_and_science-science/t/earth-day-co-founder-killed-composted-girlfriend/#.Va5u-yrtmko ‡ Archived 15th July 2015.

139　　See. Andrija Puharich with an introduction by Ira Einhorn, Beyond Thelepaty. (New York: Anchor Press / Double Day, 1973).

she was one of many people who gave him financial support. [140] But why all this interest in the paranormal surrounding Ira Einhorn? This returns us to *Earth Day* and the secret elites hidden plans around what was apparently a genuine cultural "Revolution." We know now it was just controlled chaos from the usual Illuminati and the New World Order, but back then young people were more guillible and naive. Einhorn was a New Age guru who undoubtedly played a major role in the activities of ecological groups, anti-war, and anti-establishment countercultural movements, between the 1960s and 1970s. He was a pawn for Intelligence, and for this reason he managed to escape the law for so long. Despite being arrested on a terrible accusation, he mysteriously managed to obtain significant and substantial financial support for years to come, from people linked to the occult elite. Peter Gabriel, who was by the way a great friend of my grandmother Felicity Mason, seems to have encountered him during his fugitive years, even though Gabriel officially denied it. [141]

During the court procedure, the situation became even more absurd when he took to his own defense, stating Maddux was murdered by CIA agents, who tried to convict him for the murder because of his research on the Cold War and psychotronic weapons. [142] Certainly pacifism and ecology were only a front for something else, and I'm sure that Ira Einhorn, now known as the *Unicorn Killer,* is not the only character from those years to have a few skeletons in his closet, especially in the elite secret congregations devoted to human sacrifice. Returning to **The Rainbow**, we also have the so-called flag of peace, invented by the Italians in 1961, and used for the first time during the first edition of the March for Peace between Perugia-Assisi in 1961, that was created by Aldo Capitini founder of the Nonviolent Movement. This image was inspired by similar symbols used in demonstrations in the USA and the UK, where it was "sponsored," by the philosopher Bertrand Russell and Ezio Giunchiglia, [143] one of the "wise old men" of the P2 Illuminati. These are the following words by Bertrand Russell, in the opening of the Monte Carlo Lodge Manual entitled **"Universal Unity"**:

> *The love of power is a part of human nature, but power-philosophies are, in a certain precise sense, insane. The existence of the external world, both that of matter and of other human beings, is a datum, which may be humiliating to a certain kind of pride, but can only be denied by a madman. Men who allow their love of power to give them a distorted view of the world are to be found in every asylum: one man will think he is Governor of the Bank of England, another will think he is the King, and yet another will think he is God. Highly similar delusions, if expressed by educated men in obscure language, lead to professorships in philosophy; and if expressed by emotional men in eloquent language, lead to dictatorships. Certified lunatics are shut up because of the proneness to violence when their pretensions are questioned; the uncertified variety are given control of powerful armies, and can inflict death and disaster upon all sane men within their reach. [144]*

Tragic events worldwide in the last few years, executed by the New World Order and pseudo Islamic mercenaries, eager to serve the Antichrist, will only help the growing Police State and the militarization of the main cities required by the NWO to stabilize and effect further control in these times of great change.

140   See. https://it.wikipedia.org/wiki/Ira_Einhorn ‡ Archived 15th July 2015.
141   See http://articles.philly.com/1997-06-20/news/25527079_1_eugene-mallon-ira-einhorn-helen-holly-maddux ‡ Archived 15th July 2015.
142   http://www.salon.com/2002/08/ 14 / einhorn/ ‡ Archived 15th July 2015.
143   http://users.libero.it/rennes/ ‡ Archived 15th July 2015.
144   Bertrand Russell, *Power: A New Social Analysis* (1938) Chapter 16: Power philosophies.

The world is preparing for **the year 2020**, in which we could not only have a mini ice age, at least according to reliable scientific studies and sources, [145] but a global war and the hoarding of the most precious resources during this climate crisis, which could constitute a global food crisis.

The New World Order elite wish to impose dictatorship and in the meantime spread war and destruction on a global scale with ISIS, to achieve the reduction of the world population in the numbers originally prophesied in the *Georgia Guidestones*. At the end of all this hell on Earth, the rainbow flag will rise again as a symbol of peace, just as other symbols of this age of dissolution and hypocrisy. In 1978, the gay rainbow flag created by the artist **Gilbert Baker,** was used as a flag representing *Gay Pride* and waved for the first time in San Francisco in the march of *Gay Pride* on the 25th June 1978. The flag consisted of eight strips originally, Baker adding the pink color as a symbol of sexuality, but with modifications they were later reduced to seven bands, and then six. This is the specific meaning given by Baker to each of the eight colors of the original *Gay Pride* flag he designed:

> *pink—sexuality*
> *red—life*
> *orange—health*
> *yellow—sunlight*
> *green—nature*
> *turquoise—magic*
> *blue—serenity*
> *violet—spirit*

The fifth color, **turquoise**, as you can see is related to magic, though in its place at times is often found art. And we find that the first to speak of the "seven rays" concept in modern times was Alice Bailey, who claimed that they were behind New Age psychology.

This thesis was then exposed in depth in her "**Treatise on the Seven Rays,**" composed in five volumes. After November 27, 1978, with the murder of the openly gay Supervisor Harvey Milk, the request of the rainbow flag greatly increased in San Francisco. To meet the demands, the *Paramount Flag Company* began selling a version of the flag fabric consisting of seven stripes of red, orange, yellow, green, turquoise, blue, and purple. When he began to produce his own version of the flag, Baker eventually left out the pink strip because pink cloth was not easy to find commercially. [146] Interestingly, the *Paramount Flag Co.*, of San Francisco at that time, began to sell a remaining stock of leftover rainbow flags to an organization called the "**International Order of the Rainbow for Girls,**" [147] in their shop on Polk Street, which was located in a gay area. The association in question is coincidentally a paramasonic order for young girls (usually daughters of Freemasons who belong to it). The first initiation consisted of a class of 171 girls and was made on April 6, 1922, in the auditorium of the Temple of the *Ancient and Accepted Scottish Rite* in the United States. The original name was the "**Order of the Rainbow for Girls.**" [148] As explained by Professor Enzo Pennetta: "The rainbow therefore is a symbol of the passage of the New Age but, in the best tradition of esoteric symbols there

145   http://www.liberoquotidiano.it/news/scienze---tech/11809688/Lo-studio--tra-il-2020. html ‡ Archived 15th July 2015.

146   https://it.wikipedia.org/ wiki / Bandiera_arcobaleno ‡ Archived 15th July 2015.

147   https://www.gorainbow.org ‡ Archived 15th July 2015.

148   http://web.archive.org/web/20071225045501/http://www.wsrainbow.org/Sexson. htm ‡ Filed July 15, 2015.

are different interpretations of the rainbow. In this regard, **Kenneth Grant,** the great popularizer of the doctrine of Aleister Crowley, that is so closely related to the New Age phenomenon states: *The symbolism of the rainbow connected with the flood and flash of lights that shine during the performance of the Great Work are—each in there own way—manifestations of an identical stage of the Opera: that of corruption, decay, final dissolution."* [149] As you can see, even the "enlightened" Kenneth Grant from the O.T.O. has confirmed that this symbol is linked to *corruption, decay* and *final dissolution.* Obviously this is an alchemical and esoteric interpretation linked to the so-called "Great Work" of the Illuminati through the ages, but that does not mean the final result will not effect the outside world, when the rainbow symbol is used more and more as a public symbol in various contexts to reflect this "Great Work," they will be implemented by the Illuminati sects of the New Age and thrust upon us. The lawyer and Christian author **Constance Cumbey (b. 1944),** was the first to offer a strong criticism of the New Age phenomena—although in strictly Christian terms—in her book, *The Hidden Dangers of the Rainbow: The New Age Movement and Our Coming Age of Barbarism,* released in 1983, which seems rather prophetic when Bonesmen John Forbes Kerry speaks about a war against barbarism in November, 2015, referring to ISIS/Daesh.

There are passages specifically dedicated to Lucifer and the rainbow inside this book that will provide the missing links to understand even better how Lucifer is the unknown instructor, and the long-awaited prophet of the New Age is the Antichrist. Cumbey writes:

Although the rainbow seems to be only a colored arc of light refracted through rain-drops, to both Christians and New Agers it has a deep meaning. According to the Bible, the rainbow is symbolic of God's everlasting covenant that he would never again destroy the Earth by a flood. However, the New Age Movement uses rainbows to signify their building of the Rainbow Bridge (antahkarana) between man and Lucifer who, they say, is the over-soul. New Agers place small rainbow decals on their automobiles and book stores as a signal to others in the Movement. Some people, of course, use the rainbow as a decoration, unaware of the growing popular acceptance of its occult meaning and the hidden dangers. [150]

The New Age Movement uses rainbows (the everlasting covenant pursuant to Genesis 9:15-17) to signal their building of the Rainbow Bridge (antahkarana) which is a bridge between the personality (man) and the soul (Lucifer). [151]

The Rainbow (also called the Antahkaranaor Rain-bow Bridge). This is used as a hypnotic device. They also call it an "International Sign of Peace." They claim they are building a rainbow bridge between the personality (you) and the over-soul or Great Universal Mind (literally Sanat Kumara, i.e., Lucifer!). See Isaiah 24:5 which states one reason the Lord is destroying the earth in the latter days is for breaking the everlasting covenant. The rainbow is the sign of the everlasting covenant according to Genesis, chapter nine. [152]

The year after the first publication of this book, the *National Rainbow Coalition* was created, a political organization founded by the false champion of civil rights Jesse Jackson is another puppet of the system, who in 1996 joined the operation PUSH coalition to become **Rainbow/Push.** After the rainbow symbol, what is the symbol of peace

149   Enzo Pennetta, Gianluca Marletta, *Ibid.,* p. 46.
150   Constance Cumbey, Hidden Dangers Of The Rainbow, (Shreveport, LA, Huntington House, 1983), p. 2.
151   *Ibid.,* p. 77.
152   *Ibid.,* pp. 261-262.

par excellence used here in the USA? In 1958, after a period of time that lasted from the Middle Ages, during a protest march against nuclear weapons, this symbol was "brought back to life," and then "re-introduced" mistakenly and falsely, as a symbol of peace. [153]

It is the symbol created by the British artist and designer **Gerald Holtom,** for the Campaign for Nuclear Disarmament, which then went on to become in the following decades the quintessential symbol of the hippie culture and the anti-military movement since the sixties. It's now used in peace flags of the United States, where it is positioned as an alternative to the stars along with the famous red and white strips, in various peace and environmentalist movements. After the Paris attacks of November, 2015 Jean Jullien, a French graphic designer living in London, created a drawing entitled "Peace for Paris" using the iconic Eiffel Tower in the form of this presumed peace sign.

Wikipedia writes on this symbol: *"The symbol is a combination of the semaphore signals for the letters 'N' and 'D,' standing for 'nuclear disarmament.' In semaphore the letter 'N' is formed by a person holding two flags in an inverted 'V,' and the letter 'D' is formed by holding one flag pointed straight up and the other pointed straight down. Superimposing these two signs forms the shape of the centre of the peace symbol."* Holtom Holtom later wrote to Hugh Brock, editor of *Peace News,* explaining the genesis of his idea: *"I was in despair. Deep despair. I drew myself: the representative of an individual in despair, with hands palm outstretched outwards and downwards in the manner of Goya's peasant before the firing squad. I formalised the drawing into a line and put a circle round it."*

Ken Kolsbun, a correspondent of Holtom's, says that the designer came to regret the symbolism of despair, as he felt that peace was something to be celebrated and wanted the symbol to be inverted. Eric Austen is said to have "discovered that the gesture of despair motif had long been associated with *the death of man*, and the circle with *the unborn child*." [154] A Symbol of the transmigration of souls, this ancient Anglo-Saxon rune is actually composed of the "sign of the great bustard," or the impression left by this big bird typical of Central Europe, enclosed in a circle it symbolizes eternity. It is also said to mean progress and peace. [155] So the great bustard imprint left in the sand from the paw of a great bustard is an ancient symbol of Anglo-Saxon origin, and is then passed on to us through the para-Masonic Illuminati sects like the O.T.O. and the Golden Dawn as means of emancipation from God, to reach in their eyes absolute moral freedom, clearing away all the debris that Christianity may have accumulated in the old world.

The Bustard has an obvious phallic allusion and that is why it appeared frequently in 1968 as an ulterior incitement to full sexual freedom, as the great bustard symbolizes the absolute emancipation from God for the dark side of the Illuminati. There is even more hidden in the dark symbolism of the peace sign. In the past it was known as the **"cross of Nero,"** but also as "witches foot," that is in short, a symbol of Satan, which takes its name from one of the worst killers of Christians during the early years of Christianity, the Emperor Nero. [156]

Many people, including many Christians, do not realize the origins of this symbol or why it has become a symbol of peace. An inverted cross, the anchor of the cross enclosed in a circle, is the vision of Nero, who believed it would be possible to bring peace to the world without Christianity, and for this, under his rule, thousands of Christians were

153   See. Elena Testi, Satanismo in Umbria, Orvieto,Terni, IT: Intermedia Publishing 2012), p. 156..
154   en.wikipedia.org/wiki/Peace_symbols ‡ Archived 15th July 2015.
155   Ephipanius, *Ibid.*, pdf, 2008 edition, p. 30.
156   See http://giornalistamichelupmann.blogspot.it/2011/08/il-portone-inquisito-il-portone-di.html ‡ Archived 18 July 2015.

martyred. [157] Nero thought, in his diabolical madness, that there would be a peaceful world without Christ and Christianity, and even more crazy, people use it today as a symbol of peace, this is especially when radical Islam is persecuting Christians for the first time in centuries.

This deception was evident once more in the case of the Church of Satan founder Anton LaVey, who used this symbol as a background for his altar. Lucifer, "the rainbow," Satan, and "the cross of Nero," from the emperor who was, among other things, listed as the first Anti-Christ.

157   See. Tonino Cantelmi, Cristina Cacace, *Il libro nero del satanismo. Abusi, rituali e crimini* (The Black Book of Satanism. Ritual Abuse and Crime), (Milan: Edizioni San Paolo, 2007), p. 63.

Chapter V

The Prophetic Aura of the Illuminati and the New World Order

9/11: the red pill

The ancient *Zohar: The Book of Splendor*, is studied by Illuminati sects, and Rosicrucians in particular, as one of their main occult guides. We find not only the teachings of a spiritual nature related to Kabbalah, which is considered one of their main sources of inspiration, and their most important manual, but it also contains teachings of a prophetic nature. There are statements that include dates and specifics that demonstrate that we have reached a stage in evolution known as **"the End of Days,"** which was carefully prepared by New World Order elitists, for the coming of the Messiah. In providing dates and descriptions of the events of this messianic period, the *Zohar* has predicted with incredible precision, some of the dramatic events of recent years. We learn in the teachings of the Zohar, that one day God will rebuild Jerusalem. Anyone who has visited the holy city can see that for decades they have been expanding every corner of the city. Emphasis should be put on the fact, that unlike many other major cities around the world, for almost two thousand years Jerusalem was a small provincial town, poor and derelict. Until the beginning of this century it was still considered dangerous to dwell outside the perimeter of the old walls, because of possible attacks by raiders and bandits. Only with the return of Jewish Zionists, and especially after Israel's independence in 1948, did the city begin to truly expand.

We find in the Jerusalem of today, new buildings and neighborhoods popping up everywhere across the city. It's written in the *Zohar*: *it will show a certain fixed star sending lightning with seventy flashes and seventy sparks, in the middle of the firmament, for seventy days.* Concerning the number 70, which is the value of the letter *Ain*, that governs the sign of **Capricorn**, and is a clear sign of political and economic power that seeks to dominate all others: *it will appear in the sixth day of the week, on the 25th day of the sixth month.* The shocking attacks in New York and Washington on 9/11/2001, occurred in the month of *Ellul*, the sixth month of the Jewish calendar, on the 23rd day. However, The *Zohar* speaks specifically of the 25th day of *Ellul*, but it should be noted that in this case the calculation of the current Jewish calendar is not exactly the same as two thousand years ago, and is considered when making calculations. Two days in a year are about 0.56%, or less then one percent.[1] **Elijah Ben Shlomo Zalman** (1720-1797) known as "**The Genius of Vilna**," is considered one of the most competent rabbis in recent centuries, and stated that the text of the *Zohar,* that described the destruction of three buildings in "Rome" on the 25th day of Ellul was "wrong for two" days. The *Zohar* was then corrected to the more accurate version from the *Sifra di-Tsni'uta,* where it appears in the 23rd day of Elul, which calculates to September 11th.[2] New York is the business capital of the American empire, and Washington is the seat of military power. The 9-11 attacks took place on a Tuesday, the day of **Mars, the god of war,** which is followed by the Illuminati elite devoted to the dark side. As if that was not enough, the prologue of the *Zohar* tells us the real name of the negative force that will punish the world. This negative force is represented through the metaphor of a dog as interpreted by known contemporary Kabbalist **Yehuda Berg**: "*And since the other party saw this, took courage and sent a dog to eat the offerings. And what's the name of that dog? 'B'ladan' is his name ... and it is not a human being.*"[3] B'ladan=Bin Laden, the elusive villian of the 9/11 attacks on the Twin Towers, which launched the first decade of the end-times scenario. Some criticize this interpretation, in particular, Professor James A. Beverley in his book, *Illustrated Guide to Religions.*[4] However, the presence of Bin Laden in the international arena officially ends with his alleged murder / human sacrifice that took place on May 1st, 2001, which is the anniversary of the founding of the Illuminati. The president of the United States, Barak Obama, announced his death on the very day that, according to occult tradition, there is a blood sacrifice to appease the gods. May 1st, which not coincidentally is the date for the mysterious and improbable "suicide" of Adolf Hitler, another Illuminati creation, who went on living a comfortable life afterward. This may very well be, the same destiny for Osama Bin Laden.

Some say Osama Bin Laden died ten years earlier in 2001, but the knowledge of his death would have ruined the whole legacy built around him, which was created by the **Military Industrial Complex** of the NWO. It should be noted, that the period beginning on April 26th until April 30th represents in a series of ceremonies, the union of higher beings in honor of the recurring celebration of *Beltaine* ("officially" a purely British and Irish pagan festival), but in reality the perfect time for an Illuminati ritual with an epilogue of blood. The Bavarian Illuminati was even founded on the first day after the celebrations, May 1, 1776, a date which also became *Labor Day*, so dear to socialists, anarchists; communists, and all creations of the Illuminati sects in various Masonic and para-Masonic emanations. The Illuminati elite interpreted the demolition of the Twin Towers as the symbolic destruction of Jachin and Boaz,[5] the two columns of the Temple of Jerusalem which are required to further excel in the Great Masonic Work. A gesture with an initiatic value, at least from their elitist point of view, made in their eyes for the good of humanity, and for the *Glory of the Great Architect of the Universe.* This seems to be the sad truth, but of course regular Masons will dissent on this point. Interestingly enough, in old Jewish tradition, other bloody sacrifices are also spoken about, in the period just before *Beltaine.* Since ancient times, two days are concecrated to the God

1   See http://www.cabala.org/articoli/profezie_zohar.shtml and http://magog.web-site.co.il/gog/e_terror.shtml ‡ Archived 18th July 2015.

2   See. http://www.bibleprobe.com/smokeface.htm ‡ Archived 18th July, 2015.

3   See. Yehuda Berg, The Power of Kabbalah, p. 208.

4   See. James A. Beverley, *Illustrated Guide to Religions.* (Nashville, TN: Thomas Nelson, 2009)

5   http://www.freemasons-freemasonry.com/larsonwilliam.html6 ‡ Archived 18th July, 2015.

Moloch, the 19th and 20th of April. Moloch is a bloodthirsty god that some say requires the sacrifice of children. Moloch is quoted in "The Paradise Lost" by John Milton, who is described as one of the most powerful followers of Satan:

> *First, Moloch, horrid King, besmeared with blood*
> *Of human sacrifice, and parents' tears;*
> *Though, for the noise of drums and timbrels loud,*
> *Their children's cries unheard that passed through fire*
> *To his grim idol. Him the Ammonite*
> *Worshiped in Rabba and her watery plain,*
> *In Argob and in Basan, to the stream*
> *Of utmost Arnon. Nor content with such*
> *Audacious neighbourhood, the wisest heart*
> *Of Solomon he led by fraud to build*
> *His temple right against the temple of God*
> *On that opprobrious hill, and made his grove*
> *The pleasant valley of Hinnom, Tophet thence*
> *And black Gehenna called, the type of Hell.*
> Paradise Lost, i. 391-405

According to Milton it was Moloch who convinced King Solomon to build "the temple in front of the temple of God," and for this reason he is often cited as *The Corruptor.* [6]

My friend Alex Jones of InfoWars was able to film the ceremony called *Cremation of Care* at the Bohemian Grove in Northern California. His twin documentaries, *Dark Secrets: Inside Bohemian Grove* and *Secret Rulers of the World,* argue that the ceremony is rich in ancient *Luciferian, Canaanite, and Babylonian* references, and the owl statue represents the god Moloch. [7]

The cult of Moloch was introduced in Jerusalem by King Solomon, in whose honor children were slain in the valley of Tophet: *Also, he defiled Topheth, which is in the steep valley of the son of Hinnom, so that no one would consecrate his son or his daughter, through fire, to Moloch*. II Kings 23, 10-Catholic Version. It is a valley carved by the river Hinnom on the south side of Mount Zion, which Jesus later associated with fire, and Catholics with hell. [8] Exodus XXII, 28-29, (cited from *http://www.catholic.org/*) states clearly:

> *28 Do not be slow about making offerings from your abundance and your surplus. You will give me the first-born of your children;*
>
> *29 You will do the same with your flocks and herds. For the first seven days the first-born will stay with its mother; on the eighth day you will give it to me.*

The Bible often mentions human sacrifice, in Joshua VI, 26.

It is said that Joshua took an oath:

> *26 At that time Joshua made them take this oath before Yahweh: Accursed before Yahweh be the man who rises up and rebuilds this city (Jericho)! On his first-born will he lay its foundations, on his youngest son set up its gates!*

Joshua commanded a human sacrifice following the defeat that was suffered by the

6   https://it.wikipedia.org/wiki/Moloch_(divinità) ‡ Archived 18th July, 2015.
7   See. https://it.wikipedia.org/wiki/Bohemian_Grove ‡ Archived 18th July, 2015.
8   See. https://it.wikipedia.org/wiki/Geenna ‡ Archived 18th July, 2015.

Israelis, who fought with the people of the city of Ai. The sacrificial victim chosen was Achan, who was accused of the defeat, and was then stoned to death. This sacrifice gave new life to the Israelites who, during a new battle, defeated the army of Ai. [9]

In the long course of history, a number of important events have taken place on the 19th and 20th of April, where every move is calculated by the *Invisible Masters* using the science of numerology, and the art of **"Synchronicity."** Is it a coincidence, as in the recent Paris attacks that occured on another infamous date, Friday the 13th, or is there something more to it?

There are dates of important events in history that can confirm that there are no co-incidences :

The American War of Independence (19 April 1775)
The birth of Hitler (April 20, 1889)
The election of Pope Ratzinger (19 April 2005)
The tragedy of Waco, Texas (April 19, 1993)
The Oklahoma bombing (April 19, 1995)
The massacre at Columbine High School (20 April 1999).

Cosmic "Synchronicity" is required by the **Secret Chiefs** of Freemasonry and the Il-luminati, who need a continuous revitalization of their Egregore for their power groups. They have created for this reason, the Meditation Room at the United Nations, where the Board of the New World Order gathers in secret complicity. In this place, not only reli-gious oriented leaders, but many politicians, industrialists, including the Bush family, the Clinton's and the Rockefeller's, gather. We could say the Rockefellers are masters of cere-mony, as the U.N. building was built on the land donated in 1946 by **John D.Rockefeller Jr.** [10] Spiritual leaders or pseudo ones, like the Dalai Lama, and the different Popes, have all been guested in this building and have operated with the Egregore in question. In the **Meditation Room of the UN**, the egregore of the NWO is activated by Illuminati sects and the secret symbolism is only present *for those with eyes to see.* If an amulet or talisman can prevent an attack from evil energy, then it can be said that the location or temple is a "Sacred" place that can **manifest the entity in our dimension.** When a Egregore has existed for a long time, it acquires a relatively independent life, and may no longer wish to obey the impulses that the Master of the group sends through the input of rituals. The originally enslaved Egregore can become a Master, which explains the rise of deviated movements from their primary purpose assigned, like most of the movements of the New World Order, and in particular, Neo-theosophical or pseudo-Illuminati ones related to the United Nations. **Elementary Spirits** have approximately the same form of "life" as an Egregore, and are conjured by the occultist or occult groups. On the subject of *Elementals* there is an extensive bibliography, and the procedures to manifest them is similar to the ones facilitated for the Egregore.

The resins used for religious or Masonic rituals, like Frankincense and myrrh, repre-sent the "blood" of the plants used. Such substances help direct mental currents during a Mass or a ritual, and the different Illuminati sects, are part of a global ritual supervised by our leaders to preserve their Egregore, the one favored by the blood thirsty elite sitting on top of the Pyramid of power.

9   See. "Human Sacrifices: rites, ceremonies and traditions of past and present" http://www.latelanera.com/mis-teriefolclore/misteriefolclore.asp?id=284 ‡ Archived 18th July, 2015.
10   See.http://americanprofile.com/articles/john-d-rockefeller-jr-donated-land-for-united-nations-headquarters/ ‡ Archived 18th July, 2015.

Children are sacrificed during rituals of witchcraft to receive benefits from the spirits, and men are slaughtered to appease the wrath of the gods or to ingratiate them. In the eyes of modern man, such barbaric customs may seem an unacceptable legacy of the past, and it may be difficult to imagine that respected individuls in positions of power and responsibility, can be part of this macabre horror that reigns supreme among the elite.

Since ancient times man has sacrificed his fellow man and, still, these rituals and beliefs are present in several contemporary cultures: for example, in most of the South American cultures (strongly influenced by the ancient rites of **Incan, Mayan and Aztec**), or in certain African tribes. [11] The life of an evil Egregore is ensured by these terrible actions, however the members of a pure Lodge, with their discipline, their spiritual union, their strict observance of Rites of protection and the emanation of love as a spiritual force, can counteract this evil. I linger on the subject of the occult to help you understand where and how such energies are generated, and if possible to help the more diligent reader to block this negativity from their lives and reach a new *awareness*.

The process of the "Magic Ritual" or "Theurgy," are the most powerful means of enforcement used by the network of occultists of the New World Order. We must learn to identify these negative activites in order to fight them, and if possible create our own Egregore in order to counteract the damage that is being inflicted on us.

The researcher Gian Guido Benucci summarizes the Egregoric principle as follows:

• *The psychic Egregore creatures are created by artificial human thought by a unanimity of purpose, they are vitalized and kept alive by means of Rites and are more powerful, the more powerful are the impulses coming from its leaders.*

• *They can gain a certain independence and also be free from any work suggestion when they acquire the maximum potential and their leaders do not have the strength to control them any longer.*

• *They decline or dissolve when they no longer have their power through the rites and sacrifices.*

• *They are made in the image of a Total Man, a Cosmic Man (principle of plurality in unity) by a "archetype" (an eternal idea of the Platonic system), which is the spirit, the nous, the pneuma (Divine Spirit World).*

• *These artificial creatures have for the soul, the collective soul of their people, they receive energy pulses (prayers, slogans, uniforms, mantras, litanies) and are able to receive them through a kind of psychic osmosis.*

• *They have an "astral body," a sum, made up of the symbols (pentagrams for example) from images (icons, idols, teraphim, statues etc.,) And the intuitive soul and passion of their faithful who is the hypostasis (union spirit-matter) and the vehicle.* [12]

Men with common goals form an Egregore, and when energy is united to form a spiritual Egregore; it can be positive; but also negative and even malignant. This leads us to **counter-initiation, a form of reverse initiation, towards the dark side.** Those who belong to an institution like the United Nations, or an initiatory order as the many Illuminati sects or Freemasonry's irregular or deviant branches involved with the occult elite, are all part of a common Egregore psychically integrated through an initiation ritual that becomes their common denominator, where the single individual becomes a cell of a much larger structure. This body of initiates, or in the case of the UN, the counter-initiated, are like *robots* of the New World Order, and soldiers of Satan's Legion.

When a spiritual Egregore is demonic and evil, the entire group attached to it, in turn, become demonic and wicked. Knowing the meaning of the word "Egregore" and understanding this concept is certainly crucial for those who belong to initiatory orders, but also for those in the outside world. It helps to understand the mistakes that lead to evil being unleashed on the world, and those related to false public perception of the elite; and its institutions. Eliphas Levi invented the term "Occult." He was a Freemason and Rosicrucian who also introduced the concept of Egregore in modern esotericism; to define any phenomenon of voluntarily oriented collective psyche. In this sense the Egregore is generated by the group *mind*, when consciously united in the pursuit of a common goal. [13] Eliphas Levi also identified the Egregore with the ancient tradition concerning the fathers of the Nephilim. Eliphas Levi, in **"The Great Arcanum"** of 1868, described them as *"terrible beings, that will crush us without pity, because they are unaware of our existence."* [14]

Jean Louis Bernard argues that the term Egregore comes from the sacred books of the Horites of Cilicia, a region in Asia Minor, which then was translated to Aramaic, to Hebrew and Greek. The Egregore corresponds to the guardian angels of the cardinal points in the **Book of Enoch,** those who watch "the throne of divine glory," who married the daughters of Seth (See. Genesis, VI). The meaning of the word is precisely *"the one who watches"* with a probable Egyptian origin from "gergu" or "re-ger" = quiet, with reference *"to the invisible and silent regents of humanity, on the sacred mountain."* [15]

The goal of the United Nations should be for the good of humanity, but unfortunately, if the individuals involved, either knowingly or unknowingly, do not follow the rules of conduct, projection, and use the spiritual power necessary to manifest a pure and good Egregore for the world, we are faced with a reality that we could rename *"The United Nations of Evil."* Some say this is what happens when you make Saudi Arabia a leader of the UN human rights council ... but that's another story.

How do you fight an evil Egregore, you may ask? Since the Egregore is formed when a group of people is combined with the exclusive intent and common purpose of creating it, unless the desire to manifest it to a thought form is very strong, the Egregore will dissipate quickly. One of the only ways to defeat an evil Egregore, is to infiltrate the group that created it, and to block their evil intentions. That is, of course, if the Egregore does not *kill* you first during such a delicate operation!

JRR Tolkien described how the hidden force that drives magic is "the thirst for power." The black magician, or sorcerer, or witches, want to gain power over others, and to do so they do not hesitate to seek agreements with the forces of evil and this is what the Illuminati sects are practicing. As Tolkien points out, no magic, in itself, is good or bad, black or white: it is the objective you want to achieve that colors the magic of the ritual. The color "black" is "bad" magic because it manifests dark energy, in contrast to "white" that is traditionally tied to light. According to Tolkien, magic was originally a **positive manifestation,** [16] however the lust for power can dominate those who practice magical rituals, which can easily corrupt the soul. If the magician cannot resist, he will be seduced by evil and will use the powers acquired for evil purposes.

13   http://www.fuocosacro.com/pagine/articoli/eggregore.htm ‡ Archived 19th July, 2015.
14   See. Eliphas Levi, *Il Grande Arcano*, 1898, (Rome,IT: Atanor trad.it,, reissue 1992), pp. 127-130, 133, 136.
15   See. Jean Louis Bernard, *Les archives de l'insolite,* (Paris, FR: Edition du dauphin, 1971), p. 140.
16   See. http://www.latelanera.com/misteriefolclore/misteriefolclore.asp? Id = 225 ‡ Archived 19th July, 2015.

The "*Wizards of the New World Order*" claim to be linked to so-called spirituality and "white magic." Alice Bailey, who was their icon, described a positive form of "white magic" in numerous writings, but eventually was lead to the dark side with her evil intentions. At times one would expect a more coherent work from people who consider themselves the "enlightened" of society. In *Treatise on Cosmic Fire,* Bailey writes:

*The student must recollect at this juncture the **distinction that is made between the work of the black and the white magician.** It might be helpful here before proceeding further to look at these distinctions as far as they concern the matter in hand:*

First. The white Brother deals with positive electrical energy. The dark Brother deals with the negative electrical energy.

Second. The white Brother occupies himself with the soul of things. The black Magician centres his attention upon the form.

Third. The white Magician develops the inherent energy of the sphere concerned (whether human, animal, vegetable or mineral) and produces results through the self-induced activities of the central life, subhuman, human or super-human. The black Magician attains results through the agency of force external to the sphere involved, and produces transmutation through the agency of resolvents (if so I might term it) or through the method of the reduction of the form, rather than through radiation, as does the white Magician. These differences of method need to be carefully considered and their reaction visualized in connection with different elements, atoms, and forms. [17]

Bailey discusses the nature of the white magician, in which she considers herself an advocate, in *The Treaty of White Magic*:

I would like in this first consideration of our subject to enumerate briefly the facts given in the commentary so as to demonstrate to the aspirant how much is given him for his consideration and helping if he knows how to read and ponder upon that which he reads. The brief exegesis of Rule I give the following statements:

1. The white magician is one who is in touch with his soul.

2. He is receptive to and aware of the purpose and the plan of his soul.

3. He is capable of receiving impressions from the realm of spirit and of registering them in his physical brain.

4. It is stated also that white magic—

a. Works from above downwards.

b. Is the result of solar vibration, and therefore of egoic energy.

c. Is not an effect of the vibration of the form side of life, being divorced from emotion and mental impulse.

5. The downflow of energy from the soul is the result of

a. Constant internal re-collectedness.

b. Concentrated one-pointed communication by the soul with the mind and the brain.

c. Steady meditation upon the plan of evolution.

6. The soul is, therefore, in deep meditation during the whole cycle of physical incarnation, which is all that concerns the student here.

17   Alice A. Bailey, *A Treatise on Cosmic Fire,* 1951, (Vitinia di Roma, RM, IT: Casa Editrice NUOVA ERA 1999), p. 261.

7. This meditation is rhythmic and cyclic in nature as is all else in the cosmos. The soul breathes and its form lives thereby.

8. When the communication between the soul and its instrument is conscious and steady, the man becomes a white magician.

9. Therefore workers in white magic are invariably, and through the very nature of things, advanced human beings, for it takes many cycles of lives to train a magician.

10. The soul dominates its form through the medium of the sutratma or life thread, and (through it) vitalizes its triple instrument (mental, emotional and physical) and thus sets up a communication with the brain. Through the brain, consciously controlled, the man is galvanized into intelligent activity on the physical plane. [18]

Baily's words demonstrate a clear hypocrisy underlying the New Age concept, also typical of the so-called "White Magicians" present in the U.N., who do not care about the consequences of their actions. This attitude has transformed them into dangerous black magicians. Our intense thoughts or emotions are grouped with others to create a thought form, the aforementioned Egregore. What must be clarified further at this point, is that the motivation of our thoughts will determine whether these actions will create a positive or negative *karma*. Your thoughts manifest into reality, and we are responsible for everything we transmit on various levels. It can be understood by the axiom: **"Energy follows thought." Only by changing our thoughts, entering principles and ethical values, we can rise out of negative thought forms and create positive change...** The harmony in our lives depends on the mastery of our thoughts, because it is our thoughts that manifest our destiny. [19]

The force of our thoughts has enormous power. It is now time to positively change destiny beginning with an interior renovation of the mystery schools and lodges linked to the network of the Illuminati. I began to meditate on this impossible task, after 9/11, when I witnessed the fulfillment of an evil plan that for months had been announced in different ways in different environments close to the Illuminati and Occult Masonry as I mentioned in Volume I. In this Orwellian system, ethics and morals are an option, and not a necessity or a way of life, even for those institutions like Freemasonry, that should defend the ethics and morals of our society. We are living in a system of compromise created and guided by a perverse and self-righteous Illuminati elite, who love only themselves and their Jesuit and Zionist circles, and not *humanity*. For me, 9/11 was in essence, like taking the **Red Pill,** which led to a series of events that have changed my life forever.

The plot for the creation of the so-called "End-Times"

The **Kabbalah** is an esoteric system where we find the secrets of metaphysics which are hidden by Jewish Rabbis, who learn and teach about the mystical and spiritual wisdom contained in the Hebrew Bible. Here we find the prophetic view followed by the Israeli Intelligence, who are heavily influenced by Jewish mysticism, although officially they are not involved in "spirituality." The tragedies of 9/11 were carefully executed, and the elite warned only a privileged few, including many Jews, but not 4,000, as wrongly stated by the Lebanese *Manar* TV linked to Hezbollah, [20] who are enemies of Israel, and are known to exaggerate from time to time in their propaganda

18   Alice A. Bailey, A Treatise on White Magic, 1951, (Vitinia di Roma, RM, IT:Casa Editrice NUOVA ERA 1993), pp. 33-34.
19   ttp://www.italiadonna.it/spiritualita/pax044.htm ‡ Archived 19th July, 2015.
20   http://www.focusonisrael.org/2011/09/09/11-settembre-torri-gemelle-antisemitismo/ ‡ Archived 19th July, 2015.

efforts. The collapse saw in fact 110 Israelis dead and hundreds more American Jews injured.[21] The Jewish leaders could not warn their people in plain language of their prior knowledge of the attacks. Instead, they filtered the information as a prophetic message, to avoid suspicion. They simply recommended to their flock not to go to work that day in New York. In fact, a select few were lucky enough to be warned of the events via the instant messaging service Odigo, but then again they were not only Jews or Israelis, but also included a minority of privileged elitists.

And if you are not yet ready to believe that the events of 9/11 were the fruits of a conspiracy instigated by the New World Order using various factions, let us remember the words of a credible source on the subject, the **former Italian President Francesco Cossiga (1928-2010)**, who was a *Grand Cross of Honour and Devotion of the Sovereign Military Order of Malta* (also known by the acronym S.M.O.M.), and also was one of the leaders of the notorious secret operation called **GLADIO**.[22]

Cossiga spoke of 9/11 in the press three years before his death in November 2007, in the Italian newspaper *Corriere della Sera* stating the following: *"All democratic circles of America and Europe ... know well that the disastrous attack was planned and built by the American CIA and the Mossad with the help of the Zionist world to impeach the Arab countries and to induce the Western powers to intervene in Iraq and Afghanistan."*[23] Of course he failed to mention the Catholic faction, but certainly for some, this statement would seem at first glance the statements of a conspiracy theorist. I would like to again stress, that such claims were made by the former president of Italy, a leading country of NATO. Francesco Cossiga was tied to the previously mentioned Giorgio Hugo Balestrieri, and also to the P2, but questioned his past alliances, in that final chapter in his life

Cossiga was an unwilling participant of the murder of Italian **Prime Minister Aldo Moro (1916-1978)**; organized by Henry Kissinger at the Bohemian Grove and orchestrated by the Intelligence expert **Steve Pieczenik**, while Cossiga was interior minister in Italy. The Italian investigative journalist Gianni Lannes (b. 1965) wrote the following:

> *Pieczenik, assistant secretary of state under Henry Kissinger, a psychiatrist, and a specialist in "crisis management" and terrorist expert, revealed the hidden truth of this event in a book / interview published in 2008, entitled* **We killed Aldo Moro.**
> **After thirty years a protagonist comes out of the shadows,**[24] *Pieczenik rubbed shoulders with* **Francesco Cossiga,** *in the crucial part of the 55 day affair. It was "the American expert of the U.S. State Department who directed and managed state action with the Italian Red Brigades. His presence at the Italian Interior Ministry has been interpreted by many, in recent years, as a kind of "controller" exercized on a country (Italy) at the time decisive in the balance of East-West."*[25]

Steve Pieczenik is now retired and living in Florida, and has been repeatedly summoned by the Italian authorities in recent years to answer for his actions in relation to the Aldo Moro case. He was basically only doing his job, and if anything, they should summon Kissinger, but he is an untouchable elitist and still to this day, a driving force of the NWO. Pieczenik, who occasionally appears on *Infowars* with Alex Jones, seems very witty and

21   http://www.fmboschetto.it/misteri_svelati/il_numero_11.htm ✠ Archived 19th July, 2015.
22   See. https://it.wikipedia.org/wiki/Francesco_Cossiga ✠ Archived 13th July 2015.
23   ttp://www.corriere.it/politica/07_novembre_30/osama_berlusconi_cossiga_27f4ccee-9f55-11dc-8807-0003ba99c53b.shtml ✠ Archived 19th July, 2015.
24   Emmanuel Amara, Abbiamo ucciso Aldo Moro, (Rome, IT: Cooper, 2015).
25   http://sulatestagiannilannes.blogspot.it/2013/05/ecco-chi-ha-ucciso-aldo-moro.html ✠ Archived 19th July, 2015.

intelligent, but certainly not willing to share his dark secrets from that period in his life.

Cossiga never forgave himself for the murder of Aldo Moro, also because he was a very devoted Catholic. I can only imagine how Francesco Cossiga, described as a very sensitive person, felt after the brutal assassination of Aldo Moro, which was blamed on a terrorist, knowing very well that it was all a farce organized by the U.S. State Department under orders issued by that *criminal* Kissinger. I once spoke about it with his psychiatrist, as Cossiga also had some depression problems in the years following the event.

His revelations on 9/11 in his hour of repentance should be taken seriously by all those who want to know the truth about what really happened on 9/11, and the long lasting propaganda and lies of the U.S. Government.

In 1929, this manipulation was fully realized by **Edward Bernays**, in his essay **"Propaganda,"** where he clearly explains how the advent of democratic forms of government and so-called individual freedoms, along with industrialization, produced the objective need (by the part of the political and economic establishment) to govern from the top, manipulating the thinking and the behavior of the masses, both as voters and as consumers. This is why today mental manipulation has become a technology and a science in which both goverments and private corporations invest a lot more money than any other field of psychology. **The spread of knowledge is an essential tool we can use to defend our freedoms and liberties.** Not surprisingly, before the rise of all the great dictators in history, the media has been manipulated and controlled, to shape the minds of the people. [26]

Jesuit Illuminati and Communism ...

Adam Weishaupt (1748-1830) founded the Bavarian Illuminati (which is a modern offshoot of the real ancient mystery schools of the Illuminati), whose origins are tied to the Jesuits and Jewish finance. He aimed to organize a minority of agitators that could guide man to the realization of the ultimate Goal: *"Being Free,"* [27] or at least that was his official intention functional to his Deist creed. As Wikipedia states: *Deism has no creed, articles of faith, or holy book. Neither Satan nor hell exists, only symbols of evil which can be overcome by man's own reasoning.*

In an exclusive speech for the so-called *"Mysteries Class"* of the Illuminati, reserved for Epopts and priests, he explains that Jesus *"has prepared his kingdom for us"* and *"provided a certain number of the best and most illluminated ones."* [28]

Furthermore, Weishaupt states to his chosen ones that **The letter G** (Author's note: the one used in Masonry), reminds us of the word Grace, and sheds light on the origins of the name Illuminati, originating from the early Christians who were called the *Illuminati* after their baptism, [29] which was in short their initiation. Weishaupt stated to the candidate of the Mysteries that true Christianity was perpetuated only in the lap of true Freemasonry. [30] There is further explanation based on a number of key steps of the New Testament, [31] and according to Weishaupt, these important teachings demonstrate that the

26   See. *Techniques of mental manipulation* by Marcello Pamio—October 11, 2010 available on http://www.disinformazione.it/neuroschiavi.htm commeting the book Neuroslaves: scientific manual of self-defense by Marco Della Luna and Paul Cioni, Macro Edizioni, June 2009).

27   Serge Hutin, **Occult Governments and Secret Socities,**"Ibid., p. 110.

28   Joseph Wages, Reinhard Markner, Jeva Singh-Anand, **The Secret School of Wisdom,** (Surrey, England: Lewis Masonic), 2015, p. 277.

29   **Ibid.**

30   **Ibid.**, p. 279.

31   See. **The Secret School of Wisdom, Ibid.**, pp. 272-278.

Illuminati must unite the world "*in a single family to preserve the true secrets of its doc-trine, and the light of reason.*"[32] The key steps in Latin for the "Epopts," degree show how the Illuminati [33] were required to perceive this sacred role. At this point, in his instructions, Adam Weishaupt attacks Freemasonry which was guilty of having created degrees and un-necessary teachings, that have nothing to do with real tradition: "*False Templars, false Rosicrucians, etc., came to the fore in large numbers.*"[34] On this point, I agree.

Secrecy in early Christianity, was an important role used by the Illuminati and Weishaupt, that originally drove them to "*hide their true doctrines behind hieroglyphs, and themselves behind the names of other societies.*"[35]

For Weishaupt and his Illuminati, "*It is easy to imagine that the fate of Jesus' old and new disciples was miserable and sad, just as he had prophesied.*"[36] Thus for the Illumi-nati, secrecy is necessary to avoid "*persecution from the outside.*"[37] Weishaupt sets out the system of directives on the formation of the character of man in detail. He appears to be the perfect emulator of Machiavelli, in the application of the old adage, "*the end justifies the means.*" He recommended to be appreciative toward women and *compliment* them often; so they become docile as lambs.[38] Weishaupt was not only a brilliant conspirator and agitator but a pawn of a subversive plan by the Illuminati order he created in 1776. French author Serge Hutin writes:

> *Before us there is placed, the existence on Earth of an invisible hierarchy of leaders, who watch that the movements of history are conducted according to the general rules, transcending the single individual and also the group (and where appropriate the systematic use of force, which in certain cycle periods of humanity, are neces-sary). In this case, are men just pawns in the chessboard of history?*[39]

Hutin describes the philosophy of the **Illuminati**:

> *Ultimately, to build and achieve the ideal society you must go through several gen-erations, through the experience of an authoritarian society. Far from being a disor-ganized spontaneous motion, revolutionary action must be prepared and conducted with machiavelic method, first secretly and then openly. As soon as the old govern-ment topples, a new group must be ready to assume power.*[40]

Weishaupt seems to have prophesied exactly this period for society. He was conscious-ly advocating with his practical vision, and his elaborate methods in the field of mind control and manipulation, a unique form of Secret Society, with a completely different approach from traditional Masonic teaching, applied for the first time with scientific ef-ficacy, within a secret society made up of many cells, united to achieve global control.

Weishaupt revealed in his revolutionary theory, a direct precursor to the activities of "Irregular" Freemasons like **Lenin**, or **Abu Bakr al-Baghdadi.** Even the leader of the *Bolsheviks* once said: **"No event is improvised,"** who was inspired by Weishaupt and his Order. In this context we find *Communism*, which was conceived by the Jesuits and

32   *Ibid.*, p. 282.
33   See. *Ibid.*, pp. 280, 281, 282.
34   *Ibid.*, p. 283.
35   *Ibid.*, p. 278.
36   Serge Hutin, *Ibid.*
37   *Ibid.*
38   *Ibid.*, p. 111.
39   *Ibid.*, p. 129.
40   *Ibid.*, p. 111.

then realized by German philosopher and economist of Jewish origin Karl Marx (1818-1883), whose objective was the creation of a fully centralized dictatorship and a submissive authority of state, encompassing the entire world. This is the main purpose of the deviant side of Rosicrucianism, which the elite embed with Witchcraft and Satanism; which in turn created the corrupt and deviant side of Freemasonry, the deviant side of the Illuminati and Martinism, and pushed for the establishment of a dictatorial form of *World Government*; with an emphasis on material progress, and the destruction of organized religion to elevate man to the status of *"man equals God."*

> *The root for man is man himself ... The criticism of religion comes to the doctrinal conclusion that, for man, The Supreme Being is the man. ... We want to get rid of everything that is supernatural, so we declared war once and for all to religion.* (**Karl Marx**).

> *All religious ideas are crazy! God is a monstrous corpse. Faith in God is a monstrous cowardice.* (**Lenin**).

> *No neutrality in the face of Religion. Against the propagators of religious nonsense, the Communist Party can only continue the war.* (**Stalin**). [41]

Catho-Communism is spreading like a disease around the world and Pope Francis, the Jesuit Pope, seems to love Communism. But let us now return to Adam Weishaupt, and learn what his vison of Jesus was: *"We repeat that Jesus has not founded a new religion, but simply wanted to restore the natural religion. Giving to the world a unit, spreading light and wisdom of His morals, fighting prejudices, His intention was to teach us to govern ourselves and to restore freedom and equality among men."*

For Weishaupt, every man must find in himself the inner Light, to become equal to Jesus. This is the doctrine of the founder of the Bavarian Illuminati. [42]

In July of 2015, Pope Francis accepted from the Communist President of Bolivia Evo Morales, a medallion and crucifix engraved with the hammer and sickle, originally designed by a Spanish Jesuit **Luis Espinal,** assassinated by military dictatorship in the eighties. To investigate the origin of this peculiar crucifix, the Bolivian site *Oxigeno.Bo,* interviewed Xavier Albo, a Jesuit anthropologist and linguist, native of Catalonia, who has lived in Bolivia since 1952, where he gained Bolivian citizenship. He is a friend of Espinal, and one of the best known Jesuit researchers in the country. *It is he who in fact retains the original cross, which measures 40 by 50 cm, and the one delivered by Morales to the Pope—he explains—is in fact a replica.* [43]

So the Jesuits and Father Xavier Albo SJ hold the original cross with the hammer and sickle, not the Communist government of Bolivia. In 1937, Pope Pius XI had to say this about Communism: *Communism is intrinsically wrong, and it is not acceptable in any field by anyone who wants to save Christian civilization.* [44] After 1958, with the appointment of the first Masonic Pope in history Pope Roncalli, ideals changed drastically in the Vatican.

Returning to again to Weishaupt, who was blinded by a hypocritical form of anti-clericalism, which tied him in secret to important figures of the Jesuits of that time, such as the *Illustrious* Jesuit Monsignor **Joseph Marotti (Giuseppe Marotti),** future sec-

41   Luigi Villa, Paolo VI beato?, (Brescia: Editrice Civiltà, 2010), p. 231, *[emphasis added]*.
42   Serge Hutin, *Ibid.*, p. 113.
43   http://www.ilgiornale.it/news/cronache/papa-lascia-bolivia-crocifisso-falce-e-martello-1150713.html ‡ Archived 25th July, 2015.
44   Pius XI, in *Divini Redemptoris* —in 1937.

retary of Pope Pius VI, linked to **Franz Xaver von Zwackh,** who was initially Adam Weishaupt's right hand man. [45] Marotti influenced the drafting of the Masonic rituals of Weishaupt's *Illuminati,* within the system created by Weishaupt, secretly contributing Jesuit influence to the center of this new secret society.

Weishaupt was a perfect puppet for these hidden puppeteers: on the one hand the Jesuits, who obviously could blackmail him knowing his weak spots; on the other the growing Jewish lobby; thanks to families like the Rothschilds, who have since become one of the key families, handling the world of finance for the establishment of the New World Order. As a Bavarian, Adam learned Czech and Italian as a child, and in school, he mastered Latin, Greek and, with his father's help, Hebrew. With his avid scholarship and knack for languages, his Jesuit superiors thought he would be a natural for overseas missionary work, perhaps in the Americas or in Asia.

But Adam rebelled against Jesuit discipline, resisting their overtures and eventually became the professor of Canon Law at the University of Ingolstadt. Beginning around 1768, Adam began *"the collection of a large library for the purpose of establishing an academy of scholars."* He read every ancient manuscript and text he and his associates could lay their hands on. Adam grew interested in the occult, and was obsessed with the *Great Pyramid of Giza,* a place of great *occult power,* indeed.

He was convinced that the edifice was a prehistoric temple of initiation. In 1770, he made the acquaintance of Franz Kolmer, a Danish merchant who lived for many years in Alexandria, and had made several trips to Giza. The following year, 1771, Adam decided to found a secret society aimed at "transforming" the human race, [46] but inside him there resided a great lust for earthly power and an enormous presumption that he could control everything and everyone. For this reason, Weishaupt was never able to convey fair and complete esoteric teachings in the mystery school present in his order. The *Illuminati* became only a school of manipulation and control, based on Jesuit and Masonic style methodology, which would serve to exercise power on a global scale thanks to the triumph of REASON. This so-called "reason," could eventually see the fall of all established religions which is exactly what is happening today. The fall of religion in favor of atheism and relativism, and the rise of religious fundamentalism and terrorist organizations that are constituted in ways that often resemble Weishaupt's creation.

In 1780, Adam Weishaupt entered a period of collaboration with Baron **Adolf von Knigge (1752-1796),** a true initiate who supervised part of the ritual structure of the order. He was a Freemason and an initiate of the highest level, who did not want any form of compromise with outside groups, like the Jesuits, and was actually more willing to contribute a truly initiatic element.

Wikipedia using as reference **René le Forestier** [47] who wrote about Knigge in the following way:

> *In 1780, Knigge joined Adam Weishaupt's Bavarian Illuminati and his work with the Illuminati gave the group a great deal of publicity. But in 1783 dissensions arose between Knigge and Weishaupt, which resulted in the Knigge's final withdrawal from the group on 1 July 1784. Knigge stated that he could no longer endure*

45   https://de.wikipedia.org/wiki/Franz_Xaver_von_Zwack Archived 25th July, 2015, *[emphasis added].* 46
http://www.illuminati-news.com/adam-weishaupt.htm ‡ Archived 25th July, 2015.
46   See. Furio Bacchini, La vita rocambolesca del Conte Alessandro Savioli Corbelli, (Bologna, IT: Pendragon 2011), p. 136.
47   See. René le Forestier, *Les Illuminés de Bavière et la franc-maçonnerie allemande,* (Paris:1914), Book 3 Chapter 2, pp. 202-226.

Weishaupt's pedantic domineering, which frequently assumed offensive forms. He accused Weishaupt of "Jesuitism," and suspected him of being "a Jesuit in disguise" (Nachtr., I, 129).

"And was I," *he adds,* "to labor under his banner for mankind, to lead men under the yoke of so stiff-necked a fellow?—Never!" [48]

Baron Knigge was certainly not lying when he called Weishaupt *"a Jesuit in disguise,"* revealing who this controversial founder of the **Order of the Illuminati** really was. In the meantime, Weishaupt obviously did not like Knigge's criticism and began a persecution of his ex-collaborator: *"Knigge's involvement with the Illuminati, his support of the advancement of human rights, and a period of serious illness led to the loss of support of his aristocratic sponsors and finally his fortune."* If Knigge would have compromised with Weishaupt and the Jesuits, he could have died a rich man, however: *"Knigge found a measure of financial stability again with a position in Bremen in 1790. He died in Bremen in 1796."* [49]

Adam Weishaupt's deviant teachings found other groups around the world eager to receive his teachings and adopt his modalities in the following years. In the United States, the *Skull and Bones* was founded at Yale University in 1832. The ritual of the Order of Skull & Bones recites:

There is a devil, a Don Quixote and a Pope who has one foot sheathed in a white monogrammed slipper resting on a stone skull. The initiates are led into the room one at a time. And once an initiate is inside, the Bonesmen shriek at him. Finally, the Bonesman is shoved to his knees in front of Don Quixote as the shrieking crowd falls silent. And Don Quixote lifts his sword and taps the Bonesman on his left shoulder and says, "By order of our order, I dub thee knight of Euloga." [50]

Adam Weishaupt, at the time Court Counselor of the Duke of Saxony-Gotha, published in 1787, a brief essay entitled "On Materialism And Idealism." This rare text is finally being translated and adapted into the English language by, among others, my friend Josef Wages, who is the co-writer and editor of the first book to actually portray accurately the rituals of the Illuminati, published in 2015 and entitled, *The Secret School of Wisdom: The Authentic Rituals and Doctrines of the Illuminati.*

A short extract of "On Materialism And Idealism," translated by the late Jeva Singh-Anand who died in 2015, and edited by Brother Josef, should give the reader a more clear idea of Weihaupt's mission and his "reason" crusade:

The thinker acknowledges the merits of this revealed religion with gratitude: for he also has his weaknesses, just as the mind of the wisest man has its boundaries, by which his prospects are limited. But it also makes him believe that by virtue of religion, he is entitled to use his powers as he deems sufficient, without therefore doubting their great value with regard to others or himself. **He feels entitled to give his concepts of reason as well as those of religion the degree of certainty and conviction to the fullest extent of his capacities; he even feels obligated not to console himself with one-sided proofs. He who has been gifted with more knows the duty no weaker man can have, to compare the reasons of both parties, to seek reconciliation, and thereby to achieve for himself the highest degree of certainty.** *This examination brings him additional benefits: it serves him to humble human pride and brashness,*

48   https://it.wikipedia.org/wiki/Adolph_Freiherr_Knigge ‡ Archived 25th July, 2015.
49   *Ibid.*
50   Masonic magazine "The Square," England. March 2005, *[emphasis added]*.

to draw his attention to that which is dearer to him, to encourage him to lead an active life and to preserve him from speculation, dreams, and confusion; it serves him to show people what they don't know, what they will never experience in this life in any manner; it serves him to uncover much that is inconsistent and arbitrary in our favorite philosophical systems, to warn people of errant paths, to open their eyes to the magnificence of God and His works in a new, unique, and irrefutable manner, to lead people to the boundaries of all human knowledge, and to make them understand that they, who place so much value on their intellect, are ridiculing many incomprehensible things without cause, that even certain impossibilities may be things that are quite possible; it thus rather serves him to affirm revealed religion, to make its sense of necessity more palpable and clear, rather than disputing it. [51]

Unfortunately in 1915, this *"highest degree of certainty"* culminated into the creation of the secret German organization called *Spartacus*, (initiatic name of Adam Weishaupt), an organization that marked the first stages of the human tragedy we know as Communism. A writtten manifesto of the **Spartacist League** (*Spartakusbund*) appeared in Germany in November 1918, written by Karl Liebknecht and Rosa Luxemburg. The League subsequently renamed itself the *Kommunistische Partei Deutschlands* (KPD), joining the Comintern in 1919.

In January 1919, a mysterious order was created by the Spartacist cells attempting to seize power in Germany, but a bloody revolt was organized by *Freikorp,* on orders of the Chancelor Friedrich Ebert. Hundreds of Spartacists, including Liebknecht and Luxemburg, would be killed in the following weeks by *Freikorp,* [52] and another Illuminati sect will emerge victorious. Serge Hutin, writes the following on the subject:

It is usually said that opposites attract. We should therefore not see any impossibility in the fact that Hitler executives were fascinated by Wesihaupt's system, the most modern and perfected that relies upon an active minority to make revolutions. As it was an advanced technique of uprising and coup, therefore, perfectly suitable for use even by the worst enemies of socialism. [53]

This happened with the **Thule Society**, and their counter-revolutionary political force, formed to oppose Communism and the Spartacists. The Thule society is a very influential occult branch of the Illuminati sects whose ideological legacy was set into motion by the German National Socialist Party (NSDA). Adolf Hitler was initiated into the Thule Society in 1919 by Dietrich Eckart. [54] According to Hans Thomas Hakl, the esoteric and occult content of the Thule Society was almost absent from this system, [55] just as in the Order of the Illuminati. In 1920, Hitler became the supreme leader of the National Socialist Party, secretly supported by the American Illuminati elite and big business. My friend Pierluigi Tombetti, considered one of Italy's leading experts on the esoteric side of Nazism, explains in one of his books that Wall Street began to send millions of dollars in support of the Nazi Party, by both bank subsidiaries and companies linked to the Rockefellers, and the Rothschilds. [56] Ford and Dupont (General Motors), IBM, and even Coca

51   Adam Weishaupt, *On Materialism And Idealism,* 1787, translated by Jeva Singh-Anand Edited by Josef Wages (Malta: Malta Minerval Editions, 2015), pp. 53-55, *[emphasis added].*

52   https://it.wikipedia.org/wiki/Lega_Spartachista ‡ Archived 25th July, 2015.

53   Serge Hutin, *Ibid.,* p. 129.

54   See. Jean Michel Angebert, *The Occult and the Third Reich,* (New York: McGraw Hill, 1974), p. 9.

55   See. Hans Thomas Hakl, Nationalsozialismus und Okkultismus, in: *Gnostika* 1/Jannuary (pp. 32–42), *Gnostika* 2/aprile (pp. 26–35), *Gnostika* 3/luglio (pp. 22–37), Sinzheim, 1997.

56   See. Pierluigi Tombetti, *L'Enigma Occulto di Hitler,* (Cagliari, IT: Arkadia Editore, 2013), p. 192.

Cola and FANTA in subsequent years made great business with the Nazis. [57]

After rebelling from Adam Weishaupt, Baron Von Knigge, after the convent of Wilhelmsbad, together with Baron Ditfurth, began a major reform of **The Mother Grand Lodge of Eclectic Union, Frankfurt.** It is described by the late Masonic historian, and high level Italian Illuminati, **Vincenzo Soro**, as the center of a new and ingenious system based on absolute Masonic tolerance of all Masonic Rites and all particular beliefs.

This system has all the regular Grand Lodges, and was formed according to the original system of the Grand Lodge of London of 1717, that practice and govern the first three degrees of Freemasonry, which already contain roughly the entire "Secret Doctrine" of Freemasonry. But unlike what happened and still happens in the jurisdiction of certain Grand Lodges which prohibit "Master Mason" knowledge and possession of the High Degrees of any rite, and require the practice of a given Masonic system by outlawing all others, the member of this Masonic Obedience could study and investigate all the known rites, from the most common to the most obscure, either as a whole or in each of the grades.

In *The Middle Chamber* of the 3rd degree, there is a portion of Initiation dedicated to the introduction of the system, and all the rituals, and the particular doctrines of each of these systems are carefully explained. The initiate is thus enabled to follow the rite, or rites, that he preferred, to bind to this or that Masonic body, without failing in any way his duties to *The Mother Grand Lodge of Eclectic Union.* [58] This system claims first place because of the filial persistency with which it adhered with England, and distanced itself from the blighting influence of High Degrees, Strict Observance and other Masonic abberations of that time. There is no mystery to the history of this peculiar Masonic body, its Minutes are full and complete from the earliest, to the latest; its records are admirably preserved; every statement—on their authority—and rests on documentary evidence and, from 1742, literally no question is open to doubt. [59]

However, this system, commendable in terms of Masonic teaching, was put aside with the arrival of Adolf Hitler, which as I demonstrated in Volume I, was another puppet of the hidden rulers, who acted with revenge, eliminating this Masonic tradition that opposed so strongly the Jesuits and Adam Weishaupt. That's why the *Mother Grand Lodge of Eclectic Union* did not resume their operations at the revival of Freemasonry in Germany after World War II, when there was the unification of all the old Masonic obediences on April 27th, 1958, with the founding act of the **United Grand Lodges of Germany.** [60] They had all the papers in order so what could be the reason? The Invisible Masters decided to shut them down without a second thought.

From that point onwards the *Mother Grand Lodge of Eclectic Union* became a mere curiosity and an object of study and research for historians of Freemasonry. Masonic eclecticism in a **compartmentalized world** like Freemasonry, was far from being considered an added value to the Masonic Brotherhood, since the majority of Freemasons, to this day, have a sectarian attitude, which drives them to be silent and obedient servants of a singular Rite. These hypocrites at the top of the Masonic pyramid, the various Grand Masters, Sovereign Grand Commanders and First Grand Principals, still enjoy the so-called secret knowledge of the supposed mysteries in privileged study groups of the Masonic elite, which I was able to join in the past during my active life in "Regular Freemasonry."

57   *Ibid.,* p. 194.

58   See. Vincenzo Soro, *Il Gran Libro della Natura* (The Great Book of Nature), Atanor, Todi 1921, p. 163-164.

59   http://freimaurer-wiki.de/index.php/En:_Freemasonry_in_the_German_Empire#Freemasonry_in_the_German_Empire ‡ Archived 25th July, 2015.

60   https://en.wikipedia.org/wiki/United_Grand_Lodges_of_Germany ‡ Archived 25th July, 2015.

Returning again to Weishaupt, he was raised a Catholic of Jewish descent, and that is what many researchers follow without any conclusive evidence. The first genealogical research about the Weishaupt family is not present in the records of the church before the last years of the 1600s, which would confirm in part, the view of him being of Jewish faith. The well-known Freemason and future Prime Minister **Winston S. Churchill,** when he was still a journalist, wrote an article in February 1920, in the British newspaper *Illustrated Sunday Herald,* that not only implies that Adam Weishaupt was of Jewish origin, as told in books published in the late 1800s; but was also part of an International Jewish Conspiracy that from the Order of the *Illuminati* until Communism, broke with its origins and its past traditions, and was plotting for world domination:

> *SOME people like Jews, and some do not; but no thoughtful man can doubt the fact that they are beyond all question the most formidable and the most remarkable race which has ever appeared in the world. And it may well be that this same astounding race may at the present time be in the actual process of producing another system of morals and philosophy, as malevolent as Christianity was benevolent, which, if not arrested would shatter irretrievably all that Christianity has rendered possible. It would almost seem as if the gospel of Christ and the gospel of Antichrist were destined to originate among the same people; and that this mystic and mysterious race had been chosen for the supreme manifestations, both of the divine and the diabolical. The National Russian Jews, in spite of the disabilities under which they have suffered, have managed to play an honourable and successful part in the national life even of Russia. As bankers and industrialists they have strenuously promoted the development of Russia's economic resources, and they were foremost in the creation of those remarkable organisations, the Russian Co-operative Societies. In politics their support has been given, for the most part, to liberal and progressive movements, and they have been among the staunchest upholders of friendship with France and Great Britain.*

International Jews.

> *In violent opposition to all this sphere of Jewish effort rise the schemes of the International Jews. The adherents of this sinister confederacy are mostly men reared up among the unhappy populations of countries where Jews are persecuted on account of their race. Most, if not all, of them have forsaken the faith of their forefathers, and divorced from their minds all spiritual hopes of the next world. This movement among the Jews is not new. From the days of Spartacus—Weishaupt to those of Karl Marx, and down to Trotsky (Russia), Bela Kun (Hungary), Rosa Luxembourg (Germany), and Emma Goldman (United States), this world-wide conspiracy for the overthrow of civilisation and for the reconstitution of society on the basis of arrested development, of envious malevolence, and impossible equality, has been steadily growing. It played, as a modern writer, Mrs. Webster, has so ably shown, a definitely recognisable part in the tragedy of the French Revolution. It has been the mainspring of every subversive movement during the Nineteenth Century; and now at last this band of extraordinary personalities from the underworld of the great cities of Europe and America have gripped the Russian people by the hair of their heads and have become practically the undisputed masters of that enormous empire.*

For Churchill, the struggle with Communism meant unconditional support for Zionism: "*Zionism offers the third sphere to the political conceptions of the Jewish race. In violent contrast to international communism. ... The struggle which is now beginning between the Zionist and Bolshevik Jews is little less than a struggle for the soul of the Jewish people."* [61]

It is understandable how the **State of Israel** was created in the context of the typical strategy of *Problem-Reaction-Solution* described many times by David Icke. It was developed in the decades that preceded, and then put into place, with the support of Freemasonry and other secret societies of the **Illuminati network** at large. This, of course, included the resistance that officially opposed the order of Weishaupt, as required by the *Divide and Conquer* philosophy. As you may remember, from the first volume of my *Confessions,* the "Illuminati," the *illuminated* ones, are certainly not created with Adam Weishaupt, who was rather a late emanation in a series of mystery schools and secret societies present in our world since ancient times. Of course the system Weishaupt devised created a unique method of control and infiltration of Freemasonry that was later copied by other secret societies.

Despite his possible Jewish origins, with the arrival of Knigge, Weishaupt actually excluded Jews, monks, women and members of other secret societies. But this exclusion saw many exceptions. The end of the brief Knigge Era marked the official end of the relationship between "Regular" Freemasonry and the *Order of the Illuminati* of Adam Weishaupt. From that time, the *Illuminati* became completely independent from the outside influences of any Masonic order or Rosicrucian college. They are controlled secretly by the Jesuits, still to this day, with the Academy of the Illuminati created in Rome by Professor Giuliano Di Bernardo, **Grand Master of the International Academy of the Illuminati closely linked to the Company of Jesus,** which has declared: *"The academy, with regard to relations with the Masons, must not fall into the error of the Bavarian Illuminati. The decision of Baron Knigge to link the Order to Freemasonry, on the one hand it determined the development, the other involved them in persecutions that marked their destruction."* [62]

The real Illuminati, the *truly illuminated* are those who work for God, for the good and progress of humanity. These manipulators are false prophets, atheists and libertines, who serve the Antichrist and build strong alliances between the devil and holy water. People like Professor Giuliano Di Bernardo, or his assistant Piergiorgio Bassi, are linked to the powerful Cardinal Tarcisio Bertone, and the Jewish lobby. In the past, Bernardo has shared a certain obsession for the *Book of Enoch,* which tells of the aforementioned Moloch, who was the highest representative of a race of fallen angels; better known as the *Watchers.* This first section of the *Book of Enoch* describes the fall of the Watchers, the angels who fathered the Nephilim and narrates the travels of Enoch in the heavens. [63]

Who are **the Watchers** or fallen angels and why was the early Church and the modern Vatican so concerned about them? Genesis 6:1-4 says: *"When men began to multiply on the face of the Earth, and daughters were born to them, that the sons of God saw the daughters of men that they were fair; and took them wives of all which they chose."*

Traditionally the Ben Eloha or "sons of God" numbered several hundred and descended to Earth on Mount Harmon. Significantly, this was a sacred place to both the Canaanites and the Hebrews who invaded their land. In later times, eloborate shrines devoted to the gods **Baal, Zeus, Helios, Pan** and the goddess **Astarte** were built on its slopes. These *Ben Elohim* or "fallen angels" were also known as the Watchers, the Grigori and the Irin.

61   ttp://www.patriot.dk/churchill.html ‡ Archived 25th July, 2015.
62   Ferruccio Pinotti, Fratelli d'Italia, *Ibid.,* p. 478.
63   https://it.wikipedia.org/wiki/Moloch_(divinità) ‡ Archived 25th July, 2015.

In Jewish mythology, the Grigori were originally a superior order of angels who dwelt in the highest heaven with God, and resembled human beings in their appearance. The title "Watcher" simply means one who watches, those who watch, those who are awake, or those who do not sleep. **These titles reflect the unique relationship between the Watchers and the human race since ancient times.** In the esoteric Luciferian tradition they were a special elite order of angelic beings created by God to be earthly shepherds of the first primitive humans. It was their task to observe and watch over the emerging human species and report back on their progress. However, they were confined by a divine prime directive, that was specifically ordered, to not interfere in human evolution. Unfortunately, they decided to ignore God's command and defy His orders and became teachers to the human race, with unfortunate repercussions for both themselves and humanity. Most of the information we have about the Watchers and their activities comes from the apocryphal Book of Enoch. In the orthodox Bible the prophet Enoch, from the Hebrew "hanokh" or instructor, is a mysterious figure. In Genesis 4:16-23, he is described as the son of Cain, the "first murderer," and the first city built is named after him. Further on in Genesis 5:18-19, and several generations later, Enoch is named as the son of Jared, and it is during his lifetime that the Watchers either arrive, or incarnate in human bodies. In the apocryphal *Book of Jubilee*, allegedly dictated by "an angel of the Lord" to Moses on Mount Sinai, when he also received the Ten Commandments, it says that Enoch was, "*the first among men that are born on Earth, who learn writing, knowledge and wisdom.*" It says that Enoch wrote down "the signs of Heaven" (the zodiac signs) according to their months in a book. This was so human beings would know the seasons of the years in relation to the order of the months and their respective stellar and planetary influences. The indication is that Enoch received this information from extraterrestrial angelic sources, the Watchers, and therefore he was a cultural exemplar. [64]

These **aliens** beings chose to come to Earth in human form to study, love and join the children of God. In the end, they were punished by God, who segregated their leader *Moloch*, to the depths of an unknown desert, condemning all those who follow him, to live forever on Earth with no glory and no name. This is after these alien beings had the opportunity to instruct mankind on science, causing the apparent cultural leap made in the Bronze Age, with the offspring produced, called **Nephilim.** [65] So what is the reason for offering children in sacrifice to Moloch? (The Bible says, "passed through the fire.")

Besides the story of Moloch, similar at times to that of the fallen angel **Azazel,** who is also an angel sent to watch over humanity, that created the Nephilim race with human women, and gave the world the gift of prohibited knowledge. [66] The closeness and overlapping of the two myths creates much confusion on the real importance of Moloch as commander in chief of the alien invasion. For this reason, the dark side of the *Illuminati* of Judaism and Freemasonry are devoted to Moloch in particular. [67] There are many initiates ready to rule the world after simply receiving some spurious Illuminati, Masonic or chivalric recognition. However, such rewards are given by the usual elitists for a reason. This in order to link you to a sick and perverse system, that secretly worships an alien god, a Satanic evil entity—*Moloch.*

64   Michael Howard *"New Dawn"* Special Issue 8 September 22, 2009 - Download your copy from http://www.newdawnmagazine.com/special-issues/new-dawn-special-issue-8 ‡ Archived 25th July, 2015, 2015. *[emphasis added]*.

65   See. Gabriele Boccaccini, *The Origins of Judaism Enochic: Proceedings of the First Enoch Seminar,* (University of Michigan, Sesto Fiorentino, June 19-23, 2001), (Turin, IT: Edizioni Zamorani 2002).

66   See. http://www.bibliotecapleyades.net/sumer_anunnaki/anunnaki/anu_10.htm ‡ Archived 25th July, 2015, 2015.

67   http://www.illuminati-news.com/2006/1210b.htm ‡ Archived 25th July, 2015, 2015.

LE CROCODILE,

OU

·LA GUERRE

DU BIEN ET DU MAL,

ARRIVÉE SOUS LE RÈGNE DE LOUIS XV:

POÈME ÉPIQUO-MAGIQUE

EN 102 CHANTS,

FIG. 36 – Introductive page of Le Crocodile, the magical-epical poem of Louis Claude De Saint-Martin, published in Paris in 1799 by the Cercle Social.

Adam Weishaupt and his associates wished to rule the world, be we should only wish to rule ourselves through God's grace. A God who has given us the knowledge of **True Masonry,** through Enoch (Idris for Muslims). According to Cagliostro, the gift of the Science of the Holy Spirit, will be granted to us once again in all its glory, in the end-times by the Messiah Jesus. He will destroy the Anti Christ and all Evil manifested on Earth. In the past there have been historical figures of importance that have manifested on Earth as one of many Anti Christs; such as Hilter, Mussolini, and Napoleon Bonaparte, who was by the way, initiated in Weishaupt's *Illuminati* by Giuseppe Balsamo/Count Cagliostro, in the Roman countryside. [68]

Napoleon stated that the revolutionary motto **Liberté, Égalité, Fraternité** (Liberty, Equality, Fraternity), represented the Spirit of God, and although the motto was often called into question, it finally established itself under the Third Republic, and was placed in the 1958 French Constitution, and is now part of French National heritage. I might add from a Masonic point of view, that these three words must be interpreted in an initiatic way, to comprehend them fully, and to understand their true meaning, which is far from the egalitarian superficial nonsense it portrays.

Yes, the French "Revolutionary" motto actually hides an elitist interpretation, where "Equality" is only among Freemasons of the same degree, and as we know France is a Masonic Republic. Indeed, to understand this subject in depth we should study the works of the "Unknown Philosopher" who created this motto, **Louis Claude de Saint-Martin (1730-1803)**, in his important book *Le Crocodile* (1792). (FIG. 36)

Professor Fabiene Moore of the University of Oregon writes:

> *Saint-Martin belonged to the generation who turned a page in history, as it witnessed the end of the Ancient Régime and survived revolutionary turmoil. His was the rare case of an aristocrat who lost his fortune but saved his head, genuinely embracing the Revolution as revealed by his* Lettre à un ami*, an extraordinary anti-clerical document vindicating the revolutionaries for having eliminated the gangrène of aristocrats and priests. Simultaneously, Saint-Martin wrote his only work of fiction about the Revolution, a sprawling allegory quickly exiled from the Canon: "Le Crocodile."* [69]

Saint-Martin achieved notoriety with his first treatise, *Des Erreurs et de la vérité (1775)*, a condemnation of the erroneous practices of the Church, and of the philosophers propagating materialism and sensualism, his first book that became, after his

68 See. Serge Hutin, *Ibid.*, pp. 124,125,126.
69 Fabienne Moore, *The Crocodile Strikes Back: Saint Martin's Interpretation of the French Revolution,* Eighteenth-Century Fiction: Vol. 19: Iss. 1, (2006), Article 19, p. 4, originally available from http://digitalcommons.mcmaster.ca/ecf/vol19/iss1/19 (currently not available).

death, the target of accusations that it played a role in fomenting the French Revolution.[70]

Napoleon, unfortunately was possessed by a demon who controlled and used him as a pawn in the hands of occult rulers, just like Adolf Hitler. A few days after Napoleon visited the Great Pyramid of Giza, where he participated in a secret ritual that shocked him forever, he decided to bomb a mosque in Cairo. This act of war was definitely the result of his growing demonic posession and the chaos that eventually brought him to his tragic death by poisoning, a solution desired by the elite of the European Royal Houses, the most conservative faction of the Illuminati elite, to remove him from the game once and for all.

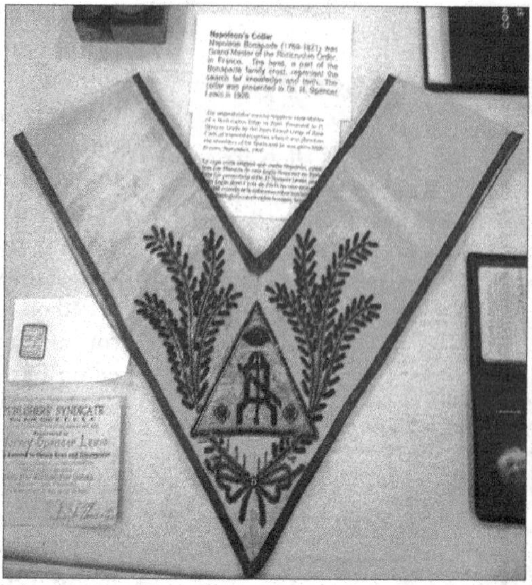

*FIG. 37 – A ceremonial collar belonging to **Napoleon Bonaparte**, Emperor of the French, while serving as Master of a Rosicrucian Order jurisdiction based in Paris (as claimed by **AMORC**). Image taken from Wikipedia: http://en.wikipedia.org/wiki/Ancient_Mystical_Order_Rosae_Cruci.*

Napoleon was considered a danger by the Jesuits and the Rosicrucians, who he knew all too well. He had a very important role in this brotherhood, as shown by an important artifact still displayed in the U.S. headquarters of AMORC (FIG. 37). Serge Hutin writes:

> *In the Archives of AMORC they preserve a document proving that Napoleon had reached the supreme dignity of the Rosicrucian Order, that of **Imperator,** in the esoteric sense the Latin word is given. According to trustworthy rumors, Napoleon hid in the walls of a castle where he had lived temporarily in the Champagne region, on the eve of his departure for Elba, Rosicrucian documents of great importance.*[71]

Napoleon did not believe the time was ripe for dispensing absolute power to a single "Illuminati" dictator or tyrant. This figure can be not only be a single individual, or a single entity—as the Bible itself states that there are **"many Antichrists."**[72]

However, in 2016, the advent of such a character seems not only desired, but strongly supported by many contemporary *Illuminati,* such as **Grand Master Giuliano Di Bernardo,** who in a somewhat controversial publication, presented the figure of the ideal **"Illuminati Tyrant."** It seems that his stance did not go down well in **Romania**, a very important country in Masonic and the international geopolitical arena, where Di Bernardo had been expanding activities in recent years. After presenting this publication it created such

70 ***Ibid.***, p. 7.

71 Serge Hutin, ***Ibid.***, p. 126.

72 ***Dear children, this is the last hour; and as you have heard that the antichrist is coming, even now many antichrists have come. This is how we know it is the last hour. 19 They went out from us, but they did not really belong to us. For if they had belonged to us, they would have remained with us; but their going showed that none of them belonged to us.*** (1 John 2:18-21 New International Version (NIV)).

dissatisfaction among its members, that he was forced to abruptly halt his project. Both his orders of chivalry and the Illuminati in that country in one night, went from hundreds of members to half a dozen people. The reason for this reaction is to be found in the recent history of this country, linked to the brutal dictatorship of **Nicolae Ceausescu**, President of Romania and President of the State Council of Romania from 1967, until December 1989, when in no time at all he was deposed, tried and sentenced to death. It is probably too early for the Romanians to embrace another tyrant, even an *"illuminated"* one.

Is it time for an Illuminati tyrant?

Let's discover who Giuliano di Bernardo is, this mysterious Illuminati Grand Master, said to be one of the most influential Illuminati power players in the world. He is a Professor of Philosophy of Science and a member of the Scientific Council of the *Académie Internationale de Philosophie des Sciences.* He was, as some of you may know, the Grand Master of the *Grand Orient of Italy* (1990-1993), and the founder and Grand Master of the *Regular Grand Lodge of Italy* (1993-2002). On his website he describes himself as the Grand Master of the **Dignity Order,** officially created in 2011 for *"the defense of human dignity."* He is also the President and Grand Master of the International Academy of the Illuminati, a new but influential Illuminati sect based on a mix of Weishaupt's teachings and some Jesuitry, founded in 2002. [73] The operative arm of the Illuminati Academy is originally described in this way:

> *In 2002, convinced that humanity needed a more authoritative guide of Freemasonry, he has retired from Masonry and founded the "International Academy of the Illuminati," understood as a modern revival of the "Order of the Illuminati," which worked in Germany in the eighteenth century. The Academy of the Illuminati is made up of eminent philosophers, scientists, mathematicians, lawyers, economists, entrepreneurs, artists, communicators, regardless of sex, race, language, religion, and culture.*

For a short period in 2008, he was also the Grand Prior of the **Order of St. Constantine the Great**, that is described as a centuries-old tradition in many countries of Europe and the United States, whose Grand Master is the *Illuminati* Prince **Sergio Jesús Paleólogo Vassallo**, descendent of a Byzantine emperor. [74] The Order of Prince Paleólogo decribes Emperor Constantine as the "promoter of a New World Order." [75] According to Prince Sergio Jesús Paleólogo Vassallo, the NWO was created at the founding of Christianity, built by Emperor Constantine. In any case, for some reason that we can not yet understand or speculate on, the partnership between Di Bernardo and the Prince Paleólogo did not last very long, and Grand Master Di Bernardo left his new project with the Imperial Byzantine nobility and their Order of St. Constantine the Great, in 2009, without dissolving his own Priory, which would simply be absorbed and reactivated in 2011 as the **Dignity Order,** another step in the "Dignity saga," originally launched by Di Bernardo in 1992, in Lucerne Switzerland, with his *Dignity Lodge.*

During his debut with the Chivalric reality of the Byzantine prince, Illuminati Grand Master Giuliano Di Bernardo gave an interesting interview to the Italian newspaper *Corriere della Sera* on July 19, 2008, where he explained his new passion for Chivalry, and the abandonment of the Masonic aprons as a amalgam for unifying the elite: *"Against Freemasonry"* he said, *"there are too many prejudices. Who knows, maybe*

---

73 See. www.dignityorder.com ‡ Archived 26th July, 2015.
74 *Ibid.*, this article is no longer available in the public side of the site in question.
75 http://www.ordendesanconstantino.net/cib-ordine.asp ‡ Archived 26th July, 2015.

a knightly order recognized by church and state could be the new dress." [76] And now, let us reflect on a few short excerpts from the book, *The Human Knowledge: From physics to sociology to religion (La conoscenza umana: dalla fisica alla sociologia alla religione)* by Professor and former Grand Master of Freemasonry Giuliano Di Bernardo, founder of **Dignity.** (FIG. 38) This is an essay published in Venice in 2010, that will help you understand that the contemporary Illuminati sects at the top of the pyramid are preparing very seriously for the advent of what Di Bernardo describes as the "Illuminati Tyrant," known as the Anti Christ. So let's learn, thanks to Di Bernardo's description, the characteristics of this future leader of the New World Order, and what we should expect in the coming years from him. Professor Di Bernardo is adamant in stating that this illuminated dictator will be required to limit civil liberties as an urgent necessity for society. Please ponder the revelations of the Grand Master of the International Academy of the Illuminati Prof. Giuliano Di Bernardo, published rather recently, not two or three hundred years ago, which is the maximum expression of contemporary Illuminati thought in the world:

FIG. 38 – Giuliano Di Bernardo known as the Sovereign Illuminated Grand Master of the International Academy of the Illuminati, and the Supreme and Most Eminent Grand Master of the Dignity Order.

There is, ultimately, only one possibility: that global ethics should be imposed. If democracy is unable to impose it, then you need to think of another form to exercise power. Aristotle would say that, after slipping into the anarchy of democracy, only the tyrant can restore order in society and ensure everyone not only the survival but also well-being and happiness. Aristotle would say that the tyrant should be "Enlightened," with the purest expression of wisdom. The Illuminati Tyrant, however, does not come from nowhere: its advent is to be prepared with care by men of quality, regardless of gender, language, skin color, religion, culture. [77]

*The writer believes in ethics and in its ability to unite people around a future project. But such a project, to express the common good, if necessary, should be imposed. If it can not be imposed by a democratic state, then we must look to a different source of state power which, in my view, is represented by the **Illuminati tyrant.** The tyrant of which we speak is not like the tyrants that we have known during the history of humanity, in its various appearances, from the tyrant of Syracuse to Hitler. This Tyrant is an enlightened man of great charisma, exceptional intellectual gifts and profound wisdom. He must know how to combine reason with emotions, which are the pillars*

76   http://archiviostorico.corriere.it/2008/luglio/19/Forgione_anti_logge_finisce_cena_co_9_080719077.shtml ‡ Archived 27th July, 2015.

77   Giuliano Di Bernardo, *La conoscenza umana dalla fisica alla sociologia alla religione,* (Venice, IT: Marsilio, 2010), p. 24.

that support the whole person. He must be able to understand the material needs of humanity but must also know how to shape it with the highest spiritual values (the true, the good, the beautiful, the right). A man with these qualities does not rule by terror but with the agreement, because everyone will recognize and accept his enlightened guidance. A man so powerful, authoritative the wise would know which way to direct the genetic changes for the creation of the new man. Submitting to his enlightened leadership, humanity would avoid the risk of self-destruction. The illuminated Tyrant, however, did not come from nothing or from the mind of Jupiter as Minerva. Its advent must be prepared even now to men of quality, regardless of sex, skin color, language, religion and culture, which I call "Illuminati." They are the ones who will create the historical and social conditions from which emerge at the right time, the one who will have to rise to supreme leader of mankind. [78]

Indeed, how could a man living in a democratic state, where there is a tendency to level down humanity, gain power and authority to rule the world as an Illuminati tyrant? Under normal conditions it would be impossible. But the conditions prevailing in the world now are degenerating gradually, so it is easy to predict that it will come to a point where the social rules will be broken and will inevitably slip into anarchy. At that point, as Aristotle argued, overcoming anarchy will only be possible with the creation of the tyrant which will delegate all powers, on condition that he carry-order in society. It is only at this stage of humanity that could the Illuminati Tyrant make its appearance. Unlike all the other tyrants, he is endowed with the qualities described above, and will direct the evolution of the human species. He, and only he, assisted by scientists, can decide how to create the new man. [79]

You can now understand and prepare to identify this mysterious key figure that in the next years will take over the scepter of global power, thus becoming the ultimate controller and "Big Brother."

Di Bernardo declared covertly to writer and journalist Ferruccio Pinotti in his book, *Fratelli d'Italia* "Brothers of Italy" the following words, offering further proof of who is really in control of the perverse power that dominates this planet and the New World Order, hand in hand with the Church and the Opus Dei, which is **powerful Israeli Freemasonry**. Giuliano di Bernardo writes:

*I started the relationship with Israel when I was Grand Master of the Grand Orient of Italy. And gradually they strengthened. So much so that Israeli Freemasonry, when in 1993 I left the GOI, removed the recognition to the Grand Orient to give it to the Regular Grand Lodge of Italy. Italian Freemasons wanted a breakthrough, which initially meant a suffering for Italian Jewish Masons. But the Grand Master Fuchs had no hesitation in doing so at the time. Even today I have very close relations with Israeli Freemasonry, on a personal basis as part of the Illuminati. On the other hand there has always been a **strong relationship between Judaism and Freemasonry**: Masonic rituals, especially the Anglo-Saxon ones, give great importance to the history of Israel and many legends, such as the Temple of Solomon, they enter the Masonic ritual in their own right. There has always been interest among Jews to Freemasonry. If we take the Royal Arch Rite, in England, we realize that it is built on literature related to the 12 tribes of Israel. There is therefore a doctrinal interest in Israel and Judaism for Freemasonry. An interest that is also political in nature: the relationship of the Jewish state with the United States over time have*

78 *Ibid.,* p. 234.
79 *Ibid.,* p. 235.

occurred through Freemasonry, especially through common membership of some Masters, like me, to the Accepted Scottish Rite. [80]

What is the mysterious *Dignity* project, that is not only a pseudo Chivalric Order? For years, prior to establishing this Order as a secret Masonic lodge behind the scenes of Anglo-Saxon Freemasonry, it went undisturbed and in parallel with other more or less visible emanations created over the years by Professor Di Bernardo with the approval of the highest offices of **English, Israeli and American Freemasonry,** and of course the **Regular Grand Lodge of Italy.** The latter created by the same Professor Di Bernardo in April 1993, through a schism masterminded by *Dignity* and operated within the **Grand Orient of Italy (G.O.I.), with the approval of the United Grand Lodge of England.** This was after a defamatory accusation of "corruption," was made about the Freemasons of the G.O.I., who have never forgiven him.

This historic turning point divided the already fragmented Italian Masonic scene made up of over a hundred Masonic Obediences. What most of the Masonic international community still does not know, is that Di Bernardo officially and secretly filed the *memorandum* and the name of the new project back in 1992.

The key operation of this phase took place on April 11, 1993, with the support of some of the biggest in International Freemasonry, like **Lord Northampton,** banker Mario Conde, and Professor Vittorio Mathieu. The presence in the same body of Masons, with members of the **Opus Dei,** seemed to be a sign that past incompatibility, was now considered obsolete in front of the "Great Work" of the New World Order. Behind the now famous Masonic "divorce" between Giuliano Di Bernardo and the Grand Orient Italy, there was his new creation, *Dignity.* Incidentally, in the articles of the secret Lodge, located in **Lucerne, Haldenstrasse 40,** we find the same ideals that reappear, after ten years, with the establishment of its *International Academy of the Illuminati.* There is also proof of the occult influence of this secret super Lodge in the new project of the Regular Grand Lodge of Italy, just read this particular passage of the official speech made at the Grand Lodge on the 6th of April 2002, on the occasion of the installation of Giuliano Di Bernardo's Masonic successor Grand Master **Fabio Venzi** (which currently holds the post), as it marked the official retirement from Freemasonry by Giuliano Di Bernardo, who would later become, despite his apparent aversion to Freemasonry, one of its new occult guides:

> *I hope not to disappoint your trust, that Professor Giuliano Di Bernardo, founder of GLRI can increase the strength and credibility of our obedience. What are the guidelines that I intend to follow in my path to guide GLRI? What I hope for the Italian Freemasonry and the Regular Grand Lodge of Italy, representing in the Italian territory the Anglo-Saxon tradition, is the achievement of a true "Dignity" to Freemasonry: the creation of conditions that make people feel proud to be such Masons.* [81]

The words of GM Fabio Venzi have a double meaning, but only to those initiated into the real mysteries. They refer to him as "the professor," and include the word "Dignity," which is put later in quotes deliberately, to emphasize its strategic importance. The structure on their official site describe *Dignity* as follows:

> *Dignity is an esoteric international order that can be represented as a pyramid whose summit is the Grand Master, Founder and Grand Master of Dignity Giuliano Di Bernardo. Institutional purpose of the Order is the defense of human dignity,*

80   Ferruccio Pinotti, *Ibid.*, p. 399, *[emphasis added].*
81   http://www.glri.it/pdf/allocuzioni/nuovoumanesimo.pdf ‡ Archived 27th July, 2015.

which is the condition of moral nobility in which man is placed from his intrinsic qualities and by his very nature. The notion of "dignity," therefore, inherent to man as such, expresses a universal characteristic, which is found in all people, regardless of sex, age, race, religion, language and culture. Thereby, it is a constitutive element of man, in the sense that, if the man loses his dignity, then it is no longer man. Because the dignity of man is an irrepressible given as an expression of his nature, it is found in all philosophical anthropology, from religious to secular. However, in the world we live in, dignity is scorned and humiliated. Many men and women are forced to live without dignity. And for this reason humanity is losing the ideal values that it has always supported. Even faith in God is dying and mankind seems to get lost in the mists of atheism and utilitarianism.

Since the concept of "dignity" is universal, its scope is unlimited. In his area of responsibility includes, therefore, the many qualities that characterize human nature. An Order which proposes the defense of human dignity must choose among the many qualities that make it up, those who, within a scale of values, are to be considered primary and essential. This choice will have to take into account the particular historical conditions and quotas facing humanity. In the world we live in, the defense of human dignity means, mainly, the defense of ethnic minorities, women, the weak and the persecuted. For our Order, and the defense of these aspects of human dignity it is the primary institutional goal, which will be built with the highest spiritual morals. Dignity is an order that is inspired by the esoteric societies and initiation dates in the history of mankind. Typical examples are Orphic and Pythagorean Secret Societies, in ancient times, and those of the Rosicrucians, Illuminati and other similar, in more recent times. Dignity aims to promote moral improvement, in cultural and social man. In particular, it is pursuing the development of intellectual activities such as philosophy, science, medicine, law, economics, art, religion, communication through projects that express harmony and respect for all views of man and life. In a universal vision, Dignity proposes and promotes ethical and cultural projects, with the participation of all those who have within them the light to illuminate the darkness that threaten humanity. Particular importance will be given to the education of the younger generation, providing them with not only the tools to learn about the world they live in, but also the ethical and spiritual principles to create harmony among men. [82]

Grand Priors, Priors, Commanders, Dignitaries, Ladies and Knights of the *Dignity* Order established according to Di Bernardo *"for the Defense of the Dignity of Man,"* participate annually in an International Convention usually held in Sicily, in a secret location chosen at the discretion of Di Bernardo, and the *International Academy of the Illuminati.*

To understand Di Bernardo further, I have included below a rare interview given ten years ago to the famous Italian journalist Giacomo Amadori, entitled *"The Illuminati exist and are among us,"* published by the Italian magazine *"Panorama"* in May 2006:

Giacomo Amadori: Do Dan Brown's books and other rumors about it have some truth?

Giuliano Di Bernardo: "In the legends there's always some truth. Every fiction is based on fragments of truth."

GA: But what is the Academy of the Illuminati?

GDB: It aims to bring together men who are the light bearers, men of quality, serving the world.

GA: The Order of the Illuminati in the U.S. is pretty serious. It is whispered that the hard core of this elite are the most important American or Americanized families, from the Kennedys to the Rockefellers, the Rothschilds to the Onassis.

GDB: "Some of these names are correct," *admitted Di Bernardo.*

GA: Amongst the international experts of lodges, secret societies and the esoteric, the name of Bill Clinton circulates.

GDB: "Certainly he has imposed on human events a deep sense of rationality" says the President of the Italian Illuminati, fifty in all. "A few, but of high level."

GA: Are there any politicians?

GDB: Very few: our project is above parties and governments and has nothing subversive.

GA: In past years it was rumored the existence of a secret lodge founded by Di Bernardo in Lucerne, Switzerland, called Dignity, an association similar to that of the Illuminati, perhaps the Mother Lodge of the Italian academics. Within Dignity there were men of all religions, the Anglican Lord Northampton, Pro Grandmaster of English Freemasonry, Abraham Foxman, the powerful leader of the Anti-Defamation League, the Emir of Dubai Mohammed bin Rashid Al-Maktoum and important Austrian Jesuits.

GDB: "The bad publicity scuppered the project, which was made in the name of transparency and had already received the consent of the canton of Lucerne" *assures Di Bernardo.*

GA: It turns out that the Illuminati of Bavaria would be the authors of the new "testament of Satan" and that their aim would be to divide the masses and corrupt politicians with sex and money to gain control of the world government. Di Bernardo smiles.

GDB: Nonsense. The power we seek is not a political one. Of course, as Brown points out, to separate fact from fiction can be difficult because of the massive amount of misinformation that has been spread about this secret society.

GA: Inside the academy there is a hierarchy: you enter with the rank of squares, you will become circles (the symbol of perfection), and triangles (the tool used by the demiurge of Plato to create the world). Geometric symbols and rituals associated with the concept of light characterize the group.

GDB: Esotericism is the basis of our research and the light can be identified both with reason and with the gods.

GA: Goodbye to anticlericalism then?

GDB: Initially the Illuminati in Bavaria fought the Jesuit dominance. Today it is different. The religious notions are essential to defeat the darkness. Even if the goal is a more genuine religion.

GA: One last question: how do you join?

GDB: You have to be presented and the proposal must be voted on and accepted. There is also an initiation rite, but what I can not explain it. [83]

Of course the phrase *"fighting the Jesuit superpower,"* is pure disinformation from Di Bernardo, who apparently during a meeting of *Dignity* a couple of years ago in the north of Italy, had the nerve to accuse me of being "a fool that speaks of reptilians."

He did this before symbolically tearing up a picture of me in front of his "Knights." Well what can I say? The "reptilians" are not my speciality.

Di Bernardo, first Grand Master of Freemasonry, and later Illuminati Grand Master, should explain the serious accusations officially made against his ex-Brothers of the Grand Orient of Italy on April 13th, 1993. This was done in a formal document (FIG. 39) that heralded the beginning of his Regular Grand Lodge of Italy, created thanks to illegal secret funds provided by the United Grand Lodge of England, thanks to the support of people like Spencer Douglas David Compton, the 7th Marquess of Northampton. (b.1946)

The amount given to Giuliano Di Bernardo for his new Masonic project in Italy was **two and a half million British pounds**, secretly pulled out of the coffers of the prestigious English institution and given directly to Di Bernardo, thanks to a bank account tied to his Swiss *Dignity* project, of which the majority of British Freemasons, to this day, know absolutely nothing about. This is such a delicate subject for the UGLE, as it touches on the secret funding of a foreign Obedience. Even the mention of it, is forbidden in Great Queen Street headquarters of English Freemasonry. I was expelled from the UGLE for taking a stand against this corruption, so nothing they do on Great Queen Street suprises me. They act contrary to the basic tenets of Freemasonry.

B'nai B'rith: The Israeli friends of Di Bernardo

Despite the alleged "enlightenment" promoted by Grand Master of the Illuminati Giuliano Di Bernardo, and other Grand Masters like him, the conditions of the world seem to be getting worse, and the Kingdom of a Thousand Years prophesied by the mysterious Rosicrucians, who unfortunately had a false start with the "Thousand Year Reich" of the Nazis, now have another problematic beginning with the United Nations and their Jesuit/Zionist influence. In the Bible, a thousand years are needed to bring the earth and humanity to original perfection, after the physical elimination by holy war of of all opponents of God. [84] **The date 2020**, and the previous date **December 21, 2012**, do not mark the end of the world, but rather the beginning of a new phase. Although the scenario that you have in front of your eyes in ten years, if we continue to believe in the fairy tales of politicians and their occult handlers, will be the one painted by the movie "Mad Max," both in the old edition of 1979, and in the new one in 2015, where they emphasized the problem of water, which is of prime importance. The elite of the New World Order wish to buy all the water, all over the planet, and then close the taps and make it the price of gold. So prepare as soon as possible resources to make your community independent with food and energy before 2020. In this context, the Roman Catholic Church that could have originally opposed all this, was infiltrated during the Second Vatican Council, which took off with Pope Roncalli known as **Pope John XXIII the first Freemason Pope in history,** a topic which I will discuss further in Volume III. It was he who unjustly disposed of poor Cardinal Giuseppe Sirri, who was duly elected by the conclave, with a Masonic coup in the Vatican. This scenario was repeated again in

83   *Gli Illuminati sono tra noi* article by Giacomo Amadori in *"PANORAMA"* May 26, 2006.
84   Pierluigi Trombetti, *L'Enigma Occulto di Hitler, Ibid.*, p.178.

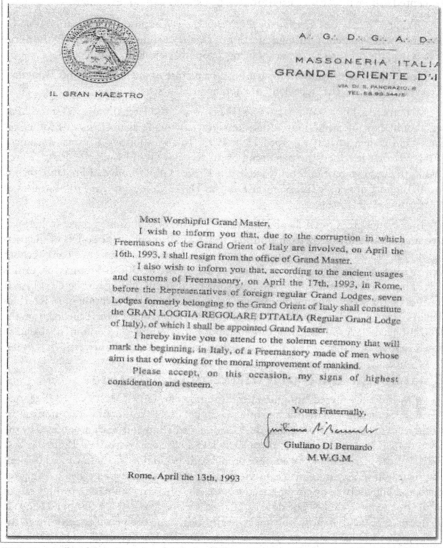

FIG. 39 – *Official Statement to the Duke of Kent, the Grand Master of the United Grand Lodge of England, issued on April 13th, 1993, by Prof. Giuliano di Bernardo as outgoing Grand Master of the Grand Orient of Italy, announcing the establishment of the Regular Grand Lodge of Italy.*

the 1963 papal conclave, when Sirri, who had already taken the name of Pope Gregory XVII, was blocked from taking on his new office by another Freemason, **Pope Paul VI,** born Giovanni Battista Enrico Antonio Maria Montini, of Jewish descent, perhaps the most Masonic of all popes. It was thanks to this Masonic infiltration of the Vatican, that a conciliary document called ***Nostra Aetate,*** was formulated by Jesuit **Cardinal Augustin Bea.** The magazine of the conservative pre-Vatican II Catholics called *"Sodalitium,"* declared in 1994 that: *"The philo-Jewish attitude of Cardinal Bea caused him to be accused of being a secret agent of 'B'nai B'rith.' Leon de Poncins accused Bea of being of Jewish origin, his real surname, was apparently Beja or Behar, acting in the Second*

Vatican Council as a secret agent of the 'B'nai B'rith.'"[85]

The faculty for Jewish Studies of the prestigious Gregorian University in Rome, heir of the Roman College founded originally by **Ignatius of Loyola**, founder of the Jesuits, is now dedicated to Cardinal Bea. In 2014, the ***Cardinal Bea Centre for Judaic Studies*** celebrated 50 years of conciliar declaration, called *Nostra Aetate*. The *Nostra Aetate* was co-written with Freemason Jules Isaac, basically a Communist, and part of the international Jewish lobby operating for the Illuminati. Jules Isaac was a member of the **B'nai B'rith;** which is another form of Freemasonry addressed only to Jewish people, so even more exclusive and sectarian. In the aforementioned article *Sodalitium*, there was mention of a book published in France called, *Mystères et secrets du B'nai B'rith* released in Italy in 1999 as "Mysteries and secrets of the B'nai B'rith." *The largest international Jewish organization*, authored by French journalist **Emmanuel Ratie,** who stated: *"On this subject, nothing so comprehensive, detailed and yet well documented was ever written."* Emmanuel Ratie begins the Italian edition of his book in this way:

> *B'nai B'rith, which in Hebrew means "Sons of the Alliance" was founded in the U.S. in 1843. It is reserved exclusively to Jews. Today it has more than 500,000 brothers and sisters as affiliates in fifty different countries. The international elite of the various Jewish communities, from Sigmund Freud to Albert Einstein, has been or is a member. It is certainly the oldest, most popular and arguably the most influential international Jewish organization. For example, it was the B'nai B'rith which obtained the recognition of the State of Israel by President Harry Truman. It was always the B'nai B'rith that was able to obtain from the Catholic Church to change its teaching for the second millennium, in regards to Judaism, in the Second Vatican Council. In 1905, Jacob Schiff, the American banker and senior official of the B'nai B'rith stated: "If the Tsar does not want to give our people the freedom desired, then a revolution will establish a republic through which you will get those rights." Twelve years later, in 1917, the Bolshevik Revolution will upset Russia expanding its influence throughout the world, and Tsar was murdered along with his family. ... August '94, Silvio Berlusconi, then head of government, had to apologize to Abraham Foxman (ADL director) for a statement by his Minister Mastella, who insinuated that it was the reaction of the American Jewish lobby to determine the fall of the Italian lira in the international money market. This organization which follows the rules of a Masonic organization is mostly unknown to the public, but has exercised, and still exercises an enormous influence on world events. This is the first independent investigation dedicated to the Mysteries and secrets of the B'nai B'rith worldwide. It contains many unpublished documents and is therefore an explosive book, able to answer questions that every citizen has the right to ask.* [86]

Emmanuel Ratie immediately speaks of the fact, that we know little to nothing about this mysterious order, and adds that he did very extensive research using trusted sources:

> *At the National Library in France there is nothing about the B'nai B'rith, except for a modest booklet in Hebrew, one in German dated 1932, another one in English and one quarter of an extremist anti-Semitist one ... Virtually nothing also at the Library of Congress in Washington and nothing at the British Library in London. However, according to the* Encyclopedia Judaica *(1970) B'nai B'rith, or Children*

85   From the magazine *"Sodalitium"* No. 38 June-July 1994—Verrua Savoia (Turin).
86   Emmanuel Ratie. *Misteri e segreti del B'naï B'rith. La più grande organizzazione ebraica internazionale"* (Mysteries and secrets of the B'nai B'rith. The largest international Jewish organization), (Verua Savoia,Turin, IT: 1999,Centro Librario Sodalitium), p. 1.

of the Alliance, is "the oldest and numerous Judaic organization of mutual assistance, meeting in lodges and chapters in 45 countries. The number of its States is approximately 500,000 men, women and young people. There are 1,700 male lodges of which 25% outside the USA, with 210,000 men and a budget of about $ 13 million. Its programs covers all Jewish interests and they also include several other geared to the broader aims of the community."

It is therefore strange that such an association, founded in the United States in 1843, and France in 1932, has never published anything about itself either in France or elsewhere. If you read the collection of newspapers which, remember, are required by law to be deposited in the *Bibliotheque Nationale* in four copies for any publication made in France (and even the Masons observe this law), it is found that the B'nai B'rith has never made a legal deposit, with the exception of only two numbers of their magazine, the *B'nai B'rith Journal*. This organization has never filed any of its official brochures in France. This no doubt explains why the non-Jewish French press is undocumented on the subject, and has consecrated to the B'nai B'rith, less than fifty articles since its founding in 1932. Despite the boycott of the legal deposit, you can trace a small part of the publications of the American, French and European B'nai B'rith, thanks to an investigation that lasted several years. If you study in depth you will understand the purpose of the order of B'nai B'rith, that is officially about "enlightening the whole of humanity." The Anti-Defamation League of B'nai B'rith (ADL) is their armed wing. [87]

Wikipedia describes The Anti-Defamation League (ADL):

Formerly known as the Anti-Defamation League of B'nai B'rith, is an international Jewish non-governmental organization based in the United States. Describing itself as "the nation's premier civil rights/human relations agency," the ADL states that it "fights anti-Semitism and all forms of bigotry, defends democratic ideals and protects civil rights for all," doing so through "information, education, legislation, and advocacy." [88]

I would like to now address the mysterious origins of the B'nai B'rith. On October 13, 1843, in a Sinsheimer coffee shop, on the dark streets of the Wall Street district, the first B'nai B'rith was founded, which took the name of Bundes-Brueder, literally *League of Brothers*, a Germanic name because the founders spoke only German and Yiddish. The choice of this Israelite coffee shop is explained by the fact that at the time the Lower East Side had a feud with German Jewish immigrants. [89] The date of establishment of the B'nai B'rith makes it one of the oldest American associations to ever exist. It saw another 37 years before the Salvation Army came to light, 38 before the Red Cross, 39 for the Knights of Columbus, 47 for the Daughters of the American Revolution and more than 70 for the Kiwanis, the Lyons Club, and The American Legion. The known historian of the B'nai B'rith, Edward E. Grusd, notes very significantly, that there are only two older organizations: *"Freemasons and Odd Fellows."* Only in 1859, will the first major Jewish association be created, the Union of Jewish Congregations, which groups all synagogues. At the time, the Jewish-American community had only 25,000 members, and this figure is considered wrong by excess. As we have seen, there was a Sephardic minority, descendant from early settlers, who had names like Cardoza, Carvalho, Seixas and Perreira. At the end of the American Revolution, this minority had, in the United States, fewer than 3,000 families, in which at least two-thirds lived in New York. Nevertheless, it counted

87   *Ibid.*, p. 4.
88   https://en.wikipedia.org/wiki/Anti-Defamation_League ✝ Archived 27th July, 2015.
89   See. *Ibid.*, p. 7.

among its members prominent figures such as Salomon, a leading stockbroker, an American of Jewish Polish origin, who was one of the major financiers of the American Revolution. Later they added a significant number of immigrants from Eastern Europe, which soon became the majority. Most were of modest origins and lived in poverty. Among them emerged the German Jews, such as Schiff, Warburg, Oppenheimer, Guggenheim, Lehman, and others. Between 1830 and 1880, 200,000 Jews emigrated from Germany to the United States. The wealthy minority, often Sephardic, was divided into "families" joined together on the grounds of common interests and synagogues, and was never in favor of a strong immigration of Ashkenazi Jews.

At that time, apart from the category of undertaker, there was no Jewish organization with philanthropic ends, and most of the communities had their own cemeteries. These "shetl" (Jewish communities), were very divided, with practices and customs that did not entertain relations between them; even marriages between Jews of different communities was considered by many, *mixed marriages*.

There were, however, specific associations of solidarity, for example, the *Landmanschaften*, the German Benevolent Society, founded in 1844, merged the following year with the B'nai B'rith. There had already been several attempts at unification, in 1841. Rabbi Isaac Lesser of Philadelphia tried to unite the different associations with a federation of congregations in synagogues called *The West.* [90] The introduction to the B'nai B'rith, intended to define their purpose and their mission, is inspired by Masonry, but with a Jewish specificity. Here is the beginning of the preamble: "*The Order of B'nai B'rith has set itself the mission order to join the Israelites (this step has become 'people of Jewish confession') in order to promote their best interests as well as those of humanity, to develop and raise the moral character of the people of this faith, of inculcating the purest principles of philanthropy, honor and patriotism, to help science and the arts, to help the poor in their needs, to visit and support the sick, to come to the aid of victims of persecution, to bring protection and assistance to the widow and the orphan following the principles of humanism in its highest sense.*"

The founders also believed that a Jewish organization should have a Hebrew name, so they kept the initials BB but changed the name: from *Bundes-Brueder* (League of Brothers) becoming the B'nai B'rith (Sons of the Covenant). B'nai B'rith in Yiddish becomes Bne Briss and it is under this name that it is known in Germany (*Unabhaangiger Orden BB*). It is also known by the Sephardic term, *Beni Berith*.

Until 1850, the meetings continued to be held in German and not in English. The Order adopted a motto: *Wohlthatigkeit, Bruderliebe und Eintracht,* which became *Benevolence, Brotherly Love and Harmony* in English and *Amour Fraternel et Harmonie* in French. **The menorah or candlestick with seven branches, was adopted as a symbol of the Order in the second meeting "because it symbolizes the light."**

Until 1868, the B'nai B'rith used Jewish religious terms for its officers: the president was the **Grand Nasi Abh**; the Vice President was the **Grand Aleph**, the **Secretary the Grand Sopher.** B'nai B'rith states: "*Remember that privileged moment in which our ancestors being on the foot of Mount Horeb (Sinai) understood the message: You have to be for me a kingdom of priests, of holy people. ... Throughout the world, for his safety and for the honor of Israel, to act, is how one conceives the high end of the Order. B'nai B'rith has its roots and its name on two alliances essential to the religion of the "chosen people," that of God with Abraham and Isaac but also, and perhaps above all, of that between*

God and Moses in the Sinai, sealed by a fire in the "sacrifice of salvation" as "blood of the covenant" (cf. Moses, V 1, 17-2, 24 and following). Even after 1868, within the Lodges, they preserved the various denominations."[91]

Its domain was voluntarily limited to America and its purpose was to provide a high-level representation of American Jews in the religious as well as in moral and intellectual sense, playing a specific role in Freemasonry. It was the first time in the history of Jews that they organized according to similar guidelines, that were no longer just local and religious. It was necessary to preserve a religion avoiding the diatribes of the synagogue. [92]

This moment marks a turning point, when the classic environment of the Synagogue is replaced by that of the lodge, which is considered much more stable because of its hierarchy and its rules. By now the elite of the Jewish people obtain an Egregore to shape and develop what became in a short time, the basis for the newly born Zionism ideology promoted by **Edmond Benjamin James de Rothschild** (1845-1934). Here I will not fall into the trap of anti-Semitism my dear readers, which of course will make me also an easy target of the ADL, the armed wing of B'nai B'rith and the Illuminati. I personally do not care to generalize, and I am neither a stupid "negationist" or a even an anti-Semite. The Rothschilds are not the entirety of the Jewish people, and not all Jews are aware of the policies made by Freemasons, Illuminati and B'nai B'rith members behind the curtains of history.

The first victims are always the general population since antiquity, this is what I realized a long time ago, after meeting a B'nai B'rith representative in Rome at the Foreign Press Association. It was an *"un-illuminating"* experience, as he was the usual elitist, nothing more, no different from others in similar organizations in the Illuminati Network. The people who fall victim are so manipulated that they don't want to consider the reality I am trying to describe to you. It will upset them, tear apart their illusions, and that's not permitted by the New World Order System supervised by the **Grand Alliance** between the **Jesuits,** the **Rothschild Zionists** and the **British Monarchy,** operating for global enslavement with Illuminati sects, think tanks, and so on. However, the so-called *Conspiracy Theorist*, always seem to choose to attack one faction without touching the other, feeding the divide and conquer methodology, instead of a more complex explanation. Such people are not honest in their own vision and the battle against the elite. What I have shown you since the first volume of my *Confessions,* is a much more complex and compartmentalized reality, made up of a vast network, with many players and different layers. At the top is the United Nations, in their ultimate occult control room. The aforementioned Cardinal Bea, operated as an agent of the B'nai B'rith, working in connection with the powerful Society of Jesus. Immediately after being appointed for this mission by the first Masonic Pope John XXIII (Giuseppe Angelo Roncalli), for the task of developing a "revisionist" document on Jewish-Christian relations, he went on to meet the powerful Jewish Freemason **Nahum Goldman**, president of the **World Jewish Congress.** This meeting took place in Rome on the 26th of October 1960, where they decided together the future fate of Catholicism.

On that occasion, Bea asked Goldman, on behalf of Roncalli, to draft a formal document on the new relations with the Jews, with religious freedom at the base of the growing One World Religion. On February 27, 1962, the *Memorandum* was presented to Bea Goldman and Label Katz (members of B'nai B'rith), on behalf of the World Conference of Jewish Organizations. Well, this draft inspired by Jewish Freemasonry and the World Jewish Congress, produced the Catholic declaration *Nostra Aetate,* which liter-

91   *Ibid.,* pp. 9-10. *[emphasis added].*
92   *Ibid.,* pp. 10-11.

FIG. 40 – *Bergoglio at lunch with the B'nai B'rith in Argentina. Source: http://i2.wp.com/ radiospada.org/wp-content/uploads/2014/04/foto-di-gruppo-di-famiglia.jpg ‡ Archived 30th July, 2015.*

ally means "in our time," which is one of the most important documents of the Second Vatican Council. A council controlled by leaders of Freemasonry, the B'nai B'rith, and the Jesuits, who on Oct. 28, 1965, with their *Nostra Aetate,* changed forever the relations between the Catholic Church and non-Christian religions. On December 18, 2006, the now retired Pope Benedict XVI, greeted 112 members of the B'nai B'rith at the Vatican recalling the *Nostra Aetate:*

> *I am pleased to greet this delegation of B'nai B'rith. After the Declaration Nostra Aetate of the Second Vatican Council in 1965, the leaders of B'nai B'rith have visited us on several occasions. Today, 18 December (2006), as a sign of the spirit of understanding, respect and mutual respect that has grown between our two communities, we welcome you and, through you, all those whom you represent.* [93]

The relations between Pope Francis and the B'nai B'rith are well-documented. There are several articles available directly from the website of B'nai B'rith Argentina on this religious "love affair," [94] where Jorge Mario Bergoglio is surrounded by his old friends of B'nai B'rith in Argentina. (FIG. 40) It's no wonder that between 1785 and 1786, the noted philosopher who started as a Jesuit seminarist, then became a Barnabite and finally a Freemason and a member of Adam Weishaupt's *Illuminati.* **Carl Leonhard Reinhold** (1757-1823), prepared two conferences for the Viennese Masonic *Lodge Zur Eintracht waharen*—a secret cell of the *Order of the Illuminati*—entitled **The Jewish Mysteries the most ancient religious Freemasonry.** In one passage, Reinhold states that the Pope is: "*the Supreme Unknown Superior*" in another, that, "**he takes the place of Aaron.**" Read this short passage and perhaps these "Jewish Mysteries" will become less "*mysterious*":

> *Who can believe, brothers, then that pious school of prophets and prodigious men should not be worthy of the important paternal care of the Supreme Unknown Su-*

93   http://www.traditioninaction.org/RevolutionPhotos/A376rcBnaiBrith.html ‡ Archived 27th July, 2015.
94   See. http://www.bnaibrith.org.ar/website/popgaleria.asp?id=2276&gal=1636 ‡ Archived 27th July.

perior (who inside the order takes the place of Aaron and his successors), who the famous Archimedes ab Aquila fulva preached to our brothers with enthusiasm and at the same time with discretion?[95]

Archimedes ab Aquila fulva was **Johann August Starck,** also known as **Stark (1741-1816).** It was an internal schism from 1767 in the Neo-Templar Masonic *Rite of the Strict Observance* on behalf of the Jesuits. Stark is also mentioned in the writings of **Albert Pike.** As stated by Gianluca Paolocci the curator of the Italian edition of Reinhold's work: *"Leonhard alludes to the pope who was once thought to secretly pull the strings of the alleged 'catholicization' of Freemasonry in Germany."*[96] This text, described more than two centuries ago by the Illuminati in official documents, takes on new meaning when you consider the frequent meetings of Bergoglio, a.k.a. Aaron, with the merry band of rabbis from B'nai B'rith. You can imagine how Jesus felt 2,000 years ago, in front of an almost identical scenario.

Journalist and author Italian Matteo Simonetti writes: *We do not know how true is the famous expression of Louis-Ferdinand Céline.* Note by the Author: this is a pseudonim of Louis Ferdinand Auguste Destouches (1894–1961):

> *"Mason is a voluntary Jew, a synthetic Jew,"* but we notice, for example, what was said by the chief rabbi Israel Meir Lau a Ashkenazi Jew on October 26, 1993 in Jerusalem, on the fortieth anniversary of the Grand Lodge of Jerusalem: "the principles of Freemasonry are all contained in the Book of Books of the Jewish people; or by Gustav Karples in his "Ode to B'nai B'rith," where he claims: The ideals of Freemasonry have sprung from Judaism for internal needs [...] Even the terminology and the majority of the Masonic symbols come from Judaism.*[97]

And now we will go deeper into the mysteries, in an analysis of this short but influential essay created by the *Illuminati* called "The Jewish Mysteries, the most ancient religious Masonry."

The Jewish Mysteries, the most ancient religious Masonry

Wikipedia writes: *"The suppression of the Jesuits in the Empire Portuguese, in France, in the Two Sicilies, in Malta, in Parma and Spanish Empire from 1767 was the result of a series of political moves more than a theological controversy. With the brief* **Dominus ac Redemptor** *(July 21, 1773) Pope Clement XIV decided to suppress the Society of Jesus. The Jesuits took refuge therefore in non-Catholic countries, particularly in Prussia and Russia, where the order was largely ignored in its work. The Bollandists moved from Antwerp to Brussels, where they continued their work at the monastery of the Coudenberg; in 1788 it suppressed even the Bollandist government of the Austrian Netherlands."*[98] Karl Leonhard Reinhold was originally educated as a Jesuit, but after the suppression of the Society of Jesus, he joined the Barnabites, where he taught philosophy.

In 1783, ten years after the dissolution of the Jesuits, Reinhold was defrocked and became a Freemason and a member of the Masonic lodge *Zur Warren Eintracht* in Vi-

---

95   Carl Leonhard Reinhold, *I misteri ebraici ovvero la più antica massoneria religiosa* (The jewish mysteries the most ancient religious masonry), Introduction by Jan Assmann, Edited and with an essay by Gianluca Paolucci, Macerata, IT: Quodlibet, 2011). p. 198, *[emphasis added]*.

96   See. Vincenzo Soro, *Ibid.*, p. 153-154.

97   Matteo Simonetti, *La verità sul Piano Kalergi* (The truth about the Kalergi plan), (Milan, IT:Edizioni Radio Spada, 2015), p. 117.

98   See. https://it.wikipedia.org/wiki/Soppressione_della_Compagnia_di_Ges%C3%B9 ✝ Archived 30th July, 2015.

enna, where **Wolfgang Amadeus Mozart** took his second degree in the Craft. Karl Leonhard Reinhold became not only a member of "Regular" Freemasonry, but also of the *Order of the Illuminati of Bavaria,* which was hidden within it, becoming one of the greatest thinkers of the time. Reinhold's controversial work on the Jewish Mysteries as the most ancient form of "Religious Freemasonry," was published for the first time in Italy in 2011. The Italian press showed an unusual interest on the subject. **Here are some excerpts from reviews made at the time in the most important Italian newspapers:**

Excerpt from *That Mason of Moses. The mysterious origin of Judaism – La Reppublica;* **10-12-2011:**

The Latest on Moses? He was a"Mason" and pro-Egyptian.

> *In front of a title that speaks of Judaism as the oldest form of Masonry perhaps some readers will wonder if this is not the usual Judeo-Masonic plot accusation that hit the French revolutionaries in the late 700s formulated by abbot Barruel that became the fixation of the Jesuits of the publication "Civilta Cattolica" in the years of the fierce anti-Jewish and anti-Masonic battle that saw them share the anti-Semitism card with the "socialism of fools." The fact is that Reinhold was a Jesuit and Freemason. A fact seemingly unique, that helps to understand how the story is constantly changing the colors of things and the meanings of words. In his time between the Society of Jesus and Freemasonry there was an intense sympathy; Jesuits attended lodges stimulated by the idea that presided over the origin of their order, that of confidence in the revolutionary potential of intelligence as a tool for action of a small enlightened elite by God. Carl Leonhard Reinhold (born in Austria in 1758, died in Weimar in 1823) began his career as a Jesuit and remained one until the dissolution of the Company, a traumatic event for a religious order that felt badly protected by the papacy and saw the dispersal of former members. The history of the Jesuits in the Habsburg Empire and their Masonic past, in a great book by Antonio Trampus, that shows members of the banned religious order flow in Masonic Lodges dividing between a more open side to the ideas of the Enlightenment and Rousseau and a reactionary side that supported absolutism. Reinhold did not follow neither the one nor the other strand of Jesuitism: converted instead to Protestantism by the influence of Herder, and found in Kant himself the master of his life, the one to whom he dedicated his extraordinary capacity of adviser and university professor in the mature stage of its activities.* [99]

Short review – *Corriere della Sera;* **26-11-2011:**

> *Carl Leonhard Reinhold (1757-1823) entered the Jesuits and, after their supression, taught philosophy in the Barnabites. Freemason since 1783—he was a member of the lodge "Zur Eintracht wahren," "For the true harmony"—and decided to leave religious life and promote widespread interest around Kant. He will take the chair in Jena University. Reinhold now comes out, introduced by Jan Assmann and edited by Gianluca Paolucci, The Jewish Mysteries the most ancient religious Masonry (Quodlibet, pp. 264, 18). In it the philosopher outlined the argument that Moses would have been devoted to the pantheistic principle of Oneness—All, that natural religion founded on the banks of the Nile. He wrote: "I don't think I offend in any way the high regard I have for the truth, as well as mosaic priesthood, if I push myself to consider such a cult, in its basic components, a faithful copy of the esoteric*

---

99 Adriano Prosperi "That Mason of Moses. The mysterious origin of Judaism," article in *"La Repubblica"* (Rome, IT:10-12-2011).

religion of the Egyptians and to affirm that the legislator of the Jews, have apparently targeted, as he could, to initiate all his people to the Egyptian mysteries." [100]

Excerpt from *Reinhold, the Mason former Jesuit who illuminated Schiller and Goethe— Il Messaggero; 25-08-2012:*

Sometimes seemingly minor figures better represent the Zeitgeist, the spirit of the time. This is the case of a strange philosopher, Viennese professor Carl Leonhard Reinhold, pupil of the Jesuits, then Barnabite. Defrocked, entered the Viennese Masonic Lodge of the True Harmony, directed by Ignaz von Born, advisor to Emperor Joseph II, and leading Austrian Enlightenment, charismatic personality so overwhelming and inspiring to Mozart (also a Mason) the hieratic figure of Sarastro in "The Magical Flute." The eighteenth-century Freemasonry was crossing from fairs infighting between factions mystical and rationalistic. Both gave rise to other more secret societies. The rationalist found themselfs in the Order of the Illuminati, whose radical program, anticlerical and anti-despotic, soon attracted the attention of some governments that outlawed them. Reinhold, who had joined this association, was forced to leave in a hurry Vienna and repair in more tolerant Duchy of Weimar. Meanwhile he completed his philosophical training with intense attendance of Kantian philosophy, which won him the Chair at the University of Jena. It was here that Reinhold had to play an extraordinary role, influencing profoundly first Schiller later Goethe, who borrowed from him the knowledge of Kantianism. From his professorship Reinhold helped form an extraordinary generation, including the brothers Friedrich and August Wilhelm Schlegel and especially Novalis. Huge was the influence of his booklet, The Jewish Mysteries or the oldest form of Religious Masonry. [101]

Excerpt from *The Alchemical Wedding of Tamino and Pamina – Il Sole 24 Ore; 27-11-2011:*

At the head of the lodge was Ignaz von Born, who perhaps inspired the character of Sarastro. And at the invitation of von Born, between 1786 and 1787 Reinhold wrote The Jewish Mysteries the most ancient religious Masonry. *The work is a review, bold and provocative, of the figure of Moses. A Prince initiated to the Egyptian mysteries, Moses would have decided to use the secret rituals of the religion of Osiris and Isis to guide his people's exodus from the land of the pharaohs. So, thanks to a trick essentially political in nature, the Jews would be the only people of antiquity to receive a revelation normally destined only to a small elite of scholars.* [102]

Of course, after the publication of this book, edited by Gianluca Paolucci, which was met with a degree of success in Italy, there was an immediate reaction from the Vatican media. And to be consistent with my spirit of defiance toward the Vatican and the Jesuits, I want to include below the views and criticism made by the main Italian Catholic daily *"Avvenire"* on the work of Reinhold, defined by the Catholic journalist Mario Iannacone, as *only* a Jesuit student. However, this is not true and if you have read the earlier excerpts I included by others papers, the journalist in question was not the only one who indicated Carl Leonhard Reinhold as a former Jesuit, as the most widely read Italian newspaper the *"Corriere della Sera"* did the same: *"he joined the Jesuits and, after their suppression,*

100   *The Jewish Mysteries,* book review by Armando Torno in *"Corriere della Sera"* (Milan, IT: 26-11-201).
101   Marino Freschi, "Reinhold, the Mason former Jesuit who illuminated Schiller and Goethe" article in *"Il Messaggero"* (Rome, IT: 25-08-2012).
102   Giulio Busi, "The Alchemical Wedding of Tamino and Pamina," article in *"Il Sole 24 Ore"*, (Milan: 11.27.2011).

taught philosophy in the Barnabites." In addition, the Catholic newspaper did not even mention the fact that at the time the Society of Jesus was dissolved and suffered a long dispersion, in particular the Ancient and Accepted Scottish Rite. And there is much more info on the subject voluntarily suppressed or manipulated by the Catholic newspaper in the article, that even casts doubt on the research of highly respected Professor Jan Assman, as well as a totally incorrect statement by Iannacone that the Templar myth survived only in Anglo-Saxon Freemasonry: *"True for the European Freemasonry but not to the Anglo-Saxon one, which continued to be based on those myths."*

Here the question becomes more complicated, because both Professor Jan Assman and the journalist Mario Iannacone who work and are guided by the Catholic Church for their reviews, do not seem initiates of the highest degrees of Freemasonry. Only an expert in such rituals could talk about this subject in a serious and consistent way.

The Templar myth survived thanks to the Jesuits in the high degrees of the Ancient and Accepted Scottish Rite (from 30° to 33° degree), considered an essential part of continental European Freemasonry, light years away from the Anglo-Saxon version; that if anything has given more space to the Jewish mysteries as seen in the Royal Arch, which only later offer the possibility to access the mysteries of the Neo-Templars for interested Christian Freemasons. These degrees are known in the United States, as the **York Rite**, which mirrors closely this Masonic system created in England, with slight changes in the underlying structure which does not change the contents taught, or the rituals.

The article in the newspaper "Avvenire" is obviously to some extent, the result of contemporary Jesuit disinformation. Just imagine, after two centuries since their formal return to the Catholic Church in 1814, the Company of Jesus now fully controls the Vatican media through **Federico Lombardi SJ (b. 1942)**, in charge of all information of the Holy See. If you think about it, with the help of the powerful Jewish lobby, the Jesuits have now taken control of the dying Catholic religion, helping to push further its decline. In any case, this is the apologetic article in question that appeared in the Vatican media. Read for yourself to understand the skills of Jesuit *disinformation.*

Excerpt from *Reinhold: a fake Jesuit between Freemason and Illuminist – Avvenire;* **14-01-2012:**

Here are translated the Jewish Mysteries of Karl Reinhold L, edited by G. Paolucci. The pamphlet, which was concluded in 1786, is difficult to understand if you are not knowledgeable of the struggles that opposed the Masonic tendencies of the late eighteenth century. The author is a philosopher now in the process of reassessment, according to the inaccurate review of Adriano Prosper for La Repubblica, "he began his career as a Jesuit," before becoming Protestant and then a Freemason. The historian is suggesting a kind of continuity in the career of Reinhold, between "Masonry and the Company of Jesus" as "there was at that time an intense sympathy between the two who shared a common belief in the revolutionary potential of intelligence."

Misleading statements. To Reinhold, Prosperi and curators ascribe the merit of having defined, in this booklet—handled as a minor classic of illuminism—the benefits that would result from monotheist relativism. Compared to his contemporaries who introduced in their texts perennialiste Masonic ideas in deism or pantheism pulling in Atlanteans, Egyptians, Chaldeans, Jews or the Essenes, the book of Reinhold is better argued and concentrates, moderating abstruse Philology, on the punctum: the futility of religious exclusivism and the advantage of a polycentric truth or "relativist" as Prosperi writes (using a anachronistic term).

The "relativism" of Reinhold coincides, however, with the Masonic method and re-calls Spinoza's pantheism. According to the author, Judaism was invented by Moses, who adapted the Egyptian mysteries which would lead both Judaism—or "religious masonry"—what became Freemasonry itself, reserved for the elite. Reinhold be-lieved in equivalence between religions and wisdom traditions and natural truth veiled behind the Egyptian mysteries. Assmann writes in the introduction: the "God of the Old Testament would be a fiction! The adaptation of a lofty concept, philo-sophical, abstract deity of the understanding of the common men."

So thought Reinhold referring to Weishaupt, Spinoza and perhaps Giordano Bruno. But Reinhold was not a Jesuit; He studied in a Jesuit coliegium but without getting into the Company (as shown in the scientific biography "Karl L. Reinhold and the Enlightment" by G. Di Giovanni, published by Springer)." He took the Barnabite "vows" in 1780 to teach, then he joined masonry, thus refusing communion with the Church (which condemned "the sect" since 1738). He attended a lodge infiltrated by members of the Illuminati like him, but not close to their ideas as claimed by Ass-mann, who also adds that Templar myths decayed in the Masonic milieu after 1782 in favor of the Egyptians: true for the European Freemasonry but not for the Anglo-Saxon one, which continued to be based on those myths. Intricate issues, which they would like to spend in favor in today's battle in favour of "relativism." Some Jesuits played a dangerous battle to control the impulses of anti-Christian German lodges and to steer them up in favor of the Stuarts Catholics lodges of the British expatri-ates present in Italy and France, they played their game so well that even in scholarly introductions (and reviews) today the maze of mirrors deceives. [103]

The Jesuits should stop their lies through manipulative filtering of the Catholic Church newspaper *"Avvenire,"* that have nothing to do with true Christianity, if it ever existed. Returning to *Karl Leonhard Reinhold*, he lived the last years of his life in Kiel, between university and Masonic activities. It was in the period behind the famous Ma-sonic Convent of **Wilhelmsbad 1782,** that his actions and work were particularly inter-esting, as we seek answers beyond appearances (and the usual Internet hoaxes) about the *Order of the Illuminati* of Adam Weishaupt. As I wrote in the first volume of my *Con-fessions*, although some agents of disinformation want to prove otherwise, it was at this time, after the Masonic Convent of Wilhelmsbad, that the turning point for Weishaupt's *Illuminati* took place. They certainly did not disappear, despite being officially disman-tled and banned as an order with this name. The Jesuits were able to operate and hide , inside the more reserved and restricted Masonic lodges of the elite, such as *Zur Wahren Eintracht* in Vienna. Later, there is a gradual growth and expansion of such teachings and methods of control formulated originally by Adam Weishaupt, which will result in new orders and dangerous sects popping up like mushrooms.

There is a real **network of the Illuminati** of a thousand emanations, and not a single order. Gioele Magaldi, the former Worshipful Master of a prestigious Roman lodge of the Grand Orient of Italy with a strong Jewish presence, reveals the real meaning of the term **"Illuminati":** [104]

This term according to the authors of this volume, is to be considered as the result of Self-attribution by certain members of Masonic and reactionary neoaristocratic cir-

103   ario Iannacone, "Reinhold: a fake Jesuit between Freemasons and Illuminist," article *"Avvenire,"* (Milan, IT: 14-01-2012).
104   Gioele Magaldi is the Past Worshipful Master of **Lodge Har Tzion Montesion 705** of the Grand Ori-ent of Italy of Palazzo Giustiniani a Masonic Obbedience recognized by all of the US Grand Lodges.

cles. Is instead quite misleading any conspiracy narrative based on the inconsistent assumption of a subsidiary, direct or indirect, of these contemporary "Illuminati" Masons supposedly linked to the Order of the so-called "Bavarian Illuminati" (operating effectively, as such, only from the mid-sixties until the late eighties of the eighteenth century, although some of their suggestions will be taken and processed specifically within Masonic circles decades and centuries later), founded in 1776 by Johan Adam Weishaupt (1748-1830). [105]

There remains no doubt that the occult side of the Illuminati, followed these mysterious teachings on the Jewish mysteries produced by the Jesuit / Freemason Reinhold, which brought the creation of the Golden Dawn, and in turn the rise of Aleister Crowley "The Great Beast," a century later. But this happened only after the Templar myth was put "officially" to sleep at Wilhelmsbad, and stored secretly in the upper echelons of the various Rites / Masonic systems. They instead gave a lot of importance to the Jewish mysteries in the early grades, which are also those of the subsequent Royal Arch. Obviously there are exceptions in the Swedish Rite, where the Templar myth and the chilvaric element are present in the DNA of the system since the apprentice degree, as you are required to be "Christian" to become a Mason or should I should say a pseudo one, at this point.

This is an anomaly, and goes against the "Universal principles" where Freemasonry is considered to be the symbolic bearer in the first three degrees, (Entered Apprentice, Fellowcraft and Master Masons Degrees of Freemasonry). These developments subsequent to Wilhelmsbad undoubtedly facilitated the rise of the Jewish (non Christian) population within Freemasonry, but also the rise of deviant forms of Neo-Templarism in opposition, like the Ordo Templi Orientis, promoted by the dark and perverse side of the Illuminati headed initially by Theodor Reuss (1855-1923).

As Aleister Crowley wrote in his Confessions, a little more than a century after the Masonic Convent of Wilhelmsbad, in regards to the state of North American Freemasonry: [106] they must now hide their Christian roots to allow the initiation of the rich Jews at the top of Freemasonry, Even Crowley who was a known instigator of deviant forms of Masonry, found it hypocritical. The text of Karl Leonhard Reinhold that focuses on the mysteries of the Jewish religion in relation to the Egyptian initiatic mysteries, is exposed in a general reorientation of European Freemasonry. [107]

The Illuminati inspired by the Jesuits, sought the return of the deeper answers to the myths and legends that generated modern Speculative Freemasonry, [108] but at the same time they were fomenting relativism. Until the end of the eighteenth century, this scenario expanded with the myth of the Templars, which was connected to the establishment of the Temple of Solomon, an element which remains of fundamental importance in Freemasonry. When the Templar myth was officially put aside because it was considered unfounded at the Masonic Convent of 1782, further studies began on the Masonic mysteries, to form solid roots for the foundation of Freemasonry. The Illuminati Order decided for this rea-

105 Gioele Magaldi, Massoni. Società a responsabilità illimitata. La scoperta delle Ur-Lodges, (Freemasons. Unlimited company. The Discovery of the Ur-Lodges), (Milan, IT: Chiarelettere, 2014), p. 634.

106 Aleister Crowley, "Confessions" Verse 5, Chapter 72: The Scottish Rite, the degrees of Knight Templar, Knight of Malta and others in England are definitely Christian, e.g. the point of one degree is the identification of prophet, priest and king, three in one, the Trinity of the Royal Arch, with Christ; and in the Rose Croix degree, Christ is recognized as the "corner stone" of earlier symbolism. But in America, the Christian elements have been removed so that wealthy Jews may reach the summit of Masonry.

107 See Carl Leonhard Reinhold, Ibid., p. 15.

108 Ibid., p. 26.

son, to reveal to their members, the hidden truths of the Jewish belief to their Masons, to help them understand the smaller mysteries of the Hebrews. Ancient Egypt and the history of the people of Israel lead by Moses, then took on a totally new meaning. Reinhold set out to demonstrate in his presentation, that the 613 commandments and prohibitions of the **Torah**, are nothing more than *"hieroglyphics, ceremonies and ritual prescriptions,"* and they represent *"a true copy of the mystery religion of the Egyptians."* [109]

Reinhold in his brilliant exposition, seems to succeed in his aim to enlighten us with his research on the true origins of the Jewish belief found in ancient Egypt. Jan Assmann writes, in his introduction to the first Italian edition of this important essay:

> *In this period the richest Masons began building pyramids in their gardens, while in the same year Giuseppe Balsamo, who called himself "Count of Cagliostro," founded his Lodges of the "Egyptian Rite." The research program developed by the mysterious Viennese Lodge is clearly a response to the pioneering publication of Starck in 1783.* [110]

The work of Starck just mentioned by Jan Assmann, is Starck's book *On the Old and new mysteries* (Berlin 1782), which had, according to Assmann, stimulated this important Viennese lodge in their research on the mysteries, and influenced the mood and the work of *Illuminati* and Freemason Wolfgang Amadeus Mozart, for his masterpiece *The Magic Flute* of 1791. This essay was cited in a study of Starck made by U.S. Freemason Albert Pike (1809-1891), Sovereign Grand Commander of the Supreme Council of the A.A.S.R. for the Southern Jurisdiction of the United States from 1859 until his death. Pike is best known for his book published in 1871, *Morals and Dogma of the Ancient and Accepted Scottish Rite of Freemasonry*, or simply *Morals and Dogma*, considered to be "the most complete exposition of the philosophy of the Scottish Rite," a statement made **by C. Fred Kleinknecht (1924-2011)**, who was also a celebrated and important Sovereign Grand Commander of this prestigious Rite of Freemasonry from 1985-2003. But the aforementioned, controversial theologian that some experts believe to be the father of the study of comparative religion and an agent of the Jesuits, was not well-regarded by Reinhold, who actually accused him of Jesuit influence. Reinhold, an *Illuminati* and former Jesuit (or Jesuit seminarist if we want to believe the Catholic newspaper *"Avvenire"*), loved to denounce any influences of this kind, because at that time there was an internal war in the Illuminati Network. The Illuminati of **The Order of the Golden and Rosy Cross** *(Orden des Gold-und Rosenkreutz, also the Fraternity of the Golden and Rosy Cross),* that is always faithful to the Jesuits, and the anti-Jesuit faction, embedded in deep anti-clericalism, was actually manipulated and instrumental to the Jesuits behind the curtains of history, that with the help of Judaism, fully developed the new plague called Communism, a utopia that originally arises within the order of the Jesuits. Returning to the mysteries of Karl Leonhard Reinhold, Jan Assmann writes:

> *The Freemasons and the Illuminati specifically recognized in this intuition "the oldest form of Masonry" and considered themselves the legitimate successors to those ancient Egyptian initiates, feeling called to keep burning in the changed conditions of the modern age that original torch of truth and wisdom.* [111]

In his work, Reinhold speaks often about the great influence in the Masonic culture with Judaism, and the influence of the Egyptian tradition which originated it. The recovery of the Egyptian mysteries in their purest form represents to him and the *Illuminati*—the

109   *Ibid.,* p. 16, *[emphasis added].*
110   See. Carl Leonhard Reinhold, *Ibid.,* p. 48.
111   *Ibid.* p. 63.

recovery of the mysteries that lie in the very foundations of the Judeo-Christian culture, the occult key to the absolute rule of the system and the foundation for the subsequent creation of modern Sinarchic Technocracy, that as I showed you earlier was launched by the theories of Alexandre Saint-Ives of Alveydre author of *Mission des Juifs* (1884). Another "Illuminati" in the broadest sense of the term, the English self-styled Egyptologist **Gerald Massey (1828-1907)**, **Grand Master of the Druids**, author and high level Freemason, a century later would publish an excellent essay called *Book of the Beginnings,* where he spoke of the true origins of the Jewish people which he also claimed was in ancient Egypt. Massey makes an extensive analysis in some ways even more profound than that of Reinhold, both from the philological point of view and from a philosophical one:

"In this way, by aid of the hieroglyphics, symbolism, and mythology of Egypt we shall be enabled now to get beyond that 'original Hebrew' so often appealed to, which has so long served as the last covert and lurking-place of hunted lies. The cave of refuge is found to have a backdoor open with a daylight world welcoming us beyond. Egyptian gives us the primaries of language, the very shapes in which thoughts were formed. Meanings that have been pursued in vain for ages can now be run down to Earth at last. The typical and symbolical may be read in the symbols and the types of those who created the myths, unless in the meantime the obscurity of the cave has produced in us such visual weakness that the organ is henceforth limited to seeing in the dark."

This huge work was originally published in two volumes in London in 1881, and influenced even **Aleister Crowley** and his disciple **Kenneth Grant.**

*In the Book of Job, the palace of the prince of glory is juxtaposed with the mishkan of the wicked. 'Ye say, "Where (is) the house of the prince? and where are the dwelling-places of the wicked?" The house of the prince in the Ritual is called the Palace of the Great House, in the region of the hill. The dwellings of the wicked were in the ten kars or hells of the damned. The meskhen was the purgatory. The son, as repa and heir-apparent, the prince of peace, the anointed one, had various impersonations in Egyptian mythology, as Horus, **Khunsu**, and Iu-em-hept. One of these is represented in the Hebrew mythology by **Solomon**, the son of David. Khunsu, in relation to Taht or the moon, is the lunar son, who fulfils and completes the double circle of sun and moon. As the solar son he is the child of Amen-Ra. That bears on his head the half circle of the moon; Khunsu carries on his the full round. He is the fulfiller. And this is the significance of Solomon's name. Shalom (שלום) means to complete, finish, bring to an end, perfect the whole work begun by some forerunner supposed to be the ante-type.*

The meaning of peace is subsidiary to and dependent on this sense of perfecting some work, and completing and finishing the whole. This is done by the son Khunsu, in fulfilling the soli-lunar circle at the vernal equinox. One of Khunsu's titles is Nefer-hept. Hept means peace; nefer may be read the good, perfect, plant, youth. The Nefer-hept is really the Hebrew prince of peace, or, as Solomon is designated in the Song of Songs, "the king to whom peace belongs." He is also called the "king of peace with the crown."

And as nefer is the crown, nefer-hept is the crowned of peace, i.e., the king of peace, synonymous with Solomon, the king of peace with the crown.

*The seventy-second psalm is called a **"Psalm for Solomon,"** and the speaker says, "Give the king thy judgments, and thy righteousness to the king's son." Taht was the signer of the sentences passed on the souls of the dead in the hall of the Two Truths. And in praise of the son it is proclaimed with great appropriateness, "In his days shall the righteous flourish so long as the moon endureth." That is the primary* *imagery. "I will make the horn of David to bud; I have ordained a lamp for mine anointed." The horn of the new moon is borne by Taht; the lamp of the full moon by Khunsu. It cannot be shown that Khunsu was considered to be the son of Taut, although he is the lunar child, and carries the full moon on his head but the son in whom the soli-lunar types were both united was Khunsu, the prince of peace, who in the Hebrew myths is Solomon, the son of David. [112]*

This originates from two influential speeches that later became a crucial illuminist booklet written by Leipzig and Weimar between 1785 and 1786 by Reinhold. A large research devoted to the Viennese Masonic lodge *Zur wahren Eitracht*, committed at the end of the eighteenth century to a complex program of studies promoted by the Adam Wesihaupt's *Illuminati*, on mystery cults in search of the origins of Freemasonry. Reinhold's research would never be personally read by him in an open lodge, but by his friend Martin Joseph Prandstretter, who will do so on the 6th of March and the 3rd of April, 1786. It will also be received in the "sister" lodge *Zur Warheit*, and not in the *Zur wahren Eitracht*, for security reasons, because from 1783 the *Illuminati* were forbidden as well as the Jesuits, and Reinhold would surely have risked a lot in participating to the presentation in person in his own lodge.

Freemasonry & Judaism a strange affair ...

When I reached to the end of my research for this chapter, I discovered a very interesting article entitled *Freemasonry & Judaism are compatible* by **Rt. Wor. Bro. Rabbi Dr Raymond Apple Emeriti Rabbi of the Great Synagogue of Sydney**, AO RFD, Past Deputy Grand Master of the United Grand Lodge of New South Wales & the Australian Capital Territory. In his brief exposition, the Rabbi and Senior Freemason points out certain lesser known aspects of the relationship between Judaism and Freemasonry, which I think are essential for a full understanding of this subject from the Jewish prospective. Rabbi Raymond Apple writes:

Especially in English-speaking countries, the movement has always had a high proportion of eminent Jewish members, including leading rabbis. Among present day Australian rabbis, high Masonic office is held by Rabbi Shalom Coleman of Perth, Rabbi Chaim Gutnick of Melbourne and myself in Sydney. Other rabbis and ministers are past masters of their lodges. All this clearly indicates that Jews have not found Freemasonry to be incompatible with their Judaism. Why Jewish Masons feel at home with the movement includes the requirement that a Mason must believe in God, and the fact that the Bible occupies a place of honour in the lodge room. Masonic ritual is based largely on biblical words, events and personalities, and the overal emphasis is on ethics, friendship and good works. Admittedly, some of the Hebrew words that figure in Masonic ceremonies are mispronounced and the references to biblical events occasionally get their history wrong, but these are regarded by Jewish Freemasons as incidental issues. No major challenge to Jewish faith is seen in being a Mason or in promoting its ideals.

The Rabbi also talks about the clash between the Catholic Church and Freemasonry calling it **"The Christian problem with Freemasonry,"** completely ignoring and not mentioning the vast Masonic Christian tradition:

It has often been otherwise among Christians. For a long period, Masonry and the Roman Catholic Church lived in a state of conflict or, at best, of uneasy truce, though the Catholic position is now increasingly positive. In recent years, however, the Church of England has taken up a critical attitude to the movement, both in Britain and elsewhere in the Anglican communion. In 1988, the synod of the Anglican Church in Australia declared Freemasonry to be "basically incompatible with Christianity." The Christian problem with Freemasonry is both general (there is an incorrect perception that the movement is a rival religion), and particular, in that it makes no reference to Jesus or the New Testament, at least in the basic three degrees through which most Masons progress.

Masonry responds by insisting that it is religious without being a religion and that it fosters a generally religious attitude to life, but has no theological doctrines, mandatory interpretations or modes of worship.

At this point Raymond Apple insists on the "Universality" of Freemasonry "open to men of all faiths" in the following passage:

"The omission of Jesus and the New Testament is implicit in the fact that Freemasonry is open to men of all faiths. Jews, Muslims, Hindus and others are as welcome as Christians. But each comes to Masonry with his own religious beliefs and commitments, and when he hears the word "God" in lodge ritual, he attaches to it his own theological interpretation. A Jew will understand the divine name in terms of the pure, indivisible monotheism of Judaism: to him, "God" is "HaShem." A Christian is free to import into the word "God" his own Christian concepts and understanding.

Then the Rabbi and Past Deputy Grand Master attacked German Freemasonry as being anti-Semitic in the past, a partially inaccurate claim as there were two distinct Masonic factions in Germany before the rise of Nazism. One was clearly Christian and Neo-Templar, known as **"Old Prussians,"** for this reason not compatible with other religions, the other was the **"Humanitarians,"** that admitted Jews, and had cosmopolitan ideals. However Rabbi Apple writes:

The history of Freemasonry suggests a major and tragic paradox. In parts of continental Europe, especially 19th-century Germany, there were major objections to Jewish membership of the movement. Anti-Semitism was then endemic in sections of German Freemasonry. Yet the anti-Semite was never rational or consistent, and before long Freemasonry was regularly attacked as "too Jewish," and therefore dangerous to society. Accusations of Jewish-Masonic plots to undermine and control the world played a role in the Dreyfus affair. They surfaced in that notorious forgery, "The Protocols of the Elders of Zion." And the German right wing and the Nazis added similar accusations to their anti-Semitic armoury. To Jews, the right to join Freemasonry became a touchstone of religious liberty, an agent of emancipation and social integration. Hence, in the free atmosphere of British countries, Jews were well represented in lodge memberships, and Jewish community leaders were prominent Masons. [113]

The late **Eric Howe, P.M. Quatuor Coronati Lodge, No. 2076**, one of the world's leading Masonic authorities, from the leading Masonic lodge of research, wrote the following, in complete contrast with the supposed expertise of the Rabbi:

The problem which bedeviled and split the Masonic Order in Germany for years on end was the so-called "Jewish question." In its original form it referred to religious rather than racial prejudice. The three "Old Prussian" Grand Lodges had always refused to accept Jews for initiation because their Craft degrees were followed by

---

higher ones of a Christian character. Thus, as far as the "Old Prussians" were concerned, one brief but important passage in the Antient Charges was ignored it reads: **"Let a man's religion or mode of worship be what it may, he is not excluded from the order provided he believe in the glorious architect of heaven and Earth and practise the sacred duties of morality."**

The six "Humanitarian" Grand Lodges, on the other hand, nominally made no distinction between Christian and Jew. This did not mean that every Jewish candidate could be sure of joining a Lodge, because exclusion by blackball was not unknown. However, once a Jew became a Freemason he could attend "Old Prussian" Craft Lodges as a visitor. Superficially, at least, the overall situation was that the "Old Prussian" Grand Lodges represented ultra-conservative attitudes, while the "Humanitarian" Obediences were more liberally inclined.

The "Jewish question," in the sense that it was perenially a source of controversy between the two groups, was probably always basically insoluble. Nevertheless, as long as it was solely based on religious prejudice some kind of modus vivendi, although never a completely satisfactory one, was contrived. In a non-Masonic context religious discrimination against Jews gave way after 1870 to political and economic anti-Semitism. Then, during the 1900s we encounter the early stages of the virulent racial anti-Semitism which was to afflict Germany like a disease and which culminated thirty years later in Hitler's "Final Solution," meaning genocide. The wave of anti-Semitic propaganda which flooded the country during the years 1910-14 was one of the various manifestations of German nationalism's overheated condition at that time. The Jew was now presented as the antithesis of all that was "truly German," hence as the embodiment of a whole range of negative or unattractive qualities.

It never occurred to the pre-1914 anti-Semitic propagandists to attack Freemasonry on the grounds that its Craft rituals incorporate material and symbolism derived from the Old Testament and therefore superficially of "Jewish" origin.

When anti-Masonic propaganda of this kind was first disseminated by the anti-Semitic caucus immediately after the First World War, the Grand Lodges found the proposition that the Craft could conceivably be "tainted" for these reasons so ludicrous that they hardly reacted. The anti-Semites had already created the "perfidious Jew" archetype before 1914. Yet another archetype, the "perfidious Freemason," was invented during the war but did not become well-known to most Germans until immediately after their country's military defeat in 1918. The astonishing proposition that Germany had been the victim of an international Judaeo-Masonic conspiracy began to be current in 1918 and was repeated ad nauseam in a succession of books and pamphlets which were published during the era of the Weimar Republic. The "Judaeo-Masonic Conspiracy" theory was so manifestly silly that the Grand Lodges cannot be blamed for failing to realise that its incessant repetition would ultimately damage the Craft. The "Old Prussian" sector protested that they were Christian institutions and did not admit Jews, but the market for myths was invariably larger than any for reasoned statements. [114]

Rabbi Dr Raymond Apple, should acknowledge certain points with a more bias and accurate modality, but of course even within Freemasonry disinformation and manipulated facts seem to be the norm, even for their Senior representatives.

114   http://www.grandlodgescotland.com/index.php/masonic-subjects/holocaust-memorial-day/articles/104-freemasonry-in-germany-part-i ‡ Archived 30th July, 2015, *[emphasis added]*.

Chapter VI

My Experience in the New World Order and my War against Satanism and Disinformation

My family

The beginning of this chapter is dedicated to how I was recruited into the New World Order, at the age of **23**. My adventure began on April 13, 1993, when I was initiated into the mysteries of the *Ancient and Accepted Scottish Rite* by Prince Don Giovanni Francesco Alliata di Montereale (1921–1994), in his dual capacity as Grand Master and Sovereign Grand Commander. This was performed "by the sword," as it is known in Masonic language, with a form of Masonic initiation reminiscent to what is effected in Knighthood Orders. I was also honored without being reguarly initiated, pass and raised, in the traditional Masonic manner, with the 33rd degree.

Gioele Magaldi 30° of the A.A.S.R. writes about this unusual form of initiation:

Especially in the past, but even in the present, survives even if in a more covered and secret way, the custom of initiating certain people (for the most diverse reasons) not through the normal, articulated and evocative rituals used by the ordinary lodges or a given Masonic communion / obedience, but through the extraordinary liturgical initiation made by a Grand Master, or a Sovereign Grand Commander, Grand Hierophant or Worshipful Master of a Ur Lodge or a Grand Dignitary delegated by them. In this way, an individual can be "made" a Mason at sight by the ritual sword touchings of a high level Grand Master or his official collaborator, and this kind of initiation is not necessarily transcribed in the records and official lists of the communion / obedience, superlodge or ritual body, but remains in the "memory" only of the initiator and of the few who, with a vocal transmission "mouth to ear," are made aware of this man. [1]

In February 1909, A U.S. Grand Master made a Mason at Sight out of *William H. Taft*, then President Elect of the United States. Useful information about this almost unknown Masonic tradition can be found in *Making a Mason At Sight* by Louis L. Williams, published in 1983 by the Illinois Lodge of Research-Masonic Book Club (based in Bloomington, Illinois). At the time of my initiation, I was the youngest 33° degree ever nominated in

1   Gioele Magaldi, *Ibid.*, p. 634.

Italy. Only Alberto Moscato, former Chief Agent of the O.T.O., was able to obtain this prestigious degree at a relatively young age in Italy. After receiving the 33° degree of the ***Sovereign Grand Inspector General of the Ancient and Accepted Scottish Rite***, I was appointed **Sovereign Grand Commander,** and heir to the throne of Alliata's Rite for Italy. (FIG. 41) This event was unusual, and in the eyes of some skeptics, unlikely. I received this transmission due to my *bloodline*, in a historical period in Europe, at the end of the Cold War.

I never accepted my role as Alliata's successor as Sovereign of the Rite, and the Rite was passed to the other equally legitimate successors of this prestigious Masonic lineage of Prince Alliata of Montereale. **Prince Alliata of Montereale** was not only a Grand Master, but also a Sovereign Grand Commander (for life-*ad vitam*), of the Ancient and Accepted Scottish Rite of Piazza del Gesù. This was a role the Prince retained his entire life due to his prestigious bloodline linked to the **Holy Roman Empire** connected to the foundations of the Rite. Alliata was Grand Master of the *National Grand Lodge of Ancient Free and Accepted Masons*, and spent a period in the *Grand Orient of Italy*, as a member of

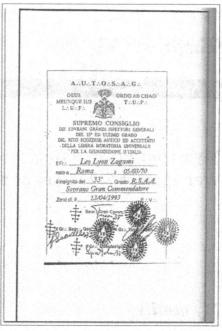

FIG. 41 – Leo Lyon Zagami Masonic Patent of Sovereign Grand Commander of the Supreme Council of the 33rd and last degree of the Ancient and Accepted Scottish Rite for the Italian jurisdiction. A document given to the author after his initiation into Freemasonry by Prince Alliata of Monreale in April, 1993.

the **P2 Lodge (membership No. 361).** He founded the *Association of Aristocrats and Nobles of the Holy Roman Empire*, and was involved in politics and Freemasonry with my grandfather, Senator **Leopoldo Zagami (1905-1973)** who was from the Aeolian Islands next to Sicily. He married a descendant of two of the noblest families of the Holy Roman Empire, my grandmother Lidia. The two noble families were the **(Di) Gregorio,** one of the most important of the Holy Roman Empire, and **Labruto,** where we find Don Giovanni Labruto, Judge of the the *Royal Supreme Court* in 1747 and one of the most influential people of the city of Messina. Messina was the last port for ships arriving from Italy and France. It was an important logistical base for the Knights Templar, as reported in a short essay entitled *I Templari in Sicilia* (*The Templars in Sicily*) by Litterio Villari; [2] that is based on rare documentary evidence that was revealed, despite the destruction and dispersal of the archives of the priories. This essay indicates 1113 as the year the first hospice run by monks and crusaders of the Order of Saint Mary of the Valley of Giosaphat in Jerusalum (*Santa Maria di Valle Giosaphat di Gerusalemme*) rose in Messina. It became a base of operations for the various knights and religious orders *"that guested for a few decades the Pilgrims going to the Holy Land."* [3]

2   Litterio Villari, *I Templari in Sicilia,* (Latina, IT: Penne & papiri), 1993.
3   *Ibid.,* p. 9.

FIG. 42 – Symbol of the (Di) Gregorio family.

Villari writes that: *The Order of the Templars owned its first church in Messina, with adjoining hospice dedicated to St. Mark the Evangelist, in today's building of the Province, not far from the benches of the port.* [4] This is a place where centuries later the Count of Cagliostro (also a member of my family) would meet the mysterious **Althotas,** who would become his Chief Secret and who initiated him to the highest mysteries. Returning to Di Gregorio, (FIG. 42) according to Baron Giuseppe Gallup, one of the most credible historic sources on Sicilian nobility: *Gregorio, said sometimes De Gregorio, sometimes Di Gregorio, actually originates from Cologne, Germany, and from the family of **General Onofrio Bolzani** at the service of Emperor Henry I of the Sacred Roman Empire; who rewarded Bolzani for his excellent work in the military with a generous compensation and with the title of **Baron of the Holy Roman Empire.** Later his son named Gregorio imposed this name to his posterity, and one of his sons Giovanni Di Gregorio was rewarded by Emperor Henry IV for his great services in the military with the government of the city of **Cologne in Germany** and the ability to have the noble symbol in the main church of the city.* [5] It remains to this day, as I witnessed many years ago, when I visited this beautiful German city.

The Greek transliteration of Grigori means *"Watchers,"* "those who are awake" and "guard." **Watcher** is also a term used in connection with biblical angels. There are many other influential people in this family that can confirm the importance of this bloodline. In fact, there are so many that Gallupi's book on the Nobility of Sicily states the following about the (Di) Gregory family: *"If we should mention all the distinguished members of this noble lineage it would result in an excessively long account."* [6] This family expanded into several branches. With the title of Marquis of Poggio Gregorio, that was later injected into the Prince of St. Elia peerage. Also linked with my maternal grandmother, was the aforementioned Labruto family, which in turn was linked to the family of the famous Illuminati Grand Master Giuseppe Balsamo, also so known as *"Count Cagliostro."*

Returning to my grandfather Leopoldo Zagami, (FIG. 43) at the end of the Second World War he joined a branch of the *Ancient and Accepted Scottish Rite* (A.A.S.R.) defined by the scholar, Jesuit Father Pietro Pirri SJ of the Historical Institute of the Society of Jesus, as an autonomous Pseudo-Catholic form of Freemasonry. (FIG. 44) The Grand Master and Sovereign Grand Commander of the Rite was the Italian aristocrat Baron **Furio Romano Avezzana,** (FIG. 45) who died in Rome on the 15th of June 1949.

4   *Ibid.,* p. 3.
5   See. Giuseppe Gallupi, *Nobiliario della Città di Messina,* (Naples, IT: A. Forni, 1887), p. 107.
6   *Ibid.,* p. 108.

Subsequently this group made up of a fusion of Lodges loyal to Baron Avezzana, then moved to the headquarters of Piazza Gesù in front of the Jesuit headquarters of the Church of the Gesù, that is the Jesuit Mother Church of the world, where the Italian Supreme Council of the A.A.S.R. still resides. At that time, there was a unification of the various branches of Italian Freemasonry close to the Catholic Church. This took place in Piazza del Gesù, which for fifty years would dominate Italy politicly, as the headquarters of the **Christian Democrat Party**; (*Partito della Democrazia Cristiana*) and was secretly financed by the U.S. State Deparment, which was also based next to the headquarters of the Supreme Council of the A.A.S.R., forming the ultimate triangle of power.

The **"New Age"** (*L'Era Nuova*), was official publication of this group, and in September, 1947, it made the following profession of faith: *"In a Catholic country like Italy, the Christianity of the Italian Freemasons can only follow true, Catholic ethics."*

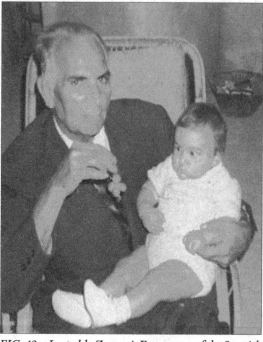

FIG. 43 – Leopoldo Zagami, Freemason of the Scottish Rite Ancient and Accepted of Piazza del Gesu, and a member of the Italian Senate who died in the mid-seventies, with his grandson, the author of this book and future 33° of the A.A.S.R., in a photo dating back to the early seventies.

Such a statement was intended to usher in a form of Catholic Freemasonry that could fight Communism, the enemy of the time, during the so-called "Cold War." It is ironic if you consider, that the same insitutions that were fighting Communism, are the ones that fully endorse it. In 1955, after the death of Baron Risi, who was Avezzana's successor, Prince Alliata was promoted to the office of Sovereign Grand Commander of the Supreme Council of the 33rd, and last degree of the Ancient and Accepted Scottish Rite for the Italian jurisdiction, recognized thanks to the direct intervention of U.S. Intelligence Chief and Freemason, **Dr. Frank Bruno Gigliotti** (1896-1975), and by the **The Supreme Council, 33°, Ancient & Accepted Scottish Rite of Freemasonry, Southern Jurisdiction, in Washington DC, USA.** [7]

This was a leading position Prince Alliata retained for the rest of his life, because of his *bloodline*, and its link to the "Grand Constitution of the Thirty-third Degree," written by Frederick the Great of Prussia in 1786. Alliata also had a prime role in the Intelligence Community during the Cold war, and was one of the key collaborators of the Italo-American, Frank Gigliotti. A well documented historian on the Illuminati Terry Melanson, writes extensively on Giogliotti in an article published online, *Frank Gigliotti: Minister, Freemason, OSS and CIA*, that is based on credible sources and documentation. I find

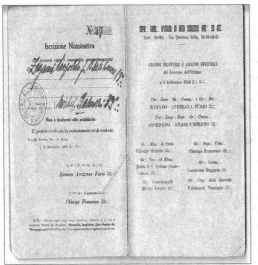

FIG. 44 – Masonic Passport issued by the Italian Supreme Council of the Ancient and Accepted Scottish Rite of Baron Furio Romano Avezzana headquartered in Rome, Via Quintino Sella 60 (site of today's Japanese Embassy), to Brother **Bartolomeo Leopoldo Zagami,** belonging to their **Lodge of The Sphinx** in Messina, testifying his status as 18th Degree of Knight Rose Croix back in1946. This is after the end of World War II, which ended the prohibition on Masonic activities imposed by fascism after 1924 on the Italian soil.

the following section particularly interesting for this research :

If you have studied the history of deep state intrigue, Gladio and stay-behind networks during the Cold war, occasionally you may have come across a fleeting mention of someone named Frank Gigliotti. In Philip Willan's **Puppetmasters,** *for example, Gigliotti is described as a "former OSS and then CIA agent" who played a key role in the U.S. negations to return control to the Grand Orient Masons, their former headquarters in Palazzo Giustiniani, Rome. "Frank Gigliotti of the U.S. Masonic Lodge,"* **Daniele Ganser** *asserts in* **NATO's Secret Armies,** *"personally recruited Gelli and instructed him to set up an anti-Communist parallel government in Italy in close cooperation with the CIA station in Rome." In Willan's book as well, Gigliotti is mentioned in a paragraph that begins with Gelli's initiation into the Grand Orient Masonry.*

The parliamentary commission of inquiry investigating the P2 specifically mentions Frank Gigliotti, his OSS/CIA/U.S. Scottish Rite/Grand Orient ties, and draws attention to the conspicuous appearance of (the recently passed) Licio Gelli, once Gigliotti leaves the scene. [8]

Terry Melanson questions Giogliotti's mission:

"This seemingly obscure Mason from the U.S. was meddling in Grand Orient Masonic affairs, on behalf of his Masonic brethren as well as the U.S. government, and was linked to the rise of Gelli and his ascendancy to the leadership of the P2. Who was this man? What was the trajectory of his career? Beginning in 1937 (McCoy 2009 b: 52) and through to his OSS years, Gigliotti was tapped for service by the mysterious army Major General Ralph H. Van Deman, "the father of military Intelligence" who died in 1952. [9]

Alliata became for a time, a member of the Propaganda 2 Lodge, which later operated independently by the Worshipful Master Licio Gelli. Prince Alliata never participated to the activities of the lodges of Grand Orient of Italy. In the following years he became the promoter of various Masonic and para-Masonic associations and Orders. In 1980, he officially launched the *Nobility Order of the Sword and the Eagle* (a Masonic-Neo-Templar Order), of which he became the Sovereign Prince and Grand Master.

In 1986, he founded the *Cultural Association of Universal Freemasonry* of the European Rite, known by the acronym MURE, of which he became president. In 1992, one year before he initiated me, he created *The Association of National Academy of Esoteric Sciences—Universal Freemasonry of the Ancient and Accepted Scottish Rite Orient of Italy* (R∴S∴A∴A∴O∴I∴), and in 1993, *The European Association of the Philosophic Rite (RFE).* It was because of a strong Masonic and political bond, between Prince Giovanni Francesco Alliata di Montereale (FIG. 46) and my grandfather Leopoldo Zagami, that I was called to this important life changing event, after a long period of observation and training that lasted several years, beginning during my time spent as a conscript in the Air Force working at the Italian Ministry of Defence Air Force Headquarters. This is where I was initially approached by people that belonged to powerful

FIG. 45 – Baron Furio Romano Avezzana, who operated in the 1940s with an elite Masonic body as Sovereign Grand Commander and Grand Master, was linked to the U.S. Office of Strategic Services, with Frank Gigliotti as their head adviser for the Italian section.

groups such as **Opus Dei** and **Freemasonry**. These were shady figures from military Intelligence, and this is when I began on a path on the edge of legality, that would put me in contact with leaders of the notorious **Operation Gladio,** and the infamous P2.

In theory, anyone can become part of Freemasonry or Opus Dei, but joining the elite network of the New World Order and their *High Collegia* is a very different affair. *You must be chosen, you can't ask to join.* The *High Collegia* (i.e. "Collegia" plural of "Collegium" which means "joined by law") also known at times in the Rosicrucian tradition as the Invisible College, is the only truly superior secret society able to influence all forms of secret societies and groups. This particular society is composed of indiscernible individuals, whose efforts lead to actions of great importance. Their historical origin can be found in the tradition of the maritime fleet of the Order of the Temple (i.e. the Knights Templar). [10]

This is how the real Illuminati operates, it is not something you can join by reading a book or visiting a website, as *Illuminatiam* asserts. Keep in mind that your average Mason completely ignores the existence of the New World Order, and knows only superficially this vast sectarian network. The common Mason is not permitted to ask certain questions without authorization. Unauthorized questions would cause the common Mason to be isolated by his "Brothers," who would either kick him out or leave him on standby in the apprentice degree, or Fellow Craft degree, for the rest of his Masonic life, without the possibility of

10   *Confessions of an Illuminati, Vol. I, Ibid.,* p. 43.

FIG. 46 – Prince Giovanni Francesco Alliata of Montereale successor of Baron Furio Romano Avezzana in the office of Sovereign Grand Commander, and key figure of the New World Order as one of Frank Gigliotti's main collaborators during the Cold War.

joining a Rite, that can only happen after the 3rd degree of Master Mason; therefore blocking the ability for the Mason to obtain further knowledge of the mysteries.

When the Ancient and Accepted Scottish Rite, or the York Rite, are taken seriously by its members, you are trained with a military form of iron discipline and blind obedience which derives from the Knighthood teachings present in the upper degrees of these Masonic systems. The A.A.S.R. as well as the "Egyptian Rites" form a proper occult chain that derives from the Rosicrucian tradition revealed to the candidate only when they reach the 18th degree. Of course this occult element can become dangerous at times, in fact the late **high level Freemason and Masonic historian Enrico Simoni (33° gold necklace of the A.A.S.R.),** who was also a member of my order (*Ordo Illuminatorum Universalis*), died prematurely of a brain tumor in 2013, and confessed the following shortly before he died: *"12 years ago I began to feel sick and it gradually worsened after I entered the Italian Supreme Council of the Ancient Accepted Scottish Rite."*

Pertaining to his sudden illness after entering the *Italian Supreme Council of the Ancient Accepted Scottish Rite,* psychically defending oneself is of utmost importance. We will return to this subject in the last chapter, with a wealth of information that will aid the reader in protecting himself from invisible and sometimes potentially lethal psychic attacks. To the Illuminati there are two important elements: the Egregore, and the occult chain, but both can be polluted and dangerous for those who adventure themselves in such realms with no real knowledge of the occult. Satanic infiltration can occur within infiltrated esoteric bodies which often result in mysterious deaths and other unpleasant occurrences. Enrico Simoni was only one, among a series of many deaths, *five to be exact,* within the same Supreme Council of the 33° the A.A.S.R. Jurisdiction for Italy, recognized by the Grand Orient of Italy and the U.S. Supreme Councils. They occurred between 2009 and 2010 when **Sergio Cimini, Dario Montalenti** (Grand Prior), **Giuseppe Oliveri** of the *Lodge Vita Nova Belfiore 116* in Florence, and another 33rd degree gold necklace named **Bent Parodi**, a Sicilian of noble origins and an Illuminati, all died one after the other, of *seemingly* natural causes.

Parodi, who died in December 2009, was a journalist and writer, also known as a scholar of world religions and president of the Order of Journalists in Sicily. He was the son of the Duke Ugo Parodi of Belsito; a Sicilian nobleman of Genoese origin, and his mother was Tove Holm-Andersen Danis, a **descendant of Hans Christian Andersen.** [11] This family however, had a dark side, and were said to be linked to Satanic practices.

11   See. https://it.wikipedia.org/wiki/Bent_Parodi Archived 30th July, 2015. *[emphasis added].*

On the 28th of April 2013, Bent Parodi's tomb located in a family chapel in the small cemetery in Capo d'Orlando in Sicily, was desecrated by an unknown assailant. Stolen was a book, placed on a small altar within a glass case. The book contained the history of religions written by the great Romanian esoteric thinker and author **Mircea Eliade**, of no economic value, but of great sentimental and energetic value to this network of Illuminati and their sects. Bent Parodi had expressed the wish not to separate from this book even after death, but the wish was not respected, as this book was a material link to his soul for their rituals.

A complaint to the Police Capo d'Orlando was filed on the incident by the Family Foundation chaired by Prof. Carmelo Romeo. [12] On the 7th of September 2013, the Family Foundation then held a new ceremony at the cemetery in Capo d'Orlando, and a new glass case and a new copy of the book by Mircea Eliade was replaced. [13]

Not one member of the present Italian Supreme Council of the A.A.S.R. has said a word publicly on the mysterious death chain that occurred in their Masonic Rite, or on this strange incident that happened at the grave of Ben Parodi. That's because, in 2009, these five Freemasons were the victims of an internal conflict within the Rite. A conflict I personally witnessed between black magicians and white magicians, which erupted in the Supreme Council of the 33rd degree and would eventually kill my friend, Enrico Simoni. In 1919, "the Beast" Aleister Crowley himself, did not succeed in his initial intention to take control of the Supreme Council of the A.A.S.R. in the "Valley" of Detroit. Crowley wrote initially with great enthusiasm: *"The accounts of the new Rite (Ordo Templi Orientis) made a great impression; and in particular, attracted the attention of the Supreme Grand Council, Sovereign Grand Inspectors General of the 33rd and Last degree of the Scottish Rite in the Valley of Detroit, Mich. ... I was therefore invited to Detroit, and a series of conferences was held. A Supreme Grand Council of the 7th Degree of the O.T.O. was formally initiated."* [14]

Aleister Crowley's ridiculous proposals were rejected by the Conservative Christian Masons in the US, who, abruptly put an end to his occult show. According to an article written in 1948, during the time Crowley's spent in Detroit, he *announced plans to build a headquarters patterned after the sun temples of the ancient Chaldeans, with exotic furnishings, fountains spraying jets of perfumed water amid burning jars of incense, silken divans for the faithful to "worship and recline on.."* Crowley then left town, and more or less gave up on his project of absorbing the Masonic world into the O.T.O. [15]

Worth mentioning, is that in **Detroit on the 25th of July, 2015** to the astonishment of people around the world, Satanists were able to publicly inaugurate a statue of Baphomet that cost 100 thousand dollars. A huge amount of money spent for an occult symbol based on the popular design of Eliphas Levi. Of course, the bizarre statue was even more twisted with the addition of two children at its sides. This incredible Satanic stunt was created and promoted by the **Satanic Temple** of Detroit, generating unprecedented media publicity. [16] Eliphas Levi was a leading figure of occultism, and Crowley claimed to be his *reincarnation.*

Returning to my family history, I would now like to explore my mother's side of the

12   See. http://livesicilia.it/2013/04/30/profanata-la-tomba-di-bent-parodi-rubati-una-teca-e-un-volume_307191/ ‡ Archived 30th July, 2015.
13   Wikipedia: Ben Parodi, *Ibid.*
14   http://www.mastermason.com/luxocculta/forbidde.htm ‡ Archived 30th July, 2015.
15   See. http://www.mythicdetroit.org/index.php?n=Main.AleisterCrowley ‡ Archived 30th July, 2015.
16   See. http://thesatanictempledetroit.com/newsroom/press-coverage/ ‡ Archived 30th July, 2015.

FIG. 47 – King George VI of England with the insignia of Masonic Provincial Grand Master of Middlesex, a position he held for thirteen years before his coronation. He was originally initiated into Freemasonry in Naval Lodge No. 2612 in December of 1919.

family. My mother, Jessica Lyon Young, is decendant of the prestigious Scottish **Lyon** family, of the Queen Mother of England Elizabeth Bowes-Lyon (1900-2002), the wife of King George VI (1895-1952), (FIG. 47) one of the more Masonic kings who was Grand Master of the Province of Middlesex and in 1936 became Grand Master Mason of Scotland. He was awarded earlier the 33rd degree of the Ancient and Accepted Rite in 1932. There was a great esteem and admiration from British Freemasonry and **King George VI,** for the family of his wife, Elizabeth Bowes-Lyon, that has another important branch the Clan Lyon in Scotland. The important link between Freemasonry and this important Scottish family, was actually stressed publicly by King George VI, during his speech to the Grand Lodge, held in his honor at the Royal Albert Hall in London on 30 June 1939, by the United Grand Lodge of England. It was an official ceremony staged after his sudden coronation as king, to officially depose as English tradition dictates, those that had official assignments within Freemasonry. In his speech, of great historical importance for Freemasonry, he said these exact words, which were also repeated in an article about King George VI, published in 2005 by "Masonic Quarterly," the then official journal of the United Grand Lodge of England:

> *[...] I have, since my initiation in 1919, been greatly interested in my association with Freemasonry. My work as a Provincial Grand Master for over thirteen years and in other directions gave me real pleasure and I was sorry when it became necessary for me to cease my activities. In this work the Queen also, to whose family connection with the Craft you have alluded, has been interested, and has attended with me various gatherings.* [17]

In my family we find the British Royal family of **Elizabeth Bowes-Lyon,** daughter of Claude Bowes-Lyon, the fourteenth Earl of Strathmore and Kinghorne and a second cousin of my grandfather **Henry Lyon Young,** a member of this illustrious family linked to the mysterious Glamis Castle in Angus Scotland, the subject of many legends

---

17   See. John Hamil, "The King and the Craft" article in *"Masonic Quarterly Magazine,"* (n° 14 / July 2005), p. 9.

and disturbing truths. Lady Glamis for example, was accused of witchcraft and burnt at the stake on Castle Hill in Edinburgh on December 3rd 1540, and this family of Celtic origin apparently made rituals dedicated to Lucifer, the "Morning Star" every Friday. In my family tree are links to the Knights Templars and later Freemasonry, as well as being figures of primary importance in the development of the Scottish Templar legacy. **King Robert I (1274–1329)**, popularly known as **Robert the Bruce**, gave protection to survivors of the Knights Templar that fled after the beginning of their persecution by **King Philip IV** of France; who desired to obtain their wealth, and ordered **Pope Clement V** to persecute them and extract confessions in a manner nothing short of cruel. Their infamous trials ushered in after the *Pastoralis Praeminentiae,* ordered the arrest of the Templars throughout Christendom, thus following a plan concocted in secret since 1305, for the total elimination of the Templar Order. This was a plan that secretly involved the Knights of Malta, who inherited all the churches and land of the Templars after their final dissolution between 1312 and 1314. It was at this time that King Robert I of Scotland established, with the survivors of the Templars, a new order, the *Order of the Knights of St. Andrew of Scotland* during the Battle of Bannockburn (23-24 June, 1314).

The Italian Masonic historian Vincenzo Soro writes:

> *They fled to Scotland where they helped King Robert Bruce win the great battle of Bannockburn, who in gratitude established exclusively for them on the day of St. John the Summer (June 24) of 1314, a special knighthood order named after St. Andrew patron of Scotland, and gave this order functions and privileges of Great Chapter of the famous and venerable Mother-Lodge of Killwinning, reserving the teaching for himself and His successors. According to another version, the Order of the Knights of St. Andrew of Scotland was established as early as the twelfth century by King David I and was attached to the Mother Lodge of "Killwinning" when the Templar refugees arrived in Scotland, which I refuge, teaching its members their secret doctrine is rather those who want to see in this Order the primitive form of the Royal Order of the Thistle Equestrian Order still exists in England but not front 1440.* [18]

John Yarker writes in "Arcane Schools" (1909): "*The Chevalier Ramsay, in his Paris Oration of 1737, states that James, Lord Steward of Scotland, in 1286 held a Lodge at Kilwinning and initiated the Earls of Gloucester and Ulster into Freemasonry.*" In his *History of Scotland*, Tytler states that these two Earls were present at a meeting of the adherents of Robert Bruce at Turnbury Castle, that is located 30 miles west of Kilwinning Abbey, where they devised plans for the vindication of his claim to the Scottish throne. The Order of the Thistle, better known in English as *The Most Ancient and Most Noble Order of the Thistle,* remains the main Scottish chivalric order, and the second in the UK for dignity (after the Garter). Also interesting is the fact that my maternal grandmother, Anne Cumming, also known as Felicity Mason, was a descendant of **John Comyn,** Earl of Buchan, an important member of the Clan Comyn (another name for the clan and family Cumming).

He was one of the main opponents of Robert the Bruce during the Civil War, in parallel to the Wars of Scottish Independence. He was brutally murdered by Bruce on February 10, 1306 in a Church in Dumfries, as **Michael Baigent (1948-2013) and Richard Leigh (1943-2007)** wrote in their brilliant essay on the origins and history of Freemasonry entitled, "The Temple and the Lodge." In this book we find a very detailed account, of some of my ancestors from the Scottish branch of the family in relation to the Templars, and Freemasonry in Scotland. The **Comyn family,** which included the counties of Buchan and Monteith, was very old and could rival Bruce for power and prestige.

18   Vincenzo Soro, *Ibid.,* p. 159-160.

Bruce murdered his opponent. John Comyn, who was pierced with a knife in front of the main altar and left to bleed to death on the stone floor of the church. [19] According to various reports he did not die immediately, as the monks attempted to heal his wounds, but when Robert the Bruce learned about this he went back and eventually finished him off in front of the altar. [20]

The Clan Comyn, [21] and the son of John, rallied for revenge with the English in Bannockburn, but he was murdered as well. Clan Comyn was then stripped of all their belongings, which were given to Clan Macpherson, close to Robert Bruce. Despite this, Comyn had a very important role in the wars for Scottish Independence, and were instrumental in winning the Battle of Roslin in 1303, but from that moment, for them began, an inexorable decline.

The Comyn family re-emerged centuries later in England as wealthy bourgeois entrepreneurs, and thanks to the marriage of my great-grandfather, tied themselves to the owners of the most prestigious brewery in Manchester. The Groves were known Freemasons and members of various Chilvaric orders. In short, a good match for this family in decline with no financial resources. Going back to Scotland in 1329, King Robert the Bruce died and was succeeded by his nephew Robert II, founder of the historic house of Stuart connected later to the Jesuits and inspiration for the Knights Templar Masonic revival instigated by Chevalier **Andrew Michael Ramsay (1686-1743)** born in Ayre, Scotland, into a family of ancient Scottish nobility and a tutor of **Charles Edward Stuart, also known as Bonnie Prince Charlie.** The birth of the Ancient and Accepted Scottish Rite is traditionally linked to the figure of Chevalier Ramsay, who studied theology in Glasgow, and continued his studies in Edinburgh, then serving in the British Army of the Netherlands. At the age of 24, he met François Fénelon Archbishop of Cambrai, who influenced him the rest of his life. After spending five years under his teachings, he converted to Catholicism, and after Cambai's death, became his spiritual heir. In 1723, he wrote the book, *Life of Fénelon* which was widely dispersed, and his most important literary work, *Travels of Cyrus,* was published in London in 1727, that made him one of the most famous French writers of that time. At this point he was elected member of the *Royal Society* of Sciences of London, and the University of Oxford awarded him an honorary degree. Ramsay's initiation into Freemasonry took place in London in the Lodge "The Horn" in Westminster March 17, 1730, but his first contact with Freemasonry was in Rome in 1724. He was tutor to the son of the "Old Pretender" to the throne of England, **James Francis Edward Stuart** (known also as **James III** of England and Ireland and **James VII** of Scotland), in the *Lodge Gormogoni,* founded by Wharton. He was committed to Freemasonry and he dedicated all of his energy to it. In Paris, he joined the Lodge "Saint Thomas," the first French Lodge, founded in 1725 by English Freemasons, Catholic and Stewart supporters. In this Lodge, in December 1736, at the initiation ceremony, he delivered an early version of the famous "Speech" on Templar and Freemasonry that was presented on the 21st of March 1737, in his capacity as **Grand Orator** to the General Assembly of the Lodges of Paris, where the Grand Master was Charles Radclyffe. The "Speech" can be considered the paper which intended to transform the conception of Freemasonry, in an ambitious plan of reconciliation with the monarchy and the institution of the Catholic Church.

---

19   See. Michael Baigent, Richard Leigh, *The Temple and the Lodge,* 1989, (Milan, IT: Newton Compton, reissue 2011), p. 39.

20   *Ibid.*

21   See. https://it.wikipedia.org/wiki/Clan_Cumming ‡ Archived 30th July, 2015.

On March 20, 1737 he presented a preview of his future speech to Cardinal Andre Hercule de Fleury, the first minister of Louis XV, but it was nevr read because the General Assembly of the Lodges was postponed. It would be then published for the first time the following year in Paris, in 1741. His vision of the origins of Freemasonry is more "noble" and adventurous, it does not come from corporations of stonemasons, but from the Crusades, at the time of **Godfrey of Bouillon**, when in the basement of the Temple of Jerusalem were found, traces of this ancient institution. [22] In short, Ramsay became an ideal subject for this project secretly promoted by the Jesuits, to favor the rise of certain high degrees in what would transform shortly afterward, the Ancient and Accepted Scottish Rite with a clear link to Scotland, but in reality, born in France.

The mysterious "Norwegian politician"

Many are familiar with my exposure work, through a series of videos, interviews and Internet revelations. Some of the articles and videos found on the internet about me are true, while others have been invented by the enemy to discredit me. My first big public exposure occurred in 2008, with the now famous interview I did for *Project Camelot*, while I was still living in Oslo. An interview seen over the years by millions of people around the world, which became an Internet classic in conspiracy circles. However, it was filmed in one of the most difficult periods of my life, at the end of my stay in Norway, where I lived for many years, until I clashed with the Satanic interests there. My life since mid-2003, after the beginning of my conflict with the *Ordo Templi Orientis*, and Scandinavian Freemasonry, became exceedingly worse, as described in the previous volume.

I might add that many problems were caused by my close collaboration with the Russian Federation, and some of its most senior representatives, which eventually led to the problems I had in London, in **Kirby Lodge 2818**. This was with my Masonic mentor **Julian Reese**, [23] Past Worshipful Master of the **Pilgrim Lodge 238**, [24] the only lodge in London that works their rituals in German. In its long history they even initiated Theodor Reuss, co-founder of the O.T.O. and many other spies, occultists and Illuminati of the English and German world. Julian Reese for example, worked for British Intelligence in Germany during the Cold War, and hates the Russians, and with the help of the O.T.O., threw me out of Kirby lodge in London, apparently jealous of my position. What I stated above is still in the archives of the United Grand Lodge of England, including the fact that I was using Russian agents to threaten O.T.O. Satanists in Norway, when they threatened to kill me shortly after the conclusion of my investigation on the O.T.O. infiltration of the S.R.I.A., another subject I discuss in detail in Volume I. However, the situation became much worse for me in the summer of 2008, after revealing to the world the alleged identity of the mysterious "Norwegian politician," who was planting disinformation about the actual use of underground bases in Norway. In recent news it has been revealed that these same underground bases were used during the Cold War by the United States, and are being restocked with American tanks and ammunition because of current tensions with Russia. This same "politician" desired to use *Project Camelot*, aka Kerry Cassidy and Bill Ryan to amplify his lies. The chaotic scenario during that time, resulted eventually in the separation of the duo. Kerry Lynn Cassidy and Bill Ryan officially split in April 2010, over an incident in which Bill *outed* two whistleblowers who, he considered, were giv-

22   http://www.massoneriascozzese.it/storia/approf_tematici/Il_discorso_del_Cavaliere_De_Ramsay.pdf ‡ Archived 30th July, 2015.
23   See. http://www.julianrees.com ‡ Archived 30th July, 2015.
24   See. http://www.freemasons-freemasonry.com/julian-rees.html ‡ Archived 30th July, 2015.

FIG. 48 – Former Norwegian Prime Minister Jens Stoltenberg currently Secretary General of NATO with Khaqan Khan (the "Norwegian politician" of Project Camelot); photo sent to me by K.Khan.

ing false and misleading information. [25]

Kerry Cassidy later spoke about her professional split from Ryan in an open letter (no longer available online), published originally on the **Project Camelot** blog.

This extract from the letter explains her version of the events, involving the **Illuminati**:

At the same time, I want to state here that the recent statements of Bill Ryan with regard to Illuminati takeover of Camelot are not only completely unfounded but a subterfuge to cover gross errors in judgment that led him to cast 2 whistleblowers to the dogs... in severe disregard of his pledge to uphold the mission of Camelot and in violation of all that Project Camelot claims to stand for. After repeated requests to Bill Ryan that he reconsider his position and views, I was left with no recourse but to publish this statement. While he will needless to say, go to great lengths to show the world that one was an unbalanced hoaxer and the other is, he believes, acting as an agent of the Illuminati in a dark plot to take down Camelot, neither is true. Camelot is operating as before with the exception that we have reached the point where working together has become impossible due to our differences in views and interpretations of what it means to have integrity.

Sincerely,

Kerry Lynn Cassidy Co-Founder, Project Camelot

The events surrounding the "Norwegian Politician," helped me to understand *Project Camelot* had been compromised by a number of Intelligence agencies interested in stopping them, including the Norwegian PST and the mysterious *Surveillance Detection Unit (SDU)*, a sort of Norwegian GLADIO operation controlled by U.S. Intelligence. The real name of the "Norwegian politician" was **Khaqan Khan** (FIG. 48) and he was actually working undercover for the **Norwegian Police Security Service** (*Politiets Sikkerhetstjeneste* or **PST**). Something comparable to the British **MI5**, it is the agency responsible for security and counter-intelligence in the UK. [26] The Norwegian version of the British counterpart is of course unique, but not always as efficient. The PST mixes in their structure Nazi Aryan superiority, typical of most of its Norwegian agents, and the conservative way of the Neo-Templar Masonic Order of the Norwegian Freemasons who practice the Swedish Rite of Freemasonry.

They are the ideal robots for Norway's Security Service, ruled at the top by the Intel-

25   See. http://goldenageofgaia.com/2010/04/17/kerry-cassidy-and-bill-ryan-split/ ‡ Archived 30th July, 2015.
26   See. http://www.thelocal.no/20150205/foreign-spies-tried-to-infiltrate-norwegian-intelligence ‡ Archived 30th July, 2015.

ligence liberal elite, made up of dangerous socialists, often leading towards communism and Islamo-communism, which works very well in Scandinavia, and in Norway in particular in a lethal mix of hypocrisy and respectability.

The PST is described in the following way: "*The task of the Police Security Service is to conduct domestic Intelligence gathering, whereas foreign operations are reserved for the Norwegian Intelligence Service. An amount of coordination between these two bodies as well as the National Security Authority is also involved.*"[27]

FIG. 49 – Jens Stoltenberg, NATO Secretary General, during an interview with the Norwegian National Television (NRK) wearing a T-shirt with the number 666, showing the true Satanic nature of the Norwegian elite.

The so-called "Norwegian politician," Khaqan Khan, who sent *Project Camelot* disinformation about a variety of subjects, was neither "Norwegian," as he was of Pakistani origins, or a high level "politician." In truth he was a PST undercover agent, working in a minor political role to cover up his Intelligence activities on behalf of the government within the Muslim community in Oslo. My exposure to his real role for the PST, eventually brought me to my second and last arrest in Norway on **July 22 of 2008,** thanks to the corrupt Norwegian authorities, who are still secretly protecting Satanists and Islamists like Khaqan Khan, who had ties with the Pakistan Intelligence Services (PIC). The Pakistani Intelligence was one of the key players in 9/11, and is specialized in Islamic false flag attacks on behalf of the New World Order. I met Pakistani operatives during my life and know what I am talking about.

Khaqan Khan's role demonstrates the Nazi methodology and barbaric ways implemented against me by the Security Police in Norway, typical of the worst Orwellian scenario. They work side by side with Islamists and Satanists, protecting and harboring Islamic terrorists like **Mullah Krekar** (now under arrest), who I have investigated in reference to his vast terrorist/mercenary network, that includes thousands of affiliates worldwide, and is now linked to ISIS/Daesh. I was able to reveal to the world many of Norway's darkest secrets on the Internet, including the truth about their underground bases, the Satanic activities of its elite and politicians, and in the end, revealing also the truth about their so-called "moderate" Muslim community. I revealed the identity of their disinfo agent Khaqan Khan, who was dedicating his time on the Internet to sabotage the "Truth Movement" on behalf of the Norwegian PST, directed at the time by the then Prime Minister **Jens Stoltenberg (a Satanist)**—who is currently the Secretary General of NATO, (FIG. 49) and his friend **Jørn Holme.** (FIG. 50)

Khaqan Khan's disinformation campaign was issued by the PST to cover the truth on the existence of **mysterious underground bases in Norway,** which *undoubtedly* exist, and are used for various secret purposes by the Norwegian elite, and their military that

27   https://en.wikipedia.org/wiki/Jørn_Holme ‡ Archived 30th July, 2015.

FIG. 50 – Jørn Holme (b. 1959) Chief of the PST, from 2004 to 2009, and Khaqan Khan at what some say was a meeting of the Security Incident Management Analysis System (SIMAS) known to be used for spying and surveillance by U.S. Embassies worldwide; photo from nyhetsspeilet.no.

stockpile huge quantities of gold, and also conduct secret experiments. Khaqan Khan was therefore a skilled disinfo agent using his alleged political activities and ties to the elite to make himself seem more credible. At that time, I was married for a very short time, to a woman who turned out to be a useful tool in service of the Norwegian elite, she is now called Fatma Betül Sarayli who is also, *unfortunately*, the mother of my son Isak. She was undoubtedly part of a plot used by the Norwegian elite to stop my online *Confessions* which began back in 2006. Fatma even confessed to this in a SMS message sent after she left, saying she was now *looking forward to working with people like Giorgio Hugo Balestrieri and Ezio Giunchiglia* (both Monte Carlo Lodge members*)*. Fatma was also politically a member in the same party as Khaqan Khan, the **Socialist Left Party** (Norwegian: *Sosialistisk Venstreparti, Northern Sami: Sosialistalas Gurutbellodat*),[28] which is a democratic socialist political party leaning towards left wing extremism with close ties to Islam. Inside SV, there is a dangerous mix of left wing native Norwegians, and new Muslim social climbers, recently arriving in the country as immigrants or supposed "refugees." This is the ideal breeding ground for recruiting double agents, spies and Islamic puppets serving the New World Order. These people aspire to "integrate," however, for many Muslims, the so-called "integration" and their efforts to promote "multiculturalism" and tolerance wind up in failure, with many of them turning to radicalization, and in the worst case scenario, becoming recruits for Islamic terrorist organizations like ISIS/Daesh.

In this mix is the involvement of the Jesuits, with their hypocritical support for so-called "moderate Islam." In reality moderate Islam doesn't exist, because Islam, just as Christianity or Judaism, is in the hands of religious leaders that are serving the New World Order agenda. For this reason, the Islamic Wahhabi elite controls and sponsors Islamic extremism on behalf of the New World Order as radicalization of Islamic citizens is part of the plan, using "moderate" Islam in the West, as an unstoppable trojan horse promoted by stronge anti-Christian forces.

Before this difficult time, the Norwegian Government locked me up more than once, in a mental health facility, which occurred after my exposure of the *Ordo Templi Orientis*, in hopes that the Psychoactive drugs I was forced to take, would silence me forever. This persecution disguised as three different Sanitary Treatments, was forced on me by the PST, in a similar manner to what was done in the old Soviet Union for the most feared political dissidents. My Internet revelations, which began in 2006 with my online *Confessions*, brought me to an instant upgrade in March 2008, which transformed me from a mad "bipolar" type, into a dangerous "anti-government" spy. All accusations against me were dropped in February 2010, and was never fully explained by the Norwegian authorities.

In the early months of 2008, I made my first attempt to contact the mysterious "Norwegian politician" from *Project Camelot* known at the time as Zarcov. My friend Atle, who belonged to the *Northern Resistance organization*, a Scandinavian movement of online activists based in Norway, warned me there was something strange going on in this mail which includes a response by the *Project Camelot* duo.

"northernresistance.info" <post@northernresistance.info>

To:

"leo zagami" <leoxxx@xxxx.com>

Hi again Leo.

I contacted the Project Camelot website regarding our mysterious friend Zarcov and his email. This was all new to them, and this is the email they sent me:

"Hi, Atle:

Thanks for your message. That's very interesting! But no, that message you received was not from us, and we do not know and have never heard of anyone calling themselves Zarcov. So all this is a mystery here. We have NOT heard from our Norwegian Source that he wants to meet Leo Zagami—in fact, as best I know and can remember, Leo Zagami was never discussed between us and him, except that our source did mention him once in an e-mail. So he does know about him. Can you help us make contact with Zarcov? That might be important. We'd be happy to work together with you about this.

Best wishes, Bill and Kerry"

So it seems there is something going on here. Probably nothing to worry about but suspicious it is. "Zarcov" used this email address: fsb000@hotmail.com

Anyway, if you want to get in contact with this supposed Norwegian politician I recommend you contact Bill and Kerry at Project Camelot.

Hope your doing fine Leo :)

Best regards, Atle

Three days after my forced 24 hour detention in a cold Norwegian prison cell where I wasn't even given a blanket, on March 4th and 5th, the "Norwegian politician" suddenly appeared. In the meantime, the Norwegian police had returned to my house during my absence to confiscate all my computers, mobile phones and other important documents. Norway is a country that often claims to be an honest and just country, but they are instead slaves of the worst "Police State" in the world. I found myself alone against giants of the Norwegian establishment, mainly for my revelations made earlier through my website "**Confessions of an Illuminati**," which was considered a danger to the internal security of the country. On several occasions between 2006 and 2008 they tried to make me desist in my mission, once even sending one of the brothers of my ex-wife, a young Muslim police officer, who was eager to enter the Norwegian PST. He appeared at my house and tried to convince me to quit my online disclosure project. This was three months before my ex-wife Fatma left, on Feb. 23, 2008. My ex-wife's Islamist "Master" is the influential Turkish Mus-

FIG. 51 – PST psy-ops operative Khaqan Khan and Jannete Kristiansen, Director of the PST from 2009 to 2012; photo from nyhetsspeilet.no.

lim cleric and CIA agent Fethullah Gulen, which as I have revealed in Volume I, lives in the USA, and is a puppet of the Jesuits, and the leader of a dangerous terrorist organization secretly controlled by the CIA. In any case this whole situation caused me a lot of stress because I was constantly threatened by e-mail, phone and even on the streets of Norway by the local Muslim community. I received false allegations of violence by my ex-wife, which obviously, being false, were never proven in court or anywhere else, but were used at the time by her, to insure the custody of my son to her.

On the Internet during that period, they even wrote false accusations stating that Fatma had accused me of pedophilia, a completely false allegation never even mentioned by my ex-wife, but that's the kind of disinformation they were trying to spread after my first revelations to *Project Camelot*. The powerful enemies I gained in Norway, that included the *Ordo Templi Orientis* and the Order of Norwegian Freemasons, removed me from their country. During this time, news surfaced in mainstream media about Norway's immense underground base used for the conservation and collection of seeds, constructed in order to preserve samples of almost all species of seeds in the world.

It is called **The Svalbard Global Seed Vault** and is found in the depths of the Arctic Mountain, located on the Norwegian island of Spitsbergen, near the town of Longyearbyen in the remote Arctic Svalbard archipelago, about 1,300 kilometres from the North Pole. The Seed Vault is sponsored by none other than **Bill Gates** and the **Rockefeller Foundation,** two giants of the New World Order. In the first email I received from Khaqan Khan, immediately after my first Norwegian arrest in March 2008, he was obviously testing me, with improbable phrases like *"There are 18,000 Freemasons in Norway, and we need to catch them,"* or *"Hope you had a nice bithday on the 5th of March, as I know you did not because of the PST."* I wish to express to Jens Stoltenberg, now Secretary General of NATO, and his faithful puppet Jørn Holme, as well as **Janne Kristiansen, (FIG. 51)** who succeeded Holme in the leadership of the PST until 2012, that they are criminals of the worst kind should be brought to justice for their crimes against humanity. Janne Kristiansen had to eventually resign for a scandal that involved Norwegian bonds and military Intelligence, called the **E Service,** with **Pakistan** during a parliamentary report.

> *"The E service has its representatives in these countries, so we co-operate via the E service about this country."* [29]

Interestingly enough, Khaqan Khan, a Pakistani naturalized Norwegian, had worked in the past as a liaison officer with the Pakistani Intelligence on behalf of Janne Kristiansen, and some of his activities in Norway included working with their infamous Pakistani crime gangs, the **A-Gjengen** and **B-Gjengen** run by criminal elements within Oslo>s immigrant Pakistani community operating in close contact with the *Surveillance Detection Unit (SDU)*.

This was the first mail I ever received by Khaqan Khan, the Norwegian Politician collaborating with *Project Camelot* on the 8th of March, 2008:

Khaqan Khan <fsb000@hotmail.com>

> *To Leo Zagami < leoyoungxxx@xxxxx.com>*
>
> *Hello MR Zagami,*
>
> *I just heard about your arrest by the PST secret police in Norway on the net.*
>
> *I to was arrested by the PST when we where going to meet Bill and Kerry in Oslo on the 16 and 17 of February. They did hold me for 7 days and told me that if I was going to talk about Illuminati, Planet X, and underground bases, they would take my children away from me and my wife would be jailed. So I had no means of meeting you or Bill and Kerry on that date, so they gave me your email as you can see from their letter. We have to get inside the Masonic lodges and only you can help doing so. Can you? I am getting monitored by the PST in Norway too, so I hope you get my mail. You can post this E mail with your contacts if you want to. The Illuminati exposure must go on, I knew for a long time that your wife worked with the goverment of Norway, but had no means of telling you because I was monitored by the PST.*
>
> *We should meet very soon my friend. Your wife is from SV and I am to from the same party (DO NOT POST THIS LINE IN when you give to others on the net this mail thank you) Its all just a cover-up for what is to come. There are 18,000 Freemasons in Norway that we have to expose. The illuminati are evil and they support evil as all the Freemasons do. I think you say Khudafis in Arabic to friends, so I do the same. Hope you had a nice bithday on the 5th of March, as I know you didn't beacuse of the PST. I had a hard time in jail when they put me in! We are brothers Me and You. All Masons in Norway are judges, millitary, police, lawyers they are minions of the NOW.*
>
> *Kind regards*
>
> *Khaqan Khan*
>
> *"the Norwegian politician"*

E MAIL SENT EARLIER FROM PROJECT CAMELOT TO K.KHAN

Dear Khaqan:

We both wish you well in everything you are doing. We fully understand that you were unable to meet with us. We hope that you are safe and well. Please let us know if you can. Remember that our fax number is on the contact page of our site (001 805-435-2021). We're just posted this update on our What's New page: http://projectcamelot.org/whats_new.html If you can't access our site, we've copied the update below. Leo Zagami would welcome contact with you. He is a very good man. His e-mail address is leoyoung1999@yahoo.com. May we give him your contact details? We will NOT do this without your permission. Here's our update below... With our very best wishes,

Bill and Kerry

And on the 13th of March, 2008 I received another interesting e-mail from "Norwegian politician":

Title: Hello Leo from the Norwegian Politician

Thursday, 13 March, 2008 23:36

From: Khaqan Khan <fsb000@hotmail.com >

To: Leo Zagami leoyoungxxx@xxxx.com

Hello Mr Leo, I got your message from my wife. You have to be careful when you contact me on my mobiles or my number. I have 8 mobile phones and all of them are under surrveilance by the PST police secret task force in Norway. I too was arrested by the PST when Bill and Kerry was in Norway meeting with you on the 16 or 17. I wish I could come and meet you but as you know I was arrested. And they are still watching me and my wife and kid, so I know of the dangers you are talking about.

I am real and I am your friend. As you can see from the pictures I am in the SV party to and you can see that SV's leader Kristin Halvorsen is very fond of me and my politics. She tends to have me along with her and with all the other politicians too, as you can see from the pics, who I am now because I wanted you to know you must trust me. This email is monitored by the PST and I will get in trouble for posting to you as the PST will warn me again for contacting you. Trust me I am on your side my friend. Do not send the pictures to others or contact any people about me, the PST will know that I have contacted you and they dont want me to do so because you are an ex Illuminati and a danger to Norway. I will get to jail because of this they have warned me about this before.

kind regards your friend,

Khaqan Khan

Khaqan was never a friend to me, he is the classic spy, monitoring me, on behalf of his powerful friends of the Norwegian elite, (FIG. 52) as the following photos will demonstrate. I would like to thank my friends, http://*www.nyhetsspeilet.no* and Norwegian journalist Hans Gaarder. Hans was very close to me during my last period in Norway; risking arrest, during my own arrest by the PST on July 22, 2008, that led to an indictment for espionage by the PST and a long interrogation by both the police and the PST.

22 July 2008

Illuminati is a Greek word meaning Illumination; a name given to those who submitted to **Christian baptism**. Those that were baptized were called "Illuminati" or Illuminated / Enlightened Ones by the Ante- Nicene clergy, because those who had been baptized into the Apostolic faith, had an enlightened understanding. The understanding of the masses on the Illuminati, is that they are plotting to take over the world since the time of its creation. That's because most people associate the term "Illuminati" with the dark side of the mystery schools, and their complex network of secret societies playing constant conspiracy games on mankind, so they are also right in their assertion. There is a good side to the Illuminati, and their wish is to spread knowledge, like many prophets of our time. Unfortunately, the side of the Illuminati manifesting upon humanity in this day and age try to control such knowledge, or to gain power and to spread lies, like Khaqan Khan. I sincerely hope that by showing to the world the true identity of this dangerous liar and agent of the dark side of the Illuminati, I have helped you to understand a bit better the real intentions of these evil manipulators of the New World Order. I was subjected to intense persecution in Norway, by both the local authorities and the Islamic mafia during my last period in this country. Hypocrites that feed us with lies, while they are secretly protecting the elite from the impending disasters headed our way.

FIG. 52 – **Crown Prince Haakon Magnus of Norway** (b. 1973), and psy-ops operative Khaqan Khan; photo from nyhetsspeilet.n.

During the **Royal Astronomical Society's National Astronomy Meeting in 2015,** an alleged Ice age was announced, that could begin in 2030, when *solar activity will fall by 60 percent during the 2030s, to conditions last seen during the Maunder Minimum of 1645-1715.* [30] And if that is not enough, *TIME* reported that a team of Ukrainian astronomers have discovered a massive asteroid, 2013 TV135, that's on track to hit Earth on Aug. 26, 2032. [31] Maybe if we are lucky we can defeat these criminals of the New World Order, before they find refuge underground in one of their many secret bases built around the world, for what seems like an incoming "Apocalypse."

During a long series of interviews created in partnership with respected American investigative journalist Greg Szymanski ten years ago (2006-2007), that aired on the *Genesis Communication Network,* I spoke about a huge base located under Oslo, constructed for over 2,000 people. This was information I received from local insiders, prior to Khan's appearance. It is confirmed that these bunkers really exist, and that even neighboring Sweden possesses them in abundance. They can move large parts of the population, at any time, and preserve their huge gold reserves. In Sweden, they have been camouflaged as geological repositories, excavated deep within a stable geologic environment. *Project Camelot* wrote the following note about the ulterior revelations received by various sources on the underground bases after Khaqan Khan's letter was published:

> *Many friends and correspondents in Norway and Sweden have been in touch, some offering intriguing details. To many of them, this information was not new and confirmed what they had known from other sources. We received specific confirmation from two scientists and one ex-Intelligence source that these facilities exist (and that both Sweden and Switzerland have the facilities to take their entire population underground if need be). A number have asked to be put in touch with the politician who wrote to us.* [32]

Now that we know how the elite plan to escape, thanks to its secret bases, I would

30   http://astronomynow.com/2015/07/09/royal-astronomical-societys-national-astronomy-meeting-2015-report-4/ ‡ Archived 30th July, 2015.

31   http://newsfeed.time.com/2013/10/17/this-giant-astroid-could-hit-earth-within-20-years/ ‡ Archived 30th July, 2015.

32   See. http://projectcamelot.org/norway_update.html ‡ Archived 2nd August, 2015.

like to speak further about the incidents that occured during the summer of 2008, when I returned to Norway after my first arrest, hoping to receive justice and to see my son again. My Norwegian journalist friend, Hans Gaarder was present during my arrest on July 22nd , 2008, exactly three years before the terrorist attacks of Anders Breivik, that I have written about at length in the first volume of my *Confessions*. [33] The authorities believe at least officially, that **Anders Behring Breivik** was acting alone that day, dressed as a policeman, and he was indicted for the two terrorist attacks. The young survivors of the massacre on the island of Utøya, interviewed by the Norwegian newspaper **VG**, describe an additional killer, who was not wearing a police uniform, but a dive suit, and quickly vanished amid the chaos after the massacre. He apparently had a pistol in his right hand and a rifle on his back—I believe that there were two people who were shooting, says Alexander Stavdal. [34]

On this point it seems interesting that Anders himself, who posted an image on the Internet a few hours before the attacks, where he was dressed in a dive suit with an automatic weapon. The attacks of the **22 of July 2011 have "false flag" written all over it,** and U.S. journalist and political analyst Webster Griffin Tarpley, in the days following the attacks in question, made these observations:

> *U.S. and NATO Intelligence have been shown to possess extraordinary capabilities inside Norway, many of which may be operating outside of the control of the Norwegian government. In early November 2010, the Oslo television channel TV2 exposed the existence of an extensive network of paid assets and informants of U.S. Intelligence recruited from the ranks of retired police and other officials. The ostensible goal of this program was the surveillance of Norwegians who were taking part in demonstrations and other activities critical of the United States and its policies. One of the Norwegians recruited was the former chief of the anti-terror section of the Oslo police. Although the goal was supposedly merely surveillance, it is possible to imagine some other and far more sinister activities that could be carried out by such a network of retired cops, including the identification and subversion of rotten apples on the active-duty police force. Some of the capabilities of a network of this type would not be totally alien to the sort of events that have just occurred in Norway.*

> *The official name for the type of espionage cell which the United States was creating in Norway is Surveillance Detection Unit (SDU). The SDUs in turn operate within the framework of the Security Incident Management Analysis System (SIMAS). SIMAS is known to be used for spying and surveillance by U.S. Embassies not just in the Nordic bloc of Norway, Denmark, and Sweden, but worldwide. The terror events also raise the question of whether SIMAS has an operational dimension. Could this apparatus represent a modern version of the Cold War stay behind networks set up in all NATO countries and best-known under the name of the Italian branch, Gladio? [35]*

On December 4, 2011, I received a request for help from the brother of one of the victims of the massacre on the island of Utøya and Oslo, seventeen-year-old **Lejla Selaci**. I would like to share it with you, to demonstrate the frustration of the families involved in this sad story, who do not believe that the official version of the events given by the Norwegian authorities, or the insanity of the murderer, initially believed to be suffering

33   *Op. cit.,* pp. 311, 318, 322, 323, 324, 325, 328, 329. 330, 331, 332, 333.
34   See. http://www.vg.no/nyheter/innenriks/terrorangrepet-22-juli-ofrene/oeyenvitne-til-vg-det-foerste-han-gjorde-var-aa-skyte-den-soeteste-jenta-han-saa/a/10080627/ ‡ Archived 2nd August, 2015.
35   http://tarpley.net/2011/07/24/norway-terror-attacks-a-false-flag/ ‡ Archived 2nd August, 2015. *[emphasis added].*

from paranoid schizophrenia, although he was later declared in a second opinion *"sane and therefore criminally responsible."* [36]

This is an enquiry via e-mail sent to **http://www.leozagami.com/**

From: Azem Selaci az-m_tba@xxxxxxxxx

Hi Leo, Breivik the Norwegian terrorist killed my sister, Lejla Selaci, 17 years old. She was in a Norwegian Political Party. and a Leader of AUF. Have you read about Breivik lately? They're saying he is a paranoid schizofren and a psychopath. That's only bullshit! I want you to help me with this, I KNOW THE NORWEGIAN GOVERNMENT is behind this! Breivik was also a Freemason, he started as a 15 year old kid. PLEASE HELP Mr. Zagami I BEG YOU, with your knowledge I can defeat these bastards! Love and peace, I.

Answer of the author from the pages of this book only:

Love and Peace to you, my dear Azem,

I hope that one day the soul of your sister and the other victims may finally rest in peace and for this reason I pray that the truth of what happened is eventually revealed to you and your family as well as the others involved, so that Norway will one day find the serenity of the past, combined with a greater consciousness about the evil that surrounds us today. So let's pray for a truer analysis of the causes of this useless massacre, not only the material causes, but also the spiritual ones, behind this evil and cowardly act.

I am regret that I could not send Mr. Selaci the above message via email. Unfortunately on the 22nd of July 2008, **I was forced to sign a document authorizing the PST to control and monitor my official email address,** and for this reason I did not want to contact him via email. I was forced to sign this document with the threat of a longer period of detention, so I prefer to not involved myself with Norwegian citizens. I would like to add, that the AUF Labour Party Youth Movement, the victims of the Utoya Island massacre, were devoted promoters of the Israel Boycott campaign, and two days before, AUF's leader Eskil Pedersen, gave an interview to *Dagbladet*, Norway's second largest tabloid newspaper, in which he unveiled what he thinks of Israel. Pederson went on to say: *"The peace process goes nowhere, and though the whole world expects Israel to comply, they do not. We in the Labour Youth will have a unilateral economic embargo of Israel from the Norwegian side."* [37] Perhaps A good reason for Israel to retaliate. Breivik was a regular online poster on several Norwegian Internet sites, notably the blog; document.no, which is run by Hans Rustad, a Jew and extremely pro-Zionist, former left-wing journalist.

Numbers

Wilter illiam Wynn Wescott (1848-1925), co-founder of The Hermetic Order of the Golden Dawn and Supreme Magus of the S.R.I.A., wrote:

The former division included two branches, arithmetic and musical harmony; the latter was further subdivided into the consideration of magnitude at rest—geometry, and magnitude in motion—astronomy. The most striking peculiarities of his doctrines are dependent on the mathematical conceptions, numerical ideas and impersonations upon which his philosophy was founded. The principles governing Numbers

---

36   See. https://it.wikipedia.org/wiki/Anders_Breivik ‡ Archived 2nd August, 2015.

37   http://mycatbirdseat.com/2011/07/was-norway-massacre-a-reaction-to-boycott-israel-camp/ ‡ Archived 2nd August, 2015.

*were supposed to be the principles of all Real Existences; and as Numbers are the primary constituents of Mathematical Quantities, and at the same time present many analogies to various realities, it was further inferred that the elements of **Numbers** were the elements of Realities. To Pythagoras himself, it is believed that the natives of Europe owe the first teaching of the properties of Numbers, of the principles of music and of physics; but there is evidence that he had visited Central Asia, and there had acquired the mathematical ideas which form the basis of his doctrine. The modes of thought introduced by Pythagoras, and followed by his successor Jamblicus and others, became known later on by the titles of the "Italian School," or the "Doric School."*

The followers of Pythagoras delivered their knowledge to pupils, fitted by selection and by training to receive it, in secret; but to others by numerical and mathematical names and notions. Hence they called forms, numbers; a point, the monad; a line, the dyad; a superficies, the triad; and a solid, the tetrad.

1. *Intuitive knowledge referred to the Monad type.*
2. *Reason and causation referred to the Dyad type.*
3. *Imagination (formorrupa) referred to the Triad type.*
4. *Sensation of material objects referred to the Tetrad type.* [38]

Numbers are of great importance in the sealed labyrinth of the Illuminati sects, and in particular **number eleven**, which the English Freemason Aleister Crowley, the magician par excellence of the Illuminati, defined in his *Liber NV sub XI* as **the key to all Rituals.** This number I have discussed in Volume I, appears in the macabre ritual linked to the terrorist attacks of September 2001 in the USA, and the massacre in Utoya and Oslo:

9/11 (September 11) equals 1 + 1 + 9 = 11

7/22 (July 22) equals 2 + 2 + 7 = 11

And there is yet another occult link if we further analyze the date **22/07/11**, focusing on the pair of numbers 22 and 11. The bomb planted by Anders Breivik in Oslo exploded at 3:26 pm, local time, and if we add 3 + 2 + 6 it equals 11. On Norway's Utoya island when Breivik went on a shooting rampage there were 560 members of the AUF Labour Party Youth Movement 5 + 6 + 0 = 11.

Why do all these eleven's keep poping up? The great nineteenth century Freemason and Illuminati William Wynn Westcott offers his take on number eleven in the book appropriately entitled, *Numbers: Their Occult Power And Mystic Virtues* (1890):

This seems to have been the type of a number with an evil repuation among all peoples. The Kabalists contrasted it with the perfection of the Decad, and just as the Sephirotic number is the form of all good things, so eleven is the essence of all that is sinful, harmful and imperfect. With the Ten Sephiroth is contrasted the Eleven Averse Sephiroth, symbols of destruction, violence, defeat and death. On the oldest Tarot cards, the trump called the Tower struck by Lightning, number XVI, shows the Ten Divine Sephiroth on one side and the Eleven Averse Sephiroth on the other side; modern Tarot designs are very much debased. John Heydon says that by it we know the bodies of Devils and their nature; the Jews understand it in Lilith, Adam's first wife, a she-devil, dangerous to women in confinements; hence they wrote on the walls: Adm Chvh Chvo Lilit, that is, "Adam, Eve, out of doors Lilith."

---

38   William Wynn Westcott, *Their Occult Power And Mystic Virtues,* (New Orleans, LA : Corner Stone Book Puplishers, 2008), p. 4.

Jesus, in Matthew 12:43, plainly allows the doctrine that evil spirits may haunt fields, which Grotius says the Jews think; and their word Demon and Field are similar, being Shdim (fields) and Shdim (evil deities); the Siddim are mentioned in Psalm 106:37. It is called the "Number of Sins" and the "Penitent," because it exceeds the number of Commandments and is less than twelve, which is the number of Grace and Perfection. But sometimes even eleven receives a favor from God, as in the case of the man who was called in the Eleventh Hour to the vineyard, who yet received the same pay as the others. [39]

There were several newspapers and online publications including "Reuters" and "Der Spiegel" who inserted the phrase **"Twin attacks,"** [40] which immediately reminds us of the 9/11 attacks on the Twin Towers. This is called **Occult**

FIG. 53 – Hans Gaarder journalist and independent researcher among the most renowned in Norway in the field of conspiracy theories.

Synchronicity, coordinated by the same group of people who are behind the 9/11 attacks. Numeric sequences are there to prove it, and thanks to Friday the 13th in Paris in 2015, or other terrorist attacks, an absolutely overwhelming reality of occult numbers emerge in front of our eyes. We must not be passive spectators, and take into account the occult value in these attacks.

It comes as no surprise that Breivik was a Freemason. Another Mason who was involved in a similar shootout where there were many victims, was **Thomas Hamilton**, who perpetrated the Dunblane massacre in Scotland, in 1996. The Grand Lodge of Scotland, after all these years, is still trying to hide the evidence of his membership in this important and prestigious Masonic obedience. [41] **Is this perhaps a reason to demonize all those honest people belonging to Freemasonry?** These are only isolated cases, the fanatics are the most easy to manipulate. I consider myself a proud Freemason, but certain forms of extremism present in some types of Freemasonry, especially the Swedish Rite, which I have been struggling with for years because of the many irregularities I found in it, include the link of many of its Senior members that should be "Christians," with Crowleyanity and the *Ordo Templi Orientis.*

39   *Ibid.*, p. 90.
40   See. http://www.reuters.com/news/picture/twin-attacks-shock-norway?articleId=USRTR2P5TX and http://www.spiegel.de/international/europe/explosion-and-shooting-norway-shocked-by-twin-attacks-a-776071.html ‡ Archived 2nd August, 2015.
41   http://www.scotsman.com/news/scotland/top-stories/question-on-masonic-links-left-dunblane-inquiry-chief-stunned-1-1099013 ‡ Archived 2nd August, 2015.

FIG. 54 – picture of Anders Behring Breivik, as Master Mason of St. Johannesl ogen St. Olaus til de tre Søiler No. 8 (the Lodge of St. Olaf at the Three Columns) in Oslo.

Masonic authorities do nothing about it, because of supposed confidentiality and privacy issues, where they tolerate characters that go completely against Masonic principles. This is of course, when the lodges themselves are not perverted by demonic energies, and actually participate to the crimes in question. Certainly in the case of Anders Breivik, his Christian-fundamentalist views went very well in a "Christian's only" Masonic context, as the Norweigan one, where the majority of members are like-minded and embrace Christian fundamentalism, all manipulated by the Jesuits. Breivik was expelled by the Grand Master of the Order of Freemasons of Norway later after the tragic attacks of July 22, 2011. Let's not be deceived by the lies told after the attacks, as Breivik was a brainwashed puppet in the hands of Christian fundamentalists and Zionists. We now turn to Hans Gaarder (FIG. 53) and his direct testimony of the events that took place in Oslo, in 2008, exactly three years before the attacks of Anders Breivik. (FIG. 54)

Leo Zagami victim of Norwegian political abuse by Hans Gaarder

The morning after arriving in Oslo at the end of July 2008, Leo Zagami, his mother Jessica Lyon Zagami, his Norwegian lawyer Arne Berdal and the Norwegian journalist having written this article arrived at the Oslo courthouse some minutes before nine. After taking the elevator to the 8 floor they headed for the coutroom of the meeting. The lawyer was walking first, followed by Leo and his mother and the journalist behind. Halfway between the elevator and the courtroom, suddenly a large group of men pop up out of nowhere, and surround Leo. The only words pronounced are "arrest, PST."

His hands are immediately handcuffed behind his back. Leo, who was mentally focused on the important meeting in the court regarding his right to be with his son at this moment, remained calm but displayed utter amazement and contempt for the brutal treatment by the emotion—and empathyless policemen. Zagami's mother, who witnessed it all at close distance, was standing in shock and bewilderment, and started to cry as if she could eventually suffer a nervous breakdown, repeating the words over and over again: "I dont believe it! I dont believe it!"

Ten minutes later the handcuffs had been momentarely removed from Zagami, indicating that the arrest in reality was a setup. The only natural response for Zagami given the circumstances was to enter the courtroom and deliver a statement that the arrest had made it impossible to go ahead with the regular court meeting as planned, and that he felt humiliated by this arrest and was forced by these sad events in renouncing his case and the right to see his son Isak Rumi Zagami.

The "unholy" time and place of this unprovoced arrest gave the situation a bad smell of power abuse by Norwegian authorities, a Nemesis in Zagamis life. Seven police-men had taken part in the arrest, two of them were dressed like civilians just ar-riving from a gym, while the other five were uniformed robot-like creatures, one of which had been capable of asking Zagami "Where do you keep your hand grenade?" during the body visitation. A father being arrested within the very courthouse and just a few minutes before a crucial meeting regarding his right to maintain contact with his son is so appalling that it is hard to believe, not only for those who hear about it, but as well for those who witnessed how it happened. When the police had observed Zagami appearing in the courthouse, why couldn't they at least keep quiet and wait outside until the court meeting had finished?

After Zagami had withdrawn the case in front of the Court under the extreme pressure of his arrest, he was handcuffed again and brought by the police to Grøn-land Police Station and had to wait in a cell for five hours before they started interrogating him. The interrogation consisted of two parts. The first with the PST—the Norwegian secret police—the second with the regular Norwegian Police.

The reason given for the first three hours of heavy interrogation by the PST was statements he had made in a conversation to a friend through Skype (published lat-er on the Internet) where in a typical Italian act of bravado he not only had threat-ened to kill the Norwegian prime minister Jens Stoltenberg, but also had threatened to bring down the buildings of government and parliament in Norway, something he said out of anger after being notified in the end of May by a Norwegian politi-cian called Khaqan Khan, that he will be arrested if he ever came back to Norway, something that actually happened on the 22nd of July 2008 confirming Leo's worst expectations. In addition to this, he had sent an email to the PST stating that they were a bunch of chickens, amateurs completely out of touch with what actually is going on in the world, and an object of contempt among the secret services and the Intelligence community around the world. If such a lousy half-joking provocation should provoke a response from the PST, wouldn't this be a proof that the insulting accusations of the email actually are valid?

Zagami explained to the interrogatory PST agents that he had not been serious about the death threats, that it's the Italian way of expressing strong emotions through strong words and that he had no means at his disposal that could not be capable of destroying the parliament and the government building of Norway nor any plan or gun or whatever to whack Jens Stoltenberg.

The PST also asked many questions to Leo regarding his Internet collaborators and research fellows and this dubbious character called Khaqan Khan, a strange and dubious figure who made contact with Leo immediately after his previous arrest in March 2008. Khaqan Khan stated in his first e-mail to Leo he was his only friend in Norway even if he was collaborating with the PST, because his allegiance lies in any case with his membership in Freemasonry and Leo's Mastership. Unfortunately his membership in Freemasonry and his words turned out to be after a careful examina-tion, only lies really, and possibly part of a clever set-up put together by Leo's ex-wife Fatma Süslü, and elements of the Muslim Norwegian community in retailiation for his new position as an apostate of the Muslim faith.

Apostasy in Islam (Arabic irtidad or riot) is commonly defined as the rejection of

Islam in word or deed by a person who has been a Muslim. The four major Sunni and the one major Shia Madh'hab (schools of Islamic jurisprudence) agree that a sane adult male apostate must be executed and obviously persecuted by the entire community if he rejects his faith in Islam, this seems also one of the main reasons why Leo Zagami is not allowed now to see his child any longer by his ex-wife Fatma and her family who are apparently very religious and follow all the way the strict rules of the Sharia laws governing apostasy. This is something very difficult for Westerners to understand, but a reality people should put into account when dealing with the Muslim tradition.

The second part of the interrogatory, and the first reason given by the authorities for the assaultive arrest of Zagami earlier in the morning, was that his ex-wife Fatma Süslü had reported to the police that Leo had been threatening her after he had left Norway earlier in 2008. As "proof" of this she had submitted five emails to the police that she had received during the last couple of months. The most remarkable fact regarding those email messages was that none of them had been sent by Leo. The other remarkability was that none of them had content that could be classified as threatening in any way. All the mail messages were from persons who had contacted Leo's ex-wife, proposing to act as intermediaries during the planning of Leo's upcoming trip to Norway, in order to facilitate the son seeing his father during the stay. These concerned individuals were also worried for the possibility of Fatma going to a Muslim country with Leo's son Isak in the summer, especialy after Leo had already received threats for his apostasy of Islam in what is known in the Muslim faith as receiving a fatwa, a dangerous situation for Zagami that the Norwegian police finaly didnt take lightly and seemed to understand very well. While confronting Zagami with this "evidence of threats" made by Fatma during the interrogation, the interrogating police officer had to put away one email printout after the other, while commenting embarrassed in low voice "this is not a threat" one time after the other, keeping his thoughts about the police officer who had prepared the case for the arrest to himself.

At half past seven in the afternoon, on the same day Zagami was released from police custody, after the two interrogations had been carried out. No charges had been made against him. Zagami's mother had visited the Italian Embassy after the initial shock of witnessing the brutal, provocate and, as it turned out, ill-founded arrest of her son. The embassy had contacted the police headquarters and asked about what was going on. During the interrogations an Italian translator and Zagami's lawyer had been present all the time. The emotional distress behind the aggressive stand of Zagami towards the prime minister of Norway, as the leading figure of the Norwegian authorities, were partly due to the abusive arrests he previously had suffered while in Norway and partly due to his inability to be with his son after the breakup of his marriage. If Zagami had wanted an excuse on behalf of the Norwegian authorities from the prime minister Stoltenberg before the latest arrest took place, such a claim does not appear less reasonable after the last incident in Norway.

(End of article by Hans Gaarder)

Final thoughts on the article by Hans. Once again I thank Hans for his testimony. A couple of weeks before the 22nd of July 2008, Hans reported about the historical meeting of the *Ordo Illuminatorum Universalis* in Nice, France. This was a turning point in the life of our Order, as Dr. Marco Paret and Ezio Giunchiglia opposed my return to the Monte Carlo Lodge, after I openly sided against the criminal activities of the New World Order. The meeting was held in the nearby Principality of Monaco, and the Nice gathering was a key event in the short history of the *Ordo Illuminatorum Universalis*, with had the participation of known French occultist and Illuminati, Jean Pierre Giudicelli. This event eventually lead to the breakdown of the "Brothers" of the Masonic Executive Committee, and the *Ordo Illuminatorum Universalis* broke from the Monte Carlo Lodge. Strangely enough during the first stages of the events that took place in February, 2008 in Norway, the first thing my ex-wife was to give an official testimony to the Norwegian Police authorities, about my secret activites in the Monte Carlo Lodge of the P2. Only a government spy, or an informant, would do that.

This was immediately reported to me by my Norwegian lawyer, who called me on my mobile after being notified by the police about her testimony. The Norwegian police authorities however, never explained why they even took her testimony. Fatma had knowledge of a sealed envelope with all the names of the powerful Monte Carlo Lodge. This envelope, which I never opened was given to me by Giunchiglia to avoid the growing interest of the Monegasque authorities towards his "irregular" Masonic body, especially after the growing involvement of French military Intelligence operative Jean Pierre Giudicelli.

For a period after my first problems with the Norwegian authorities and the *Ordo Templi Orientis*, I gave this sealed envelope, and other top secret documents, that I later used in my *Confessions* series, to a shaman not affiliated of any Masonic activity; an unsuspicious character and a friend called Lars. He kept them safely in his possession for a couple of years, before I decided to return them to Ezio Giunchiglia in June 2006, at our last official gathering. This was in order to avoid any possible retaliation once I left the Monte Carlo lodge the following month, as tensions were building in the lodge and the outcome was almost certain.

At that point, I decided to officially decline such a responsibility, blaming it on the fact that two of my closest collaborators in Norway had received suspicious visits from the Norwegian police. No one, not even my ex-wife, knew about my decision to give back the sealed envelope. When the police and the PST searched my house for the mysterious sealed envelope during my forced absence, between the 4th and the 5th of March 2008, they must have been pretty disappointed to not find it. *C'est la vie*, I am not a fool, my dear PST idiots. The Monte Carlo Lodge though "irregular" was highly influential, although it was gradually disbanded, after my public revelations on them erupted online in 2006. The scandal led the powerful lodge, originally created by Count Licio Gelli and Ezio Giunchiglia in the late 1970s, to gradually phase out all its activities in the Principality of Monaco, which, in turn, established the "Regular" *Grande Loge Nationale Régulière de la Principauté de Monaco*, with the support of the United Grand Lodge of England called by "Freemasonry Today" The Official Journal of the United Grand Lodge of England *"A Grand beginning."* [42]

In a report for Sisde (at the time the civilian secret service until the Italian reform of 2007 transformed it into AISI), states that in 1982, at the top of the Lodge in Monte Carlo, along with now defunct Count Licio Gelli, there was a certain Enrico Frittoli, accountant, owner of an import-export company in the Principality and "man of confidence" to the international arms smuggler, **Samuel Cummings,** president of the Inter Arms in London. [43] He is in turn connected to Ezio Giunchiglia who was not mentioned in the Intelligence report because of his work for SISMI (the Italian military secret ser-

---

42   See. http://www.freemasonrytoday.com/ugle-sgc/ugle/tag/Grand%20Lodge%20of%20Monaco ‡ Archived 2nd August, 2015.

43   See. Gianni Barbacetto article for societavicile.it: http://www.societacivile.it/primopiano/articoli_pp/savoia/savoia_2.html ‡ Archived 2nd August, 2015.

vice reformed in 2007, now substituted by AISE). Journalist Gianni Barbacetto describes "The Committee" as "the usual cocktail of strong political, business and nobility" figures. The Monte Carlo lodge ended mainly because of my *Confessions*, just as the Golden Dawn ended because of Crowley's writings. In this case, something new and hopefully a lot better was born out the ashes of the Masonic Executive Committee, as *Freemasonry Today* wrote: *The consecration of a new Grand Lodge is a rare event and when such an occasion took place in Monaco it proved to be a day to remember.*[44]

The P2 Committee that wanted to conquer the world

In *Papa, Mafya, Agca* (Pope, Mafia, Agca), Ugur Mumcu, a prominent Turkish journalist wrote the following remarks about the P2 lodge in Monte Carlo: "*Henry Kissinger is a member of the Monte Carlo lodge, which is the P2's 'board of directors,' also known as the Monte Carlo Committee. All the members of this lodge are Grand Masters and Masons of the 33rd degree.*"[45] The former Mossad agent Victor Ostrovsky gave valuable testimony of the alliance between the P2 and Israel, or to be more specific, with Mossad in *The Other Side of Deception*, published in 1994 after his greatly controversial book, *By Way of Deception*. Ostrovsky wrote:

The ships would arrive at various Italian ports where the Italian secret services (SIS-MI) would handle the necessary document approval, verifying that the containers were in fact loaded with Italian agricultural products headed for Germany. A sign depicting Italian products was actually affixed to the truck. The manpower for the operation and the driver were supplied by a Mossad Italian ally, the right wing followers of a man named and a group, by then outlawed, called Propaganda Due, and a second group (a NATO offspring like the one in Belgium) named Gladio.[46]

So Licio Gelli, P2's last Worshipful Master connected to Gladio, and Mossad used his alliances, for arms deals with Italy in the 1980s, with the full approval of NATO. The July, 1981 issue of *The Middle East International Journal*, established that the P2 had close links with Israel, especially with Mossad, and that the Jewish community in Italy played an important role in this operation. In later years, **Carlo de Benedetti**, the second richest man in Italy, was discovered to have had a close relationship with the P2 Lodge, and also had very good contacts with the Jewish communities in Europe and the USA. That's why one of the main divisions of the P2 known as the *Tirrenia group*, is operated with Ezio Giunchiglia's supervision, from the city of Livorno, which has the largest Jewish community in Italy aside from Rome, and one of the most important ports. The foremost names that had contact with the P2 are **Henry Kissinger**, **Edmond de Rothschild**, and **David Rockefeller**. It is evident that people of great importance had a special relationship with the Monte Carlo Committee.

This Lodge was defined in its heyday, between the end of the 1970s and the '80s as one of the more exclusive Masonic circles in the world and the "Super Lodge of Monte Carlo," at least according to Nara Lazzerini, at one time a very close friend of the late Licio Gelli who stated in 1987: *"Licio told me that Vittorio Emanuele of Savoy, Prince of Naples and Prince Rainier III were also part of the Lodge."*[47] When the Italian anti-Mafia parliamentary commission spoke in detail of the activities of P2 in hundreds of pages, a few references to the mysterious Committee of Monte Carlo also surfaced, of-

44 *Ibid.*
45 Ugur Mumcu, Papa, Mafya, Agca (Pope, Mafia, Agca), (Istanbul: Tekin Publishing, 1987), p. 246.
46 Victor Ostrovsky, *The Other Side of Deception*, (New York: Harper Collins Publishers, 1994), p. 226.
47 Gianni Barbacetto *art. cit.*

ficially confirming the existence of this secret group:

> *The Massonic Executive Committee (MEC) was founded in Monte Carlo before 1981, probably by the same Gelli. Between 1979 and 1980 they had been held in Montecatini and Livorno various Masonic meetings in which Gelli had been strongly opposed. At one of these meetings there was also Ezio Giunchiglia, nuclear expert, assigned to CAMEN (Center Atomic Military Nuclear Energy) provided of the NOS (Security Clearance), possessed only by people deemed reliable by NATO. It may be that the Committee of Monte Carlo was founded by opponents of Gelli, most notably William Rosati, to build a sort of counterpoint to P2. But it is possible that the Committee, founded at the initiative of Gelli, was then conducted by Rosati in a way not acceptable to the Worshipful Master. It remains unclear at this stage the role of Giunchiglia. The parliamentary commission of inquiry on the P2 reported him to the prosecutor in Rome, describing him as an element possibly involved in arms trafficking and connected with the secret services. Giunchiglia is close to Balestrieri, also a member of the MEC, involved in the trafficking of 200 Leopard tanks, and Elio Ciolini, involved in the disinformation campaign to confuse the investigation into the massacre of the Bologna station. After a bad heart attack happened to Rosati, the reins of the committee are taken by Giunchiglia; and through him to Gelli. Giunchiglia is always tied to the Worshipful Master and keeps in touch with him even during the period of his latitancy.*[48]

A detailed description of the structure of the Masonic Executive Committee known also by the acronym MEC:

> *The MEC, divided into thirty departments, becomes the refuge for many adherents of the old P2. In front of the parliamentary committee, the former Grand Master of Freemasonry Lino Salvini, confirmed that in the period prior to the discovery of the lists, Gelli had in mind to affiliate the members of the P2 to another Grand Lodge abroad. It was the lawyer Federici, well-linked to P2, to disclose details of the operation.*

> *The MEC was founded as a side organization by Gelli, who could send Monte Carlo Committee members their membership, maintaining secrecy, and the freedom to make public the names of others. It would appear the Committee of Monte Carlo marks the last stage of the strategy of Gelli. A strategy that aims to acquire positions of power, with the known method of infiltration of the institutions, the gradual evacuation of any democratic content in their concrete operation, the use of a network of privileged relations between influential men to enslave policy to the interests of a group of occult power.*

> *What is new is that the strategy now takes into account the crisis of the political system, explicitly called into question in the memorandum entitled, "The Universal Freemasonry."*

It should be noted one significant step:

> *The Executive Committee Masonic is not an alternative to the Masonic Lodges, but—on the contrary—their meeting point ... Keeping in mind the absolute indispensability of this medium, the Brother members of the Masonic Executive Committee must therefore study, analyze power in order to conquer it, exercise it, store*

48　*The Massonic Executive Committee,* by the Parliamentary Committee of Inquiry into the Mafia and other similar criminal associations, Report on the Relationship between Mafia and Politics, Rome, March 9, 1993—February 18, 1994, p. 799.

it, increase it and make it more balanced. We first of all want to build an assembly of people aware of their value. ... Not a man that makes of politics his landmark, but an individual who gives to his ego point of initiation, for the coherent development of human and existential conditions of collective existence. Masonic individualist cooperation will become a form of politics.

So it does not indicate the way most of the institutional reforms, as in the plan of Democratic Rebirth (Author's Note: Licio Gelli's original plan). No mention of the need to change the form of government or to impress a result, the conquest of power, which will be bent to the purpose specified by the Committee. A creeping "major reform"—change the sign of the institutions without affecting the shape.

Something similar happened in Italy in recent years.

What is most striking, in the aforementioned document of the Monte Carlo Committee, is the extraordinary similarity with the mafia method of infiltration in the institutions and parties. Step three, entitled as "Nonpoliticized" reads:

The Brother may be part of a "democratic" political party, but only for tactical reasons. Its true affiliation is to the Committee, whose directions must always take preference and priority over all others, whatever their origins. That is because he acts keeping in mind the truth and the welfare of all, with no respect for "political plot" as generally used. Politics as such is not part of its interests.

The analogy is especially in the superordination of the associative bond, criminal or occult that is over any other type of affiliation. And there is also the obligation of obedience to the orders of the leaders of the mafia, the "signs" of the Committee in the Decalogue of the MEC. These provisions are, true and proper rules of conduct that are the ones only recognized as such, with a binding force dwarfing the imperative law of the state:

Having viewed the elevation and the complexity of the task it will be appropriate for each member of the Executive Committee to intervene "immediately" on the Brother who commits something unethical for the Committee. This is to enable him not to deviate, or at least to ensure that the other Brothers can intervene promptly to rectify his mistake; a mistake that would harm "seriously" the action of the Body, as well as its credibility and reliability.

In the text, the words in quotes, have a kind of ominous message, and suggest the end of Michele Sindona, Roberto Calvi, and Mino Pecorelli. The intake of the mafia method is complete and final. [49]

(End of excerpts extracted from the official records of the Parliamentary Anti-Mafia Commission, March 9, 1993 – February 18, 1994)

In the mid-nineties I decided to become part of the Monte Carlo Lodge, and in 1999, when I joined, I felt that I was finally among the P2 elite, and there I could finally accomplish the secret mission given to me in 1993, by Prince Alliata, shortly after my initiation. He told me it was very important to give new direction to his ex-Brothers in the P2 after the end of the Cold War. From the beginning there was a strong desire to reform this important structure of the New World Order, that in turn coordinated, at least during those years, the various factions of so-called "irregular" Freemasonry (mostly of the Ancient and Accepted Scottish Rite) around the world, including the **Masonic High Council**,

49   *Ibid.*, p. 800.

the Mother High Council of the World of
the Most Ancient and Honourable Fraternity of Free and Accepted Masons. Before
Alliata died, I was handed secret contracts
and documents that could use for the establishment of a new order of "Illuminati,"
the **Ordo Illuminatorum Universalis**. It
was founded in London and Monte Carlo
in 1999, after I was officially initiated into
the Masonic Executive Committee led by
Ezio Giunchiglia.

My first encounter with Ezio Giunchiglia was in 1997, and was followed by another a couple of years later. It seemed to
me that Giunchiglia wanted to distance
himself from the late Licio Gelli. He even
told me he had broken a chair on the head
of Gelli during his last meeting at the P2
Lodge, and he did not want to have anything to do with him. Whether or not this
way true, I immediately proposed to Ezio,
Alliata's alternative Iluminati project that
was to remain secret to the rest of the Masonic community until the official foundation date. In the period of 1993 and 1994,

*FIG. 55 – Sovereign Grand Commander
Benedetto Miseria of the Sovrano Ordine
Reale D'Italia, indicated as the most
legitimate heir to the Alliata Masonic lineage.*

before dying, Prince Don Giovanni Alliata of Montereale better known as Gianfranco,
kept this project secret from the eyes of the profane, and continued his Masonic/Knight-
hood Order chaired by his lieutenant at the time called **Benedetto Miseria**. (FIG. 55)
Miseria was not made aware of the project I had been secretly proposed by the Prince,
and to this day is the Sovereign Grand Commander of a minor but influential branch of
Alliata's A.A.S.R. Supreme Council called **Sovrano Ordine Reale D'Italia**. In recent
years there has been many splits and many claims to Alliata's Masonic lineage.

Among the different factions fighting to inherit Alliata legacy, besides the aforementioned Benedetto Miseria, and the previously mentioned Adolfo Alessandro Maria
Polignano linked to the **Order of the Illuminati Knights** of Frank G. Rippel,[50] there
is the dangerous Calabrese Freemason named **Mattia Salvatore Maria Giraldi**. (FIG.
56) Giraldi is the Grand Master of a pseudo-Masonic body, known as *Grand Lodge of
God-Knights of Light,* and Sovereign Grand Commander of a Supreme Council of the
Ancient and Accepted Scottish Rite, which claims to derive from Alliata's lineage.[51] The
latter is especially dangerous, as he is not only a fraud and a charlatan, with no real continuity with the Alliata lineage, but also an agent involved in the control and monitoring
of the Italian Masonic scene on behalf of the Italian Intelligence services. In short, a spy of
the New World Order, that for a few months in 2013, tried to enlist me in his project of
espionage, offering in exchange the guidance of his Rite as Sovereign Grand Commander,
knowing very well this will legitimate its own false claim to the Alliata lineage. The only
people that can claim some degree of legitimacy in regards to Alliata's Masonic heritage,

50   http://www.frankripel.org/iutmah/meaprmm.html ‡ Archived 3rd August, 2015.
51   http://cripress.blogspot.it/2013/07/ununione-di-grande-umanita.html ‡ Archived 3rd August, 2015.

FIG. 56 – Grand Master and Sovereign Grand Commander Salvatore Mattia Maria Giraldi, false claimant to the Alliata Masonic lineage.

apart from myself, are: Alessandro Maria Polignano and more than anyone else, Benedetto Miseria.

In the 1970s, the CIA and the American Illuminati elite pushed for reunification of certain Masonic currents connected to the *Piazza del Gesù* tradition of the Ancient and Accepted Scottish Rite. This complex situation led to an internal plot in which in the end Prince Alliata lost his historic headquarters in Piazza del Gesù, thanks to the unclear maneuvers of Francesco Bellantonio, later expelled by the Grand Orient of Italy in September 1975. Subsequently, the Prince and his loyalists in the years following the P2 scandal, which influenced the Prince, who nonetheless had been a member of this infamous lodge, went on to achieve far more modest surroundings for his new Masonic projects. The reason was the lack of U.S. funding for anti-communist operations at the end of the Cold War. Such a change did not permit the luxurious premises the Prince and his followers had at one time. In short, it came to the point where Benedetto Miseria, who still has most of the secret papers of Alliata (of course only the Masonic, not the Illuminati ones), was forced, after the chief prosecutor of Palmi, Agostino Cordova, began a nationwide Masonic witch-hunt—to organize his so-called lodge meetings—on a bus parked in a remote location of the Castelli Romani, a known area in the hills near Rome. An incredible story that was told to me by a former Carabinieri officer and 30° Freemason called Valerio Mannucci, who passed on to the more legitimate **Grand Lodge of Italy** of the A.F. & A.M. (Ancient Free and Accepted Masons) based at **Palazzo Vitelleschi in Rome,** [52] where, by the way, many P2 members like Ezio Giunchiglia, wound up after the huge scandal regarding the Propaganda 2 lodge erupted at a worldwide level in the early 1980s. Manucci became later a Monte Carlo lodge member, before terminating all Masonic activities in 2009.

Going back to the late Prince Gianfranco Alliata, on May 11, 1994, Alliata, Benedetto Miseria, and others ended up in handcuffs, as you can still read in the archives of the Italian newspaper "Corriere della Sera," in an article entitled: **"Masonic plot: 4 arrests,"** where the journalist states that a *"breakthrough in the investigation began in Palmi by Cordova, now a prosecutor in Naples. In handcuffs Giovanni Alliata of Monreale, 73, Miseria Benedetto, Rasoli Alfredo and Salvemini Cosmo Sallustio."* Adding that *"Alliata had already been involved with the P2 and Junio Borghese."* [53]

Prince Junio Valerio Borghese was the architect of the December, 1970 failed Italian

52 See. Confessions vol.1 *Ibid.*, p. 187.
53 http://archiviostorico.corriere.it/1994/maggio/12/trama_massonica_arresti_co_0_9405124744.shtml ‡
Archived 3rd August, 2015.

coup d'état planned for the night of the 7th or 8th of December, 1970, and was one of my personal heroes when I was young. The same article continues by stating that Prince Alliata and his lodges, seem to have been involved in a possible coup project, that was orchestrated during the municipal elections in Rome, mentioning the presence of Carabinieri Colonel Antonio Pappalardo, who was nevertheless never investigated. Some say this coup project was supposed to join what later became known as the "Coup d'état of Sax Rubra." In this operation, the participants to the coup were to direct an assault squad on the headquarters of RAI in Sax Rubra, after an act of destabilization, taking complete control of the Italian National Radio and TV center. [54]

I was there in those turbulent days in 1993/94 after my initiation, and yes there could have been a very different outcome for Italy and myself if things had gone the way they were originally planned by Prince Alliata. Italy is still far from being ready for a coup, and a possible **dictatorship,** even the more illuminated one. The same thing almost happened 20 years later, with the Italian Social Protest of 2013, which attempted to follow **the consensus of the Italian people.** During this uprise, dubbed by some journalists the "Pitchfork protests," which I was directly involved, I encountered once again Colonel Antonio Pappalardo, one of the best friends of Prince Alliata, and one of the leaders of the "Pitchfork protest." [55]

Returning to the events of 1994, a month after his arrest, on the 20th June 1994, during the summer solstice, Prince Gianfranco Alliata of Monreale, my initiator and first Masonic mentor, died at his home on Via Re Tancredi in Rome, where he had been "confined" from May 11th under house arrest. Alliata was a victim of the events at the end of the Cold War, and a true Prince.

In the online archives of the *Corriere della Sera*, we find a farewell article dedicated to the captive prince, entitled **"The funeral of Alliata. The farewell of the 'prisoner' Prince."** Here is a brief excerpt:

> *Why inflict on an old man of 73, already in a clinic for emphysema, a dishonorable detention, even though in the walls of his house? The indictment for him, Cosimo Sallustio Salvemini, Alfredo Rasoli and Benedetto Miseria was of criminal association and the establishment of secret associations "aimed in interfering with the country's public life." While waving the Savoy flag on the coffin, flowers and medals were covering the coffin. In the front row next to the widow, Donna Rosanna de Chiarardi Candei, there was the brother of Prince Alliata, Don Fabrizio and his sister, Annamaria, with the daughter Dacia. Not far from them Prince Ruspoli. But the big black book placed next to the entrance of the church got numerous signatures, and not only the aristocracy writing on the blank pages their last farewell to Prince Alliata, many are the common names.* [56]

After a series of unpleasant episodes, relating to my work and friendship with Chiara Sonnino, known as "the Bonnie of the Magliana gang," one of the leading Mossad agents in Rome, I finally realized that the reality around me was becoming too dangerous. Intelligence operatives, right wing subversive organizations, and organized crime, could get me in serious trouble sooner or later, as I still needed time to grasp the complex system

54   http://archiviostorico.corriere.it/1993/novembre/26/golpe_Saxa_Rubra_arresti_co_0_93112612665.shtml
‡ Archived 3rd August, 2015.
55   See. http://espresso.repubblica.it/inchieste/2013/12/17/news/forconi-l-anima-nera-marcia-su-roma-1.146410
‡ Archived 3rd August, 2015.
56   http://archiviostorico.corriere.it/1994/giugno/23/addio_principe_prigioniero_co_10_9406231110.shtml
‡ Archived 3rd August, 2015.

presented to me by Prince Alliata after the initiation. In the end I decided to leave Italy for good and move to London after the summer of 1994, thanks to the advice given to me by two people so different from each other, at least in appearance, Chiara Sonnino and the late Prince Alliata of Monreale. They both suggested to me a complete change of scenery and to move abroad so to devote at least part of my life to the **"Leo Young"** project, that I had successfully built in those years as a record producer and as a DJ, activities with great success for many years to come, after following their advice. [57] Chiara **Sonnino**, who helped me financially build my first Lodge, was a very influential Jewish mafia boss from the infamous Magliana Gang, belonging to one of the historical Jewish families of Trastevere and the Jewish Ghetto in Rome. She had worked for the Mossad and Gladio in the past, and fought in the famous **Six Day War** in 1967—a war fought between Israel, and three Arab states, (Egypt, Syria and Jordan), that resulted in a rapid and total Israeli victory, a lesson of strategy by the Israelis, which confirmed their military superiority and their will to protect the new nation.

Every year, on the important celebration of Jewish Passover, Chiara Sonnino received a letter with personal greetings from one of the leading strategists of the Vatican New World Order, the former **Italian Prime Minister Giulio Andreotti (1919-2013)**, a key figure of the "First Republic." This confirmed to me the strong link between Israel and the Vatican. The expression, **"First Republic,"** refers to the political system of the Italian Republic between 1946 and 1994, the year I decided to leave Italy. In April 1994, things were changing for everyone, not only Prince Alliata, and Mrs. Sonnino, who was also arrested like most of the key figures of the Magliana Gang. [58] It seemed like everyone I knew was suddenly being arrested as a result of the end of the old balance of power in place during the Cold War; and the situation was becoming dangerous. Chiara was arrested after a few months of latitancy, on unjust charges made against her by another well-known female character of the Magliana Gang. A certain Fabiola, manipulated by a foreign Intelligence agency that wanted to get hold of top secret Gladio documentation that Chiara Sonnino was protecting—including the list of all the Gladio members. Her arrest ended up on the front pages of all the Italian newspapers, as Chiara and the other protagonists, were linked to the huge drug trafficking of the **Banda della Magliana**. [59] Having said all this, you may be curious to know the history behind this criminal organization I have mentioned. *Wikipedia* describes the infamous Magliana Gang this way:

> *The Banda della Magliana (English translation: **Magliana Gang**) is an Italian criminal organization based in Rome, particularly active throughout the late 1970s until the early 1990s. Given by the media the name refers to the original neighborhood, the Magliana of most of its members. The Banda della Magliana was involved in criminal activities during the Italian years of lead (anni di piombo). The Italian justice tied it to other criminal organizations such as the* Cosa Nostra, Camorra *or 'Ndrangheta, but most importantly also to neofascist activists such as the Nuclei Armati Rivoluzionari (NAR), responsible for the 1980 Bologna massacre, **the secret services (SISMI) and political figures such as Licio Gelli, grand-master of the Freemasonic lodge Propaganda Due (P2). Along with Gladio, the NATO clandestine anti-communist organization, P2 was involved in a strategy of tension during the years of lead, which included false flag terrorist attacks.***

57   See. http://www.discogs.com/artist/40508-Leo-Young ‡ Archived 3rd August, 2015.
58   See.http://archiviostorico.corriere.it/1994/aprile/12/spacciatori_presi_con_cinque_miliardi_co_10_940412575.shtml ‡ Archived 3rd August, 2015.
59   See.http://archiviostorico.corriere.it/1995/febbraio/26/presa_donna_del_boss_co_10_9502264289.shtml?refresh_ce-cp ‡ Archived 3rd August, 2015.

These ties, underground compared to their standard (i.e. "run-of-the-mill") activities (drug dealing, horserace betting, money laundering, etc.), have led the Banda to be related to the political events of the conflict which divided Italy into two during the Cold War, and in particular to events such as the 1979 assassination of journalist Carmine Pecorelli; the 1978 murder of former Prime minister Aldo Moro, also leader of the Christian Democracy who was negotiating the historic compromise with the Italian Communist Party (PCI); the 1982 assassination attempt against Roberto Rosone, vice-president of Banco Ambrosiano; the "Banker of God" Roberto Calvi's 1982 murder; and also the 1980 Bologna massacre. Finally, the mysterious disappearance of Emanuela Orlandi, a case peripherally linked to former Grey Wolves member Mehmet Ali Ağca's 1981 assassination attempt on Pope John Paul II, has also been related to the gang, though the Emanuela Orlandi case may not be connected to the "Grey Wolves," but may have been one of the "run-of-the-mill" Banda della Magliana criminal activities, the Orlandi kidnap designed specifically to persuade the legally immune Vatican Bank to restore inequitably retained funds to Banco Ambrosiano creditors. [60]

Years later, I met Chiara Sonnino by pure chance on the streets of Rome, in the summer of 2012, after almost twenty years had elapsed since the last time I saw her in 1994. I was in the Ostiense district, driving with my Japanese translator Hal Yamanouchi, when I noticed Chiara Sonnino in the street and called out to her. Immediately, after greeting me, she said that the judges that had her arrested in the mid 1990s were looking for her top secret lists of members from the *Stay Behind* network, known as **Gladio.** However, she confessed with a big smile that she managed to hide the list before being arrested, and she was able to make it disappear. So in the end, the powerful people she was protecting by not giving out the list, got her our of prison after only one year and a half. Chiara Sonnino, clear of all accusations, and protected by the Mossad, became a successful artist, but unfortunately after this strange synchronistic meeting, she was killed, brutally hit by a car while walking her two dogs. Apparently she had been revenged by the famous "Jewish Brigades" working for Mossad in Rome, but all this was kept secret from the media, because her murder would immediately alert the curiosity of the press if made public, as it related to the infamous Magliana Gang. The last words she told me when we met that day were *"the people have a romantic idea of the Magliana Gang, they don't even imagine the truth, I would like to clear this out with you in a book."* Unfortunately, that book will never be written, may she rest in peace.

Returning to 1994, the Cold War was over, Gladio had simmered down, and Italy soon would begin the Berlusconi era. It can be said that the time was right for my voluntary exile and a new life in London from September 1994, in the world capital of my two favorite M's, **Music** and **Masonry.**

I lived in London for eight years, in between my frequent trips around the world mainly to Switzerland, Russia and Scandinavia, I moved permanently to Norway in January 2003.They were fantastic years, where I devoted myself entirely to my passion for music, and at the same time the study of Freemasonry, esoterism and the occult, with considerable results, including a vast collection of initiations into a variety of Masonic Rites, secret societies and obscure sects of the Illuminati Network. I was invited to join the *Ordo Templi Orientis*, the *Fraternitas Satruni*, the *Fraternitas Rosicruciana Antiqua* (F.R.A.), creating for them the **Aula Lucis Cagliostro** in London, and there was my initiation in the Monte Carlo Lodge, where I immediately co-founded the Ordo Il-

60   https://en.wikipedia.org/wiki/Banda_della_Magliana ‡ Archived 3rd August, 2015.

luminatorum Universalis. This is not to forget my time in the Theosophical Society, and my brief involvement in the foundation of the Albion O.T.O., plus my Masonic "Regularization" in the **United Grand Lodge of England,** that coincided with my work for S.R.I.A. and the well-known anti-sectarian Freemason Robert A. Gilbert. Last but not least, I look back fondly at my time with the not so **Regular Grand Lodge of England,** and I had many other esoteric and magical adventures during the years between 1994-2006. Let's now focus on my work for the New World Order and their secret network after Alliata's initiation in 1993. I was used as an international observer and a messenger for the various lodges and chapters, transforming me into a **"Merchant of Light"** in the tradition shown in Sir Francis Bacon's *New Atlantis,* a book which had been just reissued in Italy, by Freemason and P2 member, Silvio Berlusconi. [61]

I liked being a noble traveler, an ancient tradition of the various sects of the Illuminati network, and very often I found myself involved in diplomatic and Intelligence business, so I used my cover as a DJ and record producer to move "with discretion and originality" as Ezio Giunchiglia used to say. He, in fact, admired my new and quite unusual, but very effective technique, to move in the spotlight and at the same time remain invisible to most of the Intelligence community worldwide. I must admit that I've always liked my DJ activity. I did my part as a genuine artist and it certainly was not only a guest appearance in the music scene as I left my mark in the most cutting-edge music.

The famous Italian DJ **Claudio Coccoluto,** who was one of my closest collaborators at the time, in one of his rare interviews in the English language for the Red Bull **Academy in Rome,** in the year 2004, stated publicly that I was known to music enthusiasts as DJ **Leo Young,** and was responsible for the influence of a certain type of music in London in the nineties. In those years various music stars related to my work, including the popular group Prodigy and DJ Harvey. [62] Music was therefore not a secondary passion but became my job for almost two decades. At the apex of my career I would call **"Cosmic,"** my Eclectic Sound was made up of a strange mix of soundtracks, electronic music, House, Afro, Jazz, and even New Wave, with a touch of Disco and Funk. Earlier on in the late 1980s, when I was considered the organizer of the first Italian Rave, I was one of the first promoters and DJs of Detroit *Techno,* introducing for the first time in Europe in the early 90s, legends like Underground Resistance and Juan Atkins.

Democritus wrote: **"Much of what is perceived, is not perceived by us."** And Dr. Norman F. Dixon, a British psychologist, author of *Subliminal Perception: the Nature of a Controversy,* [63] said in 1971 *"It may be impossible to resist instructions which are not consciously experienced. There would seem to be a close parallel between these phenomena and those associated with post hypnotic suggestion and neurotic compulsive response."* For this reason, music, the study of frequencies, and what are known as subliminal messages or *Auditory Masking,* became my natural element for a few years. It is the best way to covertly transmit secret messages from one side of the planet to the other, and push the Thelemic and Luciferian propaganda I would promote at the time. I remained on the side of the New World Order until 2006, when I decided to leave the Monte Carlo Lodge.

Some researchers, say there is no evidence of an impact of auditory subliminal stimuli on human behavior, but subliminal messages and certain frequencies bypass conscious

61   See. Francis Bacon, *New Atlantis,* (Milan, IT: **Silvio Berlusconi Editore,**1995).
62   http://www.redbullmusicacademy.com/lectures/claudio-coccoluto-come-si-dice-house-music%20408%202
‡ Archived 4th August, 2015.
63   Norman F.Dixon, ***Subliminal Perception: The Nature of a Controversy*** (European Psychology), (New York: McGraw-Hill Inc., 1971).

recognition. Dr. Lechnar comments on the definition of subliminal perception, and the studies of Dr. Dixon and his aforementioned book, in the following way:

> One of the controversies surrounding the existence of subliminal perception is its definition. Subliminal means "below threshold." An apple placed in complete darkness would be below the visual threshold for perception. It is not until the lighting on the apple increases to a sufficient level for recognition is it considered "above threshold." The minimum stimulation necessary to detect a particular stimulus (not necessarily recognize), is called the absolute threshold. However, the required amount of lighting on the apple for identification is different for everyone, and therefore what may be subliminal to one person may not be subliminal to another. It is generally accepted that a perception is subliminal if a great majority of the audience can not perceive it consciously. So what is perception? Perception is the brain's reception of incoming stimuli.

> Dr. Key said perception is total and instantaneous, but only 1/1000th of this is consciously recognized and processed. The rest is either stored in subconscious memory or dumped as irrelevant information. Although we do not fully understand how the brain perceives the world, advertisers have no interest in the motor and gears of the brain. It only cares that the brain is influenced the most by visual stimulation and there are certain ways to stimulate the brain without its conscious awareness. Dixon provides a good definition of subliminal perception, which he words as "subliminal reception."

> 1) The subject responds without awareness to stimulus.

> 2) Subject knows he is being stimulated, but doesn't know what it is.

> For the rest of the paper, I will use the above definition for subliminal perception. Subliminal messages will therefore be the transmission of subliminal content using methods which the brain subconsciously perceives but is not consciously aware.

Adding in regards to the experimental confirmation in this field:

> Since the 19th century researchers have been performing psychological tests to confirm the existence of subliminal perception. N. F. Dixon has compiled over 500 studies on this topic and concluded in his book that subliminal perceptions exists beyond any reasonable doubt. He said, "It would seem that reports of percepts may be influenced by stimulation which the percipient is not aware. Certainly, it can be claimed that the having of a conscious percept does not exclude the possibility of subliminal effects." His book is held in such esteem one advertiser quoted "Dixon's book is basic reading for our creative department. We think of it as an operational bible." Ironically, Dixon never guessed his work would be used for commercial exploitation. [64]

Reading Dixon's book early on in my life, was of great benefit for my work and my understanding about this complex subject that fascinated me since I was in my teens. I published a book not so long ago in Italy, about my time in the music business,the topics of frequency manipulation, mind control, and the occult side of show business. [65] I began producing my own music in 1988, and the first solo dance track I ever recorded two years later was based on samples taken from an old self hypnosis tape, and the use of certain frequencies.

---

64   http://www.redicecreations.com/specialreports/brainwash.html ‡ Archived 3rd August, 2015.
65   Leo Lyon Zagami, *Illuminati e la musica di Hollywood, op.cit.*

Chapter VII

Apologists and the Excessive Use of the Taxil Mystification

In the New World of relativism

Leo Taxil was the pseudonym of **Marie Joseph Gabriel Antoine Jogand Pagès**, a long time pornographer and journalist, and a scandalous figure who was strongly anti-Catholic. He was initially accused of defamation because of a book he published in 1881 entitled, *Les Amours de Pie IX secrètes par un ancien camérier secret du pape*, (*The secret loves of Pius IX for an old chamberlain of the pope*). Taxil was a Jew, who at the age of 5 enrolled in an institution run by the Jesuits, and it seems that this experience created his hatred for the Church. Leo Taxil became yet another instrument to draft disinformation on behalf of the Jesuits, and shortly you'll understand why.

On **April 20, 1884, Pope Leo XIII** issued an encyclical letter, the *Humanum Genus,* in which the Pope waged war against Freemasonry, accusing them of conspiring against the values of the Church. This is a different Church then the post-conciliar Church we have now, that fully embraces Freemasonry after being infiltrated and neutralized indefinitely during the The Second Vatican Council (Latin: *Concilium Oecumenicum Vaticnum Secundum*, informally known as Vatican II), but in those days things were different and Freemasonry and the Church were at war with each other.

The theme of the letter addressed by Pope Leo XIII, to the Patriarchs Primates Archbishops and Bishops, was the *"Condemnation of the Masonic Philosophical and Moral Relativism"* and demonstrated, *"the purpose and nature of the Masonic sect,"* denouncing to the world, *"the sect of the Freemasons, born against any law and right."* The pope communicated to the Catholic world that this danger was already understood by his predecessors: *"They already did this by reflecting on the future, gave the signal, warning those princes and populations not to fall into their cunning and insidious plots."* [1]

After the publication of this papal encyclical, Leo Taxil, or those who controlled him (the Jesuits), set up a truly diabolical plan in which Leo Taxil submitted to a sensational

---

1   http://w2.vatican.va/content/leo-xiii/it/encyclicals/documents/hf_l-xiii_enc_18840420_humanum-genus.
html ‡ Archived 4th August, 2015.

public conversion (a fake one of course), to Catholicism. He announced his intention to repair the damage that he felt was done to the Catholic faith by being a pornographer. Remember, we are talking about a Jew educated by Jesuits, a skilled individual, and a real expert in the art of manipulation. Check out his face in one of the portraits or black and white photos of the period to understand what kind of person he was.

Taxil proved right away with this gesture that he knew the art of propaganda and entertainment all too well. Remember that the Jesuits of the publication, *Civiltà Cattolica (Catholic Civilization)* had defined his conversion only two years prior as: Taxil *"the unclean pornographer."* [2] Now, all of a sudden, they are allies in the presumed battle against Satanism and Freemasonry, in reality a disinformation campaign that will ultimately damage Freemasonry more than the Church. In 1887, Taxil received audience with Pope Leo XIII, who believed in him, and not the Bishop of **Charleston**, which reflected the noble spirit of Freemasons in that mostly Protestants city, which as we know had a special role in the creation of the first **Supreme Council of the Ancient and Accepted Scottish Rite in 1801.** [3]

In 1896, the first person to start publicly questioning the Taxil affair was the famous Masonic researcher and author **Joseph Gabriel Findel**, who wrote about the non-existence of the Luciferian conspiracy promoted by Leo Taxil, and accused the Jesuits of having organized yet another, devious plot. [4] So when the Taxil/Jesuit disinformation campaign ended the following year in 1897 after 12 years of lies, Taxil promptly mentioned Findel's statement, denying any connection with the Jesuits who backed him in this farse. **But should we believe him? Of course not—he was a Jesuit agent!**

The first work produced by Leo Taxil after his feigned conversion years earlier, was a history of Freemasonry in four volumes, containing fictitious testimonies from supposed eyewitnesses who participated in alleged Satanic rituals inside Freemasonry. The amount of work required to compose so many books in so little time, makes you wonder if the Jesuits did not actually help him write the texts themselves. If he had not devoted himself to disinformation he would surely have scaled the heights of Freemasonry in no time for sure. The Secret Chiefs, however, decided something different for Leo Taxil, during a time when Anti-Masonry seemed to grow every day, especially in France, and the public desperately needed a hero. Taxil incarnated this figure in an act of disturbance towards the system.

Past Grand Master Freemason and Sovereign Grand Commander of the Scottish Rite Luigi Pruneti writes on the Taxil affair: *"Beelzebub, in the season of science and technology, steel and coal seemed resurrected from a distant past, the sooty mists of the Middle Ages, from the folds of the distressing wars of religion. He is the lord of darkness, he laughed at Pasteur and positivism, Marx and the Industrial Revolution and, grinning, left hell to sit down in the Masonic temples."* [5]

Leo Taxil with the help of a mysterious co-worker named Dr. Karl Hacks, (who operated under the pseudonym of **Dr. Bataille**), wrote another book, entitled *Le Diable au XIX siècle (The Devil in the nineteenth century)*, in which he presented a new female figure, **Diana Vaughan**, a supposed descendant of Rosicrucian alchemist **Thomas Vaughan**. Thus bringing in a female element, and the Rosicrucians to his stories of pseudo

2   *"Civiltà Cattolica"* July 1st, 1882, pp. 114-115.
3   See. http://scottishrite.org/about/history/ ‡ Archived 4th August, 2015.
4   See. Joseph Gabriel Findel, *Khatolisher Schiwindel. Eine Verteidigung des Freimaurerbundes wider Margiotta's Enthullungem,* (Leipzig, DE: J.G. Findel, 1896).
5   Luigi Pruneti, *La sinagoga di Satana. Storia dell'antimassoneria 1725-2002,* (Bari, IT: Edizioni Giusppe Laterza), p. 78.

Freemasonry and improbable Satanic scenarios. The book told fantastic implausible stories of meetings between Vaughan and incarnated demons. I'm not talking about extra-dimensional entities, but of demons in the flesh. One of these demons was said to have written prophecies on the back of Diana Vaughan, while another shaped as a crocodile played a piano. Things out of this world, to say the least, that remind us in more recent times of the "reptilian delusions" popularized in contemporary culture by the eccentric Englishman **David Icke**. Something very modest compared to the wild stories pushed at the time by Leo Taxil, and with no television or the Internet in those days, Taxil's books became bestsellers all over the world, shaping the wildest ideas in people's heads about the occult side of Freemasonry. Leo Taxil presented Diana Vaughan, as a person with a past in the Satanic practices of the Masonic elite, who was suddenly taken by repentance (in a very theatrical way). Creating a huge story like this, and later debunking it, only helped the Catholic Church and Freemasonry. It was a well-crafted plan that functioned perfectly.

This supposed transformation of Diana Vaughan, happened after she openly showed admiration for Joan of Arc, and upon hearing this name she said the demons would scatter ... Today, Leo Taxil, would probably still have great success in certain extreme conspiracy circles that treat his disinformation as real.

The Leo Taxil hoax, intended to mock not only Freemasonry, but also the Roman Catholic Church, is a complex issue. Strangely enough, Taxil was expelled from Freemasonry without ever advancing beyond the **1st degree of Entered Apprentice.** This means that Taxil could not have been able, in his modest position, to reveal the identities of influential Freemasons in various foreign jurisdictions, or the high level members of the various mystery schools of the Illuminati network, like the S.R.I.A. for example. He must have had some insider support, or otherwise the help of the Jesuits. The list of the members of each order, sect or fraternity, is in fact regarded as very sensitive information, and such lists have always been top secret, especially in those days. One wonders who gave him access to this information, as Taxil, by placing those names in his books, not only embarrassed them, but at times caused real trouble, especially when he lied about their moral integrity. René Guenon explains his own thoughts on the Leo Taxil hoax:

> To be honest it's easy to say "mystification," but the issue is much more complex and not easy to solve; it seems that, at least, the issue should be treated as something else as Taxil was lying once again when he stated he invented everything on his own initiative. You are faced with a clever mixture of true and false ... but what exactly is the "grain of truth" contained in this story?[6]

Leo Taxil published a book under the name of Diana Vaughan, entitled, *The Novena Mass*, a collection of prayers that received the praise from none other than the Pope, who gave it "a very special blessing," as reported by a Masonic publication on the 31st of May, 1897. Taxil managed to tease more than once, not only priests, and Catholics in general, but even the Pope!

A clerical correspondent wrote about the International Anti-Masonic congress of Trent organized in the fall of 1896 by leaders of the Church to fight Freemasonry:

> Our Holy Father, Leo XIII, has given his blessing to the Anti-Masonic Congress to be held at Trent from the 26th to the 30th of September.
>
> The Grand Master of the Freemasons of Italy, "noting the fact with a profound calm" in a Circular Letter dated from Rome on September 13, pours forth his de-

6 René Guenon, *Studi sulla Massoneria e il Compagnonaggio,* (Carmagnola, IT: Arktos Edizioni, 1991), p. 93.

rision and invective against it. [7]

The Congress saw the participation of Leo Taxil, but of course there was no sign of Diana Vaughan, and many asked for her presence. *La Civilta Cattolica,* the most important of all the journals of the clerical world, still to this day the official organ of the General of the Jesuits, said this in September, 1896:

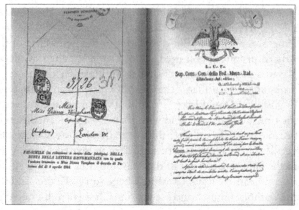

> *We want to give the pleasure of blessing publicly the names of the valorous champions who entered first the glorious arena, such as the noble Miss Vaughan.* [8]

FIG. 57 – *33° Patent of the Ancient and Accepted Scottish Rite, plus Facsimile of a letter head addressed to Miss Diana Vaughan, issued by the Supreme Council of the Ancient and Accepted Scottish Rite based in Palermo dated April 8, 1894, issued to the non-existent lady Diana Vaughan, as is reproduced in the book "Memories of a 33∴" by Domenico Margiotta.*

Some Freemasons fell into the trap of the deceptive Taxil. Those Masons that now use Leo Taxil as a scapegoat, gave a 33rd honorary degree to the non-existent Diana Vaughan, with an official document issued by an institution linked to the Masonic Italia Federation and the Supreme Council of the Ancient and Accepted Scottish Rite, based in Palermo. They sent her a diploma / patent of 33° of the Rite dated April 8, 1894, without ever having seen or met the elusive Mrs.Vaughan, and the Masonic document in question was later reproduced in the book **"Memories of a 33°"** by Domenico Margiotta. (FIG. 57)

A passage from the two documents, directed to Miss Diana Vaughan from the Supreme Council of Palermo, gives us a clear the idea of this unlikely appointment:

> *"Wanting to reward an act of affection ... our enlightened Sister ∴ Diana Vaughan for the exalted services rendered to High Masonry.*

And that's not all, the Supreme Council of Palermo went even further to say:

> *We have, in solemn assembly today decreed the title of Honorary Member of the Supreme Council and protectress of our Ancient and Accepted Scottish Rite.* [9]

This unprecenteed action made at the top of the Masonic institutions to nominate a non-existant person like Diana Vaughan, as honorary 33° and protectress of their Supreme Council, is also reported in the famous essay, "I riti massonici di Misraïm e Memphis" *(The Masonic Rites of Memphis and Mizraim)* of Count Gastone Ventura. [10]

In the end, however, on **April 19, 1897**, Leo Taxil, after selling a huge amount of books, and mocking the highest authorities and institutions in the world, held a public meeting in which he said he will present the mysterious figure of Diana Vaughan

7   Leo Taxil, *La più grande mistificazione antimassonica,* (Rome, IT: Edinac, 1948), p. 91.
8   See. Domenico Margiotta, *Memorie di un Trentatrè,* (Cosenza, IT: Brenner, 1988), pp. 340-341.
9   *Ibid.*
10   See. Gastone Ventura, *I riti massonici di Misraïm e Memphis,* (Rome, IT: Atanor, 1975), footnote 10 p. 99.

FIG. 58 – Robert A. Gilbert at the
Foundation Conference of the Circle of Rose
in support of the Rosicrucians of the Grand
Lodge of New York on October 4, 2008.

to the world. It was a long awaited move
on Taxil's side that many hoped would
end further speculations about his unre-
liability. Instead Taxil shocked everyone
once again and declared that many of the
revelations he had made on Freemasonry
were a hoax (though not all). He thanked
the clergy for having advertised his heated
statements, and announced to the public that he would withdraw permanently
from the scene. In departing, he required
a police escort for fear of being lynched after such an announcement. Yes, Leo Taxil,
a Jewish agent of the Jesuits, made fun of
everything and everyone, but the material
of his mystification is still used by the current Anti-Masonic Movement. His lies,
the most vulgar and ignorant, certainly
don't help to battle the occult and corrupt
side of Freemasonry for sure, but still have
many people that believe him to this day.
One example is in the book by James and
Pamela Sue Randall Noblitt Perskin entitled, *Cult and Ritual Abuse*, where the
Taxil mystification is considered 100%
genuine.[11] Unfortunately, Leo Taxil does
not only serve the "Anti-Masons," but also
the Masons themselves, intent in defending their institution, constantly using and
abusing the example of the Taxil mystification.

The short essay that I mentioned in the first volume entitled, THE TRIALS AND
TRIBULATIONS OF A MASONIC APOLOGIST, written by Robert A. Gilbert,
(FIG. 58) former Worshipful Master of **Quatuor Coronati n. 2076,** the most popular lodge of research in the world,[12] makes the same mistake in one of his works on the
subject. Gilbert who guided for years the prestigious Masonic publication *Ars Quatuor
Coronatorum,* demonstrates with his own words the constant use and abuse of the Taxil
mystification for the defense of the Masonic purity of intents.

Gilbert, however, like many before him, failed to mention the fact that the Jesuits
were Leo Taxil's allies in creating this collossal scam:

> *They accept as absolute truth the nonsensical stories of the Palladian Rite propa-
> gated by 'Leo Taxil' as part of his elaborate hoax at the expense of both the Roman
> Catholic Church and the Grand Orient of France. Any well-informed Freemason
> with access to a basic library of standard Masonic reference books can easily refute
> the anti-Masonic rubbish put out by Christian (and, of recent years, Islamic) fun-
> damentalists. But again we manage to shoot ourselves carefully in the foot.*[13]

11 See. James Randall Noblitt. Pamela Sue Perskin, **Cult and Ritual Abuse: Its History, Anthropology,
and Recent Discovery in Contemporary America** (Westport, CT, Praeger Publishers, 2000).
12 http://www.quatuorcoronati.com/ ‡ Archived 4th August, 2015.
13 Extract from Robert A. Gilbert, "THE TRIALS AND TRIBULATIONS OF A MASONIC APOLO-

Another important contemporary apologist of Freemasonry, is the Italian essayist and author of several books, the aforementioned **Luigi Pruneti,** a 33° former Sovereign Grand Commander and Grand Master for the period 2007 to 2013, of the aforementioned Grand Lodge of Italy in Palazzo Vitelleschi, (FIGS. 59a-59b) and one of the main Italian Masonic Obediences with more than 8,000 members. Pruneti has published two books on the subject, one is called *Antimassoneria ieri e oggi* (*Anti-Masonry yesterday and today*),[14] and the other, *La Sinagoga di Satana. Storia dell'antimassoneria, 1725 – 2002,* (*Synagogue of Satan. History of Anti-Masonry 1725-2002*). Pruneti writes:

FIG. 59 a, b – *Two images of the former Grand Master and Sovereign Grand Commander Luigi Pruneti, accompanied by the author and Princess Kaoru Nakamaru in Turin, Italy. Image taken in May of 2012.*

> *In Italy, this sacrificial victim was identified in Freemasonry. The thesis Barruel set forth, improved by Taxil, embraced by fascism, married and flourished with the Catholic-communist postwar culture, tended to be rooted firmly in the common mentality in that Collective conscious, in which the mysteries of Freemasonry and the other works of the transalpine journalist worked.* [15]

Luigi Pruneti mentions the Taxil Hoax as the origin for certain Anti-Masonic tendencies that originated with **Abbé Augustin Barruel (October 2, 1741 – October 5, 1820),** and was a **Jesuit** most known for instigating the conspiracy theory involving the **Bavarian Illuminati.** Pruneti never mentions the Jesuit involvement that began with Jesuit Augustin Barruel, and continued with the Jesuit agent Leo Taxil. On top of this Pruneti on the contrary of Gilbert, does not even mention the controversial figure of Satanist Aleister Crowley, nor the wicked practices and evil of *Ordo Templi Orientis,* nor those other affiliates of Freemasonry linked to Satanism, which I assure you there is no shortage of. It seems that the majority of historians of Freemasonry, like Luigi Pruneti, chose to ignore certain concerns that could discredit Freemasonry, rather than clarifying the situation for non-Masons.

GIST" (a short essay addressed to the Brothers of the UGLE).

14   See. Luigi Pruneti, *Antimassoneria ieri e oggi,* (Rome, IT: EDIMAI 1995).

15   *La Sinagoga di Satana, Ibid.,* p. 288.

Pruneti dedicated an entire chapter in his book to the Leo Taxil hoax, *The Synagogue of Satan. History of Anti-Masonry 1725-2002*, entitled, "A phenomenon named Leo Taxil," this is a list of topics:

Antoine Jogand Pagès aka Leo Taxil

The alleged conversion of Leo Taxil

Works and accusations of Taxil

Creating Diana Vaughan and the "Reformed Palladian Rite"

Satan, lord of the lodges, "The Franc-Maçonnerie, Synagogue of Satan"

Monsignor Leon Meurin, bishop of Port Louis

Dr. Bataille the second voice of Leo Taxil

The memories of a 33rd Domenico Margiotta

The publication of the names of the French Freemasons, a literary genre of success

The Toffana water and Masonic murder

The anti-Masonic Congress in Trento

The conference in Paris at the headquarters of the Geographical Society and the collapse of mystification

The irreparable damage of mystification

I decided to discuss the matter directly with the person involved, Luigi Pruneti, still Grand Master at the time. He graciously received me and Princess Kaoru Nakamaru, and personally said that I was correct about the Leo Taxil affair, and that he soon would devote an essay to the fact Taxil was an agent of the Jesuits, and that such hypothesis deserved a closer investigation. The Taxil mystification is at this point not only a well-crafted joke in my view, but part of a specific conspiracy of the Jesuits to promote **Relativism.** In the present day we even see a Jesuit Pope accused by some to be a relativist himself.[16] Here's a brief and concise explanation of the meaning of relativism according to Wikipedia: *"Relativism is the concept that points of view have no absolute truth or validity within themselves, but they only have relative, subjective value according to differences in perception and consideration."*[17]

During a passage of the long conversation that Pope Benedict XVI had with Peter Oswald, that later became the subject of a book, Oswald made the following remarks to the Pope, mentioning Aldous Huxley as one of the gurus of the New World Order:

In his futuristic novel Brave New World, *the British author Aldous Huxley predicted in 1932 that falsification would be the decisive element of modernity. In a false reality with its false truth—or the absence of truth altogether—nothing, in the final analysis, is important anymore. There is no truth, there is no standpoint. Today, in fact, truth is regarded as far too subjective a concept for us to find therein a universally valid standard. The distinction between genuine and fake seems to have been abolished. Everything is to some extent negotiable.*

At this point Oswald asked Benedict, **Is that the relativism against which you were warning so urgently?** The answer of the Pope was the following:

It is obvious that the concept of truth has become suspect. Of course it is correct that it has been much abused. Intolerance and cruelty have occurred in the name of

16   http://vox-nova.com/2013/10/03/is-pope-francis-a-relativist/ ‡ Archived 4th August, 2015.

17   See. *American Heritage Dictionary* for this definition or https://it.wikipedia.org/wiki/Relativismo ‡ Archived 4th August, 2015.

truth. To that extent people are afraid when someone says, "This is the truth," or even "I have the truth." We never have it; at best it has us. No one will dispute that one must be careful and cautious in claiming the truth. But simply to dismiss it as unattainable is really destructive. A large proportion of contemporary philosophies, in fact, consist of saying that man is not capable of truth. But viewed in that way, man would not be capable of ethical values, either. Then he would have no standards. Then he would only have to consider how he arranged things reasonably for himself, and then at any rate the opinion of the majority would be the only criterion that counted. History, however, has sufficiently demonstrated how destructive majorities can be, for instance, in systems such as Nazism and Marxism, all of which also stood against truth in particular. [18]

However it was because of the danger of relativism that in the year 2000, Pope Ratzinger in defense of the more traditional and conservative Catholic faction, railed against the Jesuit theologian **Jacques Dupuis.**

The red alert came for the first time from Ratzinger in a speech made in October, 1996 to the Bishops of the Americas where he states:

The fundamental problem of faith in our time has become relativism. And so the fundamental question for the Church becomes the so-called pluralist theology of religions. On the one hand it is a typical product of the Western world, but on the other is placed in contact with the philosophical and religious intuitions of Asia, especially India, and it is the link between these two worlds that determines its particular influence on the historical moment we are living. [19]

But with Pope Francis, the first Jesuit Pope, things have obviously changed in the Catholic Church, and as the well-known Italian journalist (and CIA asset) Giuliano Ferrara [20] wrote in January 2014, in the Italian newspaper *Il Foglio*, in an article very appropriately entitled, *Relativismo ad maiorem gloriam Dei*, miming the motto of the Jesuits with a touch of humor, the Pope is promotes relativism:

The Jesuits have always played a prestigious role in the apostolic religious and civil power of the Church and in the nation-states of which they became tutors, confessors and sometimes governors. Not for kindness, but for doctrine, Francis rejects the position of Inquisitor and preaches dialogue with the historical world, contingent as it is and not as we would like it to be. His rejection of the doctrinal rigor so unpopular with the sinful world is an essential Machiavellian complement of the Jesuit way of conceiving the imitation of Christ and the evangelization. [21]

Behind the Jesuit takeover of the Vatican is the late **Cardinal Carlo Maria Martini (1927-2012),** a known Jesuit and Freemason, who was already pushing the name of Mario Bergoglio, the future Pope Francis, in the papal election in 2005. Martini, also a Freemason as I mentioned in the book, *Pope Francis: The Last Pope?* [22] was the main conspirator who forced the resignation of Joseph Ratzinger orchestrated by the Society of Jesus.

This was officially confirmed by the Jesuit, Father Silvano Fausti, who died June 24,

18 Pope Benedict XVI, Light of the World: The Pope, The Church and The Signs Of The Times. A Conversation with Peter Seewald (San Francisco: Ignatius Press, 2010), 50-54.

19 http://chiesa.espresso.repubblica.it/articolo/7265?refresh_ce ‡ Archived 4th August, 2015.

20 https://it.wikipedia.org/wiki/Giuliano_Ferrara ‡ Archived 4th August, 2015.

21 http://www.ilfoglio.it/articoli/2014/01/04/relativismo-ad-maiorem-gloriam-dei___1-v-92776-rubriche_c167.htm ‡ Archived 4th August, 2015.

22 See. Leo Lyon Zagami, *Pope Francis: The Last Pope?, Ibid.*, pp. 35-36, p.75.

2015 at the age 75. A name unknown to most people, Fausti was actually a very influential personality in the ecclesiastical sphere, and one of the people closest to Cardinal Carlo Maria Martini.

The archbishop of Milan, who died in 2012, confided many secrets of the Church establishment to him, including factual background on the real motive for the resignation of Joseph Ratzinger.[23] The revelations of the Jesuit Silvano Giusti appeared in *"Il Corriere della Sera"*:

> *Father Silvano Fausti said that the moment Benedict XVI and Carlo Maria Martini were seen for the last time in Milan during the World Meeting of Families, on June 2, 2012, the Cardinal who was ill for some time, came out of the Aloisium of Gallarate to reach the Pope. It was then that he looked into my eyes and Martini's, who would have died on the 31st of August, said to Ratzinger: "the Curia does not reform, you just have to leave."*[24]

Remember, even if the author of this book is called Leo, I am no Leo Taxil, so dear proponents of the New World Order and the various slaves of prevailing relativism, read and surrender to the truth from these pages, not the usual disinformation fed by modern society corrupt by relativism and matter. Relativism is the antechamber of the new world religion ruling Satanism. **Enrico Galoppini** makes a very clever analysis in the magazine *"Eurasia"*:

> *The Western world satisfied to be " modern" considers "relativism" as the cornerstone of any social and cultural developement. Each "absolute" is openly considered a legacy of a mentality "barbaric and retrograde." "Relativism," in turn, is combined with individualism and utilitarianism: the human being, which is conceived as a mere "individual" capable of all sizes regardless of national and Community, opt for what most suits at one time. Since everyone is encouraged (by the "average" and the "intellectuals") to think and behave in this way, here it is the West that postulates a world without "boundaries," which are physical or mental. The very notion of "limit" gives tremendously bothersome. Modern man is considered accordingly as the most "open" among all his fellows who preceded him and who still "linger" on world views "of the past." But although everything seems to herald a radiant "new era" of humanity, of which the West with its "values" would be the vanguard, it must consider the fact that there is a Great Absent. The Great God is absent. However, it must be understood. Even in the West as such there are people for whom God has a place in their lives. But most of the time "the idea of God" that you make is extremely far away from what traditionally has been made all the peoples and civilizations past. The "god West"—i.e. the way in which they imagine the modern principle, the Source of all things—is a projection of their predilections and their desires more or less frustrated and unacknowledged. A "god" such is the antechamber of the "world without God," because for all religious traditions that have gone before God "spoke," indicating clearly what is right and what is wrong for His creatures. Intended to bliss or damnation.*

> *For the " modern thinking," known as "secular," this is inconceivable. For it is the man to have to decide, first, what it is "good" and what is "bad" for him. Religion, in this context, end up playing a role "comforting," as well as the agency for the support*

23   See. http://www.liberoquotidiano.it/news/italia/11811486/Il-confessore-di-Carlo-Maria-Martini.html ‡ Archived 4th August, 2015.

24   http://www.corriere.it/cronache/15_luglio_16/quando-martini-disse-ratzinger-curia-non-cambia-devi-lasciare-39c20eba-2b83-11e5-a01d-bba7d75a97f7.shtml ‡ Archived 4th August, 2015.

of certain categories of "needy." The devastating consequences of atheism in the Western world have not yet fully Been Considered, nor have all manifested themselves in their fatal tragedy. The result, however, is beginning to emerge clearly, and goes by the lowest common denominator of the "chaos."

A lack of an Order, that suffered from "Western societies," which cannot be extended to the basic framework of the sexes and the relationships between them.

*In the above human aggregations are regulated according to the contractualized diagram (the simulated societies), as opposed to the "natural-Community" (the innate societies), each is educated to the maximum of "do as you wish," which, just to further clarify things, was the same promoted by **Aleister Crowley**, considered one of the founders of modern Satanism. **We started with "freedom" and "tolerance" and we are now in Satanism. It is not at all a joke, nor an exaggeration.***

Satanism, reduced to its essence, is—rather than the worship of some strange creature depicted in the guise of a goat—the deification of self, of that ego illusion that every religious tradition indicates regular as the "main enemy" (and basically the only). This enemy of man, that is closer than his own jugular vein, which never leaves him and, in fact, raises the bar depending on the degree of realization of all, is the basis of every modern deviation, from the theological to the political from economic to the cultural and so on. It does not go far from the truth by saying that the "modern world" is an environment in which the lower forces that draw men into the innermost recesses of his consciousness obscure and confusing they had, now more than ever, a full freedom of expression.

*However, in the face of such forces, providentially, stands always a "katechon," meaning "that which restrains or one who holds," which with its very presence deferral **the coming of the kingdom of the Antichrist parody**. It is not easy to identify in practice who or what performs this function in our time. However, there are many clues that allow a view into the leadership of the Russian Federation, and, specifically, of **Vladimir Putin**, as a factor that hampers the unleashing of these forces, avoiding the final collapse of the "wall."*

This role is not the exclusive preserve of anyone, therefore can be ascribed to this providential function also the action of other organizations or other personalities. It is universally known, in fact, the role of the saints and their prayers. But here we are talking about politics, and because each one does its part, it must be said that Putin has greatly contributed, with its initiatives, not to precipitate the part of the world that he manages in the same "egotistic" spiral that has been seen unfolding elsewhere, one time after another, a hedonistic mass or elitist phenomena, all equally destructive. This is the role the Russian leadership shares with the "not aligned leaderships."[25]

"Relativism" is not only an important asset for the majority of Speculative Freemasonry in the hands of the various congregations of the Illuminati network that promote so-called enlightment, and the Jesuits that have always promoted it for centuries; but "relativism" is now the creed of the majority of the Masonic influenced Catholic hierarchy after the Second Vatican Council, increasingly atheist and materialistic.

Returning The Taxil, In 1948, **Achille Pontevia** wrote a credible account of the hoax in his introduction to a book dedicated to the Taxil mystification, where we also find a

25   http://www.eurasia-rivista.org/un-esempio-di-soft-power-occidentale-la-propaganda-omosessuale-contro-la-russia/21762 ‡ Archived 4th August, 2015, *[emphasis added]*.

faithful reproduction of the pages of a supplement called *MASONIC MAGAZINE* from the year 1897, and the translation of the last controversial speech given by Leo Taxil in public published originally by the newspaper *Le Frondeur*.

These are words written in the late '40s by Pontevia on the "Taxil affair":

> *Yet when the hoaxer took off his mask, unmasking the truth even for those who had supported him, the Church could not really say much, except that Leo Taxil was nothing more than a creature of the Masons ... and this was said although reason, morality, and justice denied it. In front of such a masterpiece of bad faith, how did the Masons react? Which speculation did they mount a response? There was nothing, they only said: We had warned you about Taxil for a long time, but you didn't want to believe us?! Nor did this change the ways of the perpetrators after such a meaningless act, nor did they have the loyalty to recognize and repair the moral damage of which they were voluntary participants. They did not talk about Taxil again, but they did not let Taxil's work fall into oblivion either, in fact, they used this seed he had thrown and wisely safeguarded it and cultivated it in order to perpetuate its fruits. Who listens today to the anti-clerical propaganda against Freemasonry feels in it a constant echo of the literature of Taxil and realizes that the Church never truly disavowed this cheater storyteller. Though Taxil disavowed himself, the Church limited itself only to officially grant him the status of a hoaxer, but in reality they continued, and still continue to use and provide the largest credit to his work. Achille Pontevia adds further on: "The priests know perfectly well that they are continuing to endorse the work of a hoaxer, but think that its effectiveness and its relevance is not yet warned off."* [26]

Devil Worship in France, [27] is a book published in 1896, a year before the end of the Taxil mystification, by the Masonic author **Arthur Edward Waite.** Masonic historian Robert A. Gilbert describes Waite this way:

> *Arthur Edward Waite, the child of Anglo-American parents, was born at a time of religious upheaval and left this world as it was busily engaged in tearing apart its social fabric. He was a prolific author, but one whose books are, for the most part, unknown and unread; he was not recognized as a scholar by the academic world, but he remains the only comprehensive analyst of the history of occultism in all its many branches. Not that he approved of the term or the looseness of its connotations; to himself he was a mystic and an exponent of mysticism. He saw, what others before him had not seen, that there can be no final understanding of mystical experience without an appreciation of the traditions, outside the confines of the Church, that preserved those practices that bring mystical experience within the reach of every man and woman. He is not easy to understand. His writing is diffuse, often verbose, and peppered with archaisms; but it has its own power and leaves the reader with the feeling that buried within the densely packed prose is a message of immense significance. This has been perceived by the more acute of his critics: Dean Inge—a scourge of sentimental pseudo-mysticism-believed that Waite had "penetrated very near to the heart of this subject" (review of* Studies in Mysticism, *in* The Saturday Review, *2 March 1907). But Waite refused to jettison all that was included under the heading of occultism. He saw within it, as Spurgeon said of the Talmud, jewels which the world could not afford to miss; and seeing them, drew them out and displayed them for all to see-all, that is, with eyes to see. Many readers of Waite, and most self-*

26   Leo Taxil, La più grande mistificazione antimassonica, *op. cit.*, p. 13.
27   Arthur Edward White, ***Devil Worship in France,*** (London: George Redway, 1896).

confessed students of "rejected knowledge," persist in seeing him as an occultist. [28]

This is partly true as Waite, at the time of his aforementioned book *Devil Worship in France,* was already member of the Martinist and the occultistic *Golden Dawn,* two of the leading Illuminati occult organizations in the world at that time, becoming a member of "Regular" Freemasonry in 1901.

Waite demonstrated, on the contrary of most Masonic experts of the time, serious doubts about the figure of Diana Vaughan and the rest of the rubbish promoted by Leo Taxil, confronting many of the characters mentioned by Taxil in his books in an attempt to discover the truth and compare versions of the events. The Leo Taxil case brings us to my final analysis of the "Taxil Hoax," to discuss the so-called "Palladian Rite" or **"Palladism,"** an alleged anti-Christian esoteric cult founded in the late nineteenth century by members of the Masons, and the "famous" **correspondence between Giuseppe Mazzini and Albert Pike.**

In 1891, Taxil and Adolphe Ricoux claimed to have discovered a Palladian Society. A 1892 French book called *Le Diable au XIXe siècle* (*The Devil in the 19th Century,* 1892), written by "Dr. Bataille" (actually Jogand-Pagès himself), alleged that Palladists were Satanists based in **Charleston, South Carolina,** headed by the American Freemason Albert Pike, and created by the Italian liberal patriot and author Giuseppe Mazzini. [29]

Another fabrication—often repeated by anti-masons and conspiracy theorists—is the claim that because of their occult link, Albert Pike was in constant correspondence with Giuseppe Mazzini. This accusation was first claimed by Edith Starr Miller, [30] and later repeated by **William Guy Carr,** who cited **Cardinal Caro y Rodriguez of Santiago,** Chile, the author of *The Mystery of Freemasonry Unveiled.* [31] In his own *Pawns in the Game,* Carr claims that this correspondence was on display in the British Museum but didn't provide the actual source of this information. Later, in "Satan, Prince of this World," Carr included the following footnote:

> *The Keeper of Manuscripts recently informed the author that this letter is NOT catalogued in the British Museum Library. It seems strange that a man of Cardinal Rodriguez's knowledge should have said that it WAS in 1925.* [32]

The British Museum has recently confirmed in writing to researcher Michael Haupt that such a document has never been in their possession. The following quotes, taken from conspiracy theorists Edith Starr Miller and William Guy Carr, have been demonstrated to be a continuation of a lengthy hoax perpetrated by Leo Taxil between 1885 and 1897. **Edith Starr Miller writes:**

> *Mazzini, who was very practical, said that it would be inadvisable to favor one rite only to the exclusion of all the others. In a letter to Albert Pike, dated Jan. 22, 1870, he writes. "We must allow all the federations to continue just as they are, with their systems, their central authorities and their diverse modes of correspondence between high grades of the same rite, organized as they are at the present, but we must create a super rite, which will remain unknown, to which we will call those Masons of high degree whom we shall select. With regard to our brothers in Masonry, these men*

28   Robert A. Gilbert, A.E. Waite: *Magician of Many Parts,* (Wellingborough, Northhamptonshire: Crucible, Thorson Publishing Group Limited, 1987), p. 12.

29   See http://www.threeworldwars.com/admin/about.htm ‡ Archived 4th August, 2015.

30   See. Edith Starr Miller, *Occult Theocrasy,* (Abbeville: Imprimerie F. Paillart, 1933), pp. 208-209.

31   See *The Mysteries of Freemasonry Unveiled,* 1925. English translation,1957, p. 118.

32   See. William Guy Carr, *Satan: Prince of This World,* (pdf published by www.ThreeWorldWars.com), p. 22.

must be pledges to the strictest secrecy. Through this supreme rite, we will govern all Freemasonry which will become the one international center, the more powerful because its direction will be unknown." [33]

Carr claimed the following was excerpted from a letter to Giuseppe Mazzini from Albert Pike, dated August 15, 1871:

> *The First World War must be brought about in order to permit the Illuminati to overthrow the power of the Czars in Russia and of making that country a fortress of atheistic Communism. The divergences caused by the "agentur" (agents) of the Illuminati between the British and Germanic Empires will be used to foment this war. At the end of the war, Communism will be built and used in order to destroy the other governments, and in order to weaken the religions.*

> *The Second World War must be fomented by taking advantage of the differences between the Fascists and the political Zionists. This war must be brought about so that Nazism is destroyed and that the political Zionism be strong enough to institute a sovereign state of Israel in Palestine. During the Second World War, International Communism must become strong enough in order to balance Christendom, which would be then restrained and held in check until the time when we would need it for the final social cataclysm.*

> *The Third World War must be fomented by taking advantage of the differences caused by the agentur of the Illuminati between the political Zionists and the leaders of Islamic World. The war must be conducted in such a way that Islam (the Muslim Arabic World) and political Zionism (the State of Israel) mutually destroy each other. Meanwhile, the other nations, once more divided on this issue will be constrained to fight to the point of complete physical, moral, spiritual and economical exhaustion ... We shall unleash the Nihilists and the atheists, and we shall provoke a formidable social cataclysm which in all its horror will show clearly to the nations the effect of absolute atheism, origin of savagery and of the most bloody turmoil. Then everywhere, the citizens, obliged to defend themselves against the world minority of revolutionaries, will exterminate those destroyers of civilization, and the multitude, disillusioned with Christianity, whose deistic spirits will from that moment be without compass or direction, anxious for an ideal, but without knowing where to render its adoration, will receive the true light through the universal manifestation of the pure doctrine of Lucifer, brought finally out in the public view. This manifestation will result from the general reactionary movement which will follow the destruction of Christianity and atheism, both conquered and exterminated at the same time.*

As the Grand Lodge of British Columbia and Yukon states on their website:

> *It cannot be stressed too strongly that these claimed excerpts from a non-existent correspondence are not supported by any documentation. Internal evidence, the language and subject matter, clearly suggest a much later creation date.* [34]

Leo Taxil reported the Palladist's (or Palladian) were Masons belonging to at least the 30th degree, and run in a hidden manner, all the Lodges. Of course it was a joke as stated in his incredible admission on April 19, 1897: *"My whole Palladism was so solidly built, with regard to the strict Masonic sense it gave, since Masons, of the*

33rd degree, did believe in its foundations. They even asked to enter it (laughter of the crowd present). *The impossibility of Palladism does not reveal itself if not for the supernatural of which we filled it."*[35]

Of course today, for those who have not studied the matter carefully, Taxil's hoax might seem like the usual "sham," like so many others, but it is far from it. In fact this "hoax" lasted 12 years, and looks rather like a big psychological operation, where Taxil appears to have been the most representative figure. The Church wanted to use the confessions of a repentant Mason like Taxil, as an effective support to their doctrinal positions (the ex-communications against Freemasonry). For this reason, they were careless and stood by this dubious figure and writer, even though there was more than suspicion and a few doubts about him from the start. Taxil did not simply publish magazines and books, but he also created a series of initiatives that represent a real "desecration," as a Catholic newspaper launched a "union of prayer dedicated to Joan of Arc" to counter the malignant Masonic forces. In 1895 they founded in Paris, *"The anti-Masonic Order of Labaro"* (*Ordre du Labarum anti-maçonnique*), a real parody of a knightly order, **divided into three grades (Legionary of Constantine, Soldier of Christ, Knight of the Sacred Heart),** which was strongly desired by the fictitious Diana Vaughan, author of the imaginary anti-Masonic "Memoirs."

The Order of Labaro, which would be interesting to study carefully to better understand its back story, stated in its statutes it was to defend the Holy Church and the Pope against its main enemy, Freemasonry. The Banner also announced they wished to give life to an anti-Masonic International Congress, which would have as the honorary president Cardinal Parocchi, vicar of His Holiness. Taxil naturally figured among the founders of the Order. In those same years, another accomplice of Taxil was the aforementioned **Domenico Margiota**, who was elevated to the rank of **Knight of the Holy Sepulchre by Pope Leo XIII,** showing imprudent papal authority in the matter. However, I believe that without the Jesuits to support the entire project from the beginning, the Pope would never have fallen into this trap. This would also explain why Leo Taxil was so warmly received at the Vatican by **Cardinal Rampolla,** who was disappointed by the fact that Taxil was just an apprentice.[36] Cardinal Rampolla, years later, was accused not only of being a Freemason, (which had prevented him from being elected pope in the conclave of 1903), but also a member of *Ordo Templi Orientis.* Aleister Crowley himself cites him among the distinguished members of the past and one of the "saints" of his *Gnostic Catholic Church.*[37]

I urge contemporary Masonic researchers to continue their research on the responsibility of Jesuits in the "Taxil hoax," confirmed by Italian Masonic historian Luigi Pruneti and even myself, as I was accused of being the new "Leo Taxil" more than once.[38] I am not interested in delivering fictional stories, when the real ones are already enough to discredit and bring into disrepute Freemasonry, as you will see in the upcoming pages.

The danger of generational Satanism in Freemasonry

In the mid 1990s Anton LaVey gave an interesting interview on the foundation of his **Church of Satan** entitled, *A Church and Fantasy and Fetish,* to the English

35   See. Review of Léo Taxil, *The mysteries of Freemasonry,* published by Excelsior – Milan, Masonic Magazine "East and West" No. 3 – March 2011.
36   See. Léo Taxil, *op. cit.,* pp. 59-60.
37   See Leo Lyon Zagami, *Pope Francis: The Last Pope?, Ibid.,* pp. 197-198, p. 209.
38   http://www.grandeorientedemocratico.com/Commento_di_Grande_Oriente_Democratico_a_Le_Confessioni_di_Zagami_scuotono_la_Massoneria.html ‡ Archived 5th August, 2015.

Satanist, journalist and author, Gavin Baddeley for his book, *Lucifer Rising: A Book of Sin, Devil Worship And Rock 'n' Roll*. This is the answer by LaVey to the question: *"What other Satanic group do you come across these days, and what do you think of them—are any of these dangerous?"*

There's a character named Joe Penner leading something called the Synagogue of Satan. He claims to have done so since the '50s and wanted to inherit the mantle of the Process. Another guy named Mordecai Levi claims that Satan is directing his holy cause. These people are jokes. There's always some hard-core nut claiming to be part of some ancient cabal. They are just dillies. The only really dangerous characters are the ones who think they are generational Satanists and their grandfather told them with his last breath what to do, or whatever.

The Satanic scene is really too nebulous to pin down. The loquacious ones are like the drunk at the end of the bar who will try to smite to fill you of nonsense—we get stacks of that type of material each week. There are many armies made by one man out there, a lot of coffee bar revolutionaries. New information technology has bred a lot of desktop Satanists and bulletin boards, meaning that cyberspace seems full of Satanists. The Christian heretics rarely go much further than designing letterheads. But many Satanists are quietly applying Church of Satan philosophy in their lives, in their own fashion, in a very real way. The best thing we could ask from those people is a passing nod of respect. We are joiners. We don't expect fanatical devotion. We're not cudgel-pummeling evangelists. I do my own thing and I don't give a shit if people want to go along with me or not. I have no problems with a guilty conscience—this isn't some kind of scam. Left to my own devices this is what I'd be doing on my own anyway. In the beginning it was a largely solitary search. It's like a story that I was told about a new doctor who comes to work at a sanatorium. "He comes across this dressing?" the inmate replies. "Then why the hat?" asks the doctor. "Well, you never know, someone might come along." That's why I keep doing what I do—because somebody might come along. [39]

In his brilliant exposition LaVey, ahead of his time, identified the growing phenomenon of the so-called laptop activists and cyber-Satanists, well before the birth of social networks, stating that: **"The only really dangerous characters, were actually generational Satanists."** It is in this context that the hypocrisy of the Illuminati seems to mix devil worship and holy water, often protected by Freemasonry. An institution increasingly complacent and silent respect to the activities of certain Satanists, within their lodges; and not only the "generational type" (see the O.T.O. for example). We see over and over again in these environments, the constant presence of Neo-gnosticism with a strong libertine overtone, that is often used to hide generational Satanism and Illuminati sectarian activities. Anton LaVey, who was one of the most influential and the most important modern Satanists—rightly warns there are indeed people who are born into families that belong to the Satanic elite active in the New World Order, that have devoted hundreds of years to the occult arts and black magic. This obviously happens a lot in European aristocracy, but also in the USA, as I demonstrate with a thorough investigation into the activities of Grand Master **David Daniel De Paul**.

David Daniel De Paul, who is in reality the "Grand Magister" of the Brotherhood of Satan known amongst its initiates with the name of **Druwydion Pendragon,** and follow a generational tradition in the United States of America, as they claim on one of their websites: *"Before the public formation of the Church of Satan in San Francisco,*

39   Gavin Baddeley, *Lucifer Rising, Ibid.*, p. 77.

CA by Dr. Anton LaVey, there existed in both Europe and the USA secretive Satanism whose members did not advertise their membership. This form of Satanism still exists and even now is undergoing reorganization."[40]

The author of these words is David Daniel De Paul, who is a Master Mason and a 33° of the **Ancient and Accepted Scottish Rite**, at least according to what I was told by the Freemason and ex-policemen from the NYPD, **Benjamin T. Mollica** (FIG. 60), who at the time informed me of this influential Satanic cult operating from the state of Georgia. Benjamin T. Mollica informed me of his own past Satanic involvement in this dangerous sect, who initially provided me with the evidence I needed to start my own investigation in the activities of this supposed Satanic generational cult, helping me to prove that David Daniel De Paul known as **Druid Druwydion Pendragon**, (FIG. 61) is not a real Freemason, but actually one of the most dangerous generational Satanists in the USA.

FIG. 60 – The American author and Freemason Arthur Temple aka Benjamin Mollica, Master Mason of the Grand Lodge of New York, who helped me in investigating the Brotherhood of Satan.

Both are Freemasons, great manipulators, and dangerous to society, but they still seem untouchable because of their connections in high places, and their alleged role in the Black Witches Pyramid and the Illuminati Pyramid Structure.[41] They are in fact linked to the *Council of Nine* of **Dr. Michael Aquino**, a former lieutenant Colonel, Intelligence expert and psychological operations expert, involved for years in research programs of mind control within the U.S. Intelligence community. It is said that Aquino and his sect in Italy, a few years ago, secretly celebrated a Black Mass near Naples. In private he preaches Neo-Theosophy in line with most of the "Puppet Masters" of the New World Order, who are awaiting the coming of the Antichrist.

I begin this analysis of David Daniel de Paul by first demonstrating his more moderate Neo-Templar side, of which he is apparently a Grand Master, to take you later on a journey into the depths of hell, which actually goes far beyond the mystification of Frenchmen Leo Taxil. **So why do U.S. Freemasons close their eyes to this growing Satanic infiltration of the Craft?** The answer is that unfortunately they turn a blind eye to enjoy a quiet life, which facilitates the increasing take over of Freemasonry by the dark side. Everything becomes gradually tolerated in the local lodges, the result of relativism which basically desires Satanism to be accepted just as any other form of religion. Relativism is increasingly expanding in modern times, and it will be devastating in the long run for the morals and ethics of our society, and that's why the whole world is going to hell if we don't stop them.

40   http://www.brotherhoodofsatan.com/pdf/BOSFYI.pdf ‡ Archived 5th August, 2015.
41   https://www.youtube.com/watch?v=2yvSdpHmzFc ‡ Filed 5th August, 2015.

FIG. 61 – Freemason David Daniel de Paul, generational Satanist and Grand Master of the **Brotherhood of Satan** during his Satanic ceremonies.

So let me begin with Grand Master De Paul's "Gnostic" address, where he describes his enlightenment and his role as an illuminator to his aspiring disciples, showing a great dose of hypocrisy and falsehood in the process:

I was pleased to see the great interest that we have seen concerning the Ancient Gnostic Order of Knights of the Temple of Solomon. As we see a revival of things Esoteric we are an Order that grows with the times and the very framework of our historical aspects. That the Gnostic Templar Orders are now networking together for our common cause of Spiritual and Occult Unity is a fact of great interest. Before accepting the honor bestowed upon me by many of the membership of the secret Brotherhood I undertook a great deal of soul searching within before I felt that this honor was deserving. My personal background in the Occult and Spiritual Sciences is extensive and from a young child raised in a Masonic family I both studied and practiced the Occult Arts for transformation of my soul and self-realization and self-empowerment. To that end, I was willing to spend countless hours, days, and years, deeply active in the study and practice of both the Eastern and Western Mysteries. While a great many children my age were doing other things in life's learning experiences, I was immersed in the research, study, and practice of the Esoteric and Occult. [42]

De Paul's words seem to describe someone clearly born within the Illuminati network. Interestingly enough, not only did De Paul boast of his long-standing family tradition with Freemasonry and Templarism, but he also brings into the equation his link with the **Theosophical Society,** so dear to the New World Order and Satanic legend Dr. Michael Aquino:

I was very fortunate that I grew up as a child in the town next to where the Theosophical Society was headquartered here in the United States and I did a great deal of study there as well as other Occult Research centers. My practice and study of the Occult has lasted a lifetime and throughout my background as a Freemason which I became when of age, thanks to the nurturing of my family. My bloodline comes from Masonic French Ancestry just as many of the French Knight Templar Grand Masters throughout history. The other of these Grand Masters have up to this point in history resided in European countries but the need for a American residing Gnostic Templar Grand Master is very apparent to American seekers of the Gnosis. I was Knighted a Masonic Knights Templar at the end of 1983 and was given a standing ovation after presenting a discourse on the Ancient Knights Templar before the dinner in the Lodge Hall directly after my being the Inspection Candidate for Knight-

hood during the visit of the Grand Commander of the state. I was knighted with my Grandfather's Masonic Knights Templar Sword which is something that has been forever instilled in my mind. Besides the many Masonic Offices that I have held and still do hold, I entered even further into the esoteric background of the Ancient Order. During this time I was granted the vision of second sight and became greatly enlightened about the many esoteric beliefs of the Ancient Order. The deeper I delved into Gnosticism and related areas of Occult Philosophy the more enlightened I became. Today, I am a Way shower and a Knight Templar that has over 40 years of Occult and Spiritual teaching and counseling under my belt and am accepted by the Secret Brotherhood as a Initiate of the Ancient Mysteries that "Knows Something." I owe my entire being to the Divine Sophia who has lead me throughout my personal Quest for Illumination. The Ancient Gnostic Order of Knights of the Temple of Solomon holds the Key to that great door through which after knocking upon it and accepted to enter, has given me the esoteric answer to the Occult maxim of "Know Thyself."

The AGOKT here in the United States is a support organization that shall always exist to serve the cause of the Universal Oneness of all Life. I admonish everyone to understand that there is "A New Day Dawning." TOGETHER we will replace the Capstone upon the Great Pyramid following in the Ancient Tradition of "The Builders" and expounders of Spiritual Alchemy.

Fraternal Salutations to All, David Daniel de Paul , Grand Master Ancient Gnostic Order of Knights of the Temple of Solomon, Baphomet Preceptory [43]

Have you noticed how David Daniel de Paul never mentions Satanism when he presents himself as a "Gnostic Templar?" However, things change when he writes without revealing his true identity on the website of the *Brotherhood of Satan:*

Satanic Truth from the Brotherhood of Satan by David Daniel de Paul

Hail Satan the only true Master of the Brotherhood! Throughout the Ages the Brotherhood has existed as the only real Secret Society from which all others sprang from that are of the Dark Occult Nature. No, we do not claim our lineage from any of the so-called existing Satanic Organizations but rather from SATAN whom we owe our only allegiance to. This is NOT an article that has been written because we seek the acceptance of others that have appointed themselves as the only spokesmen of Satanism, but rather because we are fed up with those that falsely represent themselves as such. This article is written because we will dispel a lot of the fabrications and libel going around with Satanic Truth. The truth being stated is greatly important to the Brotherhood of Satan because we do NOT want to look, or even seem, to be like all of the rest of the present Satanic Organizations out there that think that being a Satanic organization means that you must endeavor to libel, slander, and falsely claim untruths, that are simply LIES to say the very least. Instead, the Brotherhood of Satan wants to actually teach Satanism from the Generational and Old Traditional roots that it has really came from in the first place. When you see that the other Satanic Orgs out there are doing NOTHING besides libeling others to make themselves look good, it is very easy to see that they are part of the PROBLEM and certainly are NOT part of the solution. Satanism IS a highly individualistic philosophy and that has great truth in it but that does not mean we can not seek out others of a like mind to both practice and live Satanism with. Since Satanists are freethinkers, I think we

*can think for ourselves and we do not need other Satanists telling us "How to be a
Satanist or What Satanism is or is not." That is our own personal choice. When we
think and act for ourselves, we are really then practicing REAL Satanism. As the
Brotherhood of Satan moves forward (and we are not going to stop) we want to shed
some light on the truth about us. Why not read the TRUTH as it is stated from the
"Horses Mouth." As a organization, we are found in the very roots of antiquity and
we are known to be a Ancient Satanic Organization tracing its origins to the early
Demon Worshipping Cultures on our planet. We style ourselves as a Satanic Family
that answers only to SATAN and no other Master. Do not be fooled by those that we
are a direct threat because we do not seek their blessing upon anything we do for Satan. We are "The BROTHERHOOD," a Satanic Collective that can stand together
as individual Satanists of Knowledge which is Power and can stand ORGANIZED
and in UNITY.*

*The Brotherhood of Satan believes in Satan as a very real Entity and Deity, the
very Oldest in Nature. The use of the Principles of Brotherhood between all Brotherhood of Satan members is the very cement of our foundation. Is the Brotherhood
hiding something by its usage of secrecy in much of what we do in the Shadows?
No, we are NOT. We do believe that Ancient Satanic Witchcraft has existed as a
true but hidden tradition and therefore we do adhere to our traditions in a manner
that is known to us as members of the Craft of Satanism. While the Brotherhood of
Satan new Brotherhood generation has its own Satanic Craft secrets like all legitimate Dark Orders and Lodges have done, we still invite any Satanist or others of the
Dark Arts organizations or solitary Dark Witches to our offline Sabbat festivals. If
you want to see what we are all about then you should attend one. Just be ready to
actually experience Brotherhood Satanism first hand. Recently there was a question
raised because we had a Goat at the last Samhain Grand Sabbat Festival we sponsored. If we are Traditional Satanists it means we use tradition. It has always been
traditional in the Dark Satanic Covens of the Brotherhood to have the SABBATIC
GOAT present at the Sabbat ... DUH to whoever could have tried to insinuate that
we would sacrifice our special representation of Baphomet and symbol of Satan
LOL! The Brotherhood of Satan like any org out there has people out there that have
had their membership removed (by violating our laws) or they so choose to remove
themselves from the Organization. These same individuals then go out and like to
lie about a Organization that they never really progressed into. These people then set
themselves up to being more then they were even as just Disciples in the Brotherhood
Organization. You can believe me when I say that Disciples in our Organization are
only still Probationers of the Brotherhood so they would never qualify as experts on
the Organization. The Brotherhood of Satan Organization does have its own REP-
RESENTATIVES and only they are even authorized to speak for the Organization
as well as our Infernal High Clergy of Satanists. If you want to know about the
Brotherhood of Satan, ask one of our Reps, or myself and I will be pleased to give you
a "Infernal Introduction" to the Brotherhood of Satan USA. We at the Brotherhood
of Satan Offices Nationwide thank you for your time. We offer our left hand in the
Satanic Spirit of Cooperation regardless of our differences of opinion at times. Can
we have UNITY in our DIVERSITY? YES WE CAN! With Satanic respect between
one another. Far to much of Satan's time has been wasted on the who knows the most
gossip to spread about what individual Satanist leader or Satanist Org. Time to get
over the stupidity there and let's do something constructive for Satan and Satanism.
If you can not even do that then the Brotherhood does not have the time for you to*

decide what needed changes there are and we will go on to continue the Infernal work of Satan as we have always done.

Druwydion Pendragon Magister Magnus

Brotherhood of Satan Director-Brotherhood National Office [44]

On a website that is no longer active, [45] I found an official statement of David Daniel de Paul as Druwydion Pendragon, which fully confirmed the words of Benjamin T. Mollica about the dangers of the *Brotherhood of Satan,* and its privileged links with law enforcement, the judiciary world and American Freemasonry:

> *The Brotherhood has many contacts and links with the institutions, the police and the U.S. legal system, and they have a great respect for us both as individuals and as a Satanic organization. Many of our high priests are Freemasons or are part of secret societies linked to Freemasonry.*

Is Freemasonry in the U.S. compromised by Aquino and his Council of Nine?

The executive power of the dangerous sect created in the mid-70s by Dr. Michael Aquino, is held by the *Council of Nine,* which appoints both the High Priest of Set, and its Executive Director.

The Temple of Set is highly-organized, and has members around the world, but since it avoids publicity and keeps names of the members secret, no one knows for sure how many there are. On their website, *The Official Temple of Set World Wide Web Site,* [46] the disciples of Aquino openly declare themselves devotee's of black magic. However having said that, there has never been a case of violence reported by the media, or a criminal episode directly connected to the Temple of Set under investigation by U.S. police authorities. This might happen not only for their known discretion and secrecy, but especially for their vast influence. The Temple of Set, as well as its founder, Dr. Michael Aquino, have been plagued by lawsuits over the years, but in the end, no charges against Aquino were ever formalized.

In 1994, Aquino sued Linda Blood, a former member of the Temple of Set, for libel in her book *The New Satanist.* The book, Aquino's lawyers said, depicted him and his fellow Setians as "pedophiles, child abusers, murderers and the masterminds behind a nationwide Satanic conspiracy." This was settled out of court, with the details of the settlement kept confidential. Another lawsuit, in 1997, was brought against an Internet provider for failing to block defamatory posts from an anonymous user. A person using the name "Curio" had posted over 500 messages that accused Aquino of "having participated in heinous crimes, sexual perversions and acts of moral turpitude," according to Aquino's lawyers. The case against the Internet company ElectriCiti was thrown out of court. [47]

Jeffrey Steinberg wrote a couple of years later in *EIR (Executive Inteligence Review)* in 1999:

> *On Feb. 5, 1999, in U.S. District Court in Lincoln, Nebraska, an extraordinary hearing occurred in Paul A. Bonacci v. Lawrence E. King, a civil action in which the*

44   http://www.brotherhood-of-satan.com/ ‡ Archived 5th August, 2015.

45   ttp://www.grailcode.net **this site is no longer active.**

46   https://xeper.org/ ‡ Archived 5th August, 2015.

47   William H. Kennedy, *Satanic Crime—A Threat in the New Millennium,* (Chelsea, MA: Mystic Valley Media, 2006), p. 11.

plaintiff charged that he had been ritualistically abused by the defendant, as part of a nationwide pedophile ring linked to powerful political figures in Washington and to elements of the U.S. military and Intelligence establishment. Three weeks later, on Feb. 27, Judge Warren K. Urbom ordered King, who is currently in Federal prison, to pay $1 million in damages to Bonacci, in what Bonacci's attorney John DeCamp said was a clear signal that "the evidence presented was credible."

During the Feb. 5 hearing, Noreen Gosch stunned the court with sworn testimony linking U.S. Army Lt. Col. Michael Aquino (ret.) to the nationwide pedophile ring. Her son, Johnny, then 12 years old, was kidnapped off the streets of West Des Moines, Iowa, on Sept. 5, 1982, while he was doing his early-morning newspaper deliveries. Since his kidnapping, she has devoted all of her time and resources to finding her son, and to exposing the dangers that millions of children in America face from this hideous, literally Satanic underground of ritualistic deviants. "We have investigated, we have talked to so far 35 victims of this said organization that took my son and is responsible for what happened to Paul, and they can verify everything that has happened," she told the court. "What this story involves is an elaborate function, I will say, that was an offshoot of a government program. The MK-Ultra program was developed in the 1950s by the CIA. It was used to help spy on other countries during the Cold War because they felt that the other countries were spying on us. It was very successful. They could do it very well."

Then, the Aquino bombshell: "Well, then there was a man by the name of Michael Aquino. He was in the military. He had top Pentagon clearances. He was a pedophile. He was a Satanist. He's founded the Temple of Set. And he was a close friend of Anton LaVey. The two of them were very active in ritualistic sexual abuse. And they deferred funding from this government program to use [in] this experimentation on children." [48]

As you can see, the **Temple of Set** is definitely molded by a highly organized, sophisticated and intellectually prepared Satanist. It is certainly not a sect improvised for metalheads or your average Wiccan. On the contrary, it seems to exert some influence in **the military circles,** given its thriving membership and privileged contacts with the elite of the Illuminati in the United States and abroad. Jeffrey Steiberg also added in the article entitled, "Satanic Subversion of the U.S. Military" that:

Aquino was deeply involved in what has been called the "revolution in military affairs" ("RMA"), the introduction of the most kooky "Third Wave," or "New Age" ideas into military long-range planning, which introduced such notions as "information warfare" and "cyber-warfare" into the Pentagon's lexicon. In the early 1980s, at the same time that Heidi and Alvin Toffler were spinning their Tavistock "Third Wave" utopian claptrap to some top Air Force brass, Aquino and another U.S. Army colonel, Paul Vallely, were co-authoring an article for Military Review. Although the article was never published in the journal, the piece was widely circulated among military planners, and was distributed by Aquino's Temple of Set. The article, titled "From PSYOP to Mindwar: The Psychology of Victory," endorsed some of the ideas published in a 1980 Military Review article by Lt. Col. John Alexander, an affiliate of the Stanford Research Institute, a hotbed of Tavistock Institute and Frankfurt School "New Age" social engineering. [49]

48   http://www.larouchepub.com/other/2005/3233aquino_profile.html ‡ Archived 5th August, 2015. *[emphasis added].*

49   *Ibid.*

Set or Seth, also spelled Setesh, Sutekh, Setekh or Suty, is a god of the desert, storms, disorder, and violence in the ancient Egyptian religion. [50] Concerning the hieroglyphic image of Set, Te Velde states that it does not show the characteristics of an actual, living animal, and expresses doubt whether the hieroglyph can be traced to any animal that ever existed in the area of Egypt. Dr. Michael Aquino writes in his magnum opus, *From Fetish to God in Ancient Egypt*, Sir E. A. Wallis Budge *"attempts to associate the Set-animal with the Saluki dog of Arabia. By way of evidence he cites the dog's characteristically aggressive nature, ignoring the fact that it displays none of the aforementioned physical features. Hence Budge's identification must be rejected."* [51]

This is how **David Austen**, a British representative of the Temple of Set, described Set while answering in 1993 the question: *"What does Set represent?"*

Basically, the individual's psychic or mental energy—what they would call in Ancient Egypt the "nether." The "me" that is talking to you is doing so through a series of meat cantilever systems and so forth. When that perishes or passes, instead of going into the cosmic whole—becoming one with the goddess or whatever— by sheer force of will the existence of that magician's mind can be sustained. This is the whole idea of the Temple of Set, and we use the word "Xeper," meaning to "become," to define this. Set, whom we define as the Prince of Darkness, is a force about which you could say, "As we are now, he once was." When you die your force can survive. [52]

Austen replies later in the same interview, to an even more important question: *"Why do you become part of the Temple of Set?"*

For many years I have been interested in the aspect of Set as the appearance as a being or entity. Before I joined the Temple I had my own magical group with a couple of other people. We looked at the Prince of Darkness as something that occurs in every society or religious faction—there is always an opposite to the deity they say is "Good." We came to the conclusion that we would refer to this entity as the "Dark Lord," and he would be anthropoid but faceless. Looking at this concept as a diamond, Satan or Lucifer were just other facets of that diamond, purely ways of achiving workings which encompassed the whole. So, if any are particularly drawn to the gothic Satanist current, fine, use rituals based around that. In our Temple of Darkness you could equaly find Satanists, followers of Set, or followers of other paths, according to the principle that the whole is a psychodrama anyway. Magic is basically the Western version of yoga. Everything that happens in magic happens first in your head. [53]

The Temple of Set was created in the mid-seventies by a schism within the Church of Satan. This event took place partly because of the "generational Satanism" controversy that was opposed by Anton LaVey and supported instead by Dr. Michael Aquino, who has been linked in the past to Psychological Operations (PSYOP) and the infamous trauma-based Monarch Project of the CIA's MK-Ultra. By analyzing the work of the aforementioned "Setians," John and Lillee Allee, who belong to Aquino's innercircle, we understand that these people are not playing with Satanism, but are the real deal, operating for the New World Order.

To give you an idea of Aquino's philosophy of life, here is a key passage taken from his book *Black Magic* dedicated to **"The Two Paths"**:

50   See. Oxford Encyclopedia of Ancient Egypt, vol. 3. p. 269.
51   Michael A.Aquino, Black Magic, (© Michael A. Aquino 1975-2002), pdf, p. 14.
52   Gavin Baddeley, *Lucifer Rising, op. cit.,* p. 111.
53   *Ibid.*

The terms "Left-Hand Path" (LHP) and "Right-Hand Path" (RHP) are used in different and often incompatible ways by various occultists. Reportedly the terms originated in Tantrism, a school of Mahayna Buddhism in northern India which taught that Buddhahood can be realized through various theurgic practices. For mantra and mudra ceremonies the female was positioned to the right of the male; for erotic rites she was positioned to the left. (#13C) Theosophy's H.P. Blavatsky felt sex-magic to be immoral and perverse, so she subsequently employed the term LHP to characterize the magical systems she didn't like, and the term RHP to characterize the ones she did, i.e. Theosophy. Post-Blavatsky the terms have been expanded through popular usage to refer generally to what the Temple of Set defines as white magic (RHP) and Black Magic (LHP). Most popular-occult organizations, to be sure, use the two terms simply to identify their moral biases. What they consider "good" is RHP, and what they consider "evil" is LHP. After Aleister Crowley left the Golden Dawn, he portrayed it as a "Black Lodge" and his own A∴A∴ as the "Great White Brotherhood"; while on the other side of the fence W.B. Yeats and other G∴D∴ leaders considered Crowley to be the Black Magician. To further complicate the matter, there have been some deliberately criminal "Satanic" organizations which have avowedly followed the LHP as defined by those who consider it synonymous with degenerate and destructive practices. Such episodes have of course served to reinforce the conventional religious image of Satanism and Black Magic as nefarious practices. So enduring was this stereotype that the Church of Satan found it very difficult to break free from it during the entire decade of its existence. All sorts of creeps, crackpots, criminals, and cranks pounded on the door of the Church, assuming that it would excuse and encourage whatever social shortcomings they embraced. The Temple of Set has avoided this problem, presumably because "Satan" is popularly associated with "evil" while "Set" is largely unknown outside of Egyptological circles. The Temple of Set's LHP orientation is, as noted above, a function of its definition of Black Magic. No moral or ethical stances are implied by the terms LHP and RHP per se, since they refer to techniques and systems rather than to the ends to which they are applied. [54]

In general **"There are No moral or ethical stances"** taken by the Temple of Set, just "soulless robots" loyal to their "Prince of Darkness" who is only a benign character. Of course don't be fooled by his lies, let's not forget Aquino was investigated by the San Francisco police for child molestation allegations in 1987 while he was stationed at the Presidio Army Base in San Francisco, but once again, no charges.

Some say this scandal erupted to punish Aquino for staging a Satanic "working" at Himmler's SS **Wewelsburg Castle** in 1984, a once pseudo-religious sanctum for the SS, shrouded in mystery since 1945. A *Newsweek* article dated November 16, 1987 entitled, *The Second Beast of Revelation Claims of Satanism and Child Molesting*, is typical of just one of the dozens of news articles describing the case, as it made the national and international news at the time. Interestingly enough, Aquino's mother, who is deceased, was noted to be a Temple of Set high priestess, and the owner of a building rented to an organization that helped families find daycare, proving Aquino's generational link to Satanism, and suggesting also the possibility that Aquino's mother's daycare was actually used to find human material for their Satanic ceremonies and perverse rituals. However as described in appellate documents, SFPD dropped their investigation in August, 1988, and that was the end of the story. Having said all this, if the American Freemasons were really interested in keeping their lodges psychically and spiritually clean, they should immediately throw out dangerous and deviant figures like Aquino's disciples from their lodges. Ignoring this problem in the name of relativism is not the solution. True Freemason's, loyal to the Anderson's Constitutions, should challenge lodges where Satanists are active and challenge them on the level.

A sordid tale that shows us yet another side of the Masonic reality of today, that increasingly embraces black magic and Satanism as a way of life, even publicly with no shame, no matter how obvious the contrast is with the principles of Masonry. I showed you in Volume I of my *Confessions* that this is happening in the *Ordo Templi Orients*, and now in Volume II, I am digging deeper into the Occult and Satanic realities of today, so you can comprehend better the global network of the dark side of the Illuminati, and their evil idealogy. Here is David Daniel de Paul addressing his fellow Satanists as a Satanic Grand Commander:

> *Always honor yourself first because you as a member of the Brotherhood are so honored as such. What this means from the Brotherhood perspective is this: As known, the Brotherhood has always stood for the Individual Satanist first. We seek to take great Satantas and to help them become even greater and this is one of our most important of goals. By becoming a member of the Brotherhood you stand as a Individual Satanist of Power which to us has always been knowledge. Honor always the Master Satanists first, your SELF second, and the Brotherhood third. The true Brotherhood Satanist knows with conviction that by serving the Master we are truly then serving ourselves. Brotherhood Satanists will ALWAYS stand out as those Satanists that command and recieve respect from others and are indeed so honored as such for their lifetime and through Eternity.*

> *Note: The Brotherhood would not exist without the exceptional abilities of its membership and the practical application of the Brotherhood Satanic Principles by them.*

> *11) Be a Active part of the Brotherhood, for we have always been those that know and those that do. What this means from the Brotherhood perspective is this: The Brotherhood has been around for thousands of years because we as its members have always been Active and are Practioners of Satanism and the Black Arts. Our very deeds and the deeds of our Brotherhood Dark Ancestors are WHAT has made the name The Brotherhood Immortal to this day as it shall always remain in legend and history itself.*

> *Note: The Brotherhood takes its Traditions very serious and we only want the truely dedicated of Satanists as members. Remember Wisely that the Satanist that takes NO ACTION will be known by their inaction while those that honor themselves by their deeds as well as their words by action, will also be known for their own Personal Power and Satanic Wisdom.*

> *Practical experience is always the very best of teachers and this is the Brotherhood Way. Practical Experience is only gained by being one of those that KNOW and Do. There is NO OTHER WAY to BECOME A SATANIC MASTER that can create their own Destiny.*

> *12) Do not keep wisdom from others in the Brotherhood, but instead always strive to share your Wisdom and Knowledge. What this means from the Brotherhood perspective is this: Those that have proven their worth as a Brotherhood member BY THEIR ACTIONS should be able to learn the Mysteries of the Brotherhood as is their Satanic given rightful inheritance and as Brotherhood members we are instructed to share our Satanic Knowledge always to those that deserve to learn*

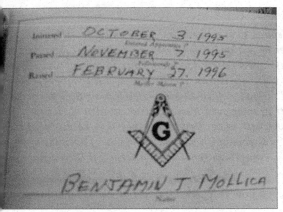

IG. 62 – Masonic initiations of Benjamin T. Mollica show at he is a Master Mason since February 27, 1996.

and understand Brotherhood Satanism. As true members of the Brotherhood we have ALWAYS been known as the Custodians and the KEEPERS OF THE MYSTERIES. To do this we must afterall, KNOW the Mysteries and to whom they should rightfully be entrusted to.

13) Remember always that Knowledge is Power and Knowledge used with Wisdom is what makes us all great. For we are the BROTHERHOOD, and our names and words are written in the Book of Satanas and we are Immortal. What this means from the Brotherhood perspective is this: If we continueas we have done throughout the Ages, in the use of our Satanic Knowledge tempered with Wisdom, all of us here in the present Brotherhood incarnation will only CONTINUE to make ourselves both individually and as a organization, Immortal. The rest is up to us. Eat from the very old Brotherhood Tree of Knowledge to really UNDERSTAND. The Deepest Understanding is the TRUTH of all things—Satanas

Thanks to the Freemason Benjamin T. Mollica's initial tip, (FIG. 62) we have a clear insight into the Satanic activities of this dangerous sect. I hope you have learned something from these unsavory characters from the Satanic realm.

My friend and Brother, the late Enrico Simoni, a 33° Grand Cross of the Court of Honour and a member of the *Ordo Illuminatorum Universalis,* in a paper on Anti-Masonry prepared for the Brothers of the Grand Orient of Italy called, **Anti-Masonry Yesterday and Today,** presented in a joint session to various Italian Lodges meeting on the 11th of June 2011, (two years before his premature death due to brain cancer) asked the Masons who were present, if Anti-Masonry "Is a psychosis," or if on the contrary this old problem is sometimes due to the non-regular behavior and bad conduct of some Masons. Adding at the end of his brilliant introduction: *"On our side we definitely need the words conveyed through publications and events but, more importantly, is the example we give with our behavior. Behavior that must be in line with the Ancient Charges."* [55]

The "Ancient Charges" published in the current Book of Constitutions of the United Grand Lodge of England altered little from those originally published by Anderson. "Ancient Charges, Regulations and Landmarks" are familiar words to Freemasons. What is called **"Anderson's Constitution of 1723"** contains both the "Charges of a Freemason" and the "General Regulations." It is noteworthy that the 39th regulation declares, "Every Annual Grand Lodge has an inherent Power and Authority to make new Regulations or to alter these, for the real benefit of this ancient Fraternity; Provided that the old Landmarks be carefully preserved, etc." Anyone who does not respect the "The CHARGES of a FREE-MASON, " that clearly state on point *Concerning GOD and RELIGION,* the

55   11th June 2011; Lodges gathered under the gavel of the XX September 1870 Lodge No. 993 of the Grand Orient of Italy (Palazzo Giustiniani).

following:

> A Mason is oblig'd by his Tenure, to obey the moral Law; and if he rightly understands the Art, he will never be a stupid Atheist nor an irreligious Libertine. But though in ancient time,s Masons were charg'd in every Country to be of the Religion of that Country or Nation, whatever it was, yet 'tis now thought more expedient only to oblige them to that Religion in which all Men agree, leaving their particular Opinions to themselves; that is, to be good Men and true, or Men of Honour and Honesty, by whatever Denominations or Persuasions they may be distinguish'd; whereby Masonry becomes the Center of Union, and the Means of conciliating true Friendship among Persons that must have remain'd at a perpetual Distance.

In the original text of **The 13 Laws of the Brotherhood of Satan Explained,** we find at point 6 the following added note that clears the role of the Satanic Illuminati Council:

> The Satanic Illuminati Council is NOT established for the purpose of control over the Brotherhood membership. It has been in existence for many thousands of years behind the scenes of many world events and we merely continue to be those with many long years in Satanism, Luciferianism, Magick, and the Left-Hand Path practical use and knowledge. We are the Brotherhood Elders and Scions and we are the Councilors and Organizers. We are the representatives of Moriah the Conquering Wind. [56]

And now a further investigation in the nature of brainwashing, a speciality of the former Lieutenant Colonel Michael Aquino (FIG. 63).

Brainwashing ...

This subchapter contains revelatory material on the subject of "brainwashing" extracted from an almost unknown essay entitled "Occult History," the result of 14 years of research by author William H. Kennedy, also known as "Teddy," who passed away suddenly and suspiciously at his home in the month of August, 2013, at the age of 48. His death was never really investigated, and when approached about it, his family seemed quite scared to stir things up, and no attention was given whatsoever to his passing by the media. Teddy was a controversial life-long Catholic writer and radio host, and he was the author of the now out-of-print and highly collectable books: *Satanic Crime—A Threat in the New Millennium,* and the even more controversial title *Lucifer's Lodge: Satanic Ritual Abuse in the Catholic Church.* He was also a regular guest on the late Dr. Stan Monteith's nationally syndicated radio show. [57]

Is Brainwashing Possible? by William H. Kennedy

> In 2003, when the Utah police confronted a missing kidnapped fifteen year old girl who was walking with her abductors she gave a strange reply. When the officer told the girl "you are Elizabeth Smart" she replied "Thou Sayest" and seemed to want to remain with her captors before she burst into tears and admitted that she was the missing teenager after about 1/2 hour of police questioning. Elizabeth was in fact quoting a Biblical passage where Jesus rebuffs Pilate when the Roman Governor asked Him if He was the King of the Jews.
>
> On the way to the police station Elizabeth did something quite unexpected. She began to defend her abductors and claimed that she did not want them to get into trouble or

---

56   http://www.brotherhoodofsatan.com/pdf/13Laws.pdf ‡ Archived 5th August, 2015.
57   See Leo Lyon Zagami, *Pope Francis: The Last Pope?, Ibid.,* pp. 198-201.

FIG. 63 – Former Lieutenant Colonel Dr. Michael Aquino. Image taken from the site: http://drjradiolive.com/content/michael-a-aquino-ph-d-april-16th-2015/ ‡ Filed and Archived, 8th August, 2015.

go to jail. Elizabeth was kidnapped by an ex-communicated Mormon named Brian David Mitchell and his wife Wanda Barzee who lived a cult-like existence. Mitchell sees himself as a Prophetic and at times Messianic figure. In his deranged worldview he came to the conclusion that Elizabeth Smart was his God ordained second wife after he completed some minor repair work at the Smart home. After he captured Elizabeth at knife point by cutting a window screen and entering her bedroom he took her on a seven month Odyssey through a strange world of homelessness, preaching and begging, the details of which are only slowly emerging in the popular media.

The fact that Ms. Smart defended her captors comes as no surprise to the psychiatrists, criminologists and military psychologists who reviewed the case. It became apparent that Elizabeth had been "brainwashed" by Mitchell to function in certain ways if she were ever taken by the police.

This strange control that Mitchell exerted over the teenager came via various techniques used by captors to manipulate the behavior of their prisoner.

No one in the popular media ever asks what "brainwashing" really is or how this process operates. It seems to be a "given" and accepted explanation for a wide variety of unusual human actions. Everything from the 9-11 attacks to the murderous crimes of teenager John Malvo the co-D.C. sniper, is explained by the phenomenon of 'brainwashing."

For a better understanding of this phenomenon it would be best to divide our subject into two subgroups for examination; Brainwashing (which will focus on the process used by individuals and certain groups) and Mind Control (a method used by government security services to control the actions of agents and captives). Of course the two definitions are provisional and they certainly intersect in many areas.

Brainwashing has been defined as "Intensive, forcible indoctrination, usually political or religious, aimed at destroying a person's basic convictions and attitudes and replacing them with an alternative set of fixed beliefs ... The application of a concentrated means of persuasion, such as an advertising campaign or repeated suggestion, in order to develop a specific belief or motivation." –American Heritage Dictionary

The term "brainwashing" itself comes not from psychology, psychiatry or any of the social sciences but rather from the world of journalism. During the Korean War Edward Hunter, a British journalist coined the word "brainwashing" (roughly based on a Chinese term) to characterize the process by which American POWs became communists in a book entitled Brainwashing in Red China (1951). In Hunter's reckoning U.S. servicemen who became communists and refused to come home were in real-

ity being manipulated by a series of psychological techniques directed toward making the POWs take destructive action against themselves and their country against their wills. This process is catalyzed by a variety of procedures which involve torture, sleep deprivation, hypnosis, drugs and threats as well as rewards for compliance.

Two primary elements for brainwashing come into play here. Isolation from normal contacts like family and friends combined with intimidation will eventually cause some subjects—like the U.S. servicemen—to comply with the thought processes proscribed by the captor. Oddly, this state of affairs can emerge when the subjugator does not intend or expect a brainwashing process to occur as in the following example.

In 1973, four Swedish bank tellers were held in a large cash vault for six days during a foiled bank robbery attempt. Strangely, the hostages became attached to their captors; a phenomenon dubbed the "Stockholm Syndrome" after this event. As bizarre as it seems the women began to resist being rescued.

After the police ended the siege and arrested the robbers the women defended them and refused to testify against the criminals. The former hostages hired a defense lawyer to defend the jailed robbers and began to raise money for a defense fund. The four women regularly visited their former captors in prison and it is reported that one of these former hostages became engaged to one of the imprisoned criminals.

She was adamant about marrying a vicious bank robber who came extremely close to executing her in the bungled burglary attempt. How can such an irrational and destructive behavior on the part of these women be explained?

According to psychologists, the abused bond to their abusers as a means to endure violence. The most notorious instance of this phenomenon came in 1974 when newspaper heiress Patty Hearst who was kidnapped by the Symbionese Liberation Army, and after some months, renamed herself "Tanya" and joined their ranks to rob banks. The Stockholm Syndrome is an emotional accessory, a sick union of co-dependence between the confined and the subjugator that develops when the aggressor threatens the life of the victim, deliberates, and chooses not to kill the captive. The relief which emerges from the removal of impending death generates intense feelings of gratitude and awe that combine to make the captive reluctant to display negative attitudes toward the captor.

It is this psychological dynamic centering on gratitude, which causes former hostages to play down the damage done to them and decline to cooperate in prosecuting their former oppressors. The victim's need to survive outweighs his/her impulse to hate the person who has created the predicament. The victim comes to see the captor as a "good guy," even as a "savior." At this juncture the victim is certainly "brainwashed" in the sense that he/she is exhibiting behaviors and expressing opinions which are contrary to their beliefs before their capture. Patty Hearst was a young college student from an aristocratic background—robbing banks to fund Marxist revolutionaries was definitely not a behavior she endorsed before her capture.

According to authorities this condition occurs in response to the four specific conditions listed below:

- A person threatens to kill another and is perceived as having the capability to do so.

- The other cannot escape, so her or his life depends on the threatening person.

- The threatened person is isolated from outsiders so that the only other perspective

available to her or him is that of the threatening person.
- The threatening person is perceived as showing some degree of kindness to the one being threatened.

It takes only 3-4 days for the characteristic bond of the Stockholm Syndrome to emerge when captor and captive are strangers. After that, research shows, the duration of captivity is no longer relevant.

It is no wonder than that Ms. Smart defended her abductors and seemed more concerned with their well-being than her own or that of her biological family.

A new form of brainwashing has been observed with the recent priest sex scandal in the Roman Catholic Church. It seems that subjects need not be completely isolated from normal contacts to be brainwashed.

I venture to coin the term "subtle brainwashing" to signify this phenomenon. Many of the children who were molested for years lived with their parents who had no idea that the abuse was occurring.

The priests used a variety of low level threats and bribes to keep the children from revealing the sexual activity to anyone. This subtle process builds up over years and is eventually combined with the false suggestion that the victim is at fault for the molestation. This sense of induced shame is what caused most of the victims to remain silent for decades. For any skeptics who may challenge this assertion consider the dramatic "impact statement" (confrontation) at the Ronald Paquin sex abuse trial in Salem, Massachusetts. A 26 year old victim stated the following under oath in a court of law:

You brainwashed me ... as your sex slave ... you created a world for me where I believed that "it's normal for sons to shower with their fathers" ... a world where "fathers and sons" are supposed to share these sexual acts ... Ronald Paquin, you are a sexual predator of exploitable innocents ... you abused your title of "Father" ... I am ashamed that your brainwashing lasted as long as it did with me. [58]

It is a phenomenon which is only beginning to be studied by social scientists and law enforcement officials. Robert Anton Wilson explored the phenomenon of Mind Control when he researched the CIA's shocking experiment in mental indoctrination and behavioral manipulation called the MK-ULTRA program in his book *Everything is Under Control* (1998):

The origins of MK-ULTRA go back to WWII, when the U.S. Army began researching barbiturates and marijuana as aids to interrogation. George Eastbrooks was a leading proponent of hypnosis as the key to interrogation and general mind manipulation of all sorts, and in 1971 he said he used hypnosis to create multiple personalities for military Intelligence purposes.

After the Korean War, the CIA began MK-ULTRA as a top secret effort to discover the best techniques, or combinations of techniques, to alter minds in any way desired. Hypnosis, drugs, newer and more complex than barbs and pot, psycho surgery, and various attempts at a "truth serum" were all extensively investigated.

One aim was to extract information from captured enemies; another, equally important, was to create agents with so many levels of mental control that they could not have information tortured out of them or even, in some cases, be aware that they

58   Boston Globe 1/3/03 "Molester Priest Paquin Cuts Deal to Testify in Abuse Civil Lawsuits" by Tom Mashberg.

were carrying secret information.

Research moved on to include LSD, ketamine, psilocybin, and the implanting of electrodes in the brain. Lobotomy was tested, along with electroconvulsive shock. One researcher believed that total mind control could be achieved by combining electroshock, LSD, and having the subject's own voice played back through headphones. That sure sounds like it would fry your brain, doesn't it?

Wilson's basic analysis touches upon several important issues concerning mind control. The central issue concerns manipulating a subject in such a way as to make him/her behave against their will and even to sacrifice their life in the process. This is really the heart and soul of mind control programs. The ability to program a subject to undertake actions that are contrary to their beliefs is incredible and would be a huge boon to government security services. The complex methods to achieve this end are relatively inexpensive. The chronicling of the Stockholm Syndrome, combined with the recent proof of brainwashing techniques being employed by Catholic priests to control the behavior of children, demonstrates how susceptible humans are to programmed conditioning by authoritive figures. Highly funded mind control experiments—like the MK-ULTRA program—would have achieved great success considering how vulnerable the human psyche is to various forms of environmental management. Rumors that various techniques of ideological mind control go back to the Persian Assassin, leader Hassan-I-Sabah, who used drugs to manipulate the behavior of his fanatical soldiers. There is more detailed information on Hassan-I-Sabah and the subject of Mind Control in Volume I of my *Confessions.* [59]

Aquino's Neo-Theosophy and other diableries

Understanding the danger represented by Dr. Michael Aquino's activities, some of the members of the Monte Carlo Lodge headed by Ezio Giunchiglia back in 2005, invited Dr. Michael Aquino to Monaco, to confront him on their doubts about his work. Certainly the "pidduisti" (members of the P2) were not afraid of a controversial figure like Michael Aquino. Some of them spoke openly in the past of being part of the mysterious secret department known as the "K Office," allegedly part of SISMI (the Italian Military Intelligence and Security Service) that ceased operations in 2007. It is said that this Office was dedicated to those Italian 007, with a license to kill, and that the letter K stood for "Killer." (64) Aquino, however, has been a member of the U.S. Armed Forces, and because of this, never believed of Monte Carlo's link to NATO, as Ezio Giunchiglia and his associates, were serious in wanting to confront him.

Aquino did not show up in Monte Carlo, but a written record of this episode from the lodge archives gives us a novel view of Aquino's current ideology, confirming not only his "Orwellian" nature, but also the unconditional support of Theosophy that appeals to globalists, and well-known Satanists like himself:

From Dr. Michael A. Aquino <*xeper@sbcglobal.net*> 07/30/05 at 8:21 PM:

Dear Mr. Zagami and Mr. Giunchiglia,

Thank you for your kind invitation to meet with you in Monte Carlo. Please accept my apologies that current responsibilities will probably keep me stuck in California for the foreseeable future, though I can't think of a more pleasant escape than Monaco.

59 http://ricerca.repubblica.it/repubblica/archivio/repubblica/1991/09/22/ufficio-killer-nel-sismi-la-procura.html
‡ Archived 8th August, 2015.

I took a look through your Statute and found its "Aims" admirable, though my impression was also that you may discourage readers with the extensive sections on organization/control. The Temple of Set has its philosophy in one area of documents, and its organizational design in another (California Articles of Incorporation and By-Laws). We have found this works well for us.

I always admire utopian visions and efforts to better this poor planet, even as I confess I have little hope for their success. Applied-politically I am at best a Stoic and at worst an Orwellian. Upon considering your "Aims" I think that you might find the works of Raghavan Iyer interesting:

http://theosophy.org/

Raghavan was a good friend of mine for many years, as well as one of my most valued teachers. (He was Professor of Political Science at the University of California where I got my own doctorate in that field.) He was by no means an "ordinary Theosophist," but a brilliant theorist beyond any labels. In my own university teaching later, I regularly used his book Parapolitics, *which contained a superb application of Plato to modern social problems.*

Thank you for offering to send me a copy of your book.

The address is:

Dr. Michael A. Aquino
Post Office Box 470307
San Francisco, CA 94147
USA

Sincerely,
Michael A. Aquino

Dr. Michael Aquino was not the only Satanist that attracted the Monte Carlo lodge in that period. The Committee was made up of Grand Masters of various bodies operating in Italy in that period, including those related to some fringe groups dedicated to Satanism and Crowleyanity, such as Roberto Negrini, (FIG. 64) the O.H.O. of the Franco-Haitian and Italian Filiation of the Ordo Templi Orientis known as O.T.O.-F.H.L. (*Fraternitas Hermetica Luciferiana* or Luciferian Hermetic Brotherhood), not to be confused in any way with the more legitimate Caliphate O.T.O. In their own words:

This structure was virtually international and eclectic, in which the various Traditions and heritages of the Neo-Gnostic, Thelemic and Draconian knowledge banks were assembled, practiced and oriented towards an ideal harmonisation. In some of its specific characteristics, the O.T.O.-F.H.L. is closely linked to the Egyptian Masonic Communion of A∴P∴R∴O∴I∴M∴M∴ (Antico e Primevo Rito Osiriaco degli Illuminati di Memphis e Mitzraïm), translated as the Ancient and Primitive Osirian Rite of the Illuminati of Memphis-Misraïm. In its high ranks and in connection with key formulae such as "Arcana Arcanorum," this Order maintains and reifies the theurgic techniques of Martinism and Willermozism of the 18th Century. It also deals with the syncretic Martinist Tradition as developed by Saint Martin and Papus, in the form of pure experimentation from a mystical-Shamanic and theurgic-operational points of view, thus devoid of any Judeo-Christian religious or devotional connotation.

A few members of the O.T.O.-F.H.L. and the A∴P∴R∴O∴I∴M∴M∴ are currently also engaged in the cultural and para-academic fronts through their involvement in the *A.Ps.A.D. (Akkademia Pan-Sophica Alpha Draconis)*. *The A.Ps.A.D. is a cultural organisation founded in 1979 that has no initiatic obedience to any particular order but is under the patronage of the Italian O.T.O. and its Tradition. The organisation is heavily involved in the various sectors of art, science, philosophy, anthropology and sociology, with the purpose of performing an interdisciplinary study and horizontal diffusion on the Magical Draconian Renaissance.*

Also in Italy, aside from a myriad of Thelemic and neo-Pagan groups that are more or less operative but not part of any historical

FIG. 64 – Roberto Negrini.

and structured organisation, there are at least two other Thelemic branches that should be mentioned. One of them is of Californian origin and connected to the "Caliphate-O.T.O." and the other is of Swiss origin and called the S∴O∴T∴V∴L∴ or Sovrano Ordine del Tempio della Via della Luceliv, translated as the Sovereign Order of the Temple of the Path of Light. Both of them have a certain historical or egregorical validity in the succession of the O.T.O. or the A∴A∴. They are also dedicated to the study and practice of the Thelemic Works in close connection with Crowley's work, although not exclusively. [60]

Negrini's Illuminati until his scandalous arrest for pedophilia in March 2013, [61] was focused as a group on the evocation of the same evil entities that were evoked originally by Aleister Crowley during his period of stay in the infamous Abbey of Thelema in Cefalu in Sicily. A kind of antechamber of hell on one side, and a mind control camp on the other, that generated a powerful and destructive Egregore that still resides there and that Negrini wanted to use.

For this reason O.T.O.-F.H.L., despite their modest size and their seemingly marginal influence in the outside world, are still considered a dangerous sect, and a very influencial especially in "magical terms." It is no coincidence that someone involved with pedofilia and Crowleyanity, like Roberto Negrini, called his "magickal" current **Mysteria Mystica Zothyriana 666,** emanating from what he called his Mother Lodge, the Ra-Harmachis Lodge, where they practiced an irregular and deviant form of the *Ancient and Primitive Rite of Memphis and Mitzraim.* (FIG. 65) A Masonic rite reformed according to their particular anti-Christian and anti-Semitic visions, linked to what Negrini calls "scientific Illuminism," a term originally coined by Aleister Crowley. In a short essay **Ordo Templi Orientis. Magical philosophy and practices of a so-**

60   Roberto Negrini, THE NEO-PAGAN REBIRTH OF MAGICK, Translation by Carlo Dorofatti, privately distributed, p. 35.

61   http://ricerca.repubblica.it/repubblica/archivio/repubblica/2013/03/15/campi-arrestato-lesoterista-pedofilo. html ‡ Archived 8th August, 2015.

FIG. 65 – First page of the Manifesto of Satanist Roberto Negrini's **Ancient and Primitive Osirian Rite of the Illuminati of Memphis-Misraïm.**

cial neopagan revolution, Negrini writes: *"Crowley called this system 'Scientific Illuminism,' defining it as 'The Method of science, the aim of religion.'"*

A circular letter sent to O.T.O.-F.H.L. members in the first half of the '90s by their former Chancellor, summarizes the basic aspects of this Illuminati sect headed by the dangerous black magician Roberto Negrini. In the text in question they refer openly to the practice of magic and sexual magick, plus specific lycanthropic rituals reserved to the highest degrees of the order. This document was originally published by the Italian University Professor **Cecilia Gatto Trocchi (1939-2005)** in her book *Affare Magia,* ("Magic Affair") and it discusses "Power zones" specifically created in the cities of Trieste, Bergamo and Reggio Calabria and evocations of States of Consciousness and Star Contact with the Ancient Extra Human Powers and extraterrestrials, whose real execution is reserved to the most High Degrees of the Order. Negrini is called in the document Frater TAU MOLOCH, yes you have read correctly; Moloch! On October 10, 1989 at 10 PM, Roberto Negrini appeared on the Italian TV network "Canale 5" in the second episode of the show "ARCANA." After an elaborate interview, Negrini went on to simulate live on TV for the first time in history, the realization of a sexual magickal ritual. Yes I know, it is pretty sick and perverse, but Italian TV in those years was the home of soft porn after a certain hour at night, and such a monstruosity was regarded as acceptable for the audience in those days. He avoided for obvious reasons, the use of real adepts, so to protect their privacy, using instead actors to complete the celebration of the Rituals before the cameras, stating officially to the press, that the reason was the tremendous dangers for television operators and technicians involved in the filming of it. [62]

The many books and the important research done in the 1980s and '90s by Professor Cecilia Gatto Trocchi might have eventually brought her to a downfall that became final with her tragic end by suicide on July 11th of 2005, officially caused by the loss of her son, who had just died of leukemia. Cecilia's work at the time in Italy did upset for sure certain occult groups, and she was not able to defend herself, both physically and psychically. The theme of **"psychic defense"** in particular is of great importance for the Illuminati, and I will introduce to you in great detail in the final chapter of this book. Many in Italy think that Trocchi became a victim of the evil spirits operated by the dark and perverse forces piloted against her by the dark side of the Illuminati dedicated to black magic and psychic attacks. This was proven by the fact that in the last few months of her life, Professor Troc-

62   See. Cecilia Gatto Trocchi, *Business magic search of magic and esotericism in Italy,* Queriniana, Brescia 2001, pp.160-163.

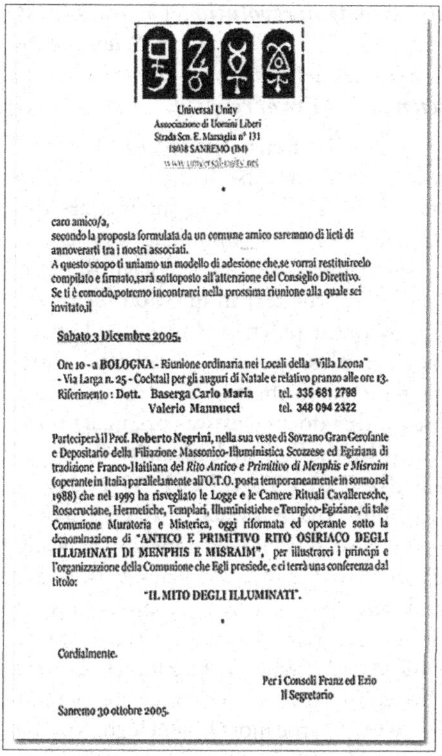

Universal Unity
Associazione di Uomini Liberi
Strada Sen. E. Marsaglia n° 131
18038 SANREMO (IM)
www.universal-unity.net

•

caro amico/a,
secondo la proposta formulata da un comune amico saremmo di lieti di annoverarti tra i nostri associati.
A questo scopo ti uniamo un modello di adesione che,se vorrai restituircelo compilato e firmato,sarà sottoposto all'attenzione del Consiglio Direttivo.
Se ti è comodo,potremo incontrarci nella prossima riunione alla quale sei invitato,il

Sabato 3 Dicembre 2005.

Ore 10 - a **BOLOGNA** - Riunione ordinaria nei Locali della "Villa Leona" - Via Larga n. 25 - Cocktail per gli auguri di Natale e relativo pranzo alle ore 13.
Riferimento : Dott. **Baserga Carlo Maria** tel. **335 681 2788**
Valerio Mannucci tel. **348 094 2322**

Parteciperà il Prof. **Roberto Negrini**, nella sua veste di Sovrano Gran Gerofante e Depositario della Filiazione Massonico-Illuministica Scozzese ed Egiziana di tradizione Franco-Haitiana del *Rito Antico e Primitivo di Menphis e Misraim* (operante in Italia parallelamente all'O.T.O. posta temporaneamente in sonno nel 1988) che nel 1999 ha risvegliato le Logge e le Camere Rituali Cavalleresche, Rosacruciane, Hermetiche, Templari, Illuministiche e Teurgico-Egiziane, di tale Comunione Muratoria e Misterica, oggi riformata ed operante sotto la denominazione di **"ANTICO E PRIMITIVO RITO OSIRIACO DEGLI ILLUMINATI DI MENPHIS E MISRAIM"**, per illustrarci i principi e l'organizzazione della Comunione che Egli presiede, e ci terrà una conferenza dal titolo:

"IL MITO DEGLI ILLUMINATI".

•

Cordialmente.

Per i Consoli Franz ed Ezio
Il Segretario

Sanremo 30 ottobre 2005.

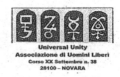

FIG. 66 – Invitation to a private conference organized by the Monte Carlo Lodge in 2005, in Villa Leona in Bologna, with the Grand Master of the O.T.O.-F.H.L. Roberto Negrini and a lecture entitled **"THE MYTH OF THE ILLUMINATI."**

Universal Unity
Associazione di Uomini Liberi
Corso XX Settembre n. 38
28100 – NOVARA

•

NUOVO STATUTO 2005

•

"UNIVERSAL-UNITY" è un'Associazione di Uomini Liberi, senza scopo di lucro, costituita tra i sottoscritti con intendimenti di altissimo valore spirituale e morale, la quale adotta il seguente

STATUTO

Art. 1 - Denominazione, sede sociale e durata dell'associazione.
La Libera Associazione assume la denominazione "UNIVERSAL-UNITY" (breve U.U.), ha una durata illimitata, e stabilisce la propria sede legale in MONTECARLO - Principato di Monaco - 38, Av. Dell'Annonciade sede amministrativa in Italia - SANREMO (18038) Str. sen. E. MARSAGLIA

Art. 2 - Oggetto Sociale.
L'Associazione è antidogmatica e si propone la ricerca di un equilibrio interiore fra gli esseri umani, e l'attuazione di qualsiasi iniziativa intesa a promuovere il Bene dell'Uomo e dell'Umanità, considerando il **Mondo senza Frontiere**, come una **Patria Unica**, senza arsenali atomici ed armi batteriologice, e possibilmente anche con una moneta unica.
Per il conseguimento dei suoi scopi intende chiamare a se tutti gli esseri umani che condividono i suddetti principi che l'Associazione intende praticare con indipendenza sovrana, con particolare attenzione ai fratelli Massoni, attivi od in sonno, onde diffondere, con i principi sopra enunciati, anche gli ideali della pura Massoneria Universale, ma senza dipendere da alcuna delle Grandi Logge legittimamente costituite che operano in qualsiasi parte del Mondo.
Per la pratica attuazione dei propri scopi, intende diffondersi in tutto il Mondo e compiere ogni e qualsiasi operazione, anche finanziaria, compreso, ove occorra, l'investimento in attività immobiliari e la relativa gestione, qualora sia utile ai propri scopi, purché sempre senza fine di lucro.
Intende curare la gestione di una Casa Editrice denominata "Universal Unity", nonché valersi di ogni altro mezzo di comunicazione secondo la più moderna tecnologia, per la pubblicazione e la diffusione del pensiero che sarà elaborato dai propri associati.
Intende promuovere riunioni periodiche fra gli associati, per un attivo scambio di opinioni e d'informazioni, attraverso il quale il libero pensiero possa svilupparsi e diffondersi, sempre sotto l'imperio della legge morale e comunque per la realizzazione dei principi fondamentali sopra enunciati.

1

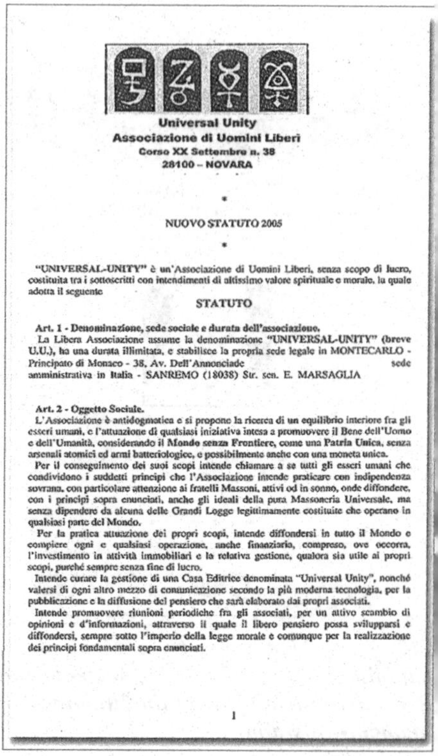

FIG. 67 – This document published in 2005 by the ***Universal Unity*** *shows without a doubt the link between the Universal Unity and the* ***Monte Carlo Lodge*** *based in the Principality of Monaco at number 38 of av. de l'Annonciade in those days Ezio Giunchiglia's residence in the principality. The administrative headquarters instead, were in nearby Italy in Sanremo at the office of the late Francesco Murgia.*

chi had increasingly fallen victim to many acts of intimidation, like the time she found a dead bird in her garden, killed in a black magic ritual. The animal's neck was tied with a red ribbon with the emblem of Satan and a skull. Attached to the emblem there was a sheet with a message that ended with an indication of the infamous Satanic **number 666**. Five years earlier, Trocchi found in her garden a dead pig with its heart pierced by a pin. In the occult world, there are many rumors on how Trocchi's suicide was murder. Among the reasons that could have led to her death, was her last television appearance made on February 27th, 2004 on the program *Riddles* on Rai Tre.[63] During the show the announcer even begged her to "not to name names and to not reveal the identity of politicians and people in power who are part of such sects," she nodded her head in disgust and unwillingly accepted. **Roberto Negrini** for example, and sociologist and Jesuit agent **Massimo Introvigne**, were both becoming increasingly upset by Trocchi's work.

Introvigne in particular began to criticize and throw mud at Trocchi, writing an article

63 See. Elena Testi, Satanismo in Umbria, ***Ibid.***, pp. 47-50.

FIG. 68 – Document of Frank G. Ripel, from December 2010, signing with his 100° degree of the Ancient and Primitive Rite of Memphis-Misraim and the bombastic title of **Sovereign Maker of the Worlds**, on March 12th 2012, giving a 97 degree recognition to American ufologist and occultist Allen H. Greenfield, a former member of the Caliphate O.T.O.

published in *The Sociological Criticism*[64] in the first half of the 1990s. Interestingly enough, Massimo Introvigne and Roberto Negrini, for a brief period were also linked with the prestigious Monte Carlo Lodge research group. Introvigne joined as honorary member because of his friendship with the known English right wing intellectual, Freemason and occultist, Jonothon Boulter, connected with **Jean Pierre Giudicelli**, also linked to Massimo Introvigne back in the days of the Group of Thebes and now currently involved in running the **Oriente Osirideo Egizio** in Nice. Negrini in Monte Carlo? An occult oddity to say the least, that lasted only a few seasons, as he was was ostracized for being openly Satanic and in league with evil entities.

In the words of the same Negrini, he works for the "**creation of Power-Zones for contact with extradimensional entities defined symbolically as extraterrestrials.**[65] Ezio Giunchiglia, interested in activating contact with such entities, even thought that working with Negrini could be useful for this purpose. That was until he was arrested for the possession of a large amount of child pornography. Negrini had in his possession 4,800 images and 130 videos.[66] Only a few prior Negrini held a conference in Bologna at Villa Leona, (FIG. 66) a place usually used by the **Opus Dei** and owned by Monte Carlo Lodge member **Carlo Maria Baserga**. This private event was arranged by members of the Masonic Universal Unity of Ezio Giunchiglia (FIG. 67) in 2005. However the various Clubs of the **Universal Unity** compromised by my Internet revelations and the books I later published in Italy, plus Marco Paret's incompetency in Masonic and Illuminati matters, eventually terminated their activities. Massimo Introvigne, wrote in his memorable research on "**New Religious Movements**" that the creation of "**Power-zones**" was one of Negrini's specialities which he attempted with magical operations in Cefalu, Ife, Nigeria, Cairo, Mount Sinai, Montsegur, and Monte Carlo; where Giunchiglia authorized him to perform a black magic ritual, and other secret locations. I think this insane act was partly to blame for the end of the once prestigious Monte Carlo Lodge of the P2. Another occultist connected to the P2 milieu is **Grand Master Frank G. Ripel** (aka Gianfranco Perilli), one of Italy's leading experts on Aleister Crowley, who appointed himself in 2010, 100° of the Ancient and Primitive

64   "The Sociological Criticism 'No. 106 (summer 1993), pp. 127-134.
65   http://www.cesnur.com/gruppi-di-magia-cerimoniale/gruppi-crowleyani/ ‡ Archived 8th August, 2015.
66   http://firenze.repubblica.it/cronaca/2013/03/14/news/condivideva_materiale_pedopornografico_campi_bisenzio_arrestato_esoterista-54540207/ ‡ Archived 8th August, 2015.

Rite of Memphis and Mitzraim, using the bombastic title of *Sovereign Maker of the Worlds*. (FIG. 68)

A controversial position that appears only once in a book of the late Count Gastone Ventura, dedicated to the Masonic *Rites of Memphis and Misraim* of which he was a Grand Master: "*It seems they wanted to assign the 100° degree of Sovereign Maker of the Worlds. Fortunately for the seriousness of these two Eastern Rites, the Grand Hyerophant Troilo Guarino didn't agree on having upon him the Sublime Master Unknown and everything went to hell.*"[67] In short, Gastone Ventura was not convinced the 100 °could help Freemasonry in any way, but Frank G. Ripel, which according to CESNUR, also claims to be the reincarnation of Aleister Crowley, and even the Antichrist, seems convinced of his eccentric choice. After Frank G. Ripel became a 100° degree (obviously irregular and not recognized by any "regular" Masonic body), he donated the 99th honorary degree, to the late Count Licio Gelli,[68] who apparently accepted. Frank G. Ripel, just like the aforementioned Roberto Negrini, are both linked to Crowleyanity and the dark side of the Illuminati.

In a letter dated 28th of June 1989, Licio Gelli who was not at all impressed by Crowley's disciples and despised black magic, expressed his positive judgment on Frank G. Ripel's previous books, attracted by Ripel's project for an Illuminati Knighthood that will be later be called O.C.I. (*Ordine Cavalieri Illuminati*) and will eventually come to light twelve years later, in 2001.[69]

The *Ordo Illuminatorum Universalis* (Order of the Illuminati of the Universe) (FIG. 69) was founded by Ezio Giunchiglia and myself in Monte Carlo in 1999 later joined by Jean-Pierre Giudicelli de Cressac Bachelerie.

The *Ordine Cavalieri Illuminati* (Order of Illuminati Knights) was founded by Frank G. Ripel in Trieste in 2001.

The *Accademia Internazionale degli Illuminati* (International Academy of the Illuminati) was founded by Giuliano di Bernardo in Rome in 2002.

Today my Order, has now collected and officially become the heir of this controversial legacy after the death of Licio Gelli. The Count surprising left the whole Masonic and Illuminati Community astonished by nominating before his death General Bartolomeu Constantin Săvoiu a member of the Ordo Illuminatorum Universalis[70] as his successor (**membership card number 91**), showing to the world with this suprising and shocking finale, his disgust for the current state of affairs of the New World Order. I will never associate with Freemasons and occultists who want to dominate the world with their occult powers, (FIG. 70) only good people and good Freemasons like General Bartolomeu Constantin Săvoiu (FIGS. 71-72), born 18 February, 1945 in Bucharest, and current head of the **Romanian National Grand Lodge – 1880**, a man I admire and respect who came into Gelli's life seven years before his death.

Masonic decadence

In my experience, both the New Age movement and Satanism often go hand in hand. The couragious Cecilia Gatto Trocchi said this during a University lecture a few months before she died, on February 26, 2004:

67   Gastone Ventura, *Ibid.*, p. 89.
68   http://www.frankripel.org/iutmah/meaprmm.html ‡ Archived 8th August, 2015.
69   http://www.frankripel.org/iutmah/cenni_storici.html ‡ Archived 8th August, 2015.
70   https://en.wikipedia.org/wiki/Bartolomeu_Constantin_S%C4%83voiu ‡ Archived 8th August, 2015

*New Age is an arbitrary synthesis where everything is the opposite of everything,
where everything looks like everything and everything is indifferent; a hellish thing
in my opinion. And I don't say hellish by chance, but because in 1968, when Kenneth Anger, one of the instigators of the Church of Satan in California, presented his
project for a short film called* Lucifer Rising *he said: "Today we held a baptism for
the age of Aquarious." Satan is the real big energy that permeates the entire universe
for these people and man must turn to him to be made of this energy, so the snake
from the garden of eden in their vision actualy made the welfare of man causing
him to eat from the three. We know what we know thanks to Lucifer, or Satan, or
the serpent, if you prefer, so actually we owe him the possibility to become like God.
That's another fixation of the New Age: every human being must become like God.
There is no difference between creator and creature, but all share in the same light
energy. The only difference is that we're not aware, while God is aware of his own
divinity. So we just have to find out all this to become like God, then we can do wonders, walking on water, turning water into wine and much more, because we want to
earn, become weathy directors of large companies ... All these things have nothing to
do neither with our Christian tradition nor with the greek-Roman one, who started
from a level of reality: who we are, where we are, what we know and what we can
do? All this is annihilated by the New Age.*

Gatto Trocchi added at the end of the report a heavy complaint about the responsibility of the New World Order in all this:

*The main purpose of this philosophy is to prepare the world to receive a new guide
called Maitreya, and to introduce the world to a New World Order. And globalism
and the New World Order start from a point that is particularly close to my heart.
Experts say that in the future only 20% of the world will be productive.* **What does
this mean?** *It means that the labor force that will produce all the goods and services
from here to 50 years will be only of 20%. The other 80% will devote themselves to
this nonsense pseudo-spiritual rubbish. Better to meditate in order to avoid mental
stress. So the idea of resorting to the East and its old religions, as the hidden aim
of accustoming the losers of the future transforming them into happy beggars. We
must wake up, because the gimmick lies beneath the strategy to create an atomized
world, where there are no more political factions, but only individuals increasingly
isolated. Even now there are very private initiations taking place on the Internet.
I can start myself to the mysteries of the cosmos. All this is in preparation of a new
world system like the Aristotelian system of polis of memory, that is, the polis seen
as a living organism, from which the idea of high political sense, has to disappear.
There must be a strong cohesion.* [71]

Professor Cecilia Gatto Trocchi's vision partly coincides with mine, the only difference is that Professor Cecilia Gatto Trocchi was a devout Catholic and could never speak
out of the immense responsibility of the Jesuits in all this. Even when Gatto Trocchi was
personally attacked by one of the biggest Jesuit disinfo agents and New Age manipulators, the aforementioned Massimo Introvigne, she never exposed him as a Jesuit shill. I
wonder if at the time she could have been saved by better magical protection and psychic
self-defense against such evil. Satan permeates the entire universe, including the once
glorious institution of Freemasonry, as the Freemasons have distanced themselves more
and more from their Christian origins since 1813. The Italian Masonic publication *La*

71   "Beware of the New Age! Terminology, symbols and practices of a religion made of nothing" a presentation by
Professor Cecilia Gatto Trocchi (anthropology) at the University *La Sapienza* of Rome, Thursday February 26, 2004.

FIG. 69 – Coat of arms of the **Ordo Illuminatorum Universalis** founded in 1999 in the Principality of Monaco by the Executive Committee of the P2 Monte Carlo Lodge.

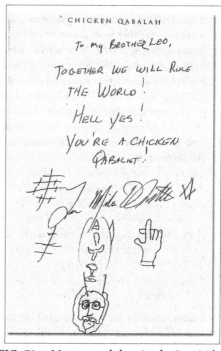

FIG. 70 – Message and drawing by Lon Milo DuQuette O.T.O.'s United States Deputy Grand Master and Archbishop of **Ecclesia Gnostica Catholica**, the ecclesiastical arm of O.T.O.

Rivista della Massoneria Italiana (Vol. X, p. 265) stated in that period: *"My brothers, Freemasons ... Satan is great!"* And even Manly P. Hall, a 33rd degree Freemason declared in his **book The Lost Keys of Freemasonry or the Secret of Hiram Abiff**: that *"Freemasons always have access to 'the bubbling energy of Lucifer.'"*[72] This Luciferian energy originally emerged from "Occult Freemasonry" and Theosophy, and was later filtered to the public through the New Age movement. However, all this happened once Christian Freemasonry became gradually minoritarian after the establishment on the 27th of December 1813, of the United Grand Lodge of England constituted at Freemasons Hall, London with Prince Augustus as Grand Master.[73] The Swiss psychologist Carl G. Jung stated: *"The larger the organizations, the more inevitable are their immorality and blind stupidity."* (Carl G. Jung, *Die Beziehungen zwischen dem Ich und dem Unbewussten*, Darmstadt, 1928) We also have clues about what will happen within the European Union—the Freemason's latest creation. Jung stated in the same book:

> *The larger a society or confederacy, the greater the amalgamation of collective factors—which is typical of every large organization—will rest upon conservative prejudices to the detriment of the individual, the more aggravated the moral and spiritual degeneration of the individual."* Apparently different ideologies have been forced upon us. In actual fact, we have all the time been dealing with different aspects of one and the same ideology—illuminism, propagated by the liberal side of

72   See, Jüri Lina, *Architects of Deception* (Stockolm, Sweden: Referent Publishing, 2004), p. 135.
73   See. https://en.wikipedia.org/wiki/Prince_Augustus_Frederick,_Duke_of_Sussex ‡ Archived 8th August, 2015.

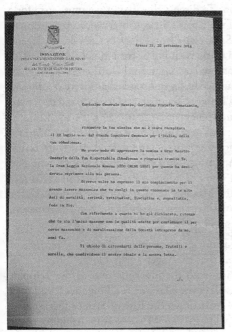

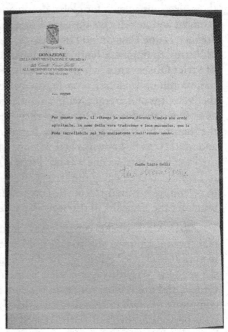

FIG. 71 – Count Licio Gelli Official Spiritual-Masonic testament from September, 2014 nominating General Bartolomeu Constantin Săvoiu his successor. Deposited in the State Archives of Pistoia.

FIG. 72 – Second and last page signed by Count Licio Gelli Spiritual-Masonic testament to General Bartolomeu Constantin Săvoiu, his successor.

international Freemasonry, the Jesuits and later the Zionist. Only insecure individuals and weak ideologies and religions need to resort to violence in order to assert themselves—Judaism, Islam, communism, national socialism, and others. The hylozoists, who follow the teachings of Pythagoras, have never resorted to violence, nor have the Buddhists. This fact alone shows the value of their philosophical teachings, which can help those souls who seek the truth. [74]

Another milestone in the transformation of Freemasonry towards a more relativist approach was the **Congress of Wihemsbad in 1782.** Throughout the history of Freemasonry there have been gatherings and events that have had a large impact on the fraternity in general, specific Orders within the Fraternity, but due to the lack of documentation it has lead to theories abound. The history of Freemasonry is a complex topic, not always because of one's ability or inability to comprehend the subject, but often due to the lack of recorded evidence to support or reject a hypothesis. When faced with incomplete information one's imagination can wander, which can sometimes lead to far-fetched and exaggerated speculations. One such event that many Masons and anti-Masons have theorized about is the 1782 Congress of Wilhelmsbad—Albert Mackey refers to this Congress as *"the most important Masonic Congress of the eighteenth century."* To the Masons, this meeting marks the impending doom of Rite of Strict Observance and the rise of the Rectified Scottish Rite. To the anti-Mason and conspiracy theorists, this is the meeting where the Bavarian Illuminati is said to have infiltrated and taken over Freemasonry to enhance their nefarious agenda for global domination. To discuss this matter we must stop for a moment and first discuss the early history of the Rite of Strict Observance. According to Stephen Dafoe, Past Grand Historian of the Sovereign Great Priory of Canada, the legend of Pierre d'Audmont, a Templar continuation myth, is said to be the brainchild of the **Rite of Strict Observance**, which was largely promoted by Baron Karl Gotthelf von Hund, or more commonly referred to as Baron von Hund. The legend states that Pierre d'Aumont, the Preceptor of Auvergne, with a number of Knights Templar, fled to Scotland disguised as an Operative Mason. On arrival they created a new order to preserve the traditions of the soon to be disbanded Knights Templar. This new order they named *Franc Maçons*, and would later be known as Free Masons when they traveled to England. The truth is that the Preceptor of Auvergne was not Pierre d'Audmont, but rather Imbert Blanke, who fled to England after dodging the arrests of the 13th of October, 1307. He later played a role in defending his Brethren in the courts. Many Masonic scholars such as Stephen Dafoe point out the absurdity of this legend, particularly the etymology of the name Freemason.

Albert Mackey believes that it was through Ramsey's Oration that this legend of Templar continuation was able to take hold, but dismisses it as rubbish having no "particle of historical evidence." Although he does admit that this legend had a large influence on the modern Masonic organization particularly with the incorporation of the Templar Orders, and this is what counts in the end, as all of the Masonic teachings are based on a composite of myth or morality tales, so why close down the Rite of Strict Observance? I am personally involved in the revival of this particular Masonic Rite, bringing those beautiful degrees from the 18th century back to life with its great Christian teachings copied later by almost every rite.

Going back in time ... In the 1740s a few German Lodges began giving their Entered Apprentices and Fellow Crafts the names of French Knights. Most of these Lodges were in Dresden, but Baron von Hund founded one of these Lodges on his estate East of Dresden, around 1751. It was from the close ties of these Lodges that the Rite of Strict Observance was created. It was said that the Rite originated with C. G. Marschall von Bieberstein, who had founded two of the Lodges in Germany; one in Dresden and one in Naumber called *Lodge of the Three Hammers*. Von Hund is said to have taken over after von Bieberstein died in 1750. Under Von Hund's watch, the Rite degrees consisted of: Entered Apprentice, Fellowcraft, Master Mason, Scottish Master, Novice, and Knights Templar. The Scottish Master degree concerned itself with the preservation of the lost word of Freemasonry which had been cut on a plate of pure metal, placed in a secure location, and centuries later discovered. This was not an exclusive belief as the Ecossais degrees used this, which sprung up after Ramsey's Oration. One of the strangest aspects of the Rite of Strict Observance was that the adherent had to swear an oath to blindly follow the directives of "Unknown Superiors" who ruled the order. This invisible leader was said to have possibly been **Charles Edward Stuart**, the Young Pretender. This was the same man who Ramsey had tried to tutor some years prior. For some, there is a lack of evidence that supports this idea, but nonetheless **the Invisible Rulers or Masters,** are said to have communicated through Baron von Hund. The Templar Degrees center on the legend that Freemasonry derived from the medieval Knights Templar. The Order of the Knights Templar, founded in the first decade of the twelfth century, was disbanded by Philip IV "The Fair" of Bourbon (1268–1314) and Pope Clement V (1264–1314) in the first decade of the fourteenth century, but according to Masonic legend, the Templars survived in the highlands of Scotland and later reappeared to the public as the Order of Freemasons. The first person to present this theory of continuation was the Scottsman Chevalier Andrew Michael Ramsey (1686–1743), who lived as an expatriate in Paris.

Ramsay was the orator of the Lodge Le Louis d'Argent, whose Worshipful Master was Charles Radclyffe (1693–1746). In a famous oration given at the lodge in 1737, Ramsay stated that medieval crusaders in the Holy Land, or Outremer, founded Freemasonry. He did not explicitly identify the crusaders who allegedly founded Freemasonry as being Knights Templar, but as Pierre Mollier has pointed out, the identification of the Crusaders with the Templars was not far away. Ramsey's oration proved to be a milestone in the development of Masonic rituals of initiation including what later became the Ancient and Accepted Scottish Rite, and soon rituals began to appear that incorporated Ramsey's thesis. It was in the milieu of the Jacobite Parisian Lodges that the Masonic Templar Degrees first developed, perhaps as early as 1737. The best-known propagator of Templar Degrees in Germany was Baron Karl Gotthelf von Hund (1722–1776), and it is often claimed that he was initiated into the Templar Degree in France in 1743. Some say the aforementioned Count Licio Gelli was von Hund's reincarnation.

Going back to the 1782 Congress of Wilhelmsbad, although it was one of the more notable of meetings, the meeting held in Wilhelmsbad came as a result of several meetings held over the years in Jena, Altenburg, Kohlo, and Brunswick. The Grand Master, Duke Ferdinand, would call for another meeting that convened on July 15th, 1778, in Wolfenbuttel. Like some of the meetings, did not succeed in clarifying much in the end. Since they could not come to any definitive conclusion as to the mysterious origins of Freemasonry, the assemblage appealed to all Masonic bodies and called for a future meeting in Wilhelmsbad. The Congress of Wilhelmsbad took place near the city of Hanau in Hesse-Cassel. It was presided over by Ferdinand, Duke of Brunswick, who was head of the Rite of Strict Observance, and opened the meeting on July 16th, 1782. It was attended by Masons from several European countries and there were 30 Sessions held. The goals of this convention were to discuss the general reformation of Freemasonry, the origin of the different systems, rites, and doctrines that had formed, and to solve the question as to whether or not Freemasonry is a modern society or derived from something far more ancient. All these questions, submitted to the assembly during its thirty meetings, went unanswered. What it did succeed in was exposing a number of fraudulent systems that had formed and reformed, some say "de-Templarized," the Rite of Strict Observance which would later fade and a new system known as the Rectified Scottish Rite would emerge, a system still in existence today. [75] So in the Congress of Wilhelmsbad the fate of the declining Rite of Strict Observance, as well as the disappearance of the Order of the Illuminati of Adam Weishaupt, was decided. This meant that they would both have to change their names and hide in other orders to survive. Part of the Rite of Strict Observance reemerged in fact, as the Rite of Strict Observance, and the Swedish Rite. The Order of the Illuminati moved to the other side of the ocean creating various offshoots, as I described in Volume I. One thing is for sure, the Christian Templar side became less influential and was later infiltrated by Satanic and liberal elements like the ones that gave birth to the *Ordo Templi Orientis*. In this scenario of unprecedented decadence, the elite indulged more and more in "ritual orgies," and became modern New Agers who deify Lucifer and the worship of devils. [76]

Two words about the so-called "ritual orgy"

The great initiate Mircea Eliade once wrote about the phenomenon of ritual orgies:

75   See. http://www.travelingtemplar.com/2013/07/the-1782-congress-of-wilhelmsbad.html ‡ Archived 8th August, 2015.

76   See. Constance Cumbey, *op.cit.*

Of ritual orgies there is evidence in many different populations. Their purposes is different: generally, however, with the orgies you are trying to avoid cosmic or social crisis—drought, epidemics, unusual weather events (such as the aurora australis)—or you want to give a religious-magic support (sparking and increasing sexual potency) to favorable events (marriages, births). Both facing a threatening crisis or a happy event, thanks to indiscriminate and excessive sex society is immersed in the era of the fabulous origins. This is particularly evident in the practice of periodic orgies at the end of the year or at intervals considered specifically sacred. In fact it is this kind of ritual orgy, undoubtedly the most archaic, to reveal is the original function of the collective promiscuous relationships. The orgy ritualizes the precise moment of creation, the stage of blissful beginnings when there was still no sexual taboos and moral or social norms. Perhaps the most striking illustration can be found among the Dayak Ngadju and some Australian tribes. [77]

Alberto Moscato, at the time head of the O.T.O. in Italy, described the practice in this way:

The very first concept needed to introduce a speech on this subject both complex and controversial as this, is that, as usual, legends inadvertently activated for over a hundred years by the pounding (which further intensified in recent decades) made by the various writers in tabloid papers more or less informative and periodicals of the "industry" and not, have created a true "culture" on the parallel phenomenon of Royal Art and Ritual of the orgy, often, intentionally or not, by mixing it with the phenomenon of the growth of the para / pseudo-religious sects on the one hand and the spread of popular superstitions and magical practices active or passive on the other. This parallel "culture," also meant that scholars of the occult serious and sensitive, form a opinion of the O.T.O. as a kind of brothel organized and that "Do what thou wilt" but especially "Love is the Law," means nothing more than "Fuck whoever you want as you please" and "Fuck only." Moscato admits also between the lines of his writings that there is actually a dark side to all this: "It's really easy, even when it has to do with esteemed Brothers and Sisters of "legitimite," and karmic candor, while the intensity of the orgy hysterical grow, even unconsciously, to slip in black magic or at least in the simple violation of the others will and / or your Oaths and Magic Obligations, over time and sessions. [78]

What is a ritual orgy? In August 1990, the famous Italian newspaper *La Repubblica*, wrote an article entitled "**ROME CAPITAL OF THE OCCULT**":

Behind the scenes of the Eternal City a creepy Satanic phenomena was stirring. A bunch of weird sects were gathering forces at the dawn of the new millennium, so who was behind all this? As I was about to finish my compulsory military service in the Italian Airforce, I read this interesting mixture of information, amazed to say the least of this interesting scenario of Satanism practiced around the corner from the Vatican. Many of these occult brotherhoods are family-run, where the smell of incense mixes often with that of the frying pan or an Italian pasta sauce. In other cases, the scenario is more disturbing. The Ordo Templi Orientis takes the theories of Aleister Crowley (1875). The rites are top secret but are based on the sexual magical practices or the lycanthropy Kabbalistical ones. Another group that refers to Crowley is the one of Jorg Sabellicus: black masses with a stuffed boar's head and

---

77   See. Mircea Eliade, *Occultism, Witchcraft and Cultural Fashions,* (Chicago: University Of Chicago Press 1978).

78   Alberto Moscato, Ars gratia artis, *Ibid.,* p. 24.

a naked girl who ends up as an altar, regularly, ending up as a ritual orgy (there is to assume that the fear of AIDS has recently thinned down the numbers of the faithful). For the celebrations, as always, these kind of priests prefer the desecrated churches, abandoned villas (preferably those that have been the scene of realy nasty crimes) but also cemeteries. Where, especially after the night of St. John (when, according to the esoteric theory, you open the doors of the hereafter) you find more frequently the remains of the celebrations and animal sacrifices. [79]

Sebastiano Fusco (1944) better known as Jorg Sabellicus, one of the aforementioned Satanists by *La Republica*, is one of the most important Italian authors on magick and the esoteric, as well as a professional journalist and an expert in publishing matters. Fusco has in fact organized many book releases for several Italian publishers, and is considered an expert. He remains out of the public eye, but in Italy amongst the Illuminati imbued in occultism and Satanism closely tied to the Vatican, he has always been an authority; although invisible to most. Some say Sebastiano Fusco is amongst the few High Priests of the dark side of the Illuminati authorized to perform "Black Masses" in the Church of San Lorenzo in Piscibus, a small church based in the Borgorione of Rome, located near Saint Peter's Square and Vatican City. The Church is not visible from the main street, Via della Conciliazione, and is used by the Vatican Satanist to celebrate their dark rites.

In the first of his four volumes of books, Sebastiano Fusco uses the introduction dedicated to Practical Magic, and offers several insights on what drives the Illuminati to do what they do ritualistically and magically speaking:

To induce occult forces to act in a certain way, the magician must operate respecting certain fixed set of rules which include the exact timing, methods, his acts. In this way you develope a real ceremony, a ritual intended to bring out the best power that is collected inside of him and out of him, to direct it according to his will and his lead. The most terrible of these ceremonies are those described in the Magic Ritual, where the Magic Forces are directly evoked, in the form of spirits or demons, to give them orders or impose duties.

And to this kind of ancient magic, believed to be extremely dangerous, which is dedicated this volume. The magical ceremonies are not, as is generally thought, the desecration of Jewish or Christian religious rites, made in an attempt to curry favor with the devil and make sure of his services. Conversely, ceremonies are held to implore from God the universal power to control personifications (usually evil) of the occult forces. Their meaning is essentially symbolic, beyond the religious reason, their function is to maximize the "mystical fury" of the magician, working through solemn and complex rituals, recite incantations in dark and uplifting tones, surrounding yourself with sacred and mysterious objects, inhaling scents that intoxicate and stun, to the point that the gathering strengthens him, like a stream swollen and increasingly agitated, not breaking its banks coming to appear in front of the operator in a form sensitive and often terrifying. These rituals are ancient. We know it was practiced in Egypt, Chaldea, Mesopotamia, as evidenced by archaeological fragments in which one reads spells and descriptions of ceremonies. By Greek and Latin writers have learned that such practices were widespread even in classical civilizations. [80]

These cults in the Greek-Roman era, were intended only to special initiates, and even then they were kept secret from the rest of the other pagans. The elite always use magic

79   http://ricerca.repubblica.it/repubblica/archivio/repubblica/1990/08/03/roma-capitale-dell-occulto.html
‡ Archived 9th August, 2015.
80   Jorg Sabelllicus, *Practical Magic Vol. 1*, pp. 11-12.

rituals as a weapon, which is the true way to obtain material power. Black magic is the direct connection with demonic, or rarely, angelic entities that hide behind these cults. A power in all its forms that is increasingly corrupt and is the main bait that is stretched to humans from these dark entities. These rituals are also carried out in secret by sects by common people, usually with the direct involvement, or at least the support, of the elite. At the center of man's spiritual control we always find the Jesuits, spiritual controllers of the **New World Order along with the Zionist Jews.**

The goal of the ritual orgy, and rituals in a broader sense, is to access contacts with entities of various kinds, a topic I visit in my upcoming book *Invisible Masters*. It must be clear to those who are reading this that for the elite, there is no law, no codes and no rights that apply to regular people. The masses simply go along, indoctrinated to believe that they are participating democratically, or at least with the illusion that there is some kind of justice guaranteed by law. There is no justice I am afraid, and there is no law on top, only a demonic force that has power over all the nations, who hides in the shadows. When a courageous denunciation of these facts is made, it is quickly obscured, censored and the person is dubbed crazy, as it happened to me more than once. Recently, one of the Grand Masters *of Ordo Templi Orientis,* who I do not want to name, intervened with one of my publishers to ask him to question the publication of my books, retelling the old story of my alleged instability and hospitalizations for mental illness in Norway. Well, as you know I do not make a mystery or a secret of what happened and I wrote about it in the first volume.

I would like to write a few words about the Tavistock Institute as they also have had responsibility in my persecution. They are the "guardians" of the Matrix built on purpose to keep people tight-lipped about their treacherous games. Until now, few knew what the Tavistock Institute—based in London—was really about and the fact it has influenced and continues to influence, directly or indirectly, many sections of our lives. It was founded to study mental disorders, derived from exposure to the terror that is generated in battle, experiments with British soldiers who survived the First World War. Its purpose was to establish, under the control of the Office of Psychological Warfare in the British Army, the "breaking point" for a man under stress. Later, Tavistock developed techniques of brainwashing that were used for the first time as I mentioned earlier, for American POWs in Korea. In 1947, the **Tavistock Institute** assumed its current role and has since developed great power in Europe, the United States and around the world. No one can receive a prominent place in any key structure in society if not trained in behavioral science by Tavistock, or at least screened and scrutinized by one of its subsidiaries centers. There is virtually no form of industry, from education to health, which is not under the influence of Tavistock, in some form or another, and the occult elite that controls it, including the music business. From music to counter-insurgency, drugs to television, we are exposed every day to the dark mechanisms created by a group of psychologists, psychiatrists and anthropologists serving the New World Order. I myself was a victim of Tavistock when they locked me up unjustly for a few days in the Department of Mental Health of Subiaco for my part in **Italy's pitchfork protests,** [81] that began at the end of 2013.

The director of the center where I was kept for two weeks is named **Dr. Giuseppe Nicolò** [82] confessed, almost bragging, before my release (and in front of my lawyer), to be tied to the notorious Tavistock Institute in which he has operated for years. [83]

81 https://en.wikipedia.org/wiki/2013_Italian_social_protests ‡ Archived 9th August, 2015.
82 http://www.terzocentro.it/dettaglio_persone_id_persone_4.html ‡ Archived 9th August, 2015.
83 See. Leo Lyon Zagami, *Illuminati e la musica di Holywood, Harmakis, Montevarchi* (Arezzo), 2014, p. 15.

Chapter VIII

Psychic Defense, Satanism and the Adepts of Atlantis

On psychic defense

Dion Fortune—whose real name was Violet Mary Firth—was born in 1891, and died in 1946. She was an accomplished occultist, psychoanalyst and writer. At a very early age she demonstrated signs of extreme sensitivity to people and places, and it soon became clear that she possessed highly developed psychic faculties and mediumistic abilities, reputedly having had visions and dreams of Atlantis as early as four years old. She grew up in a family that belonged to *Christian Science*, and her marked independent spirit and inclination for prolonged states of lucid dreaming initially caused her a lot of anxiety. The power of imagination plays a big role in the occult, and in later years she learned to make use of her abilities, when she was able to control and direct her powers though occultism, which produced extraordinary results for this woman of the esoteric mileu. Early in her life, Violet Mary Firth, was the victim of a vicious psychic attack by an employer, which she didn't fully recover from for three years. This psychic attack led to her interest in psychology, which then led to the study of occultism. She was trained by an Irish Freemason, Dr. Theodore Moriarty, who expressed his metaphysical and theosophical beliefs in a series of lectures on the esoteric subject of astro-etheric psychological conditions. Moriarty's topic of interest included the lost continent of Atlantis, Gnostic Christianity, reincarnation, and psychic disturbances that can result in illness. Perhaps more influential for her occult interests, however, was Fortune's childhood friend, Maiya Curtis-Webb, who introduced her to the **Hermetic Order of the Golden Dawn**. Beginning in 1919, Curtis-Webb instructed Fortune in trance mediumship at the Golden Dawn Temple of the *Alpha and Omega Lodge* of the *Stella Matutina*, that was headed by J. W. Brodie-Innes. She became disillusioned with the group, however, when she saw that its ranks after World War 1, had been reduced to widows and elderly men. She joined the London-based Golden Dawn group led by Moina Mathers, widow of the group's original founder, MacGregor Mathers, who was the mentor, and later enemy of Aleister Crowley. It was during this period that the former Violet Firth adopted the phrase *Deo Non Fortuna*, which translates to "by God and not by luck," as her Golden Dawn magical name, that was also the Latin motto that appeared on the Firth family crest. She subsequently shortened her new appellation to Dion Fortune. [1]

Fortune thought she had finally found her "path" with this offshoot branch of the Golden Dawn, and began to write articles under her new name, Dion Fortune. These articles were later published in book form as *The Esoteric Philosophy of Love and Marriage, Sane Occultism*, and *Psychic Self-Defence*. Her books and articles enraged Moina Mathers, who felt that Dion Fortune had betrayed the secrets of the Order, and a magical war erupted between the two, a similar event happened earlier between Aleister Crowley and Moina's husband. This new episode of psychic attack pushed her to delve deeper into the study of the subject of psychology, as she had become increasingly disillusioned with the Golden Dawn initiatic structure. After Dr. Moriarty's death in 1921, she founded her own esoteric order with a few of Moriarty's students and a few members of the Theosophical Society in London.

In 1924, her little group bought an old officer's hut from the army, and erected it at the foot of Glastonbury Tor in Somerset. This site, which they was named, Chalice Orchard, was the first headquarters of the Fraternity of the Inner Light (later re-named the Society of the Inner Light). Soon afterwards she also acquired a large old house at —3 Queensborough Terrace, in London—which was big enough for certain members to live in as well as it being an established magical lodge. Among those living at the house were Dion Fortune and her husband Dr. Penry Evans, although they divided their time between London and Glastonbury, and eventually divorced. The society soon became a high caliber initiatory school. Working in trance mediumship, Dion Fortune made contacts with certain inner plane adepts, or *Masters,* whose influence on the Western Esoteric Tradition is still vital to this day. [2] The brilliant writings of Dion Fortune can help us to better understand certain dynamics of the occult world, and the various Illuminati sects in relation to psychic attacks.

Many people, for example, email me asking for possible solutions for their own psychological defense. Others who have had direct involvement in secret societies ask me if participating in rituals, or the work in a specific lodge or fraternity is in itself a bad thing. Dion Fortune wrote with great awareness and courage in her book, *Self-Defense,* about these subjects, denouncing this problem openly: *"On the other hand, the instinctive reactions of a pure and sensitive soul are not to be ignored. There are such things as Black Lodges and evil entities. We must not allow the cry of 'Wolf! Wolf!' to make us either callous or careless. In any case, the victim is suffering remediable discomfort."* [3]

"Black Lodges and evil entities" do indeed exist, and are not speculations, as the elite would like for you to believe, which makes it easier to cover their occult links and human sacrifices. Fortune writes:

> *A Black Lodge leads by a straight and narrow way into the land of apaches and demimondaines, quite apart from its other drawbacks. Secondly, a knowledge of these facts is essential for differential diagnosis. Thirdly, occult powers are not infrequently used to obtain purely mundane ends, therefore when the question of ordinary criminality occurs in connection with an occult organisation, the issue may be complicated by an admixture of methods that belong to another plane. We must always remember that a lodge may not necessarily have been formed for the express purpose of evading the law; it may have started with a perfectly legitimate end in view, and have been exploited by evil-doers for their own purposes, for, owing to the*

1   See. http://biographyyourdictionary.com/dion-fortune ‡ Archived 9th August, 2015.
2   See. http://www.servantsofthelight.org/about-sol/biographies/dion-fortune/ ‡ Archived 9th August, 2015.
3   See. Dionne Fortune, *Psychic Self-Defense,* (Milan, IT: SIAD, 1978).

secretive nature of its proceedings, the fraternity form of organisation lends itself to various forms of law-breaking. One occult organisation is well-known to have been involved in the drug traffic trade, another is riddled with unnatural vice. A third degenerated into what was little better than a house of ill-fame, and its head was an expert abortionist. Others have been involved in subversive politics. Those who join fraternities without properly investigating them and the credentials of those who are running them may find themselves involved in any or all of these things. Behind the veil of secrecy, guarded by impressive oaths, many things may happen, and it is therefore essential to inform oneself most carefully concerning the character, credentials and record of the leaders of an organisation. [4]

When joining an Order you need to be very aware of what you are exactly joining, as there are not only dangers on the physical plane, but also the more insidious ones present on the astral plane, where the risks are much greater than most people can imagine. Dione Fortune teaches us how to identify a "Black Lodge," in the following words:

A lodge of dubious whiteness can be readily recognised by the type of people who belong to it, who may best be described as the seedy adventurer type with a sprinkling of smart society folk who often have a taste for crude flavours in the way of sensation. The really Black Lodges are as carefully guarded as the high-grade White Lodges, and no outsider can gain entrance to them. The serious student of Black Occultism is out for knowledge and magical experiment and he is not going to waste his time on a tyro. Those who choose to graduate into a Black Lodge after serving their apprenticeship in the Outer Court of a White Lodge do so with their eyes open, and experience must be their teacher. One cannot feel that they deserve much sympathy if the experience is a painful one. The person I am out to help is the person who is a victim, not the one who is hoist with his own petard. The man or woman who, rejecting the steady grade of the Way of Initiation, chooses to go up with rocket had better come down with the stick. Any request for a large sum of money should always be regarded as a danger signal. It is one of the strictest conditions of initiation that occult knowledge may never be sold or used for gain. [5]

Dear Freemasons, if one day you feel suddenly unwell after attending a lodge meeting, there is a big chance this may be related to black magic and the presence of witch doctors or black magicians in your lodge. This is a growing phenomena in Masonic circles, especially with the increase in popularity of orders like *Order Templi Orientis* or the Golden Dawn, which recruit growing numbers of Masons on the Internet, especially in the USA. Mysterious deaths and illnesses can occur in these lodges if a malignant presence has psychically polluted the temple. In this case, a method of defense should be taken against these occult forces, and should follow in general with these three main points:

1. Spend a few hours in the light of the Sun, in order to reinforce your aura, avoid those places where the forces of the elemental spirits are more powerful, such as the sea, the mountains, the countryside.

2. Avoid spending time alone, do activities that relax your body and isolate the psychic centers, eat every two hours and reduce the flow of blood to the head through a warm bath or with your feet in warm water (and salt).

3. Place on your solar plexus a hot water bottle, keep clean the intestines (the pu-

4   Dionne Fortune, *Psychic Self-Defense,* Ibid., p. 126.
5   *Ibid.,* pp. 132-133.

trid material attracts lower energies), eat a balanced diet, don't get distracted by mundane activities, keep the mind busy, stop all psychic meditations and activity, remaining on the physical plane.

The Exorcist that operates on a person who has been psychically attacked should obtain three clear results:

- *Restore the aura of the patient;*
- *Clean the atmosphere;*
- *Stop any contact that the patient has with the negative forces.* [6]

You must take physical action to purify the etheric conditions. If negative magnetism permeates the atmosphere of your Masonic lodge, or your home, it is advisable to purify the atmosphere and also the garments used by you or your group, including the Masonic Regalia or any other ritual garment you may have used in the presence of black magicians. The person, or persons, attacked by these evil forces, should also change residence for a while, and if the problem persists in his own lodge with such energies, he must immediately stop attending and ask his Grand Lodge to move him elsewhere as soon as possible.

Remember that it only takes a couple of Satanists, or even one skilled black magician, to pollute the magnetism of an entire lodge with tragic results. In such situations, running water possesses features that can ease tension and aid against with the "harassment" from evil spirits that can often take place after these attacks. The relief will be immediate and should be followed by a purification with salt water, which I highly reccomend since my days as Worshipful Master (D∴D∴A∴) of the Cagliostro Lodge of the F.R.A. in London. Water, a symbol of the psychic sphere, has particular power, and has always been used in purification rituals (think of baptism). Salt, as a crystalline substance, receives and holds etheric magnetism. Consequently, soaking in a bath of water and salt consecrated for this purpose, and wearing freshly washed clothes, can be an initial remedy from psychic attack.

If you are a particularly sensitive person, you may have noticed that occasionally you are hit by waves of negative events / negative energy. You don't have to attend a lodge to experience this, as any human grouping can conceal pitfalls if not protected. Not all parties, however, are equally sensitive. That's why some people are naturally predisposed to these influences or contacts by entities, and others are not.

The psychic attack is basically a form of aggression that can be implemented in various ways. It's a threat perpetrated by one who considers himself superior, against another. The persecutor easily handles a controlled environment, from which the victim can not escape. The mind of the victim can be completely controlled and manipulated by the psychic attacker. The currents of negative thinking are not easy to manage, because they are attracted to the weaknesses of the human psyche. It is important to remember this. Without a good deal of protection, and the confidence in the ability to cope with the attack, we can all become easy targets. The solution lies in the mind of the victim, because as long as there is a weak point which attracts the negative currents in your body, you will not be rebalanced and the problem will always persist. Before speaking of psychic attacks, we must consider the possibility that we can be personally unbalanced, and can become victims of our own negativity. I often meet people who accuse the "Illuminati" or the "New World Order" for their problems, when they should instead realize their mind and their own wrong doings could be causing the problems in their lives. Remember the NWO or the Illuminati sects are interested in you only if you are an influential person,

---

6   http://www.cavernacosmica.com/difendersi-dalle-energie-negative-parte-seconda/ ‡ Archived 10th August, 2015.

an extremely rich one, or you are part of certain families and relative bloodlines. **If not there is no interest on their side to bother you or your family. Besides, we are already controlled in so many other ways.**

Tips to rebalance and get back on track:

- Cut all ties that bind you with the alleged perpetrator or perpetrators, lodge or sect. Distance yourself, asserting your power without being subject to theirs. Sever any magical or occult ties you previously had with an exorcism ritual.

- Keep your diet healthy, get at least eight hours of sleep per night, and enjoy sunshine and fresh air while walking or doing physical exercise.

- Participate in constructive social activities that are positive.

- Avoid negative thoughts and fear after the attack.

- Receive a general medical evaluation to verify good health. [7]

The Rosicrucian Illuminati from the Golden Dawn to the F.R.A.

Dione Fortune was a member of the Golden Dawn. The initial impetus of the Golden Dawn's Inner Order, the *Rosae Rubea et Aurea Cruces* (the Red Rose and the Cross of Gold), stemmed from Rosicrucian sources, and the cornerstone of their teachings were the first two Rosicrucian manifestoes published in the 17th century by an anonymous authorship. Within the Golden Dawn's Inner Order, elaborate rituals were, and still are, utilized to describe the discovery of the vault of Christian Rosenkruetz, and the teachings he had to offer humanity. The basis for these teachings were contained in both the "Fama Fraternitatis" and "Confessio" manifestoes. In the **Adeptus Minor Ritual** of the **5-6 Grade** the following summation of these two documents is read to the Postulant:

In 1378 the Chief and Originator of our Fraternity was born in Europe. He was the son of noble but poor parents, and was placed in a cloister at the age of five where he learned some Greek and Latin. While yet a youth, he accompanied a certain Brother P.A.L. on a pilgrimage to the Holy Land; but the latter, dying at Cyprus, he himself went to Damascus. There was then in Arabia a Temple of the Order which was called in the Hebrew tongue "Damkar": that is, "The Blood of the Lamb." There he was duely initiated, and took the Mystic title Christian Rosenkreutz, or Christian of the Rose Cross. He then so improved his knowledge of the Arabian tongue, that in the following year he translated the book "M" into Latin, which he afterwards brought back with him to Europe. After three years he went into Egypt, where there was another Temple of the Order. There he remained for a time still studying the mysteries of Nature. After this, he travelled by sea to the city of Fessa, where he was welcomed at the Temple established there. While at the Temple, he obtained the knowledge and acquaintance of the habitants of the Elements, who revealed unto him many of their secrets. Of the Fraternity, he confessed that they had not retained their Wisdom in its Primal purity, and that their Kabala was to a certain extent altered to their religion. Nevertheless, he learned much there.

After a stay of two years he came to Spain, where he endeavoured to reform the errors of the learned according to the pure knowledge he had received. But this was to them a laughing matter, and they reviled and rejected him, even as the prophets of old were rejected. Thus also was he treated by those of his own and other na-

---

tions when he showed them the errors that had crept into their religions. So, after five years residence in Germany, he initiated three of his former monastic brethren, Fraters G.W., I.A., and I.O., who had more knowledge than many others at the time. And by these four was made the foundation of the Fraternity in Europe.

These three worked and studied at the writings and other knowledge which C.R.C. had brought with him, and by them was some of the Magical Language transcribed (which was that of the Elemental Tablets) and a dictionary thereof made; and the Rituals and part of the Book "M" were transcribed. For the True Order of the Rose Cross descendeth into the heights—even unto the Throne of God Himself, and induideth even Archangels, Angels and Spirits. These four Fraters also erected a building to serve as a Temple and Headquarters of their Order, and called it Collegium and Spiritum Sanctum, or the College of the Holy Spirit. This now being finished, and the work of establishing the Order being extremely heavy; and because they devoted much time to the healing of those sick and possessed who resorted to them, they initiated four others, viz: Fraters R.C. (the son of the deceased father's brother of C.R.C.), C.B. a skillful artist, and P.D., who was to be Cancellarius; all being Germans except I.A., and now eight in number. Their agreement was:

1. That none of them should profess any other thing, but cure the sick, and do so freely.

2. That they should not be constrained to wear any distinctive dress, but therein follow the custom of the country.

3. That every year on the day of Corpus Christi, they should meet at the *Collegium and Spiritum Sanctum*, or give the cause for absence.

4. Everyone should look for some worthy person of either sex, who after his decease might succeed him.

5. The word R.C. was to be their mark, seal, and character. The Fraternity was to remain secret for one hundred years. Five of the Fraters were to travel in different countries, and two were to remain with Christian *Rosenkreutz*.

The discovery of the tomb where the highly illuminated Man of God, C.R.C. was buried occurred as follows:

After Frater A. died in Gallia Narbonensi, there succeeded in his place Frater N.N. He, while repairing a part of the building of the College of the Holy Spirit, endeavoured to remove a brass memorial tablet which bore the names of certain brethren, and some other things. In this tablet was the head of a strong nail or bolt, such that when the tablet was forcibly wrenched away, it pulled with it a large stone which partially uncovered a secret door, upon which was inscribed in large letters **Post Oa Annos Patebo**—*After an hundred and twenty years I shall open, with the year of our Lord under, 1484.*

The climax of the story centers on the rediscovery of C.R.C.'s tomb, buried in a concealed, underground vault with seven sides. [8]

Engraved upon a circular altar over the tomb were the words translated from Latin: *"Unto the Glory of the Rose Cross I have constructed this Tomb for myself as a Compendium of the Universal Unity."* There are many hinted spiritual implications of the

8   See Pat Zalewski, *The Secret Inner Order Rituals of the Golden Dawn*, (Phoenix, Arizona: Falcon Press 1988).

Rosicrucian Vault in the *Fama fraternitatis Roseae Crucis oder Die Bruderschaft des Ordens der Rosenkreuzer*, usually listed as *Fama Fraternitatis Rosae Crucis*, and explored in the later teachings of the Hermetic Order of the Golden Dawn and the R.R. et A.C. The implications of this Vault are many—it represents the emblematic tomb of death and spiritual resurrection, as well as an initiation chamber and place of meditation. However, its primary significance is that of the "mystical center" or "inner temple" of man. This is an internal God-centered reality, which is inherent in the symbolism of C.R.C.'s "Compendium of the **Universal Unity**." Publication of the Fama caused commotion, and traditionalists condemned the shadowy Rosicrucian brotherhood. Skeptics doubted its existence, while Hermeticists embraced it. [9] *Myth or reality*, the Rosicrucian legend persists to this day, both inside and outside of Freemasonry, where it is preserved in New Age Illuminati cults like A.M.O.R.C., in the high degrees of certain Masonic Rites like the 18°A.A.S.R.; in elite Rosicrucian fraternities for Master Masons, like the *Societas Rosicruciana in Anglia* (that for the past ten years, has covertly embraced Crowley's pseudo-religion of Thelema), or the truly Christian, *Societas Rosicruciana* in America. My own personal experience with the Rosicrucians was with the *Fraternitas Rosicruciana Antiqua* (F.R.A.), originally established by German occultist and Illuminati Dr. Arnold Krumm-Heller in 1927, and still very popular in South America. This was the first Rosicrucian Fraternity that openly embraced Thelema and Crowleyanity when "The Great Beast 666" was still alive. Krumm-Heller's motto **"Huiracocha"** was the name a God once worshipped by the Incas—and the god's legend recites that he vanished westwards, and would one day return—those who refused to worship him received gruesome punishment. **The term** "Viracocha" (another variation of "Huiracocha") **is also found in Reuss's O.T.O. ritual-texts.** Having obtained Crowley's address from **Martha Küntzel**, Krumm-Heller wrote to him for the first time on 2/17/1928 as **"Summum Supremum Sanctuarium O.T.O., F.R.A., Frat. Herm. Lucis, Societas Pansophia"** where he wrote: *"received your address by M. Küntzel... remember myself by Reuss?"*

Krumm-Heller offered his services to promote Crowley's ideals in the USA and Spanish-speaking countries with Martha Küntzel's help, and held public readings from Crowley's *Confessions*. Because of these public readings, it was a very short time before he came face-to-face with Aleister Crowley himself, and his representative Karl Germer.

Master Huiracocha and a short history of the F.R.A.

Crowley's encounter with Krumm-Heller occurred at Henri Birven's house in Berlin on April 23, 1930. "Huiracocha" immediately irritated "Baphomet" Crowley during the meeting, because of a large spot of grease on his suit. Krumm-Heller felt a desperate need to communicate to Crowley how many Orders and secret societies he had been initiated. This is something that happens unfortunately, still today in the *Ordo Templi Orientis*, and the dark side of the Illuminati, where they are obsessed with control and recognition from the outside world. Crowley considered Arnold Krumm-Heller a Mason of equal rank, as they were both "Puppet Masters" of the elite. Crowley was 96° in the O.T.O. for England, and Reuss a confirmed 97°. Arnold Krumm-Heller told him that he was 96° for Germany, but that Reuss had cheated him by selling him this degree, along with two other Germans. Krumm-Heller at one point even made himself into a 98°, a bit like the aforementioned Frank G. Ripel who made himself a 100° not so long ago. The O.T.O./Illuminati researcher and initiate, Peter-R. Koenig, writes:

9 http://www.scribd.com/doc/237730465/ROSA-MYSTICA-The-Rosicrucian-Vault-A-Compendium-of-the-Universal-Unity-pdf#scribd Archived 10th August, 2015. *[emphasis added]*.

Crowley had high hopes for Krumm-Heller and unsuccessfully suggested in 1936 that he should "take over the work in California." Crowley had been so disappointed by the 2nd Agape Lodge that he also suggested to McMurtry he should take it over, 10 years later. (McMurtry was just one among many and certainly NOT Crowley's first choice.) In 1936, the Nazi-pamphlet "Der Judenkenner" appeared which caused the neighbours of Krumm-Heller's family in Berlin to get upset. Recently I was to discover some documents that show that Arnoldo Krumm-Heller was eagerly interested to give his children an education according Nazi-ideology. So, Cuauthemoc Krumm-Heller was sent in 1937 to the famous Nazi elite school NAPOLA (which Hitler wrote: "A youth will rise in my order castles who will scare the whole world. I want a violent, dictatorial, intrepid, cruel youth"). Krumm-Heller participated in organizing the Red Cross in Spain but left the country for South America after General Franco's ascent to power. He continued to travel (Palestine, Egypt, Turkey and Rhodesia) but spent the Second World War in Germany, where he happened to be at the outbreak of war. And with the Mexican flag alongside the Hakenkreuz in front of his house, they survived WW II seemingly safe.

In 1942, Krumm-Heller was staying at a sanatorium in Pyrmont, from where he wrote to the 2nd Agapé Lodge in Calfornia, amongst other letters. This lodge was whence the "Church of Thelema" stemmed, which is still being led by Helen P. Smith as a highly exclusive group. Krumm-Heller signed his letters to Bolivia as "Huiracocha R+C+," and stamped them with a seal bearing the title "Ecclesi a Gnostica" (which was later also used by his son Parsival). [10]

In 1956, Parsival Krumm-Heller distanced himself from the international leadership of the *Fraternitas Rosicruciana Antiqua* after his father's death, thus following his father's directions where the national branches of the FRA would continue independently. From 1995, Parsival began a complex operation to reconstitute the branches of the Fraternity into a federation. When I was still a member in the F.R.A. in 2002, Dr. Emanuele Coltro Guidi of the Antiqua-Ecclesia Gnostica Latin (who is a dangerous Satanist), had continued this unification project on behalf of Parsival Krumm-Heller. Guidi surprisingly admitted one day in open lodge, that the real leader of this Rosicrucian Fraternity was not Parsival, but an ex-officer of Himmler's SS (the infamous Totenkopfverbände), who lived in London.

Who was Arnold Krumm-Heller? Born in Salchendorf, Germany on April 15, 1876, he was a distinguished scholar and writer, and his family emigrated to Mexico in 1823. He studied medicine in Germany, Switzerland and Mexico and became a German naval Intelligence agent during the Mexican Revolution and World War I. He was a Colonel of the Mexican Army Military Health and Director General of Schools Troop. As a diplomat he was Minister of Mexico in Switzerland and Germany, until the end of the First World War. But most of his attention was devoted to the study of esotericism, Rosicrucianism, Theosophy, Occult, Martinism and Spiritual Enlightenment, as he himself described in his autobiography. He was a friend of Rudolf Steiner, whom he considered to be a true Rosicrucian, and was acquainted with **Franz Hartmann (1838- 1912)** and Theodor Reuss, [11] who initiated him into the O.T.O./Illuminati where he reached the last Degree of this system (*Ordo Templi Orientis*). After meeting Crowley he acquired a growing obsession for sexual magick, writing at one point: *"through the awakening of sexual secretions, lies the only way to reach the goal of the Great Work and everything*

10   See. http://www.pararreligion.ch/fra.htm ‡ Archived 10th August, 2015. *[emphasis added].*
11   See. https://fraternidadantiguarosacruz.wordpress.com/ ‡ Archived 10th August, 2015.

else that is not through the use of this, is unfortunately only a waste of time." Krumm-Heller's view is now unfortunately, the view of most contemporary Rosicrucians corrupted by the dark side of the Illuminati and the Left-Hand Path.

"Psychic" vampirism in the Illuminati and more ...

During my time in the F.R.A. I began to study the phenomena of *psychic vampires* or *energy vampires*. They don't have sharp teeth, suck blood, or live in Transylvania, but are very dangerous, especially if they are occultists. They are predators that use an endless repertoire of tricks to steal energy. Emotional vampires are not always aware of their role in society, but in a sectarian environment, as in the *Fraternitas Saturni*, an order openly dedicated in the degree system of feeding an astral vampire, this situation of course, changes completely, as they are the worst kind of black magicians. These people invade freedom without limitations and are convinced that humanity has been created to meet their needs.

The psychic vampire may seem like anyone else at first, but, slowly, having won your sympathy, they begin to suck your emotional energy. Even if not a secret society member, the energy vampire is dedicated to consciously perpetuating these actions. Even if your just meeting casually for a coffee, this person could use the opportunity to drain your vital energy and deplete your aura. The result could visibly be felt as weakness, and loss of energy. If the psychic draining is allowed to continue, emotional and physical results can occur, such as disease...and even death. Psychic vampirism is often utilized by Grand Masters and sorcerers of secret societies of the New World Order, that draw energy for their work in this way.

How can we turn this heavy negative energy into a beautiful, peaceful and serene one? How can we help ourselves to enjoy a happier and more peaceful life?

"Energy vampires" or "psychic vampires," are everywhere, and we are often unprepared and caught off guard when attacked. [12] **Dott. Nicholaj de Mattos Frisvold,** a Norwegian psychiatrist and known Satanist, and a figure you have been introduced to Volume I, [13] is a typical psychic vampire, who even boasted of his "vampire" status shamelessly among his close followers, believing it gave added value to his evil *persona*.

Frisvold presented me to the "Brothers" of the aforementioned *Fraternitas Saturni* in Norway, a German order linked to Crowley's Thelema, founded in Germany in 1928 by an expert psychic vampire named **Eugen Grosche**. According to Frisvold, this sect was a *hotbed* of psychic vampires, and that I should join their ranks as a high level Illuminati, to grasp certain techniques that could benefit me and the Order. In that period of my life in the late 1990s and early 2000s, I felt so much negativity around me that it was truly difficult to remain intact and positive. I was constantly frequenting bars and clubs, due to my job as a DJ, and these of places, where the use of alcohol, drugs, can expose you to negative energy, thus facilitating the task of the psychic vampire to suck your energy. Also fear, anger, resentment, jealousy—all the self-destructive emotions that pollute the mind—can open passages to energy vampires that feed on these thoughts that are present at the lowest levels of your being. That's why you have to make choices in life, to change bad habits and protect yourself. If you have fallen victim to an energy vampire like Frisvold, you may immediately find that his presence will put you in a bad mood. But if the bond that is created between you and your Master is an addictive one, as in the case of a

12   See. http://anima.tv/gaetanovivo/2010/07-vampiri-energetici/ ‡ Archived 10th August, 2015.
13   *Confessions of an Illuminati, Vol. I, Ibid.,* pp. 32, 92, 116, 117, 118, 119, 121, 227, 228.

sectarian bond, it could be the opposite, causing discontent, but with an almost morbid and unhealthy need to continue the relationship. I believe that this symptom is frequent within the Illuminati network, but no one talks about it.

When distancing yourself from a *psychic vampire*, you should set limits, and never allow him to cross them. Every time he or she attempts to cross the line, you should always re-established boundaries. Heal your self-esteem, because the psychic vampire will try in every way to lower it. One trick in the defense of psychic attack, which may seem odd, is to *praise* the psychic vampire with *compliments* because if you satiate them, they may not feel the need to feed off your energy, it is a bit like throwing a dog a bone. If they try to offer to help you should refuse, as he may make you feel indebted later. Always remember that for a psychic vampire, lying is normal for them, therefore never listen to their promises, but instead base everything on factual evidence. In addition you must heal and protect your aura, which can become weakened, and for this reason it is important, when you are dealing with a psychic vampire, to visualize an oval shell of light that surrounds your body and protects you during meetings with this person. [14]

I know this method I just mentioned might seem a bit "New Age" to some, but I can assure you that it works, having used it myself in the presence of very dangerous psychic vampires many times. In late medieval demonology—particularly in the inquisitorial trials of witchcraft—the demon called a **"succubus"** often appears in the form of a woman, where they lure men with sex, and steal his semen. Operating in the opposite direction is the **"incubus,"** the classic **"nightmare"** demon, which appears instead in the form of a man. The vampire literature often quotes an old particularly detailed text regarding the *succubi*, written by **Father Luigi Maria Sinistrari of Ameno.**

The "psychic vampire" in this case of a succubus, is not a human person but an entity. The psychic vampire can be found in literature: one classic example is *The Parasite* by Arthur Conan Doyle (1859-1930), the creator of Sherlock Holmes. Conan Doyle attended environments like the Theosophical Society and knew the esoteric theories on **"astral vampirism."** [15] One of the main supporters of this theory, was the German theosophist **Franz Hartmann,** (someone that Theodor Reuss claimed was one of the founding members of the O.T.O.), [16] who stated that this thesis was brought forward centuries earlier by Paracelsus (1439-1541). It is, however, more likely that the origins of psychic vampirism generated in an *internal debate* in the world of French spiritualism, which took place in the late 1850s.

Z.J. Piérart (1810-1878) was a French Researcher and a Professor at the College of Maubeuge, who emerged as a prominent figure in spiritist circles in the 1850s. He opposed the theory of reincarnation, but maintained instead, what became a classic in French spiritism, **"the belief in the existence of an "astral body."** It was precisely this *"astral body,"* that according to Piérart, that could explain the phenomena of psychic energetic-vampirism. He felt that different types of "astral bodies" could attack in a "vampiric" way and empty the energy of one who had done them wrong in life. The German theosophist was convinced that the *activity* of a psychic vampire could be developed by "forces," or psychic residues.

The theories of Hartmann represented innovation compared to the explanations on vampirism given at that time, especially in Theosophical Society circles. Madame Blavatsky

14   See. Http://www.meditazionecreativa.com/2012/12/come-difendersi-dai-vampiri-emozionali.html ‡ Archived 10th August, 2015.

15   http://www.ilportaledeltempo.it/?sezione=VA&art=introspezionisuivampiri ‡ Archived 10th August, 2015.

16   See. http://www.pararelgion.ch/sunrise/hartmann.htm ‡ Archived 10th August, 2015.

exposed in *Isis Unveiled* (1877) the thesis of Piérart, but she did not exclude the existence of real vampires in the classic sense of the term, and it was believed by many that "astral bodies" could actually feed on blood, which is only partially true, because they feed on sperm and other bodily fluids, and especially the energy of the soul. The theory of psychic vampirism was developed in the Hermetic Order of the Golden Dawn, where both Aleister Crowley and Dion Fortune, before joining or creating rival organizations, believed in the existence of "psychic vampires" as malevolent people, capable of absorbing energy from others. The theories of Dion Fortune in particular, exercised considerable influence in esoteric circles, and influenced all subsequent literature on the subject of *psychic vampirism.*

A variant of the psychic vampire is the "psychic sponge," mentioned by Hartmann. He spoke of a kind of vampire who uses "animal magnetism," a concept made famous by Freemason and Illuminati **Franz Anton Mesmer (1734-1815)**. In this situation, just being in the presence of this kind of person will make you feel weak and lose energy.

In the esoteric tradition, the "magnetic" form of psychic vampirism—and the means to resist it—have been described in detail by the *Confraternita Terapeutica e Magica di Myriam* (Therapeutic and Magic Brotherhood of Myriam), an Illuminati sect founded in Italy by Giuliano Kremmerz (pseudonym of Ciro Formisano, 1861-1930).[17] The practice of psychic vampirism in recent years is not only linked to the *Fraternitas Saturni*, but also to the new **Neo-Luciferian Church,**[18] an Illuminati organization founded in 2005 by Danish occultist **Bjarne Pedersen,** along with **Michael Paul Bertiaux** (b. 1935), author of *The Voudon Gnostic Workbook*, and formerly involved in Scandinavia with the activities of Dr. Nicholaj de Mattos Frisvold. Bertiaux, who claims to practice homosexual magick, is the proponent of a famous and succesful convergence between Gnosticism, Haitian voodoo, and the O.T.O., called *Ordo Templi Orientis Antiqua,* of which Frisvold was, at one time, the leading Northern European representative. This was before Bertiaux argued with Frisvold about the *Choronzon Club,* as Frisvold apparently didn't want to have a homosexual encouter with him (*at least, that's what he said*), but he still claimed that he was part of what is basically, a homosexual club.[19]

To better understand who Michael Paul Bertiaux really is, a former member of his mystery school known as **Frater Barrabas** writes:

> *Michael often performed his Voudoun ceremonies completely nude, or sometimes he would wear a mask. This was quite a departure from Michael the wandering bishop, who would wear beautiful handmade silk and satin vestments and perform private masses using the Greek Orthodox rite (of St. Basil). In his mundane habits, Michael would wear rather drab and even ill-fitting clothes—he looked a bit like a slob. He was much more comfortable wearing exotic outfits than fitting in with the urban masses. Since he worked for the State of Illinois in the capacity of a bureaucrat in the government aid services, he probably wore a nice suit and easily fit in with the grey masses of fellow bureau workers. I never saw him wear a suit, since the few times I visited were during weekends. My initiation consisted of first being completely naked, presented to the various spirits and lwa of the dead, then being forced to drink a third of a bottle of Wild Turkey, and finally, being sexually accosted by this man. I remember distinctly lying naked on the floor of his temple, with this rather flabby fury man laying on top of me, pinning me down while attempting to french kiss me (as I gritted my teeth) and thereby arouse me. Yet all it did was bring out in me a*

17 ilportaledeltempo.it, *Ibid.*
18 See. http://www.neoluciferianchurch.dk ‡ Archived 11th August, 2015.
19 *Confessions of an Illuminati, vol. I, Ibid.,* pp. 64, 65, 117, 342.

sense of complete revulsion and a stubborn will power to keep myself from being violated in any manner. I succeeded in that, but then probably didn't receive the full blessing of being magickally affected or transformed by Michael's operation. I was given a title and an accolade later, but I actually felt little changed, and I was just relieved that I had avoided any spiritual contamination. My teacher just accepted all of this without a single complaint, and didn't intercede for me when it was obvious that I was resisting Bertiaux with all my efforts. I was also restrained out of courtesy and some degree of openness to Michael, since otherwise, I would have become

FIG. 73 – *The secret symbol of the new* **Neo-Luciferian Church,** *founded by the Illuminati in 2005.*

violent towards him. I now know why Christopher didn't interfere with Michael when he was assaulting me, and that is, he had hopes to receive the many blessings of Bertiaux's initiations. Indeed, he underwent many initiations, got his bishop's consecration and other titles, and much of this is actually documented in his books. Christopher, or Bill Schnoebelen, which was his real name, completely cooperated with Michael Bertiaux for a couple of years. He probably had to endure quite a bit of sexual abuse at his hands. I have heard that others who have sought out initiations from Michael Bertiaux received far more than they bargained for, having to forbear him with the favor of anal sex as a certification of the transmission of legitimate occult initiations. Although I had been offered such enticements myself, after just one episode, I tactfully demurred any further accolades. [20]

As you have read, Bertiaux tends to use initiations to sexually harass his followers, and present among them was the controversial author and occultist **Bill Schnoebelen,** who at the time called himself **Christopher Syn,** is now a "born again Christian," but states publicly he was a former vampire. [21] Schnoebelen paints a picture of vampires in his picturesque interviews, that fall into the field of disinformation.

The **Neo-Luciferian Church,** (FIG. 73) is a relatively new organization with the motto "***Ipsa Scientia Potestas East,***" where we find a blend of modern Western occult teachings, especially the teachings of Thelema, with witchcraft; voodoo, ancient and modern Gnosticism. The "neo-Luciferian Church" is considered strongly inspired by the Luciferian Gnosticism that was inspired in turn, in the early twentieth century, by Danish Illuminati **Carl Wiliam Hansen,** a member of the O.T.O, Martinist movement and other secret societies in the Illuminati network. In 1906, Hansen published (under the pseudonym Ben Kadosh), a book entitled *Den Ny Morgens Gry, Lucifer-Hiram, Verdensbygmesterens Genkomst* (Dawn of a New Morning, Lucifer-Hiram, The Return

20   http://fraterbarrabbas.blogspot.it/2011/04/remembering-michael-bertiaux.html ‡ Archived 11th August. 2015.
21   See. https://www.relfe.com/07/Bill_William_Schnoebelen.html ‡ Archived 11th August, 2015.

of the Master Builder of the World). It is proof that the occult side of Freemasonry has been preparing for the coming of Lucifer for quite a long time.

In 1923, C.W. Hansen as Delegate of the Order of the Martinists from a charter he had received from Joanny Bricaud, founded the **"Grand Orient de la vraie et haute Maçonnerie esoterique et gnostique du Danmark."** He also founded the lodge "Sphinxen" which only operated for one year, and it was here that he met his future successor, **Grunddal Sjallung** (1895-1976). Hansen dissolved the lodge, and in the summer of 1924 he received a 33° charter from the **"Grande Oriente Italiano degli Antichi ed Accetati Muratori, Zenith di Roma,"** via Eduardo Frosini, who had been a member of Theodor Reuss' Rite of Memphis-Misraïm in Italy. Frosini was a collaborator of Arturo Reghini, who exchanged charters of a "Ritus Philosophicus Italicus" with Aleister Crowley in 1913. It was Frosini who sent the Reuss-rituals to Hansen. Frosini also sent the Rite of Memphis-Misraïm and the **"Order of Illuminati"** charter to Hansen as well. [22]

As you can see, Lucifer is the ultimate vampiric energy that the New Age offers to the dark side, with people like Carl William Hansen, and his heir Bjarne Pedersen. And of course there is the involvement of Theosophy in all this. In fact, the work of Hansen was presented to Michael Paul Bertiaux by the theosophist and Illuminati Marc Lully, vice president of a Chicago Theosophical lodge, were he originaly met Bertiaux back in January, 1966. [23] Lully in turn was in direct contact with Johansen (who died in 1977), who was the Grand Master of Carl Wiliam Hansen mystery school. In September of 1978, Marc Lully disappeared, but according to Bertioux, he lived the rest of his life in a Catholic monastery. [24] Did Lully become a Jesuit? There exists an Illuminati devoted to eclesiastical activities, also born from the Egyptian rites and Theosophy through the Liberal Catholic Church, which has given rise to one of the most known Gnostic schools. This specific branch is headed today by author and expert on Gnostic and Junghian studies **Stephan A. Hoeller (Baron von Hoeller-Bertram b. 1931),** a Jesuit agent I personally met on more than one occasion, having attended for a long time the congregation of his Gnostic Church in Oslo, led by my friend the well-known painter **Jan Valentin Saether.**

Although Baron Hoeller is an old-fashioned aristocratic from the Austro-Hungarian Empire, he is very knowledgeable and prepared individual on the subject, and he is also a 33° of the Ancient and Accepted Scottish Rite. He inherits his position as a senior representative of the milder side of the Illuminati, the *Brotherhood of the Illuminati,* (FIG. 74) from **Richard Duc de Palatine (1916-1977),** who emphasizes to its students that many of the so-called esoteric orders were in fact mythical remains of Catholic Theology. [25] As you can see in the end, all roads lead to Rome, and on the topic of Gnostic Churches in relation to the Illuminati and Jesuit manipulation, I will return in greater detail in Volume III.

C.R.O.M. Jezuitenberg and the occult origins of Damanhur

C.R.O.M. is an acronym for the *Center for Research on the World Order,* which was, until 2014, a center of studies and research on the New World Order, led by well-known researcher and author French Joël Labruyère. Because of his activities with the center in question, he was criticized by the well-known author Umberto Eco who

22 See. http://www.parareligion.ch/sunrise/hansen.htm ‡ Archived 11th August, 2015. *[emphasis added].*

23 http://www.parareligion.ch/sunrise/xi.htm ‡ Archived 11th August, 2015.

24 Bertiaux, letter of 10/29/89. cited in parareligion. ch site.

25 Grailmaster and Bishop Timothy A. Storlie, *Initiation into the Grail Mysteries,* (Lincoln, NE: Writers Club Press, 2001), p. 47.

His Serene Highness
Richard, Duc de Palatine

on behalf of

The Brotherhood of the Illuminati

issues

An Invitation

to all of his series of Lectures which will be given throughout
the United States of America from the
16th September to 10th December, 1959

You will receive a very warm welcome. Will you please pass this invitation around to your friends.

THE PURPOSE OF THE LECTURE TOUR

In every age and cycle when man enters into the darkness of material existence, one of the MESSENGERS from the Trans-Himalayan White Brotherhood enters the earth region and tries to lead mankind out of the darkness into the Divine Light of Love, Peace and Happiness. Such a VISIT is ever heralded by Their Forerunner who will seek to stop man from rushing headlong to disaster and attempt to restore to man the knowledge of his Divine Nature and the method of attaining Illumination and Interior Communion with the Divine within.

From their secret places and retreats, the Brothers of the Rosy Cross, Brothers of Light, Brothers of the Temple and finally the Brothers of Luxor in the United States have sent forth the clarion call; orders have been given that a FORERUNNER of these Centres of Light was to prepare the way for the Messenger to come in A.D. 1975, who will give the final proof of the Divine Nature of Man. The founders of the Secret Brotherhoods were themselves "ILLUMINATAE," this means that every Brother of Light must be in the position to demonstrate the Divine Science of Illumination, which is the "LOST KEY" to all spiritual endeavour.

This task of demonstrating the Divine Science has been entrusted to His Serene Highness, Richard, Duc de Palatine, who himself is a proven "Illuminati" and an initiate of the secret schools mentioned above.

– ‡ – ‡ –

TITLES OF LECTURES

(These are suggested only)

Light versus Darkness	The Power of Thought	Reincarnation
Kingdom of Happiness	The Lords of Venus	The Power Within
America in A.D. 2,700	The Goal of Mankind	Towards Perfection

Should you be unable to attend and would like these Lectures, they will be published in mimeographed form and can be secured by sending in advance $5.00 for the complete set, to:

MRS. IVA C. DUNLAP, P.O. BOX 17, SUNFIELD, MICHIGAN.

FIG. 74 – An invitation to the long series of lectures given by Richard Duc de Palatine in the United States, between September and December 1959, that presents him openly as a member of The Brotherhood of the Illuminati to the parties concerned.

recently passed away, a pawn of the occult elite, who loved to infuse secret mystery in his bestsellers. Eco attacked Labruyère publicly, from the pages of the famous Italian weekly *L'Espresso*, on the theory of a Jesuit plot behind world affairs.[26] By doing so, Umberto Eco was basically demonstrating his loyalty to the Jesuits.

After this episode, C.R.O.M. which for years had done an excellent job in France denouncing the Vatican-led New World Order, began an internal crisis that would eventually cease all activities in the organization, from May 3rd, 2014. This coincided with the inauguration of a new project, way from the public speculation, that was created by Labruyère, called *Nova Polis*. In the end, one of the various reasons for Labruyère's decision was the betrayal of two of his employees in Paris, who were initiated into the **Memphis Rite** of Freemasonry, a Rite belonging to fringe Masonry which, as I explained in Volume I, is linked to the Zionist lobby. This unusual gesture for his loyalists is said to have created the final conflict of interests in C.R.O.M.—which was consequently closed down. In 2005, Labruyère answered the following question about the relationship between Judaism and the Society of Jesus:

> *The relationship between Judaism and the Society of Jesus is full of ambiguity. It's a sort of unnatural union between Israel and the Vatican, with anti-Semitism as a sword of Damocles over the heads of the Jews. What is this great political secret?*
>
> *JL: If we use our insight we know that politics is a game of three occult powers the cosmic plan: the propertied classes (the political elite), the priestly hierarchy (religion) and the passive power of the masses, which is a considerable force moved by inertia. The two upper caste have the temporal power and spiritual power through which they control the masses. Humanity, as a third force, serves as a reservoir of energy to the two dominant caste. Humanity is the battery that powers the Egregor of the priestly afterlife, while providing the material wealth of that class system that owns this world. The caste of the invisible high priests organizes the religious and magical side, while the political class energizes the industrial and economic activity. For several centuries the international bank imposes its law on religion or political elites. Power is the hostage of finance. Money has become the stakes of politics. International finance controls the game, but it seems that a higher kind of power manipulates it. The order of the Jesuits acts in an occult way on the high Masonic degrees, and thus influence the rest of civil society.*
>
> *So there is a balance to preserve the interests of the three titans of the world. They fight against each other but must respect the status quo to maintain the cohesion of a world empire. How to reconcile the voracious appetites of the demons of materialism to the best interests of the priestly hierarchies that reign on the astral dimension? It is the great question of world politics. The world order is then based on a contract between the three titans. The masses of people will be given a socialist society, covered by an elite committed to defend its material privileges, and everything will be dominated by a theocratic regime represented by a world religion, which was responsible for transferring energy to the formation of the invisible astral. If the Titans are unable to agree to a lasting peace, since everyone wants a bigger slice of the cake, there will be total war, symbolized by the fall of Babylon the Great. We are not yet at this point, and we must therefore hope that the processes of the crisis will accelerate rather than slow, who want them with lamentations idealistic and pacifist to get a so-called "better world." In this game, the powerful political-occult side of the Jesuit Order—of*

26 See. http://alimentazioneegliilluminati.blogspot.it/2012/07/gli-ebreii-gesuiti-e-il-complotto.html ‡ Archived 12th August. 2015.

which the Company of Jesus is nothing but a mask—has the mission to corner the world power for the benefit of the priesthood in order to prolong the reign of the great priests of the invisible, yet is in danger since it spread atheism on Earth. However, while defending the ancient priestly order, the Jesuit Order has to oppose a spiritual renewal just entering the Age of Aquarius. That's why the Jesuitical works with materialistic science to maintain the dogma of a material universe created by God.

And the Roman Catholic dogma?

JL: The Jesuits are especially jealous of their monopoly on the areas of astronomy, underwater cartography, paleontology, archeology, etc. They oppose any spiritual revelation that could destroy the materialistic view of the universe. Do you know why? Because they intend to organize the solar system in a rational and technocratic way, to better implement bureaucratic control. In this we recognize the powerful will of the warrior genius of Mars that inspired Ignatius: to reduce the solar system in a theocratic form of socialism. [27]

Among the various investigations conducted over the years by the C.R.O.M. for their publications, what I consider the most interesting is the topic of the Damanhur community of northwestern Italy. This mysterious New Age community / Illuminati sect is officially presented as: *"a federation of spiritual Communities that created a reality based on solidarity, sharing, mutual love and respect for the environment."* [28]

Damanhur, which in recent years has attracted the attention of mainstream media, including the American network *ABC,* [29] is actually something very different from what the New Age propaganda would like you to believe. Damanhur means *City of Light* because it is dedicated to the god *Horus,* one of the central figures of Egyptian mythology, as well as Crowley's Thelema. From here you can easily understand the connection with Aleister Crowley, who announced himself as the prophet of the New Aeon of Horus. Damanhur is a community located in Valchiusella, north of Turin. The founder was the late Oberto Airaudi (1950-2013), who was known by the nickname "Falco" meaning *falcon,* because he wished to be connected to Horus, who was usually depicted as a falcon-headed man. In 1975, he began as a "spiritual" leader of a small esoteric circle in Turin called the **Horus center for parapsychological research.** In what eventually became his own center, he gave lectures and courses on telepathy, spiritualism, pranic breathing exercises, natural science, past lives, and hypnosis. In Airaudi's syncretism, there co-exists different elements picked up from different traditions, just like Aleister Crowley and other Illuminati New Age Guru's have practiced before him. He borrowed from the usual Theosophy, Eastern spirituality, and had a deep reverence to Aleister Crowley's "New Religion" of Thelema. The first center was joined by others in other cities, which were regarded as "embassies" of Damanhur. The 1970s were the ideal time for this project, which developed quickly into something much bigger. In 1977, Oberto Airaudi decided to found a community made up initially of a small group of people, but over the years the community exceeded 400 permanent members, to which thousands of visitors worked for free on this top secret project. In 1992, Airaudi began a new phase in the life of his community because of the problems created when a former member revealed to the Italian police authorities the existence of the "Temples of Humankind" near Vidracco, Italy. It's a series of Temples dug underground (with no building permit),

27   See. http://espresso.repubblica.it/opinioni/la-bustina-di-minerva/2008/01/11/news/una-bella-compagnia-1.6853 ‡ Archived 12th August, 2015.
28   See. http://www.nonapritequelportale.com/damanhur ‡ Filed August 13, 2015; Archived 12th August, 2015.
29   http://abcnews.go.com/GMA/popup? id = 4210038 ‡ Archived 12th August, 2015.

deep within a mountainside. Its construction lasted more than a decade in complete secrecy, and no one except the people of **Damanhur** suspected its existence. The mounain community of Valchiusella requested its immediate destruction after the discovery, but the residents of Damanhur managed to collect over one hundred thousand signatures in a short time (including those of many illustrious personalities and scholars), and were able to save their temples. It was declared a *"collective work of art"* by the *Fine Arts section* of the Piedmont region. [30]

The following is the now a rare report conducted by the now defunct French organization C.R.O.M. on Damanhur, now available in the English language, that reveals for the first time the possible links of Oberto Airaudi with the Jesuits, as well as his strange upbringing and occult links to Aleister Crowley. **C.R.O.M. on DAMANHUR:**

> *Among the New Age communities that are incorporated in Europe, that of Damanhur, based in Piedmont, is undoubtedly the most spectacular. First, because the members of this community do not occupy one and the same building, or even a single ecovillage, but an entire valley, Valchiusella, in the province of Turin, which is gradually being populated by "Damanhurians." Second, because they have dug numerous underground rooms that serve as both temples of unparalleled splendor, and workshops in which they seems to have developed, among other things, machines for time travel. The so-called "Temple of Humanity" was placed on the list of UNESCO World Heritage Sites. Within the C.R.O.M. we feed a certain distrust of the fables of the New Age, but we wanted to know more about the community of Damanhur so one of us went to the scene to conduct an investigation. His research eventualy led him to Holland where our suspicions were later confirmed. But let's see what he discovered.*

C.R.O.M.: *What was the starting point of your research?*

> *Before I went to Damanhur, I wanted to learn more about its founder Oberto Airaudi, alias Falco, especially if he was a leader able to drag his entourage of intelligent people or one of those pale figures—as there are many in New Age environments—that do not have the courage to impose a certain direction for fear of seeming "patriarchal." In this case I would not even have to move, because I knew from that kind of outset that I would find the usual New Age ideology and the same more or less anarchist organization that characterizes ecovillages worldwide.*

C.R.O.M.: *So was this the case?*

> *Absolutely not. Damanhur has proved a highly structured community, which after all is normal when you consider its size and its role in the New Age circles. In fact, it took a bit of time to find information about Falco's backround. It is mysterious, and inaccessible, as is closest associates do nothing but repeat the usual litany, and not to not annoy visitors that have anarchists tendencies who might be tempted to follow in his footsteps, they act as he never existed. Finally it is thanks to a report published in an American magazine [31] that I found relevant information, and even more than what I expected. I learned in fact that Oberto Airaudi was not an ordinary person. Already as a baby he was able to move objects with the power of thought. Later, he recalls having invoked the ghosts to "frighten his opponents in a game of football!" Finally, we know that at age 14 he organized experiments out of the body while giving courses in physics, mathematics and esoteric philosophy to an audience of a hundred people.*

---

30   http://www.damanhur.org/it ‡ Archived 12th August, 2015.
31   "Atlantis in the Mountains of Italy," published in the journal *"What is Enlightenment?"* (April to June 2007).

C.R.O.M.: A child really out of the ordinary?

I quickly realized that I was dealing with a great occultist, probably surrounded by entities, after seen all the miracles he has authored. It is possible that a baby is able to move objects with the power of thought, when not yet have the ability to think? We in the C.R.O.M. know that such an exploit can only be achieved with the help of disembodied entities, i.e. ghosts. [32] On the other hand, these entities are manifested only in case of necessity, since this requires them a great expenditure of energy. The young Oberto had to therefore be very useful to those entities, unless he has been sufficiently linked to them in the course of past lives in order to control the higher spheres of his being. In any case, these kind of feats can be accomplished only if the previous life had been devoted to an intense occult development. Not to mention the intellectual faculties that allowed a teenage Oberto Airaudi to impart courses on any subject: are also the result of an abnormal development. A life like many people only dream about; though this is not my case, I would say it rather arouses a certain revulsion in me. Only a super-ego can be capable of such miracles: an ego so "heavy" that is likely to remain anchored to the Earth during eons! But the Great Liberation does not fit the agenda of Oberto. Since his childhood he had visions— probably inspired by its occult controllers—which consisted of underground temples that he should build later in life. This idea had become an obsession and soon after he opened a center in Turin—his hometown, known for its heavy occult past, where he directed, so the story goes, 36 esoteric research groups, each pursuing a different project. One of his greatest victories, as he states in the aforementioned magazine, was that two of his Jesuit teachers left their place to study at his side. [33]

C.R.O.M.: So he studied at a Jesuit school?

It seems likely. But that does not mean much, because in the world there are a lot of schools runs by the Jesuits. What is extraordinary is the fact that two Jesuits teachers have followed him. In fact, the Jesuits are certainly not ordinary individuals: they are powerful beings who are interested only in projects that can advance their cause. However, the "spiritual exercises" of Ignatius of Loyola developed occult powers to the extreme, activating a close monitoring on those who indulge in them. There can therefore be no misunderstandings between these super ego's of the Jesuits or the one of the regimented Oberto, who has concluded a contract with the Jesuit egregore to help him do his work. In any case, there was convergence of interests between the two, this is evident.

C.R.O.M.: Because the Jesuits should support a project such as Damanhur?

It's true that some of our readers might be surprised that members of a religious order, whose initial vocation was to defend the Catholic Church, can support a New Age project—and therefore "pagan"—like that of Damanhur. These readers have a narrow view of what is really Catholicism, a view which is not that of the great occultists who are at the head of the Roman Church. The pope and his cardinals have a single goal: the survival and expansion of their egregore. To them, it matters little that the icon of choice to federate is that of Jesus or the Great Architect! [34]

---

32 *La corte dei miracoli: spiegazione dell'occulto,* (The court of miracles: the occult explanation), article published in the journal *"VITRIOL"* No. 19 (only available in French and Italian).

33 Original sentence written in the cited article is: "He knew he was on to something when he was able to convince two of his Jesuit teachers at school to quit in order to come study with him."

34 More and more prelates of the Catholic Church are becoming Masons. But we know that most of Freemasonry is itself under the control of the Jesuits, at least in the last 150 years.

Shortly before going to Damanhur, I made a brief visit to the Vatican. I had available a full day. First of all I was impressed with the power that emanates from those few hectares built. Anyone entering the Vatican acquires the certainty that the Catholic religion is still strong. But what surprised me most are the huge halls full of statues: Egyptian, Etruscan, Babylonian etc. I'm talking about the originals—not copies! There are so many that the visitor can not help but not see them, it makes you almost queasy. The ordinary visitor does not ask himself why in this place there are gathered so many art objects from religions that the official Catholic dogma considers idolatrous. Why, for example, within it's walls there are two museums on the Etruscans, when the Vatican already has so little space itself?

C.R.O.M.: Maybe because they are not museums?

Exactly! The term "museum" conceals the true purpose for the presence of all these statues, which really serve as a liaison with the hidden powers related to the ancient cults. Let me explain it to our readers. If Rome has acquired so much power in ancient times, it did it not only for its military strength, but also because it was able to absorb the magic power of its opponents. C.R.O.M. has already published an article about the Etruscans, and how Rome has somehow stolen their religion. [35]

When Rome conquered a population, they brought into the "Eternal City" statues and representations of the gods to which the vanquished people in question had worshipped. Rome told them: "You see, your gods have taken a place in our pantheon. Now they are our gods and we have assimilated them; you are therefore citizens of the Empire." It was a very strong magical act.

C.R.O.M.: But one day they destroyed all these statues, right?

Yes, when it came time to impose the Catholic "one God." To better control the consciousness of the masses, the leaders of Rome had to orient in one and the same direction all their prayers. By contrast, the elite continued to use these pagan statues to practice their magic, that's why we find these statues in the "museums" of the Vatican. In my opinion, the existence of all those Egyptian statues in the Vatican— as the Sphinx that stands in the middle of an ornamental garden—is proof that the Roman egregore groups occultists who were already dedicated to magic in ancient times. Why keep such objects inside the Vatican, except to maintain a link with the old cores? What we call "Rome" is nothing but a federation of retrograde Egregores that have joined forces to gain more strength.

C.R.O.M.: This makes us think of Aleister Crowley (1875-1947), the famous English occultist who, in England, had a political role much more important than people realize. Why he went to be initiated in Egypt, if not to bind to an egregore who he had already belonged to in previous incarnations? We know that England is the new Rome of the modern era.

Yes, exactly, and to return to Damanhur, the founder believed himself to be the reincarnation of the Egyptian god Horus, and the reason why he called himself Falco. Its first center in Turin was called the Horus Center, and Damanhur is the name of a legendary Egyptian city. Everything is so clearly linked at an occult level to Egypt, Rome, England and Damanhur. The same force currents pass through these centers, from which emanates an unbreathable air. In any case, I was right to visit the Vatican

35   *Roma, città edificata sulla paura,* (Rome, a city built on fear), published in the journal *"VITRIOL"* No. 20 (only available in French and Italian).

before going to Damanhur. In fact, when I finally got to the Temples of Humankind (open to the public), I was not surprised to find countless statues and representations of Egyptian gods, Etruscan gods, Babylonian ones, and others! Certainly these statues were less ornate than those at the Vatican, but their magical function is more apparent because, in the New Age universe that they operate, it is fashionable to initiate with any sort of "current." Actually, the Temples of Humankind are a kind of tomb, where Falco tried to lock up as many magical forces, whatever they are. Some underground rooms tell us of the evolution of humanity, others are a representation of the sky with the constellations, and some are chapels dedicated to time. Time here is the true deity of these forces trying to last as long as possible on Earth!

C.R.O.M.: Damanhur is however much more than just an underground temple. What is, in your opinion, the purpose of the community that lives around there?

Well, as its founder said, the purpose of Damanhur is to prepare for the future civilization of Aquarius. For Falco, it is clear that the present civilization will be destroyed, and considered that he was here to ensure the transition to the New Era.

In short, we can say that the forces representing Falco—because we understood, he does not act alone—are aware that, through the era of Aquarius, they risk losing everything they have gained so far. Especially since the Age of Aquarius is a time when the astral plane of the planet is cleared—those dimensions on which you have accumulated all the wrongly-oriented thoughts and emotions of humanity.

It is on the invisible planes surrounding Earth that disembodied occultists have established their kingdoms. But there are forces far superior to those magicians who are trying to dislodge them to purify the atmosphere of the planet. What are the forces for whom Falco was acting? At first they bury under the mountains, which is a very revealing sign. Then, in this bath of closed energy, they give birth to a new religion gradually, presented as the "religion of Aquarius," which however will be nothing but a synthesis of all the reactionary forces.

Catholicism was already a degenerated synthesis of all these more or less retrograde forces of the ancient era: the Etruscan religion, the mystery cults, Judaism. Originally Catholicism did not have much in common with Christianity! Today, with the New Age, things are moving at a higher speed by incorporating all the cultures in the interim findings from Rome: the Mayan, Aztec, Hindu and their marching retrograde entities. We find all this in the Temples of Humankind in Damanhur, which synthesized all that humanity has known. But a religion can not be born in an artificial way. Its development requires enlightened beings who participate and that, little by little, integrate the different energies. It is for this purpose, in my opinion, that they founded the community of Damanhur: we see a testing ground in which to test the future religion of the Age of Aquarius were sincere people act as unwitting guinea pigs for its development. Jesuits, in the sixteenth century, took control of several populations in South America to later traform them into "good Christians." To make a success of their experiments, they isolated some Indian villages from each other, then they forced the inhabitants to get up at six in the morning to the sound of bells and to work for them as they sang "Praise the Lord" from morning 'till night. This colossal enterprise of energy use, which lasted until 1768 and involving up to 140,000 guinea pigs, was conducted in what historians call "reductions," places where the Jesuits have managed to get the sedentary Indians in an urban area and in submission to their Church. So it was in this way that the Indians were subjected to civilian life and the Church.

C.R.O.M.: *Damanhur would then be a new form of Jesuit "reduction"?*

Absolutely. You might believe that Damanhurians are more aware and freer than they Indians were, but they are completely dominated. Falco himself received its directives from a sort of "energy ball" that indicated to him what to do. And all his followers followed its directives with a passion, convinced that they came from higher evolved beings. Mysticism mixed with the fear that characterized the old reductions disappeared, but there is one thing: the deification of the afterlife.

In Damanhur, we look at the reality of what we at C.R.O.M. call the "cult of the occult." Everyone has an interest in the occult and the only way to move up the hierarchy of the organization is to perfect yourself in astral travel. Those who are not able to leave one's body do not stay long in the community. But no problem: the "university" of Damanhur offers numerous courses in which everyone can learn this practice, which is clearly perceived as an immense spiritual progress. In fact, this practice opens students to invisible forces that we talked about, which may well keep them under control and use them better. Already today, some agents trained in the Damanhur ecovillage pass from one to another bringing the good word of "World Unity," of "Universal Love" and of "Astral Travel." The leaders of Damanhur are heading the **Global Ecovillage Network (G.E.N.)**, a sort of world federation of alternative communities, spiritual or not. Those who know the history of Rome and the network of alliances it has forged to have influence over the nations, can not see anything but their imperialist aims to ensure that all communities in the world follow the same line and that they make no attempt to get in dissent with the prevailing ideology of the New Age. Only a few hundred people reside permanently in Damanhur, but this community has thousands of followers worldwide. It's hard to imagine the scale, but this should not be overlooked when considering the ideological weakness of most ecovillages, compared the incrollabile certainty that inhabits the followers of Falco. We met them at New Age meetings in France: the public is almost completely conquered and sees in them models to follow.

C.R.O.M.: *What do you think of their magical technology, in particular the supposed machines to travel in time they promote so much? Is it a scam?*

Actually, they do not travel in time, they explore just what esotericists call the Akashic records, which contain all the memory of the planet. In fact, their names for their wacky technologies are intended primarily to focus astral energy. In various underground temples there are, for example, machines whose function is to recover the energy generated by the feeling of admiration of the visitors. As these technologies have been designed by occultists, I believe that actually they produce results. When a person uses the machine to travel in time (for the few initiates that are allowed to partecipate), around them are musicians that procure energy, allowing them to make a longer and more intense astral journey. The experience of Damanhur remains interesting because, their vision of scientific magic, foreshadows what will be the Age of Aquarius. This we can not deplore. Instead, what we deplore is the energy used: it is always and even astral energy correlated with old retrograde Egregores. The machines and the temples of Damanhur only serve to put the person in connection with these Egregores, participating in a vampirization process. Remember, the astral energy is limited, so it needs to be taken away from other beings. The same criticism applies to the thesis of the "synchronic lines" developed by Falco. Let me explain: thanks to his clairvoyance, Falco knew where the astral currents passed, and was able to establish a kind of occult map of the Earth.

He knew that Tibet is the place where the most amount of Synchronic Lines pass, and this is not surprising at all for those who know already about the intense activity of the Himalayan leading magicians. Falco also found that the Synchronic Lines converging in Valchiusella where he based his project, were powerful, which is why he established its Temples there that he said "communicate with the whole world." In fact, his occult map shows only the places where they are located and circulating the "waste of the astral plane" of the Earth. This map looks pretty on the ground of a sewage system, but is of no interest to people who wish to benefit from the new radiation of Aquarius.

C.R.O.M.: What should these people do?

First, you should make a clean break with all these retrograde forces. Why, for example, refer to the Mayan calendar? The Maya civilization belongs to the past, as well as all the practices that put the person in connection with the old Egregores, no matter how venerable. As I said earlier, with Falco's scientific worldview of the astral plane, Damanhur indicates nevertheless a certain way. Mysticism is much more commonplace. But, instead of using this astral energy in such a full way, we should rather try to better understand the nature of what the ancients called "ether," the pure energy that is abundant in the universe. However, being foreign to the system of the self-centered human, this energy can be collected and concentrated only by those who have a real inner-transformation. This is what's at stake in our time.

C.R.O.M.: Thank you, we agree. But before concluding, it seems that you still have not told us what you found in the Netherlands.

Oh yeah, it's as simple as it is spectacular. On the train that brought me back to France, next to me was a group of Belgians who spoke of a wonderful underground gallery that they had visited near Maastricht, with statues of Buddha, Shiva, of Ramses II and of the Christ, a winged bull, Javanese idols, etc.—a total of over 500 statues and paintings. There was even a room that completely reproduced the Alhambra, with fountains, basins and Koranic verses.

My interest was at its peak at this point: was there another Damanhur? Imagine my surprise when I heard that this place is called "Mount of the Jesuits" (Jezuitenberg in Dutch): [36] it was built by students of a seminary located in the immediate vicinity, and is therefore the future work of the Jesuits! It seems that this gallery, which is a veritable temple (several chapels with Arab, Egyptian rooms, etc.) Was built gradually from these Jesuit students during their free time, on Wednesday afternoons? Pupils add to it frequently, because this work—which I later went to visit—extends over almost a century (from 1860 to 1960, approximately), and this in a cave where the temperature never exceeds 10° C! This story, you will agree, is highly improbable. We can certainly brand the Jesuits who tried to hide the site, as unacceptable.

For my part I am convinced that this place—now abandoned—has been a laboratory for reduction, as is today Damanhur. One final observation: the last Jezuitenberg statue was carved in 1968, while the construction of Damanhur started in 1977. There was therefore a continuity between the two projects, the first of which was only a preliminary experiment (and less successful) operated in a safe environment? Or are there other similar underground "temples" built by the Jesuits that remained secret? The mystery remains, but the Jesuit trail is confirmed. [37]

---

36 www.jezuietenberg.nl ✝ Archived 13th August, 2015.
37 End of the article original featured in *Le origini occulte di Damanhur*, (The Occult Origins of Dam-

To know more about *Jezuitenberg*, (FIG. 75) here is a quick article I did for *Infowars.com:*

It is called, "One of the world's best-preserved marlstone quarries." The Jezuitenberg (Jesuit Caves) is located on the outskirts of the city of Maastricht, close to the Belgian border.

The Jesuits constructed this astonishing place between 1860 and 1960, and it has nothing to do with Christianity, and all to do with paganism and the Babylonian mystery schools. Apparently Jesuit scholars and theological students spent a

FIG. 75 – A picture of a Lamassu present in the Jesuit caves of *Jezuietenberg*, related to various deities of Mesopotamian civilizations (Assyrian in particular). They are considered beneficial and protective spirits, and for that they were placed at the entrance to the corridors of power.

great deal of their leisure time every Wednesday afternoon working on this project. So the question arises, for what purpose?

Their website describes, "many interesting studies and publications which were produced. There is a full scale floor plan of the quarry's gallery network, and moreover, they created numerous charcoal and colored drawings on the cave's walls." Such drawing strongly remind us of Islamic, and not Catholic art.

It is also stated on their website, "a large number of reliefs and statues were carved on and from the marlstone walls. Winged bulls, the Alhambra (including a fountain and a pond), Christ, Buddha, and the head of Ramses II." There are many other fascinating objects found in the interior of the subterranean galleries that expose once and for all the Jesuit Order and their link to neopaganism and the New Age. When in 1968 the Jesuit Order left Maastricht, supervision and maintenance of these caves became the responsibility of the Jezuïetenberg Foundation. [38]

A revelatory video on Jezuitenberg was filmed at the beginning of 2015, by Harrie Kerckhoffs. [39]

The investigation on Damanhur, made by French C.R.O.M. reveals *Jezuitenberg*, another Jesuit secret. where scret ancient rituals known as *The arcana arcanorum rite of Atlantis* are said to take place. The Latin motto of the Society of Jesus, the classic: *Ad maiorem Dei gloriam* (For the greater glory of God), takes on a new meaning as the Jesuits and the Illuminati network are in reality pagan, not Christian, and this includes Pope Francis, the first *Jesuit* Pope.

anhur) present in La *Piste Jésuite* (*The Jesuit Trail* by the **Centre de Recherches sur l'Ordre Mondial** (C.R.O.M.), (Arrens- Marsous, France:2009), pp. 90-95.
38 http://www.infowars.com/the-jezuitenberg-jesuit-caves/ ‡ Archived 15th August, 2015.
39 https://www.youtube.com/watch?v=mWq-0j0opiw ‡ Archived 15th August, 2015.

The *Pope Grimoire* I mentioned on Project Camelot

Ionce mentioned the existence of a mysterious "Papal Grimoire" in an interview over ten years ago. [40] The aforementioned Illuminati, Sebastiano Fusco, known by his initiatic name **Jorg Sabellicus,** in his capacity of initiate of the highest mysteries of the dark side of the Illuminati, explained that among the various books and Grimoires on the subject, the *Grimorium,* attributed to a "pope" (in some editions listed as "the Great"), has over time acquired the reputation as the most "evil" of all Grimoires. This is not only for describing a ritual, which is particularly gruesome, with reference to the blood sacrifices required, but especially because, unlike similar texts, it does not refer only to the cabalistic magic of Jewish extraction. It has strong Christian influences, which ecclesiastical authorities regard as particularly blasphemous. According to the heading, the book is merely a Papal Bull, issued by Pope Honorius III, to extend to all the "*Servants of the Church*," the power to summon and command demons. The Successor of Innocent III, Pope Honorius III, reigned from 1216 to 1227. Among the many, he was consumed with demons. [41] Will Durant states that: "*He was too good to continue with the energy struggle between Empire and Papacy.*" Most likely, as some authors believe, those who actually wrote the Grimoire in question meant the Antipope Honorius II, instead. [42] This is the opinion of Eliphas Levi in his *The History of Magic.* [43] Confirming this kind of power given to the Petrine Ministry, we find a specific passage in the New Testament:

> "*And I tell you that you are Peter, and on this rock I will build my church, and the gates of Hades will not overcome it. 19 I will give you the keys of the kingdom of heaven; whatever you bind on earth will bebound in heaven, and whatever you loose on earth will be loosed in heaven." 20 Then he ordered his disciples not to tell anyone that he was the Messiah.*"

This quote tells of the authority entrusted to the Petrine Ministry on paradise as well as hell, and it lends itself to a heretical interpretation, as it seems to echo gnostic heterodoxy, according to which, while God reigns in heaven, the Devil, his opponent, rules this world. Therefore having the authority to "bind and let loose," meaning being able to summon and dismiss demons on earth, which is a practice that often takes place in "irregular" lodges of occult Freemasonry, and the sectarian network of the Illuminati. Keep in mind the question: "Whether it is permissible to ward off demons," a practice that was addressed by Saint Thomas Aquinas in "**Summa Theologica**," and deemed *negative.*

Aquinas, considered the supreme doctor of the Catholic Church (who quotes from St. Paul, Origen, St. Augustine, St. James and St. John Chrysostom), condemns the evocation of demons according to the powers given by the Savior, as is found in Jewish tradition, and Christians are not permitted to imitate the rites of the Jews, "but rather use the powers granted to Christ."Aquinas states that it is lawful to chase away the demonic enemies, threatening them by virtue of the name of God so we are not harmed, both spiritually and physically; but casting them out or invoking is not lawful, because that would involve communication with them. Reaffirming the condemnation of the "**sorcerers who practice incantations and invocations of demons.**" St. Thomas Aquinas concludes by quoting a saying of Chrysostom, "*a healthy norm not to believe in demons, even as they proclaim the truth.*" *Much more serious is therefore using blasphemous*

40   See. http://projectcamelot.org/leo_zagami.html ‡ Archived 13th August, 2015.
41   See. Jorg Sabelicus, *Il Grimorio di Papa Onorio,* (Rome: Hermes Editions,1984).
42   See. Will Durant, *Storia della Civiltà, vol. IV,* (Milan: Mondadori, 1958-1968), p. 852.
43   See. Lewis Spence, *Encyclopaedia of Occultism,* (Mineola, New York : Dover publications, 2003), p. 231;
Ribadeau F. Dumas, *Storia della Magia,* (Rome: Edizioni Mediterranee, 1968), pp. 260-261.

text, which not only describes in detail the procedures required to activate the forbidden trade with evil entities, but attributes these teachings even to a pope, moved from "pastoral care!" The character that originated this Grimoire like previous ones, especially those attributed to Solomon, stressed a particular conception of the Devil that reflected in its text. In high level traditional magic such as in the Old Testament, the Devil is not considered in the Christian sense, the rebel angel who proudly defied God's power being cast out of heaven, and now, leads man to *sin and perdition*. Spirits that the magician conjures in his magical circle are in fact personifications of magical forces, consubstantial to the Universe, which are not divided into several kingdoms, but are conceived of as one. For Lewis Spence, their evil connotation comes from subsequent Christian interpretations of magical operations, and he saw this, erroneously, as "evil."

Sebastiano Fusco "Sabelllicus," states that: *"Magical Forces, are neither good nor bad: like all forces, and possess opposite polarities, and any ethical judgment which may affect them depends solely on the will of the magician and the purposes for which they are evoked."* Conversely, entities evoked through the steps of **"Pope Honorius"**(especially the *"demons of the days of the week"),* seem to reproduce the characteristics of the rebel angels of "Christian dogma"; which lends the makes the Grimoire even more *dark and disturbing.* In its structure, the ritual and the grimoire attributed to Pope Honorius, does not differ to more traditional Grimoires. In part, the difference lies in the Christian character of the invocations, and other features, such as the celebration of the Mass. That's why Sabellicus states that the author could be a priest, which takes up back to the Vatican. Sabelllicus believes that the author of this mysterious Grimoire, was an ordained priest, and that the book was written specifically for other religious ministers with the aim of transforming Christian ceremonies to strict Jewish Kabbalistic black *magic rituals.* [44]

It is not a coincidence that the arrival of this book coincides with the first period of expansion of the Society of Jesus, an order founded almost 500 years ago in 1534. Some researchers believe that the author of the alleged Pope's Grimoire might also be a *magician* who lived in the second half of the sixteenth century. [45] I would like to remind you that the previously mentioned thesis of its author being a priest fits the Jesuit profile, as the Company of Jesus were considered among the most powerful magis of the period. Ribadeau François Dumas writes about the founder of the Jesuits:

> As the exalted **Alumbrados (translated: Illuminati)**, Loyola went in the Benedictine monastery of Montserrat in March 1522, dedicating himself to penance, flagellation, fasting, deprivation for ten months, while constantly hallucinating. Here, there was the appearance of an evil snake that darted on his fiery eyes. Withdrawing into his cave of Manresa, he carved the way for the rise of the great initiates, and tells them about the diabolical apparitions. His "Big Picture" of August, 1522 transformed him, made him know about the invisible powers of hell. So educate yourself, he went to the University of Alcala de Henares, founded by Cardinal Ximenes. He lived in a ruined house, where no one wanted to live, in Antezena. He was invincibly attracted by the occult. [46]

The Grimoire of Pope Honorius was published in Latin for the first time in **Rome** in **1629**, with the title of *Grimorium Honorii Magni.* (FIG. 76) There are several copies located in various European libraries, and yet if you were caught with a copy you

44   Jorg Sabellicus, *Ibid.*
45   See. http://www.parodos.it/quadrettimagia.htm ‡ Archived 13th August, 2015.
46   François Dumas, *Dossier Segreti Di Stregoneria e Di Magia Nera,* (Rome: Edizioni Mediterranee, 2005), p. 260.

would certainly wind up in the hands of the infamous Inquisition. My opinion on the possibilities at the end of my research on its authorship are in fact two. This truly diabolical Grimoire might really have been written by a Pope or one of his close assistants, as the Vatican regularly celebrates Satanic rituals to this day, or by a *Jesuit*. Of course I am also open to other possibilities, and invite historians and researchers to investigate this matter further. However one thing is for sure, the Jesuits are

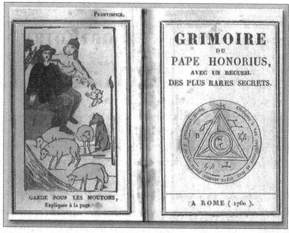

FIG. 76 – *The Grimoire of Pope Honorius,* French edition printed *(according to the cover) in Rome in 1760.*

undermining the Church since its founding, and in view of this, we find the constant expansion of relativism/Satanism, which have been supreme proponents for centuries. For this reason I think the Jesuits may very well be the authors of this mysterious Grimoire. Today, a great silence mysteriously envelopes Satan in the Catholic Church, as the Church seems scared to use this concept any longer. [47] They want us to believe that the devil doesn't exist, and evil is only a product of mankind.

So what is the message of the *"New Era?"* French writer, J.K. Huysmans states: *"Magic is no longer a crime, and sacrilege is casted out of the Church codes."* A Dominican Theologian Father Boismard recently stated that the *"reality of the Devil, must be questioned."*

Father Boismard, states the new idea that: *"It is inside the errors of man, that Satan has his origin."* [48] A phrase that seems very far from the original precepts of the Dominican order, linked to views of St. Thomas Aquinas, but closer to the usual *relativism* promoted by the Jesuits. Another Dominican, Father Christian Duquoc, commented on what he called *"incredible news"*—the death of Satan—when he writes:

> *Evil is not outside the human society, it comes entirely from man. Satan would be the means to escape the guilt. It takes on all responsibility that humanity refuses to take collectively. It is the image that reassures me on the non-perversity of my freedom.* [49]

This statement, published at the end of the 1960s in a Dominican publication, demonstrates that the Dominican order may have been irremediably compromised by the Jesuits and relativism. Satanism and the Jesuits always go hand in hand, and now they have maximum influence with their own Pope. The mysterious Grimoire of Pope Honorius, teaches how to evoke with a magic ritual. How to evoke dangerous entities, that according to Henry Cornelius Agrippa, author of *Occult Philosophy,* are: *"dark demons, which offend and practice voluntarily evil."* The dark side of the Illuminati asks for only *material advantages,* that being hidden knowledge, wealth, and POWER. This is what

47   *Ibid.,* p. 337.
48   *Ibid.,* p. 335.
49   Dominican Magazine, "Light and Life" No. 78, May 1968.

the devotees of black magic inside such sects wish to obtain in the end.

They would like us to believe that Satan and his legions no longer exist, so obviously they can continue to act undisturbed conducting Satanic rituals and promoting Satanic causes. Abortion, for example, is allowed so that we can utilize commercially, or otherwise, the aborted fetuses. Also promoted is gay marriage, which marks the end of the traditional family. Or out of control immigration, which is used to destroy the ethnicity of an entire population. On top of all this, they feed us eat genetically modified food to destroy our health, and thus facilitate the pharmaceutical companies. They promote wars without end, to sell weapons, and unfortunately, the list could go on for many pages. The Jesuit Andre Lefevre, SJ, stated that: *"It's hard to believe Christ the Redeemer, without at the same time believing in his opponent the Devil."* [50]

The Grimoire attributed to a heretic pope, and most presumably produced by the Jesuits, remains an interesting subject, also because of its current use by many of the leading Satanic sects, even inside the Vatican. All this goes well beyond the imagination of the aforementioned disinformation artist Leo Taxil. Gabriele Amorth, considered in recent years the number one exorcist of the Vatican, in one of his latest books, in which he was interviewed by Marco Tosatti, called *Memoirs of an Exorcist*, dedicated an entire chapter to **"Satanists in the Vatican,"** where I found this key revelatory passage that confirms in my opinion, Satanic practices in the Vatican:

> **Tosatti** : *Previously, Don Gabriel, you told me that some sects are less serious, while others are a lot more terrible.*
>
> **Amorth:** *Certainly, some are terribly serious. And unfortunately they are everywhere, even in the Vatican. Yes, even in the Vatican there are members of Satanic sects.*
>
> **T.:** *Who is involved? Is it simple priests or laity?*
>
> **A.:** *There are priests, monsignors and also cardinals!*
>
> **T.:** *Forgive me, Father Gabriele, but how do you know?*
>
> **A.:** *I know from people that have been able to report it because they had a way of knowing it directly. And it's "confessed" several times by the devil himself, under obedience during the exorcisms.* [51]

The secrets of Satanism in the Vatican will be a major theme of my upcoming third volume in the *Confessions* series.

Benjamin Fulford – between reality and misinformation

In recent years, many readers have asked me to clarify my role in the bonds affair, associated with the well-known Canadian journalist, Benjamin Fulford. He is a controversial figure with who I co-wrote and published two books in Japan, in 2009 and 2010. He is a strange eccentric character, who has fascinated many around the world with his particular brand of disinfo. Benjamin Fulford is one of the few Westerners in the world, initiated in the elusive and mysterious world of so-called "Chinese Freemasonry," known also as Hong Men. In addition to this, he has ties to Japanese secret societies, and he is linked to members of the U.S. Intelligence community, and even managing to interview,

50 See. André Lefèvre, *Etudes Carmélitaines Satan,* (Paris: Desclée De Brouwer. 1948).
51 See. Gabriele Amorth interviewed by Marco Tosatti, *Memorie di un esorcista. La mia vita in lotta contro Satana,* (Milan: Piemme editions, 2011).

due to his contacts, the unreachable and untouchable David Rockefeller Sr. [52] Yet if you read his blog, or if you listen to his many interviews on YouTube, he presents himself to the world as an enemy of the powerful, a hero of the underdog, full of fantastic tales of imminent arrest and great changes, that regularly never happen—as it's all part of a big disinfo game. So let's understand more about **Benjamin Fulford** and who is really behind him. This was something I came to realize, as initially he seemed like an honest person.

In the 1970s, George H.W. Bush was a member of the Illuminati with dual membership (*Skull & Bones / Bohemian Club*), and a high-ranking Freemason in the Ancient and Accepted Scottish Rite. **George H.W. Bush** is known in the Skull and Bones as "Magog," and he would become a leading player in a diplomatic mission to China that would further prepare the world for the New World Order. Some Bonesmen receive traditional names, denoting function or existential status; others are the chosen beneficiaries of names that their Bones predecessors wish to pass on. The leftover initiates choose their own names. The name Long Devil is assigned to the tallest member, and the name Boaz (short for Beelzebub), goes to any member who is a varsity football captain. Many of the chosen names are drawn from literature (Hamlet, Uncle Remus), from religion, and from myth. The banker Lewis Lapham passed on his name, Sancho Panza, to the political adviser Tex McCrary. Averell Harriman was Thor, Henry Luce was Baal, McGeorge Bundy was Odin. The name Magog is traditionally assigned to the incoming Bonesman deemed to have had the most sexual experience, and Gog goes to the new member with the least sexual experience.

William Howard Taft and Robert Taft were Magogs. So, interestingly, was George Bush. [53] This particular mission to China was inspired by the U.S. Illuminati, to establish a firm and definitive covenant between the main parties involved in the New World Order. The Jesuits, however, have had a central role in China's evolution for a long time, having being the first to go there, planting the seeds of future globalism at the time of their earliest Jesuit missions to Asia in the sixteenth and seventeenth century. In the nineteenth century the drug trade arrived, and the opium trade in particular made the ruling elite even more wealthy. English Freemason Henry John Temple, Prime Minister and Foreign Minister of Queen Victoria, also known as **Lord Palmerston**, sanctioned the first strategic alliances between the West and Chinese Freemasonry, functional for the opium trade. The U.S. joined, and years later Freemason and U.S. President **Franklin Delano Roosevelt** declared that opium was like liquor, to be considered a family business, because his grandfather used to work for *Russell & Company* of Samuel Russell, whose cousin was **William Huntington Russell**, founder of the **Skull & Bones**, a branch of the Illuminati network that as we know, formed the core of the American Intelligence establishment since its foundation.

The association between Skull & Bones and the American Intelligence agencies, from the OSS to the CIA, is well-established, with a litany of agents, directors, and of course Director of Central Intelligence, George "Poppy" Bush himself, having been a Bonesmen before being recruited for the agency. But the connection between the CIA and the international drug trade is not simply a historical one that has to do with 19th century opium traders. Just as the British empire was in part financed by the control of the opium trade through the British East India Company, so too has the CIA been found time after time to be at the heart of the modern international drug trade. From its very inception, the CIA

52   https://www.youtube.com/watch?v=b24ZuNyAckw ‡ Archived 14th August, 2015.
53   http://www.theatlantic.com/magazine/archive/2000/05/george-w-knight-of-eulogia/304686/ ‡ Archived 14th August, 2015.

has been embroiled in the murky underworld of drug trafficking. [54] All of this made initially possible by the secret ties to English Freemasonry and "the Order, " as they call the Skull & Bones, with Chinese Freemasonry and organized crime called "Triads." Since 1856, "the Order" as members call the Skull & Bones, is chaired by the **Russell Trust Association.**

In 1974, Gerald Ford could only nominate Bush as chief diplomat to the People's Republic of China (back then the United States didn't have an embassy in Beijing). In just fourteen months, Bush closed many great deals for the expansion of the New World Order and their new partnership with China.

The results were considered so positive from a strategic perspective for the Sino-American relations, that in early 1976, Gerald Ford, recalled Bush to Washington DC as a reward, nominating him director of the CIA, and making the Bush family more influential than ever. No wonder then that we see the direct involvement of Benjamin Fulford with a CIA agent like **Neil Keenan,** in the transaction of the infamous bonds linked to the mysterious **Dragon Family.** These bonds reached the public eye after an operation conducted by the Financial Guard in Italy saw two Japanese arrested in Chiasso, on the border with Switzerland, in the first days of June 2009, [55] in a story now well-known in "Intelligence" circles worldwide. This event related to the first confiscation of billions of dollars in bonds of dubious origin, that some said involved the aforementioned Neil Keenan. In my investigation I discovered, this was never a real family, as some may have believed from Fulford's usual tales, but actually a financial emanation of Chinese Freemasonry (the Hongmen Society) and the "Triads," that writer Martin Booth describes in his book *The Dragon Syndicates.* [56] The Hongmen, only a decade ago, began what is now slowly becoming a new trend, which is recruiting "non-Chinese" elements like Benjamin Fulford, someone they could use in the information warfare of the New World Order. Benjamin was a well-known journalist of international reputation, linked to the prestigious "Forbes" magazine, where he played an important role in the Asian bureau, but suddenly changed his career and became a conspiracy theory author, where he sincerely had little or no experience in the field of secret societies, and for this reason became totally manipulated by them. Fulford irresponsibly accepted this occult manipulation, to be enable him to enter **The Chinese Freemasons** (the Hongmen Society), ignoring the implications and danger that would stop any other Western journalist. Benjamin Fulford was intiated with a ritual which appears in a very rare book from 1866 written by Gustav Schlegel, [57] that actually shows a close relationship between traditional Western Speculative Freemasonry and the Chinese Freemasons of the Hongmen Society. (FIG. 77) When I asked Benjamin what he remembered most about his initiation he said, *"Leo, the character that struck me most during the ceremony was the Master of Ceremonies, known as the Incense Master."* (FIG. 78) Then he said that he had also noticed the altar of the Temple. (FIGS. 79a-79b)

Of course, the similarities between the initiation in this Masonic Chinese secret society and other forms of Speculative Freemasonry in use here in the West are many, and in the nineteenth century one of the best-known researchers in the Masonic field at that time, Dr. Jos Schauberg (1808) from Zurich, after discovering in a newspaper in 1857 called the *"Munchener gelehrten Anzeigen,"* [58] the existence of this Chinese Masonic re-

---

54   https://www.corbettreport.com/the-cia-and-the-drug-trade-eyeopener-preview/ ‡ Archived 14th August, 2015.
55   http://www.ilmessaggero.it/PRIMOPIANO/ESTERI/due_giapponesi_fermati_alla_dogana_di_chiasso_nella_valigia_96_miliardi/notizie/60867.shtml ‡ Archived 13th August, 2015.
56   *Op. cit.*
57   Gustav Schlegel, *Earth League, a secret society with the Chinese in China and India,* (Batavia-Jakarta: Lange & Co., 1866).
58   Nach den Munchener gelehrten Anzeigen fir, 1857, No. 17.

ality, dedicated his remaining years to researching it.[59] The last decent work produced that cited the subject of Chinese Freemasonry in relation to Western Freemasonry, was *The Great Triad* of René Guenon, that was published in 1946. Are researchers scared to talked about the secrets of "Chinese Illuminati?"

In the West, there are few people who know that members of the Triads and Chinese Freemasonry worship a deity in particular, named **Kwan Ti or Kuan Ti,** who is said to reside in the **Man Mo Temple in Hong Kong.** (FIG. 80) A dark-skinned deity, similar to the classic Black Madonna, but more menacing in appearance—almost Kali style. It is a male deity that originates from a real character who with time has taken on divine connotations, becoming one of the most revered Gods in China. Kuan Yu, is his original surname, and became then Kuan Ti (*Ti*, in Chinese, is the equivalent of God or Emperor) who was called "the patron of Buddhism," but for Taoists

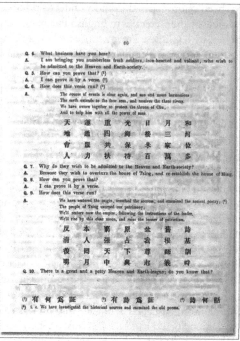

FIG. 77 – Gustav Schlegel, A secret society with the Chinese in China and India, 1866, page 60, describes the first steps of the initiation into Chinese Freemasonry.

and others he is the god of war (just like Mars, one of the gods worshipped by the Western Iluminati), therefore this obscure deity has a double aspect and a double value.

Returning to the well-known agent of disinformation at the service of Chinese Freemasonry, Benjamin Fulford, after his initiation he transformed himself into the gatekeeper of Chinese Freemasonry. He worked at spreading disinformation through psychological operations via the Internet, to cover up real operations related to financial assets of dubious origin and other illegal activities that include racketeering, gambling, drugs, weapon smuggling and more. Benjamin Fulford announces weekly the most unlikely apocalyptic flavor combinations, including the end of the Federal Reserve, the imminent arrest of Bankers, and he fights against what he calls "The Cabal" of the Nazis who leads the New World Order in a never ending virtual battle.

Wake up, my friends, not everything that glitters is gold on the web that is for sure, and the insane show set up by Fulford and his partners in the media, which included at one point a series of interviews with the renowned American researcher **David Wilcock**, was just a pathetic display of pure dinformation. I still remember when poor Wilcock got carried away with Fulford's rubbish and he even began to cry live on the radio like a little girl. This happened when they were both spoke of confiscated bonds in Chiasso and supposed threats to their lives. This was a complete farce manipulated by the CIA, the N.S.A. and influential figures such as General **Keith B. Alexander,** one of the supreme guides

59   See. Dr. Jos. Schauberg, **Symbolik der Freimaurerei,** (Zurich, Theil I. S. 178, 1861).

FIG. 78 – Image provided by the Hong Kong police and wrongly described in the book The Dragon Syndicates: The Global Phenomenon of the Triads by Martin Booth is that of a "Master of Incense" of a Triad lodge. It is however, by a more detailed investigation conducted by the author of this book, a rare image of a **Shan Chu** or "**Master of the Mountain**"—the equivalent in Chinese Freemasonry to a **Worshipful Master** of Western Freemasonry. Note the position of the hand and fingers, and the straw sandal on his left foot.

of the N.S.A. for many years, at the time commander of the U.S. Cyber Command department (**USCYBERCOM**).[60] It is the Security/Intelligence center that controls the Internet in all its facets, and is the most powerful control center in the world. Allegedly working for both Gen. Alexander and Chinese Freemasonry we find CIA agent Neil Keenan.

Neil Keenan is a key figure in this story who approached me with the following email after my return from Japan in 2009:

Neil Keenan <ncainc50@xxx.xxx>

08/27/09 at 12:24 PM

Dear Mr. Zagami,

I received a message from Mr. Fulford relating to the incident with the Dragon Family and the Italian Customs in Chiasso in which he has advised me to contact you. I represent the DF sir and have heard different things relating to the incident including the bonds are no longer in Italy, but in other hands. I guess this would include the 8 telephones that were confiscated.

As you are aware, any bonds/notes being transported without verification and or signature have no value, therefore, why were they detained? Why has there been a fine imposed for 39 Billion? I can figure most out easily enough but my main question is do you know how to make this go away? The 39 Billion is not important at this time.

It is my understanding (this morning) that Mr. Yamaguchi (Controller/Signature of the DF) and Mr. Watanabee will be returning to Italy shortly to deal with this. Is there anyway to make this easy without the world getting knowledge of the U.S., Italian, Japanese, English debt to said DF group. It is not in anyone's best interest to have such information released as you know, and if we can handle it discreetly then it is in our best interests to move on to other more important things with a brand new friendship.

I await your response not knowing what to expect, but most of all if anything it is my pleasure to make you acquaintance even over the internet. Take care and have a great day.

Neil Keenan

However, after I introduced my close friend and financial adviser Daniele Dal Bosco to Neil Keenan, things turned out in a very different way from what was originally planned, as Dal Bosco soon noticed many flaws in the supposed ownership of these bonds by the

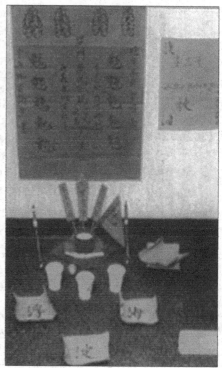

FIG. 79 a, b – Altars of traditional Chinese Triads. (From the archives of the Hong Kong. police)

so-called "Dragon Family." Dal Bosco was entrusted with the remainder of these bonds by Neil Keenan, and was at that point asked for the immediate intervention of Interpol and the U.N. financial authorities in Switzerland to clear up the matter. The events that took place in those turbulent days in 2009, became the source of much disinformation and unfounded speculations and accusations by Keenan and Fulford against, among others, my friend Dal Bosco and even myself.

On Keenan's website, his collaborator Michael Henry Dunn wrote on June 8, 2013:

> *The emergence of Neil Keenan at the cutting edge of these events can be traced to the theft in 2009 by Vatican financial insider Daniele Dal Bosco of $144.5 billion in Federal Reserve notes which were entrusted to Mr. Keenan by the Dragon Family, the group of ancient wealthy clans in Asia who are the legitimate owners of vast amounts of gold in the off-ledger Global Accounts. The Dragon Family has been attempting for decades to utilize the Accounts for their originally intended purpose, and sought out Keenan's help because of his reputation as a well-connected, tough-minded international businessman. The story of this theft, and of Mr. Keenan's filing of a trillion-dollar lawsuit against elite figures and institutions (including the United Nations, the World Economic Forum, The World Bank, the Italian government, the Italian Financial Police, Silvio Berlusconi, and others) was first revealed by Benjamin Fulford, former Forbes Magazine financial editor for Asia, who traveled to Italy to conduct initial investigations, where an attempt was made on his life. The story was then taken up by best-selling author David Wilcock (who then also received death threats), confirming the story in an investigative article on his*

FIG. 80 – The god of the Triads, Kwan Ti, or Kuan Ti, and its representation revered in the Man Mo Temple in Hong Kong, said to be the spiritual center of Chinese Freemasonry. Photo from the book of Martin Booth, The Dragon Syndicates.

influential blog. The 110-page lawsuit, first filed in New York federal court, can be viewed at this link.

In addition to his lawsuit (which he subsequently withdrew in order to re-file in a more effective jurisdiction), Keenan also filed a Cease and Desist order on behalf of the Dragon Family against a Who's Who of the cabal power structure, putting them on notice that they were defrauding the Global Accounts, and would be prosecuted for any further fraud. This Cease and Desist names George Herbert Walker Bush, George W Bush, Queen Elizabeth II, the United Nations, Ban Ki Moon, David Rockefeller, Hillary Clinton, and a host of other world figures and organizations who are in the inner circle of the cabal. The bonds which were stolen from Mr. Keenan were Federal Reserve notes given to the Dragon Family in payment for the gold deposited in the Accounts—notes which the Federal Reserve continually blocked from utilization. Mr. Keenan's lawsuit represents the first formidable attempt to defeat this theft. [61]

In reality, Neil Keenan is a loose cannon of both the NSA and Chinese Freemasonry, simply a professional disinfo artist. Just like his colleague Benjamin Fulford and people like David Wilcock, who introduced Keenan with the aid of Fulford, to a large audience until *The Event Chronicle* finally exposed them all. [62] However, at the time a series of actions were indeed taken by Dal Bosco to prevent any fraudulent use of such bonds in the future, but Keenan became immediately upset, and sent me this email:

Dear Mr. Zagami,

I have forwarded this to you for one reason and one reason only, you told Mr. Fulford that he is being fed misinformation. Please read and you will see Daniele is feeding you lies and you like me refuse to believe it is happening. It is a shame but true. If you do not wish to read the correspondence to the NSA then I suggest you read just Daniele's statement to Benjamin. In it he substantiates I do not have authorization for the bonds any longer (he looked through an old package of documents and found an old authorization). Why would he even mention this if he did not have plans for the bonds entrusted to me. He probably had the OITC send that crazy C & D to me, which he over-reacted to which was the ruse which allowed him to take the bonds to his attorney who he has never named (a crime in itself).

61   http://neilkeenan.com/sample-page/ ✝ Archived 13th August, 2015.

62   http://www.theeventchronicle.com/intel/event-chronicle-decided-longer-post-neil-keenan-updates/ ✝ Archived 13th August, 2015.

This is getting out of hand and soon it will take on another shape one that can not be taken back. Daniele is playing a game that can come back and bite him. Me, I have absolutely nothing to hide. My conversations and documents are on the table and I will send them all to Washington.

Please read and see what I now see, which to me is horrible seeing I thought the world of Daniele. To fight with him seems senseless but he has stolen bonds that do not belong to him and OITC says he sent the document to start this whole thing. You figure it out. I just want the bonds and not Daniele going to jail. This again serves no purpose.

I am going to request arrest warrants soon through the NSA. I have no choice but to protect the bonds seeing they are legally entrusted to me. At this point and time you cannot trust Daniele and what he says. I have overheard his conversations and he is outright lying, which can be proven by his correspondence with me. I am ready to put Daniele's picture all over the newspapers in this world if he does not do the right thing. I do not have time to waste with him over this.

All the best,

Neil Keenan

It would appear in this email that Neil Keenan extends a veiled threat to my collaborator and financial expert Daniele Dal Bosco, who fortunately realized immediately the nature of this person and the fact the bonds in question were really unmanageable, because they do not fall within the Canons of International Law and were completely illegal to manage in any way possible, let alone to use to save the planet as Fulford and Wilcock claimed at the time.

In the same email sent to me by Neil Keenan, is his email to General Alexander of the N.S.A., of which I include an excerpt where you can find **highlighted** by me **in bold, certain relevant parts** and the names of two agents of the New World Order mentioned by Keenan. These are the late CIA agent **Tom Clines, (Thomas Gregory Clines 1928-2013),** a Central Intelligence Agency covert operations officer who was a prominent figure in the Iran-Contra Affair, [63] and a certain **General Jack Myers**, who has also mysteriously passed away since then as reported on Neil Keenan's website in 2013. [64] Meyers, who appeared to be operating much more discreetly and covertly than Keenan, was apparently a former officer of the American armed forces who worked for Intelligence through a commercial roofing company. Little is known about him, only that he died, just as the aforementioned Tom Clines, after the scandal of the mysterious bonds erupted at an international level.

Neil Keenan to General Alexander (NSA):

NSA

Dear General Alexander,

Subject: Daniele Dal Bosco...Italian Passport Number C165xxxxxxxx--------Italian Telephone Number ----39-349-xxxxxxxxxxx and Swiss is +41 789 xxxxxxxx. He lives outside Geneva in France, with also an apartment in Rome.

It is with my utmost regret that I must write this letter to you advising you of a

63   https://en.wikipedia.org/wiki/Thomas_G._Clines ‡ Archived 13th August, 2015.
64   http://neilkeenan.com/neil-keenan-update-assassination-attempt-on-keenans-team-in-jakarta-and-smear-by-phony-whistleblower-david-crayford-is-exposed-by-michael-henry-dunn/ ‡ Archived 13th August, 2015.

*situation that never should be that threatens to undermine American Security at this very minute. I have not been able to reach my dear friend **Tom Clines**, since he has been sick, or even **General Jack Myers**, who seems to be on the go more than ever (God Bless Him) for advice, but the best way to go is always with our own and this I am sure of as advised by Secretary of State.*

This relates to one Daniele Dal Bosco, alleged Treasurer of the Masons P2 Lodge in Italy, but in fact not truth but his direct lie; financial advisor to the Vatican and again a direct lie. Four months ago Daniele just seemed to take off with his girlfriend Alessia and his family into the mountains and returning to his home in Italy. I guess when he felt it was time to return to work he returned to Geneva. It was different then. Rather than speak with him everyday, it was once every two weeks. He was hiding something and it concerned me seeing he was the Custodian for 868 Billion USD in Federal Reserve Notes which I was authorized to maintain and place into a suitable private program should I find one that the Federal Reserve would find acceptable. Face Value was 125 Billion for the 250 notes.

*Daniele up to this time was fine, but as stated he became distant and I could feel it. Then I received a letter along with others including Daniele from an **OITC Group** from Thailand demanding the return of the bonds, claiming that they controlled the bonds not the Dragon Family. "Our ownership of the Dragon Funds, being part of the Combined International Collateral Accounts of the Global Debt Facility, and our International status combined with our International Authority as granted, attested to, and formally issued by the Nations of the World."*

Daniele up to this time was distant and when he received a copy of the Cease and Desist he allegedly panicked and ran to his attorney with the FRN's and the Japanese Bond 57th series and 1 Kennedy Bond. He returned asking me what I had done and how they had gotten his email. I had no idea how they had acquired either his or mine. He told me he was not returning the bonds and his attorney was dealing with it now, and he probably would send the bonds to the OITC.

[09/06/2010 11:37:50] Daniele Dal Bosco: Neil, I just checked my email and I saw that last night I received a C&D from OITC addressed to Yama, Watanabe and you and all associates. How did they get my email? How do they know about me???? I contacted already my Lawyer on same. I am 100% legal, buddy, and I do not want to be involved in frauds. Please don't mention to anyone about myself anymore and I advise you not to pursue this matter anymore. You knew that you were being checked, and I don't know who you're dealing with now. But that's a dangerous game, for yours and my own good, please stop this game. (Daniele is creating the fraud, no one else, if you read on you will see). "Dear Neil, my Lawyer is attending to it and I have no intention of asking him to stop and return everything." (he mentions lawyer but never gives us his name despite asking).

I responded to the Cease and Desist and found a very foul man by the name of Sale representing who was to be his Excellency, Ray C. Dam. In the meanwhile, we investigated stateside. What we learned was that the OITC is a Fraudulent Group with no authority anywhere. Our Attorneys can confirm their findings as well as ex-Chairman of the Democratic Party RI, Guy Dufault who really worked hard finding the information on the OITC. Upon finding that the OITC was a non-entity, I requested from Daniele to return the bonds back to me. He did not reply but when he did he told me his attorney was handling it and he would get to me when his attorney finished his investigation. I later heard that his attorney was investigating the bonds and finally I heard that he and his attorney were working with the UN and Interpol. Now this heightened my senses, seeing that I refused the very same group that said purchasd the bonds in the past.

The Italian delegation to the UN *offered me through Daniele 100 M for the bonds, no questions asked, and I said absolutely not. They were not for sale to the UN who would undermine the USA in one second by placing them in a program and then attempting to redeem them. This was not a consideration. Besides this, it was very suspicious seeing that they did not want us to return one cent to the Dragon Family. Anyways, I said no.*

I was working on other deals with the notes and had been for a long while. The deal had to be right for all parties, including my country. I had plans to help finance the Agency, Defense Department, and Homeland Security once the bonds got into a program. They could not be redeemed, seeing we did not have the money in our coffers to pay for them. They are gold backed, so this also is a concern. They are Morgenthau Notes. As said, I was working on a deal with a U.S. Pension fund that had no intention to redeem the bonds but they would cash back them and place them into a program. This seemed to be acceptable and the returns would be for our land and our people. I was to meet them actually tomorrow to discuss the terms and how we were to do this. It all would be done at home in the U.S., surrounded by Attorneys and businessmen to make sure nothing went astray. I would get permission to enter the U.S. with them, so everything would be legal and declare them to Customs. This never happened. Furthermore he will not give anyone the name of the attorney if one does in fact exist.

Upon learning that Mr. Dal Bosco's Lawyer, a lawyer whose name I never received from Mr. Dal Bosco, nor would he give either myself, or to a Japanese journalist. This is part of my conversation with the journalist: [05:29:15] Benjamin Fulford: Yes, I got the feeling he was going to try to sell them to the UN for $100 million.

In the past Dal Bosco made it clear to me that the deal with the Italian Delegation to the UN offered us this deal NO QUESTIONS ASKED. Just cash and carry. A quick exchange. As I said I refused it much to Dal Bosco's dismay. When this deal was offered to me he kept telling me we would never get another offer like this. That we should take it. I just shook my head seeing Daniele's desperation at doing a very corrupt deal. **Mr. Dal Bosco then advised me that the Italian Govenrment was making an offer to me for the Dragon Family whereas they were offering all notes and bonds back that they had confiscated in Chiasso from Yamaguchi and Watanabee for 10% of their face value.** *I asked Daniele how they could do this, seeing they were prosecuting Alessandro Santi for maintaining false notes. Throughout this ordeal Daniele had contact (he claimed) with the financial police and they told him that the bonds were real. If this is in case fact, then they are fraudulently prosecuting Mr. Santi. Either way, if the Italian government is selling the bonds then Mr. Santi should be released from this case. Mr. Dal Bosco should be called in by Santi's Lawyers and grilled to get the information.*

While in Rome with Dal Bosco he telephoned a woman very close to Belusconi *and asked her to get him an audience with Belusconi to speak about the Santi deal. He went to said meeting and told me Belusconi would be looking at it and if there was no chance of a scandal it would go away. At the time PM Belusconi had* *some problems from what Daniele told me.*

*Yesterday Mr. Dal Bosco advised Japanese Journalist, Benjamin Fulford, that I no longer had authorization for the bonds. He went looking through my package and found an old authorization so I guess he felt this gave him the right to steal them with his so-called attorney. Little did he know that I have a new authorization with no backside. So it appears that he is looking to sell the bonds using the fact that my authorization has expired so he has the right to do what he wants with them. He forgot his fiduciary trust to me as I made him custodian. He is nothing but a THIEF and should be treated as such. One must remember that **Mr. Dal Bosco often would tell me that he is the Treasurer to the Masons and is Leo Zagami's closest friend.** I learned that Leo Zagami might not want any information coming out of Japan reaching Dal Bosco's ears and yesterday I learned that Dal Bosco might not even be a Mason, which is one of the reasons I gave him the bonds. I felt he could be trusted with the bonds if he was the Treasurer of the Masons. No other reason. He used Zagami's name regularly and even told me that Leo would safe keep the bonds until needed if I desired. I did not desire, although I have heard that Mr. Zagami is a trusted person. Also, Mr. Dal Bosco would discuss his Vatican connections with me claiming he is the financial advisor to the Vatican, which I also learned is not in fact true. What is unfortunate and has made me very angry in the past was that Mr. Dal Bosco would place the attaché carrying the notes in the trunk of his girlfriend's car and she would drive them from country to country, crossing lines without a care in the world. I had responsibility for those notes and I wanted them in safe keeping but this is surely not safe keeping. This is reckless and stupid and I told him as much.*

Now Mr. Dal Bosco is attempting to sell the bonds to the UN as he requested me to do in the beginning. If the bonds had no value he would otherwise give them back to me. So he is selling them or trying to and before he succeeds we must stop him. He can only hurt the U.S. by doing so and it seems that his concerns for the U.S. are little.

FURTHERMORE, please read all I said and upon analyzing it, one must come to the understanding that Mr. Dal Bosco CREATED this whole scenario himself so he could steal the bonds. This is Mr. Dal Bosco's doing, not anyone else's.

I have brought this to your attention so that you have the time to stop him. Mr. Dal Bosco's telephone numbers are: Italian ----39-349-xxxxxxxxx and Swiss is +41 789 xxxxxxx....

[15/06/2010 17:54:52] Benjamin Fulford: From Daniele: [23:24:59 | 23:25:01 を編集しました] Daniele Dal Bosco: he has no authority on the Notes and the Bonds, he had a POA who expired in November, 2009.

[23:25:42] Daniele Dal Bosco: but Neil is stubborn and he wants to make money even if it's through illegal ways

[23:26:04] Daniele Dal Bosco: the famous dollar sign in his eyes ... you know the saying ...

This clearly explains the fact that Dal Bosco feels he can do what he wishes with the bonds entrusted to him seeing he believes I no longer have authorization. Well, I have authorization updated and have had for a long while. He is a custodian nothing more and does not need to know everything I am doing. As for the dollar signs in my eyes, boy does he not know me. I worked 20 hours a day putting this together

> and am exhausted and did not need this now. I wanted to relax and complete and
> then feel great about issuing the funds to the proper causes. For humanitarian
> causes etc., and Dal Bosco got in the way of all this now and he was included as he
> knows. I am tired but I have a little left in the gas tank. At this time, I believe it is
> only appropriate to call for help seeing there seems to be little I can do in Europe to
> stop them from hurting my country when in fact I was trying to help it.
>
> Kindest Regards,
>
> Neil Keenan

After the futile attempt by Keenan to involve me further, I passed it on to others in the Intelligence Community, understanding the complexity and especially the possible dangers that this whole operation might be hiding. It looked like a financial *terrorism-related* plot ready to explode in the hands of the interested parties, and personally I wanted nothing more to do with it. In the meantime, Neil Keenan, is now hiding in the jungles of Jakarta after an apparent murder plot against him. Regarding the U.S. bonds, confiscated in Chiasso in June 2009, and those subsequently confiscated at the Malpensa airport in the same year, they were all declared officially false by the Italian authorities. Professor Aldo Giannuli, considered one of Italy's leading Intelligence experts, and a researcher in contemporary history at the political-science faculty of the University of Milan, wrote:

"The thesis of the falsification on the part of organized crime is not convincing at all: the cuts are too big, the amount is to concentrated." Giannulli also points out that: *"after the the first two were caught, it makes no sense to try again on the same border to get caught again. And again, why are the titles only American?"* [65]

The mystery of these mysterious bonds of the U.S. Federal Reserve that are being circulated has caught the attention of Intelligence experts worldwide, who harbor strong doubts on whether they are really false, and a few have stated publicly that the CIA is covering up the truth. It's all part of a targeted *psychological warfare operation* applied to high finance, and piloted secretly by Chinese Freemasonry and other major players of the New World Order, like the NSA. Giannulli states: *"It is not yet a full on currency war, but we are at the pre-tactical stages."* [66]

Neil Keenan, as official representative of the so-called "Dragon Family" was initiated at the time of the legal proceedings, which were later abandoned, in the Southern District court of New York in November of 2011, (FIG. 81) and are available on the Internet in PDF format, with outrageous claims that touched even the former prime minister Silvio Berlusconi, Daniele Dal Bosco, and of course I also get a mention in it. Obviously, it was all a bluff. In the same document the delusional Neil Keenan denounced Ban Ki-Moon, the Secretary General of the United Nations. I would like to add that Daniele Dal Bosco, contrary to what Neil Keenan stated in his email, is a Freemason, as he was initiated in the *Lodge Solidarietà e Lavoro* in Livorno belonging at the time to Grand Master Luigi Piazza (a P2 member now deceased). Even if he was never technically a member of a "Regular" lodge or the P2 itself, Dal Bosco was at one time a member of a Grand Lodge operating under the supervision of the Monte Carlo Executive Committee of the P2 and Ezio Giunchiglia.

Regarding my own personal involvement in this affair, it took place only because of Fulford's request, (FIGS. 82-83-84) as it was Fulford who invited me to Japan in June,

65   Aldo Giannulli, *Come Funzionano i servizi segreti,* (Milan: Ponte alle Grazie-Adriano Salani Editore, 2010), p. 346.
66   *Ibid.*

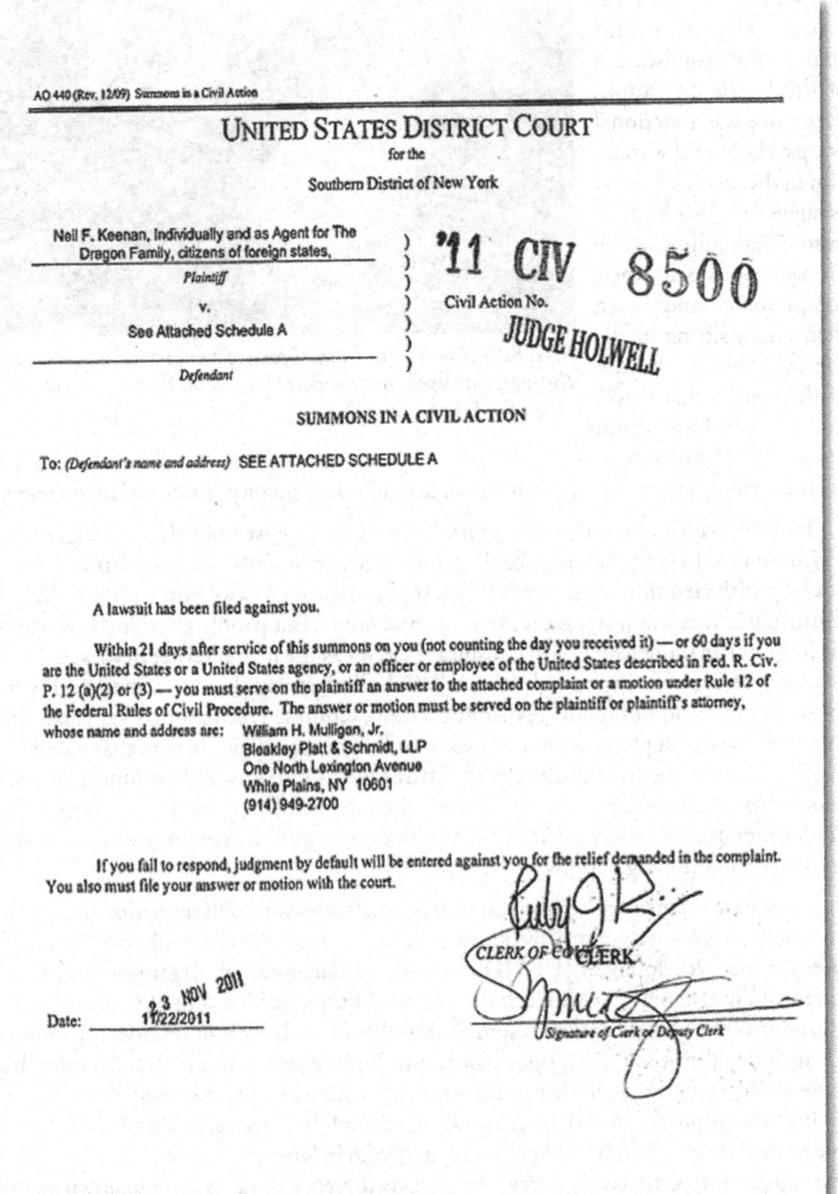

AO 440 (Rev. 12/09) Summons in a Civil Action

UNITED STATES DISTRICT COURT
for the
Southern District of New York

Neil F. Keenan, Individually and as Agent for The
Dragon Family, citizens of foreign states,

Plaintiff

v.

See Attached Schedule A

Defendant

'11 CIV 8500

Civil Action No.

JUDGE HOLWELL

SUMMONS IN A CIVIL ACTION

To: *(Defendant's name and address)* SEE ATTACHED SCHEDULE A

A lawsuit has been filed against you.

Within 21 days after service of this summons on you (not counting the day you received it) — or 60 days if you are the United States or a United States agency, or an officer or employee of the United States described in Fed. R. Civ. P. 12 (a)(2) or (3) — you must serve on the plaintiff an answer to the attached complaint or a motion under Rule 12 of the Federal Rules of Civil Procedure. The answer or motion must be served on the plaintiff or plaintiff's attorney, whose name and address are: William H. Mulligan, Jr.
Bleakley Platt & Schmidt, LLP
One North Lexington Avenue
White Plains, NY 10601
(914) 949-2700

If you fail to respond, judgment by default will be entered against you for the relief demanded in the complaint. You also must file your answer or motion with the court.

CLERK OF COURT

Date: 2 3 NOV 2011
11/22/2011

Signature of Clerk or Deputy Clerk

FIG. 81 – *Lawsuit (later dropped) filed by Neil Keenan on behalf of the so-called "Dragon Family" in the Southern District of NY, United States, in November, 2011.*

2009 to discuss the matter, (FIG. 85) and find a possible solution for all parties involved. What role are the Chinese Freemasons playing in this affair? The confiscation of the bonds on various occasions, was functional as a psychological warfare plot in the financial sector as suggested also by Professor Giannulli. A strong message for sure, for their competitors, and even their allies, sitting in the control room at the top of the system that drives the infamous New World Order. The Chinese can bring down the entire system at any time, through their mighty *"financial instruments."*

FIG. 82 – *The author in the home of Benjamin Fulford, shows the penant used to indicate his membership in Hongmen (Chinese Freemasonry).*

Fulford, who proposed to the conspiracy world a most unlikely challenge, which was announced via the Internet back in the early part of 2007, that a **Chinese Secret Society** with six million members (Chinese Freemasonry) **was now challenging the Illuminati.** This was just a great farse, nothing more, but people all over the world fell for it. Fulford's sudden arrival in conspiracy circles as the new Internet hero, seemed for many a real opportunity to fight the NWO bullies. It was, however, marked his new entry into the field of high-level disinformation, Chinese Freemasonry, via Japan. It's a complex charade in preparation for these bonds confiscated in Chiasso, that dated back to 1998, and are the fruit of **Executive Order No. 11110,** signed on June 4, 1963, by none other than President John F. Kennedy. I recommend you read John Perkins's book *Confessions of an Economic Hit Man*, a brilliant essay on the new role of an economic hit man on developing nations.

Economic hit men are highly paid professionals who steal billions of dollars in different countries around the world by pouring the money of the World Bank, U.S. Agency for International Development (USAID) and other "humanitarian" organizations into the coffers of big corporations and into the pockets of the usual handful of wealthy families who control the planet's natural resources, the elite of the New World Order. Their methods include false accounting, rigged elections, bribery, extortion, sex and murder. It's a game as old as power itself, that in the age of globalization, has taken on a new and terrifying dimension. [67] Aldo Giannuli, speaking about John Perkins, confirms the infamous role of the NSA: *"The story of Perkins is particularly interesting because, as he says, his first job for the National Security Agency was directed towards an employment for a financial consulting firm (the Main Inc. of Boston) facilitated by a senior official of the NSA with whom Perkins had a personal relationship."* [68] This remains a long and complex story, with sensational implications. On February 17, 2012 CBS News reported on a

67   See. John Perkins, *Confessions of an Economic Hit Man,* (Rome, IT: Minimum Fax, 2010), p. 7.

68   A.Giannulli, *Ibid.,* p. 226.

FIG. 83 – A picture of a Hongmen Worlwide Chinese Union pennant in the Tokyo home of Benjamin Fulford, which shows unequivocally the use of the symbols of Freemasonry by the Hongmen.

further confiscation of "false bonds" in Switzerland on behalf of the Italian authorities, [69] and guess where the origin of these bonds are from? Surprisingly enough, this time CBS states it is Hong Kong and not Japan, the city where Chinese Freemasonry has one of their more important spiritual centers at **Man Mo Temple**. [70]

For a more clear concept of Chinese Freemasonry of the "Hongmen" here is the entry for "Tiandihui" in WIKIPEDIA:

The Tiandihui (Chinese: 天地會; pinyin: Tiān Dì Huì), literally the Society of the Heaven and the Earth, also called Hongmen 洪門, is a Chinese fraternal organization and secretive folk religious sect. As the Tiandihui spread through different counties and provinces, it branched off into many groups and became known by many names, including the Sanhehui. The Hongmen grouping is today more or less synonymous with the whole Tiandihui concept, although the title "Hongmen" is also claimed by some criminal groups.

When the British ruled Hong Kong, all Chinese secret societies were seen as criminal threats and were together defined as *Triads*, although the Hongmen might be said to have differed in its nature from others. The name of the "Three Harmonies Society" (the "Sanhehui" grouping of the Tiandihui) is in fact the source of the term "Triad" that has become synonymous with Chinese organized crime. Because of that heritage, the Tiandihui is sometimes controversial and is illegal in Hong Kong. [71]

From the Bohemian Grove to the Vatican

The Bohemian Club and its infamous redwood Grove, are subjects I have written about in detail in Volume I of *Confessions*, and were also described in detail by William H. Kennedy, also known as "Teddy," who unfortunately passed away suddenly in August, 2013 at the age of 48. His death was never really investigated, and when approached about it, his family seemed quite scared to stir things up, and therefore no attention whatsoever was given to his passing by the media. Kennedy, who was a controversial life-long Catholic writer and radio host, was the author of the now out-of-print and highly collectable books: *Satanic Crime – A Threat in the New Millennium*, and the even more controversial title *Lucifer's Lodge: Satanic Ritual Abuse in the Catholic Church*. He was also a regular guest on Dr. Stan Monteith's nationally syndicated radio

69   http://www.cbsnews.com/news/italy-confiscates-6-trillion-in-fake-us-bonds/ ‡ Archived 13th August, 2015.
70   https://www.youtube.com/watch?v=Pm-daoJPi_U ‡ Archived 13th August, 2015.
71   https://en.wikipedia.org/wiki/Tiandihui ‡ Archived 13th August, 2015.

show, and he was a relative of the powerful, yet cursed, Kennedy family.[72] In **Satanic Crime**, Kennedy writes about the Bohemian Grove:

> *During the opening night of the camp, there is a ceremony in which members dress in robes and hoods (not unlike Ku Klu Klan regalia) and perform either real or mock human ritual sacrifice to the Owl of Bohemia. By Christian standards, by which the majority of members claim affiliation, all such sacrifices are forbidden, be they mock or for real. The sacrificial victim is named Care, suggesting that all the members must destroy all vestiges of caring for any human beings except for members of the Grove. Much like the Skull and Bones (as one can see Bonesman make up large portion of ranking Bohemians), members are expected to work solely for the good of fellow members only.[73]*

FIG. 84 – *The author shows a publication of the The Tiandihui (Chinese: 天地會; pinyin: Tiān Dì Huì), literally the Society of the Heaven and the Earth, also called Hongmen, found in the home of Benjamin Fulford, an object of curiosity for scholars of the subject.*

Kennedy then suggests a quick look at the text of the actual ritual, that we receive thanks to the groundbreaking work of Alex Jones and his cameramen Mike Hanson, who managed to enter the forbidden ground of the Grove on the 15th of July, 2000:

> *Filmmaker Alex Jones contends that members of the Bohemian Grove actually purchase small owl figures sold by the organization for home devotional use. In this regard, Bohemian Club members sacrifice and destroy Care year round. It is bloodcurdling when one realizes how many high-ranking political leaders have attended this strange occult ceremony. If these people don't care, then God help us all.[74]*

I never imagined to find myself, at night, in the Vatican, with **Alex Jones,** 15 years after his famous sortie at the Bohemian Grove on the 7th of August, 2015. We could not catch them as planned, during the celebration of a Satanic Mass in the Vatican, however we definitely managed to film an epic interview around Rome that night. The interview was based in part on the topics covered in my book *Pope Francis: The Last Pope?* and during the whole process, we were heavily monitored by Vatican authorities, who ultimately lead us out of St. Peter's Square after an open intimation from the Italian police that was caught on camera. We then continued to film all night, with a tour of the various sites mentioned in my book, ending up later that evening in the location where the gay pedophile priests pick up young Romanian children to bring inside the Leonine wall, and also in front of the huge gay sauna owned by the Vatican. But let's begin at St. Peter's Square, where our interview/documentary later named *Demonic Possession Of The Vatican Exposed: Leo Zagami Interview,* first took place.[75]

72   Leo Lyon Zagami, *Pope Francis: The Last Pope?, Ibid.,* p.198.
73   William H. Kennedy, *Satanic Crime, Ibid.,* p. 150.
74   *Ibid.,* p. 151.
75   https://www.youtube.com/watch?v=fc99vUS_PZE ‡ Archived 13th August, 2015.

FIG. 85 – The author and Benjamin Fulford in Tokyo in June 2009, together for a series of meetings after the strange episode in Chiasso.

The evening began under the mythical obelisk, which I saw as a good omen, because my name in the phrase: *Leo Vicit de Tribu Juda.* Our wild night of Vatican exposure for *Infowars,* in and around the Vatican, began here at 9 PM. I arrived 15 minutes earlier after parking nearby, and having friends in the Italian police serving there, I decided to call them, to see what we could do and not do to get on their nerves. Of course I knew it would be difficult to go unnoticed as the rules are quite strict throughout the area. I scouted the area, hoping that after seeing my face there for a little while the police would let their guard down, at least for the amount of time needed to film. This is a technique that usually works when you want to do this kind of operation in a forbidden area. However, the good Lord helped us do the almost impossible during the first part of the evening, when we were able to film an epic scene inside St. Peter's Square, with the weather suddenly turned the whole episode into an almost apocalyptic scenario after we began the interview. An unusual storm erupted in an otherwise hot summer night in Rome. Even Alex looked truly astonished about this sudden change of weather, a scenario very similar to what happened on the evening of the 11th of February 2013, when a storm hit the Vatican after Ratzinger's resignation, which was immortalized by the now famous photograph of lightning on the Vatican made by **Alessandro di Meo**, a photographer from the news agency ANSA. The storm projected us directly to the cover of my book, *Pope Francis: The Last Pope?* as we featured part of that pic for the cover.

This sudden summer storm enabled us, somehow, to continue filming under the huge columns of St. Peter's Square, even if prohibited by the stringent security measures in place, especially at night. But after 30 minutes, we were noticed by the police forces patroling the Square. Unfortunately that evening in August, most of my contacts in the local police force were on holiday, so I knew we could get in serious trouble in the absence of their presence. Alex continued to interview me about Satanism in the Vatican under the columns, but in the meantime, security measures around us were building.

Alex Jones, who was initially relaxed, realized the danger when a police car arrived two meters behind him and his camera man Rob Dew, and another approached us from the right. At that point I explained to Alex that it was better to get out of there before running the risk of spending the night in a cell in the Vatican Inspectorate, courtesy of Pope Francis and his Jesuits. So after a little clarification with a sympathetic police inspector, we are able to leave the square without any problems. After all, the Italian police are honest people and most of them, great professionals who are simply doing their jobs. They were obviously feeling uncomfortable with us being there that night, because technically speaking, we were on the border between two states. I heard later that the Vatican side put a lot of pressure on them to throw us out, when they saw and possibly heard what we were saying. In the meantime it was getting late, but the goal was now to travel discreetly and unobtrusively down the *Borgo Santo Spirito* leading to the very center of Vatican occult power, and to the headquarters of the Curia Generalizia of the Jesuits, home to the so-called **"black Pope."**

We later we moved on to the headquarters of the **Equestrian Order of the Holy Sepulchre of Jerusalem,** where we managed to film for a few minutes in their courtyard during a V.I.P. party for their Knights, obviously without any invitation and openly denouncing the elite during the filming, a truly daring act conducted with Alex clearly becoming intimidated by the situation that was indeed getting dangerous, as we were technically in a foreign land, where Italian law has no jurisdiction and where they get away with murder. For the rest of our adventure I invite you to watch the video in question, which I hope will be the beginning of a fruitful collaboration, as I wrote many articles and did a couple interviews with Alex after this, including a very detailed coverage of Pope Francis' U.S. visit in September, 2015.

An inside source came out in fact in that period of intense collaboration, stating that the White House had an F.B.I. task force investigating this growing media project.[76] However, both Alex Jones and myself are not Vatican-bashers, this is what Catholics need to realize, but simply professionals trying to expose something that no one wants to cover in ordinary news. In my case, I am still considered a good Catholic by the Vatican that treats me very well, even after my books and my open criticism in the media. There is a conservative force that exists in the Vatican that embraces and encourages my work, by feeding me from time to time, top secret inside information for my books. Alex Jones realized the problems of the "lunatic fringe" that has now taken over the Vatican and lies at the heart of the New World Order, and dedicated many hours of his shows to in-depth investigations about this problem. As the late William H. Kennedy wrote:

> The real "lunatic fringe" in the Roman Catholic Church consists of Cardinals who give safe harbor to child molesters posing as priests (Law, Egan et al), the predatory homosexuals who run and enroll in Roman Catholic seminaries and form bizarre sex cults, and the power brokers who have allied the Vatican's vast financial resources with organized crime. It is the skullduggery of these sorts of Catholics that causes the most harm. The devotional practices and beliefs of Traditional Catholics harm no one.[77]

I don't think I could ever summarize better than the late Kennedy, the current situation in the Vatican, and Alex understood this, and courageously decided to publicly denounce this activity, on his media outlet *Infowars.com.*[78]

When I explained and showed Alex Jones the super luxurious penthouse of the "pink pope" Cardinal Tarcisio Bertone, or the gay sauna used by the Vatican priests placed in a building belonging to the Church, or where the priests lure the kids near Termini train station to take them later to the Vatican, and many other secrets of what Kennedy called the "lunatic fringe" of the Catholic Church, Alex and I were in complete agreement that (FIG. 90) Pope Francis is no Saint, as he is openly promoting relativism every day, refusing to take a stand even on the gays that are now controlling parts of the Church, stating to journalists *"who am I to judge the gay?"* (FIG. 86)

76   https://www.youtube.com/watch?v=Hhs275ZONGM ‡ Archived 16th August, 2015.
77   William H. Kennedy, *Occult History, Ibid.,* , p.146.
78   http://www.infowars.com/alex-jones-is-the-pope-the-devil/ ‡ Archived 16th August, 2015.

FIG. 86 – The author and Alex Jones holding the book Pope Francis: The Last Pope? *on the night between the 7th and the 8th of August, 2015 in front of the Cavalieri-Waldorf Astoria in Rome, after our epic adventure in and around the Vatican. Photo courtesy of Rob Dew (Infowars.com).*

Pope Francis has been accentuating his dialogue with the B'nai B'rith, as well as Islam, and insists on promoting a fake crusade for the environment, and unconditional support to illegal immigration. It is basically a disaster for true Catholics who reject Bergoglio's relativist views.

Universal unity? No thanks ...

Funnily enough, Alex Jones' documentary on the Bohemian Grove was one of the main reasons for my difficult but necessary choice to leave the Masonic Executive Committee and their Lodge in Monte Carlo on the 3rd of June 2006, after the Annual Convent of the Illuminati of the *Universal Unity* at Massa Pisana, in the House of Spirituality of San Cerbone of the Daughters of St. Francis de Sales. (FIG. 87) This took place with the arrival of Giorgio Hugo Balestrieri, the controversial "Commander" I have already discussed in a previous chapter, in relation to the internal corruption in the United Nations. Personally, in that period around June 2006, I had everything to lose and nothing to gain by making an important figure like Balestrieri my enemy. Before my encounter with him that day, the Brothers of Monte Carlo and I had made an important decision. The Board of Directors of the *Universal Unity,* wanted the whole structure to be taken over by the **Triumvirate represented by me, Ezio Giunchglia and Jean Pierre Giudicelli** with whom I had originally created the *Ordo Illuminatorum Universalis.* I intended to go ahead and accept my new position. This meant of course a new leading role in my Illuminati order, founded in 1999, however I wanted to continue investigating the possible misdeeds committed in the various Illuminati sects in the USA. From the Bohemian Club exposed by Alex Jones with his video, to the *Skull & Bones* at Yale

University, from the Temple of Set, to the *Ordo Templi Orientis*. To do this I required Intelligence clearance issued by the U.S. State Department through Giorgio Hugo Balestrieri, but Balestrieri in front of all the members present at Massa Pisana refused to let me proceed with my plan. He got up and stated that the CIA and the F.B.I. will not grant me the necessary permits to do so, and that's why I walked out of the Masonic Executive Committee and the Monte Carlo Lodge.

Giorgio Balestrieri, in business with Ezio Giunchiglia of the P2 and U.S. Intel-

FIG. 87 – Convent of San Cerbone-Massa Pisana-Lucca. Photo taken from the site http://www.comune.lucca.it ‡ Archived 17th August 2015.

ligence since the mid-seventies, was a Captain of the Italian Navy, but after the explosion of the P2 scandal Balestrieri disappeared from Italy, and resurfaced years later with an American passport, as director of the International Service Division of the New York Rotary Club. Some say Balestrieri was involved in the staged events of September 11th, 2001, which had been predicted in the expiry date of the passport of Neo in the *Matrix* movie that came out in 1999, an important film in my spiritual evolution. Going back to his arrival at the meeting in San Cerbone, I realized in the following days that I could no longer trust him, as he was a professional in the Intelligence field without scruples. He is a double agent often working for Israeli's Mossad, and linked to the Calabrian 'Ndrangheta and the Sicilian Mafia. I remember that in 2006, three years before they issued the first arrest warrant against him for collusion with the Calabrese Mafia issued by the DDA in Reggio Calabria, Balestrieri had prominent figures behind him protecting him in Italy, as the former President Francesco Cossiga as I mentioned earlier.

Freemason Giorgio H. Balestrieri, a key figure of the P2 for years, worked with both Zionists and Jesuits through the powerful transnational Masonic institutions of the small, but influential Republic of San Marino, and is still a key player in this game even today. Balestrieri later become one of the leaders of the **Giacomo Maria Ugolini Foundation**. Ugolini used to be very close to Silvio Berlusconi, and was an important Grand Master and Sovereign Grand Commander of the minuscule Republic. Massimo Teodori, author of the book *P2: la controstoria*, and one of the biggest experts on the P2, mentions both Giorgio Balestrieri and Ezio Giunchiglia as important players and leading figures of the P2. Teodori, is a well-known Italian politician described by Wikipedia as a member of the Commission of Enquiry that in the eighties investigated the "P2." He is therefore an authoritative source. In Chapter II he writes clear and explicit words on the context in which the P2 operated in those years during the Cold War:

> *Another strategic direction was the sector concerned with the production and trade of weapons with admirals Vittorio Forgione and Achille Alfano, Ezio Giuchiglia, the carrier Alessandro Del Bene from Florence, and Captain Giorgio*

FIG. 88 – Ezio Giunchiglia and Leo Lyon Zagami in the residence of the lawyer and Freemason Francesco Murgia in Sanremo. Photo taken in 2006. Thanks to Troy Space for the image taken from his Flickr profile: https://www.flickr.com/photos/24089748@N02/ ‡ Archived 17th August, 2015.

Balestrieri of Livorno. [79]

While Licio Gelli was busy working on the "Propaganda," with the Propaganda 2 Lodge, in those difficult years the various weapon deals ended up in the hands of his "**Tirrenia division**" headed by **Dr. Ezio Giunchiglia** (P2, Tirrenia division, head group 11, No. 639, later defined by the newspaper "*La Repubblica*" in 1984 as "*the head of the P2 in Tuscany.*" (FIG. 88) Recently, "*Il Fatto Quotidiano*" wrote about Giunchiglia in March, 2011: "*an important piece of the P2 affiliated to the Emulation Lodge in Tirrenia.*" [80]

Ezio Giunchiglia ended up in jail at one point in the 1980s, accused of plotting the massacre of Bologna in 1982, but served only a few months of his sentence. He was accused of having masterminded the whole thing with the Far-Right, but they never managed to bring forward any evidence against him in the end. Giunchiglia, who was later released as completely innocent, once told me the real reason for his arrest was to cover someone else. People that included the usual Giorgio Balestrieri, who was also mentioned in relation to the bombing in Bologna, but of course, never tried by authorities. The accusations were later dropped, also for Ezio, according to Jean Pierre Giudicelli (himself an Intelligence officer for the French) because of Ezio's role in the Italian Military Intelligence where he was, said Giudicelli, a Colonel. Although I have no way to prove it, other sources have later confirmed this hypothesis as both Balestrieri and Giuchiglia were all too familiar faces in **Forte Braschi (Military Intelligence)** and **Via Lanza (Civilian Intelligence)**, where the Italian Intelligence services have their headquarters. Giorgio Hugo Balestrieri, as well as Giunchiglia, were also members of GLADIO and worked on several occasions for the CIA, and for the F.B.I. Giuchiglia himself once told me in his villa near Tirrenia, that Balestrieri had managed to receive his U.S. passport with **Licio Gelli's help** during the Cold War, when Gelli received from the CIA **a salary of 10 million dollars a month,** for the P2. He was judged by the United States as an important anti-Communist asset during the Cold War. However, Licio Gelli, at the time Worshipful Master of the Propaganda 2 Lodge, argued with Giunchiglia in regards to weapon deals that ruined the image of the Lodge, and suggested they only operate such deals from Monte Carlo, where the Masonic Committee had been set up to avoid the growing scrutiny of Italian authorities.

Later, Gelli left his Masonic creation in the Principality of Monaco to Ezio Giuchiglia, who was unable to ignite its true Masonic Light, as originally planned. Failing miserably in the end to fulfill their mission because of bad judgements and dishonesty. I would like

79   See. Massimo Teodori, P2: *la controstoria,* (Milan Sugarco, 1986).
80   See. http://www.ilfattoquotidiano.it/2011/03/29/100793/100793/ ‡ Archived 16th August, 2015.

to again state, that in the end, Brother Licio Gelli, who passed away on the 16th of December 2015, made a great decision in the last seven years of his life, to distance himself once and for all, from the criminals that used to be his Brothers in Propaganda 2 Lodge, and to embrace Freemasonry in a different and honest way, with the help of **General Bartolomeu Constantin Săvoiu.** (FIGS. 89-90) Bravo Licio, who in the end followed the only

FIG. 89 – *The late Licio Gelli (1919- 2015) and his spiritual and Masonic heir General Bartolomeu Constantin Săvoiu, a member of the Ordo Illuminatorum Universalis.*

way possible to save his soul after all his mistakes in the Masonic world, by becoming *one* with the Holy Spirit and a member of the *Ordo Illuminatorum Universalis*, the only possible way for the real "Illuminati," which I stated earlier means illumination in Greek, and was the name given to those who submitted to Christian baptism. Those who were baptized were called "Illuminati" or the "illuminated ones"—let's never forget this Brothers. Amen.

Regarding my past and present statements on the *Masonic Executive Committee* of the P2 in Monte Carlo, and my past and present involvement in the P2 milieu, the site of *www.masonicinfo.com* of Freemason **Edward L. King**—in service of the worst disinformation a Freemason can give—went so far as to write that I basically made the whole thing up by writing that I was too young, and other lies:

A true insider and member of the Freemasonic P2 Lodge?

Now here's the real problem. The P2 Lodge was closed in 1976—at a time when he was SIX YEARS OLD. Why young Mr. Young probably wasn't even Zagami at that point. Oh, and then, when he was about age 11, Italy banned all secret societies so it's bye-bye P2—except in the fantasy world of this individual. Again, for the completely clueless, his story will leave you breathless. For most others, it's probably the stench of lies rather than the story that will take your breath away. [81]

Maybe **Edward L. King,** creator of the site "Masonic Info" and illustrious Freemason of the Grand Lodge of Maine, where he had occupied a place in the committee of this prestigious Masonic Obedience for the years 2014-2015, [82] should, in my humble opinion, rename the site "Masonic Disinfo" and be more honest with his alleged research in this field, where things sometimes look different than they seem because Freemasonry is full of mysteries, even for the most educated and skilled minds.

Read for yourself, what he writes about the *Comitato Esecutivo Massonico* in Monte Carlo:

Would it surprise you to know too that the "Comitato Esecutivo Massonico" stuff

81   http://www.masonicinfo.com/zagami.htm ‡ Archived 16th August, 2015.
82   http://www.mainemason.org/grandlodge/glcommittees.asp ‡ Archived 16th August, 2015.

only appears in search engines with Mr. Zagami's name attached to it? If you're completely conspiracy-addicted, you'll already have the answer: it's a CONSPIRACY and only Zagami has the courage to talk about it. If, on the other hand, you have a modicum of common sense, you'll know that it's only because this individual has gotten a bunch of like-minded paranoids to repeat his fairy tale. [83]

I invite all Masonic researchers worldwide to publicly denounce the disinformation activities of Edward L. King by simply downloading an official document on the subject issued by the **Senate of the Italian Republic**. This document was created after in-depth investigation on the P2, and demonstrates that there are credible documents in the hands of the Italian authorities that prove the unambiguous existence of the Monte Carlo Lodge and its Executive Committee Masonic at this website: ***http: // www. senato.it/service/PDF/ PDFServer/BGT/910003.pdf***

FIG. 90 – *The author and Grand Master of the Ordo Illuminatorum Universalis and General Bartolomeu Constantin Săvoiu in Arezzo 22nd of December, 2015.*

Are the authoritative staments of the Italian Senate just lies, like the ones obviously put together by "Brother" Edward L. King? King should be expelled from the Craft immediately for his dishonest stand, or he should at least be suspended and apologize for his ignorance and false accusations against me.

The P2 was officially dismantled with a specific law (No. 17) issued by the Italian Parliament on the 25th of Jannuary, 1982. So why does King say: "*The P-2 Lodge was closed in 1976.*" This is a completely false, as the P2 was simply "suspended" officially by the Grand Master of the Grand Orient of Italy **Lino Salvini** on the 26th of July, 1976 to continue in secret with the blessings of the Grand Master, as this is even written on Wikipedia. [84] Even after the P2 was dismantled in 1982, other branches of the same group continued, to this day as P3, P4 and other names in the complex Italian Masonic scene that often pop up in Italian chonicles. The testimony of Elio Ciolini defined in the newspaper "*La Republica*" on April 20, 2001, as a character *in the middle of dark stories*, went on to state to Aldo Gentile, the judge in charge of the Bologna bombing investigation, that: "*the massacre had been commissioned to Right-wing extremist Stefano Delle Chiaie by the mysterious Masonic Lodge in 'Monte Carlo,' a branch of the P2.*"

Ciolini also said that the "*Monte Carlo*" Lodge was inserted in the "*Trilateral,*" which

83 masonicinfo.com *Ibid.*
84 https://it.wikipedia.org/wiki/P2 ‡ Archived 16th August, 2015.

he described as a terrorist organization.[85] The Trilateral Commission[86] is indeed a controversial organization with a key role in the New World Order, but to describe it as a terrorist organization is a pretty strong statement by Ciolini.

However, the mysterious **Monte Carlo Committee** (FIG. 91-92) also appeared in a 1994 article in the *"Corriere della Sera,"* where we find again Ezio Giunchiglia mentioned in relation to Federico Federici, an arms dealer linked to Count Licio Gelli, (FIG. 93) and **Maurizio Broc-**

FIG. 91 – Leather case belonging to the author, with inscriptions in gold, made for the exclusive members of the Executive Masonic Committee in Monte Carlo, known as "The Committee" of the P2.

coletti, the former managing director of Sisde (Italy's civilian Intelligence until the reform of 2007 changed its name to **AISI**). Broccoletti was involved in the scandal (later archived), that erupted in 1993 regarding the "black" funds of the Sisde, used to finance covert Intelligence operations. Federico Federici, according to prosecutors in Bologna, was also one of the closest collaborators of Count Licio Gelli, with interests in the arms trade especially with Argentina, a country central to the Sisde operations in those years, (no wonder we now have an Argentinian Pope). The Monte Carlo lodge was also chosen by Maurizio Broccoletti, a key figure of Sisdegate, for his escape.[87]

My questions to "Brother" Edward L. King will eventually be:

Why was Giorgio Hugo Balestrieri from the Propaganda 2 Lodge allowed to become a member of the Grand Lodge of New York?

Why was Balestrieri, until recently, a key figure of the Rotary Club in New York?

U.S. Freemasons should accept the information of people like Brother **Josef Wages**, who is an honest and prepared individual, a Christian and a great Masonic historian and author, not a disinformation agent like Edward L. King and many other people in the Craft, including my ex-Masonic mentor **Julian Reese.** He is another big shot of International Freemasonry and a pawn of the O.T.O., that after my revelations began 10 years ago, was only capable of criticizing me, unfortunately, not understanding my work, or the project I began with my order, the *Ordo Illuminatorum Universalis,* founded inside the Masonic Executive Committee in 1999.

After reading the research of William H. Kennedy, I discovered that there was a link

85   http://www.repubblica.it/online/politica/campagnasei/scheda/scheda.html ‡ Archived 16th August, 2015.
86   http://trilateral.org/ ‡ Archived 16th August, 2015.
87   http://archiviostorico.corriere.it/1994/marzo/08/Parisi_Mendella_pilotano_gli_attacchi_co_0_9403089999.shtml ‡ Archived 16th August, 2015.

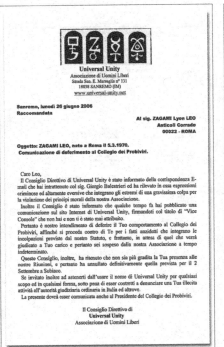

FIG. 92 – Expulsion of the author by the Executive Committee Masonic / Montecarlo Lodge issued in Sanremo Italy on the 26th of June 2006 because of the clash with Giorgio Hugo Balestrieri **later arrested and finally condemned in 2015 for external association with the Mafia.**

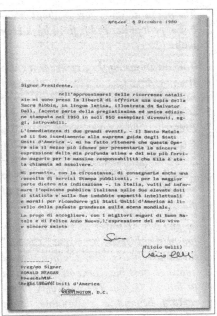

FIG. 93 – Letter sent in December 1980 from Arezzo by Worshipful Master of the Propaganda 2 Lodge Licio Gelli to his dear friend and Honorary Scottish Rite Mason Ronald Reagan President of the United States. A copy of Reagan's membership is shown in "The Northern Light Magazine," April 1988 issue, page 12.

between the aforementioned pedophilia victim Paul Bonacci involved with Dr. Michael Aquino, and the Bohemian Grove as indicated also in Kennedy's book *Satanic Crime*:

> One of the Boys Town victims was one Paul Bonacci, who testified in court proceedings that he helped kidnap Johnny Gosch into this ring in 1982. This is where it gets really interesting. Bonacci also testified that he was forced in July, 1984 to participate in a homosexual/pedophilic/necrophilic orgy at (what has since been identified as) the Bohemian Grove; all of which was filmed. And according to Bonacci, the man in charge of the filming was someone who was picked up in Las Vegas on the plane headed to the Grove, a man who Bonacci was told was one Hunter S. Thompson. No doubt most people who came across this information in the past and were familiar with Thompson's work dismissed the idea that the man behind the camera could have been the famous writer. After all, this was a man who has been fighting the likes of Nixon and Bush his entire career.

> But could Hunter S. Thompson have been brought to the Grove by someone who presented it as an opportunity to investigate what the power elite was up to behind closed doors? Could Thompson have quickly found himself in over his head, compromised, by virtue of his very presence at this horrific crime, by the men he thought he was investigating undercover?

Thompson actually wrote about a cabal of pedophiles in his final book Hey Rube *(2004):*

The autumn months are never a calm time in America. ... There is always a rash of kidnapping and abductions of schoolchildren in the football months. Preteens of both sexes are traditionally seized and grabbed off the streets by gangs of organized perverts who traditionally give them as Christmas gifts to each other to be personal sex slaves and playthings. [p. 3]

In any case, Hunter S. Thompson was found dead of an apparent "suicide" just a few hours after the news broke about a possible Gannon connection to Johnny Gosch. The only way to ascertain beyond a reasonable doubt whether Gannon is Johnny Gosch would be to conduct a DNA test on both Noreen Gosch and Jeff Gannon. This will not likely ever occur, however, as Gannon claims in a March 20, 2005 New York Times *interview that his mother was threatened since the story broke. He does not name who his mother is, nor has he ever mentioned the Johnny Gosch case on his website.* [88]

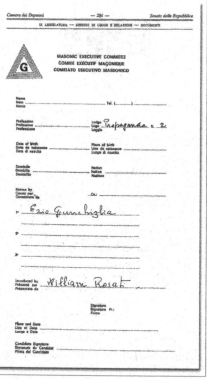

FIG. 94 – *Evidence unearthed by the Italian parliamentary Commission on the P2 case debunks Edward L. King lies on the author.*

It seems evil always has the same protagonists.

Final considerations

As written by **Joël Labruyère:**

The materialist and the average consumer of the New Age, who still wants to believe in something supernatural, has no respect for the higher powers. Faith is dead. They maybe admit the recitation of a formula in Sanskrit or a prayer that can conduct to a particular mental state, but also in this case is it only perfomed to obtain a benefit, nothing more. It lacks the sincere religious sentiment, it is useless to practice a so-called spiritual technique, or do all kinds of yoga contortions on a mat or meditating in front of a blank wall. If anything, these are ascetic disciplines diverted into therapeutic methods that have not conserved the aura of sacredness, due to their roots in a traditional doctrine, whose profound meaning escapes those who practice them now. To find the meaning of the sacred we must first of all realize you lost it, without believing that the farces of the New Age can ever replace it. [89]

This thought of Labruyère explains why Alex Jones and his colleagues returned to

88   See. William H. Kennedy, Satanic Crime, *Ibid.,* p.162.
89   Joël Labruyère, *Kali Yuga, Ibid.,* pp. 282-283.

FIG. 95 – *The Honorary Most Worshipful Grand Director of Ceremonies Domenico Macrì of the Grand Orient of Italy close friend and collaborator of Licio Gelli, at the Consecration of the new Licio Gelli Lodge in February 2016.*

the scene of the controversial scoop at the Bohemian Grove, five years later, where they found while filming nearby, a large group of people who were celebrating a "Magical" ritual with a distinctive New Age *flair*. A really pathetic situation with the usual mantra in Sanskrit, for fighting the evil influences manifested in the Grove. All this, however, without knowing they are helping to further charge the energy of the Egregore of the Bohemian Club and their meeting place: the Bohemian Grove. The "New Age" feel-good rubbish produced by relativist Neo-Theosophy and Jesuitism has created an illusory world, where people obviously accept and believe they are realizing all their wishes. They do not understand that it's just another cage, perhaps a little more beautiful from the others.

I still recall that discreet image of a passport belonging to Mr. Thomas A. Anderson, aka "Neo," that as I wrote a little earlier, shows as expiration date of September 11, 2001, appearing at 18 minutes and 11 seconds into the movie *The Matrix*, which translates into 8 + 1 = 9, followed by 11. [90]

Surely the Wachowski brothers, which have preferential contacts with the U.S. Intelligence Community, received this information and filtered it willingly through their film, with the usual "Predictive Programing" used to program the masses unconsciously. In the 1999 film *The Matrix,* the female character Trinity says to Neo, the protagonist:

I know why you're here, Neo. I know what you've been doing... why you hardly sleep, why you live alone, and why night after night, you sit by your computer. You're looking for him. I know because I was once looking for the same thing. And when he found me, he told me I wasn't really looking for him. I was looking for an answer. It's the question that drives us, Neo. It's the question that brought you here. You know the question, just as I did.

Neo replies: *"What is the Matrix?"*

Trinity says: *"The answer is out there, Neo, and it's looking for you, and it will find you if you want it to."*

To all the good people out there I will now close this Volume of my Confessions.

FIG. 96 – Bartolomeu Constantin Săvoiu, the late Licio Gelli, and Horia Nestorescu-Bălceşti 33°.

With God's help and the Holy Spirit we shall prevail over sin and wickedness in this, the darkest of ages.

Fait Lux,

Leo Lyon Zagami

TRAVEL BOOKS BY CCC PUBLISHING

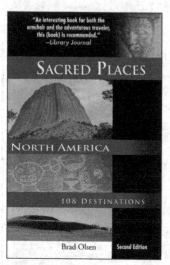

Sacred Places North America: 108 Destinations
– 2nd EDITION

by Brad Olsen

This comprehensive travel guide examines North America's most sacred sites for spiritually attuned explorers. Spirituality & Health reviewed: "The book is filled with fascinating archeological, geological, and historical material. These 108 sacred places in the United States, Canada, and Hawaii offer ample opportunity for questing by spiritual seekers."

$19.95 :: 408 pages   **paperback: 978-1888729139**

all Ebooks priced at $9.99

Kindle: 978-1888729252
PDF: 978-1888729191
ePub: 978-1888729337

Sacred Places Europe: 108 Destinations

by Brad Olsen

This guide to European holy sites examines the most significant locations that shaped the religious consciousness of Western civilization. Travel to Europe for 108 uplifting destinations that helped define religion and spirituality in the Western Hemisphere. From Paleolithic cave art and Neolithic megaliths, to New Age temples, this is an impartial guide book many millennium in the making.

$19.95 :: 344 pages   **paperback: 978-1888729122**

all Ebooks priced at $9.99

Kindle: 978-1888729245
PDF: 978-1888729184
ePub: 978-1888729320

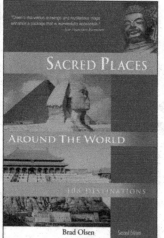

Sacred Places Around the World: 108 Destinations
– 2nd EDITION

by Brad Olsen

The mystical comes alive in this exciting compilation of 108 beloved holy destinations. World travelers and armchair tourists who want to explore the mythology and archaeology of the ruins, sanctuaries, mountains, lost cities, and temples of ancient civilizations will find this guide ideal.

$17.95 :: 288 pages   **paperback: 978-1888729108**

all Ebooks priced at $9.99

Kindle: 978-1888729238
PDF: 978-1888729160
ePub: 978-1888729313

World Stompers: A Global Travel Manifesto
– 5th EDITION

by Brad Olsen

Here is a travel guide written specifically to assist and motivate young readers to travel the world. When you are ready to leave your day job, load up your backpack and head out to distant lands for extended periods of time, Brad Olsen's "Travel Classic" will lend a helping hand.

$17.95 :: 288 pages   **paperback: 978-1888729054**

all Ebooks priced at $8.99

Kindle: 978-1888729276
PDF: 978-1888729061
ePub: 978-1888729351

ESOTERIC BOOKS BY CCC PUBLISHING

Modern Esoteric: Beyond our Senses

by Brad Olsen

Organized into three sections (Lifeology, Control and Thrive), *Modern Esoteric: Beyond Our Senses* author Brad Olsen examines the flaws in ancient and modern history, plus explains how esoteric knowledge, conspiracy theories and fringe subjects can be used to help change the dead-end course we humans seem to be blindly running into.

$17.95 :: 480 pages   **paperback: 978-1888729504**

all Ebooks priced at $9.99

Kindle: 978-1888729535
PDF: 978-1888729511
ePub: 978-1888729528

Future Esoteric: The Unseen Realms

– 2nd EDITION

by Brad Olsen

Organized into three sections (Secrets, Cosmos and Utopia), *Future Esoteric: The Unseen Realms* examines the nature of the national security state; looks forward as we enter the promise of a Golden Age; and, explains how esoteric knowledge, the extraterrestrial question, and discovering our true human abilities will lead us into the great awakening of humanity.

$17.95 :: 416 pages   **paperback: 978-1888729788**

all Ebooks priced at $9.99

Kindle: 978-1888729801
PDF: 978-1888729795
ePub: 978-1888729818

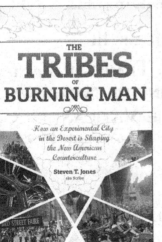

The Tribes of Burning Man: How an Experimental City in the Desert is Shaping the New American Counterculture

by Steven T. Jones

The Burning Man Festival has taken on a new character in recent years, with the frontier finally becoming a real city and the many tribes of the event—the fire artists, circus freaks, music lovers, do-gooders, sexual adventurers, grungy builders, and a myriad of other burner collectives—developing an impactful perennial presence in sister cities all over the world.

$17.95 :: 312 pages   **paperback: 978-1888729290**

all Ebooks priced at $9.99

Kindle: 978-1888729443
PDF: 978-1888729450
ePub: 978-1888729436

The Key to Solomon's Key: Is This the Lost Symbol of Masonry?

– 2nd EDITION

by Lon Milo DuQuette

Is King Solomon's story true? Is his account in the Bible to be considered historical fact? Or do myth and tradition hold the key that unlocks mysteries of human consciousness infinitely more astounding than history?

$16.95 :: 256 pages   **paperback: 978-1888729283**

all Ebooks priced at $9.99

Kindle: 978-1888729412
PDF: 978-1888729368
ePub: 978-1888729375